A HISTORY OF THE CRUSADES

Kenneth M. Setton, GENERAL EDITOR

A HISTORY OF THE CRUSADES

Kenneth M. Setton, GENERAL EDITOR

Volume V

THE IMPACT OF THE CRUSADES
ON THE NEAR EAST

Francis of Assisi before al-Kāmil, sultan of Egypt. Courtesy of Fratelli Fabri, Milan

A HISTORY OF

THE

CRUSADES

KENNETH M. SETTON
GENERAL EDITOR

Volume V

THE IMPACT OF THE CRUSADES
ON THE NEAR EAST

EDITED BY

NORMAN P. ZACOUR

AND

HARRY W. HAZARD

THE UNIVERSITY OF WISCONSIN PRESS

Published 1985
The University of Wisconsin Press
114 North Murray Street, Madison, Wisconsin 53715

The University of Wisconsin Press, Ltd.
1 Gower Street, London WC1E 6HA

First printing

Printed in the United States of America
For LC CIP information see the colophon

ISBN 0-299-09140-6

Sudor certaminis

CONTENTS

ILLUSTRATIONS

xi

MAPS

*Maps compiled by Harry W. Hazard and executed by the
Cartographic Laboratory of the University of Wisconsin, Madison*

FOREWORD

It has been a long journey. We have, however, almost reached our destination. In the foreword to Volume IV I expressed the hope that the end might be in sight, and indeed it is, for we have also turned over the sixth and final volume to the University of Wisconsin Press. From one volume to the next over a period of almost thirty years we have lost a number of our fellow pilgrims and crusaders on what has proved to be a rocky road to the Holy Land. I wish they could have lived to see the publication of the final volume. Yielding sometimes to necessity, sometimes to the possibility of improvement, we have introduced several changes into our plans for Volumes IV–VI, on the whole (we think) for the better.

Once more I express my gratitude to Dr. Harry W. Hazard, the most painstaking editor I know. In earlier forewords I have indicated his numerous and invaluable contributions to these volumes. He has generously borne a heavy load through the years. Without his stalwart, unfailing assistance, these volumes would never have appeared. Both Dr. Hazard and I are much indebted to Professor Norman P. Zacour, who has given much time and strength to this volume just as, years ago, he stepped into a breach, and helped us with the second volume. We are likewise indebted to Mrs. Jean T. Carver, who has retyped hundreds of pages in this volume, kept track of every change we have made either in planning or in the text, handled a sometimes voluminous correspondence, read proof, and helped us in numberless other ways. Dr. Susan M. Babbitt has arranged interlibrary loans, run down and corrected numerous references, and assisted us in the proof-reading. And of course we owe the most to those who have joined us in this enterprise, and who have waited so long and with such patience for the appearance of their work in print.

KENNETH M. SETTON

The Institute for Advanced Study
Princeton, New Jersey
March 14, 1983

PREFACE

This volume deals less with the cry of battle and the clash of arms than with the daily affairs of the Near East and its inhabitants — Moslems, Christians, and Jews — whose lives were wrenched this way and that by more than two hundred years of violence. It is about crusaders too: not those who came and went, but those who came and stayed, and "for the love of Christ," to quote Alexander III, "put their fighting blood at the disposal of king and magnates."[1] Among much else it examines the Arab culture of the twelfth century and the lasting impact that crusading belligerence had on Moslem lands and peoples; the social structure of the crusaders' states whose problems were as stubborn as they themselves were ephemeral; the long, tenacious exploitation of the eastern Mediterranean, especially by the Venetians, surely the most fortunate heirs of the crusading inheritance; and finally the new direction given to the European drive eastward by missionaries rather than warriors. The missionary movement drew much of its early inspiration from St. Francis of Assisi, whose brief mission to the sultan of Egypt remained green in the memory of his followers, and most of its energy from a long line of mendicants, Franciscans and Dominicans alike. Their devotion brought increased knowledge and a deeper understanding of the peoples of the east, but not, alas, any real awareness of the futility of warfare against Islam. Only time would do that.

Norman P. Zacour

The Centre for Medieval Studies
University of Toronto
Toronto, Canada
March 21, 1983

---

[1] E. Martène and U. Durand, *Veterum scriptorum et monumentorum . . . collectio*, II, col. 749: "qui . . . ibi ad defensionem terrae permanserit et sudorem certaminis ad praeceptum regis et majorum terrae pro amore Christi portaverit, remissionem iniunctae poenitentiae se laetetur adeptum."

A NOTE
ON TRANSLITERATION
AND NOMENCLATURE

One of the obvious problems to be solved by the editors of such a work as this, intended both for general readers and for scholars in many different disciplines, is how to render the names of persons and places, and a few other terms, originating in languages and scripts unfamiliar to the English-speaking reader and, indeed, to most readers whose native languages are European. In the present volume, and presumably in the entire work, these comprise principally Arabic, Turkish, Persian, and Armenian, none of which was normally written in our Latin alphabet until its adoption by Turkey in 1928. The analogous problem of Byzantine Greek names and terms has been handled by using the familiar Latin equivalents, Anglicized Greek, or, occasionally, Greek type, as has seemed appropriate in each instance, but a broader approach is desirable for the other languages under consideration.

The somewhat contradictory criteria applied are ease of recognition and readability on the one hand and scientific accuracy and consistency on the other. It has proved possible to reconcile these, and to standardize the great variety of forms in which identical names have been submitted to us by different contributors, through constant consultation with specialists in each language, research in the sources, and adherence to systems conforming to the requirements of each language.

Of these, Arabic presents the fewest difficulties, since the script in which it is written is admirably suited to the classical language. The basic system used, with minor variants, by all English-speaking scholars was restudied and found entirely satisfactory, with the slight modifications noted. The chief alternative system, in which every Arabic consonant is represented by a single Latin character (ṯ for th, ḫ for kh, ḏ for dh, š for sh, ġ for gh) was rejected for several reasons, needless proliferation of diacritical marks to bother the eye and multiply occasions for error, absence of strong countervailing arguments, and, most decisively, the natural tendency of non-specialists to adopt these spellings but omit the diacritical marks. The use of single letters in this manner leads to undesirable results, but the spellings adopted for the present work may be thus treated with confidence by any writer not requiring the discriminations which the remaining diacritical marks indicate.

The letters used for Arabic consonants, in the order of the Arabic alphabet, are these: ', b, t, th, j, ḥ, kh, d, dh, r, z, s, sh, ṣ, ḍ, ṭ, ẓ, ', gh, f, q, k, l, m, n, h, w, y. The vowels are a, i, u, lengthened as ā, ī, ū, with the *alif bi-ṣurati-l-yā'* distinguished as â; initial ' is omitted, but terminal macrons are retained. Diphthongs are *au* and *ai*, not *aw* and *ay*, as being both philologically preferable and visually less misleading. The same considerations lead to the omission of *l* of *al-* before a duplicated consonant (Nūr-ad-Dīn rather than Nūr-al-Dīn). As in this example, hyphens are used to link words composing a single name (as also 'Abd-Allāh), with weak initial vowels elided (as Abū-l-Ḥasan). Normally *al-* (meaning "the") is not capitalized; *ibn-* is not when it means literally "son of," but is otherwise (as Ibn-Khaldūn).

Some readers may be disconcerted to find the prophet called "Mohammed" and his followers "Moslems," but this can readily be justified. These spellings are valid English proper names, derived from Arabic originals which would be correctly transliterated "Muḥammad" and "Muslimūn" or "Muslimīn." The best criterion for deciding whether to use the Anglicized spellings or the accurate transliterations is the treatment accorded the third of this cluster of names, that of the religion "Islam." Where this is transliterated "Islām," with a macron over the *a,* it should be accompanied by "Muslim" and "Muḥammad," but where the macron is omitted, consistency and common sense require "Moslem" and "Mohammed," and it is the latter triad which have been considered appropriate in this work. All namesakes of the prophet, however, have had their names duly transliterated "Muḥammad," to correspond with names of other Arabs who are not individually so familiar to westerners as to be better recognized in Anglicized forms.

All names of other Arabs, and of non-Arabs with Arabic names, have been systematically transliterated, with the single exception of Ṣalāḥ-ad-Dīn, whom it would have been pedantic to call that rather than Saladin. For places held, in the crusading era or now, by Arabs, the Arabic names appear either in the text or in the gazetteer, where some additional ones are also included to broaden the usefulness of this feature.

Large numbers of names of persons and groups, however, customarily found in Arabicized spellings because they were written in Arabic script, have been restored to their underlying identity whenever this is ascertainable. For example, Arabic "Saljūq" misrepresents four of the six component phonemes: *s* is correct, *a* replaces Turkish *e*, for which Arabic script provides no equivalent, *l* is correct, *j* replaces the non-Arabic *ch*, *ū* substitutes a non-Turkish long *u* for the original *ü*, and *q* as distinguished from *k* is non-existent in Turkish; this quadruple rectification yields "Selchük" as the name of the eponymous leader, and "Selchükid" — on the model of 'Abbāsid and Timurid — for the dynasty and the people.

It might be thought that as Turkish is now written in a well-conceived modified Latin alphabet, there would be no reason to alter this, and this presumption is substantially valid. For the same reasons as apply to Arabic, *ch* has been preferred above *ç*, *sh* above *ş*, and *gh* above *ğ*, with *kh* in a few instances given as a preferred alternate of *h*, from which it is not distinguished in modern Turkish. No long vowels have been indicated, as being functionless survivals. Two other changes have been made in the interest of the English-speaking reader, and should be remembered by those using map sheets and standard reference works: *c* (pronounced dj) has been changed to *j*, so that one is not visually led to imagine that the Turkish name for the Tigris — Dijle/Dicle — rhymes with "tickle," and what the eminent lexicographer H. C. Hony terms "that abomination the undotted ı" has, after the model of *The Encyclopaedia of Islām,* been written i̇.

Spellings, modified as above indicated, have usually been founded on those of the Turkish edition, *İslâm Ansiklopedisi,* hampered by occasional inconsistencies within that work. All names of Turks appear thus emended, the Turkish equivalents of almost all places within or near modern Turkey appear in the gazetteer.

In addition to *kh,* Middle Turkish utilized a few other phonemes not common in modern Turkish: *zh* (modern *j*), *dh, ng,* and *ä* (modern *e*); the first three of these will be used as needed, while the last-mentioned may be assumed to underlie every medieval Turkish name now spelled with *e.* Plaintive eyebrows may be raised at our exclusion of *q,* but this was in Middle Turkish only the alternate spelling used when the sound *k* was combined with back instead of front vowels, and its elimination by the Turks is commendable.

Persian names have been transliterated like Arabic with certain modifications, chiefly use of the additional vowels *e* and *o* and replacing *ḍ* and *dh* with *ẓ* and *z̧,* so that Arabic "Ādharbaijān" becomes Persian "Āẕerbaijān," more accurate as well as more recognizable. Omission of the definite article from personal names was considered but eventually disapproved.

Armenian presented great difficulties: the absence of an authoritative reference source for spelling names, the lack of agreement on transliteration, and the sound-shift by which classical and eastern Armenian *b, d, g* became western Armenian *p, t, k* and—incredible as it may seem to the unwary—*vice versa*; similar reciprocal interchanges involved *ts* and *dz,* and *ch* and *j.* The following alphabet represents western Armenian letters, with eastern variants in parentheses: a, p (b), k (g), t (d), e, z, ē, i̊, t̞, zh, i, l, kh, dz (ts), g (k), h, ts (dz), gh, j (ch), m, y, n, sh, o, c̬h, b (p), ch (j), r̞, s, v̞, d (t), r, t̞s, u or v, p̣, ḳ, ō, f. Many spellings are based on the Armenian texts in the *Recueil des historiens des croisades.*

In standardizing names of groups, the correct root forms in the respective languages have been identified, with the ending "-id" for dynasties and their peoples but "-ite" for sects, and with plural either identical with singular (as Kirghiz) or plus "-s" (Khazars) or "-es" (Uzes). In cases where this sounded hopelessly awkward, it was abandoned (Muwaḥḥids, not Muwaḥḥidids or Muwaḥḥidites, and certainly not Almohads, which is, however, cross-referenced).

The use of place names is explained in the note preceding the gazetteer, but may be summarized by saying that in general the most familiar correct form is used in the text and maps, normally an English version of the name by which the place was known to Europeans during the crusades. Variant forms are given and identified in the gazetteer.

Despite conscientious efforts to perfect the nomenclature, errors will probably be detected by specialists; they are to be blamed on me and not on individual contributors or editorial colleagues, for I have been accorded a free hand. Justifiable suggestions for improvements will be welcomed, and used to bring succeeding volumes nearer that elusive goal, impeccability in nomenclature.

HARRY W. HAZARD

[Princeton, New Jersey, 1962]

Reprinted from Volume I, with minor modifications.

ABBREVIATIONS

AFP   *Archivum fratrum praedicatorum* (Istituto storico Santa Sabina; Rome, 1930–   ).

AOL   *Archives de l'Orient latin* (Société de l'Orient latin; 2 vols., Paris, 1881–1884; repr. Brussels, 1964).

BF   *Bullarium franciscanum,* ed. Johannes H. Sbaralea *et al.* (Rome, 1759 ff.).

BOF   *Biblioteca bio-bibliografica della Terra Santa e dell' Oriente francescano,* ed. Girolamo Golubovich *et al.* (9 vols., Quaracchi, 1906–1927).

BOP   *Bullarium ordinis praedicatorum,* ed. Thomas Ripoll *et al.* (Rome, 1727 ff.).

CSCO, SS   *Corpus scriptorum christianorum orientalium, Scriptores syri,* ed. Jean B. Chabot *et al.* (Paris and elsewhere, 1903 ff.).

CSHB   *Corpus scriptorum historiae byzantinae,* ed. Barthold G. Niebuhr, Immanuel Bekker, *et al.* (50 vols., Bonn, 1828–1897).

CURC   *Columbia University Records of Civilization; Sources and Studies* (New York, 1915 ff.).

IFD, BO   Institut français de Damas, Bibliothèque orientale.

Mansi, *Concilia*   *Sacrorum conciliorum . . . collectio,* ed. Giovanni D. Mansi, rev. ed. by Jean P. Martin and Louis Petit (53 vols., Paris, Arnhem, and Leipzig, 1901–1927; repr. Paris, 1960–1962).

MGH, SS.   *Monumenta Germaniae historica . . . .: Scriptores,* ed. Georg H. Pertz, Theodor Mommsen, *et al.* (Reichsinstitut für ältere deutsche Geschichtskunde; 32 vols., Hanover and elsewhere, 1826–1934).

PC, Fontes   Pontificia commissio ad redigendum codicem iuris canonici orientalis: Fontes (Vatican City, 1944–   ).

PG   *Patrologiae cursus completus: Series graeco-latina,* ed. Jacques P. Migne (161 vols. in 166, Paris, 1857–1866).

PL   *Patrologiae cursus completus: Series latina,* ed. Jacques P. Migne (221 vols., Paris, 1844–1864).

PPTS   *Palestine Pilgrims' Text Society* (13 vols. and index, London, 1890–1897).

RHC   *Recueil des historiens des croisades* (Académie des inscriptions et belles-lettres; Paris, 16 vols. in fol., 1841–1906):

   Arm.   *Documents arméniens* (2 vols., 1869–1906).

   Grecs   *Historiens grecs* (2 vols., 1875–1881).

   Lois   *Les Assises de Jérusalem* (2 vols., 1841–1843).

   Occ.   *Historiens occidentaux* (5 vols., 1841–1895).

   Or.   *Historiens orientaux: Arabes* (5 vols., 1872–1906).

RHDFE   *Revue historique de droit français et étranger* (Paris, 1855–   ).

RISS   *Rerum italicarum scriptores . . . ,* ed. Lodovico A. Muratori [1672–1750] (25 vols. in 28, Milan, 1723–1751); new ed. by Giosuè Carducci and Vittorio Fiorini (34 vols. in 109 fasc., Città di Castello and Bologna, 1900–1935).

ROC   *Revue de l'Orient chrétien* (Société de l'Orient chrétien; 30 vols., Paris, 1896–1946).

ROL   *Revue de l'Orient latin* (Société de l'Orient latin; 12 vols., Paris, 1893–1911; repr. Brussels, 1964).

Rolls Series   *Rerum brittanicarum medii aevi scriptores: The Chronicles and Memorials of Great Britain and Ireland during the Middle Ages* (251 vols., London, 1858–1896).

SOL, *SG*   Société de l'Orient latin, Publications, *Série géographique* (5 vols., Geneva, 1879–1889).

SOL, *SH*   Société de l'Orient latin, Publications, *Série historique* (5 vols., Geneva, 1877–1887).

SSRP   *Scriptores rerum prussicarum: Die Geschichtsquellen der preussische Vorzeit bis zum Untergange der Ordensherrschaft,* ed. Theodor Hirsch, Max Toppen, and Ernst Strehlke (5 vols., Leipzig, 1861–1874).

Tafel and Thomas   Gottlieb L. F. Tafel and Georg M. Thomas, *Urkunden zur älteren Handels- und Staatsgeschichte der Republik Venedig mit besonderer Beziehung auf Byzanz und die Levante* (Fontes rerum austriacarum, *Diplomataria et acta,* XII–XIV; 3 vols., Vienna, 1856–1857; repr. Amsterdam, 1964).

ZDMG   *Zeitschrift der Deutschen Morgenländischen Gesellschaft* (Leipzig and elsewhere, 1846–   ).

ZDPV   *Zeitschrift des Deutschen Palästina-Vereins* (Leipzig and Wiesbaden, 1878–   ).

ZMR   *Zeitschrift für Missionswissenschaft und Religionswissenschaft* (Institut für missionswissenschaftliche Forschungen; Münster, 1911–   ).

Volume V

THE IMPACT OF THE CRUSADES
ON THE NEAR EAST

I

ARAB CULTURE
IN THE TWELFTH CENTURY

This study of Arab culture in the twelfth century is limited to those areas in the Arab world in which the events of the crusades unfolded, and where east and west, Islam and Christendom, Arab and Frank met face to face. These areas comprise Egypt and the lands of the Fertile Crescent, although the eastern part of the Crescent remained for the most part peripheral.[1] Most of the drama was enacted on the eastern shores of the Mediterranean, from Antioch in the north to Damietta in the south. The crusaders' early thrust into the interior as far as the Tigris river was permanently arrested and pushed back before the middle of the century.

At the outbreak of the crusades, eastern Islam was divided in loyalty between the 'Abbāsid caliphate in Baghdad and the Fāṭimid imamate in Cairo. The 'Abbāsids of Baghdad were virtual prisoners of the Selchükids (Seljuks), who had, some five decades earlier, readily responded to the appeals of al-Qā'im (1031–1075) to save the caliphate from the pro-Shī'ite Buwaihids. Indeed, the Selchükids had in 1055 supplanted the Buwaihids and saved the caliphal throne; they had given the state a new lease on life, particularly during the reign of the first three Great Selchükids, Tughrul-Beg (1038–1063), Alp Arslan (1063–1072), and Malik-Shah (1072–1092).[2] The Selchükids had come as rescuers, but, as often happens, had remained as conquerors. Their domination over the caliphate continued to the last decade of the twelfth century, and their endless strife weakened the caliphate and facilitated the success of the Christian invaders. When, after the fall of Jerusalem in 1099, a Moslem delegation arrived in Baghdad

The author is indebted to his students 'Alī Hajj Bakrī, M. T. Husayn, Sa'dī Khayyāt, and Mikha'il Khūrī for help in collecting some of the material for this study.

1. Nabih A. Faris, *The Book of Knowledge, Being a Translation with Notes of the Kitāb al-'ilm of al-Ghazzālī's "Iḥyā' 'ulūm al-dīn"* (Lahore, 1962), p. 109.

2. See Claude Cahen, "The Turkish Invasion: The Selchükids," in volume I of the present work, pp. 140–154.

to seek the aid of the central government, all it received was words of sympathy from the caliph al-Mustaẓhir (1094–1118) and tears from the outraged populace. The sultan Berkyaruk (1094–1105), to whom the matter was referred by the caliph, had nothing to offer. Nine years later, in 1108, a second delegation, now from beleaguered Tripoli, appeared at the capital, but its mission fared no better than that of the first. When, at long last, sultan Muḥammad (1105–1118) bestirred himself and led an expedition against the Franks in 1111, his troops, in the words of a Moslem chronicler, "spread havoc and destruction throughout the land, far exceeding anything which the Franks were wont to do."[3]

Not only the eclipse of the power of the caliphate by the Selchükid sultans and the constant struggle among the Selchükid princes, especially after the death of Malik-Shāh in 1092, but also the deep-rooted enmity between the Sunnite 'Abbāsids of Baghdad and the Shī'ite Fāṭimids of Cairo plagued Arab society and sapped a great deal of its ability both to defend itself against the invaders and to maintain the stability necessary for development and progress. To the Sunnite 'Abbāsids it seemed more urgent to deal with the threat raised by the schismatic Fāṭimids than to face the dangers to the entire region implicit in the Christian invasion. In fact, it was not until this rival schismatic caliphate was finally liquidated in 1171 that the defenders were able to concentrate all their energies against the invaders.

Politically, the twelfth century witnessed struggles between Moslems and Franks, between Sunnites and Shī'ites, between Sunnite caliph and Sunnite sultan, between Sunnite princes in the various urban centers and those in outlying districts, between ambitious dynasts and predatory viziers, and between the mass of the population, mostly Arabs, and the foreign elements, mostly Turks. Each of these struggles was sufficient to disrupt the normal course of life and to ravage the general good of society. Together, they wrought havoc throughout the empire, rendered communications unsafe, increased lawlessness, and gave rise to various forms of brigandage. The memoirs of Usāmah, one of the best sources of information available, abound with references to highway robbers infesting the vicinities of urban centers, such as Mosul,[4] Baalbek, Shaizar, and Nablus.[5]

Perhaps the most terrifying form of lawlessness, however, was the rise of the Ismā'īlī Assassins, whose "new mission" or "new dispensa-

---

3. Sibṭ Ibn-al-Jauzī, Mir'āt az-zamān fī ta'rīkh al-aiyām (Hyderabad, 1951), p. 3.
4. Usāmah Ibn-Munqidh, Kitāb al-i'tibār, ed. Philip K. Hitti (Princeton, 1930), pp. 71–72.
5. Ibid., p. 79.

tion"[6] terrorized both invaders and defenders alike throughout the greater part of the century, and whose agents made two attempts on the life of Saladin himself.[7]

When treating of the crusades, it has been easy to make sweeping generalizations. More often than not the dichotomy of invaders and defenders, Christians and Moslems, has obscured the heterogeneous nature of each of the two groups. Actually, the crusaders, in spite of their various origins, were more homogeneous than the defenders, who were deeply divided racially, linguistically, and culturally. Within the Islamic community (al-jamā'ah) itself, the Arab elements, though always a majority in the area, had already lost their hegemony, and were bitterly pitted against such neo-Moslems as the Turks, the Persians, and the Kurds. Arab feelings, against the first two in particular, were marked by the growing resentment of the Arabs against the loss of their hegemony in the jamā'ah. Arabic literary sources invariably speak of the heretical (malāhidah) Persians and the uncouth ('ulūj) Turks. A Damascene poet, living at the time of the first four Aiyūbids, hesitates to say anything in praise of the dynasty for fear of its being lost on "mean and petty non-Arabs."[8] Another poet wonders how he could possibly eulogize any of the Turks, who are incapable of appreciating any poetry and therefore continue to neglect it.[9]

While they had their detractors, the Turks also had their defenders. According to one poet they were responsible for the glory of Islam. Another speaks of "bands of Turkish soldiers whose forays against the enemy would make the sound and fury of thunder seem like child's play. In looks, they resemble the angels; in valor and battle they match the supernatural power of the jinn."[10]

This tension runs through the course of Arab history. In the twelfth century, it seems to have gained in intensity, because of a soldiery whose debauchery and rapacity preyed upon the populace and whose leaders were unwilling or unable to curb the excesses of their followers. Except for the periods of Nūr-ad-Dīn (1146–1174) and Saladin (1169–1193), when the authority of the sultan was too strong to be contested, conflicts among the different dynasts, on the one hand,

6. Ad-da'wah al-jadīdah.
7. See Bernard Lewis, "The Ismā'īlites and the Assassins," in volume I of the present work, chapter IV.
8. Ibn-'Unain (1154–1232); see his Dīwān, ed. Khalil Mardam (Damascus, 1946), p. 33.
9. See Abū-Shāmah, Kitāb ar-raudatain fī akhbār ad-daulatain (Cairo, A.H. 1287 [1870/1]), I, 240.
10. See Ibn-Kathīr, Al-bidāyah wa-n-nihāyah fī-t-ta'rīkh, ed. 'Abd-al-Hafīz Sa'd 'Atīyah (Cairo, A.H. 1358 [1939/40]), II, 201.

and with the invaders, on the other, plunged the entire area into a state of near-chaos. To establish their authority over the various dynasts and adventurers, both Nūr-ad-Dīn and Saladin spent the greater part of their reigns in active combat against enemies both Moslem and Frank.

The constant warfare was disruptive, not only politically, but also socially and economically. Manpower was depleted, farmers left their land uncultivated rather than have their crops pillaged, public security all but collapsed, and in the face of a rising wave of brigandage and crime the populace often took the law into its own hands, organizing itself into special units for self-defense. These "youth units" (*al-aḥdāth*) were at times enlisted by the caliph himself, who issued arms to them whenever he found himself faced with danger.[11] The breakdown in security and the inability of rulers to cope with the situation threatened to disrupt the annual pilgrimage, which, as one of the divinely ordained pillars of Islam, was obligatory for every Moslem.[12] Furthermore, the frequent epidemics of plague and smallpox, and the recurrent outbreak of endemic diseases like malaria, decimated large areas. Famines of major proportion, in part caused by the forced neglect of the land, led to widespread dislocation in the population centers of the area. In 1117/1118 drought hit many areas; people left their homes and roamed the countryside in search of food, and whole villages lay desolate. To avoid starvation, people ate the flesh of dogs and cats.[13] In 1200 famine in Egypt was so severe that people were reported to have fed on dead animals and even on human flesh, only to be destroyed by the "resulting" pestilence.[14] For three years, beginning in 1178 and continuing through 1181, rain did not fall in either Iraq or Syria.[15] Prices rose abnormally, and a general famine, extending to Egypt, ravaged the entire area.[16] On top of all these catas-

---

11. (Abū-l-Farāj) Ibn-al-Jauzī, *Al-muntaẓam fī ta'rīkh al-mulūk*, X (Hyderabad, A.H. 1358 [1939/40]), 133; Ibn-al-Athīr, *Al-kāmil fī-t-ta'rikh*, ed. Carl J. Tornberg, X (Leyden, 1864), 441.

12. In 1150 beduins attacked the pilgrim caravans between Mecca and Medina and slaughtered most of them (Abū-l-Fidā', *Al-mukhtaṣar fī akhbār al-bashar*, Cairo, n.d., III, 23); in 1162 and 1166 the pilgrims found it necessary to change their return route in order to avoid beduin attacks (Ibn-al-Athīr, *Al-kāmil*, XI, Leyden, 1851, 189–190; Ibn-al-Jauzī, *Al-muntaẓam*, X, 218). In 1168 the Banū-Khafājah attacked and looted the pilgrim caravans, with the result that the Egyptians did not go on pilgrimage (*Al-muntaẓam*, X, 222).

13. Ṣibt Ibn-al-Jauzī, *Mir'āt az-zamān*, p. 68.

14. Ibn-al-Athīr, *Al-kāmil*, XII, 112.

15. "Syria" denotes not the present-day Syrian Arab Republic but Barr ash-Sha'm, the area extending from the Taurus mountains in the north to the Sinai desert in the south, and from the Mediterranean in the west to the Syrian desert in the east.

16. Ibn-al-Jauzī, *Al-muntaẓam*, X, 285; Ibn-al-Athīr, *Al-kāmil*, XI, 299; Abū-Shāmah, *op. cit.*, II, 5–6.

trophes, an earthquake hit the region in 1157, devastating "Aleppo, Hamah, Shaizar, and most of Syria and the east."[17]

In spite of these misfortunes life went on, its pleasures undiminished and its vices unchecked, as we are often reminded by the moralists. One poet, reviewing the mores of his time as reflected in the conduct of the judges of Damascus, summed up the situation in the following words:

> To drink wine in Ramadan, to play the lute
>   at the call for prayer,
> To omit prayer and to neglect the reading of the
>   Koran,
> Adultery and sodomy in the sacred house of God —
> All these are now deemed lawful and in good taste.
> You upright people of Damascus, the judge has now
>   given permission to his friends to do what they please.
> Therefore, gamble, drink, and procure,
> Pederasty practise and narcotics inhale,
> And God himself deny —
> All these you may do with impunity.[18]

In a community where heresy and treason were considered one and the same thing, it was only natural that anyone who questioned a single tenet of Islam was pronounced at once a heretic and a traitor, and that anyone who rose up against the state was declared at once a traitor and a heretic. The Islamic community was, of course, facing invasion by foreign adherents of a rival religion which Islam had from the beginning recognized as being of divine origin. The conflicts between the rising Arab state and the Byzantine empire deepened the cleavage between the two faiths and accentuated the hostility between their respective adherents. Islam had been on the offensive from the seventh century to the end of the eleventh, not only in Syria and Anatolia but also in Sicily and Spain. The reconquest of Sicily and northern Spain in the west, and the crusade in the east, represented the first successful Christian reaction against Islam. Even so, Islam could not, at least in theory, wage a holy war against Christianity as such, but only against Christians who had allegedly "ignored the teachings of their own divine dispensation."

It is this kind of distinction which explains in part the uncompromising and intense hatred which Islam reserved for its own schismatic groups, particularly the Shī'ites, who, considered at once heretics and

17. Ibn-Taghrībirdī, *An-nujūm az-zāhirah fī mulūk Miṣr wa-l-Qāhirah* (Cairo, 1935), V, 325.

18. Al-Kutubī, *Fawāt al-wafayāt,* ed. Muḥammad Muḥyī-d-Dīn 'Abd-al-Ḥamīd (Cairo, 1951), I, 123.

traitors, never ceased to be a thorn in the side of Sunnite Islam and authority. Suppression of Shī'ism, therefore, always commanded wide popular support. The spread of Fāṭimid power to Egypt and Syria in the tenth and eleventh centuries, and the rise of the neo-Ismā'īlite terror in the twelfth century, made holy war against all forms of Shī'ism one of the most urgent preoccupations of the Sunnite community. The neo-Ismā'īlites, for their part, hit back against the Sunnites by launching a series of raids on Sunnite strongholds, inaugurating a wave of assassinations, and even inviting the Franks to come to Damascus.[19]

Sectarian feuding among the Moslems was not limited to Sunnite-Shī'ite strife; it often flared up among adherents of the various Sunnite rites or juridical schools (madhāhib).[20] One of the more serious clashes took place in Baghdad in 1177–1178 between the Ḥanbalites and the Ḥanafites.[21] To reduce friction and control the feuding jurists, the caliph found himself, in 1210, compelled to license the official representatives of the four rites.[22] Besides these religious disputes, regional conflicts were not uncommon, and at times led to violence, even during the pilgrimage, the sacredness of which could not, in 1227, avert an open clash between pilgrims from Iraq and those from Egypt.[23]

Because of the incessant conflicts which rendered the twelfth century one of dissension and violence, and because of the serious setbacks to the temporal fortunes of Islam which established foreign and non-Moslem states in Moslem lands and subjected, for the first time in half a millennium, great numbers of the "faithful" to the rule of the "infidels," Moslems have seen this century as the beginning of the period of decline in Arab civilization. It is unfortunate that a number of modern scholars, both Moslem and non-Moslem, have succumbed to this oversimplification. If by "decline" is meant the drying up of the wells of creativity in Arab society, the beginnings should be pushed back at least two and a half centuries to the time of the suppression of the Mu'tazilites by the caliph al-Mutawakkil (847–861). In the tenth century, too, al-Ash'arī (d. 935/936) had established the hegemony of his scholastic theology over the dead body of Mu'tazilite thinking.

Another setback to free thought had occurred in 1017, when be-

19. Ibn-al-Qalānisī, Dhail ta'rīkh Dimashq, ed. Henry F. Amedroz (Beirut, 1908), p. 221.
20. These are the Ḥanafite, Shāfi'ite, Ḥanbalite, and Mālikite.
21. Ibn-Taghrībirdī, An-nujūm, VI, 83.
22. Abū-Shāmah, Dhail ar-rauḍatain (Cairo, A.H. 1366 [1946/7]), p. 69.
23. Sibṭ Ibn-al-Jauzī, Mir'āt az-zamān, p. 624.

cause of the growing intensity of the polemical controversy between Sunnite and Shī'ite Islam, often leading to conflict and strife, the caliph al-Qādir (991–1031) issued an edict against Shī'ites and Mu'tazilites alike, and forced their leaders to recant and return to the narrow path of Moslem orthodoxy.[24] Not long after, in 1041, al-Qā'im published in Baghdad the so-called Qādirī creed (al-i'tiqād al-Qādirī),[25] the first official statement of doctrine issued by a caliph, to which all were required to subscribe and conform. By the beginning of the twelfth century Moslem orthodoxy was already established and Moslem conformity (ittibā') was no longer challenged or contested.

In fact, except for a decline in intellectual creativity which had begun much earlier, the twelfth century was in many ways a period of revival resulting from the militant confrontation of two cultures. Indeed, the crusades seem to have delayed, for a while at least, the impending stagnation of Arab life and vigor.

As a result of the Christian-Moslem encounters of the twelfth century, the commercial activities of Italian cities—notably Venice, Genoa, and Pisa—were greatly stimulated, and the east-west trade between the ports of Syria and those of Italy enjoyed a great revival. From the point of view of the Arab east, the resulting benefits were indeed timely, for Arab trade with the Far East had already come to a standstill, primarily because of the prevailing internal unrest, which disrupted trade routes and strangled commercial enterprise. In the eleventh century, too, trade with Russia and the north had gradually diminished and all but disappeared. Therefore the revival of Mediterranean commerce, as a result of the crusades, partially compensated the Arab area for commerce lost elsewhere.

As commerce expanded, agriculture and industry shared the benefits. Furthermore, throughout the ascendancy of the two Zengid sultans, 'Imād-ad-Dīn Zengi and Nūr-ad-Dīn Maḥmūd (1127–1174), and the first Aiyūbid, Saladin (1169–1193), special attention was paid to agriculture, which had always been the main industry of the area. Ibn-Jubair (b. 1145, d. 1217), while on pilgrimage, visited Egypt, Syria, and Iraq between the years 1183 and 1185, and has left us a vivid description of life and conditions in these areas in his famous Riḥlah.[26] "Damascus was adorned with the bright blossoms of fruit trees and flowers, and resplendent in the glittering green of its gardens and or-

24. Ibn-al-Jauzī, Al-muntaẓam, VII, 287.

25. Ibid., VIII, 109–111.

26. Ibn-Jubair, Riḥlah, ed. William Wright (E. J. W. Gibb Memorial Series, 5; London, 1852); rev. Martin J. de Goeje (Leyden, 1907).

chards."[27] As he crossed through Iraq toward Baghdad, he noted the
country's "thriving villages and fertile lands, abounding with rich crops
and palm groves."[28] He expected to find Mecca, which the Koran
describes as "a valley unfit for cultivation",[29] a place devoid of everything, but instead found its markets teeming with all manner of goods
and fruits, such as figs, grapes, pomegranates, quinces, plums, lemons,
walnuts, watermelons, cucumbers, and all kinds of herbs and vegetables such as eggplants, pumpkins, turnips, carrots, beets, and cab-
bages.[30] Although these were probably not grown in Mecca itself,
but in nearby Ta'if, the account reflects a flourishing agriculture. Other
travelers were impressed by the prosperity of Tripoli. Nāṣir-i-Khusrau
describes its "suburbs which consisted of vast stretches of fields covered with billowing ears of wheat, vineyards bursting with their lus-
cious clusters of grapes, farms crowded with sugar cane, vast orchards
of trees heavily laden with oranges, and lemons and other fruits."[31]
William of Tyre (d. about 1187) mentions the sugar-cane plantations
and the sugar industry in and around his native town. Syria paid special attention to the olive tree, the fruit of which has always been
part of the staple fare of the area, and its oil the principal fat for
eating and cooking. It was also the mainstay of the flourishing soap
industry in towns like Tripoli and Nablus.[32]

The revival of trade led to a revival of industry. The major cities
of Iraq—Basra, Baghdad, and Mosul—continued to excel in weaving. Syria produced, in addition to woven fabrics, stained glass, sugar,
and paper, while Egypt's leading manufactures were cotton, woolen,
and silk fabrics, silk brocades, mattress beds, rugs, tents, sails, sad-
dles, metalwork, gold and silver jewelry, pottery, glassware, and wood-
carvings. The exigencies of war also gave impetus to shipbuilding and
the manufacture of weapons.

In spite of the disruptive effects of war and political instability,
the area retained a measure of prosperity. How widespread this was
is difficult to determine with any degree of certainty, since sources
for the most part ignore rural areas and concentrate their attention
on urban centers. The majority of the population, however, did not
live in cities; being largely peasants or seminomadic, they dwelt in
scattered villages, farms, and constantly changing campgrounds. It

27. *Ibid.,* p. 260.
28. *Ibid.,* pp. 215–216.
29. Sūrah XIV:40.
30. Ibn-Jubair, *Riḥlah,* pp. 119–120.
31. Cf. Nāṣir-i-Khusrau, *Sefer nāmeh,* Arabic tr. Yaḥyâ al-Khashāb (Cairo, 1945), p. 13.
32. See below, chapter VI.

is difficult, therefore, to generalize about their condition. Furthermore, Arab culture in general was a "palace culture." Its ramifications were not widespread, and rarely reached those segments of the
population which did not reside in urban centers.

Eyewitness reports of contemporary travelers preserve a clear picture of prevailing conditions in cities like Baghdad, Damascus,
Jerusalem, Alexandria, and Cairo. Baghdad of the twelfth century
had two parts, one on each side of the Tigris. The older part, on
the west bank, was in ruins; the newer, on the east bank, consisted
of seventeen quarters (sing., *mahallah*), each of which formed an independent unit. Though considerably run down and neglected, each
quarter had its own quota of public baths and a number of mosques.
There were thirty schools, each housed in an imposing building and
supported by its own separate endowment (*waqf*).[33] Baghdad also
had its own great hospital, which Ibn-Jubair visited. Physicians made
regular calls every Monday and Thursday, and prescribed the necessary medical treatment, prepared and administered to the patients
by regular hospital attendants.[34]

Notwithstanding civil wars and preoccupation with the holy war
against the Franks, Syria during the greater part of the twelfth century enjoyed the most brilliant period of its Moslem history since the
Umaiyad age. Under the Zengids and the Aiyūbids, particularly under Nūr-ad-Dīn and Saladin, its principal cities—especially Damascus, Aleppo, and to a certain extent Jerusalem after its recovery from
the crusaders—underwent a spectacular revival. Damascus still shows
evidence of the architectural and educational activities of these two
rulers. Nūr-ad-Dīn rebuilt the walls of the city, established the first
school exclusively devoted to the study of Moslem tradition, built
the celebrated hospital bearing his name,[35] and introduced the first
of a number of schools modeled after the famous Niẓāmīyah of
Baghdad. This enlightened patronage of learning was continued, with
added zeal, by the great Saladin, who seems to have transformed Damascus into a school city. Ibn-Jubair, who visited the city in 1184,
enumerates in it twenty *madrasahs,* two hospitals, many inns, and
numerous centers of Sūfī fraternal orders.[36]

33. Ibn-Jubair, *Riḥlah,* p. 229.

34. *Ibid.,* p. 225.

35. *Ibid.,* p. 283; Ibn-Khallikān, *Wafayāt al-a'yān wa-anbā' abnā' az-zamān,* ed. Muḥammad Muyī-d-Dīn 'Abd-al-Ḥamīd (Cairo, 1948), IV, 272; Ibn-abī-Uṣaibi'ah, *'Uyūn al-anbā' fī
ṭabaqāt al-aṭibbā'* (Cairo, 1882), II, 192.

36. Ibn-Jubair, *Riḥlah,* p. 283; Cf. Hitti, *History of the Arabs,* 10th ed. (New York and
London, 1970), pp. 659–662.

Saladin introduced the *madrasah* type of school into Jerusalem, Alexandria, and Cairo, where they became known as Ṣalāḥīyahs or Nāṣirīyahs. Under him, too, Egypt witnessed a general revival. Both Alexandria and Cairo became beneficiaries of his enlightened and energetic rule. Ibn-Jubair was especially impressed by the apparent prosperity of Alexandria, its public buildings, marble colonnades, and wide streets, and by the various *madrasahs* and the philanthropic institutions set aside for the benefit of strangers.[37]

Cairo was specially favored by the first Aiyūbid. Besides the two hospitals which he maintained in the city, he established the Cairo Ṣalāḥīyah and several similar *madrasahs,* restored the citadel and strengthened its fortifications along Norman lines, using prisoners of war in its construction, and began building aqueducts to tap the waters of the Nile for irrigation. Above all, he patronized the arts and surrounded himself with men of talent, including his two learned vizirs al-Qāḍī al-Fāḍil (d. 1200) and ʿImād-ad-Dīn al-Iṣfahānī (d. 1201), the great Jewish philosopher-physician Maimonides, and the historian-physician ʿAbd-al-Laṭīf al-Baghdādī (d. 1231).

Saladin's educational activities in Damascus, Jerusalem, Alexandria, and Cairo not only continued Nūr-ad-Dīn's educational reforms in Damascus and other Syrian cities, such as Aleppo, Homs, Hamah, and Baalbek, but also revived the practical policies of the great Selchükid vizir Niẓām-al-Mulk (d. 1092), whose main interests were to supply the rising Selchükid empire with civil servants and to combat Shīʿite teachings and propaganda emanating from the Azhar. The Niẓāmīyah type of school or academy launched by Niẓām-al-Mulk in 1065–1067 became a model for later institutions of higher learning, and the Ṣalāḥīyah type inaugurated by Saladin served the same purpose. Both were instruments of the state, but both also brought progress throughout the land.

In spite of the heroic efforts of the two Zengids and of Saladin to weld the population into one harmonious society dedicated to the task of repelling the invader and restoring Islamic solidarity, twelfth-century Arab society still lacked the attributes of a united people. Made up of heterogeneous ethnic elements not yet fused together in the crucible of time, it was further divided by its social stratifications. There were extreme contrasts of wealth and poverty, enlightenment and ignorance, comfort and squalor, refinement and crudeness. At the top of the social scale stood the caliph and his immediate family and relatives, who, being denied actual authority by the ruling sul-

---

37. Ibn-Jubair, *Rihlah,* pp. 40–45.

tans, with few exceptions took to a life of indulgence. The court of al-Muqtafī (1136–1160) required eighty mules to carry its daily supply of drinking water, which the sultan was only too willing to provide in order to divert the caliph from affairs of state toward those of his harem, where his concubines, young male slaves (*ghilmān*), and eunuchs left him little time for public affairs.[38] The personal fortune of the caliph al-Mustaḍī (1170–1180), excluding precious articles and clothes, took 170 mules to carry.[39] The relatives of the caliph "were comfortably confined in sumptuous homes from which they were not allowed to emerge or make a public appearance, but they enjoyed handsome emoluments."[40]

Next to the caliph stood the sultans and vizirs, who sometimes surpassed him in extravagance and pomp. Ibn-Jubair tells of watching the military chief of the caliph an-Nāṣir (1180–1225) emerge from the palace, "surrounded by his Turkish and Dailamite officers and escorted by about fifty men with drawn swords."[41] The predatory behavior of vizirs, who usually amassed great personal fortunes, remained unchecked except by the occasional confiscation (*muṣādarah*) of their ill-gotten property by caliph or sultan. In fact, the *muṣādarah* became a common practice during the twelfth century.[42]

Next came the learned men (*al-ʿulamā'*) and religious leaders (*al-fuqahā'*) who enjoyed great repute and special privileges primarily because they were the servants of the state and the defenders of religious orthodoxy. From the late eleventh century, under the auspices of the great Selchükid vizir Niẓām-al-Mulk, their aid was enlisted in combatting the Shīʿite "heresy" and in providing the state with its much-needed corps of civil servants. They filled teaching posts in the various Niẓāmīyah schools and academies. These functions continued to attract men of learning during the twelfth century, especially because of the surge of Bāṭinite teachings and Ismāʿīlī propaganda.

The incursion of militant Christianity placed an added burden on these scholars. They had to combat not only Moslem heterodoxy but also Christian inroads, and to exhort the believers and arouse their zeal for the defense of the faith. Both the Zengids and the Aiyūbids leaned heavily on this class and exploited their talents in various activities. From their ranks came vizirs, judges,and lecturers in the new schools. Furthermore, the state often cultivated members of the class

---

38. Ibn-aṭ-Ṭiqṭaqâ, *Al-Fakhrī fī-l-ādāb as-sulṭānīyah* (Cairo, 1945), p. 276.
39. *Ibid.,* p. 269.
40. Ibn-Jubair, *Riḥlah,* p. 227.
41. *Ibid.*
42. Ibn-aṭ-Ṭiqṭaqâ, *Al-Fakhrī,* pp. 284–285, 287.

because of their inordinate influence on the populace. Even discerning individuals like Ibn-Jubair, who criticized the people of Baghdad for their hypocrisy and deceit, exempted from this harsh judgment "their religious leaders, who were versed in the science of tradition, and their preachers, who ceaselessly admonished their followers to do right. Indeed, in the pursuit of preaching and admonishing, in warning and reprimanding, in constantly forewarning and reproving, they have attained such high stations as would win for them enough of the mercy of God to decrease their burden of sin."[43] Nevertheless, it would seem that the ranks of the learned were not infrequently infiltrated by unscrupulous men who exploited their position for material gain, and made a mockery of their calling, transforming their religious circles into meetings for illicit revels and mirth by men and women, thereby making it necessary for the *muhtasib* to intervene and lay down rules for the profession of preaching.[44]

The general public, consisting of small merchants, artisans, farmers, peasants, nomads, and slaves, shared a common adversity. Oppressed by their rulers, exploited by the wealthy few, and impoverished by war levies and marauding soldiery, they developed an attitude of callous indifference and apathy to the vicissitudes of life. Their principal interest was to ward off hunger and to survive. They were suspicious of all outsiders, whom they cheated in business dealings, or fawned over in order to gull them whenever possible.[45] Nor were the beduins better than their urban neighbors. Their much-trumpeted pride was nothing but a myth. They might feed on carrion, and still brag that they were the noblest Arabs.[46] Slavery was rampant, and traffic in slaves and concubines was popular and profitable. To forestall possible abuse, the *muhtasib* was entrusted with the task of supervising the slave market and requiring slave merchants to adhere to a strict trade code.[47]

As usual, non-Moslems continued, for the most part, to occupy a peripheral place in Arab society, and formed a distinct social group which lived in its separate quarters (sing. *ḥārah*). They were governed through their religious leaders, who were responsible to the authorities for regulating the affairs of their followers, supervising their pious

43. Ibn-Jubair, *Riḥlah,* pp. 218–219.

44. Ibn-al-Ukhūwah, *Ma'ālim al-qurbah fī aḥkām al-ḥisbah,* ed. Reuben Levy (Cambridge, Eng., 1937), pp. 179–180.

45. Ibn-Jubair, *Riḥlah,* p. 218.

46. Usāmah Ibn-Munqidh, *Al-i'tibār,* p. 12.

47. Ash-Shaizarī, *Nihāyat ar-rutbah fī ṭalab al-ḥisbah* (Cairo, 1946), p. 107; Ibn-al-Ukhūwah, *Ma'ālim,* pp. 152–153.

foundations, and adjudicating their differences in all matters of personal status. The advent of the Franks led to the tightening of governmental supervision over these *dhimmī* communities, to forestall possible collaboration with the invaders; necessary powers to carry out this supervision were granted to the *muḥtasib*. Strangely enough, however, the twelfth century witnessed little increase in Moslem hostility toward native non-Moslems, partly because of Moslem preoccupation with the struggle against Bāṭinite and Ismāʿīlī activities. In spite of the state of war existing between Moslems and Franks, some friendly relations existed between them, especially between Moslems and those Franks who had spent some time in the east and had become "domesticated."[48]

Nevertheless, as time went on intolerance grew, and expressed itself in popular uprisings against the continued employment of *dhimmīs* in government offices.[49] In 1184 an-Nāṣir ordered all non-Moslem employees removed and forbade their future employment,[50] and in 1196, while in Damascus, the Aiyūbid al-ʿAzīz (1193–1198) decreed that no *dhimmī* should be given employment in the royal service, and required that they revert to wearing distinctive garments (*ghiyār*).[51] Though these laws were directed against all *dhimmīs,* Jews and Christians alike, the Christians bore the brunt of the discriminatory treatment. They constituted a greater danger than Jews, because of their larger numbers and their obvious sympathies with their coreligionists, the Franks, to whom they extended help whenever possible. This explains why the Aiyūbids, for example, made greater use of Jewish medical talent. Saladin himself was served by three Jewish physicians, Ibn-Jamīʿ al-Isrāʾīlī,[52] Ibn-al-Mudauwar,[53] and the great Maimonides.[54] Both Jews and Christians, however, continued to play an important role as merchants, money-changers and lenders, and jewelers. Both had to pay the poll-tax (*jizyah*), each adult male appearing in person before the officer in charge and paying the tribute in the manner mentioned in the Koran.[55]

48. Usāmah Ibn-Munqidh, *Al-iʿtibār,* p. 140.

49. Abū-l-Fidā', *Al-mukhtaṣar,* III, 12.

50. Sibṭ Ibn-al-Jauzī, *Mirʾāt az-zamān,* p. 378.

51. Distinctive dress which non-Moslem subjects were forced to wear. It was first imposed by the Umaiyad caliph ʿUmar II (717–720). Among the ʿAbbāsids, Hārūn ar-Rashīd was in 807 the first to reënact some of the old discriminatory measures, which reached their culmination under al-Mutawakkil (847–861): al-Maqrīzī, *As-sulūk li-maʿrifat duwal al-mulūk,* ed. Mustafa M. Ziada, I (Cairo, 1956), 136.

52. Ibn-abī-Uṣaibiʿah, *ʿUyūn,* II, 112–115.

53. *Ibid.,* p. 115.

54. *Ibid.,* pp. 117–118.

55. Sūrah IX:29.

It has already been suggested that Arab culture was a palace culture, flourishing under the patronage of caliph, sultan, or prince, its benefits rarely reaching beyond the confines of the royal or princely court. It should be added, too, that Arab culture has been, for the most part, a masculine culture, in which women played a very minor role. By the end of the tenth Christian century Arab women had lost the greater part of their freedom and dignity. Under the Buwaihids, the system of total segregation of the sexes and stringent seclusion of women had become general. Coupled with concubinage, moral laxity, and sensual indulgence, these practices had so undermined the position of women that they had come to be looked upon as the source of all base sentiments.

Conditions in the twelfth century brought no radical change, although several unusual cases command special notice: an old woman who drew a sword and joined the men in battle;[56] another who drowned herself in a river to avoid capture by the enemy;[57] still another who killed her own husband because he collaborated with the Franks;[58] and one from Shaizar who, single-handed, captured three Frankish warriors and led them home as prisoners of war.[59] These and similar exceptions elicited from the twelfth-century Arab-Syrian gentleman and warrior who recorded them in his memoirs the observation that "it is undeniable that noble women do possess pride, courage, and good judgment."[60] Otherwise, women seem to have excelled in palace intrigues and harem diplomacy, which were to reach their climax in the middle of the following century, when Shajar-ad-Durr, widow of the last Aiyūbid, aṣ-Ṣāliḥ Aiyūb (1240–1249), assumed sovereign power and for eighty days maintained her position as sole ruler of the entire kingdom, before being forced to marry the first Mamluk sultan, Aybeg (1250–1257). The fact that a few women distinguished themselves in the field of poetry, jurisprudence (*fiqh*), and tradition was the exception rather than the rule. Arab literature, too, continued to be a masculine literature, not usually suitable for mixed company.

In art and architecture, the twelfth century was no more than a continuation of the achievements of the Fāṭimid period in Egypt and those of the Selchükids in the Arab countries of western Asia. The return to the use of stone instead of brick in monumental structures belongs to the late Fāṭimid age, and the Zengids and Aiyūbids did

---

56. Usāmah Ibn-Munqidh, *Al-i'tibār*, p. 125.
57. *Ibid.*, p. 150.
58. *Ibid.*, pp. 127–128.
59. *Ibid.*, p. 129.
60. *Ibid.*, p. 125.

no more than perpetuate the restored tradition, adding to it what they had learned of military masonry from the Franks. This influence can be discerned in the citadel of Aleppo, restored by Nūr-ad-Dīn, and the citadel of Cairo, for which Saladin was responsible. The several crusader castles and churches which still dot the length of Syria from Mt. Casius in the north to Gaza in the south, such as the Krak des Chevaliers, Belfort, the church of Notre Dame at Tortosa, and the church of St. John (now the 'Umarī mosque) in Beirut, are all of Frankish workmanship and therefore cannot be described as part of the indigenous culture.

Under the Zengids and Aiyūbids, too, the achievements of the Fāṭimids and the Selchükids in decorative art and industry were continued and in some cases refined, as in wood-, ivory-, and bone-carving, metalwork, ceramics, glassware, stained glass, and enamel. Similarly, the arts of bookbinding and illumination received great impetus, and Arabic calligraphy was fast breaking away from the angular Kūfī in favor of the cursive *naskhī,* which was to reach its finest artistic development during the Mamluk period.

It is, however, in its intellectual life and activity that the real nature of Arab culture in the twelfth century is best revealed; there its main features are best portrayed, its special characteristics depicted, and its spirit and breadth reflected. It has already been mentioned that intellectual activity lacked the luster of earlier achievements, being more concerned with preserving a glorious heritage than with adding to it. There was no real sign of creativity. Causes for this are not far to seek: the community was on the defensive, especially against persistent Shī'ite assaults, which had already become serious enough in the eleventh century to demand special refutation by al-Ghazzālī (d. 1111), whose book *Al-Mustaẓhirī fī faḍā'iḥ al-Bāṭinīyah*[61] (On the shameful actions of the Bāṭinites) represents the classic Sunnite argument and position. It did little, however, to stem the Bāṭinite movement, the "new dispensation" of which was to be pushed forward with added vigor and violence by al-Ḥasan ibn-aṣ-Ṣabbāḥ (d. 1124) and his marauding followers, the Ismā'īlī Assassins, who terrorized the world of Islam for the greater part of the twelfth century.

The Moslem community was also on the defensive against the Franks and their church militant, not so much out of fear that Islam would lose some adherents to Christianity — actually there was little to fear in that respect — but rather because of a habit of thinking character-

---

61. Dedicated to and named after the reigning caliph al-Mustaẓhir (1094–1118); ed. Ignace Goldziher (Leyden, 1916).

istic of all Moslems, who, in accordance with the religio-political nature of Islam, were unwilling and unable to separate the spiritual
from the temporal, the sacred from the profane. Any setback to the
temporal fortunes of the community, therefore, was seen as a setback
to the spiritual fortunes of Islam. This had been true of Moslem thinking since the battle of Badr (624), in which the Prophet, with about
four hundred followers, had routed some four thousand Meccans and
inflicted on them heavy losses, which was interpreted as a divine sanction of the new faith.

In the eleventh century the Selchükids had rescued a dying state
and given it a new lease on life. But by the beginning of the twelfth
century the unity they had forged was already shattered. In spite of
the efforts of the Zengids and the first Aiyūbid, the community remained religiously divided and politically splintered. Not only did the
community have to face religious schism, but it also had the task of
delivering its holy places from "infidel" control and restoring Moslem
rule over enemy-occupied territory. The community was almost completely preoccupied with survival, politically, philosophically, and
religiously. The walls of Moslem orthodoxy had to be repaired and
reinforced. Conformity in thought, belief, and conduct to the exem-
plary lives of the righteous fathers (sing., *as-salaf aṣ-ṣāliḥ*) became
mandatory for all believers. Consequently, intellectual activity turned
from innovation to compilation, from speculation to systematization.
Except for al-Ghazzālī and Maimonides, the twelfth century produced
no first-class thinker, theologian, or philosopher.

Al-Ghazzālī set the pattern for the religious and philosophical activities of the century. He viewed with horror the unbridled speculations of both the Mu'tazilites and the Bāṭinites, disdained the intellectual prostitution and sophistry of scholastic theologians, and distrusted
the collective bent of popular thinking. He dedicated his life to the
task of refuting the first, castigating the second while debunking their
"concatenations of proofs and arguments," and shielding the third
from the snares of error by urging orthodoxy upon the people. He
attached to philosophers the stigma of infidelity, pronounced scholastic theologians two-faced fakers and their discipline of little value
in healing the malady of unbelief, and consigned the general public
to the fetters of conformity and the chains of authority.[62] More serious
still, al-Ghazzālī relegated reason to a limited role, asserting that its
function was "to bear witness to the trustworthiness of prophecy and

---

62. Al-Ghazzālī, *Al-munqidh min aḍ-ḍalāl* (Cairo, 1938), tr. Claude Field, *The Confessions
of Al-Ghazzali* (London, 1909); see also *Tahāfut al-falāsifah,* ed. Maurice Bouyges (Beirut, 1927).

to confess its own inability."[63] Similarly, "it does not point the way to that which is useful [or warn against] that which is harmful in words, works, ethics, and doctrines. It does not distinguish between the propitious and the baneful. . . . When it is, however, informed, it comprehends and believes."[64]

In spite of his importance, al-Ghazzālī should not be considered a philosopher but rather a student of philosophy who used his talents to destroy philosophy. His contribution was in the field of mysticism, which he grafted onto Islam, establishing its orthodoxy. Through it he vitalized the law by making personal religion and individual experience a part of Islam. His orthodoxy safeguarded the faith against unbridled emotionalism, and his writings led Moslems back from scholastic labors upon theological dogma and minutiae to a living contact with the Koran. He freed Islam from the dead formalism of scholastic literalism, and quickened it by the warmth of the living spirit. And it was exactly this warmth for which Islam was groping. Though cursed as a heretic in Baghdad, Damascus, Jerusalem, Cairo, and North Africa, al-Ghazzālī later became "the authority of Islam" (ḥujjat al-Islām).

His most popular, though not his most important, work was the Iḥyā' 'ulūm ad-dīn (The revival of the sciences of religion), in which he preserved a summation of medieval Moslem thought. For this reason the work occupies a unique position throughout the Moslem world. In the words of an-Nawawī (d. 1272), a famous thirteenth-century Moslem scholar, "Should all other Moslem writings be destroyed, the Iḥyā', if spared, would make up for all the loss."[65] Al-Ghazzālī set the pattern for the intellectual activities of the twelfth century: preservation rather than innovation, compilation rather than creation. This trend continued throughout the century, spreading to the various intellectual endeavors of the Arabs, and would reach its climax by the middle of the fourteenth century in the encyclopedic compilations of an-Nuwairī (d. 1332) and Ibn-Faḍl-Allāh al-'Umarī (d. 1349).

Maimonides (d. 1204) was, next to Averroës (Ibn-Rushd), the greatest philosopher of his time. Averroës belonged completely to western Islam, however, where he flourished and died (1198). Maimonides, though Jewish by faith, belonged to the Arab world of both the west and the east. He was born in Cordova in 1135. His family left the city after its conquest by the fanatical Muwaḥḥids (Almohads) in 1148,

---

63. Al-munqidh min aḍ-ḍalāl, p. 174.
64. Al-Ghazzālī, Al-iqtiṣād fī-l-i'tiqād (Cairo, A.H. 1327 [1909/10]), pp. 80–81.
65. See N. A. Faris, ed., The Arab Heritage (Princeton, 1946), pp. 142–158.

and for twelve years lived in various places in Spain. In 1160 the family settled in Fez, but was soon obliged to move eastward, arriving in 1165 in Cairo, where Maimonides spent the remaining thirty-nine years of his life, and where he wrote, in Arabic, all but one of his works. His intellectual endeavors, unlike those of al-Ghazzālī, were not directed toward either preserving medieval thought or refuting earlier philosophers, but rather toward reconciling Jewish theology with Moslem Aristotelianism, in other words faith with reason, which Averroës too had successfully undertaken on behalf of Islam. In this both were in line with earlier Arab philosophers such as al-Fārābī (d. 950) and Avicenna (Ibn-Sīnā, d. 1037), both of whom were pronounced heretical by al-Ghazzālī. In spite of the fact that Maimonides' concern was with Judaism rather than Islam, his place in Arab philosophical thought has remained secure, not only because he wrote in Arabic, but also because he was an heir to Arab philosophical thought, a product of Arab society, and a beneficiary of Arab patronage.

Between al-Ghazzālī and Maimonides no Arab philosopher of note can be cited, perhaps because the main concern of the century was not in speculation but rather in systematization, as evidenced in the works of Fakhr-ad-Dīn ar-Rāzī (d. 1209) and Najm-ad-Dīn an-Nasafī (d. 1142), whose 'Aqā'id (Articles of faith) became the most popular statement of the Moslem creed, the nearest thing to a Moslem catechism, forming the basis for innumerable commentaries and glosses. The trend toward systematization is further seen in the intellectual activities of ash-Shahrastānī (d. 1153), whose Kitāb al-milal w-an-Niḥal[66] (Book of religions and sects) presents a complete and detailed statement of the various philosophical opinions and religious sects, Moslem and non-Moslem alike. Two thirds of the work is devoted to non-Moslem sects. Though not the first work of its kind in Arabic, it is far more objective than that of Ibn-Ṭāhir al-Baghdādī (d. 1037),[67] though less so than that of the Cordovan scholar Ibn-Ḥazm (d. 1064).[68] The importance of ash-Shahrastānī's work, however, rests on its being, after that of Ibn-Ḥazm, the earliest attempt in any language in the field of the history of religion.[69]

With the community thrown on the defensive by pressures from within exerted by the Bāṭinites, and pressures from without exerted by the Franks, measures to organize the faithful in face of the grow-

---

66. Cairo, A.H. 1263, 1317–1320 (1847/8, 1899/1900–1902/3).
67. Al-farq bain al-firaq (Cairo, A.H. 1328 [1910/11]).
68. Al-faṣl fī-l-milal wa-l-ahwā' wa-n-niḥal (Cairo, A.H. 1317–1320 [1899/1900–1902/3]).
69. George Sarton, Introduction to the History of Science, II-1 (Baltimore, 1931), 249.

ing danger had to be taken not only in the field of religious thought but also in that of religious organization. Inspired partly by Christian monasticism and partly by the two great military religious orders of the crusades, the Templars and the Hospitallers, Islam, which had no priesthood and no monasticism, forged their counterparts in self-perpetuating corporations organized by prominent Ṣūfīs. The first fraternal order (*ṭarīqah*) to be established on a permanent basis was the Qādirīyah order, so named after its founder 'Abd-al-Qādir al-Gīlanī (1077–1166); the second was the Rifā'ī order, named after its founder, Aḥmad ar-Rifā'ī (d. 1183) of Baghdad. Both orders still exist and claim followers in all parts of the Moslem world.

"At the beginning of the twelfth century it was impossible to become a full-fledged mathematician and astronomer without a good knowledge of Arabic."[70] This, of course, refers to Arabic mathematical and astronomical achievement in the period which began about the middle of the tenth century and had ended by the middle of the eleventh. Although the intellectual activity which produced this rich heritage had continued unabated through the eleventh century, the Arabs seem to have reached the end of their effort by the beginning of the twelfth century. While Europeans were busy translating Arabic mathematical and astronomical works—people like Adelard of Bath, Robert of Chester, Michael Scot, John of Seville, Hugh of Santalla, and, most important of all, Gerard of Cremona—the Arabs themselves were content to rest on their oars. In fact, the Arab east in the twelfth century produced no first-class mathematician and astronomer except 'Umar al-Khaiyāmī (d. 1123/4), whose main contribution really belonged to the previous century, and whose death marked the end of the golden age of Arab scientific creativity.[71] Other mathematicians and astronomers, though often cited, were either compilers and redactors, depending on earlier Arab works, such as al-Kharaqī (d. 1138/1139),[72] who leaned heavily on Ibn-al-Haitham (d. about 1039),[73] or technicians skilled in the construction of astronomical instruments, such as al-Badī' al-Asṭurlābī (d. 1139/1140),[74] or mere summarizers who abridged earlier masterpieces, such as 'Abd-al-Malik ash-Shīrāzī (d. about 1203),[75] who wrote in Arabic a summary of the

70. *Ibid.*, II-1, 7.
71. *Ibid.*, I (Baltimore, 1927), 738.
72. *Ibid.*, II-1, 204–205.
73. Ibn-abī-Uṣaibi'ah, *'Uyūn*, II, 90–98.
74. Sarton, *op. cit.*, II-1, 204.
75. *Ibid.*, II-1, 296, 400–401.

treatise of Apollonius on conics, based on the ninth-century translation of the work by Thābit ibn-Qurrah (d. 901).

In physics and technology the twelfth century was not lacking in skill. Abū-l-Fatḥ 'Abd-ar-Raḥmān al-Khāzinī, who flourished during the first quarter of the century, was the author of the Sinjārī astronomical tables, which gave the positions of the stars for the year 1115–1116, and the latitude of the city of Merv. He also wrote a remarkable book on mechanics, hydrostatics, and physics, dealing with the specific gravities of many liquids and solids, leaning largely on the works of al-Bīrunī (d. 1048). He discussed the history of the theory of gravity, the universal force directed toward "the center of the universe," that is, the center of the earth, and made some observations on capillary attraction and on the use of an aerometer to measure densities and the temperature of liquids. He also discussed the theory of the lever and the application of the balance to leveling and to the measurement of time.[76] In these things, however, al-Khāzinī was drawing on earlier Arabic translations of some of the works of Pappos, a Greek mathematician who flourished in the latter part of the third and the early part of the fourth centuries.[77]

Another technician worthy of note, illustrating Arab interest in the construction of automata and other contrivances, is Muḥammad ibn-'Alī ibn-Rustam al-Khurāsānī as-Sā'ātī (d. about 1185),[78] who constructed an elaborate clock which was placed in the Bāb Jairūn of Damascus. Ibn-Jubair mentions seeing it in his Riḥlah.[79] Riḍwān, the son of Muḥammad, repaired and improved the clock, and in 1203 wrote a book to explain its construction and use. Next to the work of his contemporary al-Jazarī on mechanical contrivances (Al-ḥiyal al-handasīyah), Riḍwān's work is the most important source on early Arab clocks.[80]

In the field of alchemy, which might be called proto-chemistry, the Arabs of the twelfth century added nothing basic to their lore, but continued the tradition of Jābir ibn-Ḥaiyān (Geber) of the second half of the eighth century, and persisted in their quest for the two alchemical will-o'-the-wisps, the "philosopher's stone" by which base metals could be transmuted into gold or silver, and the "elixir of life" by which life could be indefinitely prolonged. The most important

76. Ibid., II-1, 216.
77. Cf. ibid., I, 337–338.
78. Ibid., II-1, 298; II-2 (Baltimore, 1931), 632.
79. Ibn-Jubair, Riḥlah, pp. 270–271.
80. Sarton, op. cit., II-2, 631–632.

figure in this field in the twelfth century was aṭ-Ṭughrā'ī,[81] who was put to death about 1121 on a charge of atheism.

Several factors spurred Arab interest in geography. There was the need of Moslem communities to determine the direction of the Ka'bah both for orienting mosques toward it and for the individual faithful to face it at the time of prayer; the interest in establishing correct latitudes and longitudes for astrological purposes and practice; the practical problems of pilgrims from the whole eastern hemisphere, traveling to Medina and Mecca; and the normal demands of commerce and trade by land and sea. Nevertheless, no important additions to geographical knowledge, descriptive or astronomical, were made during the twelfth century. The works of the literary geographers of the tenth century continued to embody the bulk of geographical knowledge at the disposal of the Arabs until the end of the first quarter of the thirteenth century, when Yāqūt (d. 1229) completed, in 1228, the final draft of his monumental geographical dictionary.

The advent of the crusades increased opportunities for travel, especially for the Christians of Europe. Like their Moslem adversaries they too had their Holy Land and holy cities, notably Jerusalem, Bethlehem, and Nazareth, pilgrimage to which, though not obligatory, was considered extremely meritorious. Inevitably, the appearance of crusaders and pilgrims among the peoples of the Arab east broadened the geographical horizons of the native inhabitants. But Arab interest in lands beyond the Dār al-Islām remained limited, and whatever contribution Arab geographers and travelers made during this period was almost exclusively the work of western Arabs, such as az-Zuhrī (flourished about 1140), al-Idrīsī (d. 1166), al-Māzinī (d. 1169/1170), and Ibn-Jubair (d. 1217). One should not, however, overlook 'Alī ibn-Abī-Bakr ibn-'Alī al-Harawī (d. 1215),[82] who wrote an excellent guidebook for pilgrims entitled *Kitāb al-ishārāt ilâ ma'rifat az-ziyārāt* (Instructions for the knowledge of places of pilgrimage),[83] which deals successively with Syria, Palestine, Egypt, the Byzantine empire, Iraq, India, the Arabian peninsula, the Maghrib, and Abyssinia. Except for the last two, the information he gives, though brief, is first-hand.[84]

---

81. Yāqūt, *Irshād al-arīb ilâ ma'rifat al-adīb* (Cairo, 1936), X, 58–79; Ibn-Khallikān, *Wafayāt*, I, 438–442.

82. *Ibid.*, III, 31–33.

83. Ed. Janine Sourdel-Thomine (Damascus, 1953).

84. Sarton, *op. cit.*, II-1, 413–414.

In natural history, Arab fondness for precious stones and interest in the occult qualities of minerals prompted the production of many lapidaries. Their scientists' best efforts, however, were devoted to the study of plants for medicinal purposes. Their interest in antidotes remained undiminished, and in this they were able to make a definite contribution to knowledge during the twelfth century. Ibn-Sarafiyūn (or Ibn-Sarābī),[85] who probably flourished during the first half of the twelfth century,[86] wrote *Kitāb al-adwiyah al-mufradah* (Book of simple drugs), which was based on Byzantine and Arab sources. Another who contributed in the field of antidotes was Ibn-at-Tilmīdh (d. 1165),[87] whose *Aqrābādhīn* (Book on simples) superseded earlier Arab works on the subject. In this field, too, as in astronomy, mathematics, and geography, the contribution of western Arabs was more considerable than that of their eastern brethren.

Commerce in precious stones, drugs, and perfumes gave rise to special works or handbooks to prevent frauds and to regulate transactions. These handbooks were sometimes specially written for the benefit of the *muhtasib,* the official in charge of the supervision of markets, in which case they might be loosely described as manuals for the bureau of standards. In fact, literature on rules to govern the regulation of market practices and public morals increased, probably because of the breakdown of public morals as a result of the political and social instability characterizing the century. To this category belongs the unusual work of Ja'far ibn-'Alī ad-Dimashqī, who flourished in the second half of the twelfth century, on commerce and trade, entitled *Al-ishārah ilâ mahāsin at-tijārah wa ma'rifat al-jaiyid al-a'rād wa radīhā wa ghushūsh al-mudallisīn fīhā* (On the benefit of commerce and on knowing the good and bad qualities [of wares] and the fraudulent practices of counterfeiters). The work, however, is more than a practical manual for market inspectors. It treats of other questions such as the true meaning of wealth (*haqīqat al-māl*), kinds of possessions, the origin of money, how to preserve goods, how to determine their average prices, and how to protect

85. He should not be confused with Yahyâ ibn-Sarāfiyūn, who flourished during the second half of the ninth century.

86. Ibn-Sarāfiyūn quotes Ibn-al-Wāfid, who flourished during the middle of the eleventh century, and is himself quoted by the Hispano-Arab herbalist Ibn-al-Baitār (d. 1248). Cf. Carl Brockelmann, *Geschichte der arabischen Litteratur,* Supplementband I (Leyden, 1937), p. 887 ("um 1070"); Sarton, *op. cit.,* II-1, 229. Arab biographies make no mention of this twelfth-century Ibn-Sarāfiyūn.

87. Ibn-abī-Usaibi'ah, '*Uyūn,* I, 259; Yāqūt, *Irshād,* XIX, 276–282; al-Qiftī, *Ta'rīkh al-hukamā',* ed. Julius Lippert (Leipzig, 1903), pp. 340–342.

property.[88] In this respect the work may be considered among the earliest Arabic treatises on economics, although it draws on the *'Ilm tadbīr al-manzil,* the Arabic version of a Greek work on domestic economy, ascribed to the Pythagorean Bryson.

Although the illustrious names of Arab medical lore belong to an earlier period, the Arabs of the twelfth century retained their interest in the art of medicine (*ṣanā'ah*) and maintained their superiority over others in its practice. This is well demonstrated by the contemporary reports of Usāmah Ibn-Munqidh, who devotes a number of pages in his memoirs to this subject.[89] Nevertheless, no great medical contribution was made during the century. Furthermore, while the art remained a near monopoly of *dhimmī* physicians, those who distinguished themselves in its practice were, for the most part, Jews. The Frankish-Moslem struggle was already bearing its poisonous fruits of fanaticism, which destroyed the confidence of the public in Christian practitioners and helped make Arab medicine, from the late twelfth century through the thirteenth, largely Jewish. With the exception of Ibn-at-Tilmidh,[90] who was a Christian, all the first-class physicians of the century were Jews: Ibn-Jamī' al-Isrā'īlī (d. 1193),[91] who served as a personal physician to Saladin; Ibn-al-Mudauwar (d. 1193),[92] who served both the last Fāṭimid caliph and then Saladin as court physician; Ibn-an-Nāqid (d. 1188/1189),[93] and abū-l-Ma'ālī ibn-Hibat-Allāh al-Yahūdī (d. 1222),[94] who served Saladin and later the fourth Aiyūbid sultan, al-'Ādil (1199–1218).

While these and many others of lesser stature made no significant contribution to Arab medical lore, as practitioners they observed high standards of ethics and skill. Furthermore, stringent rules governed the profession. No person was permitted to practise the "art" unless he was first licensed by a well-known authority. He also had to take the oath of Hippocrates, and to bind himself to pay the bloodwit of any patient who might die as a result of his treatment, if it were established that it was not in accordance with the best medical practice, or that he himself had been negligent in his care for the patient. He had to be well acquainted with the anatomy and the cardinal hu-

---

88. Sarton, *op. cit.,* II-1, 462–463; for analysis of the work see Hellmut Ritter, in *Der Islam,* VII (1917), 1–91.
89. Usāmah Ibn-Munqidh, *Al-i'tibār,* pp. 132–134, 137–138.
90. See above, p. 24.
91. Ibn-abī-Uṣaibi'ah, *'Uyūn,* II, 112.
92. Sarton, *op cit.,* II-1, 432.
93. Ibn-abī-Uṣaibi'ah, *'Uyūn,* II, 115–116.
94. *Ibid.,* p. 117.

mors of the body, and familiar with the various diseases to which man is susceptible and with the medicines which should be prescribed for each. Similar conditions were required of oculists (sing. *kaḥḥāl*), who were expected to know the treatise on ophthalmology *Al-'ashr maqālāt fī-l-'ain* (The ten treatises on the eye), commonly ascribed to Ḥunain ibn-Isḥāq (d. 873). Bone-setters were required to know the exact number of bones in the human body and the shape and form of each. Surgeons were expected to know Galen's works on anatomy and physiology and to be familiar with all the members of the body and all its veins, arteries, and sinews.[95]

The tradition of caring for the sick in hospitals supported by endowments, which goes back to the ninth century, was continued, especially by the two Zengids and Saladin.[96] Almost every large urban center, such as Baghdad, Aleppo, Damascus, Jerusalem, Alexandria, and Cairo, had its own hospital. Usually the building had two pavilions, one for men and one for women. One of the Cairo hospitals visited by Ibn-Jubair had a third pavilion for the insane.[97] Some of these hospitals functioned also as schools of medicine.

As the religious and political unity of the Islamic community had already been shattered long before the twelfth century, it was natural for Arab historiography to reflect this breakdown by becoming increasingly provincial, turning its attention to local and dynastic histories, biographies, and biographical dictionaries. This trend, which would increase during the thirteenth century and reach its greatest development in the fourteenth and fifteenth centuries, reflects not only the breakdown of the political unity of the Arab and Moslem world, but also an increased tendency to look backward as an escape from the painful realities of the present. Of particular interest among the historians who flourished during this period is ash-Shahrastānī (d. 1153), whose main contribution was in the field of the history of religion;[98] he also wrote a history of philosophers (*Ta'rīkh al-ḥukamā'*). Another author exemplifying the same trend is 'Abd-al-Karīm as-Sam'ānī (d. 1167), whose *Kitāb al-ansāb* (The book of genealogies) preserves a vast number of Arabic patronymics but is chiefly valuable for what it contains about the history and proper names of Persia, Transoxiana, and Central Asia, although it seems to depend very much on the narratives of the *Ta'rīkh Iṣbahān* of Ḥamzah al-Iṣfahānī (d.

---

95. Ibn-al-Ukhūwah, *Ma'ālim,* pp. 165–169.
96. See above, pp. 11–12.
97. Ibn-Jubair, *Riḥlah,* p. 51.
98. See above, p. 20; Ibn-Khallikān, *Wafayāt,* III, 403–404.

970), the *Ta'rīkh Nīsābūr* of al-Ḥakīm an-Nīsābūrī (d. 1014), and, in particular, the *Ta'rīkh Baghdād* of al-Khaṭīb al-Baghdādī (d. 1071). With as-Sam'ānī, the age of compilation began, an age which was to reach its fullest development in the fourteenth century in works like those of an-Nuwairī (d. 1332) and Ibn-Faḍl-Allāh al-'Umarī (d. 1349). While such works preserved the Arab cultural heritage and were therefore extremely valuable, they reveal little originality or creativity.

Another compiler reflecting the same trend is 'Alī ibn-Zaid al-Baihaqī (d. 1169),[99] who is chiefly known for his biographical dictionary, entitled *Ta'rīkh ḥukamā' al-Islām* (The history of the learned men of Islam), which was a supplement to an earlier biographical dictionary of learned men, the *Ṣiwān al-ḥikmah* of Muḥammad as-Sijistānī of the second half of the tenth century. Al-Baihaqī also wrote, in Persian, a history of his birthplace, Baihaq, which he completed a year before his death.

The shift in emphasis from general to local histories is likewise demonstrated by the work of 'Umārah ibn-'Alī al-Yamanī (d. 1174),[100] who wrote the *Ta'rīkh al-Yaman* (The history of Yemen).[101] For his part in a plot to restore the Fāṭimid imamate to power with the help of Amalric, the Frankish king of Jerusalem, 'Umārah was executed on the order of Saladin.

By far the greatest Arab historian in the twelfth century, however, was abū-l-Qāsim 'Alī ibn-al-Ḥasan Ibn-'Asākir (d. 1176),[102] whose *Ta'rīkh Dimashq* (The history of Damascus) was patterned after al-Khaṭīb al-Baghdādī's history of Baghdad. In eighty volumes, the work deals casually with the history of the city, but records the biographies of celebrated learned men who either were born in Damascus or spent part of their lives there. Though abridged later by various scholars, the work, of which a complete copy is preserved in the Ẓāhirīyah library in Damascus, has never been published. Ibn-'Asākir was so esteemed by his contemporaries that, on his death, Saladin himself attended his funeral.

The trend toward dynastic histories is represented by 'Imād-ad-Dīn al-Iṣfahānī (d. 1201).[103] Persian by birth, he studied in Baghdad and wrote his works in Arabic. His best-known historical contribution is the *Kitāb al-fatḥ al-qussī fī-l-fatḥ al-Qudsī* (The Qussian interpreta-

99. Yāqūt, *Irshād,* XIII, 219–240.
100. Ibn-Khallikān, *Wafayāt,* III, 107–111.
101. Ed. & tr. H. Cassels Kay (London, 1892).
102. Yāqūt, *Irshād,* XIII, 73–87; Ibn-Khallikān, *Wafayāt,* II, 471–473.
103. Yāqūt, *Irshād,* XIX, 11–28; Ibn-Khallikān, *Wafayāt,* IV, 233–238.

tion of the conquest of Jerusalem),[104] which is an account of Saladin's conquest of Syria and Palestine. He also wrote the *Nuṣrat al-fiṭrah wa 'uṣrat al-qaṭrah* (The victory of the true faith [of Islam] and the haven of the wayfarer), a history of the Selchükids and their viziers based on a Persian original by Sharaf-ad-Dīn Anūsharwān (d. 1137). Another of his works is a seven-volume history of his own times, including his autobiography, *Al-barq ash-sha'mī* (The Syrian lightning); only one of the seven volumes, dealing with the years 1182–1184, is now extant. Al-'Imād, as al-Iṣfahānī is commonly known, was a stylist of the first order, whose literary remains are esteemed by modern critics.

An exception to the general trend toward local and dynastic histories was the work of one of the most versatile and prolific authors in Islam, the renowned abū-l-Faraj 'Abd-ar-Raḥmān Ibn-al-Jauzī (d. 1201).[105] Though he wrote many works on diverse subjects, such as biography, tradition, jurisprudence, ethics, medicine, geography, and Koranic studies, his most important contribution was a history of the world from its creation to 1180, entitled *Al-kitāb al-muntaẓam wa multaqat al-multazam*[106] (The well-arranged book of selected essentials). In spite of its comprehensive scope it contributes little new to Arab historiography. It does, however, demonstrate that the community could still produce, in times of crisis and amidst the splinter movements afflicting it, a personality capable of transcending provincial barriers and of relating his subject to the general current of Arab and Moslem history.

Though he was not a historian in the strict sense of the word, mention should be made of Usāmah ibn-Murshid, better known as Usāmah Ibn-Munqidh (d. 1188), perhaps the first Arab to produce an autobiography. In his memoirs, entitled the *Kitāb al-i'tibār* (The book of example [and reflection]),[107] he has included the earliest Arabic treatise on falconry and the chase, of which he himself was a master. The book preserves eyewitness reports and observations on Fāṭimid Egypt and Zengid and Aiyūbid Syria, as well as many details about Moslem-Frankish relations during the second half of the twelfth century.

Mention should also be made of Bahā'-ad-Dīn Yūsuf ibn-Rafi' Ibn-Shaddād (d. 1234),[108] who had a distinguished career as a teacher

104. Ed. Carlo von Landberg (Leyden, 1888).
105. Ibn-Khallikān, *Wafayāt*, II, 323–324.
106. Vols. V-2, VI–X (no more published), Hyderabad, A.H. 1357–1362 [1938–1943].
107. Ed. Hitti (Princeton, 1930); tr. Hitti, *An Arab-Syrian Gentleman and Warrior in the Period of the Crusades* (CURC, 10; New York, 1929; repr. Beirut, 1964).
108. Ibn-Khallikān, *Wafayāt*, VI, 81–98.

at the Niẓāmīyah of Baghdad, as a military judge of Jerusalem under Saladin, and as the founder of two *madrasah*-type schools at Aleppo. As a historian he turned his attention to biography and local history, writing the life of his patron and hero Saladin, entitled *An-nawādir as-sultānīyah wa-l-mahāsin al-Yūsufīyah*[109] (The celebrated words of the sultan and his distinguished works), and the history of his adopted city, Aleppo.

In Arab historiography, Ibn-Shaddād belongs to both the twelfth and thirteenth centuries and exemplifies, perhaps more than any other, the main characteristics of Arab historiography during the period under consideration, with its emphasis not on universal or general but on local and dynastic history as well as on biography.

The twelfth century, unlike the eleventh, was strikingly poor in legal studies both quantitatively and qualitatively, and those few works which come down from the period were more concerned with practice than with theory. Here again the absence of creativity is conspicuous. The sterility of the century in this vital field is exemplified by what might be called reference manuals on the conduct of state and administration. One comes from the pen of Abū-Bakr Muḥammad ibn-al-Walīd aṭ-Ṭurṭūshī (d. 1131),[110] who was by birth an Andalusian from Tortosa and by education a Hispano-Arab educated in Saragossa and Seville. After performing the pilgrimage in 1083–1084 and traveling extensively in the Near East, he settled in Alexandria, where he died. While in Egypt he wrote the *Sirāj al-mulūk*[111] (The torch of kings), a guide to royal conduct, which he completed in 1122 at Fustat and dedicated to the Fāṭimid vizir al-Ma'mūn. Another comes from the pen of Muḥammad ibn-'Alī Ibn-ad-Dahhān (d. 1194),[112] who was born in Baghdad but whose career carried him also to Syria and Egypt. Being also an astronomer, he seems to have modeled his legal work on the popular astronomical tables and called it the *Taqwīm an-naẓar fī-l-masā'il al-khilāfīyah* (The legal tables on disputed problems). The tables, preceded by an introduction, contained ten columns which gave for each question the views of the four orthodox schools of Islamic law, the principles involved, and other observations. A third work, intended as a handbook for the benefit of market officers charged with the task of verifying weights and measures and testing wares and products, comes from the pen of 'Abd-ar-Raḥ-

109. Ed. Albert Schultens (Leyden, 1732, 1755); tr. Charles W. Wilson and Claude R. Conder, *The Life of Saladin by Behâ ed-Dîn* (*PPTS*, XIII; London, 1897).

110. Ibn-Khallikān, *Wafayāt*, III, 393–395.

111. Printed in Cairo, A.H. 1289 (1872/3).

112. Ibn-Khallikān, *Wafayāt*, IV, 105–106.

mān ibn-Naṣrallāh ash-Shīrāzī,[113] a contemporary of Saladin. The most interesting of this group of works, however, is that of Ja'far ibn-'Alī ad-Dimashqī, already mentioned under natural history and commercial activities in connection with precious stones.[114] In general the value of these works lies not in their contribution to the subject matter discussed but in the light they shed on the life of the times.

Language and literature have always occupied a preëminent place in the Arab mind and, together with calligraphy, have continued to be the main instrument of artistic expression. Arabic belles-lettres (*al-adab*), which began with al-Jāḥiz (d. 868/869) in the ninth century, reached its highest level of development in the twelfth. A trend away from the simple expression of earlier days and toward a more ornate one was already discernible in the late tenth and early eleventh centuries in such works as those of Abū-Bakr al-Khwārizmī (d. about 993) and Badī' az-Zamān al-Hamadhānī (d. 1008). It reached its full development during the twelfth century and became, next to the Koran, the norm for literary excellence for all succeeding generations; its elegant style, polished expression, elaborate similes, and rhymed couplets still captivate its Arab readers and listeners even today. The style pervaded all subsequent prose writing whether belles-lettres, governmental correspondence, or even historical writings, as the *Fath al-qussī* of 'Imād-ad-Dīn al-Iṣfahānī clearly reveals.[115]

The greatest of all Arab belles-lettrists was abū-Muḥammad al-Qāsim al-Ḥarīrī (d. 1122),[116] with whom the *Maqāmāt* (assemblies), initiated by al-Hamadhāni at the end of the tenth century, reached their fullest development. Fifty picaresque stories, recounting the adventures of an amiable rascal, provided the device through which the author exhibited his mastery of the Arabic language and displayed his sophisticated literary culture. Their profound influence on Arabic letters and thought has never diminished, and a literary revival in the nineteenth century was launched with an excellent imitation of their form and style by the shaikh Nāṣif al-Yāzijī (d. 1871).

Al-Ḥarīrī also wrote on grammar, treating in particular of linguistic mistakes which educated persons make in their writings. His work in this field was carried on by a younger contemporary, abū-Manṣūr Mauhūb ibn-Aḥmad Ibn-al-Jawālīqī (d. 1144),[117] who wrote on incorrect expressions current in the vernacular. Both men seem to have

---

113. Brockelmann, *op. cit.,* I (Leyden, 1943), 603 (no. 13).
114. See above, p. 24.
115. See above, note 104.
116. Yāqūt, *Irshād,* XVI, 261–293.
117. Ibn-Khallikān, *Wafayāt,* IV, 424–426; Yāqūt, *Irshād,* XIX, 205–207.

been increasingly aware of the dangers confronting Arabic as a result of the influx of foreign elements, particularly Turkish, which came with the Selchükids. Ibn-al-Jawālīqī also compiled a list of the foreign words introduced into the Arabic language.

The influx of foreign elements into the Arab world and the transfer of authority from Arab to non-Arab dynasts whose mother tongue was either Persian, like the Buwaihids, or Turkish, like the Selchükids, or Kurdish, like the Aiyūbids, had a depressing effect on Arabic poetry. These new overlords, as Ibn-'Unain remonstrated, were incapable of appreciating poetry.[118] Indeed, the twelfth century produced few first-class poets. But the trend, which seems to have started with the Buwaihids of the tenth century, encouraged the growth of a new class of prose writers, known as court secretaries (sing. *kātib*), who displaced the court poets, and whose services gave rise to a special type of court correspondence (*rasā'il*) which, according to a favorite Arabic saying, "began with 'Abd-al-Ḥamīd[119] and reached maturity with Ibn-al-'Amīd."[120] Its full development into a flowery branch of belles-lettres, however, came in the writings of al-Qāḍī al-Fāḍil (d. 1200),[121] the famous vizir of Saladin. These *rasā'il* are characterized by verbosity and profuseness, excessive quotations, lavish use of simile and metaphor, word-play, balanced rhymed phrases, unusual words, and grandiloquent expression. In the hands of a lesser master, the style was stilted and artificial, but in the hands of the Qāḍi al-Fāḍil, the execution has the touch of a consummate artist, and the result, though formal, is nevertheless pleasing. It won considerable following, and still enjoys an eminent place in Arabic letters as the Fāḍilī style. Its genius, however, remained confined to form: a sort of literary gymnastics, displaying skill and agility, but lacking in spirit and creativity. This type of development reflects the spirit of a civilization which has reached its limit and settled down to live on its intellectual capital.

Perhaps the best embodiment of this trend toward collection rather than invention is to be found in the works of abū-l-Faḍl al-Maidānī (d. 1124),[122] whose *Majma' al-amthāl*[123] (Collection of proverbs) re-

118. See above p. 5.
119. Died 750; secretary of the last Umaiyad caliph, Marwān II (744–750); see Ibn-Khallikān, *Wafayāt*, II, 394–397.
120. Vizir of the Buwaihid Rukn-ad-Daulah (932–976); see Ibn-Khallikān, *Wafayāt*, IV, 189–197.
121. *Ibid.*, II, 333–337.
122. *Ibid.*, I, 130–131.
123. Georg W. Freytag, ed. and tr. (into Latin), *Arabum proverbia* (4 vols. in 2, Bonn, 1838–1843), I, II.

mains one of the most delightful and useful anthologies of Arabic folklore and fables. A more profound contribution to Arabic letters in the twelfth century was made by abū-l-Qāsim Maḥmud ibn-'Umar az-Zamakhsharī (d. 1144).[124] A Persian by birth, he devoted his varied talents to the service of Arabic and Islam, defending both against the Arabophobes among his countrymen. In this respect, he represents a reaction against the Shu'ūbī movement, for which the disparagement of Arabic and Islam was the main pastime. In his attitude toward Arabic he stands in striking contrast to Firdausī (d. 1021), the Dante of the Persians. Both as a lexicographer and as a grammarian az-Zamakhsharī rendered a great service to his adopted language, but his greater contribution was made as a Mu'tazilite theologian and Koran commentator. In spite of his heterodox Mu'tazilite beliefs, his commentary on the Koran, entitled the *Kitāb al-kashshāf 'an ḥaqā'iq at-tanzīl* (The revealer of the truths of revelation), still commands respect and acceptance among Moslems. Through it and through the *Asās al-balāghah* (The foundation of eloquence), he sought to resolve the problems of the matchless and miraculous (*i'jāz*) nature of the Koran, which he believed, as a good Mu'tazilite, to be not eternal but created. Although his systematic method in dealing with the subject and his positive conclusions with regard to the matchlessness of the Koran have been accepted by Moslems, his premise that it was a created Koran has been rejected. Withal, he was the last great Mu'tazilite to leave an indelible mark on Koranic studies, and all systematic studies of this problem start with the standards which he set.

Arab intellectual activity during the twelfth century shows no decline in output and productivity. In volume, the results of the intellectual activity of the Arabs remained impressive, and a goodly portion of the Arabic library has come down to us from that period. In quality, the works are less impressive, and offer little originality. Except for this slackening of intellectual creativity there were no signs of real decay. Conflict and war seem to have acted as a stimulant. The Moslem-Christian confrontation gave a petrifying culture new vigor and postponed its final hardening. Heirs of a great heritage, the Arabs focused all their efforts on the task of preserving what they had, and paid little attention to the challenge of new ideas.

124. Ibn-Khallikān, *Wafayāt*, IV, 254–260.

II

THE IMPACT
OF THE CRUSADES
ON MOSLEM LANDS

Rich in picturesque episodes and dramatic events, the crusades were poor in the contribution they made to the edification or enlightenment of the area of their operation. The chain reaction of counter-crusades and of the anti-Christian and anti-western feeling they generated has not ceased. The festering sore they left refuses to heal, and scars on the face of the lands and on the souls of their inhabitants are still in evidence. As late as the twentieth century the anticrusading ghost was invoked in connection with the mandates imposed on Syria and Iraq and the Anglo-French attack on Egypt in 1956.

At the launching of the crusading movement the religious unity of Islam had already been shattered, and its political state was fragmented. The caliphate, which personified the double unity, was then itself triple. The Umaiyad caliphate of Cordova was a traditional enemy of its counterpart in Baghdad, and both were considered illegitimate by the Shī'ite imamate of Cairo. The Baghdad caliphate had been subordinated since 1055 to newly Islamized Selchükid (Seljuk) Turks, whose loosely united—if not utterly disjointed—states and statelets had mushroomed all over the area, extending into Byzantine Anatolia. Almost every sizable city in Syria had its own Selchükid or Arab ruler, often at odds one with the other. Hostility between Rĭdvan (1095–1113) in Aleppo, who had Ismā'īlite leanings, and his orthodox brother Dukak (1095–1104) in Damascus formed, together with battles against crusaders, the central theme of their reigns. Shaizar on the Orontes near Hamah was defended by the Sunnite Arab Banū-Munqidh. Tripoli was under the Shī'ite Arab Banū-'Ammār. The Byzantines were seizing and losing towns along the coast and on Syria's northern frontier. Jerusalem, the ultimate crusading goal, was being tossed from one hand to another: in 1070 the Selchükid general Atsĭz had wrested it from the Fāṭimids; in 1096 it had reverted to their control.

33

At the advent of the crusaders, therefore, not only was the unity of Islam fundamentally impaired but the possibility of its repair under Turkish or Arab aegis looked equally hopeless.[1] In fact, throughout its history, except for a short period under the Orthodox caliphs and another under the Umaiyads, Moslem unity was more nominal than real.

Into this semichaotic politico-military situation the crusading element was injected, and to it was owed the initial success, which constituted the bulk of the total success. One after another the states in the way of the crusaders were wiped off the map. First to fall (1097) was the most substantial and consolidated, that of Selchükid "Rūm," based on Nicaea. This victory restored to emperor Alexius I Comnenus (1081–1118) his lost province and delayed the Turkish — in the event, Ottoman — invasion of Europe for two and a half centuries. Next came Edessa (ar-Ruhā', Urfa), whose large Armenian population prompted a special detour. Unhesitatingly, Armenian Christians cast their lot with crusading Catholics. With them they shared common feelings of hostility to Turks and antipathy toward Byzantines. Edessa's ruler Ṭoros of the Ṛoupenid dynasty enthusiastically welcomed Baldwin (February 6, 1098) and formally declared him son and heir. A month later the adopted son replaced the father (d. 1098). Antioch's surrender three months later, through the treachery of an Armenian officer commanding one of its towers, ended a long and arduous siege. Tripoli's Arab governor Ibn-'Ammār bought off the invaders, and contacts were established between the Franks and the Maronites, who furnished guides and forces. No serious resistance was offered until Jerusalem was reached. The fall of the third-holiest city in Islam evoked no more than an expression of regret from al-Mustaẓhir, the caliph-defender of Islam at Baghdad. But in the words of a contemporary poet:

> Tears are the least effective of weapons,
> when swords illumine the fires of war.[2]

On Christmas day of 1100, count Baldwin of Edessa was crowned at Bethlehem as ruler of the Latin kingdom of Jerusalem. A few years thereafter Tripoli was captured by Raymond of Toulouse (d. 1105). With the creation of the kingdom, to which the county of Tripoli,

---

This chapter was edited by Harry W. Hazard, after the author's death.

1. For a different view see Steven Runciman, *A History of the Crusades* (3 vols., Cambridge, Eng., 1951–1954), III, 472–474.

2. Ibn-al-Athīr, *Al-kāmil fī-t-ta'rīkh,* ed. Carl J. Tornberg (14 vols., Leyden and Uppsala, 1851–1876), I, 194.

the principality of Antioch (including Cilicia), and the county of Edessa were loosely held by feudal bonds, the mission of the cross-wearers was fulfilled, all within the compass of a few short years.

As refugees from Palestine flocked into Baghdad, a group of Sūfīs, merchants, and *faqīhs* (canon lawyers) headed by a noble Hāshimite, forced the preacher in the grand mosque to descend from the pulpit, which they tore to pieces. At last the Arab caliph al-Mustaẓhir and the Selchükid sultan Berkyaruk bestirred themselves; they sent a token contingent.

Response to the challenge came from an unexpected quarter. It started with the son of a Turkish slave, Zengi, who from Mosul spread his domain through northern Syria and in 1144 took Edessa. The first to be lost, Edessa was the first to be regained. Its restoration marked the beginning of the end of the Latin states. With it the spirit of the holy war (*jihād*) shifted to the Moslem camp. It sparked a dormant pan-Islamic spirit which materialized in counter-crusades that continued until the last crusader was thrown out of the land.

Zengi ushered in a series of counter-crusader heroes which included his son Nūr-ad-Dīn and culminated in the Kurdish Ṣalāḥ-ad-Dīn (Saladin) and the Mamluk Baybars. Nūr-ad-Dīn's capture of Damascus in 1154 removed the last barrier between his expanding kingdom and that of the Latins in Jerusalem. Saladin managed to inherit the Nūrid territory and built on the foundation of a united Syrian monarchy laid by his two predecessors. By the conquest of Jerusalem in 1187, following the dramatic victory at Hattin, the watershed in the military history of the crusades was reached and the unification of all Syria was potentially assured. Saladin's destruction of the Shī'ite Fāṭimid imamate of Cairo in 1171 was more than the ending of a dynasty; it was the destruction of the possibility of the future development there of a dissident Moslem power. Saladin's sultanate now extended from Diyār-Bakr to Nubia and included Hejaz. Thus did the crusades unwittingly contribute to reversing the centrifugal forces in political Islam and to halting sectarian expansion in religious Islam. A devout Sunnite, Saladin suppressed heterodoxy, championed orthodoxy, and more than any other Moslem hero personified the counter-crusading pan-Islamic spirit. With him the disunity, incompetent leadership, and low morale which had characterized Islam at the end of the eleventh century completed the shift to the enemy's side.[3]

This achievement, which began with Zengi and culminated in Sala-

---

3. For more details on early Moslem reaction to the crusades consult Emmanuel Sivan, *L'Islam et la croisade* (Paris, 1968), pp. 28–35.

din, may be considered the first both in chronology and in significance of the positive effects of the crusades on Moslem lands. The liquidation of the Selchükid and petty Arab states was the first of the negative effects.

Baybars resumed with telling effect the devastating blows of his great predecessor, specializing in taking Templars' and Hospitallers' castles, the main strongholds of the crusaders. His seizure of Antioch in 1268 ended the career of the second-oldest, and at this time the strongest, of the Frankish states. Not much more was left than mopping up.

The military ventures which technically began with pope Urban II's speech in 1095 and ended with the fall of Acre to Mamluk armies in 1291 had antecedents which may be traced back through Byzantine, Roman, and Alexandrian periods to earlier wars with Persians in the fifth century before Christ. Their counter-crusading sequels extended for centuries.[4]

The reawakened, vitalized combatant spirit of Islam found expression in the literature of the age. The war from the west had been waged on both hot and cold levels and had to be met accordingly. Christian propaganda was met by Moslem counterpropaganda. True, *jihād* was a basic and favorite theme in Islam, approaching the status of a sixth pillar, but now, as it stood in confrontation with a Christian counterpart, it assumed new meaning and urgency. In the new literary genre not only was the military aspect emphasized but new merits (*fadā'il*) of the places held or menaced by foreign intruders were discovered, and the promised advantages of visits (*ziyārāt*) to them were multiplied. The holy pilgrimage (*hajj*) to Mecca had been established as a pillar of faith by the Koran, but the new literature contended that to perform a complete pilgrimage the faithful must include in their visitations not only the tomb of the Prophet at Medina but tombs of his companions who fell in battle and other prophets, mostly of biblical origin, mentioned in the Koran. As Moslems wrested from Franks cities with Islamic associations, veneration of those cities was intensified. The value of holy shrines was enhanced by their temporary loss and by the struggle for their restoration. The new literary output urged visits to such cities and shrines — promising all kinds of religious rewards — and provided the pilgrims with helpful information and polemical material. New treatises served as guidebooks

---

4. Aziz S. Atiya, *Crusade, Commerce and Culture* (Bloomington, Ind., 1962), pp. 146 ff., considers even the Ottoman Turkish invasion of Europe a counter-crusade.

and counter-crusade propaganda in which Jerusalem, the most cherished city after Mecca and Medina, of course figured prominently. A Baghdad historian, Ibn-al-Jauzī (d. 1201), wrote *Faḍā'il al-Quds* (The merits of Jerusalem),[5] which served as a model for other productions. A preacher in the Umaiyad mosque at Damascus, Ibn-al-Firkāḥ (d. 1329), assured his readers that the Prophet had declared that a believer's prayer in his own home is worth but one prayer, whereas if offered in the Aqṣâ mosque of Jerusalem it becomes worth fifty thousand prayers, the exact equivalent of a prayer at the mosque of Medina and exceeded only by a prayer in the mosque of Mecca.[6] Ibn-al-Firkāḥ wrote another treatise (unpublished) entitled *Al-i'lām fī faḍā'il ash-Shām* (Information about the merits of Syria). His example was followed by a Palestinian, Muḥammad ibn-Aḥmad ibn-Ḥāfiẓ al-Maqdisī, who in 1350 entitled his book *Muthīr al-gharām fī ziyārat al-Quds wa-sh-Shām* (Arousing love for visiting Jerusalem and Syria).[7]

In 1401 as-Su'ūdī wrote *Al-kawākib as-saiyārah fī tartīb az-ziyārah fī-l-qarāfatain al-kubrâ,* in which instructions for pilgrims to the venerated tombs in Cairo and a description of those tombs are given. Abū-l-Fidā' at-Tadmurī (d. 1429), a preacher in the mosque of Hebron, wrote *Muthīr al-gharām li-ziyārat al-Khalīl 'alaihi as-salām* (Arousing love to visit [Abraham] the friend [of God], peace be upon him), in which the readers were told that the Prophet had said, "Whoever cannot make pilgrimage unto me [in Medina] let him make it unto the tomb of Abraham al-Khalīl."[8] Moslem tradition locates the tomb in Hebron. This type of literature extended to the early sixteenth century, but its excessive veneration for shrines produced a theological reaction which was first vehemently voiced by a Damascene teacher, Ibn-Taimīyah (d. 1328). Four centuries later Ibn-Taimīyah's doctrines would germinate in the puritanical Wahhābī movement of Nejd.

One other noticeable effect of the crusades on the literature of the age is the widening of the authors' horizon. Hitherto eastern Moslems had known very little indeed about western Christians, the only contact having been limited to a few pilgrims and fewer merchants. To them practically all Europeans were Rūm ("Romans", Byzantines), with a few exceptions of Saqālibah (Slavs). Now, however, a new peo-

---

5. MS. in Princeton University library, tr. as a Ph.D. dissertation by Jibrā'īl Jabbūr, Princeton, 1947.

6. "Bā'ith an-nufūs ilâ ziyārat al-Quds al-mahrūs" (Arousing souls to visit Jerusalem the Guarded [by God]), in *Journal of the Palestine Oriental Society,* XV (1935), 58; tr. Charles D. Matthews, *Palestine — Mohammadan Holy Land* (New Haven, 1949), p. 10.

7. MS. in Princeton University library.

8. *Journal of the Palestine Oriental Society,* XVII (1937), 192–193; tr. Matthews, *op. cit.,* p. 118.

ple was discovered: Ifranj,[9] Franks, whose religious background and
military practices aroused Moslem interest.

Next to the political, the economic transformation was the most
pronounced and important effect on Moslem lands. The crusader impact had its negative economic effects in the form of destruction of
life and property, but, it should be remembered, the periods of peace
were of longer duration than those of war. Trade — at least in the case
of Genoese, Venetians, and Pisans, the shrewdest money-makers of
the age — was a primary motivation in the venture.

Hitherto trade had flowed mostly from east to west, but now there
was a strong reverse current, while the east-west stream was both enhanced and accelerated. The textile industry, as old as Phoenicia, the
trade in spices, which went back to Sabaean-Roman days, the export
of pottery and glassware from Sidon and Tyre, of drugs and perfume
from Damascus, wines from Gaza, and sugar from the maritime
plain — all these activities received fresh impetus as a result of opening new markets and widening old ones. Goldwork, ironwork, the
manufacture of swords, silk, and soap, and the weaving of rugs
flourished as never before. The incoming Europeans introduced no
new techniques in industry, but crusaders, pilgrims, businessmen, and
sailors returned to their homelands with newly acquired or developed
desires and tastes for semitropical oriental products. Fabrics such as
muslin (from Mosul), baldachin (from Baghdad), damask (from Damascus), sarcenet (from Saracen), and atlas (*aṭlas*) were increasingly
in demand. New tastes, acquired for attar (*'iṭr*), sugar (*sukkar*), gin-
ger (*zanjabīl*), and other aromatics, spices, and products of India and
Arabia, had to be satisfied on behalf of returning crusaders through
commercial channels. The Syrian merchant enlarged his traditional
function as the middleman between east and west, between Europe
on the one hand, and Arabia, India, and the Far East on the other,
for the route around the Cape of Good Hope was not yet known.
After Tyre, Acre, "the rendezvous of Moslem and Christian merchants
from the four quarters of the world,"[10] became a flourishing center
of maritime trade. From their Beirut warehouse (Ar. *funduq,* from
Gr.) Venetians lost in value in one day 10,000 dinars' worth of pepper,
a figure which gives an idea of the enormous riches accumulated in
the agencies or factories of the Levant.[11]

9. This term is still used in Arabic for Europeans, especially western, and Americans.
10. Ibn-Jubair, *Riḥlah,* ed. William Wright (E. J. W. Gibb Memorial Series, 5; London,
1852); revised by Martin J. de Goeje (Leyden, 1907), p. 303.
11. See Ṣāliḥ ibn-Yaḥyâ, *Ta'rīkh Bairūt,* ed. Louis Cheikho (Beirut, 1902), p. 62.

Woolen fabrics from England, Flanders, France, and Italy went first to Venice or some other Italian port and thence on galleys to Syrian and Egyptian ports.[12] Venetians in Syria exchanged western for eastern glassware; Genoese and Florentines carried on the same kind of trade. Besides wool, linen was a desired commodity. Linen from Rheims normally passed through Marseilles on its route eastward. Pisa, Genoa, and Venice had with their fleets assisted in the conquest of the land and in return enjoyed commercial and political privileges, including the occupation of special quarters in certain cities. There their merchant colonies grew. From Syrian ports, trade found its way into the interior, into Mesopotamia, Persia, and even Central Asia.

In Cairo merchants who imported western cloth occupied a special bazaar known after them by the name *sūq al-jauwākhīn*.[13] A kind of European cloak became so popular that the "Franks imported unlimited quantities of it".[14] *Al-bunduqī* (the Venetian), for cloth imported from Venice, became a familiar word in Arabic.[15] Mamluk soldiers wore *bunduqī* cloaks. The same term was also used for a sequin struck in Venice.[16] "Sequin" comes from Arabic *sikkah,* a die or stamp.

Brisk trading and manufacturing enabled Moslem merchants, especially in the interior cities, to amass huge fortunes. Ibn-Jubair, who visited Syria in the 1180's, cites the case of two such Damascene merchants.[17] He was impressed with the uninterrupted and unimpeded march of caravans between Egypt and Damascus through the "land of the Franks."[18] His and later evidence leaves no doubt that Aiyūbid Syria enjoyed a period of unusual prosperity. By that time the shock of the invasion had abated and the two sides had evidently adjusted themselves to the strange new life. One scholar goes so far as to say that the occupation of Syria revolutionized the entire economy of commerce in the Mediterranean, helped to raise the country to the international level, and bestowed on it a prosperity previously en-

---

12. Wilhelm Heyd, *Histoire du commerce du levant au moyen-âge,* tr. Furcy Raynaud, II (Leipzig, 1886; repr. Leipzig, 1936, Amsterdam, 1967), 706.

13. Al-Maqrīzī, *Al-khitat,* ed. Muḥammad Riyādah (2 vols., Cairo, A.H. 1270 [1853/4]), II, 98; cf. R. P. A. Dozy, *Dictionnaire détaillé des noms des vêtements chez les arabes* (Amsterdam, 1845), pp. 127–131.

14. Al-Maqrīzī, *loc. cit.*

15. *Idem, Histoire des sultans mamlouks,* tr. Étienne Quatremère (2 vols. in 4, Paris, 1837–1845), I-1, 252; II-1, 81, n. 88; Fakhr-ad-Dīn ar-Rāzī, "Ta'rīkh ad-duwal," in Silvestre de Sacy, ed., *Chrestomathie arabe* (Paris, 1826), I, 87.

16. Ibn-Taghrībirdī, *An-nujūm az-zāhirah fī mulūk Miṣr wa-l-Qāhirah,* ed. William Popper (Berkeley, 1920–1929), VI, 668.

17. *Op. cit.,* p. 308.

18. *Ibid.,* pp. 287–288, 298.

joyed only under the Romans.[19] Another, however, representing the
German school, dwells on the miseries of the natives—which they
no doubt suffered in the early stages—and claims that Moslem citizens were expelled or exterminated systematically, native Christians
were put to flight, and Palestine assumed a desolate aspect.[20]

To meet the financial needs of the new situation a larger supply
and a more rapid circulation of money became necessary. The *byzan-
tinus saracenatus,* probably the earliest gold coin struck by Latins,
was minted in the Holy Land and bore an Arabic inscription. The
Templars began to issue letters of credit and perform other banking
functions. In fact, all three military orders—Templars, Hospitallers,
and Teutonic Knights—which had started as charitable religious organizations and evolved into military institutions, gradually became
to a certain extent commercial companies. The earliest consul in history was a Genoese accredited to Acre in 1180. Saif-ad-Dīn (the sword
of religion, "Saphadin") al-ʿĀdil (1199–1218), younger brother and successor of Saladin, allowed the Venetians to establish markets with
inns in Alexandria and allowed the Pisans to institute consulates there.
Al-Kāmil (1218–1238) followed in the footsteps of his father and signed
a commercial treaty with Venice. Clearly occasional military clashes
did not prevent members of the Aiyūbid dynasty from inaugurating
a series of trade treaties with Christian countries.

Uncultured though they were, the Mamluk successors of the Aiyūbids
followed the precedent of enlightened foreign relations and extended
their economic horizon beyond the Italian cities. Kalavun (1279–1290)
signed trade treaties not only with the Genoese but also with Peter III,
the king of Aragon and Sicily. The monumental manual for the secretaries of the chancery completed by al-Qalqashandī in 1412 and titled
Subḥ al-aʿshâ has preserved numerous documents relating to European trade. Thanks to this commercial intercourse Syria and Egypt
maintained their positions as transit lands for the rich Indian trade
of the Italian republics and other European states. These treaties formed
the antecedent of the capitulations later granted by Ottoman sultans,
traces of which have lingered to the present day. It was largely from
the great revenues of this international trade that the Mamluks were
able to undertake their huge building projects, including mosques,
schools (*madrasahs*), and mausoleums that rival or excel those of any
other Arab era and still attract tourists to the valley of the Nile.

---

19. Henri Lammens, *La Syrie: Précis historique* (2 vols., Beirut, 1921), I, 235.
20. Hans Prutz, *Kulturgeschichte der Kreuzzüge* (Berlin, 1883; repr. Hildesheim, 1964), pp.
93, 95, 145.

Two common words in finance testify to this international trade relationship promoted by the crusades and continued in the post-crusading period. English "check" is related to Arabic ṣakk, which appears perhaps for the first time in a geography written about 975 by Ibn-Ḥauqal.[21] This Arab geographer states that in the Maghrib he saw an I.O.U. (ṣakk) for 42,000 dinars. An Arabic word still used for a unit of currency is ghirsh (colloquial, qirsh), originally from Latin grossus (thick), but borrowed from German Groschen through Turkish.[22] The coin was first struck in France by Louis IX, himself a crusader, in 1250. It had its first official mention in Turkish in a document of Bayazid I in 1392. A Danish traveler[23] found it current in Yemen. The term occurs in an Arabic report sent by an agent of France in Mocha (Mukhā) to Napoleon.[24]

For the lower strata of Moslem society the conquest probably meant little by way of direct economic change. To them it was an exchange of one set of rulers, the Selchükids, strange in race and language, or native emirs unconcerned with their subjects' welfare, for another set of rulers, Europeans, equally strange and unconcerned. Local sultans and emirs, whether Turks or Arabs, had previously accorded territorial concessions (iqṭāʿāt) to their lieutenants for services rendered by troops under them. The mass of people lived as serfs on those feudal lands. Their daily life now went on unaffected. In country places a clearcut differentiation in treatment between Frankish-held and native-held domains hardly existed; only cities were delimited and subjected to customs duty. The crusaders belonged mostly to urban, not farming, populations, and when they lost a city to Moslems, it was usually stipulated that they evacuate it. Traces of European feudalism, however, did linger in the land, as indicated by linguistic evidence. In his encyclopedic work the Egyptian an-Nuwairī (d. 1332) remarks that Syrian fief-holders used a word faṣl (vassal) of Frankish derivation. He coins a past participle from it (mafṣūlah), applying it to lands once held as fiefs, and uses rabb al-iqṭāʿ, an obvious translation of "feudal lord".[25]

Pilgrimage, whether Moslem, prompted by the new propaganda in the aftermath of the crusades, or Christian, stimulated by the Frankish possession of the land, contributed substantially to its econ-

21. *Al-masālik wa-l-mamālik,* ed. Martin J. de Goeje (Leyden, 1872), p. 42.
22. Cf. Prutz, *op. cit.,* p. 402.
23. Carsten Niebuhr, *Description de l'Arabie* (Copenhagen, 1773), p. 191.
24. De Sacy, *op. cit.,* III, 353–354.
25. An-Nuwairī, *Nihāyat al-ʿArab fī funūn al-adab,* VIII (Cairo, 1931), 261, 260, 201.

omy. From the dawn of the Christian era there were those who felt the urge to set foot on the soil rendered hallowed by the steps of Jesus, but the practice did not develop into an institution until the mid-fourth century, after Constantine I and his mother, Helena, had marked the sacred sites with monuments and basilicas. It was then that the cult of the holy places was firmly established. The influence of St. Jerome and the rise of asceticism in the east increased interest in the pilgrimage. The eastward march of the pilgrims' caravan was hampered in the mid-seventh century, on the morrow of the conquest of Islam, but not stopped. Intensified in the days of Charlemagne, who in 800 received a delegation from George, the patriarch of Jerusalem, and the keys of the church of the Holy Sepulcher from caliph Hārūn ar-Rashīd, the practice was again checked when the Selchükids lorded it over Anatolia and northern Syria. The disabilities imposed on pilgrims by the Turks and the destruction of the church of the Holy Sepulcher in 1009 by the Fāṭimid imam al-Ḥakim (996–1021) were among the contributory causes of the crusades. What pope Urban had in mind, as he preached the first crusade at Clermont, was not a purely military expedition but a combination of pilgrimage and holy war.

With the establishment of the Latin kingdom of Jerusalem and the two principalities of Antioch and Tripoli, the cause of the pilgrimage was naturally greatly promoted and improved. Once in Palestine, the pilgrim felt Lebanon with its cedars, Damascus of Paul, and Antioch of Peter beckoning to him. Of the native shrines, Notre Dame de Sardenay (Ṣaidnāyā),[26] north of Damascus, and St. Catherine of Sinai were special objects of pilgrimage. The image of Notre Dame was said to sweat oil that had healing properties; the account of its miraculous sweating lingered for centuries. Bertrandon of La Broquière, who was shown the image and told the story in 1432, thought "it was a mere trick to get money."[27] Not only the Christians but "the Saracens" were said to be utterly devoted to this Mary.[28]

The church of St. Catherine was built in the days of Justinian I (527–565) but often altered since. No priest or layman could enter it except barefoot, as in the case of mosques. In fact this saint attracted Moslem visitors also. Then there was Notre Dame of Tortosa (Anṭarṭūs, modern Ṭarṭūs), whose cathedral is the best-preserved religious structure of the crusades. This Mary, too, achieved so many

26. On the name, consult Ḥabīb Zaiyāt, *Khabāyā az-zawāyā min ta'rīkh Ṣaidnāyā* (Ḥarīṣā, 1932), pp. 12–15.
27. "Travels," in *Early Travels in Palestine,* ed. and tr. Thomas Wright (London, 1848), p. 306.
28. James of Vitry, *Histoire des croisades,* ed. F. P. G. Guizot (Paris, 1825), p. 318.

healings that, we are told, even Saracens took their children there in great numbers to receive baptism.[29] Pilgrims who reached Antioch were often tempted to pay homage to St. Simeon Stylites, who for thirty years before his death in 459 had chosen to make his domicile atop a high pillar. The ruins of the church which was built there stand today among the most monumental of the early Christian structures. Pilgrims included prelates, priests, and laymen. Some brought guides with them from the Syrian colony in Gaul, whose origins go back to Merovingian days. Some of the pilgrims settled in the land.

The remains of churches rising in cities along the coast and of castles crowning Lebanese hills form the most conspicuous of crusader relics in Syria. The first church to be built was St. Paul of Tarsus, finished before 1102 in the Romanesque style of northern France. Later (1149) the church of the Holy Sepulcher in Jerusalem was restored in the same style, after its destruction by lightning. Many churches have since been converted into mosques. The church of Sidon, built by Hospitallers, is now al-Jāmiʻ al-Kabīr (the great mosque); that of St. John of Beirut, erected by Baldwin I in 1110, is today al-Jāmiʻ al-ʻUmarī (mosque of ʻUmar). Belmont, built south of Tripoli by Frankish monks in 1157, is at present Dair al-Balamand, a Greek Orthodox monastery and seminary. Its chapel is genuinely crusader, and its belfry the only one of its kind in Lebanon. The cathedral of Notre Dame of Tortosa, the most magnificent of all, was recently equipped with a minaret. A doorway taken from the church of Acre and incorporated in the mosque of an-Nāṣir in Cairo is the most artistic relic of those days. The extensive alterations made by crusaders in the church of the Holy Sepulcher are still traceable.

Of the castles, Ḥiṣn al-Akrād (Krak des Chevaliers) stands out as the best preserved of all medieval structures of its kind. Until a few years ago it housed an entire Moslem village. Al-Marqab (watchtower, Margat) still looks like a dreadnought perched on a crest overlooking the Mediterranean and the road between Tripoli and Latakia (Laodicea). Qalʻat ash-Shaqīf (Shaqīf Arnūn, Belfort) rises above the pass along the Litani (Leontes), linking the maritime plain between Sidon and Tyre with the inland plateau.

Many of the crusader cathedrals and castles stood on the sites of earlier Christian churches and Moslem fortresses respectively. Ḥiṣn al-Akrād perpetuates in its name the memory of a Kurdish garrison which was housed therein in precrusading days. "Krak" in its name (originally Crat) is a corruption of *Akrād* (Kurds, colloquial *Krād*)

29. *Ibid.,* p. 82.

and should be distinguished from its analogue in Krak de Montréal and Krak des Moabites (Kerak, al-Karak). This "krak" is a corruption of *karak,* originally Aramaic for town. Such Arabic words as *qaṣr* (citadel, palace, from L. *castrum*), *burj* (tower, from *burgus*) and *qasṭal* (castle, water pipe, from *castellum*), said to have been introduced into the language in this period,[30] were rather popularized now but had been introduced earlier, in the Byzantine-Roman age, into Aramaic, whence they were borrowed by Arabic. Al-Qasṭal, as the designation of a fortress in Transjordan, was used by a Moslem historian who died about 965 and who ascribes the structure to a Ghassānid prince of the mid-sixth century.[31]

Crusaders from Normandy and Italy brought with them a substantial knowledge of military masonry, but what underlay the military crusading architecture was mainly the Byzantine art of fortification, with which Arabs were already familiar. Such castles as Shaizar on the Orontes, which was defended by the family of Usāmah Ibn-Munqidh,[32] and Maṣyāf and al-Qadmūs in the Nuṣairīyah ('Alawite) region, which were occupied by the Assassins, antedate the crusades. The architecture of the citadel of Cairo, the greatest architectural monument of Saladin, betrays crusading influence. The church bell and its tower were evidently introduced into the Near East at this time from the west. Previously Near Eastern churches had used only the gong. But on the whole, in architecture as in other fields, the crusaders borrowed more than they lent.

In the minor as in the fine arts, the easterners possessed an older, richer, and more highly developed tradition, placing the westerners almost entirely on the receiving end. Likewise in science, letters, and other purely intellectual achievements the Arabs had more to give than to receive, especially since soldiers and merchants formed the bulk of the colonists. When two differing cultures stand in confrontation, the normal flow is from the higher to the lower, and this case was no exception.

In his delightfully entertaining memoirs Usāmah (d. 1188) presents the most elaborate details about contemporary social intercourse between Moslems and Franks. A warrior, hunter, gentleman, poet, and

---

30. Cf. Prutz, *op. cit.,* p. 401.

31. Ḥamzah al-Iṣfahānī, *Ta'rīkh sinī mulūk al-arḍ wa-l-anbiyā',* ed. I. M. E. Gottwaldt (Leipzig, 1848), p. 117.

32. Consult Usāmah Ibn-Munqidh, *Kitāb al-i'tibār,* ed. Philip K. Hitti (Princeton, 1930), pp. iv-vi; tr. Hitti, *An Arab-Syrian Gentleman and Warrior in the Period of the Crusades (CURC,* 10; New York, 1929; repr. Beirut, 1964), pp. 4–6.

man of letters, he defended his picturesque castle, Shaizar on the Orontes, in times of war and fraternized with the Franks in times of peace. In and around Hamah (Epiphania), in Ascalon ('Asqalān) and other Palestinian towns, in Sinai and Egypt, in Mosul and other places of Mesopotamia, he witnessed or took part in battles against Franks and Arabs, Christians and Moslems. The information he offers is often first-hand, candid, and unique. His appraisal of Frankish character no doubt reflects the then-prevailing Moslem public opinion. To him "the Franks are void of all zeal and jealousy" in sex affairs;[33] their methods of ordeal by water and duel are far inferior to the Moslem judicial procedure;[34] their system of medication appears odd and primitive when compared with the more highly developed system of the Arabs.[35] Usāmah credits them with possessing "the virtues of courage and fighting, but nothing else."[36] Again and again Usāmah draws the distinction between the outlandish, rude "recent comers" and the "acclimatized" Franks in Moslem lands.[37] One knight was on such intimate terms of friendship with Usāmah that he began to address him as "my brother."[38]

Many crusaders must have realized that baggy clothes and heavy headgear were preferable in a warm climate, and they consequently adopted native dress.[39] Their preference for native dishes is also attested. A Frank in Antioch who shunned European dishes employed an Egyptian cook, and never had pork in his kitchen,[40] but we know of no cases of Arabs adopting European clothes or preferring western food. For one thing, Islamic dietary laws involving pork and the manner of slaughter would stand in the way. Nor do we know by name any Moslem attracted by a visit to Europe. When the knight who called Usāmah "brother" asked Usāmah to permit his fourteen-year-old son to accompany the knight to Europe, Usāmah felt as if there fell upon his ears words which would never come out of the mouth of a sensible man.[41] Nevertheless, he apologetically told his friend that the only reason for rejecting the request was the unusual attachment of the grandmother to her grandson.

---

33. *I'tibār*, p. 135; *Arab-Syrian Gentleman*, p. 164.

34. *I'tibār*, pp. 138–139; *Arab-Syrian Gentleman*, pp. 167–168.

35. *I'tibār*, pp. 132 ff.; *Arab-Syrian Gentleman*, pp. 162 ff.

36. *I'tibār*, p. 132; *Arab-Syrian Gentleman*, p. 161.

37. *I'tibār*, pp. 134–135, 140–141; *Arab-Syrian Gentleman*, pp. 163–164, 169–170.

38. *I'tibār*, p. 132; *Arab-Syrian Gentleman*, p. 161.

39. Emmanuel G. Rey, *Les Colonies franques de Syrie* (Paris, 1883), pp. 11 ff.; Gustave Schlumberger, *Numismatique de l'Orient latin* (Paris, 1878; repr. Graz, 1954), p. 45.

40. Usāmah, *I'tibār*, pp. 140–141; *Arab-Syrian Gentleman*, pp. 169–170.

41. *I'tibār*, p. 132; *Arab-Syrian Gentleman*, p. 161.

Physicians served at times to bridge the social gap between the two peoples. Some of these were native Christian doctors, as in the case of one Thābit, of whom an anecdote is charmingly told by Usāmah.[42] So impressed was king Amalric, when on a visit to Egypt, by the skill of an Arab physician, abū-Sulaimān ibn-abī-Fānah, that he offered him through the reigning caliph the position of court physician and took him back with his five children to Jerusalem.[43] But when the "king of the Franks in Ascalon" sought the services of a physician from the Egyptian court, and Maimonides was offered the position, he flatly refused.[44] It was a Saracen who cured John of Joinville (d. 1319) of a malady contracted while captive in Egypt.[45]

Knighthood was another social link. It is reported that early in his career Saladin was consecrated knight by the lord of Krak de Montréal (ash-Shaubak).[46] His nephew al-Kāmil was knighted with full ceremony by Richard the Lion-Hearted. It is probable that more than one emir sought the privilege. The order of *futūwah,* through which Islamic chivalry antedated in its origin the crusades, was reformed and patronized by the 'Abbāsid caliph an-Nāṣir (d. 1225), who might have been impressed by reports about Templars and Hospitallers. The caliph granted the hereditary rank of *futūwah* to various persons and elaborated the ceremonies of initiation, which included wearing spread trousers (*sarāwīl* or *libās al-futūwah*)[47] and drinking the *fityān's* cup (*ka's al-fityān*). The catechisms of initiation show degrees of *futūwah* which roughly correspond to degrees of European chivalry. The *futūwah,* however, was and remained a Moslem institution with a deeply rooted religious basis, and it participated in the character of the guild, whereas European chivalry was based on a regulated system of land grants.

Intermarriage is a fair criterion of social equality and relationship, but such marriages were contracted mostly between European men and native, generally Christian, women. Baldwin I set an early example by marrying (1098) an Armenian princess, Arda. Armenian princesses figured in the courts of Antioch and Jerusalem.[48] One of these,

42. *I'tibār,* pp. 132–133; *Arab-Syrian Gentleman,* p. 162.

43. Ibn-abī-Uṣaibi'ah, *Uyūn al-anbā' fī ṭabaqāt al-aṭibbā',* ed. August Müller (Königsberg, 1882), II, 121.

44. Al-Qifṭī, *Ta'rīkh al-ḥukamā',* ed. Julius Lippert (Leipzig, 1903), p. 318.

45. *Histoire de St. Louis,* ed. Natalis de Wailly (Paris, 1868), cap. 324 (p. 176).

46. Ernoul and Bernard le Trésorier, *Chronique,* ed. Louis de Mas Latrie (Paris, 1871), pp. 35–36.

47. Ibn-al-Athīr, *op. cit.,* XII, 268; Ibn-aṭ-Ṭiqṭaqâ, *Al-Fakhrī,* ed. Wilhelm Ahlwardt (Paris, 1860), p. 370; Ibn-Jubair, *op. cit.,* p. 280.

48. William of Tyre, *A History of Deeds Done beyond the Sea,* tr. Emily A. Babcock and August C. Krey (*CURC,* 35; 2 vols., New York, 1943), I, 415–416, 461.

Isabel (Zabēl), daughter of the last Ṛoupenid prince Leon II, married the Latin Philip of Antioch, who in 1222 was elevated to the Armenian throne on condition that he accept the Armenian faith. Especially in the principalities of Antioch and Edessa mixed marriages were numerous. Richard the Lion-Hearted proposed a marriage between his sister Joan and Saladin's brother al-ʿĀdil with the hope that the wedlock might contribute to ending the strife between east and west. The half-caste progeny of native mothers, designated *poulains* (young ones), lived mostly in cities, jealously secluded their wives, and often followed the mothers' religion rather than the fathers'.[49] Moslems on rare occasions married Christian wives but often used female captives as concubines. Usāmah's father, Murshid (d. 1137), once presented a friend of his, the lord of Qalʿat Jaʿbar, with a beautiful captive maid. The son of this union succeeded his father, but the mother ran away and married a Frankish shoemaker.[50]

After the annihilation of the crusading power in Syria, some families no doubt settled in the land and were ultimately fully assimilated. Names and traditions of certain Christian families — such as Ṣalībī (crusader) and Faranjīyah — suggest European origin.[51] Among place names Ṣanjīl (or Ṣinjīl, Saint Gilles), ar-Rainah (Reynaud), both in Palestine, and Sabkhat Bardawīl (Baldwin) in Sinai perpetuate Frankish names.

Two serious barriers to social intercourse and cultural cross-fertilization were, and remained, language and religion. We know of several crusaders' studying and mastering the Arabic tongue but we know of no Syrian or Egyptian Moslem by name who controlled Latin or French. For one who spoke the "tongue of the Angels," studying such a foreign language was not only useless but sheer condescension. Some native Christians, especially among the clergy and merchant class, were no doubt versed in European tongues. Bar Hebraeus (d. 1286) mentions a Jacobite physician from Antioch who mastered Latin, migrated to Europe, and settled in the court of Frederick II, but later became so homesick that he fled on a ship bound for Acre.[52] A number of Syrian-born Europeans, such as William of Tyre and William of Tripoli, knew not only the colloquial but the classical Arabic, too. In their writings they used Arabic historical and literary works. A Pisan named Stephen translated in Antioch (1127) ʿAlī ibn-al-ʿAbbās

49. James of Vitry, *op. cit.,* pp. 137–138; see below, chapter IV, note 1.

50. Usāmah, *Iʿtibār,* p. 130; *Arab-Syrian Gentleman,* pp. 159–160. The lord was Mālik ibn-Sālim, the son Badrān.

51. Hitti, *Lebanon in History,* 2nd ed. (New York and London, 1962), p. 319.

52. *Mukhtaṣar ad-duwal,* ed. Anṭūn Ṣāliḥānī (Beirut, 1890), pp. 477–478.

("Haly Abbas", d. 994) al-Majūsī's *Al-kitāb al-malakī* (The royal treatise) into Latin. This medical work was the only known major scientific text rendered into a western tongue throughout the crusading period. Masters of the Templars and Hospitallers, high officials in the courts of Jerusalem, Tripoli, and Antioch, and envoys to native rulers could communicate in Arabic. Reginald of Châtillon, lord of Kerak (d. 1187), who audaciously made an attempt on Mecca and Medina, was especially facile in the use of Arabic. Saladin's biographer reports a visit to the sultan by Reginald Grenier, the lord of Belfort, "who knew Arabic and was able to speak it; he also possessed some knowledge of history."[53] Joinville singles out certain compatriots who could express themselves in Arabic.[54]

Certain Moslems, no doubt, made it a point to acquire control over the French tongue. This was especially true of the Assassins, dissident Moslems, who entertained friendly relations with the Franks and at times allied themselves with them. When Saladin was pressing the siege against Acre he received from the Old Man of the Mountain, Rāshid-ad-Dīn Sīnān (d. 1193), two messengers who spoke "Frankish" (*faranjī*) and offered their services to kill the king of the Franks.[55] But when Louis IX in Acre received a friendly delegation from the Old Man, two knights served as interpreters.[56] We know of no Latin or French work rendered into Arabic at this time.

About 1172 Sīnān had sent an envoy named abū-'Abd-Allāh to Amalric to negotiate the possibility of conversion to Christianity on the part of his Assassins in consideration of the remittance of the 2,000-gold-piece annual tribute which the Assassins were then paying the Templars. As ultra-Shī'ites, Assassins could practice dissimulation in religion. The king agreed, but the envoy was killed by the knights after passing Tripoli on his way back.[57] The ranks of both religious camps were recruited from slaves and prisoners of war who found it to their advantage to be converted. Among the Frankish captives who fell into the hands of Usāmah's father was a lad with his mother and sister. The youth accepted Islam, was offered a home and a wife by his master, and produced two sons. When they were about six years old the father took them with their mother and the

53. Bahā'-ad-Dīn, *Sīrat Ṣalāḥ-ad-Dīn* (Cairo, A.H. 1317 [1899/1900]), p. 80; tr. Charles W. Wilson and Claude R. Conder, *The Life of Saladin by Behâ ed-Dîn* (PPTS, XIII; London, 1897), p. 142.
54. *Op. cit.,* caps. 354, 361, 444 (pp. 192, 196, 242).
55. Stanislas Guyard, "Un Grand Maître des assassins," *Journal asiatique,* 7th ser., IX (1877), 408–411, 463–466.
56. John of Joinville, *op. cit.,* cap. 454 (p. 248).
57. William of Tyre, tr. Babcock and Krey, II, 392.

furniture of the house and joined the Franks in Apamea (Afāmiyah), where they all reverted to Christianity.[58] Joinville relates the story of a knight from Provins who embraced Islam and established himself in Egypt.[59] *The Arabian Nights* (no. 895–896) tells the story of a Frankish woman captive of Acre bought by an Upper Egyptian linen merchant; a ransom was later offered to secure her return to her knight husband, which she spurned. A Mamluk sultan, Lājīn (1296–1298), is said to have been originally a Teutonic Knight who fought in Syria. James of Vitry (d. 1240) reports some Saracens who took refuge in the grace of the baptism of Jesus Christ.[60] But such cases were undoubtedly sporadic. On the whole, it may be assumed that the typical attitude of the Moslems was that expressed by Usāmah when a Frank in Jerusalem exhibited a picture of Mary with Jesus and offered to show Usāmah "God as a child" and Usāmah remarked: "God is exalted far above what the infidels say about him!"[61]

The Christian military venture left Islam more militant, less tolerant, and more self-centered. In its formative stage Islamic culture enthusiastically entered upon the Greek heritage through the intermediacy of Syrian (Syriac-speaking) Christians. But the lowering of the crusading curtain shut it off entirely from that source. The venture created another barrier between Moslems and their Christian countrymen. The alienation between the two societies has lingered to the present.

But whereas Islam can show some items on the credit side of the balance sheet, eastern Christianity has hardly any to show. Its followers, upholders of a tradition more venerable than that of Rome or Byzantium, entrepreneurs of classical science and philosophies, liaison officers between east and west, were by the end of the crusading period weakened to the point of impotence. The enterprise which had its inception in the urge to defend Christendom came near to destroying Christendom's eastern wing.

We have thus far treated the area as a Moslem land with a Christian minority. But in Syria-Lebanon-Palestine the Christian minorities in total must have amounted to a majority at the dawn of the crusades, though not a united one.[62] In the aftermath of the crusades they

---

58. Usāmah, *I'tibār*, pp. 130–131; *Arab-Syrian Gentleman*, p. 160.

59. *Op. cit.*, caps. 395–396 (pp. 214–216).

60. *Op. cit.*, p. 31.

61. *I'tibār*, p. 135; *Arab-Syrian Gentleman*, p. 164.

62. Consult Claude Cahen, *La Syrie du nord à l'époque des croisades et la principauté franque d'Antioche* (IFD, BO, I; Paris, 1940), pp. 190–191.

dwindled into an insignificant minority. Especially strong were the Armenian and Greek Orthodox elements in Antioch, Edessa, and the rest of northern Syria, extending through Cilicia. In Palestine the Greek Orthodox alone probably formed half the total population. The western branch of the Syrian (Suryānī) church, commonly called Jacobite and once based in Edessa, was spread all over the area. Maronites controlled northern Lebanon. Copts were not numerous but did figure in the Egyptian population and manned high administrative and government positions. True, all these Christians were second-class citizens in the Moslem state, but their rights and obligations were clearly defined by the Koran and Islamic law and the adherents were generally reconciled to their status. The crusaders' advent introduced a most disturbing factor. It gave Moslems occasion to suspect their Christian neighbors of sympathy with their western coreligionists, and offered native Christians the temptation to turn collaborationists.

The Latins considered eastern Christians as schismatics, and Rome considered it its duty to "reunite" them with the mother church. Through pressure or persuasion and for political reasons certain groups yielded to the new disruptive force, were then cut off from their respective denominations, and became separate "Uniate" sects. But Moslems, rulers and ruled, were not fully cognizant of that fact and of its implications. To them Gregorian Armenians, Syrian Jacobites and Nestorians, Lebanese Maronites, Egyptian Copts, and Latin Franks were all simply Christians. They had to pay a heavy price after the restoration of Moslem control. Certain communities were decimated, others converted. With the exception of Lebanon, the area began to assume the Moslem aspect it still maintains.

First among the Christians to establish close relations with crusaders were the Armenians. This community in Cilicia and northern Syria cherished nationalistic memories of an Armenian kingdom farther east and yearned for independence from Selchükid and Byzantine yokes. Even before the crusaders' advent an Armenian bishop had gone to Rome to seek help from pope Gregory VII (1073–1085). The first arrivals from the west found Armenians ready to make common cause against their Christian and Moslem enemies; hence the welcome accorded Baldwin on his entry into Edessa in 1098.

In Antioch, it will be recalled, it was through the treachery of an Armenian officer that the city fell into the hands of storming knights in June 1098. Two years later a Latin patriarch was installed[63] in the

---

63. William of Tyre, tr. Babcock and Krey, I, 297; he was Bernard of Valence (1100–1135).

city where the Christians were first so named. The gradual extension of Latin ecclesiastical domination over native Christian churches was consequent upon the establishment of Latin patriarchates first in Antioch and then in Jerusalem.

Eighteen years before the first crusaders entered Edessa, Armenian refugees fleeing Selchükid destruction of their kingdom had sought safety behind the Taurus and established a principality under a Ṛoupenid. From the hills Ṛoupenid princes had extended their control to the plains and laid the basis of Lesser or Cilician Armenia. Friendly intercourse characterized the relations of the principality with the Franks on both the religious and the secular levels. Though Monophysite in its theology, the Armenian church was not now treated by Rome as heretical. Negotiations for recognition were initiated early by the catholicos Gregory II (d. 1105), who received the pallium from the pope.[64] Certain Armenian bishops of Cilicia in common with those of Edessa advocated full union with Rome. Nersēs of Lampron, archbishop of Tarsus (d. 1198), an eloquent and persuasive champion of the movement,[65] received support from the ruling prince, Leon II, whose main ambition was to obtain a royal crown, which he did in 1198 under Frankish aegis. The establishment of this kingdom may, therefore, be considered a direct result of the crusades. The rapprochement between the two communions culminated in the acknowledgment (1307) by the synod of Sis, the Armenian capital city, of Roman supremacy. But the action, to a large extent politically motivated, was so unpopular that serious riots broke out.

In 1342, when the male succession of the Hetoumids came to an end, the crown passed to Guy de Lusignan of Cyprus, whose mother, Isabel (d. 1323), was the daughter of king Leon III (1269–1289); Guy ruled as Constantine III (1342–1344). Thirty-three years later (1375) the last Armenian fortified city, Sis, fell to the Egyptian Mamluks, who in 1266, 1273, and 1275 had subjected the country to punitive expeditions for its alliance first with the crusaders and later with the Mongol invaders. Armenian independence therewith ended, though for a few years thereafter the kings of Cyprus continued to bear the title king of Armenia, and down to the present the Armenian word for "mister" (master) remains our word for baron, a relic of borrowed feudal institutions.

The West Syrians (Jacobites), who once formed the basic Christian

---

64. Henry F. Tournebize, *Histoire politique et religieuse de l'Arménie* . . . (Paris, 1910), p. 164; John T. McNeill *et al.*, eds., *Environmental Factors in Christian History* (Chicago, 1939), p. 261.

65. Nersēs of Lampron, in *RHC, Arm.,* I, 576 ff.

element of northern Syria, were at the advent of the crusaders dispersed over the whole area extending to Palestine. Like their Armenian neighbors, Jacobites courted closer relations with the Roman church as a measure of self-protection if not self-preservation. The crusaders, on their part, reciprocated and for reasons of policy allowed them to practise their religious rites in peace. When the crusaders took possession of Jerusalem, they found the Jacobite metropolitan seat vacant, bishop Cyril and other high clergymen having fled to Egypt before Selchükid fury. When the metropolitan returned he claimed and was given back the vacated ecclesiastical properties. The renowned Jacobite patriarch of Antioch, Michael the Syrian (d. 1199), asserts that the Franks "never raised any difficulty on the subject of faith."[66] A successor of his, Ignatius II (1222–1252), visited Jerusalem in 1237 and offered his submission to Rome in the presence of the Dominican provincial, a submission reiterated ten years later in a letter to Innocent IV,[67] but this was not considered binding by his church as a whole. The union was evidently as insincere and unpopular as that of its Armenian precedent.

The Greek Orthodox was the largest eastern denomination and, by virtue of its Byzantine associations, the least responsive to Latin advances. When the crusaders seized Jerusalem they found the patriarchal seat vacant, its incumbent, Symeon II, having retired to Cyprus under Selchükid oppression. The higher clergy had followed him into exile, where he died. Arabic-speaking parishioners were not reluctant to accept the ecclesiastical jurisdiction of the newly established Latin patriarchate. But years later the conquest of Jerusalem by Saladin included among its results the restoration of the Greek patriarchate, which to the present day maintains its seat in Jerusalem with a Greek-speaking occupant.

In Antioch, which with its Greek-speaking settlers had remained a stronghold of orthodoxy, even under the Selchükids, union with Rome presented more difficulties. After prolonged negotiations the Latins offered the maintenance of the autonomy of the Orthodox church with its own hierarchy and Greek ritual. In the 1240's the patriarch David accepted these terms, but his successor, Euthymius, rejected papal authority and was excommunicated by the Latin patriarch of the city and banished.[68] Damascus became the new seat, whose

66. Michael the Syrian, *Chronique,* ed. and tr. Jean B. Chabot (4 vols., Paris, 1899–1924), III, 222.

67. Rey, "Les Dignitaires de la principauté d'Antioche," *ROL,* VIII (1900–1901), 155.

68. For further details consult Runciman, *op. cit.,* III, 281. The Latin patriarch was Opizo Fieschi (1247–1268).

incumbent has since the end of the nineteenth century been an Arabic-speaking native of the land.

In their inter-Christian relations in the Near East the Latins achieved no enduring results except among the Maronites of Lebanon. For a time the Armenian and Jacobite communions professed interest in or full union with Rome, but the ultimate failure of the crusading venture radically changed the situation. Centuries had to pass before French Catholic missionaries succeeded in detaching sufficient members to form two new Uniate communions.

As the first crusaders wound their weary way along the eastern Mediterranean coast they passed through the territory of the Maronites, who furnished them with guides and later provided the Latin kingdom of Jerusalem with a contingent of archers. The Maronites formed then the largest and certainly the most cohesive Lebanese Christian community. James of Vitry (d. 1240) found them established in Lebanon and Palestine, to which they must have drifted as a result of the crusades. This French prelate, who became bishop of Acre and a cardinal, was impressed by their skill in battle and in the use of the bow and arrow. Referring to their religion he calls them followers of "one Maro, a heretic, who taught that Christ had one will and one energy."[69] In this charge of monothelitism he was preceded by William of Tyre. William goes on to say that in 1180 the Maronites repudiated their heresies and returned to the Catholic church.[70] They were subsequently accorded all the privileges of the Latins, both ecclesiastical and civil, and enjoyed the juridical rights of the Latin bourgeoisie.[71] Maronite scholars, however, have claimed continuous orthodoxy for their church throughout the ages. The fact remains that it was during this period that the rapprochement between Rome and the national church of Lebanon was inaugurated, a rapprochement which culminated in union in the eighteenth century.

The first Maronite patriarch to visit Rome was Jeremiah of 'Amshīt (Irmiya al-'Amshītī) in about 1213.[72] On his return, he undertook several "reforms" relating to liturgy and ordination. Through his legate, pope Innocent III (1198–1216), who brought papal power to its height, prescribed baptism with three immersions. This marks the beginning of the Romanization of the Maronite rite. Since then several pontifical letters have highly commended this church of Lebanon, likening

69. James of Vitry, *op. cit.*, p. 156. This Maro flourished about 700.

70. William of Tyre, tr. Babcock and Krey, II, 459.

71. René Grousset, *Histoire des croisades et du royaume franc de Jérusalem* (3 vols., Paris, 1934–1936), II, 758.

72. Pierre Dib, *L'Église maronite* (Paris, 1930), p. 192.

it to a rose among thorns and to a firm rock in the midst of dashing waves. In 1584 pope Gregory XIII founded in Rome a seminary designed to train Maronite students for clerical life. The seminary graduated a number of men who distinguished themselves as historians, bishops, and patriarchs and who contributed to the process of Romanization. The final touch came when a graduate of this institution, the renowned as-Sam'ānī ("Assemani"), in 1736 participated in the Maronite synod in Lebanon as a delegate of the pope. This church of Lebanon, however, has retained to the present its Syriac liturgy and noncelibate clergy. Its friendship with the French, dating from the crusading period,[73] is still cherished. Louis IX is still popular in Lebanon. A Maronite family, al-Khazin, supplied France with a number of consular agents for Beirut, beginning with abū-Naufal, who was appointed in 1655 by Louis XIV.[74] This *amitié traditionelle* has since been repeatedly invoked by both sides and was strengthened in 1860, when Napoleon III sent troops to halt the civil war, and at the close of the first World War when the French mandate was established over Lebanon.

In their Christology Copts, like Jacobites, embraced the Monophysite doctrine. For both sects it was one way of expressing their independence from Byzantium and Rome. Under the Fāṭimids Egyptian Christians had two disastrous experiences, first under al-Ḥakim (996–1021), who imposed humiliating disabilities on *dhimmīs,* and later under al-'Āḍid (1160–1171), by whose vizir's orders 20,000 pounds of naphtha were poured over the old capital Fustat and set ablaze to save it from falling into the hands of Amalric, king of Latin Jerusalem. The incredible conflagration rendered thousands of Copts destitute overnight.

Saladin inaugurated his regime by replacing high government officials —Moslems and Christians—with relatives and friends from Syria. As clerks, secretaries, tax collectors, and treasurers, Copts had filled a national need in the country. Under Saladin's successors, Arabic began increasingly to replace Coptic. The worst was yet to come under the Mamluks, who in 1250 superseded the Aiyūbids. Not only did they follow the policy of discrimination against Coptic employees but whenever the government treasury needed replenishing, as it frequently did, they found a ready source to tap in the cash or property

---

73. René Ristelhueber, *Les Traditions françaises au Liban,* 2nd ed. (Paris, 1925), pp. 42 ff.; Kamal S. Salibi, "The Maronites of Lebanon under Frankish and Mamluk Rule (1099–1516)," *Arabica,* IV (1957), 288.
74. Ristelhueber, *op. cit.,* pp. 143 ff.

of their Christian subjects.[75] Conversions to Islam mounted. When in 1249 Louis IX landed in Egypt and gained possession of Damietta, he found the Coptic element of its citizens ready to welcome him. In turn he treated them with special consideration. But when a later crusade was directed against Alexandria (1365) and temporarily occupied it, its Christians were pillaged by the Franks no less than were their Moslem neighbors. The ninth Mamluk, Muḥammad an-Nāṣir, reactivated the discriminatory laws against *dhimmīs,* and the end of his reign in 1341 may be considered as marking the extinction of an effective Christian presence in the valley of the Nile. Between 1279 and 1447 no less than forty-five churches and unnumbered monasteries in the Cairo region were reportedly destroyed.

As the Sunnite Mamlūks began to establish their ascendancy over Syria, the day of reckoning came not only for the Christians but also for the schismatic Moslem minorities. It should be recalled, however, that at times native Christians fought side by side with Moslems against crusaders, and Sunnite Moslems fought on the side of crusaders against fellow Moslems. Several Moslem cities of Syria and many beduin tribes on more than one occasion sought Latin aid, and more than one native state allied itself with a Latin state.[76] At one time the Assassins (Ismāʻīlites), whose fortresses in the north formed a frontier between crusaders and Moslems, ceded their stronghold in the south, Banyas (Bāniyās), to the Franks. The Latin kingdom had in its service a body of light cavalry, Turcopoles (sons of Turks), recruited mainly from Moslems.

As new professors of Islam, the Mamluk sultans were eager to impress their subjects with their zeal. They also endeavored to keep aflame the spirit of *jihād.* In their hostility toward their Christian subjects they may have been reacting against the contemporary treatment of Moslems in Spain by rising Christian states. On the Lebanese coast the Egyptian sultans followed a scorched-earth policy and methodically ravaged Lebanon, razed its forts, and deported its population; even the earth was to be punished. They also insisted on conformity on the part of all dissident Moslems. Ismāʻīlites and Nuṣairīs, who had compromised their loyalty, were now systematically decimated. Baybars (1260–1277) forced the Nuṣairīs (ʻAlawites) to build mosques in their villages, but could not force them to pray in them. Large

75. Atiya, *A History of Eastern Christianity* (London and Notre Dame, 1968), p. 97.

76. Ibn-al-Qalānisī, *Taʼrīkh,* ed. Henry F. Amedroz (Beirut, 1908), pp. 289–290, 314, 316; Ibn-Khaldūn, *Kitāb al-ʻibar wa-dīwān al-mubtadaʼ wa-l-khabar fī aiyām al-ʻArab wa-l-ʻAjam wa-l-Barbar* (Cairo, A.H. 1284 [1867/8]), VI, 7–8.

numbers of Nuṣairīs had been slaughtered by the first crusaders. Even the Druzes, who had generally cast their lot with the Moslems, were now enjoined to conform. Between 1292 and 1305 three punitive expeditions were directed against the Maronites and heterodox Moslems in Kasrawān. The last, by Muḥammad an-Nāṣir, practically annihilated the Shī'ite population of Kasrawān.[77] This sultan's reactivation of the anti-*dhimmī* laws was applied in the area; thousands of Maronites fled to Cyprus. They had begun their migration earlier, at the time of Saladin's occupation of Beirut. Documents establish their existence in Cyprus even earlier.[78] After the occupation of the island by Guy of Lusignan in 1192 more Maronite refugees flocked to it. An estimated 80,000 Maronites once flourished in Cyprus; some 4,000 still do, mainly in Kormakiti, which today has a Maronite cathedral. Their colloquial speech, a mixture of Syriac and Arabic, is reminiscent of their twelfth-century ancestral tongue. Northern Syria, Lebanon, and Palestine, which for a time had been oriented westward, reassumed the general cultural aspects that they maintained till the early nineteenth century.

Not only the territories of minorities but the entire maritime coast felt the disastrous effects of the aftermath of the crusades. Fearing the return of the Franks, some of whom had simply moved to nearby Cyprus, the Mamluks undertook the dismantling of such cities as Ascalon, Acre, Arsuf, Caesarea, Tyre, and Tripoli. The Mongol invasions of Syria, which began with Hulagu after the destruction of Baghdad (1258), added to the disastrous effects upon the country in general and the minorities in particular. In the battle of Homs (1299) Armenians and Franks fought in the ranks of the Mongol army. In the following year Druze bowmen from Lebanon harassed the Mamluk army on its retreat. Ibn-Jubair in 1185 found Tyre a fortified town;[79] abū-l-Fidā' (d. 1331) a century later found it utterly desolate.[80] Especially striking are the observations of Ibn-Baṭṭūṭah, who traveled in that area in 1326: "I journeyed to the fortress of Ascalon, now a heap of ruins. . . . Then I arrived in Acre, once capital of the Franks in Syria but today a ruin. . . . Thence I journeyed to Tyre, which is a ruin, with a populous village outside it. Next I went to Tiberias, once a large imposing city of which nothing remains today

77. Ṣāliḥ ibn-Yaḥyâ, *op. cit.,* p. 136.

78. Dib, *op. cit.,* p. 259.

79. *Op. cit.,* p. 304.

80. *Taqwīm al-buldān,* ed. Joseph T. Reinaud and MacGuckin de Slane (Paris, 1840), p. 243; he was twelve years old at the time.

but vestiges witnessing to its former size and glory."[81] Bertrandon of La Broquière, who visited Syria in 1432, reported in Jaffa nothing but tents covered with reeds, in Acre not more than three hundred houses, and Beirut "has been more considerable than it is now."[82]

One interesting and enduring byproduct of the crusades was the initiation of missionary work among Moslems. With the failure of Christians to subdue the "infidel" by force, the theory prevailed that his soul might be subdued by persuasion. The possibility of substituting peaceful, spiritual conquest for a military one took root as a reaction from the crusading methods and as a result of the newly generated interest in the east. Launched in the early thirteenth century, the missionary activity, with its many ramifications, has persisted down to the present time.

The two earliest missionary organizations were the Franciscan and the Dominican, both originating in Syria. Francis of Assisi himself started the mission named after him when in 1219 he arrived in Acre and sent eleven disciples across the land. This city became the headquarters of the Franciscan effort. He also presented himself before the Aiyūbid al-Kāmil, nephew of Saladin, in Egypt and discussed religion with him. About the same time the Dominican mission was launched; it established a convent in Damascus and another in Tripoli. The Carmelite order, monastic and contemplative rather than missionary, also had a Syrian origin; it was organized earlier by a veteran crusader and took its name from a Palestinian mountain. Ṣāliḥ ibn-Yaḥyâ (fl. about 1437) refers to a Franciscan convent and church in Beirut which his ancestors had converted into a stable.[83]

The results of this early missionary effort among Moslems were disappointing. The protagonists thereupon sought new channels directed toward native Christian communities. The creation of the Uniate churches, Syrian and Greek, in the seventeenth and eighteenth centuries was the crowning achievement of Catholic missionary activity.

As the idea of converting Moslems was germinating in Christian minds, Mongol hordes were pouring into western Asia, thus providing the missionaries with a wider field for their activity. The victorious march of the Mongols landed them in Syria, where they and the crusaders found themselves facing a common enemy—the Moslems.

81. *Tuḥfat an-nuẓẓār fī ghara'ib al-amṣār wa-'ajā'ib al-asfār,* ed. and tr. Charles Defrémery and Beniamino R. Sanguinetti, 3rd ed. (4 vols., Paris, 1893), I, 126, 129, 130, 132.

82. *Op. cit.,* pp. 286, 292.

83. *Op. cit.,* p. 149.

Negotiations were carried on for concerted action. Embassies were exchanged with popes and kings. For a time these heathens from Central Asia flirted with Christianity. Hulagu, whose wife, Toqūz Khātūn (d. 1265), was a member of the east Syrian church, sympathized with this faith. His general Kitbogha, who had led the army triumphantly into Palestine, professed the same form of Christianity. But the routing of the Mongol army in 1260 at 'Ain Jālūt, the first major check the Mongols experienced, and the subsequent expulsion of the Franks from the land must have convinced these heathens that Islam was the more powerful religion.[84] In 1295 their seventh īl-khān, Ghazan, adopted the Arabic name Maḥmūd and declared Islam to be the Mongol state religion.

In Europe the champion of the policy of peaceful penetration was a Catalan, Raymond Lull, who persuaded the king of Majorca to found a school of Arabic studies to train missionaries whose only weapons would be "love, prayers, and the outpouring of tears." Acting on Lull's plea the Council of Vienne in 1312 ordered the teaching of Arabic in the universities of Rome, Paris, Oxford, Bologna, and Salamanca. The study of Arabic led to the study of other oriental languages. In the course of the thirteenth and fourteenth centuries, Catholic bishoprics were established not only in Syria, Armenia, and Persia but also across Central Asia to eastern China.[85]

In the wake of the missionary went the trader. Travelers and merchants, especially from Italy, penetrated by land from Acre to Peking. Others circumnavigated southern Asia from Basra to Canton. Both of these land and sea routes had been known to Moslems and frequented by them for centuries; but to Europeans the experience amounted to a discovery of anterior Asia and the Far East, resulting in an expansion of geographical knowledge that ranks in importance second only to that entailed by the discovery of the New World two centuries later.

---

84. Laurence E. Browne, *The Eclipse of Christianity in Asia* . . . (Cambridge, Eng., 1933), p. 154.
    85. See chapter X, below.

III

SOCIAL CLASSES
IN THE CRUSADER STATES:
THE "MINORITIES"

"Minority" is used in this chapter in the sense of "a group of people, differentiated from others in the same society by race, nationality, religion, and language, who both think of themselves as a differentiated group and are thought of by the others as a differentiated group with negative connotations. Further, they are relatively lacking in power and hence are subjected to certain exclusions, discriminations, and other differential treatment."[1] This definition is particularly useful, since although the "minorities" dealt with formed in total an overwhelming numerical majority in the areas conquered by the crusaders, their legal, social, and economic position was determined by the European conquerors who settled in Syria and Palestine. We shall be concerned, however, with more than a single minority. The term as applied to the crusader states covers many groups quite varied in culture, although the conquerors paid little attention to distinctions among them, looking upon the entire non-Frankish population of whatever kind as a single entity. Despite the efforts of some modern historians to distinguish different policies followed by the crusaders respecting natives who were Christians and those who were not, in law—as distinguished from practice—no such difference existed.

Contemporary sources written by Europeans are very much aware

In general see Hans Prutz, *Kulturgeschichte der Kreuzzüge* (Berlin, 1883; repr. Hildesheim, 1964); Claude Cahen, *La Syrie du nord à l'époque des croisades et la principauté franque d'Antioche* (IFD, BO, I; Paris, 1940), esp. pp. 176–204. For more particular studies regarding Palestine see Joshua Prawer, *The Latin Kingdom of Jerusalem: European Colonialism in the Middle Ages* (London, 1972), pp. 46 ff.; Jean Richard, *Le Royaume latin de Jérusalem* (Paris, 1953); and Hans E. Mayer, *Geschichte der Kreuzzüge* (Stuttgart, 1965), tr. John Gillingham as *The Crusades* (Oxford, 1972). The sources and secondary bibliographies for the different minorities are given below at the appropriate places throughout the chapter.

1. Arnold M. Rose, in *International Encyclopaedia of the Social Sciences*, X (1968), 365, *s.v.* "Minorities."

of the kaleidoscopic variety of peoples, something almost unknown in the west. Wilbrand of Oldenburg describes the city of Antioch in 1212 as follows: "It has many rich inhabitants: Franks and Syrians, Greeks and Jews, Armenians and Moslems, all of whom are ruled by the Franks and each of whom follows his own laws."[2] A few years later, in 1217, Thietmar lists "Greeks, Jacobites, Georgians, Armenians, Nestorians, Jews, Sadducees [probably the Jewish sect of Qaraites], Samaritans, and Assassins."[3] As time passes, the list grows. James of Vitry (d. 1240) adds the forgotten Maronites,[4] and Burchard of Mount Sion (1283), having already mentioned Moslems, Syrians, and Greeks, adds "Armenians, Georgians, Nestorians, Jacobites, Chaldeans, Medes, Persians, Ethiopians, Egyptians, and many other people who are Christians."[5] Even a Jewish native of Moslem Spain, Benjamin of Tudela, far more familiar with varieties of people of different languages and religions, says of Jerusalem about 1167 that it "has many inhabitants; and the Ismaelites [Moslems] call them Jacobites, Aramaeans [Armenians or Syrians], Greeks, Georgians, and Franks."[6] To get a clearer view of the different communities involved, however, it will be necessary first to draw a rough picture of their geographical distribution in the Syro-Palestinian area held by the crusaders.

In the narrow stretch of land running some 530 miles in length from the confines of Cilicia to the Red Sea the crusaders met with a variety of races, religions, and languages. The aim of the First Crusade, to destroy the "infidel" and liberate oriental Christendom and the Holy Land, came up against hard realities, the existence of which could not have been suspected. It was one thing to lump all "infidels" together for general condemnation and destruction, but how to deal with eastern Christians? It was well known in the cultural and political centers of Europe that the Greek church was not in communion with Rome, but as for other Christian denominations, the Franks had never encountered them before. Among scholars there was some historical knowledge of their heresies, but none whatsoever of their identity as "nations" or, as the crusaders would sometimes call them,

2. Wilbrand of Oldenburg, in *Peregrinatores medii aevi quatuor,* ed. J. C. M. Laurent (Leipzig, 1873), p. 172.

3. *Mag. Thietmari peregrinatio,* ed. Laurent (Hamburg, 1857), p. 52 (repr. bound with *Peregrinatores medii aevi quatuor).*

4. James of Vitry, "Historia Iherosolimitana . . .," cap. 74, in Jacques Bongars, ed., *Gesta Dei per Francos* (Hanau, 1611; repr. Jerusalem, 1972), I, 1090.

5. Burchard of Mount Sion, in *Peregrinatores,* ed. Laurent, p. 89.

6. *The Itinerary of Rabbi Benjamin of Tudela,* ed. and tr. Marcus N. Adler (2 vols., London, 1907), I, 35.

"languages"; and there was no idea that some areas were densely settled by them, or that indeed they even formed a numerical majority in some places. As for knowledge of Islam in general, let alone its internal divisions, it was practically nil. Though merchants of Amalfi and Venice were in contact with the Levant, their knowledge had little diffusion in Europe. Only in the second half of the twelfth century did the image of Islamic peoples become clearer. It was a permanent loss to European cultural history that the first Latin history of Islamic peoples, by one who lived in the Levant and had an intimate knowledge of its inhabitants, namely William of Tyre, did not survive.

It is not easy to draw an accurate picture of the Moslem inhabitants of the crusader states. They disappeared almost entirely from all the fortified cities and fortresses during the ten years of conquest (1100–1110). Almost all sieges which ended in victory for the crusaders were followed by the massacre of Moslem and Jewish inhabitants (and occasionally also of eastern Christians, whose external appearance did not differ from that of the others). Moslems remained in only a few places, usually those taken without fighting, such as Nablus in Palestine. Even where the city capitulated, as did Tyre in 1124 and Ascalon in 1153, the Moslems to whom the Franks guaranteed their lives preferred to abandon their homes. After the initial conquest, however, with greater security and the economic development of the coastal cities, Moslems began to return. Some were probably former inhabitants,[7] others migrated from the countryside, but in what numbers we cannot say. Certainly the Turkish garrisons of northern Syria and the interior of Palestine disappeared completely, as did the *mamlūk* garrisons of the Fāṭimids in the coastal towns. The Moslem city element seems to have been stronger in the north than in the south. Beirut and Sidon in the kingdom of Jerusalem, Jabala in the county of Tripoli, Jubail and Latakia in the principality of Antioch, all seem to have had large Moslem populations — indeed a majority, according to one Moslem source.[8] There were probably large Moslem concentrations in other crusader ports such as Antioch, Tripoli, Tyre, and Acre. But there were none in Jerusalem. Both western and Jewish sources attest to the fact that immediately after the conquest the crusaders promulgated a law barring Moslems and Jews from the holy city.[9]

7. As late as 1136, after Zengi's recapture of Ma'arrat an-Nu'mān, the Moslems who had titles to property were allowed to recover it. Others had to find their titles in the dīwān of Aleppo (Ibn-al-Athīr, in *RHC, Or.,* I, 423).

8. 'Imād-ad-Dīn, in Abū-Shāmah, "Livre des deux jardins," *RHC, Or.,* IV, 309.

9. The relevant sources are analyzed in Prawer, "The Jews in the Latin Kingdom" (in Hebrew, with English summary), *Zion,* XI (1946), 38–82.

Though the Moslems abandoned the cities during the period of conquest they did not abandon their farms and villages, although there were refugees from Syria and Palestine in Damascus as well as in Egypt. After a period of silent hostility, the most spectacular expression of which was the abandonment of their farms,[10] the Moslem peasants, with some exceptions,[11] and the Frankish seigneurs established a *modus vivendi*.

Whatever had been their historical background, the Moslem peoples of the crusader states formed a linguistic and ethnic bloc by the twelfth century. Arabic was spoken by everybody,[12] and former ethnic differences in Syria ceased to be important (they had never been important in Palestine, which had hardly been colonized by the Arab invaders of the seventh century). Within the frontiers of the Latin states there were virtually no Turks or nomadic Turcomans. Only the beduins, called "Arabs" in Moslem sources, stood out as a separate group.

Within this Moslem bloc, however, there were religious differences, in particular between the Sunnites, who acknowledged the 'Abbāsid caliphs of Baghdad, and the Shī'ites, who accepted the Fāṭimid imams of Egypt. In addition there were sectarian Shī'ites, unimportant within the crusader states but numerous along the frontiers. During the last quarter of the eleventh century when the Selchükid Turks, the secular arm of the 'Abbāsids, pushed the Fāṭimids out of Syria and Palestine, there probably followed some strengthening of the Sunnah. Turkish garrisons in the newly conquered territories were Sunnites. Local emirs, qadis, and ra'ises who lost their independence or their links with Cairo, pronounced the *khuṭbah* or Friday prayer in the name of the 'Abbāsid caliphs. It is doubtful, however, that the allegiance of the mass of the local population changed. On the other hand Fāṭimid rule lasted for only a hundred years, during which Sunnite elements certainly continued to exist. On the whole, it seems that the Shī'ites were predominant in northern Syria, whereas southern Syria and Palestine were to a large extent Sunnite,[13] but there were exceptions. By the end of the tenth century, the northern parts of Palestine and Transjordan

---

10. William of Tyre, IX, 19 (*RHC, Occ.,* I, 393). Cf. Prawer, "The Settlement of the Latins in Jerusalem," *Speculum,* XXVII (1952), 490–503.

11. On Moslem refugees escaping the hard treatment of a Frankish lord in Nablus, see Emmanuel Sivan, "Réfugiés syro-palestiniens au temps des croisades," *Revue des études islamiques,* XXXV (1967), 135–147.

12. Abraham N. Poliak, "L'Arabisation de l'Orient sémitique," *Revue des études islamiques,* XII (1938), 35–63. Cf. Cahen, "Un Document concernant les Melkites et les Latins d'Antioche au temps des croisades," *Revue des études byzantines,* XXIX (1971), 285–292.

13. Cahen, *Syrie du nord,* p. 188.

were overwhelmingly Shī'ite (especially Tiberias, Kadesh in Galilee, Nablus, and 'Ammān).[14]

The Shī'ah underwent many schisms. Only the Druzes, however, who accepted the eccentric imam al-Ḥākim (996–1021) as the last incarnation of divinity, were to be found, at least partially, within the borders of the Latin states. They were in Jabal as-Summāq and Buzā'ah in northern Syria, though their special area was on the confines of the kingdom of Jerusalem and the county of Tripoli. "Some ten miles outside Sidon," writes Benjamin of Tudela, "there is a nation fighting those [Franks] of Sidon. This nation is called Druzes and they are pagans and have no religion. They inhabit the high mountains and the recesses of the rocks and there is no king or judge over them. And they stretch as far as Mount Hermon, some three days' march."[15] This is the earliest description of the Druzes which has come down to us. In all probability there were also other heretical communities in this area near Belfort (Qal'at ash-Shaqīf), Banyas,[16] and Wādī-t-Taim. A contemporary Moslem source describes the area as a concentration point of Nuṣairīs, Druzes, Zoroastrians, and other sects.[17] The most spectacular of the Ismā'īlite sects was the bāṭiniyah (esoteric) sect of Assassins (Hashīshīyūn) organized by the Persian Ḥasan-i-Sabbāḥ (al-Ḥasan ibn-aṣ-Ṣabbāḥ, d. 1124) at the end of the eleventh century in the stronghold of Alamut. From their fortresses at al-Kahf and other places near the Frankish frontiers, they menaced the lives of Moslem and Frankish leaders from time to time, but they can hardly be considered part of the local population.

On the fringes of the cultivated area and the desert, as often within the Latin states as without, were the nomadic beduins.[18] The main tribe, of which the others were branches or related clans, were the

14. Al-Maqdisī (al-Muqaddasī), "Description of Syria . . . ," tr. Guy Le Strange, in *PPTS*, III-3 (London, 1892), 6; Nāṣir-i-Khusrau, "Diary of a Journey through Syria and Palestine," tr. Le Strange, in *PPTS*, IV-1 (London, 1893), 9, 11–12.

15. Benjamin of Tudela, *Itinerary*, ed. Adler, p. 18.

16. In 1126 the city of Banyās was handed over by Tughtigin to the Ismā'īlīs who had to flee from Damascus. They in turn handed it over to the Franks in 1129; Ibn-al-Athīr, in *RHC, Or.,* I, 366–368, 385; Mayer, "Latins, Muslims and Greeks in the Latin Kingdom of Jerusalem," *History,* LXIII (1978), 175–192.

17. Ibn-al-Athīr, in *RHC, Or.,* I, 383; on the Druzes see Philip K. Hitti, *The Origins of the Druze People and Religion* (New York, 1928); O. H. Thompson, "The Druzes of Lebanon," *Moslem World,* XX (1930), 270–285; and Kamal S. Salibi, "The Buḥturids of the Ġarb: Mediaeval Lords of Beirut and of Southern Lebanon," *Arabica,* VIII (1961), 74–97. On the Nuṣairīs see below, note 122.

18. The major sources (slightly late, but based on tradition or earlier sources) are al-Qalqashandī, *Ṣubḥ al-a'shâ* (Cairo, 1914), I, 324; IV, 203–215; az-Zāhirī, *Zubdat kashf al-mamālik* (Paris, 1894), p. 105; al-Maqrīzī, *As-sulūk li-ma'rifat ad-dulūk,* ed. Étienne Quatremère (2 vols., Paris, 1837–1844), I, 79–80, 83. Cf. Arthur S. Tritton, "The Tribes of Syria in the

Banū-Ṭaiy, who roamed the large expanses between Egypt, Palestine, and southern Syria. In northern Syria and Iraq they met with other tribes: the Kilāb, Uqail, and others. East and north of Egypt there were the Darmah and the Banū-Ruzaiq on the Egyptian border, some suspected of coöperating with the Franks. In the half-deserted area between Gaza and Hebron were branches of the Banū-Ṭaiy, namely the Jarm Quḍā'ah and, on the coast to the south of Gaza and Darum, the Banū-Ghaur (suggesting the valley of the Jordan) and Banū-Buhaid. In the area between Sinai and Transjordan, the sources also mention the Banū-Ṣadr (perhaps connected with Wādī Ṣadr in western Sinai), Banū-Ā'id, Banū-Fuhaid, and Banū-Ubaiy, the last having a reputation as eaters of dead animals, located in the al-Jafr and Ḥismah area.[19] Southern Transjordan was a place much favored by the beduins, who found a prosperous market for their horses and cattle at the great annual fair in the plain of Maidān,[20] near Muzairib, in the Hauran. Around 1115 the Banū-Rabī'ah roamed here, from around Petra to 'Ajlūn. Then they moved to the Hauran and broke up into the powerful Faḍl, who moved to the north, and the Ḥamah and Mīrah, who remained in the Hauran. In southern Transjordan there were other tribes from Egypt, seemingly colonies of frontier defenders. They included the Banū-Kinānah, the Banū-Ḥaubar, and the Banū-Khālid. To the north, near the crusader castles of Krak de Montréal (ash-Shaubak) and Kerak, were the Banū-'Uqbah and Banū-Zuhair. Farther north still, near 'Ajlūn, were the Banū-'Auf, who gave their name to the high plateau of the area. Here they joined with the powerful Banū-Rabī'ah of the Ṭaiy, the successors of the Banū-Jarrāḥ, former rulers of central Palestine with their capital in Ramla (tenth-eleventh century), who roamed as far as the Hauran. Unspecified nomadic tribes pressed on the northern borders of the kingdom near the sources of the Jordan, and in the Marj 'Uyūn and Wādī-t-Taim, drawn by their excellent pastures.[21]

14th and 15th Centuries," *Bulletin of the School of Oriental Studies,* XII (1948), 567–573. Additional material is in *An Arab-Syrian Gentleman and Warrior in the Period of the Crusades: Memoirs of Usāmah ibn Munqidh,* tr. Hitti (*CURC,* 10; New York, 1929; repr. Beirut, 1964); and Ibn-al-Qalānisī, *The Damascus Chronicle of the Crusades,* tr. H. A. R. Gibb (London, 1932). See also the excellent studies by Max von Oppenheim, *Die Beduinen* (Leipzig, 1939), I, 280 ff.; II, 7 ff., 82–83; Karl V. Zettersteen, *Beiträge zur Geschichte der Mamelukensultane . . . nach arabischen Handschriften* (Leyden, 1919), p. 38–39; and Poliak, *op. cit.*

19. Usāmah Ibn-Munqidh, *An Arab-Syrian Gentleman,* p. 36. The coöperation of the Banū-Ruzaiq with the Franks (1112–1113) is mentioned by Ibn-al-Qalānisī, *op. cit.,* tr. Gibb, p. 130. He also mentions the Arabs of the Ṭaiy, Kilāb, and Khafājah tribes as participating in the attack on Tiberias in 1113.

20. On the Maidān fair see Prawer, *Histoire du royaume latin de Jérusalem,* I (Paris, 1969), 380.

21. Among them were certainly the Banū-'Āmilah; see below, note 120. Cf. Maurice Godefroy-

It is a remarkable fact that the beduins never threatened the security of the crusader kingdom. Until the Selchükid conquest of Palestine, the beduins were often its real rulers, but their raids and invasions then ceased for over two hundred years; only with the decline of Mamluk power in the late fifteenth century do the beduins reappear in force.

As we shall see, the Franks, faced with the problem posed by these nomadic tribes, soon found a way to deal with them.

The second most numerous element among the minorities were the eastern Christians, living in solid groups, but often, especially south of Tripoli, in enclaves amidst a mixed population. As a whole they were more numerous in Syria, in the principality of Antioch and in and around Edessa, than in Palestine, although there was an important Christian enclave, the Maronites, in the mountains of Lebanon.

In the city of Antioch, and in the countryside almost as far as the eastern frontiers of the Orontes river, the Christian element probably comprised a majority of the local population.[22] Byzantine domination of Anatolia well into the eleventh century, the renewed Byzantine rule in Antioch during the century which preceded the First Crusade, the strong position of the Greek church under Byzantine rule, and the strengthening of the position of the non-Chalcedonian creeds after the Moslem conquest — all these factors had helped to preserve Christianity in Antioch and Edessa.[23]

Demombynes, *La Syrie à l'époque des Mamelouks d'après les auteurs arabes* (Paris, 1923), p. 23, note 4. On the Wādī-t-Taim cf. Prawer, *Royaume latin,* I, 291, 309–310, 320, 334, 510–511.

22. Cahen, *Syrie du nord,* p. 343; Hitti, "The Impact of the Crusades on Eastern Christianity," in *Medieval and Near Eastern Studies in Honor of Aziz Suryal Atiya,* ed. Sami A. Hanna (Leyden, 1972), pp. 211–217.

23. There are a large number of studies relating to eastern Christians which occasionally deal with the period of the crusades, but there is no special study of the problem as a whole. Of the greatest importance is Gilbert Dagron, "Minorités ethniques et réligieuses dans l'Orient byzantin à la fin du Xe et au XIe siècles: L'immigration syrienne," *Travaux et mémoires du Centre de recherche d'histoire et civilisation de Byzance,* VI (1976), 177–216. For summaries and bibliographies see *Religionsgeschichte des Orients in der Zeit der Weltreligionen* (Handbuch der Orientalistik, ed. Bertold Spuler, I: Der Nahe und der Mittlere Osten, vol. VIII: Religion, part 2; Leyden and Cologne, 1961); Georg Graf, *Geschichte der christlichen arabischen Literatur* (Studi e testi, XXXV; 4 vols., Vatican City, 1944–1953); Stephan E. Assemani, *Biblioteca orientalis clementino-vaticana,* II: *De Scriptoribus Syris Monophysitis* (Rome, 1721); Anton Baumstark and Adolf Rücker, *Die syrische Literatur* (Handbuch der Orientalistik, II–III, 1954); Raymond Janin, *Les Églises orientales et les rites orientaux* (Paris, 1926); Donald Attwater, *The Christian Churches of the East* (2 vols., Milwaukee, 1961); Aziz S. Atiya, *A History of Eastern Christianity* (London and Notre Dame, 1968); and Anna D. von den Brincken, *Die "Nationes Christianorum orientalium" im Verständnis der lateinischen Historiographie von der Mitte der 12. bis in die zweite Hälfte der 14. Jahrhunderts* (Cologne and Vienna, 1973), with copious bibliography, pp. 463–501.

There were also significant Christian elements farther east. The Nestorian church was the dominant Christian community in Mesopotamia and Persia, and had branches reaching into Central Asia and even farther.[24] Their patriarch was the only Christian prelate allowed a see in the 'Abbāsid capital of Baghdad. The geographic area of Nestorianism lay for the most part well beyond the area of the crusader states and their immediate Moslem neighbors. Driven eastward by early persecution, the Nestorians found a home in the Persian empire, there to develop the famous Nestorian missions, the first to penetrate eastern Asia. The Moslem conquest did not bring about any significant return of Nestorians to Syria, Lebanon, and Palestine. Consequently, by the time of the crusades they were not numerous in these areas, although they were to be found in the county of Edessa, both in the cities and in the countryside.

Whereas Nestorians, Orthodox Georgians (often confused by the crusaders with Monophysites), Monophysite Armenians, Copts, and Abyssinians formed an outer Christian periphery, within the area of the crusader states the major Christian groups were the "Syrians" or Melkites, the Jacobites, and the Maronites of Lebanon. The overwhelming majority of eastern Christians were the "Syrians" and the Jacobites. Both were in large measure indigenous, going back to the native populations converted to Christianity during the fourth and fifth centuries. The "Syrians"—whose name led some crusaders to fanciful etymologies, connecting them with "Assyrians"—were Greek Orthodox in creed, and used Greek in their liturgy, although their normal language of communication was Arabic. The generic name *Suryānī* sometimes led to confusion, with some sources using it indiscriminately to denote all the eastern Christians of Syria and Palestine.[25]

In contrast to the Greek Orthodox and "Syrians," called by their adversaries "Chalcedonians," and in Syria "malkānī" (Arabic: *malkīyūn*) and so Melkites, were the Monophysite Jacobites, whose creed was

24. There were virtually no Nestorians in the crusader states other than Edessa. A Nestorian monastery near Jericho existed between the fifth and ninth centuries, but was later abandoned; see Heinz Stephan, "A Nestorian Hermitage between Jericho and the Jordan," *Quarterly of the Department of Antiquities of Palestine,* IV (1935), 81–86. A Nestorian scholar in Tripoli in the thirteenth century was the teacher of the great Jacobite Bar Hebraeus; see his *Chronicon ecclesiasticum,* ed. and tr. (into Latin) by Jean B. Abbeloos and Thomas J. Lamy (3 vols., Paris and Louvain, 1872–1877), II, 670. It is very likely that the "Mousserins" of the *Assises de Jérusalem* were Nestorian merchants who had connections with Acre; see Richard, "La Confrérie des Mosserins d'Acre et les marchands de Mossoul au XIIIème siècle," *L'Orient syrien,* XI (1966), 451–460.

25. Cf. Frédéric Macler, "Notes latines sur les Nestoriens, Maronites, Arméniens, Géorgiens, Mozarabes," *Revue de l'histoire des religions,* LXXVIII (1918), 243–260; Wilhelm de Vries, S.J., *Der Christliche Osten in Geschichte und Gegenwart* (Würzburg, 1951).

that also embraced by the Armenians, Copts, and Abyssinians. But while these last were ethnic groups with what were in effect national churches, the Jacobites were never such. They were stronger in the north than in the south, but their communities could be found in all the crusader cities as well as in the countryside.

The relative numbers of "Syrians" and Jacobites are impossible to estimate. In the area of the principality of Antioch the Byzantine or Greek Orthodox church was important, although it has been alleged that even here the Jacobite church was stronger. It has been estimated that by the end of the tenth century the Orthodox hierarchy had lost a third of its former 152 episcopal sees, while the Jacobites counted some 160. In Antioch itself the Jacobites were apparently more numerous than the Orthodox when the city fell to the crusaders.[26] In the south, in Lebanon and Palestine, the Byzantine church was certainly weaker, but it controlled the great sanctuaries, such as the churches of Nazareth, Bethlehem, and the Holy Sepulcher. The number of Byzantine Christians was of course small, their clergy probably recruited in the Byzantine empire. But the protection given by the basileus was tangible enough. In the eleventh century, formal treaties were concluded between the empire and the caliphate to ensure the safety and property of the Byzantine church in the Holy Land. As a matter of fact, the last reconstruction of the church of the Holy Sepulcher before the crusades was the outcome of such an agreement.

26. For the Byzantine church see Bernard Leib, *Rome, Kiev et Byzance à la fin du XIème siècle* (Paris, 1924); *idem, Deux inédits byzantins sur les azymes au debut du XIIème siècle* (Rome, 1923); Walter Norden, *Das Papsttum und Byzanz: Die Trennung der beiden Mächte und das Problem ihrer Wiedervereinigung bis zum Untergange des byzantinischen Reiches* (Berlin, 1903); Steven Runciman, *The Eastern Schism: A Study of the Papacy and the Eastern Churches during the XIth and XIIth Centuries* (Oxford, 1955); Ferdinand Chalandon, *Les Comnène: Étude sur l'empire byzantin au XIe et au XIIe siècles* (2 vols., Paris, 1912; repr. New York, 1960); W. de Vries, Octavian Bârlea, Joseph Gill, and Michael Lacko, *Rom und die Patriarchate des Orients* (Freiburg and Munich, 1963); George Every, *The Byzantine Patriarchate 451-1204* (London, 1947); Carlo Gatti and Cyril P. Karalevskij, *I Riti e le chiese orientali,* II, *Il Rito bizantino e le chiese bizantine* (Genoa, 1942); Hans G. Beck, *Die byzantinische Kirche im Zeitalter der Kreuzzüge (Handbuch der Kirchengeschichte,* ed. Hubert Jedin, V-2; Freiburg, 1968). See also the detailed introduction by Theodosyj T. Haluščynskyj in his edition of *Acta Innocentii III (1198-1216) e registris Vaticanis aliisque fontibus* (PC, Fontes, ser. 3, vol. II; Vatican City, 1944). Of basic importance is Karalevskij, "Antioche," in *Dictionnaire d'histoire et de géographie ecclésiastiques,* III (1924), cols. 563-703. The Greek Orthodox view is presented by Aleksandr Popov, *Latinskaja Jerusalimskaja Patriarkhya epoki Krestonoscov* (St. Petersburg, 1903); A. Papadopoulos-Kerameos, *Analecta hierosolymitikes stachyologias e sylloges anecdoton,* II (St. Petersburg, 1894); cf. Chrusostomos A. Papadopoulos, *Historia tes ekklesias Hierosolymon* (Athens, 1970). Meliaras Kallistos, "Hoi hagioi en Palestne kai ta ep antu dikaia tu helleniku ethnes," *Nea Sion,* XX (1925), 677 ff.; C. Charon [i.e., C. P. Karalevskij], "L'Origine ethnographique des Melkites," *Échos d'Orient,* XI (1908), 35–40; and Venance Grumel, "La Chronologie des patriarches grecs de Jérusalem au XIIIe siècle," *Revue des études byzantines,* XX (1962), 197–201.

The Armenian church enjoyed a somewhat similar position in the county of Edessa, where autonomous or semi-autonomous Armenian communities preserved their identity and their own hierarchy. Outside this area, however, Armenian communities were small, probably consisting only of collegiate chapters and monastic communities, although around these there sometimes gathered secular communities. Such was the case, for example, in Jerusalem under the Moslems and later under the crusaders, with its Armenian sanctuary of St. James.[27]

The Jacobites, who had successfully opposed Byzantine pressure, preserved a well-developed church organization.[28] It was the persistence of their church which to a large measure kept the community alive, preserving it from annihilation through conversion to the Orthodox or to the ruling Moslem creed. From the Jacobite point of

27. On the Armenians see below, note 90, but cf. Dagron, "Minorités ethniques."
28. In addition to the general studies indicated above, note 23, see Gabriel Khouri-Sarkis, "Introduction aux églises de langue syriaque," *L'Orient syrien,* I (1956), 3-30; Martin Jugie, "Monophysite (église syrienne)," in *Dictionnaire de théologie catholique,* X (1928), cols. 2216-2251; I. Ziadé, "Syrienne église," *ibid.,* XIV (1939), cols. 3017-3088; George Every, "Syrian Christians in Palestine in the Early Middle Ages," *Eastern Churches Quarterly,* VI (1945-1946), 363-372; *idem,* "Syrian Christians in Jerusalem, 1183-1283," *ibid.,* VII (1947), 46-54; and Joseph Nasrallah, "Syriens et Suriens," *ibid.,* VII (1947), 487-505. The history of the Jacobites (and incidentally that of the Armenians and Melkites also) under crusader rule is better known than that of other eastern denominations, owing to the Jacobite literature (written in Syriac and Arabic) of the period. See Graf, *op. cit.,* II, 263 ff. Of great importance are three chronicles: Jean B. Chabot, ed. and tr., *Chronique de Michel le Syrien, patriarche jacobite d'Antioche (1166-1199)* (4 vols., Paris, 1899-1924); Gregory abū-l-Farāj (Bar Hebraeus), *op. cit.,* and *The Chronography of Gregory Abû'l Faraj, Commonly Known as Bar Hebraeus,* ed. and tr. E. A. W. Budge (2 vols., London, 1932); and *Anonymi auctoris chronicon ad annum 1234 pertinens,* ed. Chabot (*CSCO, SS,* ser. 3, vols. XIV-XV; Paris, 1920), Syriac text ed. Chabot (*CSCO, SS,* 37; Louvain, 1952), first part tr. Chabot (*CSCO, SS,* 56; Louvain, 1937); the French translation stops before the crusade. A partial translation of other parts by Chabot is in *Mélanges offerts à M. Gustave Schlumberger . . .* (2 vols., Paris, 1924; corresponding to the Chabot ed., II, 118-128), and one by Tritton and Gibb is in the *Journal of the Royal Asiatic Society* (1933), pp. 69-101, 273-305 (corresponding to the Chabot ed., II, 54-162); there is an excellent summary by Rücker in *Oriens Christianus,* XXXII (1935), 124-139. Later part tr. Albert Abouna, with introduction and notes by Jean M. Fiey (*CSCO, SS,* 154; Louvain, 1974). Cf. an evaluation by Fiey, "Chrétiens syriaques entre croisés et mongols," *Orientalia Christiana analecta,* 197: *Symposium syriacum, 1972* (Rome, 1974), pp. 327-341.
For secondary works see Peter Kawerau, *Die jakobitische Kirche im Zeitalter der syrischen Renaissance: Idee und Wirklichkeit* (Berlin, 1955); Paul Krüger, "Das syrisch-monophysitische Mönchtum in Ṭūr-'Abdīn von seinen Anfängen bis zur Mitte des 12. Jahrhunderts," *Orientalia Christiana periodica,* IV (1938), 5-46; Ernst Honigmann, *Le Couvent de Barsaūmā et le patriarcat jacobite d'Antioche et de Syrie* (Louvain, 1954); Spuler, "Die west-syrische (monophysitische) Kirche unter dem Islam," *Saeculum,* IX (1958), 322-344. Cf. Chabot, "Les Évêques jacobites du VIIIème au XIIIème siècle d'après la chronique de Michel le Syrien," *ROC,* IV (1899), 444-452, 512-542; V (1900), 605-636; VI (1901), 189-220; and Judah B. Segal, *Edessa: "The Blessed City"* (Oxford, 1970).

view, even the Moslem conquest of the seventh century was advantageous, for it allowed them to spread into predominantly Nestorian Mesopotamia and Persia. Likewise the Selchükid conquest of Antioch freed them from the dominance of the Byzantine church.

The various Christian communities formed solid blocs in the north, but were little more than small enclaves in the predominantly Moslem population of the south. "Syrians" and Jacobites might be found in all crusader cities; there were some villages entirely of Christians of one or the other denomination.[29] Elsewhere they lived side by side with their Moslem neighbors in the villages, as they had for many generations in the cities before the crusader conquest. It is remarkable that, despite the poverty of eastern Christian sources, Frankish sources mention some twenty villages with an eastern Christian population in addition to the important communities in the cities, their monasteries, and some seminomadic Christian tribes living in Transjordan. Some areas seem to have had a special attraction for eastern Christians, especially the neighborhood of shrines, such as Bethlehem, Nazareth, and Mount Tabor. It is possible that these enclaves survived because the churches of the Orthodox and other Christian denominations had landed possessions in these areas and thus could more effectively shelter their Christian inhabitants from Moslem pressure for conversion than in areas where the Christian peasant had to face a Moslem landlord or a Moslem official alone.

In addition to Moslems and Christians, almost every city of importance in Syria, Lebanon, and Palestine had its Jewish inhabitants, although the Samaritans, who as late as the seventh century could still rise against Byzantium, were no more than a small community in the city of Nablus. The Jews suffered greatly during the First Crusade and the following period of expansion. There was a flourishing Jewish community when Ramla, the capital of the province, and Jerusalem, with its "Academy of the Holy Land" or "Yeshīvat Gaōn Ya'akōv," were the major centers of the Fāṭimids and their schismatic brothers, the Qaraites. It withered with the Selchükid invasion. The crusader conquest destroyed all the urban centers, among them Jerusalem and Haifa, where the Jews took up arms in their defense together with Moslems. Yet the Jews did not disappear. Some two dozen villages in Galilee preserved their Jewish communities as did the two cities, Tyre and Ascalon, which were not taken by storm but

---

29. See Prawer, *Latin Kingdom*, p. 225, no. 21. With the completion of the new archeological survey the list will certainly be enlarged.

capitulated. Moreover, once the conquest was over, the Jews again
settled in the cities although, as has been mentioned, they were barred
from Jerusalem.

The variety of ethnic groups and religions posed problems of which,
naturally, the crusaders had no knowledge before they arrived in the
east. The situation varied in the different states; the population of
the two northern principalities was to a great measure Christian,
whereas from Tripoli southward the Moslem element was by far the
dominant one. The law books which enshrine the "official" policy
respecting minorities pertained to the kingdom of Jerusalem proper,
rather than to the principalities. But it was a policy which probably
applied to the entire conquered area, namely to treat all the natives
as a single legal class of second-rate subjects, with fatal results for
ultimate Latin survival.

Although the crusaders soon became aware of the internal divisions of the native Christian population, they lumped them all into
a single category of people "who do not obey Rome."[30] To these they
added the Moslems, Jews, and Samaritans, all in the same legal class.
In contrast to these were those who were obedient to Rome, that is,
all Latin Europeans. Though themselves subdivided into distinct classes
—nobility, burgesses, and nationals of the communes—they all belonged to the dominant group, the conquerors.

There is no better evidence of the relative legal position of the Franks
and the minorities than their respective money compositions for criminal offenses. If a Frankish burgess is convicted for assaulting another
burgess, "he has to give the court 100 bezants and to the assaulted
man 100 sous."[31] If the assailant is a Syrian, however, "the court has
to have from the Syrian 50 bezants and the assaulted Frank 50 sous,
because the Syrian does not pay for assault but half the law and does
not receive but half the law."[32] We may compare this with the fines
for a similar offense involving a knight and a burgess. A knight who
assaults a burgess pays him 100 sous, and forfeits to the lord's court
his horse, mule, and harness.[33] A burgess who assaults a knight loses
his right hand or can redeem it by payment of 100 bezants to the

---

30. Philip of Novara, cap. 28 (*RHC, Lois,* I, 502): "Grés et Suriens et tous autres Crestiens
qui ne sont de la ley de Rome."

31. *Livre des Assises de la Cour des Bourgeois,* cap. 295 (*RHC, Lois,* II, 221).

32. *Ibid.,* cap. 296 (p. 222). This is also the general rule applied to *dhimmīs* in Moslem
lands. Their *diyah,* which corresponds to the *wergeld,* is half that of the Moslems. See Cahen,
s.v. "Dhimma," in *The Encyclopaedia of Islam,* new ed., II (Leyden and London, 1965), 226–231.

33. *Livre au roi,* cap. 19 (*RHC, Lois,* I, 619).

knight and 1,000 bezants to the court.[34] If he cannot pay the latter (roughly the annual income of two average villages, or two years' income of a knight's fee), he is to remain in prison at the mercy of the court.

The compositions for assault make no distinction even between native Christians and non-Christians.[35] In everyday life the crusaders may have felt a greater affinity for eastern Christians, and showed them more favor, but the law made no such distinction. Although the legal treatises, with one exception, date from the mid-thirteenth century, there is no doubt that the general policy toward the natives was fixed at an early period, probably during the first two decades after the fall of Jerusalem. Moslems, Jews, and Samaritans were left complete freedom of worship, but the Moslems, and in some measure the Jews, saw their sanctuaries destroyed or converted into Latin churches. This happened in Jerusalem where the two great Moslem sanctuaries, the Dome of the Rock (the mosque of 'Umar) and the al-Aqṣâ mosque, became the Templum Domini and Templum Salomonis respectively. It happened in all the maritime cities, like Ascalon where the mosque called al-Khiḍr (the Green One; or possibly connected with the prophet Elijah) became Sancta Maria Cathara. In many cases the mosques, which the crusaders called *mahumeria,* became simple lodgings. With the disappearance of the Moslem population from those cities taken by force, their mosques disappeared as well, and we do not know if any were reëstablished under crusader rule. On the other hand, mosques remained in villages and possibly in some cities. With the reconquest by Saladin in 1187 there followed a complete reconversion of churches to mosques; in the process even churches founded by the crusaders became mosques or pious foundations.[36]

A similar process, but on a smaller scale, probably took place with regard to the synagogues. The most numerous community of Jews and Qaraites was that of Ramla, although it had diminished in importance almost a generation before the First Crusade. The synagogues of Jerusalem were burned down together with the Jews who had sought within them a last refuge in prayer. This must also have happened

34. *Ibid.,* cap. 17 (pp. 617–618). There was no money composition between nobles: *ibid.,* caps. 40–41 (p. 635).

35. A Moslem who assaults a Christian pays living expenses and medication; otherwise he is beaten and expelled. If he is accused again of a similar offense, he is hanged; *Livre des Assises de la Cour des Bourgeois,* cap. 241 (*RHC, Lois,* II, 173).

36. Cf. Saladin's inscription of 1192 converting the church and nunnery of St. Anne into a Shāfiʻite madrasah, preserved in the tympanum of the church. For Acre and Jerusalem see Prawer, *Royaume latin,* I, 659, 676 ff.

in other places.[37] However, with the great waves of Jewish immigration into Palestine at the end of the twelfth century and during the thirteenth, synagogues were rebuilt or houses were converted into places for prayer. There were academies in Tyre and especially in Acre. By the time of Saladin's reconquest, Jewish prayer places had been rebuilt in some cities, foremost among them in Jerusalem about 1190 and again in 1267.

What might have been expected to happen to mosques and synagogues surprisingly happened to Christian churches also, though for different reasons and in a different way. Urban II's call at Clermont clearly included as a major aim the liberation of eastern Christians from the Moslem yoke. Yet three years later the leaders of the army of liberation, having captured Antioch and refused to hand it over to the Christian basileus of Constantinople, could write to the pope: "We conquered the Turks and pagans, but we could not defeat the heretics, the Greeks, Armenians, Syrians, and Jacobites." They then invited the pope to join them, "and all the heresies, whatever they might be, you will eradicate and destroy by your authority and our valor."[38] Clearly, crusading ideology had not survived confrontation with the Christian east. Eastern Christians might very well be liberated from the Moslem yoke, but voices in the army also demanded the eradication of the schismatic and heretical churches. No such policy was pursued, but the attitudes revealed had a fatal impact on the social and political organization of the crusader states, and quite possibly on their political destiny.

The attitude to these different Christian denominations, though the same in principle, was not so in practice. Generally speaking, the "schismatic" Byzantine and the "Syrian" or Melkite churches found themselves worse off than under the rule of Islam, whereas the "heretical" churches were better off than before.[39] The establishment of

---

37. Benedict of Alignan, bishop of Marseilles, mentions the ruins of a synagogue in the place where the Templars built their castle in Safad; see R. B. C. Huygens, "Un Nouveau texte du traité 'De constructione castri Saphet'," *Studi medievali,* 3rd ser., VI-1 (1965), 355–387; cf. *BOF,* I (Quaracchi, 1906), 249–253.

38. *Die Kreuzzugsbriefe aus den Jahren 1088–1100,* ed. Heinrich Hagenmeyer (Innsbruck, 1901), p. 164 (ep. 16).

39. The position of the Greeks and Melkites can be gathered from some Orthodox itineraries: "Vie et pèlerinage de Daniel, hégoumène russe, 1106–1107," in *Itinéraires russes en Orient,* ed. and tr. Sofia de Khitrovo (Khitrowo) (SOL, *SG,* V; Geneva, 1889), pp. 1–83; tr. Charles W. Wilson in *PPTS,* IV-3 (London, 1895); and John Phocas, "A Brief Description of the Holy Land, 1185," tr. Aubrey Stewart in *PPTS,* V-3 (London, 1896). It is unnecessary to discuss here the partisan literature regarding the attitude of the crusaders to the Greek and Melkite church. Of the western descriptions, those of James of Vitry and Burchard of Mt. Sion pay more attention to the eastern churches than do the others.

the Latin church in Syria and Palestine was accompanied by the destitu-
tion of the Greek and Melkite hierarchies and by an almost wholesale
spoliation of the Byzantine sanctuaries. The holiest places, such as
the church of the Annunciation at Nazareth, the church of the Nativity at Bethlehem, and the Holy Sepulcher, became the property of
the Latin church, though the Byzantine and other denominations preserved the right to celebrate offices there.

The Greek patriarchs John of Antioch and Symeon II of Jerusalem
were replaced by the Latins Bernard of Valence and Daimbert of Pisa,
respectively. The Byzantine church continued to appoint patriarchs
who lived in Constantinople. This was more true for Jerusalem than
for Antioch, not only because in Antioch there was a large Byzantine
population, but also because the claims of the Byzantine emperor
to the possession of the city of Antioch sometimes resulted in the
acceptance there of a Greek patriarch.[40]

Although the Byzantine church was not in communion with Rome,
the idea of one church and one faith was never abandoned. It would
have been scandalous, therefore, to have two bishops, one Greek and
one Latin, in the same place, a practice which had been rejected by
the church from the earliest times of Christianity. In effect, this meant
that Byzantine bishops were replaced by Latins, and the lower Byzantine clergy subordinated to the jurisdiction of Latin prelates. This
was put into practice almost immediately, although more thoroughly
in Jerusalem than in Antioch, and had consequences far beyond the
frontiers of the kingdom. When Greek Cyprus was captured, and
later when the Byzantine empire became the Latin empire of Constantinople following the Fourth Crusade, the same principles were
applied to these new areas, where there were few Moslem inhabitants
and the population was overwhelmingly Orthodox.[41] The policy had
already become one of long standing when explicitly defined in a canon
of the Fourth Lateran Council: "Since in many places in the same
city and diocese there are people of different languages, who have
different rites and customs under one faith, we order strictly that the
bishops of such cities or dioceses should appoint suitable men who

40. In 1137 Raymond of Poitiers, prince of Antioch, promised to invest a Greek patriarch
(Chalandon, *Les Comnène,* I, 132, note 3); so did Reginald of Châtillon (regent 1153–1160;
ibid., II, 445, 449). In 1165 Bohemond III installed the Greek patriarch Athanasius (*ibid.,* II,
531); the Greek Symeon II was installed in 1206–1207. David and Euthymius followed in the
middle of the century (Karalevskij, in *Dictionnaire d'histoire et de géographie ecclésiastiques,*
III, cols. 616–620).

41. The decisions of Honorius III for Cyprus expressly cite the customs of the crusader
mainland; see Aloysius L. Tăutu, ed., *Acta Honorii III (1216–1227) et Gregorii IX (1227–1241)
e registris Vaticanis aliisque fontibus* (PC, Fontes, ser. 3, vol. III; Vatican City, 1950), nos. 108, 140.

will celebrate the divine offices and administer the sacraments according to the diversity of rites and languages, instructing them both in words as by example. But we prohibit entirely that one and the same city or diocese should have different bishops, like one body with many heads, as though a monster."[42] In the case of grave necessity, however, the local bishop might appoint a prelate to such "nations" as his vicar, who would be directly subject to him.

This was generally applicable also to the Syrians or Melkites. Since they were of the same rite as the Greeks, they should have been dealt with in the same way. In fact, however, we do not know how things worked out. There may have been "Syrian" bishops in cities and in the countryside, perhaps a remnant of the once-numerous hierarchy of the Byzantine church.[43] With the disappearance of the Byzantine population proper, the "Syrians" may have continued the tradition. But we do not find their bishops in the great sees, while those we know about were subject to the patriarchs of Antioch or Jerusalem.

The policy of replacing Greek patriarchs and bishops, like the removal of Greeks in Nazareth and Sebastia, could not be imposed on the lower clergy. Nor were the monastic establishments affected. The lower clergy and monasteries were required to recognize the supremacy of the Latin prelates; this was mere lip-service.[44] The "Syrians" had to have their own Arabic-speaking clergy as well as their Greek liturgy. Consequently, despite wholesale spoliation, they succeeded in hanging on to some churches and property. We have already mentioned Greek services in the Holy Sepulcher and in Bethlehem. On Mount Tabor the Greek monks kept the monastery of St. Elijah when

---

42. *Acta Innocentii III,* ed. Haluščynskyj, pp. 483–484; Karl J. von Hefele, *Conciliengeschichte,* tr. Henri M. Leclercq, *Histoire des conciles* (12 vols., Paris, 1907–1952), V-2, 1339, canon 9.

43. From signatures on an act of the order of St. John we learn of the Greek archbishop of Gaza and Bait Jibrīn, one Meletos, as well as of Greek clergy of the chapter of the Holy Sepulcher with the titles *heiereus* (abbot), *deuterarius* (prior), *protodecanos* (archdeacon), and *decanos* (dean) (J. Delaville Le Roulx, "Trois chartes . . .," in *AOL,* I [1881; repr. Brussels, 1964], 413–415; Reinhold Röhricht, *Regesta regni Hierosolymitani 1097–1291* [Innsbruck, 1893; repr. New York, 1960], no. 502). As our document states, the Melkite bishop was spiritually affiliated with the order. The Greek bishop of Pharan (Faran, on Mt. Sinai) was dependent on the Latin archbishop of Philadelphia ('Ammān); John of Ibelin, cap. 266 (*RHC, Lois,* I, 417); Mayer, "Die Laura des hl. Sabas und die orthodoxe Klerikergemeinschaft am hl. Grabe," *Bistümer, Klöster und Stifte im Königreich Jerusalem* (MGH, Schriften, 26; Stuttgart, 1977), pp. 406–409.

44. Latin prelates like James of Vitry, bishop of Acre, often complained of their insincerity, a complaint so often repeated in itineraries and histories and by the popes that we can be sure there was passive resistance. See *Acta Honorii III,* ed. Tăutu, pp. 116–117 (nos. 86–87) and *passim.*

the Benedictines took over their former house.[45] In the greater cities
there were Greek parish churches and hospices, for example, the
monastery of St. Catherine in Acre, and the hospice of St. Moses,[46]
the church of St. Abraham,[47] and the monasteries of St. Sabas and
St. Chariton in or near Jerusalem.[48] It was a small remnant of what
had belonged to the Orthodox church before. A considerable amount
of landed property was taken over by the newcomers, some thirty
villages with the Holy Sepulcher, and twelve villages belonging to
Mount Tabor.[49]

The position of the Greek church under the crusaders was precarious. In the principalities of Edessa and Antioch it was almost permanently on the brink of revolt. Yet the Greek and "Syrian" churches
had their moments of triumph, almost always as a result of Byzantine
military, or sometimes political, intervention. In Antioch there were
times when Greek patriarchs were allowed to take over the cathedral
of St. Peter and were accepted by the prince, though naturally excommunicated by the Latin clergy. When Byzantino-Frankish diplomacy allowed, as under Manuel I Comnenus (1143–1180), imperial
support was made available to Greek churches and the great common
Christian sanctuaries. Thus Manuel covered the tomb in the Holy
Sepulcher with gold and installed marvelous mosaics in the chapel
of Golgotha.[50] At the same time Byzantine artists and money embellished the church of Bethlehem with mosaics where bilingual inscriptions, Latin and Greek, testified to a kind of medieval ecumenism
of convenience.[51]

The basileus also helped the Greek monasteries to hold their own
when other ecclesiastical establishments were disappearing. These were

45. Cf. Daniel, in *Itinéraires russes,* ed. Khitrovo, p. 67, and Phocas, in *PPTS,* V-3, 14.

46. St. Catherine and St. Moses belonged to the abbot of Mt. Sinai; *Acta Honorii III,*
ed. Tăutu, pp. 35–37 (no. 17) and cf. no. 148; Röhricht, *Regesta,* no. 897.

47. Near the Damascus gate; it belonged, it would seem, to the Melkites or Jacobites. An
eighteenth-century Georgian itinerary mentions St. Abraham in Jerusalem as a Georgian foundation: Marie F. Brosset, *Histoire de la Géorgie depuis l'antiquité jusqu'au XIXe siècle* (2 vols.,
St. Petersburg, 1849–1858), I, 197–209. See also John B. Hennessy, "Preliminary Report on
the Excavations of the Damascus Gate, 1964–1966," *Levant,* II (1970), 22–27.

48. Röhricht, *Regesta,* no. 409.

49. As late as 1140 the chapter of the Holy Sepulcher was claiming possessions in Antioch
which had originally belonged to it under Byzantine and Moslem rule: "qua temporibus Graecorum deservierant": Eugène de Rozière, ed., *Cartulaire de l'église du Saint-Sépulcre de Jérusalem* (Paris, 1849), p. 179 (no. 90), repr. in *PL,* 155 (Paris, 1880), cols. 1105–1262.

50. Phocas, in *PPTS,* V-3, 19. A beautiful mosaic of this period, an apotheosis, is still
preserved in the Latin part of the Golgotha.

51. Cf. Robert W. Hamilton, *Guide to Bethlehem* (Jerusalem, 1939), and Bellarmino Ba-
gatti, *Gli Antichi edifici sacri di Betlemme* (Jerusalem, 1952).

venerable institutions, some going back to the earliest period of Christian monasticism. Latins did not replace Greek monks in the monasteries, which were often in almost inaccessible places of the desert of Judea or on the banks of the Jordan, some surviving to our times.[52] Moreover, even literary activity continued in them under crusader rule.[53]

There is no doubt that the relative situation of the non-Greek denominations was more favorable. In the northern principalities, there were the two Monophysite groups, Armenians and Jacobites; only the latter were really important in the county of Tripoli and in the kingdom of Jerusalem, although there was an important Armenian sanctuary in Jerusalem, and churches and hospices in Tripoli, Acre, and other places.

Though never accepted by or integrated into Frankish society, these communities were accorded better treatment for various reasons. The Armenians were a political factor in Byzantino-Frankish relations, especially in the thirteenth century in the principality of Antioch. As the Armenian state, and even more their church, had long suffered from Byzantine persecutions, they were, in a sense, natural allies of

52. The following Greek monasteries are mentioned in contemporary sources: St. Elijah (Mār Elyās), on the road from Jerusalem to Bethlehem, destroyed by earthquake and rebuilt by Manuel Comnenus; St. Euthymius, St. Sabas (Mār Sābā), St. Chariton, Calamona, St. George of Khoziba in the Wādī al-Qilt, St. Gerasimus (Qaṣr Ḥajlah), and St. John (Qaṣr al-Yahūd) on the banks of the Jordan, also restored by Manuel Comnenus. The list is based on the itineraries of the Russian abbot Daniel, *PPTS,* IV-3, and Phocas, *PPTS,* V-3; cf. Otto F. Meinardus, "Notes on the Laurae and Monasteries of the Wilderness of Judaea," *Liber annuus,* XV (1964–1965), 220–250; *idem,* "Wall Paintings in the Monastic Churches of Judea," *Oriens Christianus,* L (1966), 46 ff. Cf. Siméon Vailhé, *Répertoire alphabétique des monastères de Palestine* (Paris, 1900; republished from *ROC,* IV [1899]); Robert Devreesse, "Les Anciens évêchés de Palestine," *Mémorial Marie Joseph Lagrange* (Paris, 1940), pp. 217–227. In addition to St. Sabas (on which see Vailhé, "Le Monastère de Saint-Sabas," *Échos d'Orient,* III [1899], 168 ff., and Albert Ehrhard, "Das griechische Kloster Mar Saba in Palästina," *Römische Quartalschrift,* VII [1893], 32–79), the most important monastery was that of St. Theodosius. A papal confirmation of its possessions mentions the church of St. Theodosius in Jerusalem with hospice, *apotheca,* and bakery; the monasteries of St. John the Baptist and St. George; property in Ascalon and Ramla; the church of St. Jonah outside Jaffa with *apotheca* and hospice; a church in "Zevel" (Jubail?) and another (in the same place?) of Sts. Peter and Paul with hospice; see *Acta Honorii III,* ed. Tăutu, pp. 1–2 (no. 2). One wonders if "Laberia" in the title Sanctus Theodosius Cenobiarcha de Laberia might not refer to La Berrie, the southern desert of Judea in crusader terminology.

53. This can be gathered from twelfth-century MSS. today in the library of the Greek patriarchate; Ehrhard, "Die griechische Patriarchat-Bibliothek von Jerusalem," *Römische Quartalschrift,* V (1891), 217–265, 329–331, 383–384; VI (1892), 339–365; cf. *idem,* "Das griechische Kloster Mar Saba," *ibid.,* VII, 32–79; Kenneth W. Clark, *Check List of MSS. in the Library of the Greek and Armenian Patriarchates in Jerusalem* (Washington, 1953); Prawer, *Latin Kingdom,* p. 224, note 20; p. 226, notes 24, 26.

the Franks. The Jacobites were in a somewhat similar position. They never played any political role and had no military value, but the fact that they had been persecuted by Greeks and Melkites, which had led them to favor the Selchükid invasion, brought them the favor of the Franks. The Jacobites would emphasize the fact that Monophysite blood ran in the veins of the royal dynasty (from Melisend's mother Morfia). As "heretics" rather than just "schismatics" they retained their own hierarchy, simply recognizing their subjection to the Latins. Their patriarch at Antioch, Athanasius VII, and their bishops were neither expelled nor replaced by Latins. The Latin hierarchy and the papacy deplored the situation[54] but, in fact, required only a nominal obedience from them. Of course the relatively favorable attitude of the Franks, well attested by the great churchman and historian Michael the Syrian (d. 1199), Jacobite patriarch at Antioch, did not prevent the confiscation of property in the early years of the kingdom, or later spoliations in the county of Edessa.[55]

Yet on the whole the Jacobites, with bitter memories that in the eleventh century their patriarch had been expelled by the Greeks from Antioch, now enjoyed freedom of worship. Given the particular structure of the Jacobite church, it was the patriarch at Antioch who was in direct contact with the Franks, whereas the realm of his vicar, the "Maphrian" (from *Prj,* fertilizer—that is, the ordainer of bishops) was in the east. The Franks often showed the patriarch favor, but not without a good deal of condescension.

The area of heaviest Jacobite population seems to have been between Antioch and Edessa in the north and in Palestine in the south. Jacobite bishops functioned in Acre, in Tripoli,[56] and in Jerusalem with its churches of St. Mary Magdalen and St. Simeon the Pharisee. Although built by a Copt, Macarius of Nabruwah, under the patriarch of Alexandria Mar Ya'qūb (810–830), the former became Jacobite under the benevolent Selchükids, through the exertions of a Jacobite in their service, Manṣūr al-Balbayī (the reading of the name is not

54. *Acta Honorii III,* ed. Tăutu, pp. 117–118 (no. 88): "Suriani, Jacobini, Nestoriani . . . nec archiepiscopo et praelatis, nec ecclesiis obediunt Latinorum, sed tamquam acephali evagantes, suis sectis antiquis et erroribus innituntur." Consequently the pope orders: "quatenus Surianos, Jacobinos et Nestorianos . . . ad obedientiam . . . archiepiscopo et suffraganeis eius . . . impendendam, monitione praemisso, per censuram ecclesiasticam, appellatione remota, cogatis." The bull pertains to Cyprus, but was sent to Ralph of Mérencourt, the patriarch of Jerusalem, Peter of Limoges, the archbishop of Caesarea, and bishop Renier of Bethlehem.

55. Jean P. Martin, "Les Premiers princes croisés et les syriens jacobites de Jérusalem," *Journal asiatique,* XII (1888), 471–490; XIII (1889), 33–80. For Joscelin's plundering of the monastery of Bar Ṣaumā in 1148 see Michael the Syrian, *op. cit.,* III, 283 ff.; Bar Hebraeus, *Chronicon,* II, 510; Fiey, "Chrétiens syriaques," pp. 327–345.

56. Bar Hebraeus, *Chronicon,* I, 681, 708.

clear). It was consecrated in 1092, in the presence of the delegates of Cyril II, the Coptic patriarch of Alexandria.[57] Here lived the Jacobite bishops of Jerusalem, with a hospice and a residence for the patriarch when he visited Jerusalem. In a sense it was a Monophysite center where Jacobites mixed with Copts. The church was built in what had been the old Jewish quarter, colonized through the efforts of Baldwin I (about 1115), who brought in eastern Christians from Transjordan.[58] It is therefore possible that, although the inhabitants are described as "Syrians",[59] they were really Jacobites, perhaps with an admixture of Greeks and Melkites who probably kept to their own old quarter near the Holy Sepulcher. Not only was the monastery of St. Mary Magdalen an administrative center, but there was some literary activity there also.[60]

Contacts between Jacobites and Franks were frequent, more so in Antioch than in Palestine. On the whole they were friendly, but internal ecclesiastical quarrels brought about the intervention of Frankish rulers and clergy. The Frankish authorities, whether lay or ecclesiastical, were called on to confirm ecclesiastical elections, which opened the way to bribery.[61] Bar Hebraeus (d. 1286) goes so far as to accuse the west Jacobite church of simony "like that practised by the Armenians".[62] No doubt the custom inherited from the earlier Moslem period, the confirmation of election by the local emirs, which continued now under the Franks, encouraged simoniacal practices.

---

57. Our knowledge of the Copts under the crusaders depends largely on Syrian Jacobite sources. For Coptic sources of the period see Sawīrus ibn-al-Mukaffa', *History of the Patriarchs of the Egyptian Church . . .*, ed. and tr. A. S. Atiya, Yassa 'Abd-al-Masīh, and O.H.E.K. Burmester (Cairo, 1948–1959); earlier part tr. B. T. A. Evetts in *Patrologia orientalis,* I-2/4; V-1; X-5; a Latin summary by Eusèbe Renaudot, *Historia patriarcharum Alexandrinorum Jacobitarum a D. Marco usque ad finem saeculi XIII* (Paris, 1713). Al-Maqrīzī's study of Christian churches and monasteries deals mainly with Egypt. For the building and restoration of the Jacobite St. Mary Magdalen, see *Patrologia orientalis,* X, 461, and Sawīrus ibn-al-Mukaffa', *op. cit.,* pp. 364–365; Hugo Duensing, "Die Abessinier in Jerusalem," *ZDPV,* XXXIX (1916), 98–115. Cf. Enrico Cerulli, *Etiopi in Palestina: Storia della communità etiopica di Gerusalemme* (Collezione scientifica e documentaria dell' Africa italiana, 12; Rome, 1943), I, 10–13, and Meinardus, *The Copts in Jerusalem* (Cairo, 1960), pp. 11 ff.

58. Cf. Prawer, "The Settlement of the Latins in Jerusalem," pp. 490–503.

59. Between the street of Josaphat and the city walls, up to the gate of Josaphat (today the Gate of the Lions): "a rue ausi come une vile. La manoient li plus des Suriiens de Iherusalem. Et ces rues apeloit on la Iuerie. Et en cele rue de Iuerie avoit j. Moustier de Sainte Marie Madelaine"; *Itinéraires à Jérusalem et descriptions de la Terre Sainte . . .*, ed. and tr. Henri Michelant and Gaston Raynaud (SOL, *SG,* III; Geneva, 1882), pp. 27, 160–161.

60. Cf. Meinardus, *Copts in Jerusalem,* p. 15.

61. Bar Hebraeus, *Chronicon,* II, 470, 476–478, 498, 656–664, 668, 710–712. Cf. Michael the Syrian, *op. cit.,* III, 197, 211, 385–386: the rebellious Jacobite monk Bar Wahbūn bribed Heraclius, the corrupt Latin patriarch of Jerusalem, to get possession of St. Mary Magdalen.

62. Bar Hebraeus, *Chronicon,* II, 516. Cf. Michael the Syrian, *op. cit.,* III, 379: Amalric

The relations between the Monophysite denominations were on the whole very friendly. This was the result in part of their common hatred for the Greeks, the "Chalcedonians," in part of their creed, which, despite minor differences in ritual, was virtually the same for them all. Their leaders played down the differences; this did not prevent the writing of critical interdenominational tracts, but the polemical tone was less sharp than when they dealt with Franks and Greeks.[63]

The Jacobite patriarch and the Armenian and Coptic prelates announced their elections to one another, and customarily received mutual congratulations, sometimes with pious exhortations. Their elections were also announced in the different patriarchates.[64] The only important quarrel under crusader rule was the interference of the Coptic patriarch of Alexandria in Jerusalem and that of the Jacobite patriarch of Antioch in Ethiopia. Ethiopia's bishops were usually ordained by Alexandria, and were Egyptians. But Ignatius II in a dispute with Cyril III, the patriarch of Alexandria, appointed a black named Thomas for Ethiopia, after Cyril in 1236 appointed a Copt named Basil as archbishop of Jerusalem, even though Jerusalem depended on Antioch. The new archbishop, appointed it seems under the pressure of Copts who visited the holy places, was confirmed by the Franks when he promised to unite his church with that of the Franks.[65]

Friendly relations with the Franks not only allowed the repair and enlargement of the church of the Magdalen in Jerusalem, but also the erection of a new church in Antioch in 1156, the consecration of which was celebrated in the presence of the Frankish patriarch Aimery of Limoges.[66] There was even a rumor that the Maphrian Ignatius IV, who died in Tripoli in 1258, had left half his fortune to

---

(1163–1174) as well as Baldwin IV (1174–1185) confirmed the Jacobite patriarch. Joscelin, who played the role of protector of the Jacobites, insisted that the consecration of the new patriarch Athanasius, though he was elected in Kesoun, should be celebrated in his presence at Tell Bashir; Michael the Syrian, *op. cit.*, III, 231; Bar Hebraeus, *Chronicon*, II, 484.

63. For polemical tracts written by Joannes Bar Andreas, bishop of Mabūj, against Armenians and Franks, see Michael the Syrian, *op. cit.*, III, 238; Bar Hebraeus, *Chronicon*, II, 484. Cf. Michael the Syrian, *op. cit.*, III, 256, 344–345.

64. *Ibid.*, III, 331, 354–355.

65. This famous quarrel is described in detail by Bar Hebraeus, *Chronicon*, II, 656–664. There is reason to suppose that this began a permanent rift among the Monophysites and the establishment of an independent hierarchy of Copts in Jerusalem. Saladin seems to have later confirmed the Copts and Abyssinians in their places in the church of the Holy Sepulcher; see Timotheos P. Themeles, *Les Grecs aux lieux saints* (Jerusalem, 1921), p. 68, cited by Meinardus, *Copts in Jerusalem*, p. 16.

66. Bar Hebraeus, *Chronicon*, II, 667; Michael the Syrian, *op. cit.*, III, 303–653.

the Frankish churches and half to Jacobite churches and monasteries. In some cases Jacobites baptized their children in Frankish churches in Edessa,[67] in the light of which the plundering in 1148 of the great Jacobite monastery of Bar Ṣaumā by Joscelin II of Edessa[68] with the participation of Armenian troops seems to have been a sad episode, though local chicanery was never wanting.

Despite the seemingly amicable relations, and despite the efforts of Michael the Syrian to emphasize the friendliness of the Franks, something not too apparent in the chronicle of Bar Hebraeus, it was all very superficial. As for the Anonymous Syrian Chronicle of 1234, it is clear that the chronicler's Christian perspective did not lead him to favor the crusader establishments. He judged Moslems and Latin Catholics according to their attitudes toward and relations with the "orthodox" (non-Chalcedonian) nation of the Syrians.

The great Jacobite church, comprising in the eleventh and twelfth centuries some seventeen metropolitans and thirty bishops in the west (and some eighteen under the Maphrian in the east), never accommodated itself to the new conditions of a crusader state on the coast. Though the patriarchal see was Antioch, no Jacobite patriarch, except Mār Ignatius II (1222–1252), ever stayed there. Amida, Ḥiṣn Ziyād (Kharput), Bar Ṣaumā, and Mardin were the normal places of residence. The great centers of Jacobite learning remained the monasteries of Bar Ṣaumā in the west and Bar Mattai (near Mosul) in the east, though Bar Hebraeus studied rhetoric and medicine with a Nestorian in Frankish Tripoli.[69] Other than in times of war, Jacobite patriarchs moved so freely between Moslem and Christian lands that one has the impression of a single region peopled by the Jacobite or Syrian "nation."[70] Frankish Syria and Palestine had no attraction for them. Their focus of religious and community life remained in the lands of Islam. Whatever hopes they might have entertained at the moment of the crusader conquest, the event had no meaningful impact on their customary organization. When Jerusalem became a center of western Christendom, and the Jews, as always in times of

67. Bar Hebraeus, *Chronicon*, II, 668. It is quite possible that the testament of the eastern Christian who left money to Latin and non-Latin establishments was that of a Jacobite (*ibid.*, II, 478). For a Jacobite church built on Frankish property in Antioch after a miraculous healing of a child, see Michael the Syrian, *op. cit.*, III, 304.

68. Michael the Syrian, *op. cit.*, III, 283 ff.

69. Bar Hebraeus, *Chronicon*, II, 670.

70. Patriarch Michael, after his election, visited the centers of his community in Edessa, the Holy Mountain, Kesoun, Barīd, Cilicia, Antioch, Latakia, Tyre, and Jerusalem; Michael the Syrian, *op. cit.*, III, 331–332.

crisis, turned their eyes in expectation to Jerusalem, the holy city never ranked as a Jacobite patriarchate, but only as a bishop's see. Bar Ṣaumā remained their great sanctuary, and even Michael the Syrian wrote in the shadow of the great saint.

This attitude, whether dictated by experience or by a detached, unsentimental appreciation that the majority of Jacobites lived in Moslem lands, led to an ambivalent view of the crusades and of the Franks. Jacobite writers, despite their "official" hatred of Moslems, judged events and people, Moslems and Christians alike, from a particular Jacobite perspective. This is true even with a Francophile like Michael the Syrian or the Armenian Matthew of Edessa (d. about 1136). They praised the Selchükids, for example, for allowing the construction of two Jacobite churches (St. Mary and St. George) in Antioch after its capture from the Byzantines.[71] The liberality of the Selchükids was put on the same level as that of the Franks in allowing complete religious freedom to the Jacobites. The former drove out the Greeks, who could "no longer force the Orthodox [the Jacobites], as was their cruel custom, to be converted to their heresy." The Franks "never created difficulties in the matter of faith . . . in arriving at a single formula for all the nations and languages of the Christians, but regarded as Christian everyone who adored the cross, without further inquiry or examination."[72]

This did not prevent the Syrian patriarch from condemning Joscelin II and his Armenian soldiery for the spoliation of the monastery of Bar Ṣaumā,[73] or Nūr-ad-Dīn for renewing discriminatory legislation against Christians and Jews.[74] On the other hand, when Kîlîj Arslan II, the Selchükid sultan, in 1181 invited the Jacobite patriarch Michael to meet him at Melitene, Michael heaped praises upon him, while "all the Christians lit candles, raised crosses on high, and lifted their voices to sing the office."[75]

The Jacobite point of view was a function of the local attitudes they met as a minority. Their precarious position is clear from an episode, described by the Jacobite patriarch, which occurred in 1141 in Melitene. The Turks invaded the monastery at Zabar and sacked it. In May 1142 the crusaders decided on vengeance: "They robbed the goods of the Christians, but did not confront the Turks. And when

71. *Ibid.,* pp. 170, 174.
72. *Ibid.,* p. 222.
73. *Ibid.,* pp. 283 ff.
74. *Ibid.,* pp. 342 ff.
75. *Ibid.,* p. 351.

the Franks left, the Turks came again, pillaged, and departed. Thus the Christians were robbed by both sides."[76]

In times of tension, the Moslem population often gave vent to anti-Christian feelings, even though the Jacobites were in no way involved. Thus, after the battle of Hattin, the repercussions were felt by the Jacobites. "How much outrage, injury, and contempt the Moslems then heaped on the persecuted Christians in Damascus, Aleppo, Harran, Edessa, Amida, Mardin, Mosul, and in the rest of their dominion, no words can describe,"[77] complains the Jacobite patriarch.

For the Jacobites there was only one consolation, the providence of God. No words are more illuminating than those of Michael the Syrian: "if, because of our sins, God has allowed Arabs or Turks to rule over us, nevertheless in his mercy he has never abandoned us and never will, at no time and in no way. By his providence he watches over us and delivers us from all our enemies, because of his love for his church."[78] The Franks did not consciously favor the Jacobites. Their attitude was one of toleration mixed with suspicion. As our sources are often one-sided it is not easy to judge events. Yet in some cases not much is left in doubt. Armenians of Albistan, calling in Moslems in 1106 against the Franks, and shouting the equivalent of "Franks go home!" is a revealing incident; it led the pro-Frankish Armenian Matthew to explain that the great Frankish warriors of the time of the conquest were dead and their principalities were in the undeserving hands of their descendents.[79] Earlier, in 1101, we are told that the holy fire (a pious fraud) did not appear on time, to punish the Franks "because they chased from their monasteries the Armenians, the Greeks, the Syrians, and the Georgians," and established nunneries. The Franks then repented (the holy fire having appeared after the prayers of the Jacobites) and "reinstated each nation in what belongs to them".[80]

In 1104, after the defeat of the crusaders at Harran, when Chökürmish of Mosul attacked Edessa and Rîdvan of Aleppo Antioch, the Christian population opened the gates of the surrounding cities to Rîdvan.[81] The same thing happened less than a generation later after

76. *Ibid.,* p. 249.
77. *Ibid.,* p. 404.
78. *Ibid.,* p. 345.
79. Matthew of Edessa, in *RHC, Arm.,* I, 81.
80. *Ibid.,* I, 54–55; Hitti, "The Impact," pp. 211–218.
81. Prawer, *Royaume latin,* I, 286.

the crusaders' defeat at Darb Sarmadā (the "ager sanguinis").[82] In 1148 the Jacobites (though not the Armenians) were ready to accept Zengi in what was left of the county of Edessa.[83] In 1182, when Ḥabīs Jaldak in Transjordan fell to Farrūkh-Shāh of Damascus, its commander Fulk of Tiberias was accused of having left the place to a native Christian garrison.[84] All this culminated in the famous accusation in 1189 that the eastern Christians had connived at turning over Jerusalem to Saladin. The Coptic chronicler of Alexandria pointed an accusing finger at the Jerusalem-born Melkite Joseph al-Batiṭ, who moved to Damascus and entered the service of the Aiyūbids. In Egypt he met Saladin and tried to ensure the status of his community. Saladin used him as an envoy in his dealings with the Franks, but also as a spy and agent. In this latter capacity he was sent with bribery money to Jerusalem in return for Saladin's favor for his community.[85] It is impossible to know what really happened, but the story spread to the Franks and to Europe.[86]

Quite possibly Zengid, Aiyūbid, and Mamluk attitudes toward eastern Christians explained Frankish suspicions, although in some cases there is no doubt about their pro-Moslem sentiments. Zengi tried to drive a wedge between the Franks and the eastern denominations. On his order the massacres in Edessa in 1144 were stopped. The Jacobite bishop Basil Bar-Shumnā became his adviser. The same favor was shown to Ananias, the Armenian bishop of Edessa. The churches and their spoils were restored and former Latin churches were handed over to them.[87] Saladin's proclamation that Christians who wanted to remain in the formerly Frankish cities would be allowed to do so was clearly aimed at the eastern Christians, since no Frank would have thought to remain. In fact, eastern Christians and Jews remained in Acre, Nablus, and Jerusalem. In the last, like the Franks, they had to pay ransom, and also the *jizyah* which they had earlier paid as *capitatio* to the Franks.[88] There is no reason to suppose that they evacuated other places. Strangely enough, when the Moslems and Jews abandoned Jerusalem in 1219 after the destruction of its walls by al-

---

82. *Ibid.,* p. 301.

83. *Ibid.,* pp. 398–399.

84. *Ibid.,* p. 601.

85. *Histoire des patriarches,* quoted by Edgar Blochet in his translation of al-Maqrīzī, *Histoire d'Égypte,* in *ROL,* IX (1902) 29–32, published separately (Paris, 1908), pp. 124–127.

86. Röhricht, *Regesta,* nos. 661, 664a.

87. *Syrian Anonymous Chronicle,* tr. Tritton, *Journal of the Royal Asiatic Society* (1933), pp. 282–286. Cf. Michael the Syrian, *op. cit.,* III, 262–268.

88. 'Imād-ad-Dīn, in Abū-Shāmah, *RHC, Or.,* IV, 340, 301–302.

Malik al-Mu'aẓẓam of Damascus, the eastern Christians remained behind.[89]

While the Melkites were often held suspect, and the Jacobites were treated, or mistreated, more or less according to local circumstances, the Armenian church enjoyed a more privileged position.[90] The presence of independent principalities and later of an Armenian state had a decisive influence on Franco-Armenian relations. Furthermore, the Armenians and Maronites were the only local Christians whom the Franks appreciated as excellent warriors.

Within the boundaries of the Latin states the Armenian community was to be found mainly in Antioch and in Edessa. In the latter, on the eve of the crusade, they enjoyed a kind of precarious independence under both the Byzantines and the Selchükids. Together with the Jacobites they formed the majority of the local population. It was the Armenians who elevated Baldwin to the throne in place of their local Armenian ruler Ṭoros (d. 1098), and they kept faith with the Franks until the fall of Edessa and even afterward.

There was a marked difference in their position in the north and in the south. In Edessa Frankish rule was based on their coöperation. In Antioch their standing was bolstered by the Armenian principalities and later on by the kingdom in Cilicia and was thus often a function of interstate relations. Farther south their numbers diminished, but Armenian communities were to be found in the greatest of crusader ports, Acre, as well as in Jerusalem. According to an ancient Armenian tradition, they had some seventy monasteries at the end of the

89. Al-Maqrīzī, *Histoire d'Égypte,* tr. Blochet, *ROL,* IX (1902), 483 (ed. Paris, 1908, p. 277). Giles of Lewes, in a letter written on November 10, 1219, after the Frankish conquest of Damietta, says: "Civitas autem Sancta Jerusalem post destructionem murorum recedentibus Sarracenis, ex toto a solis Surianis et aliis cristicolis habitatur"; Röhricht, *Studien zur Geschichte des fünften Kreuzzuges* (Innsbruck, 1891), p. 43.

90. The Armenian chronicles of the period are published in *RHC, Arm.* Of special interest here are the chronicles of Matthew of Edessa and Gregory the Presbyter, published in translation by Édouard Dulaurier in the Bibliothèque historique arménienne (Paris, 1858); Armenag Salmaslian, *Bibliographie de l'Arménie* (Paris, 1946); Henry F. Tournebize, *Histoire politique et religieuse de l'Arménie . . .* (Paris, 1910); Macler, "Les Arméniens en Syrie et en Palestine," *Congrès français de Syrie,* II (Marseilles, 1919), 151–688; L. Hugues Vincent and Félix M. Abel, *Jérusalem: Recherches de topographie, d'archéologie et d'histoire,* II, *Jérusalem nouvelle* (by Abel; Paris, 1926), 529–561; Anneliese Lüders, *Die Kreuzzüge im Urteil syrischer und armenischer Quellen* (Berlin, 1964); G. Ter-Gregorian Iskenderian, *Die Kreuzfahrer und ihre Beziehungen zu den armenischen Nachbarfürsten bis zum Untergange der Grafschaft Edessa* (Weida, 1915); Erwand Ter-Minassiantz, *Die armenische Kirche in ihren Beziehungen zu den syrischen Kirchen bis zum Ende des 13. Jahrhunderts* (Leipzig, 1904); Arshag Ter-Mikelian, *Die armenische Kirche in ihren Beziehungen zur byzantinischen vom IV. bis zum XIII. Jahrhundert* (Leipzig, 1892); K. Hintlian, *History of the Armenians in the Holy Land* (Jerusalem, 1976); and Prawer, "The Armenians in Jerusalem under the Crusaders," in *Armenian and Biblical Studies,* ed. Michael E. Stone (Jerusalem, 1976), pp. 223–236.

Byzantine domination, clearly an exaggeration.[91] Still, there is no doubt that Jerusalem had an Armenian and Georgian community at a very early period (mid-fifth century) centered around the Georgian monastery of St. Menas, which later became the great sanctuary of St. James. Beautiful mosaics outside the walls of Jerusalem near the so-called grotto of Jeremiah, and mosaics on the Mount of Olives, with tombs of Armenian abbots, testify to the high artistic level of these establishments.

On the eve of the First Crusade, almost contemporary with the reconstruction of St. Mary Magdalen, the Georgian monk Prokhorë rebuilt the church of St. James the Elder (1072–1088). The Spanish legend about the miraculous voyage of the head of St. James to Santiago de Compostela (known since the ninth century), was commemorated in crusader Jaffa, where a *perron* marked the place of his alleged embarkation.[92]

Before the middle of the twelfth century, relations between Franks and Armenians were friendly enough for a great pilgrimage of the Armenian catholicos, Gregory III Bahlavouni (1133–1166), to Jerusalem. Received with pomp in Antioch, he participated in the church council of 1142, where he is supposed to have accepted the Latin dogma and the supremacy of Rome. This was the opening of a long series of promises to be given by the heads of eastern communities during the two hundred years of crusader domination.[93] It was possibly on this occasion that the catholicos received permission to reconstruct the cathedral and to add an Armenian hospice to it. This may have happened, however, a few years later during the visit of prince Ṭoros II (1152–1168) of Cilician Armenia at the court of Amalric.[94] Whatever the case, the new Armenian cathedral in Jerusalem in the rue des Arméniens (*Hermins*) was functioning by 1165, its architecture a mixture of Armenian and Frankish romanesque styles.[95]

Armenian pilgrims, the "*Mahdeci*" (*Muqaddasī*), those visiting the

91. Leone M. Alishan, ed., "Deux descriptions arméniennes des lieux saints de Palestine," *AOL*, II-2 (1884), 394–405. After the Moslem conquest the number fell to fifteen. Cf. Charles Clermont-Ganneau, *Archaeological Researches in Palestine during the Years 1873–1874*, II (London, 1899), 329–339.

92. *Itinéraires à Jérusalem*, ed. Michelant and Raynaud, p. 92: "le perron Saint-Jacque de Galisce"; cf. pp. 181, 191.

93. Brosset, *Deux historiens arméniens: Kiracos de Gantzag, Histoire d'Arménie; Ouktanes d'Ourha, Histoire en trois parties* (St. Petersburg, 1870–1871), p. 61; Michael the Syrian, *op. cit.*, III, 256. On the synod of 1142 in Jerusalem, see Mansi, *Concilia*, XXI, 505–508, 583, 584.

94. *Chronique d'Ernoul et de Bernard le Trésorier*, ed. Louis de Mas Latrie (Paris, 1871), pp. 27–29. The exact date of the visit of prince Ṭoros II is not known, but it was during the reign of Amalric, after 1162.

95. Abel, *Jérusalem nouvelle*, II, 522.

holy places, were quite numerous. The Armenian mosaics near the grotto of Jeremiah in Jerusalem still have an inscription: "To the souls of all Armenians." Among the pilgrims was prince Toros II. A Frankish chronicler tells an illuminating story of how the Armenian prince, very much aware of the problems of population and security facing the Franks, proposed an Armenian immigration of 30,000 peasants to colonize the country. The plan fell through when the Latin clergy insisted that the new settlers should pay the ecclesiastical tithe.[96]

The Armenians certainly regarded the kingdom as a haven. When Saladin and his Kurdish and Syrian troops became lords of Egypt, the Armenian patriarch of Alexandria left Egypt (1172) and settled in Jerusalem, bringing with him seventy-five codices, among them a marvelous illuminated gospel. Thus were probably laid the foundations for the rich library of the Armenian patriarchate of Jerusalem. He established the monastery of St. Sharkis (Abū-Sirjah) with twenty monks, in the vicinity of Jerusalem. This initiative was supported by the Franks. He died soon afterward, and it was rumored that he was poisoned by the Armenian bishop of Jerusalem.[97] An Armenian bishop officiated in Jerusalem, and besides the cathedral he was in charge of some other places which belonged to the Armenians, such as the chapel of St. Mary in the Holy Sepulcher and a chapel in the courtyard of the property of the Holy Sepulcher on Mount Sion.[98]

The fall of Jerusalem to Saladin was lamented in far-off Cilician Armenia, where the catholicos Gregory IV Dgha (the Child, 1173–1193) wrote a dirge to commemorate the event.[99] Saladin, pursuing a policy of favoring the eastern Christians in the crusader kingdom, confirmed the Armenians in their possession of the cathedral of St. James after the fall of the city (1187).[100] The Armenians also kept their property in Bethlehem, and in 1227 a magnificent carved wooden

96. It is not clear on what basis the Latin clergy demanded the tithe, which was paid by the Franks only — by the peasants from their crops, by the landlords from their incomes. Possibly Toros stipulated that they were to be landowners, and not tenants from whom the Frankish lord would probably exact a part of the tithe. This may explain Toros's answer: "The Armenians will not come to another man's land to be serfs."

97. *The Churches and Monasteries of Egypt and Some Neighbouring Countries Attributed to Abū Ṣāliḥ the Armenian,* ed. and tr. Evetts (Oxford, 1895), pp. 6–7. The catalogue of the Armenian patriarchate in Jerusalem now in print does not mention any MSS. originating in the place during the crusader period.

98. Theoderic, "Description of the Holy Places," tr. Stewart, in *PPTS,* V-4 (London, 1896), 15, 20. There is some confusion regarding the monastery of St. Chariton in Jerusalem, which Theoderic, *ibid.,* p. 43, assigns in 1172 to the Armenians, but which belonged to the Jacobites. Similarly, the monastery of St. Sabas is erroneously assigned in 1165 by John of Würzburg to the Armenians, *PPTS,* V-2 (1896), 29, whereas in reality it belonged to the Greeks.

99. *RHC, Arm.,* I, 272 ff.: cf. *ibid.,* I, 686, no. 2.

100. *Ibid.,* I, 820.

door with Armenian and Arab inscriptions was brought as a gift to the church of the Nativity from the Armenian king Heṭoum I,[101] son of Constantine of Lampron. The only other Armenian community in the kingdom was in Acre, with a hospice for the needs of their pilgrims.[102] But it was in Jerusalem[103] and Bethlehem (and later Jaffa) that Armenian sanctuaries assured the survival of the community.

A very similar position to that of the Armenians was enjoyed by the less numerous Grusinian (Georgians, Iberi) community.[104] Their distant homeland in the Caucasus had long-standing connections with the Holy Land, almost since their conversion to Christianity. It is more than probable that the first "Armenian" monastery in Jerusalem, St. Menas, was really Georgian. Some monasteries were founded in the second half of the fifth century and later rebuilt by emperor Justinian. Their number in the crusader area was rather small, but they are mentioned in various western and eastern descriptions of the Holy Land. According to Georgian tradition, king Bagrat IV of Georgia received from the Byzantine emperor Constantine IX half of Calvary and established a Georgian hegumen (bishop) in Jerusalem (about 1050). Whatever the case, the Georgian center under the crusaders was the church of the Holy Cross on the main road which led to the Jaffa gate in Jerusalem. It was a Georgian monk, Prokhorë, who built the sanctuary (1036–1055). It was probably at that time or slightly later that the two famous versions of the legend which explained or justified the name of the Holy Cross (the place where the tree grew from which the cross was made) came into being.[105] Some

---

101. Melchior de Vogüé, *Les Églises de la Terre Sainte* (Paris, 1860), pp. 112–114 (repr. with introduction and bibliography by Prawer, Toronto, 1973); and Prawer, *The World of the Crusaders* (London, 1972), p. 56.

102. Röhricht, *Regesta*, no. 696. An Armenian monastery is also mentioned near Jerusalem, *ibid.*, no. 590.

103. *Itinéraires à Jérusalem*, ed. Michelant and Raynaud, p. 104: "apres j. petit est l'Eglyse des Hermites [sic: Hermines], ou saint Iaque de Galicie fu declés."

104. See the eighteenth-century itinerary of the archbishop of Tiflis, Timothy Gabachwili, in Brosset, *Histoire de la Géorgie*, II, *Additions et éclaircissement* (St. Petersburg, 1851), pp. 197–209. Cf. Janin, "Les Géorgiens à Jérusalem," *Échos d'Orient*, XVI (1913), 32–38, 211–219; Aleksandr A. Zagarelli, "Historische Skizze der Beziehungen Grusiens zum heiligen Lande und zum Sinai" (tr. from Russian, originally published by A. Anders in St. Petersburg, 1888, pp. 27–88), *ZDPV*, XII (1889), 35–73; Ehrhard, "Das Kloster des hl. Kreuzes und seine Bibliothek," *Historisches Jahrbuch der Görresgesellschaft*, XIII (1892), 158–172, with detailed analysis of sources and bibliography; Gregory Peradze, "An Account of the Georgian Monks and Monasteries in Palestine as Revealed in the Writings of Non-Georgian Pilgrims," *Georgica*, I (1937), 181–246.

105. According to one version, Adam asked to plant here a branch of the forbidden tree from Eden. Stuck into his mouth, it implanted itself in his head. The True Cross was cut from its branches, and thus the blood of the Savior washed the skull of Adam. According to another version, it was Lot who planted these trees here; a cypress, a cedar, and a pine. They became

Georgian traditions have it that king David II (1089–1125) sent presents to the Holy Sepulcher and built a monastery on Mount Sinai. His daughter, or a widow of a Georgian king, became a nun in Jerusalem and with the consent of the patriarch Gibelin of Sabran (1108–1112) established a Georgian nunnery there.[106]

It is not clear if the isolated monastery outside Jerusalem suffered from the Selchükid conquest (1071) or was partially destroyed by the Moslems a generation later in preparation for the defense of the city against the crusaders (1099), or both. However, when the English pilgrim Saewulf visited Jerusalem (1102), he saw it damaged, but a few years later (1106–1107) the Russian hegumen Daniel of Kiev merely mentioned it as belonging to the Georgians without referring to any damage.[107] It is possible that king David II of Georgia restored it. The monastery is mentioned in every crusader itinerary of the twelfth century, and some eastern itineraries also mention Georgian hermits, usually near monastic establishments of other rites.[108]

The Georgians did not disappear with the conquest of Saladin. Their monks remained in Jerusalem, and a crusader source has it that when Christian pilgrims hardly dared to go to the holy city, the Georgians were allowed to enter it with pomp carrying their banners.[109] This seems rather a strange statement, but apparently the Georgian queen Tamar (1184–1212) actually established friendly relations with Saladin.[110] It was during her rule that the Georgian monk Shoṭa Rusṭveli went to Jerusalem and wrote the greatest of the Georgian national epics, *Vepkhis Tqaosani* (The man in the leopard's skin), celebrated throughout Georgia in 1937 at the 750th anniversary of its composition. The monastery, which proudly stands now on the road to the Hebrew University, became the property of the Greek patriarchate

one, and the True Cross was cut from it. Cf. Janin, *op. cit.*, pp. 215–216. About 1110 a cantor of the Holy Sepulcher sent a particle of this cross to Galo, bishop of Paris (*PL*, 162, cols. 729–732). It was still being shown in the early nineteenth century; cf. Richard, "Quelques textes sur les premiers temps de l'église latine de Jérusalem," *Recueil de travaux offerts à M. Clovis Brunel*, II (Paris, 1955), 423–426; Prawer, "The Monastery of the Cross," *Ariel*, no. 18 (1967), 59–64; Zourab Avalishvili, "The Cross from Overseas," *Georgica*, I (1936), 3–11.

106. *PL*, 162, col. 730: "Congregatio sanctimonialium Georgianarum."

107. *PPTS*, IV-2, 21; IV-3, 82–83.

108. Johannes Phocas (fl. 1185) mentions Iberian monks in St. Sabas, St. Gerasimus, and St. Chrysostom. A curiosity to be noted is the Iberian monks shut up in a building which stood on the rock called "Kukumos" near Gethsemane. This possibly refers to the monument of Absalom in the valley of Josaphat.

109. James of Vitry, *PPTS*, XI-2 (1896), 84, repeated by Marino Sanudo, *Liber secretorum*, III, viii, cap. 3, in Bongars, *Gesta Dei per Francos*, II, 184.

110. Behâ ed-Dîn, tr. Charles W. Wilson and Claude R. Conder, in *PPTS*, XIII, 384.

in the nineteenth century. Some years ago, a Grusinian archaeological expedition discovered a magnificent painting of the national poet in a seventeenth-century fresco of the monastery.[111]

There are few histories more obscure than that of the Maronites in Lebanon. Since the sixteenth century, when the ties between the Maronites and Rome became stronger and scholars of Maronite origin began writing their history, their early history has been a subject of controversy.[112] There has been little agreement either on the question of Maronite orthodoxy or heterodoxy (in the Latin sense) or on their relations with the crusaders, or even on the area in which they were settled at the time. What makes the study difficult is the fact that the documentation regarding Maronites is extremely poor, some scattered remarks in the chronicles which cannot be assigned with any certainty to the Maronites. Given such little evidence one can dismiss such notions as the continual preoccupation of the Franks with their fate. As a matter of fact nowhere in the rich literature of crusader jurisprudence are the Maronites even mentioned. As for the chronicles, they sometimes mention Christians in the mountains of Tripoli, or Syrians, or inhabitants of the mountainous regions of the

111. The plan of the church is in *Survey of Western Palestine,* III (London, 1883), 379; Irakliy Abashidze, *The Monastery of the Holy Cross* (in Russian; Tiflis, 1962), reproduced in Prawer, "The Monastery of the Cross," pp. 59–64, and *idem, The World of the Crusaders,* p. 129; Thinathin Virsaladze, *Les Peintures murales du monastère de la Sainte-Croix à Jérusalem et le portrait de Chota Roustaveli* (in Russian, with French summary; Tiflis, 1973).

112. The poet Ibn-al-Qilā'ī (d. 1516), the great scholar as-Sam'ānī (S. E. Assemani) (1742), through P. Duwaihi, P. Chebli (1903), T. al-'Anaïsī (Tobias Anaissi, 1927), and Pierre Dib, who took a very partisan stand on the question of orthodoxy, in contrast to Siméon Vailhé, Henri Lammens, and more recently Robert W. Crawford, Kamal S. Salibi, and Philip K. Hitti. For a general introduction see Hitti, *Lebanon in History* (London, 1957); *idem, History of Syria, Including Lebanon and Palestine* (London, 1951); Richard, *Le Comté de Tripoli sous la dynastie toulousaine, 1102–1187* (Paris, 1945); Salibi, *Maronite Historians of Mediaeval Lebanon* (American University of Beirut, Oriental Series, XXXIV; Beirut, 1959). The most detailed study is by Dib, in the *Dictionnaire de théologie catholique,* X (1928), cols. 1–142, *s.v.* "Maronite, église"; republished with corrections as *L'Église maronite,* I, *L'Église maronite jusqu'à la fin du moyen-âge* (Paris, 1930); now see his *Histoire de l'église maronite* (Mélanges et documents, I; 2 vols., Beirut, 1962); see also Vailhé, "Les Origines religieuses des Maronites," *Échos d'Orient,* IV (1901), 96–102, 154 ff.; V (1902), 287 ff.; IX (1906), 143 ff.; Crawford, "William of Tyre and the Maronites," *Speculum,* XXX (1955), 222–229; Salibi, "The Maronites of Lebanon under Frankish and Mamluk Rule, 1099–1516," *Arabica,* IV (1957), 288–303; and *idem,* "The Maronite Church in the Middle Ages and Its Union with Rome," *Oriens Christianus,* XLII (1958), 92–104. The favorable attitude of the crusaders to the Maronites is alleged by Emmanuel G. Rey, *Les Colonies franques de Syrie aux XIIème et XIIIème siècles* (Paris, 1883), p. 76, often repeated and expanded; cf. René Ristelhueber, *Les Traditions françaises au Liban* (Paris, 1925), pp. 58, 61, cited in René Grousset, *Histoire des croisades et du royaume franc de Jérusalem* (3 vols., Paris, 1934–1936), II, 758.

county of Tripoli, without specifying ethnic group or religion. There is certainly no reason to think that the majority of the inhabitants of the county of Tripoli were Maronites.

One reason it is so hard to establish the most elementary facts about the Maronites is that the mountains and deep valleys lying east of the narrow coastal plain were for hundreds of years an asylum of persecuted denominations under both Islam and Christendom. On the other hand religious propaganda might find there an undisturbed area almost cut off from the outside world. Renan has described the mountain of Lebanon as a tomb of history, and Philip Hitti writes of "the mountains . . . honey-combed with schismatics,"[113] which is close enough to what was said by the Moslem chronicler Ibn-al-Athīr, a contemporary of the crusades.[114]

Since the tenth century, following al-Mas'udī (about 950) and his contemporary Sa'id ibn-al-Biṭrīq (Eutychias), it was believed that the Maronites had been Monothelites and from the seventh century a heterodox denomination. William of Tyre introduced this view to the crusader world. It was then repeated by James of Vitry, bishop of Acre, and Marino Sanudo (d. 1337), and became accepted in the west. Since the sixteenth century Maronite scholars have energetically combatted this view.[115] An interesting explanation of this question has recently been suggested, namely that we are dealing not with two Maronite saints, St. Maro (d. 410) and John (Yuhanan) Maro (about 707), the organizer of the church, but with a Nestorian Maro of Edessa (d. 580), whom William of Tyre confused with his namesake, the first patriarch of the Maronites.[116] If this thesis is accepted then the famous union of the Maronites during the patriarchate of Aimery of Limoges at Antioch (about 1182) must have another meaning—not the forswearing of heretical views, but the recognition of the supremacy of Rome by an orthodox church under its own primate or patriarch. The reforms mentioned then, and a generation later by Innocent III (1198–1216), were more in the nature of a unification of rites and

---

113. Hitti, *Lebanon in History,* p. 281.

114. *Ibn al-Athīr,* in *RHC, Or.,* I, 583.

115. Possibly none more vehemently than Dib; see above, note 112.

116. Crawford, "William of Tyre and the Maronites," pp. 222 ff. This ingenious explanation also suggests that the sixth ecumenical council, which, according to William of Tyre (XXI, 8; *RHC, Occ.,* I, 1017–1019) excommunicated the Monothelites, in fact had nothing to do with it. Although this seems to be a very plausible explanation, one wonders how William of Tyre, who wrote two or three years after the Maronites were united with the Latin church, could have been so mistaken. For what it is worth, we may note that the French translator of William of Tyre left out the item on the council. Of course, he may have shortened the text, or perhaps used another version.

customs than of a union through acceptance of the orthodox dogma of the two wills in Christ.

It is in connection with this occasion that William of Tyre describes the Maronites as a Christian nation, 40,000 strong, living in the mountains of Lebanon.[117] This would be repeated a generation later by James of Vitry, who adds a comment on their prowess as archers.[118] The unsolved question is the area of Maronite settlement. It is usually accepted that in the seventh century they migrated southeastward from the Orontes valley and its tributaries into the mountains. They are mentioned by al-Mas'ūdī in the tenth century as being not only in the mountains, but also in Homs, Hamah, and Ma'arrat an-Nu'mān. The area is badly defined.

In the southern part of Lebanon, on the confines of the county of Tripoli and the Latin kingdom, the mountains seem to have been occupied partly by the Druzes. According to Benjamin of Tudela, the only available source,[119] they stretched from the mountains east of Sidon to Mt. Hermon, which means that the area included the Wādī-t-Taim, Marj 'Uyūn, and the sources of the Jordan. It is quite possible that they here met with the beduins of the 'Āmilah tribe.[120]

The Druzes adjoined to the north another heretical Moslem sect, the Nuṣairīs,[121] and it is this problem of the Nuṣairīs which seems to be crucial in demarcating the Maronite area. Unfortunately the question cannot be easily resolved. It has been convincingly argued that the Nuṣairīs were probably among the Persian Shī'ites on the Lebanese coast and that they were the predominant factor in the mountains of Lebanon, not only in Jabal 'Akkār but also at Botron and 'Aqūrah; moreover, that the whole of the Kasrawān area was Nuṣairī and not Maronite.[122] If this is so, then the Maronites were in reality north of the Nuṣairīs and moved into southern Lebanon only after

117. William of Tyre, XXII, 8 (*RHC, Occ.,* I, 1076).

118. James of Vitry, *op. cit.,* cap. 81.

119. Benjamin of Tudela, *Itinerary,* ed. Adler, p. 18.

120. The wandering of the Banū-'Amilah, who gave their name to upper Galilee, is not very clear. In Galilee they fused with the Banū-Judhām and at the beginning of the eleventh century moved into the Bilād ash-Shaqīf in southern Lebanon; cf. Lammens, in *The Encyclopaedia of Islam,* new ed., I (Leyden and London, 1960), 436, *s.v.* "'Amila," in opposition to the view that they moved far more to the north. Cf. Lammens, "Notes de géographie syrienne," *Mélanges de l'Université de Saint-Joseph . . .,* I (Beirut, 1906), 275.

121. Hitti, *Lebanon in History,* p. 281.

122. On the Nūṣairīs see René Dussaud, *Histoire et religion de Nosairis* (Paris, 1900). The crucial problem of relations between the Maronites and Nūṣairīs was dealt with very convincingly by Lammens, "Les Nosairis dans le Liban," *ROC,* VII (1902), 452–477. In his later *La Syrie: Précis historique* (2 vols., Beirut, 1921) the problem is not mentioned; strangely enough, the most recent studies do not refer to it. See Matti Moosa, "The Relation of the Maronites of Lebanon to the Mardaites and al-Jarājima," *Speculum,* XLIV (1969), 597–608; Cahen, "Notes

the destruction of the Nuṣairīs' power. The Maronites, as far as can be ascertained, probably occupied a part of the coastal plain outside the maritime cities and the area from Jubail through Botron to Tripoli and the Besharrī area in the mountains to the east.

This not only suggests that the Maronites, far from being the majority of inhabitants of Lebanon, were in reality pressed into a relatively small and well-defined area (although some groups were probably to be found outside), but it may help in explaining the paucity of notes preserved by chronicles contemporary with the crusades. Christians are occasionally mentioned as giving help to the army of the First Crusade making its way along the Lebanese coast. Again, we find local Christians helping Raymond of St. Gilles (about 1102) in the siege of Tripoli.[123] We do not hear specifically about Maronites from crusader sources until their contact with Antioch around 1182.[124] Still we know that the Maronite community existed, and it is possible to establish a list of their patriarchs as well as the villages which they settled. The names of villages are almost always linked with monasteries which, with the titles of Maronite prelates, show that the monks were the solid core of their church, probably performing parish duties. There were patriarchal sees at St. Mary in Yānūḥ, St. Mary in Maifūq, St. Elijah in Lihfid, St. Mary in Habil, St. George in Kafar, all in

---

sur les origines de la communauté syrienne des Nuṣayris," *Revue des études islamiques,* XXXVIII (1970), 243–249.

123. Raymond of Aguilers, in *RHC, Occ.,* III, 288. The native Christians gave the Franks advice about the road to Jerusalem during the siege of 'Arqah. Their number is given as 60,000. This was probably used by William of Tyre, VII, cap. 21 (*RHC, Occ.,* I, 310). According to him, the Christians lived in the mountains between 'Arqah, Tripoli, and Jubail. In his chapter on the Maronite union William gave 40,000 as the size of their population. In discussing the siege of Tripoli Ibn-al-Athīr speaks about "the inhabitants of the mountains [*ahl al-jabal*] and those of the *sawād* [countryside] who were mostly Christians" (*RHC, Or.,* I, 212). Lammens understands this as being the majority of inhabitants of the plain, whereas the mountain region was settled by Nūṣairīs; "Les Nosairis dans le Liban," p. 455.

124. The well-known episode of the defeat and capture of Pons of Tripoli in 1136 caused many difficulties for historians. William of Tyre (XIV, 23, in *RHC, Occ.,* I, 640) says: "et prodentibus eum Surianis, qui in Libanicis super eamdem civitatem [Tripoli] habitant jugis, occisus est." This was followed by a bloody punitive expedition under Raymond. He brought back captives with women and children to Tripoli: "ubi in praesentia populi, in ultionem sanguinis eorum qui in acie cediderant, eos variis affecit suppliciis, et durissima mortis genera . . . compulit experiri." This passage, if applied to the Maronites, would be rather exceptional, given their relations with the Franks. In fact, nothing of the kind happened to any Christian denomination. William of Tyre does not say that they were Christians, although "Suriani" would normally apply to them. The passage embarrassed the French translator of William of Tyre, who wrote: "li Surien qui abitoient el mont Libane le traïrent. Ses genz furent descomfiz et tornerent en fuie. Il fu pris après par la bone volenté as Suriens. Li Turc traitors l'occistrent." It is more than likely, as already assumed by Lammens, that these Lebanese were not Maronites but Nuṣairīs.

the diocese of Jubail, and Kafarḥai and St. Maro in Kafarḥai in the diocese of Botron.[125] There were also the monastery of Sts. Basil and Luke, called Mār Nuhrah, in the diocese of Jubail, and the monastery of St. Sergius near Hardīn in the diocese of Tripoli;[126] the monastery at Kaftūn (northeast of Botron) and the monastery of Ḥālāt (southeast of Jubail).[127] There were other villages such as al-Munaiṭirah, Dimilṣā (north of Jubail), and Bnahrān and Ḥadath (in the Besharrī mountains, southeast of Tripoli).[128]

There is no proof that before the union with Rome around 1182 there had been direct contacts between the Maronites and the Latin church.[129] The act of union occurred in Antioch. It did not satisfy everyone; there was a popular movement against it, even accompanied by acts of violence.[130] We do not know the reaction of the local Latin clergy, but in 1203 the papal legate, cardinal Peter, met in Tripoli with the Maronites, who promised adherence to Rome.[131] Ten years later Innocent III invited the Maronite patriarch, Jeremiah of 'Amshīt (1199–1230), to participate in the Fourth Lateran Council.[132] Before he left Rome in 1216, a papal bull gave instructions to the Maronites regarding dogmas, rites, and customs. It remains a moot question how far the bull of Innocent III refers to real heterodoxy, but there is no doubt that he imposed Latin usages on the Maronites. He also tried to establish unity in the community between Uniates and anti-Uniates. This situation seems to have persisted throughout the thirteenth century and beyond. Frankish ecclesiastical and lay authorities tried to strengthen the Uniate party. As with other denominations,

---

125. Assemani, *Biblioteca medicea-laurentiana* (Florence, 1742), pp. 16–18; cf. Dussaud, *Topographie historique de la Syrie antique et médiévale* (Paris, 1927), pp. 69–72.

126. *Ibid.*, pp. 26–27.

127. Mentioned in the autobiographical note of the Maronite patriarch Jeremiah; see below, note 132.

128. Cf. Salibi, "Maronite Church," in *Oriens Christianus*, XLII, 97.

129. Although a Maronite tradition has it that Alberic of Beauvais, cardinal-bishop of Ostia, who presided over a synod in Jerusalem in 1140 with the participation of the Armenian catholicos, contacted the Maronites in Tripoli and they declared their submission to Rome.

130. This is indicated in a bull of Innocent III; Anaissi, ed., *Bullarium Maronitarum, complectens bullas, brevia, epistolas, constitutiones aliaque documenta a Romanis pontificibus ad patriarchas Antiochenos Syro-Maronitarum missa* (Rome, 1911), pp. 2–5 (no. 2).

131. *Ibid.*

132. Due to a misprint or mistranslation in Assemani, *Biblioteca orientalis clementino-vaticana*, p. 17, whereby he gave the year as 1490 of the Greek calendar instead of 1590, the patriarch Jeremiah of 'Amshīt (1199–1230) was confused with his namesake Jeremiah of Dimilṣā, who lived nearly a hundred years later. This was incorporated by Dib in *Dictionnaire de théologie catholique*, X, which confused the entire picture. He later corrected it in his *L'Église maronite,* and the correct text was used by Salibi in *Oriens Christianus*, LXII (1958), 92–104, who straightened out the chronology. See Anaissi, *Bullarium Maronitarum.*

the Frankish princes intervened in the elections of the Maronite prelates; the patriarch Jeremiah of Dimilṣā states clearly that the Embriaco lord of Jubail took part in his election.

The opposition to the union brought about the election of rival
patriarchs supported by the *muqaddams* or local Maronite ra'ises.
The Uniates were stronger near the coast, that is, nearer the Frankish
strongholds and cities, whereas the opposition was stronger to the
east, in the mountain regions. The papacy tried to strengthen the contacts with the Maronites. Their prelate Jeremiah of Dimilṣā, abbot
of Kaftūn, elected after the death of Daniel of Ḥajīt in 1282, was
invited to Rome, leaving the pastoral duties to a prelate named
Theodore.

It was at the end of the Frankish rule and the fall of Tripoli[133]
that a major change took place in Lebanon, the punitive expeditions
of the Mamluks in 1292 and 1305 against the Nuṣairīs. Their destruction allowed a Maronite migration into the south and Kasrawān and
the redrawing of the ethnic map of Lebanon.[134]

The Jews could not expect any better treatment than the rest of
the native population;[135] if anything, they could expect worse. The news

133. As late as 1282 Jeremiah witnessed a crusader document at Nephin, together with some
other Maronite prelates, the archbishop of "Villejargon" ('Arqah) and the archbishop of "Resshyn"
(Ra'ashīn): L. de Mas Latrie, *Histoire de l'île de Chypre,* III (Paris, 1855), 662–668.

134. The expeditions are described by Ṣāliḥ ibn-Yaḥyâ, *Histoire de Beyrouth et des Bohtors,
émirs du Gharb* (Beirut, 1902); republished by Francis Hours and Salibi (Beirut, 1969); Arabic
text: *Ta'rīkh Bairūt wa akhbar al-umarā' al-Buhturīyīn . . .,* ed. Louis Cheikho (Beirut, 1927);
readings corrected by Jean Sauvaget, "Corrections au texte imprimé de l'histoire de Beyrouth
de Ṣāliḥ b. Yaḥyā," *Bulletin d'études orientales de l'Institut français de Damas,* VII–VIII (1937–
1938), 65–82. They are also mentioned by abū-l-Fidā' (d. 1331) and later by al-Maqrīzī (d. 1442).
The texts were thoroughly analyzed by Lammens, "Les Nosairis dans le Liban," and compared
with late Maronite historiography, which saw in them an expedition against the Maronites and
turned the episode into a national heroic epic.

135. The main collection of sources regarding the history of the Jews under crusader and
Mamluk rule will appear in *Sefer ha-Yishūv,* III, ed. Yitzhak F. Baer, J. Prawer, and Chaim
H. Ben-Sasson. The number of sources grows each year with the publication of the Genizah
material. The latest publications are recorded in the *Bibliography of Jewish Studies,* ed. Issa-
char Joel, published by the National Library in Jerusalem. Four monumental collections of
sources and studies are basic for our period: Jacob Mann, *The Jews in Egypt and in Palestine
under the Fāṭimid Caliphs* (2 vols., London, 1920–1922; repr. New York, 1970); *idem, Texts
and Studies in Jewish History and Literature* (2 vols., Cincinnati, 1931–1935); Solomon D. Goitein, *A Mediterranean Society* (3 vols., Berkeley, 1967–1978); and E. Ashtor-Strauss, *History
of the Jews in Egypt and Syria under the Mameluks* (in Hebrew; 3 vols., Jerusalem, 1944–1970).
Rich material was recently published in the collection of texts and studies by Goitein, *Palestinian Jewry in Early Islamic and Crusader Times in the Light of the Genizah Documents,* ed.
J. Hacker (in Hebrew; Jerusalem, 1980). An important collection of excerpts from sources is
Ben-Zion Dinur, *Israel in the Diaspora* (in Hebrew), new ed. (Tel Aviv, 1960–), II, 1; tr. Merton
B. Dagut (Philadelphia, 1964). For a general study of the period, with extensive bibliography,

of the horrible massacres of Jews in the Rhineland in 1096 reached the east almost a year before the crusading armies appeared. The Jewish communities from Antioch in the north to Raffiyaḥ in the south prepared themselves for the worst in the event of a crusader victory. Some tried to find refuge in the larger cities and fortifications.

The conquest was as much a calamity for the Jewish communities as it was for the Moslems. The Jews defended and died for Jerusalem (1099) and Haifa (1100).[136] In other places like Antioch, Jubail, and Beirut, they were exterminated together with the local population. Those who escaped tried to reach the Moslem lands of the ʿAbbāsid caliphate or Fāṭimid imamate.

Yet, after this period of calamity, which lasted some ten years, things began to change. Except in Jerusalem, where neither Moslems nor Jews were allowed to live,[137] there was no specific discrimination against the Jews in the sense of distinguishing between them and other natives. This remained so until the end of the crusader states on the coast of Syria and Palestine, a remarkable fact if we remember that it was precisely at this time that Europe initiated anti-Semitic legislation which for eight or nine centuries controlled the fate of the dispersed nation. Moreover, when every crusade from the first to that of Louis IX was accompanied by new pogroms, whether in France, England, or Germany, we hear of no excesses of this kind in the lands of Christian domination in the Levant. This does not mean that the crusaders were in any sense tolerant, but simply that they looked on all natives as a single legal class. This prevented specific discrimination against the Jews, although in daily affairs relations were certainly more nuanced. Thus William of Tyre complained that the crusader princes preferred Jewish and Moslem doctors to

see Salo W. Baron, *A Social and Religious History of the Jews,* III–V (New York, 1957). Among studies directly dealing with our problem are Prawer, "The Jews in the Latin Kingdom of Jerusalem" (in Hebrew with English summary), *Zion,* XI (1946), 38–82; *idem,* "The Jews," chap. 13 of *The Latin Kingdom of Jerusalem,* Hebrew ed. (Jerusalem, 1974) (with up-to-date bibliography); Goitein, "Contemporary Letters on the Capture of Jerusalem by the Crusaders," *Journal of Jewish Studies,* III (1952), 162–177; *idem,* "A Report on Messianic Troubles in Baghdad, 1120–1121," *Jewish Quarterly Review,* XLIII (1952), 57–72; Benjamin Z. Kedar, "Notes on the History of the Jews in Jerusalem in the 13th Century" (in Hebrew with English summary), *Tarbiz,* XLI (1972), 82–94; *idem,* "On the History of the Jews in Palestine in the Middle Ages" (in Hebrew with English summary), *Tarbiz,* XLII (1973), 401–418. See also Zvi Ankori, *The Karaites in Byzantium* (New York, 1953). Special attention is paid to the history of the Jews in the crusader period in Prawer, *Royaume latin.*

136. E.g., Gilo Parisiensis, VI, vv. 305 ff. (*RHC, Occ.,* V, 798); Albert of Aachen, I, vii, 22 (*RHC, Occ.,* IV, 521).

137. William of Tyre, XI, 27 (*RHC, Occ.,* I, 500–501); Abraham bar Hiyiā, *Megillat ha-Megale,* ed. Julius Guttmann (Barcelona, 1929), IV, 99; al-Ḥarīzī, *Taḥkemonī,* ed. Armand Kaminka (Warsaw, 1899), cap. 28. Cf. Prawer in *Speculum,* XXVII, 77 ff.

Christians, and James of Vitry accused the crusaders of being too tolerant of Jews.[138]

The conquest created conditions which reshaped the map of the Jewish communities. They were exterminated in the cities, mainly on the coast, but as there was no real fighting for control of the countryside we find in the twelfth century some two dozen villages (there were possibly more) in Galilee with a Jewish population.[139] Moreover, the Jews, like the Moslems, soon settled again in the maritime cities. In two, Tyre and Ascalon, which capitulated rather than be taken by force, there is good reason to assume that the Jewish communities survived and continued to exist under crusader rule.

At the end of the first kingdom there were important changes in the Jewish community, bringing a kind of renaissance in the thirteenth century. Jewish pilgrimages to the Holy Land continued without any difficulties during the whole of the twelfth century. If anything, they were more frequent than before. Moreover, if the pilgrimages before the crusades were mainly restricted to Jews from the Moslem Near East, the development of commercial routes linking the Levant and Europe now brought Jews from western Europe. Some, like the Spanish Jew Benjamin of Tudela or the German Petaḥiyah of Regensburg (fl. 1190), left "Itineraries" not unlike their Christian contemporaries', but naturally with a different perspective.

This pilgrimage movement began to change in size and in character at the time of Saladin's conquest (1187). The occurrences which had focused attention on the Holy Land created repercussions among Jews everywhere. Soon messianic stirrings made their appearance from Spain to Baghdad and far off Khurasan.[140] Some were directly linked with the crusades, others were due to local circumstances, still others grew out of forces within the Jewish community, but all had in common the background of the wars of cross and crescent.

When the ideology of holy war transferred Europeans to the east and rekindled the Moslem *jihād* in reaction, the Jewish community reacted with their own interpretation of events. As early as the First Crusade there is recorded, in a letter which originated in the Balkans, a messianic movement centered on Thessalonica (1096) and spreading

---

138. William of Tyre, XVIII, 34 (*RHC, Occ.,* I, 879–881); James of Vitry in Bongars, *Gesta Dei per Francos,* cap. 81. His characterization of the Jews in Palestine was the one current in contemporary Europe but had hardly any application to the Jews of the Levant.

139. See the list of Jewish settlements in cities and villages in Prawer, *Latin Kingdom,* Hebrew ed., chap. 13.

140. Mann, "Jewish Messianic Movements at the Time of the Crusades" (in Hebrew), *Hatekufa,* XXIII (1925), 253 ff. Cf. Goitein, "Messianic Troubles," *Jewish Quarterly Review,* XLIII, 57 ff.

into Anatolia and Syria. Since the real causes of the crusade were unknown, the description is a mixture of fantasy and wishful thinking. The crusaders were conceived of as the ten lost tribes shut up by Alexander the Great behind the mountain of darkness. Now, moved by God's order, they were proceeding to the east. The prophet Elijah had appeared; and in some communities the Jews sold their property and waited for the Messiah who would bring them to Jerusalem.[141] The whole aim of the crusade, according to the anonymous author of this letter, was "to gather them as on a threshing floor and then God will say to Israel: 'Stand up and thresh, O daughter of Zion'" (Micah 4:13).

The calamities associated with the crusades interrupted speculations for a time, although the messianic expectations did not cease.[142] The new security offered by the crusader states on the coast brought about the reëstablishment of Jewish communities there, and in the 1170's a flourishing Jewish community existed in Tyre. Although the Palestinian Gaonate ceased to exist in the Holy Land, the sages of Tyre were in contact with the great leader of the period, Maimonides (d. 1204), who settled in Fustat in Egypt. He praised them for their learning, which was renowned even outside the boundaries of the country. Another community of importance was that of Acre.[143]

The fall of Jerusalem to Saladin had far-reaching consequences for the Jewish community. Crusader legislation prejudicial to Moslems and Jews was naturally abolished, and the few Jews who had lived under royal tolerance near the citadel of Jerusalem[144] became a fair-sized community. As a matter of fact, three Jewish groups settled in the place: the Ascalonites, whose city was dismantled on the order of Saladin (September 1191), Jews from the Maghrib who fled the persecutions (1198–1199) of abū-Yūsuf Ya'qūb al-Manṣūr and his son Muḥammad an-Nāṣir, and finally Jews from France and the Plantagenet dominions on French soil. This last was a migration of some 300 families with their rabbis, moving to Jerusalem in two groups in 1209 and 1210.[145]

This sudden revival of Jewish community life in Jerusalem after

141. See above, note 139.
142. The rich apocalyptic literature begins at the time of the wars between Byzantium and the Sāsānid empire. The rise of Islam, the emergence of the Umaiyads, 'Abbāsids, Selchükids, and crusaders until the great onslaught of the Mongols in the thirteenth century, then found their expression in the different chapters of this literature. The texts were published by Even Shmuel, *Midrasheī Geūla [The Exegesis of Salvation]* (Tel Aviv, 1954).
143. *Responsa of Maimonides* (in Hebrew), ed. Alfred Freimann (Jerusalem, 1934), par. 105.
144. Benjamin of Tudela, *Itinerary,* ed. Adler, p. 35.
145. Solomon Ibn Verga, *Shevet Iehūda,* ed. Azriel Shohet (Jerusalem, 1946/7), 147.

three generations of being barred from the city seemed providential. When al-Harīzī, the Jewish poet from Spain, visited Jerusalem in 1216, he was told by a Jewish inhabitant of the city: "And God moved the spirit of the king of [the] Ismaelites [Moslems] in the year 4950 of creation [1190] and the spirit of good counsel and right moved him and he and all his host went out from Egypt and laid siege to Jerusalem. And God gave it into his hands. And he ordered to be proclaimed in every city, to old and young, as follows: 'Speak ye to the heart of Jerusalem, let everybody from the seed of Ephraim, from the Diaspora of Ashur and Egypt, from all those dispersed in the four corners of the world, come to her.' And so they gathered from all horizons and settled inside her boundaries."[146] One cannot exclude the possibility of such an official proclamation by Saladin. There was the earlier example of Zengi, who after the capture of Edessa settled 300 Jewish families there, who would later be extremely loyal to the Moslems.[147] But on the whole this seems rather an explanation *ex post facto,* made some twenty-five years after the renewal of Jewish life in Jerusalem.

From then on the movement bore more the character of an immigration than a pilgrimage to the holy places. Some of the greatest Jewish luminaries of the period settled in the Holy Land. Suffice it to mention the leader of French Jewry in the middle of the thirteenth century, rabbi Yeḥiel of Paris (d. 1286), that of Spanish Jewry Naḥmanides in 1267, and rabbi Meir of Rothenburg, caught in 1283 by emperor Rudolph I of Hapsburg in northern Italy, while on his way to the Holy Land with his family.[148]

Though certainly influenced by the general deterioration of the position of the Jews in Europe, the new attitude was mainly the outcome of Jewish reaction to the great events in the Holy Land. When the messianic expectations of the First Crusade were followed by massacres, the creation of the crusader kingdom was perceived by Jews as an act of injustice. How did it happen, asked the great Hebrew poet in far-off Spain, Yehūdah ha-Levī (fl. 1140), that "the Edomite [crusader] became resident in my palace, that the hands of the Arabs reign and that the red one ["Edomi," Esau, Christian] rules my sheep with his dogs?" And a twelfth-century German poet, who also wrote the "Chronicle of the Massacres" of the crusades in Europe, Ephraim

---

146. Al-Harīzī, *Taḥkemonī,* ed. Kaminka, cap. 28.

147. Tritton and Gibb, "The First and Second Crusade from an Anonymous Syriac Chronicle," *Journal of the Royal Asiatic Society* (1933), p. 291.

148. For Meir see the notice in the Jewish Community Book of Worms, in *Shem ha-gedolīm,* ed. Ben-Yaakov (Wilno, 1856), p. 84b.

of Bonn (fl. 1180), prays: "Let him turn Edom into Sodom and the cursed Ismāʿel into Gomorrah. Let him return the power, which was once given to us, and let him give back to us the whole land [of Israel]."[149]

The European Jew saw little difference in the land of his fore-fathers being in Christian or Moslem hands. Both were unjust, both were unlawful, and providence would presumably soon take vengeance and restore the promised land to its legitimate heirs. It is in this frame-work that we should envisage the Jewish immigration to Palestine in the thirteenth century. The war between Islam and Christendom, in which defeat or victory on one side or the other never seemed deci-sive, and major battles in the Holy Land inexorably brought about its destruction, gave rise to a particular Jewish view of events. This is clearly expressed in the biblical commentary of Naḥmanides, begun in Spain but completed in Jerusalem, where he created a school of wide repute. The basic ideas of Naḥmanides are summarized in his exposition of Leviticus (22:36): "And I will bring the land into desola-tion and your enemies which dwell therein shall be astonished at it." Naḥmanides comments: "This is the message of glad tidings through-out the countries of the Exile, that our land does not accept our foes. It is also a decisive proof and a promise to us, for in all the inhabited world there is no land so fair and large, settled from time immemorial and which is as desolate as it is now. For ever since we departed from it, it had not accepted a single nation. They all try to settle it, but it is beyond their power."

The thrust of this interpretation was that the time of salvation was near. Moreover it would not do just to wait for the decree of provi-dence and the coming of the Messiah. The legitimate right of the Holy Land was not prescriptive, and every generation, including Naḥmanides' own, was ordered to take hold and inherit the land. "It is a divine precept to inherit the land which God gave to our fore-fathers . . . and we shall not leave it either to the foreign nations nor to desolation." This right to the heritage is considered to be tangibly proved by the existing situation, which Naḥmanides sums up in a suc-cinct phrase: "Great is the desolation in this rich and wide land, be-cause they do not deserve you and you are not fit for them."

Naḥmanides not only expounded a theory, but what he preached he put into practice. He left his Catalonian birthplace, migrated to the Holy Land in 1267, and established himself among the ruins of Jerusalem, where soon a synagogue and a school made their appear-

149. Dinur, *Israel in the Diaspora*, II-1, 444–445.

ance. Yet it was not Moslem Jerusalem but crusader Tyre and Acre
which became the centers of the Jewish community. Jerusalem suffered many vicissitudes in the thirteenth century, and life there was
extremely insecure. When in 1229 al-Malik al-Kāmil handed it over
to Frederick II, anti-Jewish legislation was reëstablished. Following
some negotiations, however, a Jewish family was allowed to live in
Jerusalem and so to assure a halting place for Jewish pilgrims, who
were allowed to visit the city.[150] The Khwārizmian invasion of 1244
and the Mongol raids of 1260 in the vicinity of Jerusalem made life
almost impossible, and many who had tried to strike roots in the holy
city left for the coast. Consequently Acre, the richest of the crusader
cities, became the great Jewish center from the second quarter of the
thirteenth century on. Security was greater in the cosmopolitan city
and so were the economic means of subsistence.

The Jewish community in Acre became a cross-section of the different communities of the Diaspora. The leading elements were Jews
from Spain and from northern and southern France, in addition to
eastern Jews, whether Palestinian-born or from neighboring Moslem
countries. Each element brought its own traditions in ritual and liturgy, but also its own attitudes to the great intellectual problem common to Judaism, Christianity, and Islam—the relation between philosophy and religion. Jewish Spain and southern France represented
in this sense a more liberal attitude than the Diaspora of Ashkenaz
in northern France and Germany, although a new trend, that of Spanish mysticism (the Kabbala), was quickly finding adherents. The focus of tension was the philosophical works of Maimonides ("The
Guide of the Perplexed"). Vehement discussions between their admir-
ers and those who condemned them stirred unprecedented troubles
and even led to mutual excommunication of the contending factions.
Acre became a battleground of the opposing views, where European
and eastern Jewish centers, like Damascus and Mosul, intervened.
The latter, who fanatically adhered to Maimonides, took a strong
view against those who calumniated his memory, an attitude also to
be found in Egypt and in crusader Acre. Here a Talmudic academy
continued the tradition of the French Tosafists, whereas rabbi Salo-
mon Petit (fl. 1280) expounded the Kabbala and Spanish Jews continued their own tradition. The flourishing community of Acre lived
its great days in the last quarter of the century, but was wiped out

---

150. Goitein, "New Sources on Palestine during the Crusader Period," *Eretz Israel*, IV (1967),
155.

during the massacre which followed its capture by al-Ashraf Khalīl in 1291.[151]

There were two major factors which directly influenced the existence and the way of life of the minorities: the European traditional social structure imported by the crusaders and the organization of political and social life of the minorities in the previous Moslem period.[152] The European feudal system offered a model of human interdependence; Moslem society at the turn of the eleventh century was evolving in the same direction, though one would hesitate to call it feudal. At no time before or after did the two societies so much resemble each other as at the beginning of the twelfth century. On the other hand, although minorities were not entirely unknown in Europe, it was the Moslem east which, during the previous four hundred years, had developed methods of rule over and coexistence with minorities. With the conquest of the Levant, and the problem of ruling a local population made up of heterogeneous groups, the crusaders took over the existing system and adapted it to their own needs and assumptions. They also accepted with some modification the system of social and economic dependence, which met their material needs and conformed to their image of society. The Franks had no wish to disrupt local groups and institutions; as a matter of fact they were happy to preserve them as the basis of their own feudal superstructure. The model seems to have been common to the northern principalities and the Latin kingdom, but different demographic patterns led to some variety.

The most striking change affected the Moslems. From rulers they became subjects, losing in the process their urban and rural aristocracy, their intellectual elite, and their political institutions. Relegated to the class of the conquered, their organization did not differ from that of the other non-Frankish communities.

The feature common to all the minority groups was their autonomous organization as religious communities. In some cases they were identified with territorial units—villages or quarters in cities. Some preserved a larger organizational framework, like the ecclesiastical

151. On the Jewish community in Acre see Prawer, *Royaume latin,* II, 397–419.

152. Cahen, *Syrie du nord, passim;* the question has been treated in more detail by the same author: "Le Régime rural syrien au temps de la domination franque," *Bulletin de la Faculté des lettres de Strasbourg,* XXIX (1950–1951), 286–310; *idem,* "La Féodalité et les institutions politiques de l'Orient latin," *Oriente ed Occidente nel medio evo* (Accademia nazionale dei Lincei, Fondazione Alessandro Volta, Atti dei convegni XII; Rome, 1957), pp. 167–191. See also Prawer, *Royaume latin,* I, 461–537; *idem, Latin Kingdom,* pp. 46–60, 126–159, 214–233.

organizations of Christians and Jews, but in everyday life it was the smaller units of tightly organized local communities which played a major role in the life of their members.

The independence of the communities was reflected in the jurisdictional rights of their religious leaders, including questions of marriage and inheritance. In many cases there was a mixed leadership of local clergy and lay notables, a feature common to Christians and Jews, but possibly also to Moslems. This was a legacy of the former Moslem period with its notion of *dhimmīs,* clients of the Moslem state. Basically applied to the ʿAhl al-Kitāb (the people of the Holy Scriptures of Revelation), it guaranteed life and property as well as the right to live according to one's own laws and customs.[153] This notion of second-class subjects, distinguished from the ruling group by religion, was taken over by the crusaders.

John of Ibelin, count of Jaffa (1250–1266), recounts somewhat naively how autonomy was granted to the minorities, and attributes it to Godfrey of Bouillon. The "Syrians," he says, came to Godfrey and asked for the privilege of being judged by their own courts and their own laws. Their request was granted. The story is an episode in a larger narrative about how the laws of the kingdom were created, the details of which are partly legendary, although there was nothing extraordinary in the Syrian request.[154]

The crusaders granted autonomy not only to "Syrians" but also to Moslems and Jews. The institutional expression of this autonomy, according to John of Ibelin, was the court of the *raʾīs,* the headman of the community. Crusader documents furnish us with a number of cases in which such ra'ises (though not their courts) appear. In addition to the rural or village ra'ises there were ra'ises in cities, whose position was to some extent different from that of their rural namesakes.[155]

153. In addition to the studies in the previous note see Tritton, *The Caliphs and Their Non-Muslim Subjects* (London, 1930); *idem,* "Non-Muslim Subjects of the Muslim State," *Journal of the Royal Asiatic Society* (1942), pp. 36–40; Goitein, *A Mediterranean Society;* Neophytos Edelby, "Essai sur l'autonomie juridictionnelle des Chrétiens d'Orient," *Archives d'histoire du droit oriental . . .,* I (1952); Cahen, *s.v.* "Dhimma," in *Encyclopaedia of Islam,* new ed., II, 227–231; *idem,* "Indigènes et croisés," *Syria,* XV (1956), 351–360; Sivan, "Notes sur la situation des chrétiens à l'époque ayyūbide," *Revue de l'histoire des religions,* CLXXII (1967), 117–130; Jonathan Riley-Smith, "The Survival in Latin Palestine of Muslim Administration," in *Eastern Mediterranean Lands in the Period of the Crusades,* ed. Peter M. Holt (Warminster, 1977), pp. 9–22.

154. John of Ibelin, cap. 4 (*RHC, Lois,* I, 26). On Godfrey as lawgiver see Prawer, "The *Assise de tenure* and the *Assise de vente:* A Study of Landed Property in the Latin Kingdom," *Economic History Review,* ser. 2, IV (1951–1952), 77–87.

155. Cahen, "La Féodalité," pp. 185 ff.; Riley-Smith, "Some Lesser Officials in Latin Syria," *English Historical Review,* LXXXVII (1972), 1–26; *idem, The Feudal Nobility and the Kingdom of Jerusalem, 1174–1277* (London, 1973), pp. 90–91, 47–49.

The term *ra'īs,* transcribed as *raicius* (and the office as *raisagium*), must have meant different things depending on place and community. In the city of Antioch it seems to have corresponded to the *iudex,* a title taken over from the former Byzantine administration or derived from the Norman Sicilo-Byzantine administration;[156] in the Moslem and eastern Christian villages it must have corresponded to the headman of the village, the *mukhtār* of modern eastern villages. In the majority of cases, however, we may assume that it really corresponded to the head of the *ḥamūlah,* the extended family. The *ra'īs* was probably the head of the dominant *ḥamūlah* of the village. This explains why in several villages we find more than one *ra'īs,* who must have represented several village *ḥamūlahs;*[157] these were extraordinary cases, as the villages as a rule were relatively small and not many *ḥamūlahs* lived in a single village.

The *ra'īs* of the village, head of a *ḥamūlah,* was by definition a notable, and exercised a traditional kind of patriarchal jurisdiction over the inhabitants. He was certainly not chosen by the Frankish lord, although he was acknowledged and confirmed by him. Some were quite important, being ra'ises of a district or a group of villages (possibly inhabited by the same clan), and therefore exercising considerable influence. In such a case, the Frankish lord took care to safeguard his rights, and although the post was certainly hereditary, at least in the notable's family, the confirmation was formal. A good example is that of the Hospitallers who "conceded to *raicius* Abet ['Abd] a number of villages to hold, till and guard as long as it will please the masters and brothers of the order."[158] This kind of native overlordship must have been more common in the thinly populated and less accessible mountain areas, hence the *raisagium montanae* to be found in a crusader document.[159] In similar cases, particularly in the mountains of Lebanon in the county of Tripoli, the Franks looked on the *ra'īs* as a *regulus,*[160] kinglet or chieftain, possibly corresponding to the local chieftains of the mountains of Tripoli, the *muqaddams.*

Head of the village community, notable of the district with traditional rights of jurisdiction, the *ra'īs* was also the Frankish lord's representative in his dealings with the community.[161] As such he might

---

156. Cahen, *Syrie du nord,* pp. 461–462.

157. E.g., Röhricht, *Regesta,* no. 1220.

158. *Ibid.,* no. 1237.

159. *Ibid.,* no. 212.

160. J. Delaville Le Roulx, ed., *Cartulaire général de l'ordre des Hospitaliers de S. Jean de Jérusalem (1100–1310),* I (Paris, 1894), 320 (no. 467).

161. Other officials, not necessarily natives or connected with the native community, were the *drugeman* and *scriba;* see Riley-Smith, "Some Lesser Officials," pp. 15–26.

be called a bailie, although this could also mean a Frankish supervisor, a kind of steward, like the Venetians' *gastaldio* in their rural domain in Tyre.[162] As the lord's representative he was important, because the Franks drew their revenue as a rule not from individual peasant lots, but from the entire village community or some part of it.

In both his responsibilities, the traditional and the official, the *ra'īs* took counsel with the elders of the village, whom we see on occasion participating in the symbolic act of transferring the lordship of their village from one Frank to another or taking a form of oath in a mixed Frankish-oriental ceremony.[163]

The problem of autonomy for minorities was far more complex in the cities. There had existed native courts headed by the *ra'īs,* but these disappeared in time, to be replaced by the *Cour de la Fonde,* or court of the market.[164] Though our sources speak only of "Syrians", possibly meaning Melkites and Jacobites, other minorities, Moslems and Jews, were undoubtedly affected. *Prima facie,* one has the impression that the replacement of the court of the *ra'īs* by the *Cour de la Fonde* was tantamount to the abolition of the autonomy of the non-Frankish communities. But Jewish sources prove beyond a doubt that Jewish autonomous jurisdiction not only continued to exist but, if anything, became stronger in the course of the thirteenth century. The rabbinical courts and the "good man of the city" (*tuveī ha-'ir*) or the "presidency of the community" (*rosheī ha-qahal*) functioned even in smaller communities divided one from another because of their different liturgies, with their own religious and lay leadership.[165] Besides religious questions they took care of education, ritual baths, ritual slaughterhouses, synagogues, schools, the ransom of prisoners, and a multitude of welfare problems.[166]

What is certain for the Jewish community was probably no differ-

---

162. Some of these officials bear distinctly eastern names, like Botros (Peter), Semes (Shams). Cf. Delaville Le Roulx, *Cartulaire,* II, 784–785; Tafel and Thomas, II, 371: "preposicius casalis, quem nos appellavimus Gastaldiones [sic];" Prawer, "Étude de quelques problèmes agraires et sociaux d'une seigneurie croisée au XIIIe siècle," *Byzantion,* XXII (1952), 5–61; XXIII (1953), 143–170.

163. Delaville Le Roulx, *Cartulaire,* II, 764–767, 786–787.

164. *Livre des Assises . . . des Bourgeois,* cap. 241 (*RHC, Lois,* II, 171–173).

165. E.g., decisions of the rabbinical court in Acre in the second half of the twelfth century; *Responsa of Maimonides,* ed. Freimann; the decisions of the "Qahal of Acre" in 1234, *Responsa of R. Abraham, Son of Maimonides,* ed. Freimann and Goitein (Jerusalem, 1937), par. 8 (p. 25). For more details see Prawer, "The Jews in the Latin Kingdom."

166. See the letters from Jerusalem by rabbi Yeḥiel ha-Zarfatī in Mann, *The Jews in Egypt and in Palestine under the Fāṭimid Caliphs,* vol. I. The most up-to-date study is that of Goitein, *A Mediterranean Society,* vol. II, which deals with such problems in the Fāṭimid and Aiyūbid empire. Cf. Ashtor-Strauss, *History of the Jews in Egypt and Syria, passim.*

ent for other minorities. The silence of the sources respecting the court of the *ra'īs* in the cities (only larger cities with their own *Cour de la Fonde* are in question) should not be regarded as implying their abolition. It is reasonable to suppose that the native courts continued to function, catering to the needs of the members of the community. Their activity depended on the cohesion of the community, and its willingness to bring the cases of its own members before its own court. This had long been the case, certainly for the past four centuries, since the Arab conquest, and possibly much earlier, given the fact that Jewish autonomy had existed at least since the second century. The members of minority communities could bring cases involving their own members before the public court of the lordship, but this was always looked upon askance by every community, since it opened the door to outside interference. The invocation of the state was often formally prohibited by secular or ecclesiastical authorities' threatening the offender with anathema. This was as common as the official prohibition against invoking outside intervention in the election of ecclesiastics of the different communities. There were always jurisdictional problems regarding members of the same community, but the courts of the ra'ises or the ecclesiastical courts continued to act according to their own customs and laws.[167]

However, Syrian and Palestinian cities were extremely heterogeneous in their ethnic and religious composition, to which there was now added a new ruling class, the Franks, whose economic life was interwoven with that of the local population. This created a new problem, that of jurisdiction in mixed cases involving members of different communities. Moreover, there was a wide range of criminal cases involving members of minority groups which were never in the hands of the *ra'īs*. This belonged to the local Court of Burgesses.[168] The same is true for civil cases involving property held in burgage tenure (*borgesie*).[169] However, the supplanting of the court of the *ra'īs* by the *Cour de la Fonde* was linked with the commercial traffic of the

---

167. The same rules existed in the contemporary Moslem state. A relevant case is that of Saladin, who called for legal advice regarding the jurisdiction of the *dhimmīs*. He received an answer from abū-dh-Dhāhīr ibn-'Aūf al-Iskandarī of the Malikite rite, subscribed to by abū-dh-Dhāhīr as-Salafī of the Shāfi'ites. According to this decision Jews should be judged by their own customs (*'ādah*) and their own *ḥakīms*. Only if both parties agree could the suit come before a Moslem judge, who could still refuse to hear the case. The decision is recorded by Tāj-ad-Dīn as-Subkī, *Tabaqāt ash-Shāfi'īyah al-kubrâ*, in Martin Schreiner, "Notes sur les Juifs dans l'Islam," *Revue des études juives*, XXIX (1894), 208–213.

168. *Livre des Assises . . . des Bourgeois*, cap. 241 (*RHC, Lois*, II, 171–173).

169. Non-Franks were excluded *de jure* from holding *borgesies*, but in practice they were often proprietors of city land and city houses; cf. *Abrégé du livre des Assises de la Cour des Bourgeois*, cap. 24 (*RHC, Lois*, II, 254).

sūqs and bazaars and the coexistence of different communities in restricted areas. This created intercommunity agreements and litigation mentioned in crusader sources, respecting debts, mortgages, rents, loans, sales, purchases, and the like.

In the *sūqs* and bazaars, buyers and sellers often belonged to different communities. In Acre or Tyre the seller might have been a Moslem, eastern Christian, or Jew, often a peasant bringing his products or wares from the countryside; the buyer was usually a Frank. In litigation involving a Frank, the *raʾīs* of the community would hardly be acceptable to the crusaders as judge. The same would also be true in commercial cases involving members of different minorities. Such cases came before the *Cour de la Fonde*. Its president, the bailie, was a Frank, noble or burgess; two of its jurors were Franks, the other four were "Syrians," Melkites or Jacobites.[170] If the suit involved a sum greater than one mark of silver, the competent authority was not the *Cour de la Fonde* but the Court of Burgesses.[171]

Thus the emergence of the *Cour de la Fonde* left the court of the *raʾīs* intact, as far as its own community was concerned, its effectiveness depending on the willingness of its members to use it. A state court, royal or baronial, came into being for those who, for various reasons, preferred a public court, while the *Cour de la Fonde* was the institution competent to judge cases which involved Franks and natives.[172]

Religion was at the basis of the crusaders' attitude to the minorities, but the legal and social standing of a member of any minority was additionally circumscribed by where he lived and his occupation. The major distinction was that between city and country dwellers. Religious affiliation had little to do with economic occupation, and consequently a Melkite or Jacobite, to mention the largest group of non-Latin Christians, or a Moslem or Jew, enjoyed several privileges when he lived in a city which he lost if he lived in a village or on

---

170. *Livre des Assises de la Cour des Bourgeois,* cap. 241 (*RHC, Lois,* II, 171).

171. At the beginning of the fourteenth century, one mark of silver equaled 25 bezants of Cyprus.

172. The standard procedure was that witnesses had to be produced by the defendant; *Livre des Assises . . . des Bourgeois,* caps. 59–65 (*RHC, Lois,* II, 53–56): "Car le dreit comande que de cele lei, don celui est don l'on se clame, de cele lei deivent estre les garens" (cap. 65, p. 56); an exceptional case is *ibid.,* cap. 140 (p. 96). This often created legal difficulties, for example, the impossibility of church establishments' claiming their property. The papacy intervened several times on such occasions; e.g., *Acta Honorii III,* ed. Tăutu, no. 80, pp. 108–109: "ut non tantum Graecos, vel Surianos vel Armenos et generaliter fideles omnes ad testificandum idoneos pro vobis et ecclesia vestra in testimonium inducere valeatis."

a farm. Basically, there were no serfs in the cities. The expression *servus* in the sense of serf is almost never to be found in crusader documents, though it does appear (with another meaning) in the writings of the jurists. In crusader acts, all non-Frankish peasants are *villani* or *rustici*.[173] The feudal vocabulary of the crusaders is manifestly that of northern France (with some exceptions in Antioch and Tripoli) and one wonders if the use of *villanus* rather than *servus* reflects the European legal distinction, foggy as it often was, between the two. Yet the *villanus* in the crusader kingdom was for all practical purposes a serf. If we had only the legal treatises to go by, the picture would seem clear enough, though not very detailed. Only John of Ibelin paid any attention to the problem. From him we learn about the existence of legislation and legal institutions dealing with villeins. A special assise, called *L'assise et l'établissement des vileins et des vilaines,* was promulgated to deal with some aspects of the problem. Unfortunately the precise date of promulgation, apparently in the first half of the twelfth century, is not stated. The aim of the assise was to establish the rights of feudal landlords over their villeins. At the same time, it ordered the establishment of special courts to deal with fugitive villeins.[174] The members of this special court are variously called *juges, enquereors,* or *ciaus qui tenent l'assise.* Their appointment was the responsibility of the overlord (it is not clear whether this meant the king or the holder of the lordship). There had to be "three liegemen to hold the assise," to be established *par les contrés et par les seignories.* If one of them failed to act or changed his place of residence, he had to be replaced by the overlord.[175]

The procedure of the court is reminiscent of the Carolingian *inquisitio* or the Anglo-Norman inquest. Its main function was to decide questions of lordship over villeins as well as to call for the pursuit of fugitives and their restoration to their legal owners. In disputed cases the ownership of a villein could be decided by an *enqueste* using the testimony of other villeins.

Thus the peasants were *ad glebam adscripti.* They were not allowed to leave their farms without permission of their lords. *Formarriage* was also prohibited, but if it took place with the connivance of another lord, the latter had to replace the loss of the female serf by another woman of the same age and condition. In some cases peasant

173. The noun *rusticus* is for some reason more frequent in the colonial Venetian documents; cf. Tafel and Thomas, II, 371. See Prawer, "Serfs, Slaves and Bedouin," in his *Crusader Institutions* (Oxford, 1980), pp. 203 ff.

174. John of Ibelin, caps. 251-255 (*RHC, Lois,* I, 403-406).

175. *Idem,* cap. 253 (*ibid.,* p. 405).

families, or rather their heads, were called *homliges*. Despite the noble origin of the designation they do not seem to differ from other villeins, and the noun does not seem to mean more than "subjects," people dependent on an overlord.[176]

All this sounds very much like feudal European legislation. Although links of dependence, even strict dependence, had existed before, Islamic law, which sanctioned slavery, did not recognize the status of serf. Moslem legislation made a distinction between Moslems and the non-Moslem clients of the Moslem state, but this reflected their position as subjects of the state, not personal servitude.

Still, the crusader conquest did not sensibly change the position of the Syrian and Palestinian peasantry. By the eleventh century, free and independent peasants were rare in the Moslem Near East. There was a proliferation of large domains belonging to pious institutions (sing., *waqf*), a process probably accentuated by the Selchükids. In addition, the spread of the *iqtā'ah,* a benefice or fief, made the peasant dependent on an overlord. Finally, the private usurpation of payments to the state also contributed to the same development, the disappearance of small independent properties. The Frankish lords merely generalized the existing system of servitude.

The legal position of villeins can also be deduced from the legal acts of the period. Land is alienated "cum omnibus terris, villanis et pertinentis suis";[177] or with the land there also go "praedicti villani cum eorum posteritatibus";[178] or land is transferred "cum omnibus villanis Surianis sive Sarracenis, ubicunque sint,"[179] or "cum vineis et olivetis et iardinis, cum omnibus terris suis cultis et incultis, cum omnibus villanis terre et cum omnibus pertinenciis et divisionibus suis."[180]

Serfdom, being a personal condition, went with the villein wherever he might be. Thus land is alienated "cum rusticis quoque, qui de eisdem casalibus sunt nati, ubicumque sint";[181] or "simul cum rusticis omnibus qui in predicto casali habitant presentialiter, et quicum-

---

176. I do not see any special reason, though there are opinions to the contrary, to regard these *homliges,* to be found in a Venetian inventory of the middle of the thirteenth century, as anything but serfs. In the Tyrian village of Theiretenne the *homliges* represent all the peasants who belonged to the Venetians: "sunt in dicto casali XII homliges"; Tafel and Thomas, *op. cit.,* II, 373–374. A clear proof is given by the village of Homeire (Humairah) in the same territory; "Habemus in dicto casali nostro tres homliges. Nomina rusticorum sunt hec: primus Raysinegid, Couaha, Habdeluaif"; *ibid.,* II, 374.

177. Rozière, *Cartulaire,* no. 44, p. 81.

178. *Ibid.,* no. 48, p. 88.

179. Ernst Strehlke, *Tabulae ordinis theutonici* (Berlin, 1869; repr. Toronto, 1975), p. 3 (no. 3).

180. *Ibid.,* pp. 13–14 (no. 14).

181. *Ibid.,* p. 15 (no. 16).

que convinci potuerint inveniri fore de predicto casali."[182] Possibly
this applies to fugitive villeins. In some cases Frankish lords entered
into special agreements with their neighbors to prevent villeins' running away and settling in other villages. Thus in 1186 Bohemond III
of Antioch, when selling al-Marqab to the Hospitallers, specifies that
if "my villeins, or those of my men, who are Saracens, by any chance
come into the territory of Valanie or Margat . . . the brothers of the
Hospital will return them to us according to the *assise* and the customs of the land. But if they are Christians, the Hospitallers will rec-
ompense us (*pacificabunt*) within fifteen days or will release them
from their land. But if their villeins by chance come into my land
or the land of my men, we shall likewise give them back to the brothers
of the Hospital."[183] A curious agreement, from the neighborhood
of Beirut, stipulates that the Buḥtur emirs of al-Gharb will hand all
fugitive villeins from Beirut over to the Frankish lord of the city within
eight days.[184]

The flight of villeins was not uncommon in the early years of the
existence of the kingdom, though this was more the result of political
circumstances. In one case, however, in the middle of the twelfth century, Moslem peasants, because of maltreatment in the vicinity of
Nablus, set up an organization to enable fugitives from Frankish
lands to escape and join their Moslem coreligionists.[185]

One peculiarity of this rural regime deserves looking at. Many documents mention the sale or gift of individual villeins or villein families. Thus in a generous grant of villages to the Hospitallers, Pons
of Tripoli (1112–1137) adds: "And I give the right to all my men, who
hold land from me, that if they are willing, they may give one villein
to the Hospital . . . anyone whosoever in his fief. I likewise approve
their giving more, if done after consulting me."[186] A confirmation
of the Hospital's privileges in 1154 reads like a strange inventory of
donations of single villeins: "one rich villein who lives in Nablus . . .
three villeins given by the bishop of Nazareth [Achard], one given
by William de Tenchis, another by Pagan Vacca, another given by
Drogo," and so on.[187] There are many similar donations which prove
such procedure to be customary in the Latin east. The frequency of

182. Delaville Le Roulx, *Cartulaire,* II, 135 (no. 1372).

183. *Ibid.,* I, 495 (no. 783).

184. Cf. Clermont-Ganneau, "Deux chartes des croisés dans les archives arabes," *Revue
d'archéologie orientale,* IV (1905), 5–31.

185. Sivan, "Réfugiés syro-palestiniens au temps des croisades," *Revue des études islamiques,*
XXXV (1967), 135–147.

186. Delaville Le Roulx, *Cartulaire,* I, 77 (no. 82).

187. *Ibid.,* I, 172 (no. 225).

this type of donation, though not unknown in the west, seems to be a product of the Frankish agricultural regime. In theory, the sale or gift (which was more common) of a villein meant the transfer of the man, his family, and his descendants into somebody else's power. It also meant the transfer of his tenure and of its dues and services to the new lord. However, our documentation points to the transfer of economic rights only, while jurisdiction over the person remained with the former lord, unless a whole village or a larger territory was transferred. This is understandable if we remember that the crusaders did not create a manorial system, or at least had little or no demesne land. Consequently, payments in kind or cash, and dues in kind on special occasions, were the main villein obligations. Other than the *xenia,* the bulk of these dues was paid by the village as a whole.[188] Corvées were almost entirely nonexistent or very limited and in such cases concentrated on special crops (olive groves, vineyards) or occupations (fishing).[189] Since the Frankish overlord was rather a *rentier* than a squire with land in the village, it was simpler in making an economic donation, therefore, to mention the villein and his family rather than describe his property.

Economically and socially a number of villein families enjoyed considerable local prestige. Such were the families of the *ra'īs,* as well as the richer villeins, forming a class similar to the European *villici.* Such, for example, was the villein given in 1154 by Paganus II, lord of Haifa, to the Hospitallers, together "with lands and houses in Haifa and Capharnaum" (Shiqmōna to the south of Haifa),[190] obviously a man of some standing, as was the *divis villanus* in Nablus.[191] Sometimes villeins came into more property or income by performing special duties. In such cases they held service tenures, such as an eastern Christian 'Abd-al-Massīḥ (Abdelmessie), the *ra'īs* of Margat, who possessed three fourths of a village,[192] or Guido Raicius, who seems to have held a large tract of land near Nablus.[193] In Antioch the care of the mill of the Holy Sepulcher belonged to three Syrians, Nicephor, Michael, and Nicholas; their office was hereditary and is described as

188. E.g., "Quicquid reddunt, acumulatur; et postea dividitur ita, quod terciam integram habemus." The same argument applied to fines. See the Venetian inventory of their possessions in Tyre, in Tafel and Thomas, *op. cit.,* II, 373.

189. Rozière, *Cartulaire,* p. 149 (no. 74): "angaria et auxilium piscatorum" in the Sea of Galilee.

190. Delaville Le Roulx, *Cartulaire,* I, 172 (no. 225).

191. *Ibid.*

192. *Ibid.,* I, 314 (no. 457): 1174.

193. Henri F. Delaborde, *Chartes de Terre Sainte provenant de l'abbaye de Notre Dame de Josaphat* (Paris, 1880), p. 91 (no. 43): 1185.

feodum villanie and *villania*.[194] Others received real fiefs, like the Arab knight or warrior (*Arabicus miles*) who possessed two villages,[195] or the Turcopole who held land near Nablus.[196] The Barda Harmenus who in 1154 gave a whole village near Acre to the order of St. John[197] may also have been a military warrior. Still, such cases were exceptional, and one cannot draw the conclusion that Moslems served the Franks in a military capacity.

In addition to the villeins, the legal treatises also mention "serfs." Their appearance is so rare that we feel we are dealing not really with serfs but with slaves. It was a crusader rule that no Latin Christian could become a slave. The only slaves were Moslems, eastern Christians, or Jews, usually captured in conquered cities or bought in the market.[198] If a slave ran away, the *ban* was called throughout the city. The hiding of a fugitive slave was a criminal offense punishable by hanging.[199] The ransoming of captured Jews from the Franks is as well attested as the ransoming of eastern Christians and Franks from the Moslems.[200]

When dealing with villeins and slaves, one must also deal with enfranchisement. The jurists have almost nothing to say about it; only the mid-thirteenth-century compilation known as *Livre des Assises des Bourgeois* furnishes some details. Unfortunately it is not the most reliable source, since the chapters dealing with enfranchisement can be traced back to the Provençal *Lo Codi,* and indirectly to Roman law.[201] Still, some of the customs were certainly part of crusader law. Freeing a slave could be done in one of three ways: before three witnesses, by charter, or by testament.[202] By leaving property at death to a slave the latter is automatically enfranchised and becomes *libertin*.[203] But there was still another way of being liberated, namely con-

---

194. Rozière, *Cartulaire,* p. 179 (no. 90): 1140.

195. *Ibid.,* pp. 110 (no. 56), 120, (no. 60), 128 (no. 63): 1155–1158.

196. Delaborde, *Chartes . . . de Notre Dame de Josaphat,* pp. 80–83 (nos. 33–35): 1159–1161.

197. Delaville Le Roulx, *Cartulaire,* I, 173 (no. 225).

198. In Acre the selling of a slave was taxed one bezant; Tafel and Thomas, II, 398.

199. *Livre des Assises . . . des Bourgeois,* cap. 210 (*RHC, Lois,* II, 142).

200. The ransoming of Jews from the Franks by Jewish communities in Apulia and the different communities of Syria, Palestine, and Egypt is well known from the Genizah documents; cf. Kedar, "Notes on the History of the Jews in Palestine in the Middle Ages," *Tarbiz,* XLII (1973), 405 ff. For the ransoming of eastern Christians, for example after the capture of Edessa by the Moslems, see Matthew of Edessa, in *RHC, Arm.,* I, 329 ff. Ransoming of noble Franks by their vassals was a feudal obligation. The aim of a special congregation, that of the Holy Trinity, was the ransoming of Christian prisoners from Moslem captivity.

201. Prawer, "Étude préliminaire sur les sources et la composition du 'Livres des Assises des Bourgeois'," *RHDFE,* ser. 4, XXXII (1954), 358–382.

202. *Livre des Assises . . . des Bourgeois,* cap. 207 (*RHC, Lois,* II, 140).

203. *Ibid.,* cap. 206 (pp. 139–140); cf. cap. 16 (p. 29).

version: "Because the Christian law and the people are called 'the land of Francs' they [the baptized] should be entirely free."[204] Thus a fugitive Moslem slave who returns and accepts conversion is freed from the power of his former lord. Strangely enough, if the fugitive slave was a Christian he was not free on his return because he acted through *male fei*. His former lord can even sell him, but only to a Christian.[205]

The relations of the *libertin* to his benefactor are strictly prescribed and follow the rules of Roman law.[206] He cannot plead against his former lord or he will be fined or even run the danger of mutilation. If the enfranchised slave dies without testament, his property goes to his benefactor or the benefactor's children.[207] If he offends his former lord, he can be returned to slavery, although he cannot be sold, and his children are to be free. While the *Assises des Bourgeois* use the terms *serf, serve,* and *servage,*[208] they undoubtedly meant slave and slavery, modified in translating from *Lo Codi,* since the Roman *servus* meant slave.

Conversion and enfranchisement of a villein are incidentally dealt with in one of the typical hairsplitting chapters of Philip of Novara (fl. 1243). Among those excluded from sitting in a seigneurial court because of religion or former offenses he includes the villein whom the lord has married off to a free woman, and *ipso facto* enfranchised. The defendant could claim that the enfranchised serf should not sit in court, by addressing the lord: "He is your man, you keep faith to him, but you cannot make him our peer."[209]

The problem of conversion was a difficult one. Whatever the ideology of the First Crusade, the crusaders in the east never became a missionary establishment, if "missionary" is taken in the sense of seeking the conversion of individuals. They were for the most part indifferent to the problem, or in some cases actually opposed to conversion. Nothing is more revealing than the complaint of the bishop of Acre, James of Vitry. Leaving aside his claims about his effectiveness as a preacher before eastern Christians and Moslems, we have his explicit statement that Franks, and even the order of St. John, were opposed to preaching and conversion.[210] Frankish opposition to conversion must have been strong if even the papacy had to intervene—

204. *Ibid.,* cap. 255 (p. 191).
205. *Ibid.*
206. *Ibid.,* cap. 16 (p. 29).
207. *Ibid.,* cap. 204 (p. 138).
208. *Ibid.,* cap. 205 (p. 139).
209. Philip of Novara, cap. 28, (*ibid.,* I, 502).
210. *Lettres de Jacques de Vitry,* ed. Huygens (Leyden, 1960), p. 88 (II, 206–210): "Christiani servis suis Sarracenis baptismum negabant, licet ipsi Sarraceni instanter et cum lacrimis

though rather mildly, which suggests that the curia was aware of the attitudes of the crusaders. Thus Gregory IX, in a letter to patriarch Gerald of Jerusalem (1237) mentions the fact that Moslem slaves (*sclavi*) are refused baptism because it would lead to their enfranchisement. The pope orders that they should be baptized if they promise "to remain in the state of their former serfdom."[211] Some efforts were made in this direction, and the Latin clergy was ordered by Urban IV in 1264 to seek converts among the poorest Jews and Moslems by offering them food, shelter, and baptism.[212]

Thus for the great majority of the population their status as second-rate citizens, the former *dhimmīs,* was compounded by their status as villeins.

Moving from the countryside to the city, the picture changes. Once the period of conquest was over, the native population, not only eastern Christians, but also Moslems and Jews who had left the cities before the siege or escaped the massacres which accompanied the conquest, returned and settled in them again. The only exception, as already mentioned, was Jerusalem. The non-Frankish inhabitants of the cities were not regarded as villeins. They were not bound to city soil; not only were their movables their own, but it seems that they were also proprietors of land and houses. They paid rent and probably a recognition tax, *cens,* and were bound to some specific payments obligatory on non-Latins only. Such was the *capitatio,* doubtless a descendant of the Moslem *jizyah,* paid by every male over fifteen. It was paid to the *seigneur justicier,* not to the landowner. So, for example, the Venetians in Tyre collected a poll-tax from Jews and Syrians,[213] a privilege every *seigneur justicier* enjoyed over the villeins on his estate.

It was in connection with taxation that the non-Latins were discriminated against. In Acre, after the Third Crusade, the non-Latins, at least those under royal jurisdiction, were barred from living in the older part of the city and relegated to the new, not yet fortified, suburb of Montmusart. Moreover it is very likely that they were compelled to use a special market, which belonged to the king, not to

---

postularent. Dicebant enim domini eorum . . . 'si isti Christiani fuerint, non ita pro voluntate nostra eos angariare poterimus'." Cf. Prawer, *Latin Kingdom,* pp. 507 ff.

211. A baptized Moslem is immediately freed, according to the *Livre des Assises . . . des Bourgeois,* caps. 204–212 (*RHC, Lois,* II, 138–144). The quotation is from *Acta Honorii III,* ed. Tăutu, no. 228, pp. 307–308.

212. See the letter of Urban IV to patriarch William of Jerusalem (1264), in Kedar, "Notes on the History of the Jews," *Tarbiz,* XLII, 416: "Sarraceni pauperes et Judei, converti ad unitatem ecclesiae cupientes, ad civitatem Acconensem accedunt et postulant baptizari."

213. Tafel and Thomas, *op. cit.,* II, 359.

the communes.[214] Though we do not know of any special taxation in Jerusalem, the fact that the non-Latins lived in a special quarter and had their own counters in the bazaars of Jerusalem would have facilitated such taxation.[215]

Members of minority groups who lived in a city were personally free and could move from place to place, acquire possessions (basically burgage tenures), or rent property. Yet a number of documents point to the existence of another class among them, at least in the northern principalities, though we do not find them in the Latin kingdom proper. There were individuals who, while they lived in cities, might be granted away by the lord of the place. So a Syrian Ben Mosor was given by Bohemond III to the Hospitallers (1175) in Jubail together with "his children and all their rights and possessions" (*cum omni eorum jure et rebus*). In Latakia a Jew, called by the Franks Garinus, was also given away.[216] Again in Latakia in 1183 Bohemond III gave the order of St. John a number of Greeks (6), Armenians (5), and Jews (7). The document concludes: "And those men mentioned above, Latins as well as Greeks, Armenians, and Jews, the house of the Hospitallers may have, hold and possess in perpetuity, in peace and without appeal, free and quit of all *tallea*. And these are all that belong to the Hospital in Latakia; they shall not have others unless I myself have donated them."[217] There were only a few donations of this type, all in the northern principalities.[218]

It is not easy to interpret these texts. Obviously those so donated were henceforth bound to make payments to their new lord. Possibly they were former serfs who had lived in the countryside and retained their former status after moving into the city. In a donation of Bohemond III to the Hospital in 1194 one such man, George the notary, son of Vassilius, son of Uardus, is described as *homo peculiaris*. His

214. Prawer, "L'Établissement des coutumes du marché à Saint-Jean d'Acre," *RHDFE,* ser. 4, XXIX (1951), 329–351, unconvincingly opposed by Cahen, "À propos des coutumes du marché d'Acre," *ibid.,* XLI (1963), 287–290, who agrees on the space limitations but argues against the term "ghetto." The difference of taxation in different markets was proposed by Richard, "Colonies marchandes privilégiées et marché seigneurial," *Le Moyen-Âge,* LIX (1953), 325–340. Cf. Prawer, *Latin Kingdom,* pp. 412 ff. A decision of the *maggior consiglio* of Venice of 1271, ordering all its Jewish subjects in Acre to live inside the Venetian quarter, has hitherto escaped the attention of historians; see *Deliberazioni del maggior consiglio di Venezia,* ed. Roberto Cessi, II (Bologna, 1931), septima rubrica, I, 15–16. It is thus possible that after the recapture of Acre by the crusaders in 1191 the communes kept "their" *dhimmīs* and that the legislation ordering their seclusion in Montmusart referred to the royal *dhimmīs* only.

215. Prawer, *Latin Kingdom,* p. 410.

216. Delaville Le Roulx, *Cartulaire,* I, 324 (no. 472).

217. *Ibid.,* I, 436–437 (no. 648).

218. A similar case for Tibnīn (1183) may possibly be regarded as not dealing with a city; Strehlke, *Tabulae,* p. 10.

property (*hereditas*) at the time of alienation was to remain with Bohemond III, but new acquisitions after this date would belong to the Hospital.[219] The adjective *peculiaris* points to the *peculium,* the property of a serf. Thus George the notary, despite his social standing, inherited the legal position of his ancestors even though living in the city.[220] Whatever the case, we have very few examples of this kind suggesting serfdom in the cities; we are inclined to regard them as the outcome of particular circumstances.

A few words should be said about the legal status of the beduins. Several documents which enumerate beduins inside the borders of the kingdom point to the fact that the crusaders found a legal formula for dealing with them.[221] By definition neither city inhabitants nor serfs, they had a special legal status, being considered the king's property. This meant that they paid for their pasture rights, probably in horses, camels, or sheep, and were under royal jurisdiction rather than that of a particular lordship. This rule was well adapted to their mode of existence as nomads; the crown, theoretically at least, was the only force which could assure them protection in all parts of the kingdom. It needed a special royal grant to alienate a tribe or its branch to a lordship.[222] Still, we find beduin tribes in the possession of the Templars,[223] and in a special grant king Baldwin IV permitted the order of St. John to allocate areas in Galilee to a hundred beduin tents on condition that they came from beyond the frontiers of the kingdom and had never been under the king's or any other lord's domination.[224]

219. Delaville Le Roulx, *Cartulaire,* I, 613 (no. 966).

220. The presence of Latins in the donation of Bohemond III is puzzling, and we may regard it as a slip of the scribe. As a matter of fact, in the detailed enumeration of names no Latin is mentioned.

221. A detailed description of a beduin tribe and its branches or families is furnished by a deed of Baldwin IV to the Hospitallers in 1178. The tribe was once given by queen Melisend and her son Baldwin to Amalric, viscount of Nablus. They were sold to Baldwin of Ibelin, lord of Ramla, for the sizeable sum of 5,500 bezants. All in all there were 103 tents (families). It seems that the tribe was called Banū-Karkas or Banū-Kargas; Delaville Le Roulx, *Cartulaire,* I, 372–373 (no. 550).

222. When Baldwin III invested Philip of Milly, lord of Nablus, in 1161 with Transjordan, he added: "salvis eciam Beduinis meis omnibus, qui de terra Montis Regalis nati non sunt"; Strehlke, *Tabulae,* p. 4 (no. 3).

223. In 1179, in a peace agreement between Templars and Hospitallers, the document mentions a "querela de quadam predacione Biduinorum Templi, facta a turcopolis Gibilini"; Delaville Le Roulx, *Cartulaire,* I, 378–379 (no. 558).

224. ". . . dono . . . centum tentorum Beduinorum . . . quos ab alienis partibus convocare poteritis, et qui in regno meo sub meo vel hominum meorum potestate nunquam fuerint"; *ibid.,* I, 395 (no. 582).

Jerusalem. From a fourteenth-century French illuminated manuscript in the collections of the Bibliothèque nationale

IV

SOCIAL CLASSES
IN THE LATIN KINGDOM:
THE FRANKS

A. *Social Stratification*

During the eleventh century, when social distinctions tended to become sharper in the west, two areas recently added to Christendom revealed a different pattern of social stratification. These were Spain and Sicily, the former slowly pushing back the frontiers of Moslem domination, the latter falling into the hands of the Norman conquer-

There are three categories of sources pertinent to the subject of social classes in the Latin east: legal treatises; acts and deeds; and the chronicles written either in the east or by westerners who had participated in the crusades or had visited the crusading states, including itineraries with descriptions of the Holy Land and its neighboring countries.

The legal treatises have been published by Auguste Beugnot, *RHC, Lois* (2 vols.). These include (vol. I): *Livre de Jean d'Ibelin; Livre de Geoffroy le Tort; Livre de Jacques d'Ibelin; Livre de Philippe de Navarre; La Clef des Assises de la Haute Cour du royaume de Jérusalem et de Chypre;* and the *Livre au roi;* (vol. II): *Livre des Assises de la Cour des Bourgeois; Abrégé du Livre des Assises de la Cour des Bourgeois; Bans et ordonnances des rois de Chypre; Formules; Documents relatifs à la successibilité au trône et à la régence; Document relatif au service militaire; Les Lignages d'Outremer;* and *Chartes.* These are all private collections and, with the exception of the *Livre au roi,* belong to the thirteenth century. The *Livre au roi* is apparently the earliest, written between 1197 and 1205. Besides the lengthy introductions by the editor, Beugnot, the fundamental study of these treatises is that by Maurice Grandclaude, *Étude critique sur les livres des assises de Jérusalem* (Paris, 1923). His attempt to assign a more official character to the *Livre au roi* is not entirely convincing: see his "Caractère du *Livre au roi*," *RHDFE,* ser. 4, V (1926), 308–314. Philip of Novara's treatise was badly edited and needs redoing. No treatise on the laws of Tripoli is preserved, but the customs of Antioch survive partially in an Armenian translation; see *Assises d'Antioche, reproduites en françois,* ed. Leone M. Alishan (Venice, 1876); cf. the remarks in a review by Marius Canard in *Arabica,* IX (1962), 112. For Greek and Latin translations of the various treatises see Grandclaude, *Étude critique,* and Dimitri Hayek, *Le Droit franc en Syrie pendant les croisades* (Paris, 1925). There has been no recent general study of Frankish law in the crusader states.

For a reconstruction of the early royal legislation see Grandclaude, "Liste d'Assises remontant au premier royaume de Jérusalem (1099–1187)," *Mélanges Paul Fournier* (Paris, 1929),

ors. These two areas were rather similar to the Latin states in the east. The distinctive features of social stratification in all of them lay in the fact that they began their history with the same kind of decisive event: a Christian conquest of a non-Christian country. And yet the Latin states in the east would tend to create a special type of society, different from the others. In the course of time Spain would be entirely colonized by its Christian conquerors (expelling or converting in the process the Moslem and Jewish population); the Norman conquerors of Sicily would merge with the heterogeneous local population. But during their two-hundred-years' rule on the eastern shores of the Mediterranean, followed by another two hundred years in Cyprus, the Franks never really succeeded in colonizing their conquests.

---

pp. 329–345, to be supplemented by Joshua Prawer, "La Noblesse et le régime féodal du royaume latin de Jérusalem," *Le Moyen-Âge,* ser. 4, XIV (1959), 41–74; and *idem,* "Étude sur le droit des *Assises de Jérusalem:* Droit de confiscation et droit d'exhérédation," *RHDFE,* ser. 4, XXXIX (1961), 520–551; XL (1962), 29–42. A general study of the royal legislation remains a desideratum.

An excellent guide to the rich treasure of acts and deeds is Reinhold Röhricht, *Regesta regni Hierosolymitani, 1097–1291* (Innsbruck, 1893; repr. New York, 1960) and *Additamentum* (Innsbruck, 1904; repr. New York, 1960). See also Hans E. Mayer, *Bibliographie zur Geschichte der Kreuzzüge,* 2nd ed. (Hanover, 1965), pp. 75–76, together with his "Literaturbericht über die Geschichte der Kreuzzüge," *Historische Zeitschrift,* Sonderheft 3 (Munich, 1969), pp. 641–731, and his "Aspekte der Kreuzzügeforschung," *Geschichte und Gegenwart: Festschrift für Carl Erdmann* (Neumünster, 1980), pp. 75–93. The bulk of these documents were preserved in the archives of ecclesiastical institutions (churches, monasteries, military orders) and communes, whereas the royal and seigneurial archives seem to be entirely lost. See Paul Riant, "Les Archives des établissements latins d'Orient," *AOL,* I (1881; repr. Brussels, 1964), 705–710.

For papal letters see Mayer, *Bibliographie,* pp. 72–74, and Eugène de Rozière, ed., *Cartulaire de l'église du Saint-Sépulcre de Jérusalem* (Paris, 1849; repr. in *PL,* 155 [Paris, 1880], cols. 1105–1262); *Chartes de Terre Sainte provenant de l'abbaye de Notre Dame de Josaphat,* ed. Henri F. Delaborde (Paris, 1880), supplemented by Charles Kohler, "Chartes de l'abbaye de Notre-Dame de la vallée de Josaphat en Terre-Sainte (1108–1291)," *ROL,* VII (1899), 108–222; Emmanuel G. Rey, "Chartes de l'abbaye du Mont Sion," in *Mémoires de la Société nationale des antiquaires de France,* VIII (1887), 31–56; *Cartulaire général de l'ordre des Hospitaliers de Saint Jean de Jérusalem (1100–1310),* ed. J. Delaville Le Roulx (4 vols., Paris, 1894–1906); *Chartes du Mont Thabor,* in Delaville Le Roulx, *op. cit.,* II, 897–914; *Codice diplomatico del sacro militare ordine Gerosolimitano oggi di Malta,* ed. Sebastiano Paoli (2 vols., Lucca, 1733–1737); and *Cartulaire général de l'ordre du Temple, 1119?–1150: Recueil des chartes et des bulles relatives à l'ordre du Temple,* ed. Marquis (Guigue) d'Albon (Paris, 1913; only one vol. published). The huge collection of copies made by d'Albon is in the Bibliothèque nationale in Paris: see Émile G. Léonard, *Introduction au cartulaire manuscrit du Temple (1150–1317) constitué par le Marquis d'Albon* (Paris, 1930). See also *Tabulae ordinis theutonici,* ed. Ernst Strehlke (Berlin, 1869; repr. Toronto, 1975); Erich Joachim and Walther Hubatsch, *Regesta historico-diplomatica ordinis Sanctae Mariae Theutonicorum, 1198–1525* (4 vols., Göttingen, 1948–1950); "Fragment d'un cartulaire de l'ordre de Saint Lazare en Terre Sainte," ed. Arthur de Marsy, in *AOL,* II-2 (1884), 121–157; "Tîtres de l'hôpital des Bretons d'Acre," ed. Delaville Le Roulx, in *AOL,* I (1881), 423–433. Sources of documents for the commercial communes are noted below, note 155.

They neither became a majority in the territories they seized, nor merged with the native population. Consequently the social stratification of the crusader states reflected a division between conqueror and conquered which lasted as long as the Franks remained in the east.

From the legal as well as from the sociological point of view, the population of the crusader states falls into two major categories:

It would be superfluous to list again the principal chronicles, which are noted in the first two volumes of the present work. An excellent guide to the itineraries is Röhricht, *Bibliotheca geographica Palaestinae* (Berlin, 1890; repr. with supplements, Jerusalem, 1963). The major collections of itineraries are *Itinera Hierosolymitana et descriptiones Terrae Sanctae, bellis sacris anteriora et latina lingua exarata,* ed. Titus Tobler, Augustus Molinier, and Kohler (2 vols., Geneva, 1879–1885); *Descriptiones Terrae Sanctae ex saeculo VIII, IX, XII et XV,* ed. Tobler (Leipzig, 1874); *Itinéraires à Jérusalem et descriptions de la Terre Sainte rédigés en français aux XIe, XIIe et XIIIe siècles,* ed. and tr. Henri Michelant and Gaston Raynaud (SOL, *SG,* III; Geneva, 1882); and *Peregrinatores medii aevi quatuor,* ed. J. C. M. Laurent, 2nd ed. (Leipzig, 1873). English translations and some original texts are in *PPTS.*

For Arabic descriptions see *Bibliotheca geographorum Arabicorum,* ed. Martin J. de Goeje (8 vols., Leyden, 1870–1894); German translations by Johann Gildemeister in *ZDPV,* IV (1881), VI (1883), VII (1884), and VIII (1885), and *ZDMG,* XXXVI (1882); translation of excerpts in Guy Le Strange, *Palestine under the Moslems: A Description of Syria and the Holy Land from A.D. 650 to 1500, Translated from the Works of the Mediaeval Arab Geographers* (London, Boston and New York, 1890; repr. Beirut, 1965), and A. Sebastianus Marmardji, *Textes géographiques arabes sur la Palestine* (Paris, 1951).

For Hebrew collections see Abraham Ya'ārī, *Igrōth Eretz-Israēl* [Letters from Palestine] (Jerusalem, 1953); *idem, Masa'ōth Eretz-Israēl* [Voyages to Palestine] (Jerusalem, 1956).

There are few secondary works dealing with the subject as a whole. Basic work, although often erroneous and now out of date, was done by Beugnot in his long introductions to the two volumes of *Lois* cited above. We should also mention the excellent essay by Louis Madelin, "La Syrie franque," *Revue des deux mondes,* LXXXVII (1917), 314–358. The best study, although dated, is by Hans Prutz, *Kulturgeschichte der Kreuzzüge* (Berlin, 1883; repr. Hildesheim, 1964), to which should be added the works of Rey, *Les Colonies franques de Syrie aux XIIe et XIIIe siècles* (Paris, 1883); "La Société civile dans les principautés franques en Syrie," *Cabinet historique,* XXV (1879), 167–186; and *Essai sur la domination française en Syrie durant le moyen-âge* (Paris, 1866). See also Jean Longnon, *Les Français d'Outremer au moyen-âge* (Paris, 1929), and Charles R. Conder, *The Latin Kingdom of Jerusalem, 1099 to 1291 A.D.* (London, 1897; repr. New York, 1973).

Almost all general histories of the crusades have chapters on society in the crusader states. To be specially noted are Claude Cahen, *La Syrie du nord à l'époque des croisades et la principauté franque d'Antioche* (IFD, BO, I; Paris, 1940); Richard, *Le Comté de Tripoli sous la dynastie toulousaine, 1102–1187* (Paris, 1945); *idem, Le Royaume latin de Jérusalem* (Paris, 1953); Hans E. Mayer, *Geschichte der Kreuzzüge* (Stuttgart, 1965), tr. John Gillingham as *The Crusades* (Oxford, 1972); Prawer, *Histoire du royaume latin de Jérusalem* (2 vols., Paris, 1969–1971; 2nd ed., 1975), especially I, 461–537, and II, 215–257; *idem, The Latin Kingdom of Jerusalem: European Colonialism in the Middle Ages* (London, 1972); *idem, The World of the Crusaders* (London, 1972), and *Crusader Institutions* (Oxford, 1980); Jonathan Riley-Smith, *The Feudal Nobility and the Kingdom of Jerusalem, 1174–1277* (London, 1973); and Raymond C. Smail, *The Crusaders in Syria and the Holy Land* (London, 1973).

"Franks" and "non-Franks." Franks is the all-inclusive name for all western Europeans who came with the crusades to the east. The name was ultimately applied not only to the crusaders but also to their descendants, comprising the entire conquering and ruling population. It was only natural that the French descendants of the first settlers found it too inclusive, and consequently used *pullani* or *poulains*[1] for their offspring to distinguish them from members of the various Italian communities. On the other hand, the Arabic-speaking Christians, Moslems, and Jews used the name *al-Ifranj* for all who were not indigenous members of the population. In this sense the word was equivalent to "invaders." As far as we can ascertain, the native population did not use the expression "Christians" (*an-Naṣārah*) for the conquerors, to avoid confusing native Christians with Europeans. But the Franks were often called "crusaders" (*Ṣalibīyah*), whereas western sources used *crucesignati* to denote not all those who went to the east but only those who had taken the cross and enjoyed the lay and ecclesiastical privileges of crusaders. These semantic distinctions underline the fact that, as far as the indigenous population was concerned, the most relevant feature of their relations with the Franks was a strict legal and social segregation.

The entire population of the Latin kingdom consequently falls into two categories — conquerors and conquered. The European conquest not only changed the conditions existing in the conquered territories, but also cut deep into the web of social relations and legal status of

---

1. The origin of the name is obscure. Contemporaries derived it from Apulia, suggesting that the native-born Franks were descended from marriages between crusaders and women brought over from southern Italy because of the lack of women among the settlers. Another explanation connected it with Latin *pullus,* young animal, in the sense of newcomer. See James of Vitry, *Historia orientalis,* I, i, cap. 67, in Jacques Bongars, ed., *Gesta Dei per Francos* (Hanau, 1611; repr. Jerusalem, 1972), I, 1086 (lines 14–17): "Pollani autem dicuntur, qui post praedictam terrae sanctae liberationem ex ea oriundi extiterunt: vel quia recentes et novi, quasi pulli respectu Surianorum reputati sunt; vel quia principaliter de gente Apuliae matres secundum carnem habuerunt." Still another connects it with an offensive Arabic expression, *fulān ibn-fulān,* meaning literally "X son of X," a man whose father was unknown — in short, a bastard. One wonders if ultimately the word might not have been derived from the Greek *-poulos,* son. It may be recalled that the crusaders' light cavalry was called *turcopuli.* Margaret R. Morgan, *The Chronicle of Ernoul and the Continuations of William of Tyre* (London, 1973), pp. 194–195, has questioned the general opinion that it was used in the derisive sense of "half-caste," as has Prawer, *The World of the Crusaders,* p. 83. On the *turcopuli* see *idem, The Latin Kingdom,* pp. 340–341. Cf. also Henri Diament, "Can Toponomastics Explain the Origin of Crusader French Lexemes *Poulain* and *Turcople?" Names: Journal of the American Name Society,* XXV (1977), 183–204; and Morgan, "The Meaning of Old French *Polain/*Latin *Pullanus,"* *Medium Aevum,* XLVIII (1979), 40–54.

the conquerors themselves, changing European notions as they existed at the time of the founding of the kingdom. Two cases will suffice to illustrate the difference between European and crusader notions of social and legal status. In eleventh-century Europe, being a peasant meant, with few exceptions, to have the legal and social status of a serf or villein. In the Latin states in the east a peasant was a villein only if he belonged to the native population. A Frankish peasant working his own land, or his holding, or settled in one of the newly established Frankish villages, was under no circumstances a villein. He was always called a "burgess" (*burgensis*). Despite being a peasant he preserved his legal status and social standing as a member of the ruling class, well above the status of villein or serf. From the point of view of the general stratification of society his occupation was of no consequence. The decisive factor was his European origin. Conversely, a Syrian Christian, Moslem, or Jewish peddler, artisan, or small shopkeeper, often living in a street neighboring that of a Frank pursuing the same occupation, was neither socially nor legally his equal. Any Frank, even the poorest and the lowest, ranked well above the wealthiest of the native population.

Another factor which helped to delineate the two main divisions of society was the social tradition brought over from Europe with the first settlers and strengthened by later waves of immigration. The armies of the First Crusade did not reflect in their composition an accurate cross-section of European society. Not only were some strata of society hardly represented, but all marks of servility ceased to exist for any man who went to the east. From the outset, the crusading army was composed of "nobles" of different degrees and freemen, or to use the terms found in our sources, *milites* and *pedites*. What in the first instance denoted a way of fighting, on horseback or on foot, in reality marked the basic distinction between "noble" knights and simple free men, including those who became free by joining the crusading army. To these two main classes of *milites* and *pedites* we have to add the clergy. The crusading clergy reflected in its composition the clerical establishment of Europe, from great lords like Adhémar of Monteil, bishop of Le Puy, through the more modest chaplains serving princely households, down to the simple priests who hardly differed at all in social status from the *pedites*. These three elements— *milites, pedites,* and *clerici*—formed the nucleus of the European society transplanted to the east. It is here that we have to look for the future classes of nobles and non-nobles, or to use the Frankish terms, nobles and burgesses, the two main groups of Frankish lay society.

Still another element was provided by the natives of Italian, Provençal, and Spanish communes. Their original class distinctions were of no consequence in determining their legal status in the crusader states. With the exception of a few families, like the Embriachi of Genoa who became lords of Jubail, and as such entered the ranks of Frankish nobility, their social and legal position resulted from agreements between the representatives of the respective European communes and the authorities in the crusader army and later the kings and princes of the crusader states. The natives of the western communes can be regarded as an occupational group, as indeed they were. It was not the fact that they were merchants, however, which assured their place in society, but rather the particular privileges they acquired. Although each commune obtained for its members somewhat different sets of privileges, they were on the whole still regarded by their contemporaries as a distinct class.

B. The Nobles[2]

"Among all the vocations [*mestier*] which should be taught as early as possible in childhood there are two, the highest and the most hon-

2. For the early period there are few documents, and we must rely for the most part on the chronicles of the First Crusade. Besides the legal treatises we may cite C. du Fresne Du Cange's *Les Familles d'Outremer,* ed. Rey (Paris, 1869), supplemented by *idem, Sommaire du supplément aux Familles d'Outremer* (Chartres, 1881), and Röhricht, *Zusätze und Verbesserungen zu Du Cange* (Berlin, 1886). A new edition of *Les Familles d'Outremer* is needed. Copious materials were collected by Louis de Mas Latrie and are preserved in the Bibliothèque nationale: MSS. fr., nouv. acq., 6793–6803. An important outline may be found in John L. LaMonte, "Chronologie de l'Orient latin," *Bulletin of the International Committee of Historical Sciences,* XII-2 (Paris, 1943), 141–202.

Several studies deal with the different local dynasties: L. de Mas Latrie, "Les Comtes de Jaffa et d'Ascalon," *Revue des questions historiques,* XXVI (1879), 181–200; Mary E. Nickerson, "The Seigneury of Beirut in the Twelfth Century and the Brisebarre Family of Beirut-Blanchegarde," *Byzantion,* XIX (1949), 141–185 (which supersedes the study by Rey in *ROL,* IV [1896], 12–18); LaMonte, "The Lords of Le Puiset on the Crusades," *Speculum,* XVII (1942), 100–118; cf. Richard, "Un Évêque d'Orient latin au XIVe siècle: Guy d'Ibelin, O.P., évêque de Limassol, et l'inventaire de ses biens (1367)," *Bulletin de la correspondance hellénique,* LXXIV (1950), 98–133; LaMonte, "The Lords of Caesarea in the Period of the Crusades," *Speculum,* XXII (1947), 145–161; *idem,* "The Lords of Sidon in the XIIth and XIIIth Centuries," *Byzantion,* XVII (1944–1945), 183–211; LaMonte and Norton Downs, "The Lords of Bethsan in the Kingdoms of Jerusalem and Cyprus," *Mediaevalia et humanistica,* VI (1950), 57–75; LaMonte, "The Rise and Decline of a Frankish Seigneury in the Time of the Crusades," *Revue historique du sud-est européen,* XV (1938), 301–320; *idem,* "The Viscounts of Naplouse in the 12th Century," *Syria,* XIX (1938), 272–278; Harry Pirie-Gordon, "The Reigning Princes of Galilee," *English Historical Review,* XXVII (1912), 445–461; L. de Mas Latrie, "Les Seigneurs d'Arsur en Terre Sainte," *Revue des questions historiques,* LV (1894), 585–597; Rey, "Les Seigneurs de Montréal et de la Terre d'Outre le Jourdain," *ROL,* IV (1896), 19–24; W. H. Rüdt de (von) Collenberg, "Les Premiers Ibelins," *Le Moyen-Âge,* ser. 4, XX (1965), 433–474. Cf. René Grousset, *Histoire des croisades,* II (Paris, 1935), appendix. Many genealogical tables are to be found in the works of Grousset and Steven Runciman. For the dynasties in Antioch, Tripoli, and Edessa see Cahen, *Syrie du nord,* and Richard, *Comté de Tripoli,* cited above in the bibliographical note, and Marshall W. Baldwin, *Raymond III of Tripolis and the Fall of Jerusalem, 1140–1187* (Princeton, 1936); Robert L. Nicholson, *Joscelyn III and the Fall of the Crusader States* (Leyden, 1973); and Mayer, "Die Seigneurie de Joscelin und der Deutsche Orden," in *Die geistlichen Ritterorden Europas,* ed. Josef Fleckenstein and Manfred Hellmann (Sigmaringen, 1980), pp. 171–216.

Some useful information is to be found in Gustave Schlumberger, *Numismatique de l'Orient latin* (Paris, 1878–1882; repr. Graz, 1954), to be supplemented by Dorothy H. Cox, *The Tripolis Hoard of French Seignorial and Crusaders' Coins* (New York, 1933). See also Henry Longuet, "La Trouvaille de Kessab en Orient latin," *Revue numismatique,* ser. 4, XXXVIII (1935), 163–181; Paul Balog and Jacques Yvon, "Monnaies à légendes arabes de l'Orient latin," *Revue numismatique,* ser. 6, I (1958), 133–168 (superseding older studies by De Saulay, Blancard, and La-

orable to God and the world, that is, clergy and chivalry; because
he cannot be a good clerk who did not start from childhood, and

voix); Yvon, "France, Italie et l'Orient latin," *A Survey of Numismatic Research, 1960-1965,*
II, *Medieval and Oriental Numismatics,* ed. Kolbjørn Skaare and George C. Miles (Copenhagen,
1967), pp. 216-256; David M. Metcalf, "The Templars as Bankers and Monetary Transfers between West and East in the Twelfth Century," in *Coinage in the Latin East,* ed. Peter W. Edbury
and Metcalf (Oxford, 1980), pp. 3-17; Peter W. Edbury, "The Baronial Coinage of the Latin
Kingdom of Jerusalem," *ibid.,* pp. 59-72. Some interesting material can also be found in G.
Schlumberger, F. Chalandon, and Adrien Blanchet, *Sigillographie de l'Orient latin* (Bibliothèque
archéologique et historique, XXXVII; Paris, 1943); cf. Mayer, *Das Siegelwesen in den Kreuzfahrerstaaten* (Bayerische Akad. der Wissenschaften, philosophisch-historische Klasse, Ab-
handlungen, n.s., 83; Munich, 1978). Epigraphic materials were recently collected and published by Sabino de Sandoli, *Corpus inscriptionum crucesignatorum Terrae Sanctae, 1099-1291*
(Jerusalem, 1974).

Works on the territorial composition of the various lordships are of special importance.
Although mostly dealing with topography, the basic studies are those of Gustavus Beyer: "Das
Gebiet der Kreuzfahrerherrschaft Caesarea in Palästina," *ZDPV,* LIX (1936), 1-91; "Neapolis
und sein Gebiet in der Kreuzfahrerzeit," *ibid.,* LXIII (1940), 155-209; "Die Kreuzfahrergebiete
von Jerusalem und S. Abraham," *ibid.,* LXV (1942), 165-211; "Die Kreuzfahrergebiete Akko
und Galilea," *ibid.,* LXVII (1944-1945), 183-260; "Die Kreuzfahrergebiete Südwestpalästinas,"
ibid., LXVIII (1946-1951), 148-192, 249-281; and "Civitas Ficuum," *ibid.,* LXIX (1953), 75-87.
See also Dan Barag, "A New Source Concerning the Ultimate Borders of the Latin Kingdom
of Jerusalem," *Israel Exploration Journal,* XX (1970), 107-217; Peter M. Holt, "Qalāwūn's
Treaty with Acre, 1283," *English Historical Review,* XCI (1976), 802-812; Richard, "Les Listes
de seigneuries dans le *Livre de Jean d'Ibelin:* Recherches sur l'Assebèbe et Mimars," *RHDFE,*
ser. 4, XXXII (1954), 565-577; Mayer, "Die Kreuzfahrerherrschaft 'Arrābe," *ZDPV,* XCIII (1977),
198-212; Marie Louise Favreau, "Die Kreuzfahrerherrschaft 'Scandalion' (Iskanderūne)," *ibid.,*
XCIII (1977), 12-29.

On the general status of studies of Latin society in the east see Cahen, "La Féodalité et
les institutions politiques de l'Orient latin," *Oriente ed Occidente nel medio evo* (Accademia
nazionale dei Lincei, Fondazione Alessandro Volta, Atti dei convegni XII; Rome, 1957), pp.
167-191. Studies dealing with different aspects of the knightly class are not numerous: Richard,
"Pairie d'Orient latin: Les quatre baronnies des royaumes de Jérusalem et de Chypre," *RHDFE,*
ser. 4, XXVIII (1950), 67-88; Prawer, "The *Assise de tenure* and the *Assise de vente:* A Study
of Landed Property in the Latin Kingdom," *Economic History Review,* ser. 2, IV (1951-1952),
77-87; *idem,* "Les Premiers temps de la féodalité dans le royaume latin de Jérusalem," *Tijd-
schrift voor Rechtsgeschiedenis,* XXII (1954), 401-424; *idem,* "La Noblesse et le régime féodal
du royaume latin de Jérusalem," *Le Moyen-Âge,* ser. 4, XIV (1959), 41-74 (these three studies
were translated and updated in Prawer, *Crusader Institutions,* pp. 343-357, 3-19, and 20-45
respectively); Runciman, *The Families of Outremer* (Creighton Lecture in History, 1959; London, 1960); Mayer, "Studies in the History of Queen Melisende of Jerusalem," *Dumbarton
Oaks Papers,* XXVI (1972), 93-182; *idem,* "Ibelin versus Ibelin: The Struggle for the Regency
of Jerusalem 1253-1258," *Proceedings of the American Philosophical Society,* CXXII (1978),
25-57; Edbury, "The Disputed Regency of the Kingdom of Jerusalem 1264/6 and 1268," *Camden
Miscellany,* XXVII (London, 1979), 1-48; Prawer, "Étude sur le droit," *RHDFE,* ser. 4, XXXIX,
520-551; XL, 29-42, expanded and tr. as "Roman Law and Crusader Legislation: The *Assises*
on Confiscation and Disinheritance," in *Crusader Institutions,* pp. 430-467; Edmond Meynial,
"De Quelques particularités féodales dans les Assises de Jérusalem," *RHDFE,* XVI (1892), 408-
426; Richard, "Le Statut de la femme dans l'Orient latin," *Recueil de la Société Jean Bodin,*
XII (1948), 377-388; Smail, "Crusaders' Castles of the XIIth Century," *Cambridge Historical
Journal,* X-2 (1950-1952), 133-149; and Prawer, "Étude de quelques problèmes agraires et sociaux d'une seigneurie croisée au XIIIe siècle," *Byzantion,* XXII (1952), 5-61; XXIII (1953),

he will never ride well who did not learn it when young."[3] Thus wrote
Philip of Novara, knight, writer, jurist, and, at the end of his life
(about 1260), moralist at the court of the Ibelins. Looking back over
his own career, this Frankish nobleman of obscure origin from tiny
Novara in northern Italy summed up the possibilities open to a young
man of good birth: "A good knight by the fame of his valor . . .
very often came to acquire riches and great property. And many became crowned kings and others had great riches and great seigneuries."[4]
Giving good advice to that younger generation which would witness
the fall of the kingdom, Philip goes on to emphasize the traditional
ideals of knighthood and nobility: "Besoigns est que il soit cortois,
et larges et hardiz et sages." Significantly enough a woman need only
preserve her chastity ("prode fame de son cors"). This would cover
all other requirements and allow her to walk everywhere with her head
held high.[5] He then goes on: "The young man of high origin and
the knight and other people bearing arms should work to gain honor
so as to become famous for their valor, and to have earthly property
and riches and land, from which they might live honorably and so
might their children, if they have any, and so they might help their
friends and those who serve them and be able to retire in their old
age."[6] There is a rather pedestrian sound to the ideals of knighthood
as expressed by Philip, and the phrase just quoted is not an isolated
one. Again and again the attainment of wealth, as an end in itself
or as a means of living according to a given standard, jars our ears,
perhaps because often we still see the crusaders through the eyes of
novelists and romantic historians. But Philip of Novara, whose work
is original and free of the usual moralizing banalities,[7] was simply
summing up his own personal experience.

Philip mentions three different orders of nobles in the crusader states:
"Haut home et li chevaliers et les autres gens d'armes"—magnates,
knights, and other people bearing arms. This tripartite division, which
we find in other sources in such expressions as *riches hommes ou
terriers, barons, chevaliers,* and so on, makes it clear that the ruling
class of the kingdom was not monolithic, but was made up in Philip's
time, as indeed a century earlier, of different categories: a high nobil-

143-170, expanded and tr. as "Palestinian Agriculture and the Crusader Rural System," in *Crusader Institutions,* pp. 143-200.

3. *Les Quatre âges de l'homme: Traité moral de Philippe de Navarre,* ed. Marcel de Fréville
(Paris, 1888), p. 10.

4. *Ibid.,* p. 11.

5. *Ibid.,* p. 20.

6. *Ibid.,* p. 39.

7. Charles V. Langlois, *La Vie en France au moyen-âge,* 2nd ed. (Paris, 1926), pp. 205-240.

ity, a baronage,[8] and simple knights. All of them were noble and as such belonged to the highest estate of the kingdom, within which, however, there were marked distinctions. It was the economic standing of the individual coupled with his origins which classified him within the noble hierarchy of the crusader states. Philip of Novara himself hardly belonged among the magnates. He was one of the baronage who did well for himself, rising in the service of the Ibelins and of the court to the rank of an influential baron in the kingdom. The ideals which he expressed fit that middle group among the nobility who rose from the ranks of the knights to become barons. The crusader states, though hardly a land of unlimited possibilities, sometimes offered opportunities which contemporary Europe, less fluid and more established, seldom presented to the young and the enterprising. Philip, mentioning knights who became kings, probably had in mind Guy of Lusignan. He might also have thought of Reginald of Châtillon, whose remarkable career inflamed the imagination. But did he also think of his own benefactors, the Ibelins? Their origin was obscure, possibly minor officials in Chartres or even Pisan merchants established in the east. Yet they became the uncrowned rulers of the kingdom, kingmakers intermarrying with the royal houses of Jerusalem and Cyprus and even with the imperial dynasty of Constantinople. At the time of Philip of Novara the family had already succeeded in forgetting, and making others forget, its origins.

What, then, is the nobility of the crusader states? Its first layer is to be sought among those warriors who took part in the First Crusade and stayed on in Syria and Palestine afterwards. A scrutiny of the names to be found in chronicles and documents up to the end of the rule of Baldwin I (1118) throws some light on this early group. A salient feature is the particular ethnic groupings in the three principalities of Antioch, Tripoli, and Jerusalem. This was foreshadowed by the composition of the armies of the First Crusade, when the various ethnic groups were led by their traditional local leaders. Vassals of Godfrey of Bouillon in Lower Lorraine made up the main part of his army, and the same can be said for the Flemings, the Provençals, and the Normans, including those from Sicily and southern Italy. It can also be shown that individual knights or groups of knights, not

---

8. The connotation of "baron" in the sources is not very precise. It was often used to connote "noble," but more frequently, it seems, was used to stress the notion of vassalage; cf. *Livre au roi,* cap. 2 (*RHC, Lois,* I, 608): "don de roi ni de roine ni des barons dou reaume ni des terriers qui don fassent par prevelige . . .;" and *ibid.,* cap. 16 (p. 617): ". . . se aucun home lige ou terrier ou baron dou reaume. . . ." We shall use the word in the sense of a class between the magnates and the simple knights. See below, note 44.

belonging originally to the feudal family of the leader but living in
his neighborhood, joined his army for reasons of convenience, familiarity, or identity of speech and customs. This loose ethnic grouping
became stronger during the march to the east, when necessities of
command and provisioning made for greater cohesion. New links of
vassalage were forged. True, some of the leaders changed their allegiance, as did Tancred, who started with Bohemond, went on with
Raymond of St. Gilles, and finally took service for better pay under
Godfrey of Bouillon.[9] But in this case it was not just Tancred, but
his whole army, that accepted a new overlord and commander.

Since the various crusader states were captured by different commanders, it was natural that the knights of Antioch, under Bohemond I and later Tancred, would be predominantly Norman,[10] while
Tripoli would have a population of knights originally from southern
France. The kingdom of Jerusalem proper, south of Tripoli, though
it may have had a pronounced north French knightly class (roughly
speaking from north of the Loire, except Normandy), had a more
heterogeneous composition. One of the reasons was probably the fact
that different ethnic groups participated in the siege of Jerusalem;
later pilgrimages and waves of immigration brought more elements
of diverse origin to Jerusalem than anywhere else. Such additions were
of course not limited to Jerusalem. Southern families, possibly originally connected with Raymond of St. Gilles, can be found in Antioch. The presence of Raymond of Poitiers in Antioch (1136-1149) also
brought some non-Norman elements to the principality. Still, the
predominance of the respective ethnic groups was strong enough to
leave their mark on the customs and organization of the different
states. A German pilgrim in the second half of the twelfth century
complained bitterly that the merits of his own people, not to mention
his language, were obliterated in the east.

Whereas the names of knights allow us a glimpse into their ethnic
origin, our sources fail us almost completely when we inquire into
their social position before leaving Europe. The reason does not lie
in any lack of documentation, but rather in the fact that most of
the crusaders we know anything about went home again. Of the men
from the great noble families who went with the First Crusade only
a few—Raymond of St. Gilles, Bohemond, Tancred, and Godfrey
of Bouillon and his brother Baldwin—stayed on in the east. The others
left, some before the conquest of Jerusalem, others immediately after.

9. Raymond of Aguilers, cap. 16 (*RHC, Occ.,* III, 278).
10. They were certainly Normans, but it is not clear whether from Normandy or Sicily.

The great mass of *milites* who went on the crusade, and the small remnant[11] who settled in the east after the conquest, belonged neither to the upper nobility nor to the middle nobility whose records are preserved in the deeds and annals of their countries of origin. Those who stayed on in the east after their leaders returned home had been household knights and petty vassals. These provided the major element from which grew the new class of Latin nobility.

The modest origin of the early nobles in the Latin states of the east remains, however, a hypothesis, though a plausible one, since it fits in with several phenomena which would otherwise remain unexplained. One, for example, is the important role played by an anonymous group of knights called *domus Godefridi*[12] in connection with the coronation of Baldwin I. The term is a typical expression for household knights (probably connected with Godfrey when still in Lorraine) who remained in the service of the *advocatus Sancti Sepulcri*. They were still a coherent group as late as 1105, five years after the accession of Baldwin I. It is likely that had there been any among them of prominence, our sources would have pointed out the fact and mentioned their names.

Another clue is the fact that neither in Jerusalem, nor in Antioch, nor in Tripoli do we find, among the first holders of fiefs, surnames pointing to connections with European castles or seigneuries. Moreover, later local dynasties bear the names of their Syrian and Palestinian fiefs, whereas European family names (like Grenier in Jerusalem and Mazoir in Antioch) are exceptions, and even then hardly indicate noble origins.[13] In a feudal age, people proud of their origins would hardly have foregone the occasion to mention their ancestral names, if such had been of any consequence.

Under the princes who became rulers of the crusader states, therefore, the knightly class was of modest background. Their loyalties were to the man or house which they had served in Europe or took service with in the course of conquest and settlement. Their well-being

---

11. The numbers given in our sources for the early period of the kingdom are small; e.g., October 1100: 200–400 knights; September 1101: 260–300 knights; summer 1105: 500 knights. Cf. Fulcher of Chartres, *Historia Hierosolymitana,* ed. Heinrich Hagenmeyer (Heidelberg, 1913), II, i, 2; II, xi, 2; II, xxxii, 3.

12. Albert of Aachen, VII, 57; IX, 3 (*RHC, Occ.,* IV, 545, 592). On the different numbers see William B. Stevenson, *The Crusaders in the East* (Cambridge, Eng., 1907), pp. 33, 35, 39, 44; and Prawer, "The Settlement of the Latins in Jerusalem," *Speculum,* XXVII (1952), 490–503 (in *Crusader Institutions,* pp. 85–101). Riley-Smith argues that Godfrey never bore the title "advocate of the Holy Sepulcher."

13. For Jerusalem see Prawer, "La Noblesse et le régime féodal," pp. 41–74; for Antioch see Cahen, *Syrie du nord,* genealogical tables, pp. 543 ff.; for Tripoli see Richard, *Comté de Tripoli,* pp. 71 ff.

and future depended in large part on the success of the conquest and
the good will of their lord. The economic situation of the crusader
states was critical for many years. Sometimes it was so bad that the
finances depended on a successful raid on a Moslem caravan.[14] The
simple knights from whom emerged the later nobility often complained
because of arrears in payment of their salaries, and even threatened
open revolt.[15] When Baldwin I forced the patriarch Daimbert of Pisa
to take thirty knights on his payroll, it was considered a great achievement.[16] During this early period the mass of *milites* was no more than
a salaried army, composed of knights receiving salaries or assigned
fixed revenues.

The first signs of development appear under Baldwin I. Godfrey
of Bouillon had not distributed any land fiefs but had contented himself with assigning his men revenues from land or cities. Under Baldwin the growing mass of conquests was organized and the expanding
frontiers were defended according to feudal practices. Seigneurial fiefs
were created and granted to some of the king's companions, although
the salaried knight was still very much in evidence.[17] But a higher
baronage was emerging. A closer look at this early class of upper
nobility proves that local conditions and historical circumstances
created in the Latin east a type of nobility and a pattern of organization differing from that known in Europe. The most salient feature
is that the nobles and knights were predominantly city-dwellers, whereas
nowhere in Europe can we find a knightly class wholly located in
cities. The reasons are not difficult to identify. The normal habitat
of the earlier Moslem ruling class was the fortified city or the citadel.
The crusaders did not besiege castles, but cities. With their conquest
the adjacent territory also fell into their hands. The isolated castle,
as a place of defense and administration, was introduced by the crusaders only later under the pressure of circumstances.[18] Being a small

14. In 1108 Baldwin I captured a caravan making its way from Egypt to Syria—thirty-two
camels bearing sugar, pepper and spices, oil and honey, "quorum abundantia tota regio
peregrinorum relevata et confortata est": Albert of Aachen, X, 36 (*RHC, Occ.,* IV, 648).

15. In 1101, "a militibus suis in urbe Japhet [Jaffa] pro pecunia angustiatus est [Baldwin
I], quam illis debebat pro conventione solidorum, qui etiam fratri eius Godefrido, principi
Jherusalem, multum obsequii impenderant, et nunc eius causa et honore non minori studio
militaris operis laborabant": Albert of Aachen, VII, 58 (*RHC, Occ.,* IV, 545). Baldwin abandoned the siege of Sidon when offered money: "anxius et sollicitus de conventione solidorum
quos debebat militibus, totus pecuniae intendebat": *ibid.,* X, 4 (*RHC, Occ.,* IV, 632–633).

16. *Ibid.,* VII, 49, 58, 61 (*RHC, Occ.,* IV, 540, 545, 547).

17. On his deathbed Baldwin I left his property "militibus quoque domesticis et advenis,
et cunctis qui sibi in auxilio militari servierant in conventione solidorum": *ibid.,* XII, 23 (*RHC,
Occ.,* IV, 703–704).

18. Smail, "Crusaders' Castles." Obviously in Transjordan the crusaders settled in castles,

minority surrounded by a hostile majority, the crusaders concentrated their numbers in the conquered cities, often strengthening their fortifications, or erecting strong-points around the cities where such did not already exist (as in Bethsan and Tiberias). This strengthened their military position; it also facilitated the continuity of the earlier pattern of administration which, under the Byzantines and Moslems, centered on the cities. At the same time, the city offered not only security but also accommodations for the new settlers, who took over houses according to the famous "law of conquest," which accorded ownership of a given property to the first person who put his sign on it.[19]

Amid the general insecurity,[20] nobody risked leaving the shadow of the city walls without an armed escort, let alone taking up residence in the rural area. These early conditions changed in the course of time. Life became more settled, security was more assured, but even as late as 1179, when the crusader states were well established, Frankish rule in some parts of Galilee was still more nominal than real.[21]

Despite the growth of security there was no exodus of the knightly city dwellers to manor houses in the country. The crusaders established a manorial system entirely different from that prevalent in Europe. It was a predominantly *rentier* system based on rents and taxes collected directly from the villages and assessed on the peasants' holdings.[22] As a rule the Frankish landowner did not retain demesne lands of any importance, and his income came almost wholly from the *tenurae* held from him by his peasants. There was, then, little interest in the direct management of rural estates and no incentive to live in a manor house in the village or in the fief. The administration was handled by local representatives of the lord, chosen from among the native population or specially appointed, like the *gastaldiones* in Venetian properties.[23] The holders of fiefs, more *rentiers* than anything else, remained in cities, there receiving and consuming the incomes from their fiefs. The city-dwelling fief-holder remained the predominant type of knight in the crusader states.

---

the only exception being some villages which they tried to colonize; see Prawer, "Crusader Security and the Red Sea," in *Crusader Institutions,* pp. 475–477.

19. See below, note 80.

20. Cf. the descriptions of Palestine by Saewulf and the Russian abbot Daniel in *PPTS,* IV-2, 3 (London, 1896, 1895).

21. William of Tyre, XXI, 26 ff. (*RHC, Occ.,* I, 1049 ff.).

22. Prawer, "Étude de quelques problèmes agraires et sociaux," *Byzantion,* XXII (1952), 5–61; XXIII (1953), 143–170; *Crusader Institutions,* pp. 143–200.

23. *Gastaldiones,* a word of Lombard origin, seems to have been used only by the Venetians as a name for their bailies. See the report of Marsiglio Zorzi (Giorgio) in Tafel and Thomas, II, 351 ff.

The erection of castles changed this general pattern somewhat, with some knights fulfilling garrison duties in castles though seldom making them their normal abode. Still, the crusaders' castles, with very few exceptions (smaller fortifications or observation points), were usually surrounded by real cities, as for example the mighty fortresses in Transjordan: Krak de Montréal (ash-Shaubak) and Kerak of Moab (al-Karak). Other castles, which might have been for a short time centers of lordships, became real city settlements (Ibelin, Gaza, Darum, Mirabel). On the other hand, after the middle of the twelfth century the newly built castles were almost systematically handed over to the military orders, which garrisoned them with their own knights. Even allowing for these exceptions, there is no doubt that the bulk of the knightly class lived in cities, differing basically from the nobility of contemporary Europe.

In this early period of formation of a knightly class, social mobility seems to have been characteristic. The breaking down of class barriers may have owed something to the four years' march to the east. Battles, sieges, and calamities, when horses were killed by enemy action or eaten by the starving army, often turned *milites* into *pedites*. Nor is it difficult to believe that under circumstances of chronic warfare and varying fortunes some of the *pedites* became knights. The fact that at any given moment almost everyone in the army was paid by a leader also had a leveling effect. The "law of conquest" probably had the same result. In some cases we may suspect that some of the witnesses of early royal documents were of non-noble origin,[24] who some years later signed their names among the *milites* on royal charters. In the fluctuating state of society, of war and death, immigration and emigration, social mobility existed *de facto* if not *de jure*.

To round out this description of the early Frankish nobility a few remarks should be made about their economic status. As suggested above, Godfrey of Bouillon and Baldwin I were tight-fisted about creating fiefs, especially seigneurial fiefs. They preferred to assign city revenues rather than territory to their vassals. This was probably also true, though to a lesser degree, with respect to the creation of fiefs out of the royal domain. It is more than likely that the simple knight living in Jerusalem, Acre, or Tyre preferred to receive his salary directly from the royal exchequer or from one of the royal revenues (market tolls, city gate taxes, or the like), than to bother supervising and collecting dues from an outlying farm or village. Hence

24. See below, p. 159.

the characteristic money-fief, *fié en besanz,* was the usual type of feudal tenure. What had once been a salary on a contractual basis became in time the normal type of fief. Such an arrangement suited lord and vassal alike. The former, especially in the maritime cities, could easily pay his knights out of revenues from the port, market, or other monopoly. The latter, living in cities in surroundings of an evident money economy, must have found such an arrangement most welcome. The crusaders' feudal jurisprudence accorded the same social standing to the holders of a *fié en besanz* as to those of land fiefs,[25] and consequently no sense of degradation, because of being salaried rather than enfeoffed, disturbed the knight.

Another kind of property also came into the hands of the knightly class. City property, courtyards and houses, are often found in their possession. Some were held as allodial property, some as *borgesie,* some as parts of fiefs. The same is true of land in the immediate vicinity of the cities. This strange occurrence of allodial holdings in a land supposed to be a "paradise of feudalism" was one of the results of the original "law of conquest."[26] It reflects an early stage of organization when property could be had for the asking, especially in the depopulated cities.[27] As for the *borgesie* tenures in the hands of knights, well attested by our sources, they may have been the result of intermarriage between knights and non-nobles, the consequence of a shortage of women in the early settlement as well as the coexistence of the two classes in the cities. The *borgesies* probably constituted parts of the dowries of burgesses' daughters which passed with the hand of the heiress to her husband.[28] This suggests less a rigid class distinction than a fairly high social mobility in the population of the crusader states.

Under Baldwin II (1118–1131), however, and even more so under Fulk (1131–1143) and Baldwin III (1143–1163), a group of knights began to be distinguished from their erstwhile fellows. The necessity to rule the country in a feudal framework led to the creation of lordships granted by the king and princes to some of their vassals. Some lordships probably represent independent conquests, which the crown

---

25. Noted by Prutz, *Kulturgeschichte der Kreuzzüge,* pp. 182 ff; cf. LaMonte, *Feudal Monarchy in the Latin Kingdom,* pp. 143 ff.; Prawer, *The Latin Kingdom,* pp. 126 ff.

26. Prawer, "The *Assise de tenure* and the *Assise de vente,*" pp. 77–87. Burgage tenure may have been created by the same process; see Prawer, "Burgage-Tenure," in *Crusader Institutions,* pp. 250–262.

27. Prawer, "The Settlement of the Latins in Jerusalem," pp. 490–503.

28. The knights naturally tried to acquire *borgesies,* since they were not burdened with military service; see above, note 26, end.

then incorporated into the framework of the feudal state as fiefs held from the crown.[29] The result was the emergence of a baronage distinct from the general body of knights. It was some time in the making. For more than a generation we cannot trace any regular succession in the great fiefs, either in Jerusalem, in Tripoli, or in Antioch.[30] Deaths from warfare and disease were common, and the newly conquered and thinly occupied lands could not yet boast large families. Fiefs were allotted to men of merit but often escheated to the crown when there were no heirs to claim them. In these circumstances, although a baronage was evolving, it had not yet crystalized into a class. The real power remained with the royal house, still the only real dynasty in a fluid society. It was the king who enfeoffed lordships acquired by conquest or escheat, creating a baronage dependent upon his authority.

By 1130, however, there were signs of a process of stratification within the nobility as this baronage became more coherent. It comprised the great tenants-in-chief, who soon succeeded in becoming hereditary holders with the status of *seigneurs justiciers* in their respective lordships. It is not clear whether there were any principles which determined the status of a fief as being an independent barony with its own seigneurial jurisdiction or as a fief within the domain of the crown. It was probably a matter of common understanding that any large fief with a city as capital was in fact a barony. In the middle of the twelfth century more than two dozen such baronial fiefs existed in the kingdom, and their tenants can be regarded as a baronage, an upper nobility.

A whole set of assises promulgated at this time definitely served the interests of the new class. Early legislation of the first half of the twelfth century had aimed at creating a large and solid knightly class to assure thereby the existence of a strong military class owing service to the king and the princes. Women had been allowed to succeed to fiefs almost immediately after the conquest.[31] Fiefs became hereditary very early even in the collateral branches of a family,[32] but could not pass to an already enfeoffed knight if his younger brother

29. Thus Bethsan and Tiberias were private conquests of Tancred (as was Bethlehem). He tried to create an independent principality of Galilee with Tiberias as its capital and Haifa as its main port. This conquest was incorporated into the kingdom under Baldwin I. Its holders continued, however, to hold the title of "prince."

30. The difference between the king's authority in Jerusalem and the prince's in Antioch has often been stressed, but is certainly exaggerated as far as the early period is concerned.

31. Philip of Novara, cap. 71 (*RHC, Lois,* I, 542).

32. *Idem,* cap. 66 (*ibid.,* I, 537); John of Ibelin, cap. 15 (*ibid.,* I, 233, 235).

or any other member of his family in line of succession was not yet
provided for.[33] The emergence of a new baronial class was accompanied by far-reaching changes in this early legislation. It is possible
that a twelfth-century assise which cannot be dated with more preci-
sion, requiring that a lord should retain a greater portion of his whole
fief than the total of its subinfeudated parts,[34] is already a sign of
the growing power of the baronial class. The purpose of the assise
was to prevent the fragmentation of family holdings. It may have
been the first step toward creating entailed estates. Even more important was the assise that changed the rules of succession, permitting
the concentration of an unlimited number of fiefs in the hands of
one person.[35] This laid the basis for accumulating landed property
and concentrating power in the hands of an upper nobility. The results were immediately felt in the kingdom of Jerusalem, although
we do not know the effect in Antioch or Tripoli. As a matter of fact
we do not even know whether this assise was ever adopted by the
principality or county.

Even more remarkable was the curtailing of the royal prerogative
in noble wardships. A noble widow was usually married off to a
knight proposed to her by the king, who could thereby assure himself
of the feudal services. Probably around the middle of the twelfth
century—we cannot be more precise—under the pressure of the nobility, the king agreed to propose to a widow three candidates for
her hand and fiefs. The upper nobility, or magnates, would not accept even this conciliatory step. The lady might refuse all three candidates if there was the danger of a *disparité*.[36] In other words, the
magnates now regarded a marriage to a knight less wealthy than the
heiress as a *mésalliance*. There was therefore not only the growing
self-consciousness of a nobility, exemplified in such assises as that
which prohibited the arrest of a knight for debts (whereas a burgess
could be not only arrested but compelled to work in prison to pay
off his debts),[37] and the assise of Bilbais (probably 1168), which allowed a noble to remain on horseback when besieging a city,[38] but
there was also the growth of a particular self-consciousness on the
part of the magnates. The new laws of succession and wardship aimed

33. Philip of Novara, caps. 68, 71 (*ibid.,* I, 538, 542); John of Ibelin, caps. 148, 187 (*ibid.,*
I, 223–224, 297–299).
34. *Livre au roi,* caps. 38, 46 (*ibid.,* I, 633–634, 640); Philip of Novara, cap. 81 (*ibid.,*
I, 553–554); John of Ibelin, caps. 142, 143, 148, 150, 182 (*ibid.,* I, 216–217, 223–227, 284–285).
35. Philip of Novara, caps. 67–70 (*ibid.,* I, 538–541).
36. *Idem,* cap. 86 (*ibid.,* I, 558–560).
37. John of Ibelin, cap. 188 (*ibid.,* I, 300–301).
38. *Ibid.,* I, 455, note c.

at creating an exclusive class, in a position to bar from its ranks both the simple knight and the immigrant from abroad.

The emergence of this baronial class is emphatically signaled as early as 1132 by the first baronial revolts against the crown. The attempts of Hugh II of Le Puiset, lord of Jaffa, and Roman of Le Puy, lord of Transjordan, to rebel against the king, although unsuccessful, indicate a major change in the standing and attitude of a class of nobles previously homogeneous. In the middle of the twelfth century this upper nobility actively intervened in the quarrel of succession between Baldwin III and his mother Melisend, and became a strong political faction during the reign of Baldwin IV (1174–1185).

The status of the simple knights was not unaffected by all this. They certainly did not gain in power or position — quite the contrary. Their dependence on seigneurial power became increasingly marked. This may have been partly because the generation of conquerors who could boast of participating in the First Crusade and the conquest was gone; it was also because a stronger organization of fiefs inside the baronies brought a stricter organization of vassalage. The economic position of the knights was never a comfortable one. The inventory of the fiefs of the kingdom, which dates from about 1170, gives a total number of 675 knights serving the king.[39] About forty percent came from the royal domain, the remaining sixty percent from the different lordships. It is only for the royal domain that the details of service are indicated. Excepting the fiefs of the great officers (chamberlain, constable), and the fiefs of important persons which remained in the domain (the viscount of Nablus and the fief of Balian II of Ibelin in Nablus), we find 59 knights serving "with their body," possessing fiefs *unius militis*; 16 knights serving with one vassal each; 8 knights with two vassals; 6 knights with three vassals; 2 knights with four vassals; 2 knights with six vassals; and one knight with seven vassals. The predominance of simple knights, those serving *de leur corps* or with a single companion, is a typical feature of the class. No less distinctive is the truncated feudal pyramid. In most cases there is a direct enfeoffment from king to simple knight, or in some cases a subinfeudation of two degrees. In both cases there is an almost direct contact between king and knight. Although we have no such statistics for the independent lordships, there is no reason to suppose that the situation was much different. One example which we know in detail, the lordship of Arsuf in the middle of the thirteenth century, reveals

---

39. John of Ibelin, cap. 271 (*ibid.*, I, 422–426). The estimate is that of Smail, *Crusading Warfare, 1097–1193* (Cambridge, Eng., 1956), p. 89.

a similarity of pattern between the organization of the royal domain and that of the lordships.[40]

Another feature was important in defining the status of the knightly class. It is impossible to say how many knights held land fiefs and how many were in fact salaried warriors.[41] It is hardly imaginable, however, that the possession of a money-fief did not have an effect on the knights as a class. In the first place, it was small. The value of a money-fief was between 400 and 500 bezants a year,[42] rather modest if we consider that the daily pay of a mercenary knight was 1 bezant (365 a year).[43] On the other hand, the possession of a territorial fief tended to create a type of "squire," a landowner ruling his peasants and possessing what Marc Bloch has called the *droit de commandement*. The continuous exercise of this right created a particular type of aristocracy in the west, contributing to a sense of independent judgment and behavior, and giving reality to the notion that the lord and his vassals were peers with reciprocal duties, allowing for the special respect due the lord from his vassal. In the east, however, the prevalence of money-fiefs, their smallness, and their concentration in cities must have minimized the economic differences between the simple knight and the burgess, and diminished the political importance of the simple knights as a class.

Given Philip of Novara's three classes of nobles, one might well ask if there was a distinguishable group of nobles midway between the magnates and the simple knights. The great majority of enfeoffments were made directly by the lord possessing a barony to simple knights.[44] An intermediate class of barons certainly existed, but it

40. Delaville Le Roulx, *Cartulaire*, III, 6–7 (no. 2985). Cf. Prawer, "Étude de quelques problèmes," pp. 23 ff.

41. In the above-mentioned case of Arsuf, only one man out of six knights and twenty-one sergeants held a territorial fief. Moreover, a large number of money-fiefs were paid not in money but in agricultural produce.

42. Philip of Novara, cap. 67 (*RHC, Lois*, I, 538); cf. *L'Estoire de Eracles empereur*, XXVI, 12 (*RHC, Occ.*, II, 192); *Livre au roi*, cap. 34 (*RHC, Lois*, I, 629–630).

43. Cf. Prawer, "La Noblesse et le régime féodal," pp. 60 ff.

44. The word "baron" is often ambiguous. Take, for example, the three documents written on the same day by the same clerk dealing with the alienation by Hugh of Ibelin of a village which he held from Amalric, count of Ascalon (the future king of Jerusalem), to the canons of the Holy Sepulcher. The deed of alienation, Amalric's confirmation, and king Baldwin III's confirmation are witnessed by almost the same people. But whereas in Hugh's deed all nobles are classified as *de baronibus,* and in Amalric's confirmation *de baronibus regis,* we find in the royal confirmation a distinction between *de baronibus regis* and *de hominibus regis,* both groups including individuals who in the other documents were described as barons; Rozière, *Cartulaire,* nos. 62, 59, 56 (January 1155 or 1156, in Ascalon). In another royal confirmation the witnesses are grouped under the common heading *de baronibus vero et de hominibus regis; ibid.,* nos. 57, 51 (1160). On the other hand, there seems to be a clear distinction between liege-

was very small and its position did not assure it any influence in the feudal hierarchy.[45] Generally speaking, there were only two major elements in the nobility: the seigneurial class, or magnates, comprising in the middle of the twelfth century some two dozen families, and the great mass of simple and dependent knights.

A major change in the social position of the nobility as a whole and of its two major components took place in the second half of the twelfth century. The famous *Assise sur la ligèce* of king Amalric (1163–1174)[46] represented an attempt on the part of the crown to strengthen its position by bringing it into closer contact with the knights of the kingdom. But the attempt to weaken or circumvent the power of the baronage came too late, and the dependence of the knights was already too great to permit a major change. The assise theoretically should have enabled the subvassals, usually simple knights, to participate in meetings of the high court, previously a monopoly of the great tenants-in-chief, and should also have prevented arbitrary confiscations of their fiefs by their immediate lords. It did not have the expected results. In fact, it was the crown which lost its own prerogative to confiscate fiefs without judgment of the high court.[47] From then on the king was forced to bring such cases before the peers of the accused, and it would have to be a flagrant case of treason or breach of feudal contract before they would pronounce confiscation. On the other hand, the great lords were strong enough to prevent a knight's plea against themselves from being brought into the high court. The ultimate result of the assise was the opportunity it gave the nobles to present a common front against the crown. By "conjuring" all vassals and subvassals of the crown they could request a debate of their real or imaginary grievances before the high court. Under

---

men (holding land or money-fiefs) and mercenaries (who may not all have been knights); a document of Amalric mentions, among others, two sets of witnesses: *de hominibus meis* and *de stipendiariis meis; ibid.,* no. 60 (1158).

45. The status of men in this intermediate class was rather modest, e.g., a knight, one Isambert, who in 1135 sold a village, Arthabec, in the seigneury of Caesarea, received 500 bezants. Walter Grenier, lord of Caesarea, his overlord, received 150, but his immediate lord, Arnulf of Haynis, received only 60; Delaville Le Roulx, *Cartulaire,* I, 97 (no. 115).

46. Philip of Novara, cap. 51 (*RHC, Lois,* I, 526–527); John of Ibelin, caps. 140, 199 (*ibid.,* I, 214–215, 319–320). On the whole problem see Prawer, "La Noblesse et le régime féodal," pp. 41–74.

47. *Establissement dou roi Bauduin segont,* in *Livre au roi,* cap. 16 (*RHC, Lois,* I, 616–617); *Les Livres des Assises et des usages . . .,* ed. Eduard H. von Kausler, vol. I (Stuttgart, 1839), caps. 234–235. On this legislation see Prawer, "Étude sur le droit des *Assises de Jérusalem,*" pp. 520–551, tr. in *Crusader Institutions,* pp. 430–470. These *établissements,* usually attributed to Baldwin II, may in fact belong to Baldwin III; see Prawer, *RHDFE,* ser. 4, XL (1962), 29–42.

the circumstances the simple knights, despite their numbers, were a negligible entity with no power whatsoever. If Amalric's assise aimed to create a separate "estate" of knights, it failed completely. The knights were too dependent on their immediate lords to be able to unite in an estate. It can rather be said that the *Assise sur la ligèce,* with its procedure of judgment by peers and its "swearing-in" of all vassals and subvassals, contributed to the formal establishment of an "estate of nobles." Its mouthpiece was the high court, where the simple knights could not raise their voice except against the king at the instigation of their immediate lords.

The failure of Amalric's assise brings us to the last quarter of the twelfth century and to the end of the first kingdom. The remarkable feature of this rather short period is the strengthening of the position of the baronage of the kingdom and at the same time a marked change in its composition. The high court was at this time entirely ruled by the baronage. In times of crisis it was the decisive body intervening in matters of royal succession. If necessary, it represented the opinion of the nobility against the will of the crown. At the same time, the baronage itself was changing. Through succession to fiefs and through marriage the baronage was more and more closing its ranks. The social mobility of fifty years earlier had disappeared and the chances of a knight entering the enchanted circle of *riches hommes ou terriens* had become almost nil. Moreover, the upper nobility of the kingdom defended more or less successfully its positions against newcomers, who by the grace of the king tried to enter its ranks.

In the final years of the first kingdom the upper baronage was composed of not more than half a dozen families, all intermarried or otherwise connected with each other, to whom belonged the greater part of the kingdom. The crown tried to counter by introducing into the baronage nobles recently arrived from Europe. As the local baronage never succeeded in making the court offices hereditary, the crown still had the option of conferring these on whom it chose. But the great offices were not of paramount importance in the later history of the kingdom, when the lordships became more and more independent of the crown. The possibility left open to the king of marrying off royal daughters and heiresses of great fiefs to his favorites was curtailed by the baronage, which claimed that the king had no right to force an heiress into a *mésalliance.* The barons even went so far as to sabotage military and political efforts just to prevent the intrusion of newcomers into their ranks. In some cases they did not stop at murder to eliminate an undesirable intruder. The entrance of an alien did not always disrupt their ranks. Some of these were of modest origin, often owing their career to the crown, but identifying themselves in the course of time with the magnates. A conspicuous example is Reginald of Châtillon, a noble of undistinguished background who reached the top of the feudal hierarchy through consecutive marriages with the heiresses Constance of Antioch and Stephanie of Transjordan. At the end of this period he was already an important member of the local baronage, and was accepted as such by the barons. And it would be precisely Reginald of Châtillon who would make the haughty answer to the king: "Que ausi estoit-il sires de sa terre come il [Guy of Lusignan] de la soe"![48] This is, in a nutshell, the new position of the upper nobility of the kingdom on the eve of the disaster of Hattin.

The fall of the kingdom and its revival following the Third Crusade created a new geopolitical framework for the Latin states in the east. Except for short periods the kingdom and the northern principalities consisted of only a long, narrow strip of the coast, which would be attacked and cut up piecemeal by Baybars and his successors, Kalavun and al-Ashraf Khalīl, until its complete disappearance in 1291.

Some of the tendencies, already strong in the first kingdom, now became paramount. The city, the main residence of the conquerors even in the twelfth century, came to be their only residence (with the exception of a few castles). The European farmer disappeared entirely, although some efforts at colonization were still being made. The kingdom and its lordships comprised the cities and their immediate areas, more reminiscent of a European city *Bannmeile* than of a lordship. The thirteenth-century kingdom was the only one in Christendom where the entire ruling population was urbanized. The muddled politics of the thirteenth century can be partially explained by the fact that state politics had become city politics, not unlike the factious strife in the cities of contemporary Italy.

The growing importance of the burgesses and the communes is in some measure explained by the fact of urbanization of the entire society, and even more so by the impoverishment of the seigneurial class. The nobles lost their rural fiefs and domains, the knights their holdings. With some slight exaggeration it might be said that in the feudal system of the Latin kingdom of the thirteenth century there were neither landed nobility nor landed gentry. There were naturally differences between the lordships. While the prince of Galilee conserved his title but lost his principality (except for a short period between 1240 and

---

48. *Eracles*, XXIII, 23 (*RHC, Occ.*, II, 34).

1244), lesser lords like those of Arsuf, Beirut, Tyre, and Caesarea kept their castles and a few villages, or just the adjacent farms. But even their position was weakened and became precarious, especially after the middle of the thirteenth century. Financial difficulties forced many of them to sell out to the military orders, a practice already present in the twelfth century but more prevalent in the thirteenth.[49] Others found refuge and support in the new kingdom of the Lusignans in Cyprus. Some even used their revenues from Cyprus to maintain their mainland possessions.[50]

At a lower level the small group midway between the highest nobility and the simple knights found itself deprived of resources. Their standing depended entirely on their connections with the higher nobility. A man like Philip of Novara is a typical representative of this group. Through connections and services to the party in power, he had his debts paid by royal bounty and received revenues—city revenues—for his living. Finally, the simple knights, already very much dependent on their lords in the twelfth century, would now become little more than salaried knights, not to say simple mercenaries. The original feudalism based on land possession became what Max Weber would have called *Pfründefeudalismus,* based on direct payments. Nor did the payments come regularly. The knights had to use the extreme weapon of "conjuring their peers," invoking the *Assise sur la ligèce* to assure their payment.[51] They were recruited and paid in the expeditions against Damietta and in the crusade of Louis IX. They were courted and recruited by the different parties during the war against the "Lombards" and during the fratricidal wars of the communes. Their maintenance was better assured during times of war than times of peace.

The general penury, especially felt in the lower echelons of the knightly class, at times must have blurred the distinctions between classes. The insistence of the thirteenth-century lawyers upon the exclusion of knights from holding *borgesies*[52] suggests that renting a

49. Beyer, "Die Verschiebung der Grundbesitzverhältnisse in Palästina während der Kreuzfahrerzeit," *Palästinajahrbuch des deutschen evangelischen Instituts für Altertumswissenschaften des Heiligen Landes zu Jerusalem,* XXXII (1936), 101 ff.

50. Philip of Novara, *Estoire de la guerre,* in *Les Gestes des Chiprois,* ed. Raynaud (SOL, SH, V; Geneva, 1887), pp. 41–42.

51. John of Ibelin, cap. 239 (*RHC, Lois,* I, 383–384); cf. caps. 236–237 (*ibid.,* I, 376–382).

52. *Borgesies* in the hands of knights were already known to the twelfth-century *Livre au roi,* cap. 20 (*ibid.,* I, 619), in which there was a tendency to regard all small property as *borgesie* tenure: "chans ou vignes ou maisons"; and again (caps. 37, 43): "maisons et terres et jardins et vignes." The Cypriote *Abrégé du Livre des Assises de la Cour des Bourgeois,* cap. 21 (*RHC, Lois,* II, 251), written between 1325 and 1350, gives a clear definition, probably no different

borgesie, almost free from payments to say nothing of services, was an even safer and easier way of making a living than holding a money-fief. But buying *borgesies* legally had to be done through the "court of burgesses," which with the growing spirit of legality and the interests of city lords made it difficult. Still, we do find *borgesies* in the hands of the nobility, and one of the ways of getting them was through marriage.

As has been said, the general situation of knights must have blurred class distinctions. Immediately after the restoration of the second kingdom a great jurist, Ralph of Tiberias, scion of the princes of Galilee, when asked to preside over a committee of codification, disparaged the legal knowledge of Raymond Anciaume and other "clever bourgeois and low-born men of letters."[53] This would change in the thirteenth century; a burgess, Raymond of Conches, would often be heard in the high court.[54] Marriage could also stimulate social mobility. We do not find burgesses marrying into the highest nobility, but we may assume that they intermarried with the lesser nobles. There may have been some lesson derived from this in Cyprus which led Henry II de Lusignan, king of Cyprus (1285–1324) and lately king of Jerusalem, in 1297 to prohibit the holding of *borgesies* by anyone other than burgesses.[55] In 1298 he issued a similar ordinance directed against the communes and the clergy.[56] Even more significant is an ordinance of May 1296 which proclaimed: "No bourgeois and no bourgeoise and no merchant, whoever he may be, or of whatever nationality, should marry off his sister, daughter, or relative, which he has, to a knight or a son of a knight. And whoever does so, his body will be at the will of the king. And he will pay a fine to the amount of the dowry."[57] Such legislation was unknown in the kingdom of Jerusalem, where there was greater social mobility. In a country where knights and burgesses lived together and differences in wealth were slight, class distinctions tended to become blurred.

---

from that used in the Latin kingdom: "borgezies qui sont dedens ville, si come sont heritages de maizons, et jardins et chans." A knight might invoke the *retrait des voisins* regarding a *borgesie* if he happened to be a neighbor of the property; if successful, however, he had to alienate it again within a year and a day after its acquisition (*ibid.,* cap. 33); cf. Prawer, *Crusader Institutions,* pp. 250–263, 327 ff.

53. "Et messire Rau respondi que de ce que il savoit ne i feroit il jà son pareil Remont Anciaume ne autre soutil borgeis ou bas home letré": Philip of Novara, cap. 47 (*RHC, Lois,* I, 521–523). Philip mentions another jurist, Nicholas Antiaume, apparently a knight (cap. 49, *ibid.,* I, 525). On the Antiaumes see Prawer, *Crusader Institutions,* pp. 280–290.

54. *Idem,* cap. 38 (*ibid.,* I, 515–516); John of Ibelin, cap. 239 (*ibid.,* I, 383–384).

55. *Abrégé du Livre des Assises de la Cour des Bourgeois,* cap. 16 (*RHC, Lois,* II, 315).

56. *Bans et ordonnances des rois de Chypre,* cap. 9 (*RHC, Lois,* II, 361).

57. *Ibid.,* cap. 5 (*RHC, Lois,* II, 359).

Not only did the political situation and its financial implications
tend to bring simple knights and burgesses closer together; it also
polarized the two extremes of the noble estate. Whereas the simple
knight became increasingly dependent on his lord, the highest stratum of the nobility assumed effective leadership in the country. The
absentee kingship of the Hohenstaufens left the kingdom under the
thumb of the high court, dominated by the great families, for more
than a generation. These great families, which intermarried among
themselves and even with the royal house of Jerusalem and the imperial house of Byzantium, became a closely knit elite with common
political and social interests. Legally there was no difference between
these few families and the rest of the class of knights, but inevitably
the higher nobility sought to abandon what by now was a fictitious
equality and legitimize their superiority. John of Ibelin, one of the
great jurists in an age of legal luminaries of law all over Christendom,
invented a body of "four baronies," which never really existed, as
a kind of superior estate, with the extraordinary privilege that its
members could be judged only by one another, as they were the only
real peers of each other.[58] In so doing, he perpetrated a historical
crime, not the only one to be found in his treatise. At the same time,
he reflects the ambition of these few select families to preserve for
themselves a place unattainable by others in the kingdom.

The new situation of the kingdom influenced the general outlook
of the nobility. During the two hundred years of its existence, this
class could boast of a good number of real warrior heroes, but no
great men of state. The realms of culture, letters, and philosophy
had no representatives among them despite their contact with the
Moslem world. The truly great historian of the twelfth century, probably the greatest of his time, William of Tyre, was of bourgeois origin. No schools of any importance were ever founded in the east and
the contact with the eastern churches inspired neither polemics nor
theology.

It was the more material side of civilization which was cultivated.
The excellent military and religious architecture, erected to the glory
of God and knighthood, reveals the influence of eastern models and
is in many ways far in advance of European architecture. The Ibelin
palace of Beirut, which took away the breath of a German ambas-

---

58. John of Ibelin, cap. 269 (*ibid.*, II, 417–419). See the excellent study by Richard, "Pairie
d'Orient latin."

sador to the east, shows Moslem and Byzantine influences.[59] The
descriptions of luxurious houses, the soft and rather loose ways of
living, the lovely romanesque sculptures of twelfth-century Nazareth,
the paintings of Bethany, the sculptured flowers of Caesarea,[60] the
mosaics of Bethlehem, all suggest an appreciation of the arts, but
at the same time indicate that the great lords, lay and ecclesiastical,
had either to import architects, painters, and sculptors from Europe
or recruit them from among the Syrians and Greeks. The nobles, if
not fighting or hunting, enjoyed the good things of life and in times
of peace indulged in the leisurely rhythm of life in the Levant. The
ideal nobleman described by Philip of Novara rose early, said his
prayers, attended mass (and did not leave in the middle), provided
charity, and then attended to his business until noon, when all work
stopped. Lunch was followed by an hour's siesta. Then came some
light entertainment, after which he received others, or was received
by others, until bedtime.[61]

There was one branch of culture, however, which not only was
represented and cultivated in the Latin east, but reached an extremely
high level there — feudal law. It may be said without exaggeration that
all the resources of the best minds among the nobility were devoted
to the study of law. True, no schools were founded. Legal lore was
orally transmitted from one noble to another, and was illustrated by
the functioning of the courts. Although some noblemen took to the
law even in Europe (to mention only Beaumanoir, a contemporary
of John of Ibelin), the Levant provides a unique example in the medieval world of an entire class addicted to the study of law. The
medieval state has been called by an eminent German scholar *Rechts-
staat,* and it is certainly true enough that the specific aim of the nobility in the Latin east was the preservation of a state based on law.

This praiseworthy aim, however, consciously or unconsciously, served
deeply rooted selfish interests. Constitutional law, as expounded by
John of Ibelin, was distorted and deformed to tell a tale of an elected
monarchy — we might even say a social contract — of a republic of
nobles, of a high court ruling the country. As private law it dealt
with procedure, where the knowledge of formulas and the use of debatable points of law, subterfuge, and artifice made the adjective *sub-*

---

59. Wilbrand of Oldenburg, in *Peregrinatores medii aevi quatuor,* ed. Laurent, pp. 165 ff.

60. Discovered during the excavations of 1959–1962. On the other hand, the most beautiful
Corinthian capitals, marble columns, and stones bearing Roman inscriptions (one containing
the name of Pontius Pilate) were used as foundations for houses and streets.

61. *Les Quatre âges de l'homme,* ed. de Fréville, pp. 86 ff.

til the highest praise for the lawyer. As personal and property law it specified in the most systematic way, far beyond anything known in contemporary Europe, the law of fiefs, but at the same time it safeguarded their possession and their possessors. This mental background, this ideology, one may say, of the feudal law as expounded by John of Ibelin, is the best expression of feudal thinking. It is the ideology of the "feudal paradise," never quite realized even in the crusaders' kingdom.

On a different level we have the work of the Gallicized Italian Philip of Novara. Lower in the social hierarchy than John of Ibelin, he describes feudal law and its procedure as it really existed in his time. Constitutional history and political theory are clearly beyond his interests. He describes his work in the third person: "And he wrote another book on the procedure of pleading [*forme de plait*] and the usages and customs of the *Assises d'Outremer* and of Jerusalem and of Cyprus."[62] Significantly he has to justify himself, as the counsels he gives may serve personal interests rather than the cause of justice. It is evident that a good many of his *avisées* simply facilitate evading the law. Lesser treatises, those of Geoffrey le Tort and James of Ibelin, are only convenient abridgments for everyday use, the first written by a knight of modest origin. True, the great noble houses never deviated from the common code of chivalry. Their ideas were those of their time and class. Concern for family honor appears frequently in their utterances, inspiring and regulating their actions and behavior. But the repute of their houses was often confounded with the welfare of the state.[63] The anarchy which prevented the rule of any monarch, whether a Hohenstaufen, or the aging Alice of Champagne, or her husband, Ralph of Nesle (or "of Soissons"), was instigated by the great *lignages* dominating the high court.[64] But everything had to be done in the most legal way, according to the customs, usages, and assises of the kingdom. Even a revolutionary movement like the "commune of Acre," which we may look upon as the crusaders' equivalent of an assembly of estates, took shelter under a royal privilege. The state went to pieces in a blaze of legal oratory in the high court of Acre. They were *sans peur et sans reproche,* but *prudhommes* only in the narrowest circle of their peers.

62. *Ibid.,* p. 123.

63. *Les Gestes des Chiprois,* cap. 161 (*RHC, Arm.,* II, 702–703); see Prawer, *Histoire du royaume latin,* I, 215–257.

64. Cf. a different assessment by LaMonte, "John d'Ibelin, the Old Lord of Beirut, 1177–1236," *Byzantion,* XII (1937), 417–448.

C. *The Burgesses*[65]

Social realities and crusaders' jurisprudence excluded from the noble "estate" all Franks who were not already noble, as well as members of the Italian, Provençal, and Spanish communes. This large mass of people, who formed a broad base for the colony of European conquerors, was called *burgenses* in Latin, *bourgeois* in French. It is important to note that no chronicle of the First Crusade uses the noun or adjective *burgensis*. The perspective of their authors was defined by military matters. The social composition of the armies was indicated by references to *milites* and *pedites*. It is among the thousands of *pedites* in the First Crusade that we have to look for the elements which would later form the class of *burgenses*. Historians of the nineteenth century accepted as self-evident that the *burgenses* had originally been European city inhabitants, who came with the First Crusade, settled in the east, and were reinforced in the course of time through successive waves of immigration, generally recruited

65. The main sources are indicated above in the general bibliographical note. Of special importance is the *Livre des Assises de la Cour des Bourgeois,* ed. Beugnot, *RHC, Lois,* II. A better edition is that of von Kausler, *Les Livres des Assises et des usages dou reaume de Jérusalem,* vol. I (Stuttgart, 1839; no more published); a new edition is needed. On the *Livre des Assises . . . des Bourgeois* see Prawer, "Étude préliminaire sur les sources et la composition du *Livre des Assises des Bourgeois,*" *RHDFE,* ser. 4, XXXII (1954), 198–227, 358–382 (bibliography, p. 202, n. 2); revised, expanded, and translated in *Crusader Institutions,* pp. 358–407 (bibliography, pp. 408–412). See also *idem,* "L'Établissement des coutumes du marché à Saint-Jean d'Acre et la date de composition du *Livre des Assises des Bourgeois,*" *RHDFE,* ser. 4, XXIX (1951), 329–351; Richard, "Un Partage de seigneurie entre Francs et Mamelouks: Les casaux de Sur," *Syria,* XXX (1953), 72–82; Cahen, "À propos des coutumes du marché d'Acre," *RHDFE,* ser. 4, XLI (1963), 287–290.

There are few special studies regarding the burgesses, but see now Prawer, "Burgage-Tenure," in *Crusader Institutions,* pp. 263–295; "Burgage-Tenures of the Communes and Ecclesiastical Establishments," *ibid.,* pp. 315–326; and "The Burgesses and Their Seignors," *ibid.,* pp. 327–339. See also E. Derazé, *Le Mariage d'après les Assises de Jérusalem* (Poitiers, 1910); Pierre Christin, *Étude des classes inférieures d'après les Assises de Jérusalem* (Poitiers, 1912); Hayek, *Le Droit franc en Syrie pendant les croisades: Institutions judiciaires* (Paris, 1925); LaMonte, "The Communal Movement in Syria in the 13th Century," *Anniversary Essays in Mediaeval History by Students of Charles Homer Haskins,* ed. Charles H. Taylor (Boston and New York, 1929), pp. 117–131; Cedric N. Johns, "The Attempt to Colonize Palestine and Syria in the Twelfth and Thirteenth Centuries," *Journal of the Royal Central Asian Society,* XXI (1934), 288–300; Prawer, "Colonization Activities in the Latin Kingdom of Jerusalem," *Revue belge de philologie et d'histoire,* XXIX (1951), 1063–1118; *idem,* "The Settlement of the Latins in Jerusalem," *Speculum,* XXVII (1952), 490–503.

from among the same social elements. The name "burgesses," coined in Europe, was thought to have been imported into the Latin east along with European townsmen. The theory is difficult to accept. The sources of the First Crusade hardly ever mention the *pedites* in any way that might suggest their origin. They are referred to in general terms,[66] the purpose being to impress the reader by the immense number of crusaders, and perhaps also to stress the fact that all classes of society and many nations participated in the movement.[67] Furthermore, the general condition of the countries from which the crusaders came hardly suggests an urban origin for the non-noble participants. Two factors contradict such an assumption. First, the number of urban agglomerations of any size in the eleventh century in Europe was extremely small. Aside from northern and central Italy, which contributed only a few small contingents from Lombardy[68] besides those who participated in the expeditions of the communes and consequently were not included among the burgesses, only Flanders and Provence had urban centers of any importance. This alone makes it unlikely that any appreciable proportion of the thousands of *pedites* could have originated in a few dozen urban centers. Moreover, only a very few western towns could boast of a population exceeding several thousand inhabitants. At the end of the eleventh century the populations of most western towns could be counted in hundreds. It is therefore out of the question that these towns could have furnished thousands of emigrants to the east.

We must also take into account that the end of the eleventh century and the beginning of the twelfth witnessed a spectacular social and economic evolution, the rise of cities. Underlying this was a demographic growth in the countryside and the integration of the surplus population either in the movement of internal agricultural colonization or in the new movement of urbanization. The growth of cities was an uninterrupted process lasting something like two centuries. In these circumstances it is rather doubtful that they were centers of emigration. For two hundred years cities would draw people from rural areas; it is difficult to assume that they lost population in any great numbers through emigration at the same time. It hardly seems likely, therefore, that any sizeable European city population went to the east during the two hundred years of the Latin kingdom's existence, and certainly not during the First Crusade. Of course, there

66. Cf. Ekkehard, IX (*RHC, Occ.,* V, 18): "tot legiones equitum, tot turmas peditum, totque catervas ruricolarum."
67. Typically, Fulcher of Chartres, I, 13 (ed. Hagenmeyer, pp. 4–5).
68. The great expedition from the Lombard cities in 1101 did not reach the kingdom.

was some sporadic participation of townsmen in the crusades, but it was not from these that the great crusading armies were recruited, nor they who contributed significantly to the movement of emigration to the east. Finally, the popular element, the armies of Peter the Hermit, Gottschalk, and their companions, did not contribute much to the actual settlement in the east. These armies were destroyed in 1096 before reaching Syria. The majority of those who in fact reached the future lands of the crusaders came with the great barons. While there were urban groups which joined the Peasants' Crusade during its march along the Rhine and the Danube (in several cities the townsmen participated in the Jewish massacres), the proportion of townsmen in the baronial hosts was too small to mark the early crusading settlements with a European urban imprint.[69]

We have then to imagine the earliest non-nobles in the crusading army and in the newly conquered lands as having an essentially rural, peasant background. Here and there household servants of the nobility or servants of knights went with their lords to the east. Others came from villages and manors in the neighborhood of the centers of crusading propaganda. The predominance of the rural element in the host goes far to explain the lack of craftsmen, carpenters, and smiths during sieges of cities. For example, the army besieging Jerusalem was unable to build siege towers and machinery until the arrival at Jaffa of Genoese ships bearing materials and craftsmen experienced in the more complicated skills of construction.[70]

During the crusade itself the *pedites* were not organized or dealt with in any special way. Repression of excesses must have been made summarily by the leaders of the different armies, which would have been sufficient to meet the needs of an army on the march. Only with the first conquests and settlement did the problem of the non-noble Frankish population as a class become pressing. The sheer weight of numbers, combined with traditional European class attitudes, necessitated some kind of organization. But it would be wrong to suppose that there existed any consciousness of the Frankish non-

---

69. Those known to us as *burgenses* almost never have city patronymics. They often have a bizarre or ridiculous surname, sometimes the name of the province of origin. Normally, the Christian name is followed by the father's name, usually in the genitive, which sometimes becomes a surname.

70. Caffaro di Caschifellone, *De liberatione civitatum orientis*, IX (*RHC, Occ.*, V, 57); Raymond of Aguilers, cap. 20 (*RHC, Occ.*, III, 298); William of Tyre, VIII, 9 (*RHC, Occ.*, I, 338): "Erant enim viri prudentes, et, nautarum more, architectoriae habentes artis peritiam . . . . Sed et alia multa . . . secum attulerant argumenta; ita ut quod ante eorum adventum vix et cum difficultate sperabatur effectui posse mancipari, per eorum operam facile compleretur."

nobles as a class or "estate." The kingdom was *in statu nascendi* as late as the time of Baldwin II. Private conquests, like those of Tancred, had only just been integrated with some difficulty into the general framework of the kingdom. Although the basic distinction between nobles and non-nobles was clear, there was little feeling of dealing with a corporate "estate" within the framework of a state. Whereas feudo-vassalic organization was the basis of the state structure, there remained the problem of assigning to the Frankish non-nobles an appropriate status in the different places conquered and held by the Franks. What probably happened was that solutions first tried and empirically established in Jerusalem were later transferred to royal cities like Acre, and finally copied in other cities that became centers of lordships.[71]

Whereas the *milites* found their earliest organization and consolidation in the traditional baronial court, to which they owed obedience through their oath of homage and fealty, no such organization or tradition existed for the others. The only tradition which the crusaders brought with them for dealing with such people was that of the manorial court. This kind of court was hardly satisfactory in the new circumstances, although some of its principles might have influenced the organization of the special burgesses' jurisdictions. The new needs were perhaps neither very urgent nor very clear at the outset. For more than ten years (1099–1110) the colonies of the crusaders were in a state of continual warfare, when any battle might easily have ended with the destruction of the entire kingdom. A special jurisdiction regarding *pedites* in the army probably remained more urgent than the kind of organization more appropriate to a settled society at peace.

The earliest legislation, as far as is known to us, deals with feudal matters, although some royal ordinances, like that about property laws in the city of Jerusalem, deal with vassals and burgesses alike.[72] Such an ordinance seems to be symptomatic for the early period. It is essentially a city bylaw, to use a modern notion, relating to Jerusalem alone, which did not prevent it, because of its royal origin, from being called an assise. But in the course of time, there arose the need

71. The tendency to see a corporation or "estate" derives from the *Livre des Assises . . . des Bourgeois*. These assises were not composed, however, before the middle of the thirteenth century, in Acre. By that time there may actually have been an "estate," but such is not the case for the early period of the kingdom. It may have been different in Antioch, where the great cities belonged to the prince and a general conception of dealing with an "estate" may have originated in the court of the principality, but I doubt it.

72. Cf. Prawer, "The Settlement of the Latins in Jerusalem," pp. 490–503; *idem*, "The *Assise de tenure* and the *Assise de vente*," pp. 77–87.

to define the standing of the burgesses as a social and juridical entity. Three factors seem to lie at the basis of defining the place of Frankish non-nobles in society: their number; the fact that they lived alongside nobles within the city; and their particular occupations—in crafts, commerce, and services which lay outside the interests of seigneurial courts. We do not know when the earliest burgesses' jurisdiction was established. But although the tradition reported by John of Ibelin of two courts, feudal and burgess, established by the legendary law-giver Godfrey of Bouillon, has to be rejected, it seems likely that the first special non-noble courts were established very early in the twelfth century.

These courts probably grew up around the first castellans or vis-counts (the term for the lord's representative ruling the city) of Jerusalem and the principality of Antioch. Their composition, though not their functions, could not have been a matter of doubt. They had to follow the rule, common to the Romano-Germanic worlds, of judg-ment by peers as a matter of principle. This principle, common to baro-nial and manorial courts alike, may well have been followed from the very beginning. It is a matter of conjecture when courts for non-nobles came into existence.[73] We may suppose that around 1110, at the end of the great period of expansion, it became a matter of necessity to organize city life within the framework of a specific organization.

The specific notion of a non-noble class, the class of burgesses, appears for the first time in a privilege of Baldwin I granted to the canons of the Holy Sepulcher. The king granted his *optimates, mili-tes,* and *burgenses* the right to concede freely their revenues to the Holy Sepulcher.[74] This first appearance of the name *burgenses* seems to coincide in time with the first coalescence of a distinct class.

More often than not the appearance of a name is a clue to the ori-gin of a class or institution, but this cannot be said about the name *burgenses.* The designation, not attested to by our sources before 1110, was not coined for urban emigrants from Europe, although the word itself was imported from Europe. Why was it used? The first reason seems to be the new social and legal status acquired by non-nobles. To join the armies of the First Crusade or a later crusade, or merely to emigrate to the east, brought about a marked change in the legal

73. On this whole problem see Prawer, "The Origin of the Court of Burgesses," in *Crusader Institutions,* pp. 263–295.

74. William of Tyre, XI, 12: ". . . Concedo quod quicumque meorum optimatum, vel ali-quis militum, seu burgensium . . . de suis redditibus . . . dare eidem ecclesiae voluerit, libera sit sibi piae voluntatis executio. . . ." (*RHC, Occ.,* I, 472–474).

status of the participant. Whereas in the knightly class new links of vassalage were created, which sometimes replaced traditional connections, the basic relationship of lord and vassal did not in itself change. Among the lower echelons of society, however, a real revolution took place. The peasant, villein or serf, who joined the host became *ipso facto* a free man. All marks of servitude disappeared; the heterogeneous mass of villeins became entirely free. The great host of *pedites* were consequently called *liberi homines* or *franci*. This last term was already used to designate everyone in the army, witnessing to its ethnic origin. On the other hand *liberi homines,* although juridically correct, quite often at the end of the eleventh century meant not only free men, but sometimes knights, people free from any kind of servitude.

It might have been to avoid confusion that the name *burgenses* was used. This was the usual designation of the inhabitants of *burgi* or *borcs,* new urban agglomerations just coming into being and inhabited by a new free but non-noble population. As a matter of fact the *burgi* were almost the only places in western Europe where such a population could be found. Drawing upon European traditions and experience, in all probability from France (Normandy and Flanders, but also Norman Italy), such a designation seemed to be appropriate and acceptable. Then, too, the entire Frankish population in the east settled in cities, which, if they were not *civitates,* bishops' sees, would be called in European usage *burgi,* as opposed to *urbes* or *oppida.* Consequently, as a designation for a free, non-noble class the name *burgenses* was quite appropriate. But from the outset it had a different meaning from the one it had in Europe. It not only excluded nobles, as it was meant to from the beginning, but it also excluded all non-Franks, even if they were city-dwellers. The "burgesses of Jerusalem" never included the local Syrian Christian population, but was a term applied only to the Franks.[75] The *cour des bourgeois* was a strictly Frankish court, judging Syrians only in exceptional and well-defined cases.

Later sources, although probably reflecting earlier legislation, pro-

---

75. Whenever we meet Syrian Christians having the status of *burgenses,* we must assume that they were converts to the Roman creed, e.g., Ṣalibah, *civis Acconensis,* whose testament (1264) proves that he was a Catholic and indeed a *confrater* of the Hospitallers; Delaville Le Roulx, *Cartulaire,* III, 91–92 (no. 3105). See Richard, "La Confrérie des Mosserins d'Acre et les marchands de Mossoul au XIIIe siècle," *L'Orient syrien,* XI (1966), 451–460. See also a Latin inscription bearing the name of an eastern Christian, in Johns and Naʿim Makhouly, *Guide to Acre* (Jerusalem, 1946), p. 92; Cahen, "Une Inscription mal comprise concernant le rapprochement entre Maronites et croisés," in *Medieval and Middle Eastern Studies in Honor of Aziz Suryal Atiya,* ed. Sami A. Hanna (Leyden, 1972), pp. 62–63.

claimed as a fundamental principle that the burgesses were excluded from holding fiefs.[76] This meant that they were restricted to owning non-feudal land, land owing no military service. This legislation, following European usage and answering local needs to reserve enough land to provide for military service, reflected a chronic shortage of fighting manpower. The military obligations of the burgesses were met in a different way, without infringing on the limited land resources. The typical landed property of the burgess, therefore, was city land and some very small holdings in the immediate vicinity of the city. These holdings were called *borgesie* (*burgisia*). The characteristic feature of this kind of tenure was its complete freedom from any kind of feudal service, the land being burdened only with a quit-rent (*cens*) payable to the lord from whom it was held. Its alienation by sale, gift, or exchange required the approval of the lord, represented by his viscount or chatelain, who had a right to a customary small payment on such occasions. Free from feudal service and from servile exactions alike, the *borgesie* was, with the exception of the allod, the nearest thing to free property that existed in the central period of the Middle Ages. Its standing in the hierarchy of land tenures corresponded to the social and juridical status of the burgess, neither knight nor serf. One is even tempted to ask if the *borgesie,* well known in the early twelfth century in Normandy, Flanders, and Sicily,[77] preceded the name *burgenses* in the east—if the tenure itself suggested the name—but this is a hypothesis that would be difficult to prove or disprove.[78]

The emergence of the *borgesie* is important as providing the earliest economic basis for a burgess class. The massacre or expulsion of the natives during the conquest had left the cities almost empty, and the conquerors had the greatest difficulty in providing for their settlement and defense. We know that in Jerusalem the new Frankish population settled in one quarter of the city only, the quarter around

---

76. John of Ibelin, cap. 249 (*RHC, Lois,* I, 397–399).

77. Cf. Robert Génestal, *La Tenure en bourgage dans les pays régis par la coutume de Normandie* (Paris, 1900); Guillaume Desmarez, *Étude sur la propriété foncière dans les villes du moyen-âge et spécialement en Flandre* (Paris and Ghent, 1898); Morley de Wolf Hemmeon, *Burgage Tenure in Medieval England* (Cambridge, Mass., 1914).

78. Cf. John of Ibelin, cap. 24 (*RHC, Lois,* I, 47): "De quoi [borgesie] l'on ne deit plaideer que en la Court de Borgesie." He defines the rights of a seigneur as: "court, coins, justise," as compared to the "court de borgesie et justise": cap. 270 (*ibid.,* I, 419–421). In both cases, it seems, it is the type of tenure rather than the status of men that is important. Cf. also *Abrégé du Livre des Assises de la Cour des Bourgeois,* cap. 21 (*RHC, Lois,* II, 251): "Tout premierement en ladite court se uze et se doit uzer de toutes manieres de bourgesies; et je crois que ce est unes des chozes pourquoi ceste court a esté apelée la Court de la Bourgezie, volés la Court de Borgois."

the Holy Sepulcher, not being able to populate the city as a whole. As late as 1115–1116 king Baldwin I of Jerusalem brought in settlers from Transjordan, assigning to them the old, now empty Jewish quarter, which under the crusaders became the Syrian quarter. The situation was no different in places like Ramla, where only part of the ancient city was inhabited,[79] although it was better in some coastal towns where it was easier to make a living.

It is against this background of half-empty cities immediately following the conquest that the first tenures were created. The first city property was created through the "law of conquest," which was still in use as late as the middle of the thirteenth century. The first person to put up a sign on a house or property in a captured city automatically became its proprietor.[80] This is probably the origin of the Provençal quarter, near the gate of Zion, which had been captured by the army of Raymond of St. Gilles.[81] In the vicissitudes of war many a former serf suddenly found himself the proprietor of houses and land.[82] Some of them did even better; like some knights of modest origin, they acquired not only houses and city property, but even villages. A number of villages and farms in the vicinity of Jerusalem are known by the name of their Frankish occupants, who were petty knights and burgesses well known in the city itself.[83] We should not, however, exaggerate the value and importance of these holdings. We have to remember that at a time when land and houses were to be

79. Prawer, "Colonization Activities," pp. 1063–1118.

80. The creation of seigneurial property is described by Raymond of Aguilers, cap. 20 (*RHC, Occ.,* III, 292): "Erat enim consuetudo inter nos, ut si aliquis ad castellum vel villam prior venisset, et posuisset signum cum custodia, a nullo alio postea contingebatur"; cf. *ibid.,* cap. 14 (p. 275). Fulcher of Chartres, I, 29, describes the taking possession of city property: "ingressi sunt domos civium rapientes quaecumque in eis reppererunt: ita sane, ut quicumque primus domum introisset, sive dives sive pauper esset, nullatenus ab aliquo alio fieret iniuria, quin domum ipsam aut palatium, et quodcumque in ea reperisset, ac si omnino propria, sibi assumeret, haberet et possideret. Hoc itaque jus invicem tenendum stabilierant. Unde multi inopes effecti sunt locupletes." Cf. Albert of Aachen, VI, 23 (*RHC, Occ.,* IV, 479).

81. Porta Belcayre (Beaucaire). Cf. L. Hugues Vincent and Félix M. Abel, *Jérusalem: Recherches de topographie, d'archéologie et d'histoire,* II, *Jérusalem nouvelle* (by Abel; Paris, 1926), p. 945.

82. This may have inspired the comment by Fulcher of Chartres, III, 37 (about 1124–1128): "hic iam possidet domos proprias et familias quasi iure paterno et hereditario. . . . Qui erat alienigena, nunc est quasi indigena, et qui inquilinus est, utique incola factus."

83. West of Jerusalem we find among the villages that later belonged to the Hospitallers "casale Huldre [Hulda] et de Porcel et de Gaufrido Agulle et de Anschetino et de Bacheler et de Girardo Bocher" (1141); Delaville Le Roulx, *Cartulaire,* I, 139. Porcel, Agulle (Acus), and Bacheler were without doubt burgesses. In a confirmation of Baldwin II (1129) to the Hospitallers we find other benefactors: "Ainaldus cognomine Barba dimidiam partem casalis Jebetzah [Khirbat Jabatah] et alteram dimidiam donavit Aldeburgis, soror Lamberti cambiatoris": Delaville Le Roulx, *Cartulaire,* I, 84.

had for the asking, and the population was extremely small, the worth of the new property lay more in the provision of comfortable quarters and shops than in its monetary value. It was only with the growing immigration of the first half of the twelfth century that city real estate rose in value.

With political stability and the establishment of an administration, the burgess holdings in the city were integrated into the larger scheme of seigneurial and urban administration. This came about through listing city property as paying a rent to the lord of the city, and making the proprietor and his property dependent on the city authorities, the viscount or chatelain (often both offices in the same hands), and the court of burgesses. This process of integration was not complete. Many *borgesies* paid no *cens* to the lord and were in fact allodial possessions. This kind of property is known in our sources as *franc borgesie* and is defined as not owing services or rents to anybody.[84] These allodial possessions probably represent the first property acquired through the "law of conquest." As greedy as they were, the conquerors had no use for empty spaces. They took possession of houses in a small part of the city, which they settled and defended. Some of this allodial property escaped being listed, while whatever remained unoccupied was considered the lord's property, to be donated or rented to new settlers. Such grants would be subject to a payment for *borgesie*. The lord might also keep the property, letting the houses to new settlers without alienating either his seigneurial rights or his ground rent.[85] By this time the *franc borgesie* had become an anachronism kept alive only by Frankish legists and in the courts.

That burgesses held city property should not lead us to look for an affluent society in the early period of the kingdom. The general poverty, marked by the precarious position of the knights who waited, often in vain, for their salaries, affected the burgesses as well. A city like Jerusalem was almost emptied by mass emigration to the coastal ports because the inhabitants could not make a living in the capital. Undoubtedly the burgesses depended largely on seigneurial bounty. The hundreds of *pedites* who took part in military expeditions were paid by the king or his vassals. A number entered the domestic service of the king, nobles, and churchmen. Military spoils provided an additional source of livelihood.

---

84. *Livre des Assises . . . des Bourgeois*, cap. 31 (*RHC, Lois*, II, 36):" . . . se celuy heritage est en la terre dou rei et en rende cens. . . . Mais ce la terre ou la maison est franche, ce est qu'ele ne rende point de cens au rei ne à autre, qui que se soit." Cf. Philip of Novara, cap. 78 (*RHC, Lois*, I, 550).

85. The lord will then be both *seigneur justicier* and *seigneur foncier.*

It was only later, roughly after 1110 when almost all coastal cities but Tyre and Ascalon had been taken, that the young state entered upon a period of stability. The spectacular victory of the crusading armies and the slow but steady extension of the frontiers set off a growing immigration from Europe. Religious aspirations, economic calculation, social expectations, and, last but not least, public opinion directed settlers to the Holy Land. The non-noble immigrants seem to have been largely recruited from the southern parts of France, probably because newly opened maritime lines of communication facilitated emigration from areas adjacent to the Mediterranean.[86] The growing stability and the increase in population were reflected in the economic activities of the burgesses, including the arts and crafts, and a local commerce in food, baking, cooking, and so forth. The burgesses became real city dwellers, fulfilling economic functions typical of city life. For the great majority this was a revolutionary change in occupation and habits. Coming predominantly from rural areas, they possessed some knowledge of such primary crafts as carpentry and forging, but what was good enough for small villages in Europe looked primitive indeed when compared with the skills of easterners. Some crafts common in the east, like mosaic paving, were almost entirely unknown to the newcomers. Masonry, in demand in the west only for palaces and churches, was now needed for the simplest buildings, because of the scarcity of wood and the abundance of stone. But the Franks were quick to learn and to adapt. We shall probably have to look to the Christian Syrians (since the Moslem and Jewish populations in the cities were generally exterminated) for the teachers of the new crafts developed by the Franks. In some arts they would do better than their teachers; their ironwork would be admired by the Moslems. Other occupations developed with the growing immigration and pilgrimage. In Jerusalem there was a whole street taken up by cooks catering to the bachelors and pilgrims in the city.

Yet the class of burgesses achieved no real position of influence before the middle of the thirteenth century. Though their starting point was more propitious than that of their European contemporaries, owing to the flourishing coastal cities and ports and the fact that the kingdom implanted itself in the midst of an advanced money economy, the burgesses as a class never reached economic or political preëminence. This was because of the dominating presence of the commer-

---

86. A list of burgesses in one new settlement, Mahumeria (al-Bīrah, La Grande Mahome-rie), near Rāmallāh, to the north of Jerusalem (about 1156), included a substantial number of southerners from Auvergne, Provence, Burgundy, Gascony, Limoges, Poitou, Tours, Bourges, Catalonia, Valencia, Lombardy, Venice, Barletta, etc.; Rozière, *Cartulaire,* no. 131.

cial communes. It was almost inevitable that the merchants of Italy,[87] and later of Provence and Spain, would monopolize almost at once the most lucrative occupation, international maritime commerce. Experienced merchants and almost the only shipowners among the Franks, they extended their commercial activities, which already connected the Byzantine empire and Egypt with Italy, to the Syrian and Palestinian coasts. This may have been more important to Syria and Palestine than to the Italian communes themselves. Their main activities, growing in unprecedented measure during the twelfth and thirteenth centuries, remained essentially centered in the great emporia of Constantinople and Alexandria. Relative newcomers to the eastern part of the Mediterranean, like the Genoese and Pisans, may for a time have favored the crusaders' ports, but economic realities made them come to realize that fortunes could more easily be made in Byzantine and Moslem than in Latin ports. But although Mediterranean commerce remained based on the old centers, the communes in the Latin ports monopolized the commerce reaching the crusaders' states. The local burgesses had to resign themselves to the local market only, and even here they were generally handicapped by Italian competition.

The Italians boasted a long list of political and economic agreements with the kings of Jerusalem, the princes of Antioch, and the counts of Tripoli, and later on with the different city lords, which assured them exceptional privileges in customs and market tolls. As far as we can determine, the local authorities never made the distinction, current in Europe, between wholesale and retail trade. Both were consequently left in the hands of the Italian merchants, enjoying low customs duties and city tolls. This undermined the burgesses even in the retail commerce of imported goods. Their business shrank to local traffic in products of daily use, to buying and selling foodstuffs and supplying the everyday needs of a growing city population and a knightly consumer class which drew little but primary foodstuffs from its landed possessions. This modest economic position was not improved by the rise in value of city real estate. The burgesses often had their own houses, for which they paid a modest rent,[88] but they

---

87. In particular Pisa, Genoa, and Venice. Amalfi, the great power in Levantine commerce before the crusades, had very few privileges in the kingdom. Later Marseilles, Montpellier, and Barcelona succeeded in getting a foothold in the Latin east.

88. Several rent-lists are preserved in our sources. Cf. an inventory of the canons of the Holy Sepulcher in Jerusalem; Rozière, *Cartulaire,* no. 185 (pp. 329–330); of Hospitallers in Jerusalem in Paoli, *Codice diplomatico,* I, 235–236 (no. 190). According to this inventory, written about 1170, the very modest sum of 224 bezants was paid annually by 42 inhabitants. Other inventories are preserved for the city property of the communes in Acre and Tyre.

would hardly have seized houses and lands, when such was still possible, not needed for immediate use. Formerly empty spaces and unoccupied houses belonged to the lord of the city. If anyone became rich because of the rise in land values, therefore, it was not the burgesses, but the various city lords. Still, it may be assumed that some initial capital in the hands of the burgesses was created by their possession of *borgesies;*[89] the rise of land values, the direct outcome of a growing city population, would give them the means of either acquiring additional property or establishing shops and businesses.

Acquisition of city property was facilitated by the fact that the holding of *borgesies* was restricted to burgesses. Communes, military orders, and knights were barred from such holdings. There was even legislation to prevent alienation of *borgesies* to non-burgesses.[90] In Cyprus, but still during the lifetime of the Latin kingdom, Henry II forced on non-burgesses the immediate sale of their *borgesies.*[91] Although the aim of this legislation was to ensure that knights would owe feudal duties for their possessions, which was not applicable to *borgesie* tenure, and that church establishments would not convert *borgesies* into *franc-almoign,* the result was to favor the burgesses. We know that Henry II of Cyprus angrily left the Latin kingdom when the Templars acquired a village near Acre, which had the status of *borgesie,* without his permission.[92]

By the end of the first quarter of the twelfth century a number of burgesses had risen above the normal status of their class. As far as we can see, this upward movement was effected through court ser-

89. Which they could alienate by observing some slight seigneurial restrictions; the lord had the right of preëmption and the right to a small payment, a kind of *laudemium* or *lods et vente,* in case of alienation. The European *lods et vente* was a fiscal remnant of the old rule that alienation required the lord's agreement. As far as we know, the lord never had a right of refusal in the east, which suggests that the institution was brought from Europe in its developed form; *Livre des Assises . . . des Bourgeois,* caps. 31, 302 (*RHC, Lois,* II, 36, 224); cf. Delaborde, *Chartes,* no. 80; Rozière, *Cartulaire,* nos. 105, 110; Delaville Le Roulx, *Cartulaire,* II, 261, 782; *AOL,* I, (1881), 427.

90. *Livre au roi,* cap. 43 (*RHC, Lois,* I, 637–638). The prohibition is included in several deeds: cf. Rozière, *Cartulaire,* no. 105 (A.D. 1160); Delaville Le Roulx, *Cartulaire,* I, 491, 502 (A.D. 1186). See Prawer, "Burgage-Tenures of the Communes," in *Crusader Institutions,* pp. 315–326.

91. *Bans et ordonnances des rois de Chypre,* IX (*RHC, Lois,* II, 361). Cf. *Abrégé du Livre des Assises . . . des Bourgeois,* caps. 24, 17 (*ibid.,* II, 254–255, 249).

92. *Eracles,* XXXIV, 28 (*RHC, Occ.,* II, 474–475): "por un contens qu'il ot au Temple; por le casal de La Fauconerie [not identified], que li maistres dou Temple avoit achetté sanz seu et sanz congié dou roy d'un chevalier d'Acre . . . qui tenoit le dit casal de borjoysie, dont il ne devoit homage ne servise." Cf. Marino Sanudo, I, iii, par. XII, 4, in Bongars, *Gesta Dei per Francos,* II, 226.

vice of the various city lords. In Jerusalem, where we find the first traces of a burgess elite, we see them in the entourage of the king or his city representative, the viscount, or in the retinue of the patriarch, the lord of an autonomous quarter in the holy city with a court of his own.[93] Several names of burgesses appear again and again among the signatories of royal and patriarchal deeds and official proclamations.

The legal distinction between nobles and non-nobles, and the traditional European principle of judgment by peers, made a special jurisdiction for burgesses imperative. It was usual for quarrels between burgesses to come before a court composed of burgesses and presided over by the chatelain or viscount. This court also had jurisdiction in cases of alienation of *borgesies*. Even supposing that a special court of burgesses did not exist in the earliest period of the kingdom, and consequently that in the beginning a seigneurial court (perhaps with the participation of some burgesses) was the competent authority, it still would be normal for alienations to be made before burgesses, who would witness the act and attest to its legality.[94] There were no official registers of a court of burgesses until the crusade of Louis IX,[95] but any document which includes a list of witnesses provides a record of the names of those competent to testify before the court. Preceding, therefore, the first appearance of a court of burgesses as such, from 1120 on we meet with people styling themselves *idonei viri* (1120), *conventionis testes* (1134–1135), *regni testes legitimi* (1136), *pacti testes* (1136), *legitimi viri* (1144), *probi homines* (1150), and *de viris Jherusalem* (1174).[96] These appellations in written deeds prove that alienations of *borgesies* were recorded before a body of burgesses by 1120 and probably earlier. On the other hand, such titles as *regni testes legitimi* or *regie maiestatis iurati*[97] indicate a consciousness of a privileged standing in the social hierarchy of the country. This feeling is also indicated by such a title as *boni homines et legalitatis et justitie executores* (about 1146–1150),[98] which, as a matter of fact,

---

93. Prawer, "The Patriarch's Lordship in Jerusalem," in *Crusader Institutions,* pp. 296–314.

94. The earliest document of alienation of city property dates from 1125. It is a kind of memorandum written by one Oger, clerk of the Tower of David (i.e., the castle) in Jerusalem. The sale was made before the viscount Anschetino, who received a payment (*rectitudo*). It was signed by twenty-one witnesses, among them the son of the viscount and a son of the seller, "qui fuit ad potationem huius rei": Rozière, *Cartulaire,* no. 103.

95. *Abrégé du Livre des Assises . . . des Bourgeois,* caps. 13 ff. (*RHC, Lois,* II, 246 ff.).

96. In the order of citation: Rozière, *Cartulaire,* no. 45; *ibid.,* no. 109; Delaville Le Roulx, *Cartulaire,* I, 97 (no. 116); Rozière, *Cartulaire,* nos. 65, 107, 115; Delaville Le Roulx, *Cartulaire,* I, 318 (no. 464).

97. Rozière, *Cartulaire,* no. 108 (A.D. 1155).

98. Delaville Le Roulx, *Cartulaire,* I, 145 (no. 184).

is an exact description of the competence and standing of the *jurés* of the court of burgesses.

The term "court of burgesses" appears for the first time in a document dated 1149 in Jerusalem,[99] followed in 1166 in Antioch,[100] 1167 in Caesarea,[101] and only very late, not before 1184, in Acre.[102] It is certainly due to chance that relatively few and rather late documents mention the court by name. But we have to remember that a register of proceedings of the court did not come into being before 1251, and even this register is lost. Our documentation derives from deeds regarding property, which later came, with the property itself, into the hands of church establishments or of communes. The court of burgesses, or the court of the viscount, was in some measure an expression of the specific needs of the burgesses, although it never became an instrument to voice their demands. Still, the judgment by peers, the special procedures, and a number of assises or customs satisfied the most urgent needs and provided some sense of a distinctive class. The court enjoyed considerable prestige and heavy penalties were imposed for contempt of the court, its viscount, and its jurors.[103] The city ruler would not appoint a viscount without the formal assent of the burgesses, and was also supposed to take their advice in proclaiming city ordinances.[104]

The court did not lead to city autonomy, but in a sense it acted as a force for consolidation. Its general supervision and policing of the city gave it the appearance of a ruling body. Its competence *ratione personae,* over burgesses, gave it the appearance of an autonomous body politic, and its competence *ratione materiae* brought before it even knights and nobles who held city property defined as *borgesies.*

The early *boni homines,* or people bearing equivalent titles, mark the first signs of a class distinction among the burgesses. It is of some interest to note that, as far as we can learn about their occupations, they are very often money-changers and goldsmiths,[105] that is, people of means and liquid capital. At least in the thirteenth century, the

99. Rozière, *Cartulaire,* no. 112.
100. Delaville Le Roulx, *Cartulaire,* I, 251–252 (no. 367).
101. *Idem, Les Archives,* no. 27.
102. *Idem, Cartulaire,* I, 445–446 (no. 663).
103. Philip of Novara, cap. 87 (*RHC, Lois,* I, 561).
104. *Livre des Assises . . . des Bourgeois,* cap. 6 (*ibid.,* II, 23). A specific feature of the court of burgesses is its relationship both with the lord who appointed the court and with the city itself. If two cities belong to the same lord, each will have its own court of burgesses; cap. 224 (*ibid.,* II, 551).
105. *Cambiatores, nummularii, aurifabri;* e.g., a deed regarding Jerusalem signed by seven people, after whose name we read: "omnes isti aurifabri": Rozière, *Cartulaire,* no. 82; cf. *ibid.,* nos. 101, 104, 84, 105; Delaville Le Roulx, *Les Archives,* nos. 25, 26.

jurors sat three days a week in court and were not salaried; this in itself presupposes that they were people of some economic standing. On the other hand it was quite customary for the lord of a city to appoint to the court men enjoying prestige among city inhabitants. Some, of course, could have acquired such prestige from the very fact of their being nominated. That some viscounts were of burgess origin[106] indicates how well burgesses could do for themselves through seigneurial service. Similar advances were made by burgesses in the patriarch's court, where some were designated by the title *iudex,*[107] not known in later sources or treatises on law.

It is from among these notables that the first jurors (*jurati*) of the court of burgesses were recruited. In Jerusalem, where there were two distinct courts, the king's and the patriarch's, each competent, it would seem, in a different part of the city, we can trace the emergence of an official burgess elite through a series of documents. The burgesses possessing villages around Jerusalem probably rose in status from that very fact. The more usual way of social advancement, however, was to move from the privileged position of juror in the court of burgesses to the noble class of knights. A few examples may illustrate this social mobility. One man appearing frequently in the early documents of the kingdom is Godfrey Acus. Beginning in 1120, when he witnessed a royal decree of Baldwin II partially abolishing taxes on food brought to Jerusalem, and up to the eve of the Second Crusade, we find him in the entourage of the kings of Jerusalem, of the patriarch and the canons of the Holy Sepulcher.[108] About 1125 Ralph of Fontanella, a knight, left him a vineyard on the road leading from Jerusalem to Bethlehem "because he served me well and with devotion for a long time."[109] But whereas his signature as late as 1136 is among the witnesses described as *de burgensibus,*[110] in 1144 and 1147 he is listed among the *barones regni* of Baldwin III.[111] It is pertinent to note that a village near Emmaus (Amwās), which belonged to the order of St. John (1141), was called *casale de Gaufrido Agule.*[112] That such cases

---

106. E.g., Godefridus filius Reubauth (Raimbaldi) signs in Antioch in 1133–1134 (Rozière, *Cartulaire,* no. 85; Röhricht, *Regesta,* no. 149) as *de baronibus;* in 1135 (Rozière, *Cartulaire,* no. 86; *Regesta;* no. 157) as *de burgensibus;* in 1140 (Rozière, *Cartulaire,* nos. 88, 90; *Regesta,* nos. 195, 194) as *vicecomes.*

107. Cf. Rozière, *Cartulaire,* nos. 82, 107, 135 (1135–1136).

108. E.g., Röhricht, *Regesta,* nos. 128, 129, 141, 130, 164.

109. Rozière, *Cartulaire,* no. 121.

110. Röhricht, *Regesta,* no. 164.

111. *Ibid.,* nos. 226, 244.

112. *Ibid.,* no. 205. Röhricht has incorrectly identified it with *castrum Gaucefredi de Agolt,* which was in the county of Tripoli; *ibid.,* no. 78.

were not restricted to Jerusalem is clear from the career of one Gerald, son of Arnald, in the city of Ramla, who in 1167 signed as a burgess, but in 1169 as a knight.[113]

Social mobility through royal service did not stop with the first kingdom. A famous burgess family like the Antiaumes, prominent throughout the thirteenth century, would see one of its members called *miles Acconensis* (1288).[114] Another example of the same type, although not leading as far as knighthood, is that of Godfrey of Tours, closely connected with the patriarch's household. He signed documents (1153–1186) pertaining to the canons of the Holy Sepulcher, and appeared from 1161 as the patriarch's seneschal (*dapifer*),[115] head of the patriarch's household, and perhaps even fulfilling some military functions. He witnessed a charter of Baldwin III among the *burgenses regis* and also served as a juror of the court of burgesses of Jerusalem.[116] In this last capacity we find him again and again between 1161 and 1186.[117] These random examples prove the existence of an upper group among the burgesses, which came to prominence in the administrative service of the kings, patriarchs, and lords of the kingdom. Naturally, some would also become prominent through successfully run businesses. For example, Theobald of Tyre gave a loan to a knight, James of Sidon, of 500 bezants, taking as security a village called Gyps and receiving, to pay off the loan, 150 bezants' worth of agricultural produce annually during the next twelve years.[118]

The frequent appearance of burgesses in royal and seigneurial documents does not mean that there was a blurring of the clear-cut distinction between nobles and burgesses. The latter often signed documents where nobles were concerned, but this was because they dealt with *borgesies*. Their signatures had legal importance should a dispute come before the court of burgesses *ratione materiae*. Still, we sometimes find their signatures on royal and seigneurial documents where it is impossible to assign to them any legal significance. We should remember, however, that the court of burgesses of Jerusalem was a royal court, and there is nothing extraordinary in the fact that the jurors or eminent burgesses of the city might witness a royal document.[119] In other cases it was the solemnity of the act that led the ruler to

113. *Ibid.,* nos. 432, 472.
114. *Les Registres de Nicolas IV,* ed. Ernest Langlois (2 vols., Paris, 1886–1905), I, 48 (no. 266).
115. Röhricht, *Regesta,* no. 391.
116. *Ibid.,* nos. 545, 643, 651.
117. *Ibid.,* nos. 299, 300, 301, 332, 333, 531, 534.
118. Delaville Le Roulx, "Chartes de la Terre Sainte," *ROL,* XI (1905–1908), 181–183: 1158.
119. Rozière, *Cartulaire,* nos. 62, 59, 56, 63, 60, 57.

invite their signatures. Such, for example, is the case of a donation by Robert of St. Gilles to the Hospitallers. It was made in the presence of the patriarch and with the consent of king Fulk. The patriarch (William of Messines) sealed it "in the presence of the lawful witnesses of the three orders".[120] Such instances are not very frequent, but they do occur in the kingdom as well as in the principalities.[121] The burgesses were lawful men, the good citizens of the king or lord, and their signatures were an additional adornment. As to their importance, however, we may concur with the writer of the documents by which Raymond III of Tripoli transferred Rafanīyah and Montferrand to the Hospitallers, who, after noting the signatures of the clergy, nobility and some burgesses, then added: "and all the rest of the names of which it would be more boring than profitable to tell."[122]

While some burgesses moved upward, another kind of distinction emerged within the class. By the middle of the twelfth century the kingdom had reached its zenith. Military successes had pushed its frontiers to their maximum extent. The cities were densely settled, in the north by the local Christian population and new European immigrants, in the south predominantly by Europeans. It is at this time that new social groups were discernible in the cities. One of these, of a rather formal character, was connected with church establishments, especially the Holy Sepulcher. A large number of men and women declared themselves *confratres* of the Holy Sepulcher. These were very poor people. One couple promised to resign their "fief" to the Holy Sepulcher at death, but their son was to receive from the canons *victum et vestimentum*.[123] A woman sold a garden to the canons and promised to leave them her house when she died, while in turn the canons promised to supply her with "every day one loaf, like that eaten by the canons, and half a liter of wine, a dish of cooked

120. Delaville Le Roulx, *Cartulaire,* no. 139: "sub legitimis trium ordinum confirmetur testibus."

121. Fulk restored property to the Holy Sepulcher in Jerusalem: "habito consilio domini patriarchae et episcoporum et baronum simulque burgensium": Rozière, *Cartulaire,* no. 86 (1135). His privilege to the Hospitallers was made "tocius regni tam cleri quam populi hortatu" and was signed by burgesses; Delaville Le Roulx, *Cartulaire,* no. 116 (1136). A donation to the Hospitallers of Tripoli bore the signatures of nobles "et aliorum virorum qui huic dono adfuerunt, clericorum scilicet et militum et burgensium": *ibid.,* no. 210 (1152). Bohemond III confirmed the sale of Margat in the presence of many "clerics, knights and burgesses": *ibid.,* no. 783 (1186).

122. Delaville Le Roulx, *Cartulaire,* I, 116: "et ceteri omnes quorum nomina tedius esset magis quam proficium enarrari." See Prawer, "The Burgesses and their Seignors," in *Crusader Institutions,* pp. 327-339.

123. Rozière, *Cartulaire,* no. 77 (1129); see Riley-Smith, "A Note on Confraternities in the Latin Kingdom of Jerusalem," *Bulletin of the Institute of Historical Research,* XLIV (1971), 301-308; and Prawer, note 93, above.

meat (?), and on Sundays and feast days a piece of meat or other food as eaten by the canons."[124] People promised to leave their property to the canons at their death, or to give them all their property immediately on condition that they be fed and clothed.[125] Although technically the *confraternitas* allowed for participation in the spiritual and ecclesiastical privileges of the canons,[126] it seems obvious that economic motives were a strong incentive to such association. Thus, elderly couples and lonely old people with limited means came under the jurisdiction of the canons. People of higher status also declared themselves *confratres* either of the Holy Sepulcher or, as was often the case, of the military orders, which knights joined for a limited period. In the case of the Hospitallers, even burgesses associated themselves as *confratres*. But in most cases we are dealing here with the lower stratum of burgesses, looking to church establishments for help and protection.

The case is different, however, with those burgesses connected with the canons of the Holy Sepulcher who are described in the sources as *clientes*. Whole families, possibly even villages, are to be found in this category. The village of Saint Lazarus, near Jerusalem, which belonged to the canons, seems to have been settled by *clientes*.[127] The *clientes* held property from the canons called *feuda*, "fiefs";[128] we can be sure that these were not knights' fiefs. An act of 1129 mentions a holder of such a "fief," a *confrater* of Saint Lazarus whose daughter was to marry a *nutritus famulus* of the canons.[129] In all probability it was property granted in this way to burgesses who produced the service of 500 sergeants which the canons were obliged to provide the kings of Jerusalem.[130] That such was the use of the term *cliens* is clear from a passage of Fulcher of Chartres, where the army of Baldwin I is described as being composed of *300 milites lectissimi et clientes advectitii 400 probissimi*.[131] The monastery of Mount Tabor followed the same example to ensure its own military services.

124. Rozière, *Cartulaire,* no. 106 (1132).

125. *Ibid.,* nos. 102, 103.

126. *Ibid.,* no. 101: "Participes omnium bonorum . . . spiritualium."

127. A widow of one *cliens,* remarried to another, and her daughter who was also married to a *cliens,* had to live with their husbands on the property of the canons either in Jerusalem or in Saint Lazarus: *ibid.,* no. 109.

128. *Ibid.,* no. 110.

129. *Ibid.,* no. 77.

130. John of Ibelin, cap. 272 (*RHC, Lois,* I, 426–427). The canons had a special officer called *magister clientum Sancti Sepulchri:* Rozière, *Cartulaire,* no. 107.

131. Fulcher of Chartres, III, 11 (*RHC, Occ.,* III, 447). In the confirmation of the sale of Margat to the Hospitallers by Bohemond III in 1186 there is a clear distinction between *burgesia* and *de feodo vero militis vel clientis:* Delaville Le Roulx, *Cartulaire,* I, 491 (no. 783).

A long list of witnesses to a deed of Mount Tabor is headed: "from among the lay brothers," but the same people appear in another document as *turcopuli,* light cavalry.[132] As the military service due from church institutions was rather heavy, we can assume that hundreds of burgesses were hired for military service. Naturally, not all of them received "fiefs" as did the burgesses of Saint Lazarus. Some were content to receive food or quantities of crops from church properties, or simply money. And it was money which was paid to the sergeants in times of emergency, when additional soldiers were needed. They were simply *stipendiarii,* mercenary soldiers.

Lords of cities also hired burgesses for military, administrative, and domestic services. Ties of dependence were strong, especially in places where the burgesses served as mercenaries of the lord. Often they identified themselves with the head of the local dynasty and, according to accepted feudal ideas, became a class traditionally serving a great house, belonging to its "family" (*maisnie*).[133]

By the middle of the twelfth century new developments were making distinctions among the class of burgesses. Political stability and relative security favored colonization. There was a migration from the cities to the small semi-urban agglomerations and to newly founded villages. A Frankish class of peasants and inhabitants of small towns, in the main agricultural, was in the making. The population of these communities, in the shadow of a fortress or citadel, was recruited from among the burgesses. They settled in what would be called in Europe, and in at least one eastern source, *borcs.*[134] Some of these settlements became real towns mushrooming beneath the fortifications and almost always surrounded with low walls, not strong enough to withstand a regular siege but good enough to repel marauding beduins or Moslem peasants.[135] Other places never developed into towns, but remained villages settled by a Frankish peasantry. We know of at least half a dozen cases of colonization undertaken by kings, church institutions, military orders, and lay lords.[136] The new villages differed entirely from the native ones, which they often replaced. They were fortified and far more populous. While the native village

132. Röhricht, *Regesta,* nos. 389, 594.

133. Cf. *Les Gestes des Chiprois,* cap. 164 (*RHC, Arm.,* II, 705): "chevaliers et sergens et valès, qui tous furent de la maihnee et de la noreture dou lignage d'Ybelin."

134. *Chronique de Terre Sainte:* "[Escalone] quy est un mout fort chastiau sur mer et un grant bourc come une cité": *Les Gestes des Chiprois,* ed. Raynaud, p. 5.

135. William of Tyre, XVII, 12; XX, 20 (*RHC, Occ.,* I, 777–779, 975–977).

136. Prawer, "Colonization Activities," pp. 1063–1118; Riley-Smith, *The Feudal Nobility,* index, *s.v.* "colonial settlements."

population might be estimated at ten or twenty families, the new Frank-ish settlements included fifty families or more. There is no doubt that the settlers came from among the poorest of the burgesses, those who could not make a living in the cities.[137]

Settlement outside the cities, although it created a class of Frankish peasantry, did not create a class of Frankish serfs. The Frankish in-habitants of the newly colonized village of al-Bīrah, although peas-ants, did not lose their status as *burgenses*. They attended public courts, and their property, for which they paid only a small rent, was free land. The rent was established along the lines of the *champart* or similar tenures without personal servitude, at a fixed amount of the produce, but the property was otherwise hereditary, unburdened by servile dues. The holder had the right to alienate it without restric-tion (except for the lord's preëmptive right).

That these peasants were looked down upon by their peers in the cities is probable. Nor was the danger of their subjection an imagi-nary one.[138] But legally and socially the Frankish farmer was a bur-gess, well above the richest Syrian or Moslem peasant of the coun-tryside. Wherever burgesses settled, they had a right to their own court and to the judgment of their peers. An inventory of such courts, in-dicating the diffusion of the Frankish population, is preserved by John of Ibelin. He lists thirty-seven places for the kingdom, but the list is incomplete. If we may assume that a viscount is to be found in all places which had a civil Frankish population, we can add another four.[139] If we add localities which we know were colonized by Franks, it gives us a total of about fifty places where the burgesses settled and had their own form of organization in a court of burgesses.

In the principality of Antioch courts of burgesses existed certainly in three localities—Antioch, Jabala, and Latakia—and there were prob-ably more. In the county of Tripoli courts of burgesses existed in Tripoli and Rafanīyah, and probably also in Tortosa, 'Arqah, and Jubail. The fact that a relatively small number of such courts are known to us in these principalities may be due partly to our lack of sources

---

137. *Eracles*, XX, 20 (*RHC, Occ.*, I, 976), speaking about the settlement in Gaza: "povres gent gaengneor et marcheant vindrent après qui se herbergierent autour ce chastel." William of Tyre, XX, 19 (*RHC, Occ.*, I, 973–975), on the settlement in Darum: "Erat enim locus com-modus, et ubi tenuiores homines facilius proficerent quam in urbibus."

138. Cf. Rozière, *Cartulaire*, no. 132 (*c.* 1151). The canons of the Holy Sepulcher agreed that Robert of Retesta should use the Frankish colonists established by the monks in al-Bīrah, if they were willing, but "super burgenses vero prefatos nullam dederunt . . . potestatem vel dominium exercere, nec violentiam inferre aut forifactum vel exactionem exigere."

139. John of Ibelin, cap. 270 (*RHC, Lois*, I, 422–426). We may add Qalansuwā, Qāqūn, Majdal (Mirabel), and al-Lajjūn (Legio, Lyon).

(there being no inventory like that for the kingdom of Jerusalem), but even more to the relatively meager colonization of the northern principalities and the concentration of their Frankish populations in the great cities.

The burgesses of Jerusalem enjoyed a privileged position among those of the kingdom. Not only were they the burgesses of the holy city, the capital of the kingdom, but they were the "burgesses of the king." During the coronation they participated in the ceremony and served the king the coronation meal at the *templum domini*.[140] The burgesses of Acre, the royal city on the coast which became the capital of the kingdom in the thirteenth century, enjoyed a similar position. But it was a position of precedence, with no legal sanction. Naturally the fact that some of the burgesses of Jerusalem, especially during the time of Baldwin III and Amalric, were in constant attendance on the king might have given them some special prestige, but it is impossible to discern any practical results.[141]

The existence of courts of burgesses and a common law of burgesses (differing from one principality to another, but the same within each), did not lead, generally speaking, to the creation of an "estate" or a corporative body of the burgesses of the crusader states. What is even more striking is the fact that they never took over any city government,[142] and their participation in such government was far more limited than in any contemporary European city. Only once in Jerusalem do we find them opposing the king, one of the Baldwins, for having proclaimed an ordinance about cleaning the city streets without their advice and counsel.[143] Nowhere do we see them act as an "estate" with its grievances and demands. At a time when European cities were becoming "collective vassals" and taking over city administrations, such a feature of city life was entirely nonexistent in the Latin east.

The main reason lay in the fact that the city population included not only burgesses but almost the entire knightly population. This gave a particular coloring to city life and organization. Although economically well defined, the city was neither a community nor a corporation. It never became a center of burgess independence or self-government, since it was never a burgess city. Nor did knights and

---

140. *Eracles*, XXIII, 3 (*RHC, Occ.*, II, 5–6); John of Ibelin, cap. 8 (*RHC, Lois*, I, 51–52).

141. Documents emanating from Melisend, Baldwin III, and Amalric were frequently witnessed by burgesses, even in cases, such as the confirmation of franc-almoigns and fiefs, where their signatures were not legally necessary. See Prawer, note 122, above.

142. For the so-called communal movement see below, pp. 167–169, 188–192.

143. *Livre des Assises . . . des Bourgeois*, cap. 303 (*RHC, Lois*, II, 225).

burgesses merge into a formal community. There can be no comparison with Italian cities where nobles, having once entered the city commune, identified themselves with the city, fighting its wars against empire and neighbors alike. City autonomy, in the sense of self-government or civic privileges, even on the economic level alone, was entirely unknown.

It is even more remarkable that no guilds or similar corporations were created.[144] This is more difficult to explain. It might be partly because the first burgesses, originally peasants, did not bring with them any corporative traditions. But this did not preclude a later development of guilds. It might be suggested, however, that the normal course of European development, the creation of a merchant guild which ruled the city and set off a counter-movement of craft organizations to defend their own interests against the ruling city oligarchy, could find no place in the east. No Frankish merchant guild was ever created, because the lucrative commerce was a monopoly of the Italian communes.

Furthermore, the most characteristic feature of the kingdom, at least in the twelfth century, was that it was a country of immigrants. In more than one sense the existence of the state depended on the continued flow of immigrants and their economic absorption into the kingdom. On the other hand, guilds were exclusive bodies. The regulated system of apprenticeship, examinations, and advancement, let alone the later policy of limiting the number of masters, was suited to a stable economy and society. It could hardly flourish where the population fluctuated and had to be continually renewed. Moreover, such a policy would have caused difficulties in the economic integration of the immigrants.

There is another factor that might have played some part in handicapping guild organization. The native population, mainly local Christians living in the cities, pursued the same occupations as Frankish burgesses. As there was a deep abyss between the two, it was hardly thinkable that they could coöperate on the basis of common occupations. The only possibility was to have parallel guild organizations, and somehow this never happened.

What served as a rudimentary substitute for guild organization was created by the living together of people of the same occupation. Thus there were streets of cooks, of spice merchants, of malt or ale makers, skinners, tanners, money-changers, and so forth. Membership

144. Although physicians were sufficiently organized to require the examination of a newcomer wishing to exercise their profession in the kingdom; *Livre des Assises . . . des Bourgeois,* cap. 298 (*ibid.,* II, 223).

in an ethnic or linguistic group provided another basis of social cohesion. Scanning the names of streets in the major cities of the kingdom, we find not only the members of Italian communes but also Provençals, Spaniards, Germans, Englishmen, and Bretons living in special streets or quarters. Quite often there will be a church under a patron saint popular in a European province to indicate the origin of the inhabitants of a quarter. It is again the fact of immigration which led newcomers to seek out compatriots speaking their own language or dialect and sharing familiar customs and rules of behavior. This huddling together replaced family and community ties severed by emigration.

The anarchy of the second quarter of the thirteenth century and the rise of independent jurisdictions, especially those of the communes, which has led one historian to call the kingdom "le royaume des marchands,"[145] created a situation of insecurity and instability. One of its results was the emergence and the growing importance of new types of social cohesion and political dependence. These appear in the second quarter of the thirteenth century in the form of *fraternitates* or *frairies*. The fraternity, or brotherhood, was an association that recruited its members on a voluntary basis for the common pursuit of religious and social goals.[146] Just as in Europe, the authorities were suspicious of associations where an oath had to be taken by each member on entrance, which possibly explains why the rules of the brotherhoods had to be confirmed by the lord of the city. A brotherhood had its patron saint, its own rules, and its seal to legalize acts. In a sense they took the place of guilds in fulfilling social and religious functions.

In the middle of the thirteenth century, when political factions ruled Acre, it was almost inevitable that any corporation which grouped

145. Richard, *Royaume latin*, pp. 274–275.
146. There were certainly more than the two whose names we know, the brotherhood of St. Andrew and the Pisan *Societas Vermiliorum;* cf. Georg E. Müller, ed., *Documenti sulle relazioni delle città toscane coll' Oriente cristiana e coi Turchi fino all' anno 1531* (Florence, 1879; repr. Rome, 1966), nos. 27–28 and p. 33; see Riley-Smith, note 123, above. The location of the *societas vermiliorum* is not very clear, and Müller's explanations are not satisfactory. It seems to have been a corporation which, after taking part in the defense of Tyre under Conrad of Montferrat, took over the responsibility of administering Pisa's property in Acre. The property assigned to it was hereditary and might even have been divided among its members. In an anti-Pisan move, Henry of Champagne abolished the status and reduced the privileges granted to the commune by Conrad and Guy of Lusignan, at which time we lose all trace of the *societas;* see Prawer, *Latin Kingdom*, p. 490. The existence of many other brotherhoods is proved; e.g., by Philip of Montfort's promise to the Genoese in 1264 in Tyre, that property in their quarter will not be given to other communes or brotherhoods: "Et quod dominus Tyri non possit dare hoc quod sibi remanet de barrigisia [sic], communitatibus, nec frareriis pro hospitando, neque pro alio re facere": *AOL,* II-2 (1884), 226.

a large number of people together should become the object of competition between the contesting parties. It was hardly politics which
drew the brotherhoods into the conflict, but rather their coherence
in a time of general anarchy. Their support of this faction or that
often depended on chance, the proximity of a powerful neighbor, or
the dependence of its members on a given power such as a church,
monastery, or military order. It was one of these brotherhoods, that
of St. Andrew,[147] that became the focus of Ibelin opposition to the
rule of the "Lombards." The fact that a baronial revolutionary movement connected itself with a brotherhood is not symptomatic of any
privileged standing of the burgesses or their semipublic corporations.
The brotherhood of St. Andrew was chosen because its rules were
such that virtually anyone could join. Whoever was willing to swear
the oath of membership was readily accepted.[148]

Later the brotherhood of St. Andrew became the nucleus of the
"commune" of Acre, a revolutionary movement directed against Hohenstaufen rule.[149] Neither the "commune" of Acre, however, nor the
"communes" of Antioch and Tripoli had anything in common with
a communal movement in the usual sense of the term. They were
not urban movements aimed at city independence from an ecclesiastical or secular lord, nor did they seek economic or legal guarantees.
They aimed, rather, at legalizing opposition to an established rule
which they declared to be illegitimate. All of them were led by members of the upper nobility who sought power through the selection
of the ruler. These movements were more akin to contemporary European assemblies of estates.[150] If the nobility chose the form of a commune, the reason was the example of the existing Italian communes
in their cities and the impossibility of converting the high court into
any kind of parliament or estates general for the purpose. The legal

147. Probably connected with the port of Acre; Saint Andrew the fisherman is connected
with the sea. During the war in Acre there were *poulains du port* as members and supporters
of the brotherhood.

148. The essential facts about the brotherhood of St. Andrew are given by *Eracles,* XXXIII,
26 (*RHC, Occ.,* II, 391-392): "en la terre avoit une frarie qui estoit nomée la Frarie de Saint
André, la quel estoit otroiée dou roi Baudoin et confermée par son prevelige. Et apres la con-
ferma le conte Henri et en fist prevelige. Et en cele frarie si avoit establissemens, devises et
motiz es preveliges, et entre les autres establissemens estoit ce que tuit cil, qui en la frairie
se voloient metre, le poeent faire, et que cil de frairie les poeent recevoir." Cf. Marino Sanudo
in Bongars, *Gesta Dei per Francos,* II, 214 (who wrongly calls it *fraternitas S. Iacobi*).

149. See chapter VI, below.

150. The idea is correctly expressed by Jean Colson, "Aux Origines des assemblées d'états:
L'exemple de l'Orient latin," *Revue des études byzantines,* XII (1954), 114-127, but his assessment needs qualification, as it does not take into account the machinery of the crusaders' regime.

mentality of the nobility preferred to graft a revolutionary movement onto a legitimate body already in existence, in Acre the brotherhood of St. Andrew, which by its rules allowed the coming together of nobles and burgesses, possibly even members of the Italian communes. There were no elections, no appointed representatives. The general meeting of the brotherhood, like the *parliamentum* of an Italian town, was a meeting of the entire body politic. But although the frontiers of the commune were the city walls, it did not aim at ruling Acre alone; it aimed at ruling the kingdom.

In Antioch it was a different legal problem which led to the adoption of the revolutionary commune of 1193. It was an attempt to find a formula that would unite the Latin and Greek inhabitants of the city. As we have seen, the common danger was the establishment in Antioch of an Armenian principality and an Armenian church hated by Greeks and feared by Latins. The Greeks, probably a majority of the population, by definition were not burgesses. A commune gave them the opportunity of participating in the government of the principality.[151]

These communes were short-lived. The brotherhoods themselves, however, did not dissolve, but rather grew in influence. In 1243 princess Alice was accepted as the ruler of the kingdom with the support of the barons, the patriarch, the Genoese, the Venetians, "and also the brotherhoods of the city."[152] Hugh III de Lusignan left Acre in 1276 "because of many quarrels which he had with the military orders and the communes and the brotherhoods which he could not dominate or govern at his will." And again, he was asked to come back to Acre by "prelates, military orders, other Knights Hospitaller, Teutons, Pisans, burgesses of the country, Genoese, brotherhoods, and all other kinds of people."[153]

While the burgesses never developed as an estate, some individuals became quite influential in the kingdom. In a society obsessed by legal forms, knowledge of the law became an important asset for advancement. The burgesses known to us as influential in political life are those to be found in the courts of burgesses. John Valin, William of Conches, and Philip Baudoyn[154] were at one time or another among

---

151. See below, p. 230; for the sources, see Cahen, *Syrie du nord*, pp. 653–660. On the communes of Tripoli, see below, note 155.

152. *Les Gestes des Chiprois*, cap. 226 (*RHC, Arm.*, II, 731): "et toutes friairies de la ville ausy."

153. *Eracles*, XXXIV, 28 (*RHC, Occ.*, II, 474–475).

154. *Les Gestes des Chiprois*, caps. 221, 225 (*RHC, Arm.*, II, 728, 731); all fl. *c.* 1240. On the Antiaumes see above, note 53.

the jurors. Some of them were accepted in the circles of nobility, even appearing in the high court. A fraternity of legists could have been founded despite the social differences between nobles and burgesses.

On the whole, however, the role of the burgesses in the kingdom bore no relation to their numbers as a whole or to the achievements of a few individuals. Rather, it reflected the position of a middle class in a country colonized by immigrants. Sharing a privileged position as conquerors, they were barred from further advance by the traditional nobility. They attained power as a class neither in the city nor in the country. The collapse of the central power prevented their becoming an estate, while city-dwelling nobles prevented them from taking over city governments. They never acquired great wealth because the greatest source of wealth, international maritime commerce, remained in the hands of the real European burgesses, the commercial communes of the west.

D. The Communes[155]

A special place among the social classes of the crusader states was reserved to the natives of the great European mercantile cities, primarily the maritime cities of Italy but also, to a lesser degree, some cities of southern France and Spain. Among the Italian cities the most important were Genoa, Pisa, and Venice. Although cities like Amalfi

---

155. The main sources are the privileges accorded the different European commercial cities and commercial contracts. A list of the principal privileges is to be found in LaMonte, *Feudal Monarchy in the Latin Kingdom of Jerusalem, 1100 to 1291* (Cambridge, Mass., 1932), appendix D, pp. 261–275. See also Robert H. Bautier, "Sources pour l'histoire du commerce maritime en Méditerranée du XIIe au XVe siècle," in *Les Sources de l'histoire maritime en Europe du moyen-âge au XVIIIe siècle,* ed. Michel Mollat (Paris, 1962), pp. 137–179; Prawer, "Economic Life and Commerce," *Latin Kingdom,* pp. 352–415 (with bibliography, pp. 552–557); and *idem,* "The Italians in the Latin Kingdom," in *Crusader Institutions,* pp. 217–249.

The main collections are Tafel and Thomas; *Liber iurium reipublicae Genuensis,* ed. Ercole Ricotti in *Historiae patriae monumenta,* VII, IX (Turin, 1854–1857), partially superseded by C. Imperiale di Sant' Angelo, *Codice diplomatico della repubblica di Genova* (3 vols., Rome, 1936–1942); Müller, *Documenti,* partially superseding Flaminio dal Borgo, *Raccolta di scelti diplomi pisani* (Pisa, 1765); Louis Méry and F. Guindon, *Histoire analytique et chronologique des actes et des délibérations . . . de la municipalité de Marseille* (2 vols., Marseilles, 1841–1843); and Matteo Camera, *Memorie storico-diplomatiche dell' antica città e ducato di Amalfi* (2 vols., Naples, 1876–1881; repr. Salerno, 1972).

Commercial contracts are preserved in notarial registers, the richest being those of Genoa. The registers which furnish materials directly bearing on our subject are *Il Cartolare di Giovanni Scriba,* ed. Mario Chiaudano and Mattia Moresco (2 vols., Turin, 1935; repr. Turin, 1970), replacing the older edition of *Historiae patriae monumenta, chartarum II* (Turin, 1853); *Lanfranco, 1202–1226,* ed. Hilmar C. Krueger and Robert L. Reynolds (3 vols., Genoa, 1951–1953); *Liber magistri Salmonis, sacri palatii notarii, 1222–1226,* ed. Arturo Ferretto (Genoa, 1906); Cornelio Desimoni, "Actes passés en 1271, 1274, et 1279 à l'Aias . . . et à Beyrouth par devant des notaires génois," *AOL,* I (1881), 434–534; Raimondo Morozzo della Rocca and Antonino Lombardo, eds., *Documenti del commercio veneziano nei secoli XI-XIII* (2 vols., Rome and Turin, 1940); Lombardo and Morozzo della Rocca, eds., *Nuovi documenti del commercio veneto dei secoli XI-XIII* (Venice, 1953); Louis Blancard, ed., *Documents inédits sur le commerce de Marseille au moyen-âge* (2 vols., Marseilles, 1884–1885); and Mayer, *Marseilles Levantehandel und ein akkonensisches Fälscheratelier* (Tübingen, 1972).

The notarial registers have not yet been fully exploited, expecially those of the thirteenth century. For an analysis of the contents of Genoese registers see Moresco and Gian P. Bognetti, *Per l'Edizione dei notai liguri del secolo XII* (Turin, 1938) and Archivio di Stato di Genova, *Cartolari notarili genovesi* (Publ. degli Archivi di stato, XXII, XLI; Rome, 1956, 1961).

There are many studies regarding the commercial activities of the Italian cities. The most important general works are still Wilhelm Heyd, *Histoire du commerce du Levant au moyen-âge,* tr. Furcy Raynaud (Leipzig, 1885–1886; repr. Leipzig, 1936, Amsterdam, 1967); Adolf Schaube, *Handelsgeschichte der romanischen Völker des Mittelmeergebiets bis zum Ende der Kreuzzüge*

(which had played an important role in east-west commerce before the crusades) and Ancona in Italy, Marseilles, St. Gilles, and Montpellier in France, and Barcelona in Spain should be mentioned, it is among the nationals of the three great maritime powers of Venice, Genoa, and Pisa that we find the typical commune in the crusader states.

Socially the settlers and merchants of the Italian communes belonged to the same class as the town-dwelling Frankish burgesses. Their living quarters and their places of business were in the cities, their main occupation was commerce. They were certainly not classed among the knights and nobles. One may postulate that they formed a higher, because far richer, stratum in the class of burgesses, but this would be misleading. The fundamental factor which defined their standing was not their economic function but primarily their legal standing as defined by a long list of treaties, privileges, and agreements. The treaties did not grant the same status to all communes, or even to different colonies of the same commune. Not only did the communes vary in status between the kingdom of Jerusalem, the principality of Antioch, and the county of Tripoli, but even within

---

(Munich and Berlin, 1906); Robert S. Lopez, "The Trade of Medieval Europe: The South," in *The Cambridge Economic History of Europe,* ed. Moise M. Postan and Edwin E. Rich, II (Cambridge, 1952), 257–354; Irving W. Raymond and Lopez, *Medieval Trade in the Mediterranean World* (*CURC,* 52; New York, 1955). Cahen, "Orient latin et le commerce du Levant," *Bulletin de la Faculté des lettres de Strasbourg,* XXIX (1951), 328–345, indicates future lines of study.

Studies of the communal movement include LaMonte, "The Communal Movement in Syria"; Mayer, "On the Beginnings of the Communal Movement in the Holy Land: The Commune of Tyre," *Traditio,* XXIV (1968), 443–457; *idem,* "Zwei Kommunen in Akkon?" *Deutsches Archiv für Erforschung des Mittelalters,*" XXVI (1970), 434–453; Riley-Smith, "The *Assise sur la ligèce* and the Commune of Acre," *Traditio,* XXVII (1971), 179–204; *idem,* above, note 123; *idem, Feudal Nobility,* pp. 194 ff.; Prawer, "The Earliest Commune of Tripoli," in *Studies in Memory of Gaston Wiet,* ed. M. Rosen-Ayalon (Jerusalem, 1977), pp. 171–179; and *idem,* "Estates, Communities, and the Constitution of the Latin Kingdom," in *Crusader Institutions,* pp. 46–82.

Despite the titles of works on colonization, they are more concerned with privileges and political problems than with settlement as such. The latter subject is dealt with in part in studies on the social aspects of commercial activity. The best guide to Genoese studies is Vito Vitale, *Il Commune del Podestà,* in *Storia di Genova dalle origini al tempo nostro,* III (Milan, 1951). On Amalfi see Vsevolod Slessarev, "*Ecclesia Mercatorum* and the Rise of Merchant Colonies." *Business Historical Review,* XLI (1967), 177–197. The principal studies on various aspects of colonization are Camillo Manfroni, *I Colonizzatori italiani durante il medio evo e il rinascimento,* I, *Dal secolo XI al XIII* (Rome, 1933); Roberto Cessi, *Le Colonie medioevali italiane in Oriente* (Bologna, 1942); Lopez, *Storia delle colonie genovesi nel Mediterraneo* (Bologna, 1938); *idem, Genova marinara nel Duecento: Benedetto Zaccaria* (Messina and Milan, 1933); Bruno Dudan, *Il Dominio veneziano nel Levante* (Bologna, 1938); Lamberto Naldini, "La Politica coloniale di Pisa nel medio evo," *Bolletino storico pisano,* n.s., VIII (1939), 64–87; Giuseppe Rossi-Sabatini, *L'Espansione di Pisa nel Mediterraneo* (Florence, 1935); Guido Astuti, "La Posizione giuridica

the same state. Despite these variations, however, we are justified in viewing the communes in the east as a whole; in fact, they were so viewed at the time.

In a society based fundamentally on feudo-vassalic relations, the commune seemed an anomaly to the jurists. Small wonder, then, that Philip of Novara, John of Ibelin, and, what is even more significant, the *Assises de la Cour des Bourgeois* have so little to tell us about them. Had we been left with these legal sources alone we could hardly have known that we were dealing with major economic powers in the east, powers which, from the middle of the thirteenth century on, directly influenced the destinies of the crusader states.

We do not know how these communes were regarded by the Frankish burgesses, but we know something of the feelings of the knights. One young knight, disappointed that his fiancee had been given in marriage to a rich merchant-prince of Pisa, expressed the sentiments of his class when he complained that "he [Raymond III of Tripoli] gave her away to a *vilain.*" "Because," we are told, "those of France despise those of Italy. And may they be as rich as possible, they will still always regard them as *vilains.* Because most Italians are usurers,

delle colonie di mercanti occidentali nel Vicino Oriente e nell' Africa settentrionale nel medio evo: Le colonie genovesi," *Rivista di storia del diritto italiano,* XXV (1952), 19–34; Pietro S. Leicht, "La Posizione giuridica delle colonie . . .: Le colonie veneziane," *ibid.,* pp. 35–59 (both were lectures delivered at the International Congress of Comparative Law, London, 1950); Eugene H. Byrne, "Commercial Contracts of the Genoese in the Syrian Trade in the 12th Century," *Quarterly Journal of Economics,* XXXI (1916), 128–170; *idem,* "Genoese Trade with Syria in the 12th Century," *American Historical Review,* XXV (1919–1920), 191–219; *idem,* "The Genoese Colonies in Syria," in *The Crusades and Other Historical Essays Presented to Dana C. Munro,* ed. Louis J. Paetow (New York, 1928), pp. 139–182; *idem, Genoese Shipping in the Twelfth and Thirteenth Centuries* (Cambridge, Mass., 1930); Gino Luzzatto (originally published in 1941 under pseudonym A. Padovan), "Capitale e lavoro nel commercio veneziano dei secoli XI e XII," *Studi di storia economica veneziana* (Padua, 1954), pp. 89–117; *idem,* "Capitalismo coloniale nel Trecento," *ibid.,* pp. 117–123; *idem,* "Les Activités économiques du patriciat vénitien (X–XIV s.)," *ibid.,* pp. 125–165; David Jacoby, "L'Expansion occidentale dans le Levant: Les Vénitiens à Acre dans la seconde moitié du treizième siècle," *Journal of Medieval History,* III (1977), 225–264; André E. Sayous, "Le Commerce et la navigation des Génois au XIIe et XIIIe siècles," *Annales,* III (1931); *idem,* "L'Activité des deux capitalistes-commerçants marseillais," *Revue d'histoire économique et sociale,* XVII (1929), 132–155; *idem,* "Aristocratie et noblesse à Gênes," *Annales,* IX (1937), 366–381; Lopez, "Aux origines du capitalisme génois," *Annales,* IX (1937), 422–454; *idem,* "La Colonizzazione genovese nella storiografia più recente," *Atti del terzo Congresso di studi coloniali* (Florence, 1937), 247–261; Reynolds, "In Search of a Business Class in Thirteenth Century Genoa," *Journal of Economic History,* supp. V (1945), 1–19; Krueger, "Genoese Merchants, Their Partnerships and Investments, 1155–1164," in *Studi in onore di Armando Sapori* (2 vols., Milan, 1957), I, 257–271; Bautier, "Les Grands problèmes politiques et économiques de la Méditerranée médiévale," *Revue historique,* CCXXXIV (1965), 1–28; *idem,* "Les Relations économiques des occidentaux avec les pays d'Orient au moyen-âge: Points de vue et documents," *Sociétés et compagnies de commerce en Orient et dans l'océan indien,* ed. Mollat (Paris, 1966), pp. 263–331.

or pirates, or merchants, and because the others are *chevaliers,* they despise them."[156] Such a comment is natural for the young squire Ernoul, who elsewhere describes the inhabitants of Damascus as "soft people and bad people (*mauvais pueple*), as are always those who are merchants and artisans."[157] Legal status and public opinion combined, therefore, to define the members of the communes as a class apart, reinforced by their economic standing, rivaled neither by noble nor by burgess. Although we dispose of a rather rich documentation regarding the privileges accorded by the crusader states to the different communes, and have hundreds of entries in notarial registers and copies of agreements to facilitate the description of the commercial activities of the communes, we are left with very few sources regarding the actual settlements of the communes in the east. So far, only one register kept in the east, with a few entries dealing with Beirut,[158] has come to light. The registers of the local courts of the communes, which existed[159] and could have served as the main source for the life of the communes in the east, seem to have been definitely lost, probably during the sack of Acre in 1291.

The first privileges accorded the different communes are not always explicit enough to allow us to determine what kind of settlements or colonies were envisaged. Moreover, experience in colonization, even for Venice, was very limited. As a matter of fact, the communes in the crusader states represent the first colonial enterprise by the maritime cities, as distinct from land colonization by peasants, outside the frontiers of European society. The Italians, it seems, did not think in terms of emigration and colonization, but rather in terms of dominating the lines of communication and commerce between the eastern shores of the Mediterranean and Europe. Lodgings in the ports, warehouses for merchandise to be transported to the west, a number of people on the spot to guard property, to protect privileges against outside encroachments, and to arbitrate quarrels between merchants and sea captains—these were the immediate aims of the merchant adventurers at the dawn of the twelfth century. Often the privileges brought more than was foreseen and certainly more than was needed. There are constant references to large spaces in the newly

156. Ernoul, *Chronique,* ed. Mas Latrie, p. 114, developed in *Eracles,* XXIII, 34 (*RHC, Occ.,* II, 51–52).

157. *Eracles,* XXXIII, 59 (*RHC, Occ.,* II, 432).

158. Desimoni, "Actes passés en 1271, 1274 et 1279 par devant des notaires génois," *AOL,* I (1881), 434–534.

159. E.g., Statut de Marseille de 1253 à 1255, I, 17, in Jean M. Pardessus, *Collection de lois maritimes,* IV, 256 ff.; repr. in Gustave Fagniez, *Documents relatifs à l'histoire de l'industrie et du commerce en France,* I (Paris, 1898), 180.

conquered cities. Often the merchants claimed and were given a third of a city; sometimes they were allotted quarters in all cities to be conquered or all cities of the kingdom. These privileges, if carried out to the letter, would have left hardly any city in the kingdom to the king or his vassals. The lavishness of grants and privileges not only reflects the urgent needs of the crusaders, but also, on both sides, ignorance of the real needs and possibilities. The princes may have hoped to locate Italian merchants in all their cities. The Italians, who were in a good bargaining position, demanded as much as possible. But experience soon proved that quarters in inland cities, like the capital, Jerusalem, were of no practical use to merchants whose main interest was in the *catena,* in the customs-office of the port, where ships anchored and cargoes were exported to Europe. As a matter of fact, the communes were concentrated in only a few ports. Cities like Caesarea, Ascalon, and even Jaffa, although some communes had privileges in them, never housed any communal colony. Antioch, Tripoli, Tyre, and Acre dominated commerce and their economies in turn were dominated by the communes.

Consequently it was the purely commercial clauses in the privileges, added to the physical arrangements for lodgings, warehouses, and bazaars, which were of importance at the outset. The status of extraterritoriality was at this stage of secondary importance.

The early communal population underwent continual change. These were not settlers and colonizers, but merchants on the move, seeking a foothold in the port and customs franchises to assure preferential status to their commerce. Their families and properties remained in Genoa, Pisa, or Venice. The ports of the crusader states were only so many stopping places on their voyages. True, the exigencies of commerce made their stops rather prolonged. Genoese or Venetians embarking for a crusaders' port in the last days of September, so as to arrive before Christmas, usually remained for several months, until Easter,[160] although the bulk of their business seems to have been transacted during the first fifteen to thirty days after their arrival.[161] Business itself, almost to the end of the twelfth century, primarily took the form of exchange of precious metals from the west in return for eastern products. Not until the middle of the century was Europe able to export its own half-finished or finished products for eastern goods. During the months of stay in the east the Italian merchant found his compatriots, neighbors, and business associates from the Rialto in

---

160. Byrne, "Commercial Contracts of the Genoese," p. 133.

161. This was the normal delay for paying off loans contracted in the metropolis; cf. Morozzo della Rocca and Lombardo, *Documenti,* I, nos. 48, 53, 81, and *passim.*

Venice, or the neighborhood of San Lorenzo in Genoa or San Pietro in Pisa, living in common lodgings, very often the chambers (*camerae*) of the huge warehouse, above the shops and stores in his national quarter.[162] The commune in the east supplied a social framework of life, replacing family and neighbors in far-off Italy. Compatriots spoke their local Italian dialects among themselves, and wrote their commercial agreements in barbarous Latin stuffed with Italian commercial terms. They had their own bakery and their own bath. The church of their quarter, subordinated to the cathedral in the metropolis but with a familiar rector, took care of their spiritual needs and, at death, of their testaments and burials. Only those who know the sorrow of exile can appreciate the importance of transplanting familiar institutions to a foreign country.

These "trans-hibernating" early colonies in the east, if we may so describe the merchants who remained in the east from December to April, were predominantly societies of sea captains, sailors, and merchants. Combining seafaring and commerce, money-changing, importing, exporting, and piracy when conditions were propitious, they moved back and forth from Venice or Genoa to Alexandria, Acre, or Constantinople, sometimes to Cyprus and Crete. Once a year or once every two years, they would make a longer stay in the east, for four or five months. They had no real home other than in Italy.[163] Their numbers were not large. The cartulary of John Scriba proves that as late as the middle of the twelfth century, not more than one merchant ship went annually from Genoa to the east.[164] The number of merchants in their eastern emporia should consequently not be counted in hundreds but in scores.

The merchants of the different communes, though belonging to the same class, in everyday life competed with one another. The neighborhood of their quarters or warehouses was marked by rivalry rather than coöperation. Transactions between one group and another seem to have been exceedingly limited. This might have been because it was easier and safer to do business with one's own compatriots, who could be summoned to one's own city court when back in Italy. But it is likely that from the beginning the rivalry between Genoa and

---

162. See the description of the Venetian quarter in Tyre in the 1243 report of Marsiglio Zorzi, in Tafel and Thomas, II, 351 ff.

163. A typical captain and merchant was the Venetian Romano Mairano (mid-twelfth century). The study by Reinhard Heynen, *Zur Entstehung des Kapitalismus in Venedig* (Stuttgart, 1905; repr. New York, 1971), ridiculed by Max Weber, has been vindicated by Luzzatto, "Capitalismo coloniale nel Trecento," pp. 117–123. The Mairano family awaits a biographer.

164. Byrne, "Commercial contracts of the Genoese," p. 134.

Pisa and later between Venice and the other two mercantile cities, and their fickle alliances which turned into war on land and sea, created barriers between the nationals of the different colonies. They might have been regarded by everyone else in the kingdom as a class apart, but the class was composed of bitter rivals.

This early communal phase in the east roughly coincided with the first decade of the history of the crusader states, the period of conquest. The respective communes engaged in varying degrees and in different places and times in the capture of the coastal cities of Syria and Palestine. Transportation of crusaders and food, warfare, and spoils were at this time more important than commerce. We find Italians, as late as 1110, massacring the native population of Sidon (although the barons wanted, for understandable reasons, to keep the city and its population intact), despite the fact that they were accorded privileges in the place.[165]

It is probably only in the second decade of the kingdom, when all the coastal cities, from Antioch southwards, had been captured (with the exception of Tyre and Ascalon, which fell in 1124 and 1153 respectively), that commerce acquired a more regular rhythm. The Moslem danger on the seas was diminishing, immigration from Europe was growing and turning the exceedingly small crusader settlements into sizable colonies, more stable conditions favored the extension of commerce and the growth of the merchant colonies. The result was a transition from a sporadic or seasonal fair of wandering merchants to a fixed market, favoring the emergence of a permanent merchant class. It was a slow process whose main feature was the transition from prolonged stays in the east to permanent settlement. This took place in the second quarter of the twelfth century, a generation after the conquest. The well-known *Pactum Warmundi* signed in 1123 by Gormond of Picquigny, the patriarch of Jerusalem (in the absence of Baldwin II, taken prisoner by the Moslems), to assure Venetian help in capturing Tyre, indicates a new phase in the life of the communes beyond the sea. The *Pactum Warmundi*[166] not only assured the Venetians commercial privileges and a third of Tyre, but a kind of autonomy, which one might be prompted to call a real state within the state.[167] It was only the belated intervention of Baldwin II which assured some

---

165. On the massacre in Beirut see Albert of Aachen, XI, 17 (*RHC, Occ.,* IV, 670–671).

166. Tafel and Thomas, I, no. 40.

167. See the report of Marsiglio Zorzi, *ibid.,* II, 351 ff. The position of the Venetians is succinctly stated in a privilege accorded by John of Montfort (1277) in Tyre: "Quod . . . habeant tertiam partem civitatis . . . legaliter et regaliter, sicut consortes et veri domini ipsius tertiae partis": *ibid.,* III, 150.

semblance of reciprocal obligations between the commune and the state, in the form of the service of three knights owed by the Venetians to the king.[168]

The Venetians now claimed not only full jurisdiction (the limitation to civil cases only must have been a later royal interpretation, because there is nothing about it in the *Pactum*) over their own nationals and in mixed cases, but also complete authority over all inhabitants of their third of the city, the Venetian quarter in Tyre. The formula used to describe the new prerogative is explicit and very significant: "Besides, the Venetians will have the same rights of jurisdiction and taxation over burgesses of whatever origin, living in the quarter and the houses of the Venetians, as the king has over his own."[169] This seems to be a new departure, which we find again when the Venetians sum up the treaty in regard to Tyre (later put into practice), and Ascalon and Jerusalem (not implemented, because of no special interest to the Venetians). The Venetians would hold their third of Tyre and Ascalon *libere et regaliter, sicut rex alias duas [partes]*.

At this time no other commune enjoyed such privileges. It is even more striking that no baron of the kingdom, either in Jerusalem or even in Antioch, could claim such an independent status. The "collective seigneur," if one is allowed to apply a late legal fiction to the Venetian quarter in Tyre about 1124, was more independent than any contemporary vassal of the king. The only exception was perhaps Jubail, where a third of the city was granted in 1104 to the Genoese, and later the whole city, which the commune finally enfeoffed to the Embriachi (after a period of administration of its third by one Ansaldo Corso).[170]

The *Pactum Warmundi* is not only important in establishing an extraterritorial colony. No less significant is the privilege which it accorded the Venetians of a third of "all lands belonging to it [Tyre]."[171] Earlier treaties sometimes gave the communes land "one mile" around the city.[172] This might have been a deliberately vague phrase or a precaution to assure food and provision to be sold to the commune or

168. Confirmation by Baldwin II in 1125: *ibid.,* I, no. 41 (pp. 90–94).
169. *Ibid.,* I, 88.
170. Imperiale di Sant Angelo, *Codice diplomatico,* no. 14, quoting Caffaro. The original agreement is lost and the terms of Caffaro, although explicit enough, do not allow a more detailed analysis.
171. Tafel and Thomas, I, 68.
172. E.g., in Baldwin I's grant to the Genoese of a third of Arsuf "cum tertia parte illius terre usquequo distenditur leuga una et unum casale in eadem." The same is granted in Caesarea, Acre, and elsewhere: "One third of all cities captured with their help and a third of the revenue from land in the radius of one mile": Müller, *Documenti,* no. 15.

even grown for it. In Tyre we meet with a different approach. A whole third of a rich seigneury which, despite its narrow frontiers, counted some 120 villages,[173] from then on belonged to the Venetian commune. It was a logical demand on the part of the Venetians. Having created an independent lordship, they demanded, and were granted, a seigneury of the normal Palestinian type, comprising a city serving as capital and a surrounding rural area, with its villages and peasants, as its domain. But we may suppose another factor which influenced the Venetian demand. It is hard to believe that the Venetians claimed jurisdiction over all the inhabitants of their quarter, and sought a rural area nearby, which would need constant care and the establishment of an administration, solely for the benefit of a changing population of sailors and merchants. Nor could the Venetians have thought as early as 1123 to exploit their possessions on the later colonial pattern. Certainly, any income accruing from these possessions would profit the metropolis, but it seems more likely that the Venetians began to think in terms of colonization and settlement following the experience gained in the Latin kingdom itself. While the main occupation of Venetian settlers was commerce, the enfeoffment of a part of their property, the establishment of a local administration to supervise and exploit the rural area and to collect dues and customs from the inhabitants of the quarters—in brief the establishment of an organization to create and run a lordship—reflects a major change in the social and demographic composition of the commune in the east. Although it might be debatable whether this change has already taken place before the signing of the *Pactum Warmundi,* or whether it was the *Pactum* which created the necessary conditions for such a change, the second quarter of the twelfth century witnessed the formation of a real Italian settlement, a real colony in the ports of the kingdom.[174]

The basis of this somewhat sedentary population was an abundance of communal land and city possessions. Somebody had to administer these and keep an eye on rulers who tended to forget the original terms of the privileges.[175] Meanwhile, commerce was getting more

173. Prawer, "Étude de quelques problèmes," pp. 5-61; tr. as "Palestinian Agriculture and the Crusader Rural System," in *Crusader Institutions,* pp. 143-200.

174. The success of the colonizing efforts is eulogized in a well-known chapter of Fulcher of Chartres written (fourth redaction) about 1124 (ed. Hagenmeyer, III, 37) and in a passage of Ekkehard of Aura's *Hierosolymita* (ed. Hagenmeyer [Tübingen, 1877], cap. 36), written between 1114 and 1117 as an exhortation aiming to stimulate greater support for the new state; cf. Prawer, "The Settlement of the Latins in Jerusalem," pp. 490 ff.

175. The Genoese went so far as to erect a monument in the church of the Holy Sepulcher with an inscription recording their participation in the crusades and the contents of their privileges. See the facsimile in Caffaro's *Annali,* ed. Luigi T. Belgrano, I (Rome, 1890), p. 114.

voluminous[176] and more people settled in the east. The advantages of establishing business headquarters in a communal quarter in Antioch, Acre, or Tyre were evident. Until the middle of the thirteenth century no riots or pogroms against the communes, like those in Constantinople, no seizures of property, were ever witnessed in the crusader states. Merchants arranging to go to the east knew beforehand that they would stay there for three to five years. Some would even bring their wives and children. The contracts show names with eastern patronymics, like Bertrand from Syria, John Andrew of Tripoli, John of Acre, Bonvassal of Antioch. Some introduced clauses into their contracts like "if I stay overseas," "if I do not come back from Syria."[177] These are Genoese examples, but Venetian contracts of the same period, or even somewhat earlier, mention merchants as "inhabitant of Acre" or "inhabitant of Tyre," and we even find a Venetian, William Scriba, from Genoese Jubail.[178] These examples illustrate the fact that in the middle of the twelfth century the communes had entered a new phase. Merchants were no longer occasional residents for the duration of a business voyage, a winter, or even a year, but genuine colonists, subjects of their mother-cities but settled in the crusader states. No wonder then that at the end of the first kingdom we find Italian families which had lived in the east for three generations. An example, preserved in a Venetian contract, shows one Peter Morosini as an inhabitant of Acre in the second half of the twelfth century, his son James, who established himself in Tripoli, and his grandson Nicolino, who lived in Acre in 1203, when he signed an agreement with one of the merchant-captains.[179] Peter Morosini still possessed property in Venice when he was described as *Petrus Maurocenus de Acris,*[180] but his descendants probably sold their property in Venice before finally settling in the east.

A different view is taken by Mayer and Favreau, "Das Diplom Balduins I. für Genua und Genuas goldene Inschrift in der Grabeskirche," *Quellen und Forschungen aus den italienischen Archiven und Bibliotheken,* LV/LVI (1976), 22–95. This is contested by Benjamin Z. Kedar.

176. Although, as suggested by Cahen, "Orient latin et commerce du Levant," pp. 328 ff., the trade with Alexandria and Constantinople surpassed by far that with the crusader states, there is no doubt that the absolute volume of the latter was continually growing. Byrne has estimated the volume of trade for the years 1156–1164 at 10,075 Genoese pounds for Syria, but 9,031 for Alexandria. In 1191 alone Syrian contracts reached the sum of 6,000, and in 1205, 8,000; see Byrne, "Genoese Trade with Syria," pp. 202 (note 37), 211.

177. Quoted from Genoese registers by Byrne, *ibid.,* p. 213 (notes 83–84).

178. Morozzo della Rocca and Lombardo, *Documenti,* I, nos. 158, 171: "habitator Achon, habitator Acres"; no. 321: "Guilielmo Scribano de Çebeleto [Jubail]"; no. 373: "habitator in Tyro."

179. *Ibid.,* II, no. 463: "Manifestus sum ego quidem Nicolinus Maurocenus filius quondam Jacobi Mauroceni habitator Tripoli, quod Jacobus filius fuit quondam Petri Mauroceni habitatoris Acconis. . . ."

180. Lombardo and Morozzo della Rocca, *Nuovi documenti,* no. 17 (June 1162).

The sources, so rich in what regards commerce, fail to tell us much about the Italian colonists themselves. They did not as a rule include the patriciate of their native cities, with one notable exception, that of the Genoese "Visconti" family of the Embriachi, administrators of one-third and then lords of the entire city of Jubail. The wealthy nobility, at least in Genoa, controlled the eastern trade, but as far as we can see, did not settle in the east. In Venice, however, there was no patrician monopoly of the eastern trade. From the beginning the average Venetian investment surpassed by far the Genoese individual investment, possibly because Venice had more experience in eastern trade, possibly also because there was more liquid capital to be had in Venice than in Genoa.[181] The Della Voltas of Genoa had just enough liquid capital from city incomes to be able to invest in eastern trade. In Venice the diffusion of capital was greater, and already in the early twelfth century more people than the aristocracy alone could engage in trade.

The aristocracy, as said before, did not settle in the east. Even when participating in military expeditions they would hastily collect their share of the spoils, sometimes substantial,[182] and return to Italy.[183] Those who stayed behind to supervise the communal property were modest people of whom we know nothing but their names, an Ansaldo Corso in Genoese Jubail (1104), or Siegbald in Genoese Acre (1104).[184] Besides these officials the earliest settlers were probably recruited from among the sailors manning the ships going to the east. We know that sailors often invested in commerce that part of their salary paid to them before embarkation. This required knowledge of the east, its population, needs, markets, and commercial privileges. On a different level we find merchants, who often started with a small capital or no capital at all other than their skill and knowledge, and who made their living and sometimes fortunes by joining people of means in the Levant trade. These people, the *socii tractantes* or *portitores,* "factors" specializing in the eastern trade, gradually

181. The Genoese investments were rather small. In Venice the earliest contract (1104) for shipping food from Venice to Otranto and Antioch shows an investment of 150 pounds. Sums of 50, 100, and 200 pounds are frequent at the beginning of the twelfth century. An agreement (*colleganza*) between Henry Contarini and Domenico Giustiniani's widow in 1138 has the latter investing 1,000 pounds in a venture to Acre and elsewhere: Morozzo della Rocca and Lombardo, *Documenti,* I, no. 71.

182. Individual Genoese who took part in the capture of Caesarea in 1101 came away with sizable fortunes: Caffaro, *De liberatione civitatum orientis,* cap. 18 (*RHC, Occ.,* V, 65). For additional data see Prawer, *Latin Kingdom,* pp. 391–402.

183. After the capture and division of Tyre, the Venetians "recesserunt omnes ad sua": Fulcher of Chartres (ed. Hagenmeyer), III, 36.

184. Siegbald, the first Genoese viscount, was a canon of the church of San Lorenzo.

abandoned the sea to settle in one of the crusader ports, either as
agents of Italian merchant houses or doing business on their own.
Some sea captains, often proprietors of ships, might also establish
their home port in Syria, without discontinuing their voyages to Moslem and Byzantine ports.

Settlement in a foreign country was probably less of a change for
navigators and merchants than for the great mass of European peasants who overnight became burgesses in the crusader states. To settle
among fellow countrymen made adaptation easier; lodgings were rented
or bought from the communal authorities, and maritime commerce,
despite its risks and dangers, remained lucrative. Genoese documents
show profits of thirty percent per voyage or per year. Venetian documents tell us that the customary profit was twenty percent,[185] although
we find profits of thirty percent[186] and even more.[187] These still seem
modest when compared with the "sea loan," in which the interest to
be paid for a single voyage might reach one hundred percent, to offset the greater risk.

It seems that the Venetian colonies had a social structure somewhat
different from those of the Genoese and Pisans. We discern among
the Venetians a higher class of society established in the east, a feature unknown in the colonies of other communes. We know for example that a Vitale Pantaleone, called Malvoisin, son of John Pantaleone, had property in Tyre. Roland Contareno was richly enfeoffed
in the same place, and we can trace the same family for three generations in Tyre. William Jordan might have been a Venetian or a Provençal knight who married a Pantaleone and held rich property in
the place.[188] The existence of this element in the Venetian colony can
be explained by the fact that the Venetians, as masters of a third of
the lordship of Tyre, organized their administration by infeodating
part of their land and income to Venetians of patrician origin for
rent and military services. But whereas a similar practice by the Genoese
in Jubail ended with the full independence of the Embriachi,[189] the

185. Morozzo della Rocca and Lombardo, *Documenti,* II, no. 463:". . . ad racionem de
quinque sex per annum, secundum usum patrie Venecie [in 1202]."
186. *Ibid.,* I, no. 53 (1129): an investment of 50 bezants was supposed to return 65; the
investor gave final quittance, however, for only half that amount.
187. Whenever only the sum to be paid back (not the sum invested) is indicated, we may
safely assume that this was deliberately done to evade the anti-usury legislation.
188. All mentioned in the report of Marsiglio Zorzi describing the commune's property
in Tyre and Acre.
189. In 1147 the Embriachi were already twenty years behind in their payments. However,
the authorities reëstablished them as nominal vassals of the commune; Ricotti, *Liber iurium,*

Venetians, far better organized, kept an eye on their nationals, although some losses were inevitable.

Another reason the Venetians had settlers of a higher social class probably stems from the fact that some of the Venetian representatives in the east who were of knightly origin stayed on. Some had commercial connections before being appointed and then remained in the place. As an example we may cite Domenico Acontano, who in 1184 administered the possessions of St. Mark in Tyre.[190] He later served as bailie of Venice, although not a very successful one.[191] One member of the same family, Guy, witnessed an act of Philip Corner, bailie of Venice in 1222 in Acre, and another, John, served in the same year as ambassador of the Venetian bailie in Acre to the consul of Pisa in the same city.[192] The commercial contracts of the Venetians show a number of noble families not only investing in trade with Acre and Tyre, but actually staying on and doing business in the Latin east.[193] We find, for example, James Dandolo doing business in Acre at the time of his death about 1186. His son John was acting as viscount of Venice in Tyre and Acre in 1209.[194] Since he had guaranteed the loans of his brother Mark, he found himself in an embarrassing position when, as viscount, he had to announce his own insolvency in the court over which he was presiding.[195] Another family was the Dulce (Dulcis, Dous). Manasseh Dulce was viscount of Venice in Tyre, a Thomas Dulce had property in the city and was administrator of the property of St. Mark, a Peter Dulce was known in Acre from

---

I, no. 137. In 1154 the commune enfeoffed its possessions in Antioch and Acre to the Embriachi: *ibid.,* I, nos. 173, 196. Alexander III in 1180 and Urban III in 1186 tried to intervene on behalf of the privileges of the commune: Röhricht, *Regesta,* no. 580.

190. Morozzo della Rocca and Lombardo, *Documenti,* I, no. 350.

191. He was accused of losing possessions through negligence.

192. Röhricht, *Regesta,* nos. 956, 961.

193. The following are from vol. I of Morozzo della Rocca and Lombardo, *Documenti:* Domenico Michiel, possibly in Antioch, 1104 (no. 31); Marino Michiel and Otto Falier in Acre, 1129 (no. 53); Otto Falier in Syria, 1130 (no. 56); Viviano da Molin in Acre, 1130 (no. 59); Marino Michiel in Tyre, 1132 (no. 62); Henry Contarini in Acre, 1138 (no. 71); Marino Michiel in Acre, 1147 (no. 90); John Dandolo in Acre, 1161 (no. 155); for the three generations of the Morosini, see above, note 179; Peter Ziani in Acre, 1178 (nos. 289, 292); James Dandolo in Acre, 1186 (no. 376); Marco Contarini in Tyre, 1190 (no. 385); Domenico Contarini in Tyre, 1192 (nos. 411–412); and II: James Dandolo in Acre, 1192 (no. 463); John and Marco Dandolo in Acre, 1209 (no. 509); Marco Giustiniani in Tyre and Acre, 1209 (nos. 510, 514, 521); Leonard Querini in Acre, 1209 (no. 514); one of the Nenni, a priest, in Acre, 1209 (no. 514); John and Marco Dandolo in Tyre, 1211 (no. 529). These examples prove that the theory of Sayous regarding capitalists and factors in Venice is untenable; cf. Luzzatto, "Capitale e lavoro nel commercio veneziano," pp. 117–123.

194. Morozzo della Rocca and Lombardo, *Documenti,* I, no. 376; II, no. 513.

195. *Ibid.,* II, no. 521.

1209,[196] a Domenico Dulsi in Tyre in 1211.[197] Another case is that of the knightly family of the Falieri. They appear as early as 1129 and 1130 transacting business in Acre, although we do not know if Otto Falier,[198] mentioned in these early documents, had any fiefs in Tyre. Members of the family, some still in Venice, others in Syria, appear again in 1206, when at the death of Leo Falier his brother Vitale, still living in Venice, was enfeoffed by the doge of Venice, Peter Ziani, with his late brother's property.[199]

As has been said, the settlement of patrician families in the east seems to have been characteristic only of the Venetian colony. Despite a far richer Genoese documentation we can seldom discern any such trait in their eastern colonies, although it was not entirely unknown. The Genoese viscount in Acre in 1212, Simon Rufferio, left his son a fief in the kingdom after his departure from Syria. Belmusto Lercario, consul in Syria in 1203, secured a fief which was still in his family in 1253. On the other hand Simon Malocello, consul in Acre in 1249–1250, who engaged actively and profitably in the eastern commerce just before and after his tenure of office, invested the profits from his large enterprises not by founding a family fortune in the east but by buying up landed property in Genoa,[200] to which he ultimately returned.

We have few sources regarding the Pisan colony in the east. There was a wealthy Pisan in Tripoli with the non-noble name of Plebanus, who rose to the lordship of Botron by marrying the heiress, Marguerite (or Cecilia) Doral, and paying her guardian, Raymond III of Tripoli, her weight in gold.[201] Of Pisan origin also were the members of the "Fraternity of the Vermiliores" participating in the Third Crusade and richly endowed by Conrad of Montferrat (d. 1192). They were probably an essentially knightly brotherhood.[202] Unfortunately neither the origin nor the later activities of this brotherhood are known.

Below this element composed of members of noble families, consular families, or families holding lesser offices at home, and below the ship captains and factors or agents of European houses who set-

196. Thomas and Manasseh are mentioned in the report of Marsiglio Zorzi; Peter Dulce witnessed an act in October 1209, in Acre; Morozzo della Rocca and Lombardo, *Documenti,* II, no. 513.

197. *Ibid.,* II, no. 529.

198. *Ibid.,* I, nos. 53, 56, 57.

199. Tafel and Thomas, II, 11–13. In 1209 Angelo Falier was procurator of St. Mark: Morozzo della Rocca and Lombardo, *Documenti,* II, no. 513.

200. See Byrne, "The Genoese Colonies in Syria," pp. 171–172.

201. *Eracles,* XXIII, 34 (*RHC, Occ.,* II, 50–52).

202. Müller, *Documenti,* nos. 27–28.

tled in the ports of the kingdom, the bulk of the colonists came from the *popolani* of the respective metropolis. Unfortunately no cartulary of any court in the east, nor any register of a notary, makes this anonymous mass more articulate.

The size of the different colonies cannot be statistically estimated, although some impressions can be gathered from the inventories of the different communes. These inventories give some idea of the size of the Italian settlements, and also reveal an interesting feature. The Venetian quarter in Tyre counted some fifty houses (*domus, habitationes*), besides a great number of shops (*stationes*) and warehouses.[203] The Genoese inventory for Acre lists no less than forty-eight houses,[204] which makes it a very substantial quarter. The interesting feature is that some of these buildings, especially the larger ones, the *palazzi,* remained empty during the greater part of the year. While the permanently occupied houses of the Genoese in Acre brought in no more than 358 bezants, the seasonally rented buildings produced more than 1,000 bezants a year. This seasonal renting was done on the arrival of the European ships with the *passagium* or *caravana* once or twice yearly. Then all the palazzi, loggiae, stalls, and storehouses with their small rooms above were immediately rented to the highest bidder.[205] There is a typical entry in the Venetian inventory: "Two small shops [*stationes*] with a small room above them, which are empty. If rented they pay 24 bezants each per month. But for the greater part of the year they stay empty."[206]

This particular feature is indicative of the nature of the Italian colonies. The colony expanded immensely once or twice yearly with the arrival of the ships from the homeland. The colony was composed, as a rule, of a permanent nucleus, by now substantial in size, and a transient merchant population which stopped in the place to transact its business under the protection of its quarter and then embarked for other ports of the Levant or to Italy.

The interests of these two categories of Italians were not always identical. The transient element was primarily interested in commercial privileges, while the settled colonists were concerned with their

---

203. Tafel and Thomas, II, 534 ff.

204. Published by Desimoni in *AOL,* II-2 (1884), 215 ff.

205. Marsiglio Zorzi: "Omnes predicte [11] domus incantantur cum caravana Venecia in Accon": Tafel and Thomas, II, 393. "Est una domus . . . que non locatur nisi mercatoribus, qui venerunt de Venecia. Que, cum est garavana in Accon, consuevit incantari in mense Bis. XII": *ibid.,* II, 391. Genoese inventory of its property in Acre: "Possessiones quae ad passagium apautantur": *AOL,* II-2 (1884), 215.

206. Tafel and Thomas, II, 364. The rent is extremely high. On the number of houses and their income, see Prawer, *Crusader Institutions,* pp. 234 ff.

possessions, their business, and their general standing in the kingdom. Holding vineyards and courtyards, and with homes and shops on their own land,[207] they were citizens of the city, not to say of the kingdom, enjoying extensive commercial privileges, giving little in return. Their Frankish co-citizens, paying taxes and owing military service, to say nothing of market tolls and port customs, were in comparison at a distinct disadvantage. Fifty years after the conquest it was easy to forget the services that the Italians rendered in the first decade of the existence of the crusader states. It is not surprising, therefore, that attempts were made to abrogate their privileges. But this was not easy to do; even the Holy See intervened on their behalf. Still their position must have been annoying to the local population. If transient Italians bringing in ships and merchandise might claim to serve the kingdom in some way, this was not true of the permanent Italian settlers. If they paid any taxes on their land in the cities and their neighborhood, it was to their own curia only.

This anomalous situation, of settlers exempt from all obligations yet enjoying all the privileges of burgesses, prompted Amalric, one of the most vigorous kings of Jerusalem, to decide on a new course. In a privilege to the Pisans in 1168, he was careful to indicate that their autonomous jurisdiction excluded "all those who are my men and have houses, income, or real estate in my kingdom."[208] These were to fall under the jurisdiction of the royal court. Raymond of Tripoli followed suit in his privilege to the Pisans in 1187.[209] Bohemond III of Antioch would specify in his privilege to the Genoese in 1189: *exceptis meis burgensibus Januensibus de Antiochia et Laodocia et Gabulo.*[210] Ten years later, in 1199, repeating this exception, he would add a significant prohibition, that the local Genoese could not be accepted into the "commune of Antioch."[211] But even this solution was only a partial one, for the local Genoese could easily arrange with their compatriots resident elsewhere in the crusader states to do their business for them, thus enjoying, as no local residents could, the commercial privileges of the commune. It was to prevent this abuse that Bohemond IV of Antioch extended the earlier prohibitions to

207. In 1154 Pisans received land in Latakia to build their houses: Müller, *Documenti,* no. 4. The privilege of Amalric as count of Jaffa, accorded to the Pisans in 1157, is typical: "plateam unam . . . ut in ea componant sibi domos et faciant ibidem forum sibi . . . [et] locum unum ad fabricandum sibi in eo ecclesiam": *ibid.,* no. 6.

208. *Ibid.,* no. 11: "praeter illos qui homines mei sunt et mansiones seu redditus et possessiones stabiles in regno meo habent."

209. *Ibid.,* no. 22.

210. Imperiale di Sant Angelo, *Codice diplomatico,* II, 184.

211. Ricotti, *Liber iurium,* I, 433: "quos in eorum communione recepi non permitto."

make them more effective. In his privilege to the Genoese in 1205, he excluded "the burgesses of the kingdom of Jerusalem, the county of Tripoli, Cyprus, and the principality of Antioch."[212] At the same time Plebanus, the Pisan who became the lord of Botron, limited his own compatriots in the same way. In an exemption from almost all customs in his lordship of Botron, he stipulated: "From this privilege are excepted all those who took the oath of citizenship of Pisa and live in the land of Tripoli and all our men who live in the land of Botron."[213] The aim of this new legislation is best expressed by Henry of Champagne (1192–1197) who, when renewing (and limiting) the privileges of the Pisans in Tyre, added: "If any Pisan holds from me a *burgisia,* then either he leaves it to me and will be free as other Pisans, or if he wants to hold my *burgisia,* he will be obliged to me as are other burgesses."[214]

The purpose of these limitations was to confine the commercial privileges to those whose commerce brought in revenue and business, and to ensure that services in taxes or otherwise should be paid by those who earned their living in the country, and who until then had been exempted from obligations by virtue of privileges accorded to their communes two or three generations earlier. Furthermore, it also meant the abrogation of extraterritoriality of Italian settlers in the east. They would have to become burgesses of the different lordships, juridically on a par, although living in their own quarters, with other burgesses in the cities. The need for such a reform is self-evident; we can assign the innovation to Amalric's privilege to the Pisans of 1168. Together with the *Assise sur la ligèce,* which was intended to bring the subvassals into immediate contact with the king, the leveling of the status of the nationals of the communes would go far to integrate Frankish society in the kingdom. It is quite possible that Amalric received his inspiration from the Byzantine empire, where some years earlier Manuel I Comnenus had curtailed the Venetian (and possibly other Italian) privileges, introducing the distinction between traveling Italian merchants and those permanently established in the empire. The latter were to become, as our Greek source indicates, *bourgesioi* of the basileus.[215]

The constant recurrence of the limitation clauses in the privileges

212. *Ibid.,* I, 522.

213. Müller, *Documenti,* no. 53 (1202): "excepimus omnes illos qui iurebunt amodo honorem Pisane civitatis et habitantes sunt in terra Tripolis, et omnes nostros homines, qui habitant in terra Botroni."

214. *Ibid.,* no. 37.

215. Joannes Cinnamus, *De rebus gestis . . . Ioannis et Manuelis Comnenorum* (Troyes, 1652), p. 307; cf. Heyd, *op. cit.,* tr. Raynaud, I, 200.

suggests, however, that it was the colonies which triumphed and not the Frankish rulers, whose legislation came too late. It was not until seven years after the fall of the Latin kingdom that we find general legislation in the kingdom of Cyprus regarding *borgesies* in the hands of Italian settlers. By an ordinance of 1298 Henry II ordered the nationals of the communes to get rid of their *borgesies* within six months under threat of confiscation. Only with the king's assent were they to be allowed to hold *borgesies*.[216]

The economic power of the communes and their political standing were strengthened during the thirteenth century because of the disintegration of Frankish society. The support needed by rulers or those who claimed to rule strengthened the bargaining power of the communes and their settlers in the east. In times of crisis the communes were courted and received privileges, such as those accorded to the Pisans by Conrad of Montferrat in October 1187, granting them full jurisdiction over Pisans of whatever status, excluding only holders of fiefs and money-fiefs.[217] Another example is the privilege of Guy of Lusignan of November 1189, which was probably worded in a fraudulent way, so as to make any royal taxation of Pisans impossible.[218] Henry of Champagne tried to reverse this development in his privilege of May 1198, but such efforts were the exception and of no avail. The communes regarded themselves as part-lords of cities with full jurisdiction over the land and inhabitants of their quarters. An arbitration of 1212 shows the viscount of the Genoese in conflict with the consul of Pisa respecting the jurisdiction over a woman who had a *burgisia* in the Genoese quarter.[219]

The relative importance of the communes grew continually after the Third Crusade. The diminishing immigration from Europe, the internal political strife, and the financial situation brought into prominence those groups of society which, because of foreign affiliation, could take advantage of these difficulties. This was true both of the military orders and of the communes, who became controlling powers in the kingdom. The physical bases of their strength were the inhabitants of their quarters in the ports of the country and their navies controlling the seas.

With the end of the crusade of Frederick II we enter the gravest

---

216. As a matter of fact, Henry II's privilege (1291) to the Pisans of Nicosia says: "salvo di facto di giustitia et di borgesia": Müller, *Documenti,* no. 73.

217. *Ibid.,* no. 23.

218. *Ibid.,* nos. 23–25, 31–32.

219. *Ibid.,* p. 439 (*illustrazioni*).

period in the history of the kingdom. The state virtually disappeared as a political unit, and society was in chronic turmoil. The rival factions of nobility, the rivalries of the military orders, and the wars of the communes made the kingdom in the middle of the thirteenth century the most unedifying spectacle in Christendom. In these conditions any organized group became a power to be courted by the different factions. One has only to read the report of the Venetian viscount in Acre, Marsiglio Zorzi, in 1243–1244, when offering his commune's help to enthrone princess Alice against the claims of the Hohenstaufens, to realize that state and society were entirely atomized, and that there was no state interest to preserve unity or prevent decadence and collapse. We should like to know more about the Italian colonies in the period following the murderous war of St. Sabas in the middle of the thirteenth century, when Acre became the battlefield of Italian rivalries and jealousies, when whole city quarters were destroyed and stones and columns were taken as trophies of war to Italy.[220] We know far more about political events and the everyday fratricidal battles fought from the walls and ramparts of the city than about the lot of the population inhabiting the commercial quarters.

One feature seems to be clear, that the numbers of Italians permanently settled in the kingdom had grown. More and more people bearing such eastern patronymics as Bonvassallo of Antioch,[221] Ribaldus of Antioch,[222] Conrad of Acre,[223] and Roger de Ultramare[224] are mentioned in the national notarial registers. Not only professional merchants but also artisans engaged in the Levantine trade. One may assume that these *fabri, scutarii,* or *taiatores (tagliatores)*[225] borrowing money to trade in the east and carrying with them their own products, would stay on in the east, although a good many artisans invested their money only, themselves remaining in the west. Wealthy colonists bestowing large dowries, even of 1,000 bezants,[226] on their

220. The *colonni acritani,* two of which still adorn, rather incongruously, the Piazza San Marco in Venice, and which were traditionally linked to this event, came, it is now claimed, from Constantinople; see R. Martin Harrison and Nezih Firtali, "Excavations at Saraçhare in Istanbul," *Dumbarton Oaks Papers,* XIX (1965), 231–236.

221. *Lanfranco,* nos. 46, 87, 141, 330.

222. *Ibid.,* nos. 550, 610, 1299, 1312.

223. *Ibid.,* no. 1087.

224. *Ibid.,* no. 1111. Among those involved in a process in Genoa (1224) about debts and the sale of a ship in Acre, there were: "Obertus de Sancto Donato qui est Ultramare, Guillielmus de Sto. Donato qui est Ultramare et frater eius qui est Ultramare, Ugo de Campo qui est Ultramare, Bonvassalus et Rainerius eius cognatus qui sunt Ultramare, Jacobus magister axie qui est in Baruti": *Liber magistri Salmonis,* ed. Ferretto, p. 739.

225. *Lanfranco,* nos. 1130, 1181, 747.

226. The average income from a fief in the kingdom was 500 bezants a year.

daughters to secure a good marriage in the mother-city, and sons following their fathers to the east and later settling in the place despite the remonstrances of their families,[227] occur frequently.

Another indication of the increased number of colonists in the Latin east is the emergence of institutions enabling the colonists to impose control in some measure over officials sent from the European metropolis. The *consules* and *vicecomites* were appointed in the mother cities in Europe, usually from among men who had experience in the east. But they were appointed for a short term, usually not more than a year. Consequently an institution grew up which guaranteed that the management of local affairs would be based on knowledge of local conditions and would ensure the continuity of local policies. This institution was the *consilium,* mentioned several times after the middle of the thirteenth century, but without doubt existing earlier, perhaps from the beginning of the century.[228] The nature of this body is not very clear. It might have been a general assembly of the settlers, a kind of *magnum consilium,* but in all probability it was a select body of the leading members of the colony, more or less formally elected by the settlers. The scarcity of published documents does not permit us to say more.[229]

An indication of the cohesion of these colonies is the use of oaths, which in medieval usage gave the colony a corporate entity. We read that the inhabitants of the Venetian quarter of Tyre were obliged (1243) to take an oath of allegiance to Venice, which was also required of non-Venetians buying houses in the Venetian quarter.[230] An oath was imposed on the Genoese of Tyre in 1264. Whenever a change of officials occurred the new consuls and their counselors had to swear to keep the agreement with the lord of Tyre. But in addition, an oath of allegiance (worded in feudal terms) to the lord of Tyre was required of all Genoese staying in Tyre.[231]

In comparison with Venice and Genoa, the commune of Pisa had fewer possessions in the kingdom, and one has the impression that

227. Byrne, "Genoese Colonies in Syria," pp. 162 ff.

228. Expressly mentioned in Tyre (1206): "in palatio communis Januae ubi regitur consilium": Tafel and Thomas, III, 40. The agreement of 1264 between Philip of Montfort and the Genoese is signed on behalf of the latter by the *consilium Januae: AOL,* II-2 (1884), 225.

229. Among the Genoese witnessing an inventory of the commune's possessions (1249) was Peter Straleria, whose family, a branch of the Visconti, later related to the Malloni, was for some three generations connected with the east. The tombstone of John Straleria (d. 1203) is preserved in the museum of St. Anne of Jerusalem; cf. Belgrano, "La Lapide di Giovanni Stralleria e la famiglia di questo cognome," *Atti della Società ligure di storia patria,* XVII (1885), 198–225; and de Sandoli, *Corpus,* pp. 146–147.

230. Tafel and Thomas, II, 360–361.

231. *AOL,* II-2 (1884), 228.

the size of its colonies was smaller. The commune of Pisa, as we learn from a lengthy document, embraced Tuscans — people from Florence, Lucca, San Gimignano, Siena, and other such localities — who declared themselves Pisans in order to benefit from the privileges enjoyed by the Pisans (for which they probably paid), at the same time recognizing the authority of the consul of Pisa.[232] The same attitude of suspicion, noticeable in Genoa and Venice in regard to their representatives in the east, can also be found in Pisa. As late as 1286 the elected consul was barred for life from holding the same office again; the same was true for the official notary. Even the *consiliarii,* one a lawyer and the other a well-known merchant, were appointed in the mother city.[233] But in practice things worked out differently. A document from San Gimignano (1245) tells us that "the Pisans who are in Acre agree among themselves as to the consul and then send to the commune of Pisa, so that they should send the man proposed by them, and the commune of Pisa sends them the man they require."[234] If this was the practice regarding the consul, it is more than likely that it was also the practice in electing the counselors. Still, the mother city took care first and foremost of its traveling nationals, curtailing the right of the eastern Pisans to tax them in any but exceptional cases.[235]

Smaller communes like Marseilles do not seem to have created any large permanent settlements. Even the late statutes of the city (1253–1255) give the impression that the *fundacum,* the warehouse, and its guardian, the *fundegarius,* were the pivot of the commune's interests. The *rector* of Marseilles appointed the consul from among merchants going to Syria; he also appointed the counselors. The commune took a realistic view of its foreign representatives, requiring consuls to swear

232. "Si dixerint dictos consules preesse omnibus de Tuscia in Accon . . . dicant quomodo sciunt et si coguntur Florentini, Luccenses, Sangeminiacenses, Senenses et omnes alii de Tuscia dictis consulibus subesse si nolunt"; and again: "Quia homines de Tuscia, qui sunt in partibus ultramarinis libenter confitentur se Pisanos et gerunt se pro Pisanis, quia sunt franchi ad cathenam"; Robert Davidsohn, *Forschungen zur Geschichte von Florenz,* part II, *Aus den Stadtbüchern und Urkunden von San Gimignano* (Berlin, 1900), pp. 297, 298.

233. *Breve Pisani communis* (1286), 177, in Francesco Bonaini, *Statuti inediti della città di Pisa dal secolo XII al secolo XIV,* vol. I (Florence, 1854).

234. Davidsohn, *Geschichte von Florenz,* II, 298.

235. *Breve Pisani communis,* 177, in Bonaini, *Statuti inediti:* "Datam vel tinam aut collectam seu aliquid aliud, quocumque nomine censeatur, dictus consul, consiliarii et universitas Pisanorum in Accon non possit exigere . . . ab aliquo cive Pisano, nisi solum pro guerra communium alicuius mansionis, aut domini, vel baronis illarum partium christiani." The practice of taxation was current, as we learn from Genoese notarial registers. It was stipulated, for example, that loans contracted in Genoa to be paid back in Acre at a given rate, should be done "mundos a curia Janue et omnibus dispendiis et avariis" and "mundos a consulibus": *Lanfranco,* nos. 1150, 1175.

not to establish prostitutes in the *fundacum*. The *fundegarius* received his orders directly from the rector and the consul had no right to countermand them. In emergencies, ten or fifteen merchants had the right to elect a consul until the rector appointed one.[236] In the last quarter of the thirteenth century Marseilles's settlements in the east are reminiscent of those of the Italian communes 150 years earlier, in the first phase of their expansion in the Mediterranean.

The first outburst of colonizing fervor came to an end in the last quarter of the thirteenth century. By that time French written privileges were showing unmistakable influences of Italian; a Mediterranean "lingua franca," a mixture of French, Italian, and Greek, was spoken in the ports, making its way into written deeds. By that time, too, the Italian settlements had undergone profound changes. Despite their autonomy, despite their independent jurisdiction, they had adopted local customs even in their personal affairs. Nothing is more revealing than a Genoese marriage contract written in Acre in 1273, in which the marriage settlement was drawn up *secundum morem et consuetudinem civitatis Accon.*[237] The facts of intermarriage, and daily contacts with other Italians and the *pullani,* created conditions where social distinctions and differences in customs were slowly disappearing. But this process, which might have created a Levantine society in the modern sense of the word, was not allowed to continue. The Latin kingdom disappeared, and colonization of Syria and Palestine stopped, to be continued elsewhere in the Mediterranean and later on across the Atlantic in the New World.

---

236. *Statut de Marseille de 1253 à 1255,* I, cap. 17, in Fagniez, *Documents relatifs à l'histoire de l'industrie et du commerce en France,* I, 176-194; "De consulibus extra Massiliam constituendis," in *Les Statuts de Marseille,* ed. Régine Pernoud (Monaco and Paris, 1949).
237. Müller, *Documenti,* no. 102.

V

THE POLITICAL AND ECCLESIASTICAL ORGANIZATION OF THE CRUSADER STATES

Historians of the First Crusade have been unable to decide with certainty if, at the time the expedition set out, its promoters foresaw the establishment in the Holy Land of a colony of "Franks" charged with the duty of occupying the conquered territories and defending the holy places. We do know, however, that some crusaders at the time of their departure contemplated the possibility of settling in the east.[1] This might have referred, however, to becoming vassals of

The institutions of the Latin states in the east, especially the kingdom of Jerusalem, have given rise to a large literature because of the interest taken in the writings of the great jurists (conveniently edited by Auguste Beugnot, *RHC, Lois,* 2 vols.). There are some chapters devoted to institutions in works on particular crusader states: Claude Cahen, *La Syrie du nord à l'époque des croisades et la principauté franque d'Antioche* (IFD, BO, I; Paris, 1940); Jean Richard, *Le Comté de Tripoli sous la dynastie toulousaine, 1102–1187* (Paris, 1945), supplemented by "Le Comté de Tripoli dans les chartes du fonds des Porcellet," *Bibliothèque de l'École des chartes,* CXXX (1972), 339–382; *idem, Le Royaume latin de Jérusalem* (Paris, 1953); Hans E. Mayer, *The Crusades* (Oxford, 1972); Joshua Prawer, *Histoire du royaume latin de Jérusalem,* 2nd ed. (2 vols., Paris, 1975); *idem, The Latin Kingdom of Jerusalem: European Colonialism in the Middle Ages* (London, 1972); and *idem, Crusader Institutions* (Oxford, 1980), a collection of his articles.

Works more directly devoted to the history of institutions in the crusader states are Gaston Dodu, *Histoire des institutions monarchiques dans le royaume latin de Jérusalem* (Paris, 1894); John L. LaMonte, *Feudal Monarchy in the Latin Kingdom of Jerusalem, 1100 to 1291* (Cambridge, Mass., 1932); Cahen, "La Féodalité et les institutions politiques de l'Orient latin," *Oriente ed Occidente nel medio evo* (Accademia Nazionale dei Lincei, Fondazione Alessandro Volta, Atti dei convegni XII; Rome, 1957), pp. 167–191; Prawer, "Estates, Communities and the Constitution of the Latin Kingdom," *Proceedings of the Israel Academy of the Sciences and Humanities* II, no. 6 (Jerusalem, 1966); and Jonathan Riley-Smith, *The Feudal Nobility and the Kingdom of Jerusalem, 1174–1277* (London, 1973). Other studies, many of them important, as well as works on ecclesiastical institutions, will be cited in the notes which follow.

For the many political events which are frequently alluded to below, the reader is referred to the relevant chapters in the first two volumes of the present work.

1. Such a plan has been attributed to Godfrey of Bouillon and Raymond of St. Gilles; see John H. and Laurita L. Hill, *Raymond IV de Saint-Gilles, comte de Toulouse* (Toulouse, 1959), p. 26. Achard, lord of Montmerle, who was killed in 1099 (William of Tyre, VIII, 9;

the Byzantine emperor Alexius I Comnenus (1080–1118); Bohemond of Taranto was happy to receive a Byzantine title and an important fief in anticipation of lands which the crusaders might take from the Moslems.[2]

The reality must have quickly dispelled whatever plans the crusaders might have had. During the crossing of Anatolia, the emperor's representative Taticius entrusted the defense of conquered strongholds to certain Franks, probably as garrison commanders rather than as vassals. Such was the case with Peter of Aulps at Comana.[3] Bohemond himself got Taticius to give him the care of the fortresses of Cilicia when the Byzantine general left the crusading army.[4] And Raymond of St. Gilles appears to have persuaded the Byzantine officers to hand over to him Latakia and some places on the nearby coast.[5]

But when Taticius left, and Alexius Comnenus did not join the crusaders, the question was put in a new light. When Bohemond established himself at Antioch, having outmaneuvered the other barons who could claim to occupy the city with him, he did not seek to reconcile this occupation with the rights of the Byzantine emperor. When Baldwin of Boulogne established himself at Edessa, which the Moslems had never occupied during the Turkish conquest, he did not bother asking Alexius Comnenus to invest him with it. Still less would the Latins concern themselves with Byzantine claims on Jerusalem, which the Byzantines had not held for more than four centuries.

We know that Byzantium did not accept the *fait accompli*. Alexius tried to reoccupy by force the plain of Cilicia and even Antioch. In 1108, he imposed on Bohemond the treaty of Devol (Deabolis), which corresponded almost to what Bohemond himself had requested in 1096–1097: the Norman prince, accorded the title of *sebastos,* was to receive Antioch and Aleppo as a fief, while giving up Cilicia and the Syrian coast.[6] But the treaty remained a dead letter. Tancred and his successors refused to recognize the suzerainty of the emperor. John

---

in *RHC, Occ.,* I, 336–338), mentions in the donation which he made to Cluny before his departure the case where "quoquomodo illis in partibus remorari voluero" (Alexandre Bruel, ed., *Recueil des chartes de l'abbaye de Cluny,* V [Collection de documents inédits sur l'histoire de France, XVIII; Paris, 1894], 52 [no. 3703]).

2. Ralph B. Yewdale, *Bohemond I, Prince of Antioch* (Princeton, 1924); François L. Ganshof, "Recherches sur le lien juridique qui unissait les chefs de la première croisade à l'empereur byzantin," in *Mélanges offerts à M. Paul-E. Martin* . . . (Geneva, 1961), pp. 53–54.

3. *Gesta Francorum,* tr. Louis Bréhier, *Histoire anonyme de la première croisade* (Les Classiques de l'histoire de France au moyen-âge, IV; Paris, 1924), p. 61. Was the Burgundian knight Welf, who occupied Adana, a representative of the basileus?

4. Cahen, *Syrie du nord,* p. 214.

5. Hill and Hill, *Raymond IV,* pp. 127–130; Richard, *Comté de Tripoli,* pp. 10–11, 27–28.

6. Cahen, *Syrie du nord,* pp. 251–252; Yewdale, *Bohemond I,* pp. 124–130.

II Comnenus (1118–1143) intended to take Antioch back, granting the prince a fief to be conquered from the Moslems. It was only Manuel I Comnenus (1143–1180) who accepted a compromise: the prince would acknowledge himself to be a vassal of the empire, but keep his whole principality except Cilicia.[7] This state of affairs lasted from 1158 to 1182, but the decline of Byzantine power which resulted from the usurpation of Andronicus Comnenus (1183–1185) rendered the rights of the emperor over the principality meaningless. However, Bohemond IV, at the beginning of the thirteenth century, must have had these rights in mind when he claimed that he was the vassal of the Latin emperor of Constantinople, but that was an argument fashioned for the occasion.[8]

As for the county of Edessa, it accepted Byzantine suzerainty in 1137 at the time of the expedition of John Comnenus, and in 1150, when the countess Beatrice had to resign herself to abandoning what remained of the county, it was in fact to the emperor Manuel that she offered her castles, as prescribed by feudal law, which stipulated that when a vassal was forced to sell his fortresses he must offer them to his lord.[9]

The attempts aimed at recovering the territories conquered by the crusaders in the Byzantine empire were slow and hardly extended beyond the lands that the Turks had taken away from Byzantium at the end of the eleventh century. The excellent relations that Raymond of St. Gilles had maintained with the basileus were not enough to make the empire's rights over the county of Tripoli more effective.[10] It was above all the right of conquest, not imperial investiture, which gave rise to the new states. Moreover, this right of conquest was sometimes crowned by a decision of the council of barons who directed the *christiana militia*.[11] Bohemond asked for the agreement of his peers to legitimize his taking possession of Antioch. These were the barons who entrusted bishop Robert of Lydda with the government of Ramla and Godfrey of Bouillon with the government of Jerusalem.

---

7. Cahen, *Syrie du nord,* pp. 359–363, 399–402.

8. *Ibid.,* p. 619. Bohemond IV at the time (1213) was trying to avoid being judged by patriarch Albert of Jerusalem, who had been appointed by pope Innocent III to settle the question of the succession in Antioch.

9. Cahen, *Syrie du nord,* pp. 387–389.

10. I have concluded that there was a Byzantine suzerainty over the region of Tortosa and Maraclea, occupied by Raymond of St. Gilles with Byzantine assistance (Richard, *Comté de Tripoli,* pp. 26–30; cf. LaMonte, "To What Extent Was the Byzantine Empire the Suzerain of the Latin Crusading States?" *Byzantion,* VII [1932], 253).

11. Cf. Hill and Hill, "Justification historique du titre de Raymond de Saint-Gilles: 'Christiane milicie excellentissimus princeps'," *Annales du Midi,* LXVI (1954), 101–112.

However, neither Baldwin in Edessa nor Raymond in Albara[12] and later in Tripoli seems to have asked the other crusaders to acknowledge his rights.

From the very first, those who had taken possession of the towns regarded themselves as also possessing the territory that depended on them: Godfrey, in 1099, refused to allow Raymond to settle either at Ascalon or at Arsuf, and in 1102 Tancred got Raymond to withdraw from fortresses that he had occupied on the coast and in the Syrian interior, including Albara, which the Provençaux had occupied in 1098.[13] The division of the conquered territories among four lordships — Antioch, Edessa, Tripoli, and Jerusalem — was thus soon looked upon as final, and each of these powers considered itself qualified to occupy certain of the large towns still in Moslem hands. Further, the attempt of the Second Crusade to establish count Thierry of Flanders at Damascus (1148) and the plan to form, for his benefit, an independent principality around Shaizar (1157) ran up against the hostility of those princes who were already established.[14]

In this division, some of the rulers were led to take into account the boundaries which had existed before the crusade. The princes of Antioch, especially, appear to have wished to claim everything that had constituted the old Byzantine duchy of Antioch. They claimed the homage of the counts of Edessa, even resorting to open war,[15] and in 1109 Tancred won recognition of his suzerainty over the northern part of the county of Tripoli, along with the homage of its count, Bertrand of St. Gilles.[16]

This respect for preëxistent boundaries took a peculiar turn in the case of the districts disputed between Franks and Moslems. It reached the point where the two sides would agree to adopt a rule of condominium. Whoever occupied the fortress would guarantee the policing of the territory; the revenues were to be divided in half, and travelers would be guaranteed against all aggression while they

---

12. Cf. Richard, "Note sur l'archidiocèse d'Apamée et les conquêtes de Raymond de Saint-Gilles en Syrie du nord," *Syria,* XXV (1946-1948), 103-108.

13. Cahen, *Syrie du nord,* p. 233; Hill and Hill, *Raymond IV,* pp. 123-124.

14. William of Tyre, XVII, 7 (*RHC, Occ.,* I, 768-770); Cahen, *Syrie du nord,* 395-398.

15. Robert L. Nicholson, *Joscelyn I, Prince of Edessa* (Urbana, 1954), pp. 16-24. Joscelin II acknowledged himself vassal of the prince of Antioch, and dated his acts by the prince's regnal year; cf. Reinhold Röhricht, *Regesta regni Hierosolymitani* (Innsbruck, 1893; repr. New York, 1960), no. 206, and William of Tyre, XV, 2 (*RHC, Occ.,* I, 657-658).

16. The circumstances were unusual. Tancred had supported William Jordan against Bertrand of Toulouse, who claimed the county. Arbitration gave the north of the county to William, who then paid homage to Tancred because of his support (Richard, *Comté de Tripoli,* pp. 30-31).

crossed the territory, which was thus neutralized within its traditional boundaries.[17]

It was, nevertheless, the right of conquest which determined both the birth and the configuration of the Frankish states. In 1097 Tancred, Baldwin, and other leaders began the occupation of Cilicia. In 1097–1098 Baldwin established himself in various places of upper Mesopotamia and eliminated Ṭoros, the Armenian *curopalate* of Edessa; hence the birth of the county of Edessa. Bohemond assured himself the exclusive possession of Antioch in 1098, took over the places occupied by other barons in the neighborhood during the summer of 1099, and undertook the occupation of the Byzantine places on the coast and in Cilicia. Thus was born the principality of Antioch. Raymond constituted his county of Tripoli by occupying Tortosa (1102) and by immediately blockading Tripoli, which fell only in 1109, four years after his death.[18]

With Jerusalem the situation was more complex. After a rather confused debate the *christiana militia* seems to have duly decided to form an ecclesiastical seigneury for the benefit of the Holy Sepulcher (as had just been done at Ramla for the bishop of St. George), placing it under the protection (*advocatia*) of a great baron already established at Jerusalem and endowed with territories around the holy city. Godfrey of Bouillon, *advocatus Sancti Sepulcri,* did not exercise temporal power in the city, but he was ready to establish a state within the boundaries of Palestine, and he showed great resolve in refusing to Raymond the right to occupy Ascalon and in maintaining his own right to oversee the conquests that Tancred would undertake in Samaria and in Galilee. He left to Baldwin I the task of making sure of Jerusalem and of Jaffa; Baldwin put an end to the plan of forming them into an ecclesiastical seigneury, and had himself crowned "king of the Latins of Jerusalem."[19] The kingdom of Jerusalem was thus established.

17. Cf. Richard, "Un Partage de seigneurie entre Francs et Mamelouks: Les *Casaux de Sur*," *Syria*, XXX (1953), 72–82.

18. The title "count of Tripoli" seems to have been used even before the city was taken; cf. Richard, "Le Chartrier de Sainte-Marie-Latine et l'établissement de Raymond de Saint-Gilles à Mont-Pèlerin," in *Mélanges d'histoire du moyen-âge dediés à la mémoire de Louis Halphen* (Paris, 1951), pp. 605–612.

19. On all this cf. Joseph Hansen, *Das Problem eines Kirchenstaates in Jerusalem* (Luxemburg, 1928), pp. 18–22, 44 ff. It was Daimbert who first claimed the Tower of David and Jaffa in the name of his church; these had not been included in the seigneury of the Holy Sepulcher which had been established in 1099. As for the title *rex Jerusalem latinorum,* it might have meant that the king of Jerusalem belonged to a Latin dynasty rather than one descended from David; but we sometimes meet with the term *rex Latinitatis Jerusalem* in the twelfth century, which might have meant that he was the king of the Latins in Jerusalem rather than king of the holy city.

A. The Sovereigns

The adoption of the royal title did not confer on Baldwin supremacy over the other crusader states, nor did the title king of Jerusalem limit the new kingdom to the Holy Land. Baldwin I (1100–1118) did not forbid conquests which would have made him master of Egypt or of the Syrian interior and Damascus.[20] First he availed himself of Tancred's departure to bind the principality of Galilee more closely to the crown. Then in 1109 he secured the homage of Bertrand of Toulouse for Tripoli and the southern part of the county. The count of Edessa, Baldwin of Le Bourg (or Bourcq; king 1118–1131), had already received his county from Baldwin's hands, thus acknowledging himself the king's vassal.[21] However, the texts attest to the liege homage only of the count of Tripoli to the king;[22] Fulk (1131–1143) and Baldwin III (1143–1163) tolerated the recognition of Byzantine suzerainty by the prince of Antioch and the count of Edessa.[23]

In fact, royal authority over the three Frankish states of the north was limited. We find the prince and the two counts calling the king to their aid. When they were taken prisoner, or when they died leaving young children, the king was to take over the government of their states. Fulk was *rector et bajulus Antiocheni principatus* in 1133; Amalric was *Tripolis comitatus procurans* in 1170.[24] But the king seems primarily to have played the role of head of a league of Frankish states, especially when the prince of Antioch lost much of his power after the death of Tancred (1112) and the disaster of the *ager sanguinis*

---

20. This seems to be the sense of the expression *regnum Babylonie atque Asie disponens* applied to Baldwin I in an act of 1102–1103 (Eugène de Rozière, *Cartulaire de l'église du Saint-Sépulcre de Jérusalem* [Paris, 1849; repr. in *PL*, 155, cols. 1105–1262], no. 36. Cf. Richard, *Royaume latin*, p. 32).

21. Albert of Aachen, *Historia Hierosolymitana*, VII, 31 (*RHC, Occ.*, IV, 527): "hanc in beneficio suscipiens." In 1118 Baldwin II bestowed his county on Joscelin I of Courtenay.

22. William of Tyre, XI, 10 (*RHC, Occ.*, I, 467–469). Moreover, Bertrand's son Pons refused service to the king, and Baldwin II had to force his submission (Richard, *Comté de Tripoli*, pp. 31–38). In August 1198 king Amalric tightened the dependence of the count of Tripoli on the crown by giving him the *catena* of Acre as a fief-rent worth 4,000 bezants (Röhricht, *Regesta*, no. 743).

23. Moreover, feudal law of the twelfth century allowed a vassal to pay homage to different lords, provided that only one of these was liege homage, and that the same fiefs were not involved.

24. LaMonte, *Feudal Monarchy*, pp. 187–202.

(Darb Sarmadā, 1119). The prince and the two counts pursued their own policies, making treaties with their Moslem or Greek neighbors without troubling themselves about the policies of the king. And our sources are ambivalent: John of Ibelin classes the count of Tripoli among the barons of the realm of Jerusalem, but Ernoul writes "La tiere de Triple ne d'Antioch n'est mie dou reiaume."[25]

Jerusalem's master alone bore the royal title, from 1100 on. Did he owe this title to election? The question has been much discussed. Gaston Dodu wrote that "the kingdom of Jerusalem was originally a feudal republic presided over by an elected king," and John La-Monte believed that inheritance replaced election only after Baldwin V's designation as the heir of his uncle Baldwin IV (1174–1185).[26] To be precise, however, Godfrey was designated not by his future vassals but by the council of barons who directed the crusade. These persons did not settle down in the kingdom, and the barons of the kingdom owed all their fiefs and their titles to the king:[27] they had no legal right to proceed to the election of a sovereign. And, after 1100, the kings succeeded one another by virtue of the strictest rules of inheritance. However, on the death of Baldwin I, in 1118, it was necessary to decide whether they would accept the king's brother, Eustace III, count of Boulogne, or his cousin Baldwin of Le Bourg, count of Edessa. At the urging of Joscelin I of Courtenay the barons summoned Baldwin, and it was claimed that Baldwin I had designated him as his successor. Eustace agreed to step aside. This precedent appeared sufficient to establish that the crown should pass to the nearest heir of the deceased king provided that he was present to take up his inheritance. This allowed the barons in 1243 to keep out king Conrad, the son of Frederick II and queen Isabel of Brienne (Yolanda). But a clever lawyer, Philip of Novara, succeeded in establishing that Conrad had to be allowed the chance to assert his rights by coming to claim the throne. The queen of Cyprus, Alice of Champagne, who based her claim on the traditional rule, thus could not get herself crowned.[28]

The royal office could pass to women. In 1131, Baldwin II's daughter Melisend inherited the crown and transmitted it to her husband

25. *Livre de Jean d'Ibelin,* cap. 269 (*RHC, Lois,* I, 417–419); *Chronique d'Ernoul et de Bernard le Trésorier,* ed. Louis de Mas Latrie (Paris, 1871), p. 27.

26. Dodu, *Histoire des institutions,* p. 150; LaMonte, *Feudal Monarchy,* p. 8 ("the accession of Baldwin de Burg came about purely through election") and p. 33.

27. The question has been thoroughly studied by Mayer, "Studies in the History of Queen Melisende of Jerusalem," *Dumbarton Oaks Papers,* XXVI (1972), 93–182.

28. LaMonte, *Feudal Monarchy,* pp. 70–74; Richard, *Royaume latin,* pp. 257–259; Riley-Smith, *Feudal Nobility,* pp. 209–212, has emphasized that this is the application of the rule giving the succession to the "plus dreit heir apparant."

Fulk of Anjou. But she intended to remain queen and to exercise the prerogatives of the office, on the grounds that her father had left the kingdom to her just as much as to her husband and her young son. Not only did she endorse her husband's acts during his lifetime (not unusual in the twelfth century), but after his death in 1143 she refused to turn over the crown to her son Baldwin III when he came of age. She accepted his coronation only with the agreement that she could keep the royal title and the government of half the kingdom. Later, in 1151, Baldwin III had recourse to war and forced his mother to settle for a dower.[29]

When the kingdom was transmitted by a woman to her husband, he held it only during her lifetime or during the minority of the children she left him. This allowed the barons of the kingdom to refuse to recognize Guy of Lusignan when queen Sibyl and her children died in 1190, and allowed Frederick II to eliminate John of Brienne in 1225 by marrying the daughter John had had by Mary of Montferrat. The uncertainty of the position explained, perhaps, why Henry of Champagne, in 1192, refused to accept the royal title when he married Isabel of Jerusalem. By her previous marriage Isabel had had a daughter, Mary, who would take the royal title when she became of age. But Aimery of Lusignan, who married Isabel on Henry's death in 1197, took the title king of Jerusalem.

Baldwin IV tried to change the rules of succession in order to keep his brother-in-law Guy of Lusignan off the throne. Guy had married Sibyl of Jerusalem. Baldwin chose as heir the son that Sibyl had had by a first marriage, and had his barons swear that, if the boy died, they would look to the pope, the kings of France and England, and the emperor, to decide the respective rights of his two sisters, Sibyl and Isabel.[30] When Baldwin V died in 1186, however, Sibyl had recourse to force and had herself crowned, and the consent of Isabel's husband Humphrey IV of Toron to this coronation rendered inoperative the arrangements made by Baldwin IV. Inheritance thus triumphed over a notion recognized elsewhere, according to which the king of

---

29. LaMonte, *Feudal Monarchy,* pp. 11 ff.

30. Sibyl, like Baldwin IV, was born of Amalric's first marriage, to Agnes of Courtenay, which had been annulled; Isabel, of his second marriage, to Maria Comnena. Baldwin IV had been designated Baldwin III's heir as his godson (the king had promised him the kingdom *in filiolagio*); see William of Tyre, XVIII, 29 (*RHC, Occ.,* I, 870–871). Although the legitimacy of Sibyl's birth was not disputed, Baldwin seems to have looked upon the rights of his sister and his half-sister to the throne as equal. See Marshall W. Baldwin, *Raymond III of Tripolis and the Fall of Jerusalem* (Princeton, 1936), p. 58; Nicholson, *Joscelyn III and the Fall of the Crusader States, 1134–1199* (Leyden, 1973), p. 58.

Jerusalem would have been only "the lieutenant of the kings of Outre-mer".[31]

In fact, the king of Jerusalem enjoyed complete sovereignty; he had no secular suzerain, and it is not certain that he recognized the suzerainty of the Holy See.[32] Baldwin I had ignored the claims of the patriarch to receive the king's homage. The king held his crown only from God, and this assured to the barons of the kingdom, who looked upon themselves as the high court of the kingdom, the ability to play a role in the succession to the throne. In 1118 it was they who summoned Baldwin II to take the crown, in preference to Eustace of Boulogne.[33] In 1243 they decided to give their homage to Alice of Champagne rather than to king Conrad. In 1264 Hugh III of Antioch-Lusignan and Hugh of Brienne submitted their claims to the throne to the judgment of the high court; the barons decided in favor of the former and gave him their homage. And the barons also intervened in the marriages of royal heiresses.[34] Though we cannot properly speak of election by the barons, they had nevertheless considerable influence on the choice of the sovereigns.

As in the kingdom, the succession to the other thrones of the Latin east was regulated by the principle that the inheritance passed to the nearest relative, of whatever sex, of that person who had last exercised the *saisine* of the principality or county.[35]

We are poorly informed of the succession crises of the county of Tripoli. In 1148 Alfonso Jordan, count of Toulouse and son of Raymond of St. Gilles, seems to have wanted to contest the county with his grand-nephew Raymond II. In 1187 Raymond III prevented the

31. The description applied to Conrad of Montferrat in 1189 by Abū-Shāmah in the *Livres des deux jardins* (*RHC, Or.,* IV, 400), when Conrad refused to open the gates of the city to Guy of Lusignan; Conrad called himself "lieutenant des rois d'outre-mer" and seems to have attributed to the kings of the west the right of recognizing royal authority in the Holy Land.

32. LaMonte, *Feudal Monarchy,* p. 4, speaks of "the Pope's claim to Jerusalem as a state of the Church," which is quite debatable. That there was recognition of papal suzerainty over the kingdom of Jerusalem has not been established; see Baldwin, "The Papacy and the Levant during the Twelfth Century," *Bulletin of the Polish Institute . . . in America,* III (1945), 277–287.

33. One party summoned Eustace, possibly the same group of barons who, according to Galbert of Bruges, had invited the count of Flanders, Charles the Good, to come and receive the crown of Jerusalem (Dodu, *Histoire des institutions,* pp. 141–142; Richard, *Royaume latin,* p. 69).

34. Often turning to western sovereigns to choose a husband for the heiress (as in the case of John of Brienne). In 1192 they forced Isabel of Jerusalem to separate from Humphrey IV of Toron and marry Conrad of Montferrat.

35. This was the basis for the claims of Mary of Antioch against Hugh of Antioch-Lusignan. She claimed to be more closely related to Isabel of Jerusalem, the "deraine saisie dou reiaume," whose granddaughter she was (Richard, *Royaume latin,* pp. 323–328).

succession of his relatives of Toulouse in the interests of his godson Raymond of Antioch.[36] But in 1201, at Antioch, Bohemond IV claimed the principality against his nephew Raymond Roupen, Raymond of Antioch's son, arguing that Raymond of Antioch had died (1197) before their father Bohemond III (1163–1201), and so had not been *en saisine* of the principality.[37]

Possession of the kingdom was complete from the moment the king was consecrated and crowned. Baldwin I received his crown from the patriarch Daimbert in the basilica of Bethlehem.[38] From 1118 to 1197, the coronation took place at the Holy Sepulcher. After the fall of Jerusalem (with the exception of Frederick II who crowned himself at the Holy Sepulcher in 1229) it took place in the cathedral of Tyre. This ceremony did not imply that the king became the vassal of the patriarch, but the patriarch was supposed to ask those present if the new sovereign was indeed the *dreit heir* of the kingdom, and crowned him after their acclamation.[39] It was at this moment in the ceremony in 1269 that Mary of Antioch proclaimed before a notary her refusal to recognize the rights of Hugh of Antioch-Lusignan. Enough importance was attached to the ceremony that Baldwin III refused to allow his mother, Melisend, to be crowned at the same time he was, and that in 1186 Sibyl made her coronation the essential element of her *coup d'état,* while Conrad of Montferrat, murdered in 1192 before he could be crowned, was called simply *rex electus.*[40]

The princes of Antioch also turned to their patriarch to be consecrated. Claude Cahen has suggested that this ceremony was instituted in 1112 by the regent Roger of Salerno, a rather distant relative of

---

36. Richard, *Comté de Tripoli,* pp. 45–48; Baldwin, *Raymond III,* p. 138. In the event, Raymond's brother, Bohemond (IV) of Antioch, became count (1187–1233). The counts of Toulouse seem to have maintained their claims to *totum principatum Tripoli de Suria,* as a text of 1259 reveals: Claude de Vic and Jean J. Vaissète, *Histoire générale de Languedoc,* ed. Édouard Dulaurier, *et al.* (15 vols., Toulouse, 1872–1893), VIII, 1445–1446.

37. Cahen, *Syrie du nord,* pp. 591–595. I have interpreted the statement of William of Tyre's continuator, that Bohemond III died "saisis et revestus et tenant," in a different sense than has Cahen.

38. It has been assumed that the choice of Bethlehem was made in order not to prejudice the grant of Jerusalem to an ecclesiastical lordship (Hansen, *Das Problem,* pp. 83–85). It has also been suggested that it preserved the tradition established by Godfrey of Bouillon, who refused to wear a crown of gold where Christ had worn a crown of thorns. But it might also be that Baldwin had himself crowned in Bethlehem simply because Christmas, being the first great feast day following his accession to the throne, was celebrated in Bethlehem.

39. John of Ibelin, cap. 7 (*RHC, Lois,* I, 30). See Mayer, "Das Pontifikale von Tyrus und die Krönung der lateinischen Könige von Jerusalem," *Dumbarton Oaks Papers,* XXI (1967), 141–232.

40. The title is reminiscent of a bishop who has not yet been consecrated, but it does not imply that the choice of the king had been the result of an election.

Bohemond II, the legitimate heir to the principality, in order that his accession to the principate be thenceforth undisputed. His successors continued to have themselves consecrated by the patriarch.[41]

The history of the crusader states is noteworthy for the problems caused by regencies. In the twelfth century this was especially so at Antioch, whose princes often died violent deaths. In the thirteenth the same was true at Jerusalem, because of difficulties over the succession. At the beginning of the twelfth century, the barons, deprived of their head, appealed to a neighboring prince, as in Edessa where Tancred was called on to replace Baldwin of Le Bourg, who had been taken prisoner. But soon the idea of calling on the nearest relative of an incapacitated prince prevailed: Tancred was summoned to Antioch to replace the captured Bohemond I;[42] Roger was chosen to replace the minor Bohemond II. Or else they turned to their suzerain:[43] kings Baldwin II, Fulk, and Amalric were called upon to govern the counties or the principality when their leaders died, until their heirs came of age. We frequently see a conflict between the king and the princess of Antioch, the latter claiming to exercise the regency and refusing it to the king of Jerusalem, who nevertheless took it over each time.[44]

In the kingdom of Jerusalem queen Melisend, on the other hand, effectively carried on the government during the minority of Baldwin III. The arrangement was different, however, when Amalric died:[45] the dying king entrusted the regency to one of the great officers, Miles of Plancy. But Miles was murdered in 1174, and Baldwin IV's nearest relative, count Raymond III of Tripoli, took over the government (1174–1176). Baldwin IV was debilitated by leprosy, and sought to entrust the government to someone he could trust (count Philip of Flanders, who refused, and then Reginald of Châtillon), but when his sister Sibyl remarried in 1183 he gave the regency (*baill*) for Sibyl's infant son Baldwin to his brother-in-law Guy of Lusignan. Then he deprived Guy of the regency and entrusted the protection of the child to his

41. Cahen, *Syrie du nord*, p. 312. However, the princes Bohemond IV and Bohemond V, in conflict with their patriarch, were not consecrated.

42. Moreover, he was required to take an oath of fealty to Bohemond before the gates were opened to him (Continuation of Peter Tudebode, in *RHC, Occ.*, III, 228).

43. Although Tancred claimed suzerainty over Edessa, demanding the homage of Baldwin of Le Bourg before giving him his land in 1107.

44. The nobility of the principality seems to have been opposed to female regencies (Cahen, *Syrie du nord*, p. 440).

45. Baldwin IV's mother, Agnes, had been repudiated by Amalric, and she was not, as Melisend was, the heiress of the kingdom.

uncle, count Joscelin III of Courtenay, while Raymond III was again charged with the government with the title of regent.[46] Thenceforth it was conceded that the regent should be the nearest relative of a king who either was a minor or was prevented from ruling effectively.[47]

The regent governed the kingdom, received the homages due the king, and took over the royal domain.[48] His position was hardly different from that of the king himself. Aimery of Lusignan, queen Isabel's husband and regent for princess Mary of Montferrat, actually took the title of king, while Henry of Champagne, in the same position, called himself "lord of the realm." Frederick II, after the death of his wife Isabel in 1228, was also regent for the young Conrad. But at Conrad's coming of age the barons refused to continue accepting Frederick as regent. They were unable to give homage to Conrad, who had not come to the kingdom. It was then that they decided to recognize the regency of Conrad's nearest available relative, Alice of Champagne. Arguing, however, from a precedent in the Morea, they refused to hand possession of the fortresses of the royal domain over to the regent, although giving her the homage due the crown.

From 1243 to 1268 the kingdom was thus governed by a regent or "lord of the kingdom" with limited powers: first queen Alice (1243–1246), next her son Henry I of Lusignan (1246–1253),[49] then Hugh II, Henry's son. But since he was a minor, the "lordship of the kingdom" was filled in succession by his mother Plaisance of Antioch (1253–1261), represented by her brother Bohemond V of Antioch, next by his aunt Isabel of Lusignan (1263–1264), and then by her son, Hugh III de Lusignan (1264–1269). The death of Hugh II in 1267 made Hugh III king of Cyprus, and that of Conradin, legitimate heir to the throne, in 1268, allowed Hugh III in 1269 to exchange his title of regent for that of king of Jerusalem.[50]

The regent himself might be absent from the kingdom (as were the rulers of Cyprus from 1243 to 1268). In this case, as also when the king of Jerusalem was absent, a bailie was established "sur le fait de la seignorie." At the time of the captivity of Baldwin II, it seems

46. Baldwin, *Raymond III*, pp. 57–59. See also Nicholson, *Joscelyn III*, pp. 118–127.
47. "Ne l'on n'en apelle baill que ciaus à qui le reiaume peut escheir": cap. 249 (*RHC, Lois*, I, 398). On the regency see Riley-Smith, *Feudal Nobility*, pp. 184–228.
48. It is debatable whether he could administer the domain as he wished without an accounting when the heir reached the age of majority. Raymond III was required to render such an accounting; Aimery of Lusignan took care to separate the administration of the kingdom, which he governed in the name of his wife Isabel, from that of his own kingdom of Cyprus.
49. Pope Innocent IV recognized his title on April 17, 1247: Georg H. Pertz and Carl Rodenberg, eds., *MGH, Epistolae saeculi XIII e regestis pontificum romanorum*, II (Berlin, 1887), 244 (no. 324); see also p. 299 (no. 411) and p. 401 (no. 568).
50. It was only then that he was in a position to reclaim the royal castles at Acre and Tyre, thitherto held by the commune of Acre and Philip of Montfort.

that the barons designated Eustace Garnier, lord of Sidon (1123).[51] But it was Frederick II who named Thomas of Acerra bailie of the kingdom in 1226; then, in 1228, Balian I Grenier of Sidon and Warner the German, whom Richard Filangieri later replaced.[52]

John of Ibelin, whose account is open to criticism (he omitted to mention the designation of Filangieri),[53] affirms that the liege men had the right to choose the bailie themselves. In fact, it was Frederick II to whom the pope would suggest in 1236 (when the emperor would make Bohemond V regent of the kingdom) that he designate two bailies, one at Acre, the other at Tyre.[54] And in 1241 the Guelf barons themselves asked the emperor to replace Filangieri with Simon of Montfort.[55] It was only after 1243, when king Conrad reached his majority, that the barons refused his representative Thomas of Acerra, and themselves designated a bailie whose nomination was confirmed by the "lord of the kingdom."[56] This procedure became thenceforth the normal way of designating the bailie. But his powers were limited;[57] he could not hear cases relating to fiefs and he had to take an oath to the liege men. He appeared thus as much their representative as that of the king or of the "lord of the kingdom."

51. One might well ask, however, whether Eustace Garnier was not closely related to the family of Baldwin I and Baldwin II (Charles Moeller, "Les Flamands du terroir au royaume latin de Jérusalem," *Mélanges Paul Frédéricq* [Brussels, 1904], p. 189).

52. John of Ibelin says (cap. 249) that Thomas of Acerra's powers expired on the death of queen Isabel of Brienne, and that the liege men then elected the old lord of Beirut and Balian of Sidon "estre sur le fait de la seignorie jusque à la venue de l'empereor" (*RHC, Lois,* I, 399). For the designation of Balian and Warner see *L'Estoire d'Eracles empereur et la conqueste de la terre d'Outremer (RHC, Occ.,* II, 384). For the seal of Richard Filangieri as bailie of the kingdom see Gustave Schlumberger *et al., Sigillographie de l'Orient latin* (Bibliothèque archéologique et historique, XXXVII; Paris, 1943), p. 66.

53. He says (cap. 249) that when Frederick II wanted to substitute Philip of Maugastel for Balian of Sidon and Odo of Montbéliard (who had taken Warner's place), the liege men refused to accept him (*RHC, Lois,* I, 399).

54. *MGH, Epistolae saeculi XIII,* I (Berlin, 1883), 571–572 (no. 674); cf. LaMonte and Merton J. Hubert, *The Wars of Frederick II against the Ibelins in Syria and Cyprus (CURC,* 25; New York, 1936), pp. 49–50, 168. This solution had been envisaged in 1233 by Frederick II: "si il voloyent que son baill qui estoit a Sur fust lor baill, il lor otroyeroit bien qu'un de ses homes de la terre fust lor bail a Acre [Philip of Maugastel], et Richart Philangier fust a Sur" (*Les Gestes des Chiprois,* cap. 205, in *RHC, Arm.,* II, 722); Riley-Smith, *Feudal Nobility,* pp. 201–204.

55. *AOL,* I (1881), 402–403.

56. They chose Odo of Montbéliard, constable of the kingdom, according to John of Ibelin (caps. 249, 250, in *RHC, Lois,* I, 399–400). However, in 1258 it was the regent Bohemond V who named the bailie, John of Arsur (Arsuf: "Continuation de Guillaume de Tyr, de 1229 à 1261, dite du manuscrit de Rothelin," *RHC, Occ.,* II, 634–635).

57. "Les hommes dou reiaume se deivent assembler ou le greignor partie d'iaus, et eslire un d'iaus, celui qui lor semblera qui seit plus proufitable, et là où le plus des homes s'accorderont à estre sur le fait de la seignorie, por faire et tenir dreit à la gent et assembler court et faire esgart ou conoissance à ciaus qui li requeront," according to John of Ibelin (cap. 249, in *RHC, Lois,* I, 398).

B. The Feudal Regime

The crusader states were formed at a time when the feudal system was at its height in western Europe. Furthermore, possibly with some exceptions,[58] all the conquered lands were embraced within the feudal structure of the new states. The prospect of a Moslem reconquest, moreover, would give to this structure a very particular force: the rulers sought to retain in their service on a permanent basis the knights whom they employed by giving them fiefs; later, when a network of fortresses would ensure the security of the frontiers as well as the interior, these fortresses too were used as fiefs.

The granting of fiefs seems to have gone on from the very beginning of the conquest.[59] The princes often kept within their own domain the main towns, which were the first to be conquered. But already Godfrey had invested Tancred with what would become the principality of Galilee, and promised a knight of Forez, Gaudemer Charpinel, the investiture of Haifa in anticipation of its capture. Baldwin I, when his brother died, reinvested the knights and barons with the fiefs which had been established for them out of the town revenues. Many fiefs were thenceforth money-fiefs.[60]

The feudal organization of the kingdom of Jerusalem was famous for the strictness of its principles. But this strictness exists primarily in the writings of thirteenth-century jurists.[61] The documents preserved in church archives allow us to modify its rigidity. The kinds of fief varied. There were important lands, some of which carried the title of county (Jaffa) or principality (Galilee), and lands of less importance, or simply money-fiefs, the *fié en besanz* in contrast to the *fié*

---

58. See above, p. 153, with respect to the allods. Were these allods, or *fiefs francs,* an outgrowth of the right of occupancy given to the first occupants? On the existence of allods or *fiefs de reprise* in the county of Tripoli, see Richard, "Le Comté de Tripoli dans les chartes des Porcellet," pp. 360-363.

59. Prawer, "La Noblesse et le régime féodal du royaume latin de Jérusalem," *Le Moyen-Âge,* LXV (1959), 41-74.

60. Albert of Aachen, VII, 37: "beneficia vero, prout cuique statuta erant de reditibus civitatum, protulerunt" (1100: *RHC, Occ.,* IV, 532).

61. On the controversy over this matter between Carl Stephenson and LaMonte, cf. LaMonte, "Three Questions Concerning the Assises of Jerusalem," *Byzantina metabyzantina,* I (1946), 201-204.

en casau or *en terre.*[62] Most of the holders of fiefs lived in towns or fortresses, not on their lands, limiting themselves to collecting the revenues of their villages. A village usually belonged to a single lord, but occasionally it might be divided. Such division stopped, however, at the point where a holding assured the maintenance of one knight, the *caballaria* or *chevalerie.*[63]

The most important fiefs were endowed with rights of justice or command. The *Livre de Jean d'Ibelin* gives a list of them; though incomplete, it reveals that the lords of simple villages were able to exercise certain rights of justice over the inhabitants who were their tenants.[64] The *barons et terriers* had the right of punishing their men,[65] inflicting mutilation on them if caught red-handed, as is indicated by a canon of the council of Nablus (1120):[66] this was *justise.* They held a *cour,* made up of their vassals, in order to decide feudal matters. Finally, they had *coins,* that is, molds for impressing their seal and counterseal on a lead *bulla,* and this right allowed them to *faire prevelige donatif,* to grant a piece of land without the confirmation of their suzerain.[67] These prerogatives seem to have been acknowledged as belonging to the holders of those lordships which included an important castle, the center of an extensive territory and the residence of a group of knights bound to the lord of the castle by ties of vassalage.

Some of these lords claimed special privileges. One discerns in the thirteenth century an attempt on the part of the principal lord high justiciars to form a group of four "barons," which John of Ibelin sought to define on the basis of the exceptional importance of their

---

62. John of Ibelin, cap. 166 (*RHC, Lois,* I, 255).

63. Their division was forbidden (*idem.,* caps. 148, 150, *ibid.,* I, 224–225; Richard, *Comté de Tripoli,* p. 79). Some fiefs were made up of a certain number of *carracatae* (such as that of John Bannier at Caymont: Röhricht, *Regesta,* no. 614). Beduin tribes might also form the basis of a fief; cf. *Regesta,* no. 562, and John of Ibelin, cap. 271 (*RHC, Lois,* I, 424): "Baudoyns de Ibelin, por II lignées de Bedoyns," owed the service of four knights "en reconoissance do fyé."

64. There is a list of seigneurs having "cour et coins et justise" in John of Ibelin, cap. 270 (*RHC, Lois,* I, 419–421); cf. Richard, "Les Listes de seigneuries dans le Livre de Jean d'Ibelin," *RHDFE,* ser. 4, XXXII (1954), 565–577. The existence of seigneuries endowed with rights of low justice has been alluded to by Cahen, "Notes sur l'histoire des croisades et de l'Orient latin; II, Le Régime rural syrien," *Bulletin de la Faculté des lettres de Strasbourg,* XXIX (1950–1951), 304–306; and John of Ibelin (cap. 207, in *RHC, Lois,* I, 332) refers to the concession of rights of justice.

65. *Livre au roi,* cap. 39 (*RHC, Lois,* I, 634).

66. Mansi, *Concilia,* XXI, col. 262, canon 35.

67. Raoul Chandon de Briailles, "Le Droit de 'coins' dans le royaume de Jérusalem," *Syria,* XXIII (1942–1943), 244–257; John of Ibelin, cap. 189 (*RHC, Lois,* I, 302). The lords who did not have this right used a wax seal (which the great lords began to use at the end of the thirteenth century), and had to have their donations confirmed by the lord from whom they held their fiefs, who affixed his seal (e.g., Röhricht, *Regesta,* no. 594).

seigneuries. The baron was to furnish a contingent of one hundred horsemen for the royal army and to be accompanied by a lord high constable and a marshal. The four barons were to enjoy the privilege of being justiciable only in the court of barons, when it was a question of their bodies, their honor, or their fiefs. But this theory seems to have been introduced rather late, perhaps in imitation of the *cours des pairs* in the west.[68] Only the kingdom of Jerusalem appears to have experienced an attempt of this kind, echoed neither in Antioch nor in Tripoli, where the lord high justiciars enjoyed prerogatives similar to those of the kingdom.

The fief was normally burdened with a service that its holder was supposed to render to the one who had given it to him. There were, however, fiefs which owed no service,[69] somewhat similar probably to the allods which we find in the towns.[70] The service varied greatly: they called fiefs the tenures of sergeants who fought on foot as well as those of seigneurial officials (scribes, native interpreters).[71] The fiefs of knights, however, required them to perform military service under carefully defined conditions.

The lord called them up by sending a sergeant, the *bannier,* who brought them the summons. The vassal had to go unless wounded or sick (in which case a doctor's or surgeon's certificate might be required), or if the lord had not yet paid him what he owed.[72] The king's men were at his disposition for a whole year throughout the length and breadth of the kingdom; they had to serve him with horse and arms, stated precisely in 1168 by the assise of Bilbais, which exempted knights from serving in the sieges of towns.[73] A vassal under forty had to serve in person; if older, he need merely *tenir hernois,* put his arms at the disposition of his lord.[74] In fact, a vassal had to own a war horse and a complete suit of armor, and the king stopped his pay when the armor was incomplete, although he had to re-

68. Richard, "Pairie d'Orient latin: Les quatre baronnies des royaumes de Jérusalem et de Chypre," *RHDFE,* ser. 4, XXVIII (1950), 67–88. On the other hand, the four baronies were not to be partitioned among sisters (John of Ibelin, cap. 177, in *RHC, Lois,* I, 280).

69. Cahen, *Syrie du nord,* pp. 530–531; John of Ibelin (cap. 249) mentions the "fié franc qui ne doit point de servise ne d'omage ne de redevance" (*RHC, Lois,* I, 399); he points out (cap. 141) that the king could grant a fief "à servise et sans servise" (*ibid.,* I, 215).

70. Prawer, "The *Assise de tenure* and the *Assise de vente:* A Study of Landed Property in the Latin Kingdom," *Economic History Review,* ser. 2, IV (1951–1952), 82–83.

71. Cahen, *Syrie du nord,* p. 534 (the fief of a "client"); Prawer, *Historie du royaume latin de Jérusalem,* p. 129.

72. This last excuse was not accepted when it was necessary to assist a threatened stronghold; cf. John of Ibelin, caps. 212, 213, 214, 223 (*RHC, Lois,* I, 338–343, 354).

73. *Gestes des Chiprois,* cap. 202 (*RHC, Arm.,* II, 721).

74. John of Ibelin concluded that after the age of sixty a woman holding a fief could refuse the king's right to have her married again, on the grounds that at this age a knight no longer owed the service of his body (caps. 226, 228, in *RHC, Lois,* I, 358, 362).

place a horse worn out or lost in his service.[75] The requirement to
serve in person brought with it a prohibition against leaving the kingdom without handing over the fief to the lord. Failure to serve was
punished by confiscation of the fief for a year and a day.[76]

However, it was anticipated that the obligations of certain fiefs might
be fulfilled by someone other than the vassal. In his list of the "ser-
vises que les cités dou reiaume de Jerusalem doivent" (c. 271) John
of Ibelin noted that John of Rheims owed the king "un chevalier
pelerin," and that other holders of fiefs owed the service of two to
five knights. In such a case, the vassal could subinfeudate portions
of his fief to rear-vassals, but it was assumed that he would keep
for himself a more important part than that allotted to a rear-vassal.[77]

The requirement of military service limited the possibility of
alienating the fief. It was forbidden to sell it to a minor or to an
unmarried young woman. But the inheritability of fiefs was soon
widely recognized; the legitimate son of a knight and his lady could
not be prevented from holding a fief, even if incapable of proper
service ("vil, recréant, coart, bossu, mahaignié de aucun de ses mem-
bres, yvroigne, entechié de aucun mauvais ou vilain vice").

Even inheritance through a collateral line was allowed in Jerusalem,
up to the middle of the twelfth century.[78] However, the partition of
a fief was not allowed. Only the first born succeeded to the fief of
a father who had only one fief, and he could subinfeudate only a
part to his brothers. Daughters, on the other hand, divided the fief
among themselves if there were no male heir, provided that the fief
comprised several *chevaleries;* only in 1171 was it decided that the eldest would receive the homage of her sisters.[79] If the heir was a minor
the fief was placed under the care of the lord, who could grant it
(sometimes in return for money) to anyone he chose, so long as the
care of the child himself was entrusted to his nearest relative.[80]

At fifteen the young man asked for his fief, and he was allowed

75. *Livre au roi,* cap. 10 (*ibid.,* I, 613).

76. John of Ibelin, caps. 180, 184 (*ibid.,* I, 282–283, 287).

77. *Idem,* cap. 182; cf. cap. 148 (*ibid.,* I, 284–285, 223–224).

78. *Idem,* cap. 187 (*ibid.,* I, 297–299); Cahen, *Syrie du nord,* p. 534; Prawer, "La Noblesse
et le régime féodal," pp. 48–49, 62–63.

79. *Livre au roi,* cap. 34 (*RHC, Lois,* I, 629–630); John of Ibelin, caps. 148–153 (*ibid.,*
I, 223–231).

80. John of Ibelin, caps. 169–170 (*ibid.,* I, 259–262). Philip of Novara, cap. 20 (*ibid.,* I,
494), explains that this measure was intended to prevent the holder of the regency from getting
rid of the heir, quoting the adage:

> Ne doit mie garder l'aignel
> Qui en doit avoir la pel.

For the sale of a regency in 1179 see Röhricht, *Regesta,* no. 588.

to swear homage to the lord, an indispensable formality without which the fief could be confiscated by the lord for the lifetime of the defaulting vassal. Homage forbade him to strike his lord, to bear arms against him, to give counsel that might harm him, to injure his honor or that of his wife, his daughter, or his sister; it obliged him to give up his horse to his lord in the course of battle if the lord had been unhorsed, and to give himself up as a hostage to free his lord from captivity. On the other hand, the lord was forbidden to strike his vassal or to take his fief, and had to arrange his deliverance when the vassal had given himself up as a hostage in his place.[81]

The heiress of a fief could be required by the lord to marry on reaching the age of twelve. Theoretically she had a choice among three candidates of a rank compatible with her own. Her parents, who might wish to arrange her marriage, were often forced to offer the lord a sum of money to get his approval of the match which they themselves proposed. Raymond III of Tripoli, for example, let himself be tempted by the attraction of a large sum to marry off the heiress of Botron to someone other than Gerard of Ridefort, to whom he had promised her.[82]

When a fief changed hands there was no transfer tax except at Antioch, where it amounted to a ninth, possibly the equivalent of the "relief" in the west.[83] But alienation was controlled; the fief could be sold, even at auction, provided that it be to a person capable of holding it. This excluded not only minors but churches, religious orders, communes (such as the Italian republics), and burgesses. Where a sale to a buyer of this sort had to be made (for example, when the vassal had to pay a ransom), the lord had to authorize it or else the fief might be forfeited.[84]

The fief could be taken from a vassal not only for failure to swear homage or perform service (which entailed only a temporary forfeiture) but when the vassal denied God or betrayed his lord, according to John of Ibelin. A twelfth-century text, the *Establissement dou roi*

81. John of Ibelin, caps. 184, 195 (*RHC, Lois,* I, 287, 313–314). Amalric succeeded in imposing an income tax of one percent on his vassals, and in having some of them sell fiefs which they held in the names of their wives in order to ransom their lord, who had been taken by the Saracens, following an event which is obscure. This was the "assise dou rei Amauri, qui fu faite à Sur, por la desconfiture . . . des Crestiens ou fait de Naples" (John of Ibelin, cap. 249, in *RHC, Lois,* I, 398).

82. *Idem,* caps. 177–179 (*ibid.,* I, 279–282); Richard, *Comté de Tripoli,* p. 80; cf. above, p. 184. According to Prawer, "La Noblesse et le régime féodal," p. 51, it was about 1130 that the king extended his right to impose a husband of his choice to include widows.

83. Cahen, *Syrie du nord,* p. 532.

84. John of Ibelin, cap. 143 (*RHC, Lois,* I, 217). For the sale in 1161 of the fief of John Gothman see Röhricht, *Regesta,* nos. 368–369.

Bauduin segont, numbers twelve cases in which forfeiture occurs, including apostasy, treason, armed revolt, the coining of false money, the usurpation of regalian rights (coinage, port and highway tolls), and refusal to obey the lord.[85] But under Amalric a new text was adopted, the *Assise de la ligèce,* which limited considerably the right of forfeiture.[86]

This assise established a principle favorable to royal authority, the swearing of liege homage to the king by all vassals and subvassals as well as an oath of fealty by the inhabitants of cities, towns, and castles held in fief of the king. Previously, liege homage and the oath of fealty, mentioned in texts of 1144 in Tripoli, 1149 in Antioch, and 1155 in the kingdom, were required of the vassals of the king and princes, and of burgesses of the cities in their domains. The new arrangement would require rear-vassals and burgesses to abandon their immediate lord if he rebelled against the king.[87]

On the other hand, this assise created a bond between all the king's liege men; if an injustice was committed against one of them by their immediate lord, it was their duty to support one another, demanding of the lord that he have the vassal in question judged by the court before laying hands on his fief. If the lord refused the "esgard et connoissance de sa cour," the vassals could refuse the service due from their fiefs, and the king was to intervene on their behalf.[88]

The king himself was required to provide justice in his court to any vassal he might wish to dispossess or imprison. In this way the

---

85. *Livre au roi,* cap. 16 (*RHC, Lois,* I, 616–617). Cf. Prawer, "Étude sur le droit des *Assises de Jérusalem:* Droit de confiscation et droit d'exhérédation," *RHDFE,* ser. 4, XXXIX (1961), 520–551, esp. 522–532, and XL (1962), 29–42. In view of the references to a well-developed regalian right, Prawer has suggested that the *Establissement dou roi Bauduin segont* was adopted later, during the reign of Baldwin III.

86. John of Ibelin, cap. 140 (*RHC, Lois,* I, 214–215); cf. caps. 197–201 (*ibid.,* I, 317–323); on the ceremony of liege homage see cap. 195 (*ibid.,* I, 313). The standard interpretation by LaMonte, in his *Feudal Monarchy,* p. 24, has been discussed by Prawer, who proposes another view in his "La Noblesse et le régime féodal," pp. 64–73. Elsewhere ("Estates, Communities and the Constitution") Prawer has pointed out that the *Assise de la ligèce,* by giving the nobility a horizontal structure, with the right of forming a *conjuratio,* turned the nobility into a veritable "estate," and brought about the control of the high court by the greater nobility. Other social groups were also led to establish internal ties.

87. John of Ibelin is explicit on this point (cap. 197, in *RHC, Lois,* I, 317). However, Prawer has refused to accept it ("La Noblesse et le régime féodal," p. 73) because we know of no example of such a coalition of rear-vassals supporting the king against their immediate lord.

88. Tradition has it that this assise was adopted on the occasion of a war between Amalric and Gerard of Sidon, which broke out "par ce que le dit Girart deserita un sien home, sans esgart et sans conoissance de court, dou fié que il tenoit de lui"; Prawer has dismissed this (*ibid.,* p. 65): "il est difficile d'imaginer Amaury, homme d'Etat réfléchi et prince cupide, guerroyant pour une *iusticia* abstraite." In any case, it would appear that Amalric's assise assured the king above all a guarantee against future revolts.

Assise de la ligèce made the strict application of the *Establissement dou roi Bauduin segont* impossible. Aimery of Lusignan succeeded in reimposing it, but after him the liege men of the kingdom used the *Assise de la ligèce* against arbitrary acts of the royal will;[89] John of Ibelin could write of this text that "les seignors et les homes se doivent plus pener de savoir la" than any other assise, and LaMonte has shown that it ensured the supremacy of the high court of the kingdom.

There was a "high court" in the kingdom and in the principalities[90] just as there was a court in seigneuries of less importance. The lord usually surrounded himself with his vassals to give judgment, since they owed him their counsel. He could even ask a vassal to furnish advice through a third party, just as he could ask him to go to conduct an inquiry on the spot, or transmit a summons or a message. But service of court consisted above all in "faire esgars et conoissans et recors de cort."[91]

By their presence, on the other hand, the vassals brought a guarantee to the acts of the lord. Further, the vassals of the prince of Antioch refused to recognize the validity of the transfer of the principality to the emperor John Comnenus (1142) which had been made without the consent of the prince's court.[92] This guarantee ceased to appear in the acts of western princes by the end of the twelfth century, but it would persist in the Latin east.

The judicial competence of the high court of Jerusalem began to be defined at the time of the assembly of Nablus (1120), which attributed to it the cognizance of cases in which two barons opposed each other, or one baron and the man of another. Usāmah Ibn-Munqidh saw how it worked in receiving the complaint of a Moslem prince against a Frankish baron. On this occasion the king selected some knights to discuss and draw up the verdict, which he then put into effect.[93] But the composition of the court remained fluid; new crusaders occasionally sat with royal vassals.

89. Cf. Prawer, "La Noblesse et le régime féodal"; Riley-Smith, *Feudal Nobility*, pp. 145–184.
90. Cahen, *Syrie du nord*, pp. 441 ff.; Richard, *Comté de Tripoli*, pp. 71–73; La Monte, *Feudal Monarchy*, pp. 87–104.
91. John of Ibelin, cap. 217 (*RHC, Lois*, I, 347).
92. William of Tyre, XV, 20 (*RHC, Occ.*, I, 690–691); Cahen, *Syrie du nord*, pp. 366–367.
93. Mansi, *Concilia*, XXI, col. 262; Hartwig Derenbourg, *Ousâma ibn Mounḳidh, un émir syrien au premier siècle des croisades*, I, *Vie d'Ousâma* (Publications de l'École des langues orientales vivantes, ser. 2, XII; Paris, 1889–1893), pp. 185–186; Richard, *Royaume latin*, pp. 68, 70. On the delimitation of judicial competence between the court of the prince of Antioch and that of the patriarch, see below, p. 248.

The composition and procedure of the high court became increasingly defined later when the *Assise de la ligèce* came into force, bringing new cases before the court. But the members of the court were not so specialized as to form a body like the *parlement* of the kings of France. As early as 1250 the high court considered keeping a register of decisions, but the idea was abandoned.[94] However, the high court was normally made up of men having some legal competence. The law that was being applied became so complicated that it was necessary to make collections of customs such as the *Livre au roi,* the *Livre en forme de plait* of Philip of Novara, the *Livre des assises et des bons usages* of John of Ibelin, and still others. But it is especially the political role of the high court which has attracted attention. The *Assise de la ligèce* led it to intervene in the difficulties between the king and his liege men. The succession crises which allowed the vassals to judge the right of a claimant to receive their homage and service, required the high court to judge who was to receive the crown or the legality of the nomination as regent. A doctrine was elaborated by which this right allegedly went back to Godfrey of Bouillon's election by those who were to be his vassals. And the high court had the means of making its decisions respected by the king, the *conjuratio* of the liege men, who could withdraw their service from their lord.

Did the adoption of the *Assise de la ligèce* at least make feudal revolts impossible? The kingdom of Jerusalem had known such revolts before; Roman of Le Puy, lord of Transjordan, rebelled against Baldwin II, who had confiscated his barony before 1128;[95] Hugh II of Le Puiset, count of Jaffa, after having been accused of scheming against the life of king Fulk, took up arms and appealed to the Egyptians for help, but his barons abandoned him and he had to submit (1132).[96] The affair of Gerard of Sidon seems to have been more complicated: in 1160 he fought against Baldwin III, who besieged his cas-

94. *Abrégé du Livre des Assises de la Cour des Bourgeois,* caps. 13–19 (*RHC, Lois,* II, 246–250).

95. I have attempted to connect the adoption of the *Establissement dou roi Bauduin segont* with this revolt, as being the manifestation of a too independent vassal usurping royal rights (*Le Royaume latin de Jérusalem,* p. 90); but if the *Establissement* (or at least the part relative to the regalia) is to be attributed to Baldwin III, as Prawer has suggested (see above, note 85), this hypothesis must be abandoned.

96. LaMonte, "The Lords of Le Puiset on the Crusades," *Speculum,* XVII (1942), 100–118. Mayer, "Studies in the History of Queen Melisende," pp. 102–113, sees the revolt of Hugh II of Le Puiset as revealing the refusal of a party of the nobility to accept the claims of king Fulk to govern without the queen's being associated in his decisions, since she was the daughter of Baldwin II and the true holder of the kingdom.

Young king Baldwin III refuses the tutelage of his mother, queen Melisend. From the collections of the Bibliothèque nationale

tle of Belhacem, and he appealed to Nūr-ad-Dīn;[97] but, though it is possible that this war broke out because of the plundering of the lord of Sidon, it is certain that he did not die at the stake as Michael the Syrian wrote.[98] We know that tradition linked the adoption of the *Assise de la ligèce* to a conflict betwen Amalric and Gerard, without being able to say whether or not it had to do with the affair.

These rebellions of vassals did not have the same character as the conflicts which pitted Baldwin III against his mother, Melisend, or Raymond III of Tripoli against Guy of Lusignan.[99] These were problems of succession which ended in civil wars in which the barons participated. It was the same when Guy of Lusignan faced the barons who supported Conrad of Montferrat. On the other hand, Guy's revolt against Baldwin IV, who had stripped him of his regency in 1183,[100] and Reginald of Châtillon's refusal of obedience when Guy asked him in 1187 to surrender the spoils that he had taken from the Moslems (though it did not come to armed conflict),[101] were true acts of insubordination of vassals toward their lord.

After 1192 there were conflicts between the king and his vassals from time to time, but without degenerating into open revolt.[102] Even when Frederick II tried to take Beirut away from John I of Ibelin and confiscate his fiefs, the old lord of Beirut knew enough to avoid battle, preferring to rely upon the high court. Thus the use of force by Filangieri allowed John of Ibelin to enlist the help of most of the barons of Acre. The civil war which broke out in 1232 and which led to a take-over of Acre by John's partisans had a firm juridical base, and took a form much different from that of the feudal rebellions of the twelfth century. Now the sovereign appears as refusing to observe the *Assise de la ligèce* under which the barons took shelter. Thenceforth the royal authority became incapable of asserting itself.

The other crusader states also experienced difficulties between the princes and their vassals. In Edessa, Baldwin of Le Bourg had to strug-

---

97. Michael the Syrian, in *RHC, Arm.,* I, 354; Ibn-al-Athīr, in *RHC, Or.,* I, 522–523; Röhricht, *Regesta,* no. 344.

98. Richard, *Royaume latin,* p. 81.

99. In this case, Guy of Lusignan demanded an accounting from Raymond III for the administration of the kingdom, of which he had been the regent, and seized Beirut, which was Raymond's possession. The count of Tripoli got a promise of military aid from Saladin should the king attack him; cf. Baldwin, *Raymond III,* pp. 81–85.

100. *Estoire d'Eracles,* in *RHC, Occ.,* II, 2, 5; Baldwin, *Raymond III,* pp. 55–56.

101. At this time Reginald declared to the king that "ausi estoit-il sires de sa terre comme il de la soe" (*Estoire d'Eracles,* in *RHC, Occ.,* II, 34).

102. Tradition preserves a record of the abuse of power committed by Henry of Champagne against Aimery of Lusignan, and by Aimery against Ralph of Tiberias, who was accused of plotting against him and could get no hearing before the high court (1198).

gle against the independent aspirations of Joscelin I of Courtenay, lord of Tell Bashir, whom he stripped of his land. In Antioch, the barons appealed to the king of Jerusalem to stop princess Alice from reaching agreement with the Moslems or the Byzantines (1130–1136); they took part in the conflict between two claimants to the princely throne, Bohemond IV and his nephew Raymond Roupen, from 1201 on, and most of the great vassals, having sided with the latter, had to flee to Cilicia. In 1181 Bohemond III had been in conflict with the patriarch, Aimery of Limoges, and those of the barons who had supported the patriarch also had had to go into exile in Cilicia.[103]

The county of Tripoli was especially troubled by feudal revolts in the thirteenth century.[104] A war broke out in 1203–1206 between Bohemond IV and Renart, lord of Nephin, who was supported by king Aimery, over the marriage of an heiress of a fief. Renart had married Isabel, the daughter of Astafort, lord of Gibelcar ('Akkār), without the count's permission. The court of the barons of Tripoli decided in the count's favor, but Renart refused to accept this judgment.[105] In 1258 Bohemond VI was embroiled with his vassal, Bertrand Embriaco of Jubail, in the course of the war of Saint Sabas, in which Bertrand had taken the side of the Genoese against the count; the favor that the latter showed to the relatives of his wife Lucienne of Segni stirred up a revolt, led by Bertrand, of most of the lords of the county, notably Guy II of Jubail, John of Botron, and Meillor of Maraclea; Bohemond overcame it only with difficulty.[106] In 1276–1282 there was another conflict, provoked again by the marriage of an heiress (the daughter of Hugh l'Aleman, who married John Embriaco, the brother of the lord of Jubail); Guy, supported by the Templars and the Genoese, held Bohemond VII in check, but was

103. Cahen, *Syrie du nord,* pp. 350–357, 423, 534, 595, 634. In 1208, again with the concurrence of the patriarch, Peter of Angoulême, the knights hostile to the prince tried to turn the commune of Antioch against him (*Gestes des Chiprois,* cap. 65, in *RHC, Arm.,* II, 664).

104. In the twelfth century, we do not know if the count's vassals took part in the intrigues which led to the assassination of Raymond II in 1152, or in the conflict between Raymond and his cousin Bertrand, son of Alfonso Jordan, in 1148.

105. Cahen, *Syrie du nord,* pp. 604–605; Röhricht, *Geschichte des Königreichs Jerusalem (1100 bis 1291)* (Innsbruck, 1898), p. 697, note 1; W. H. Rudt de (von) Collenberg, "Les Raynouard, seigneurs de Nephin et de Maraclé en Terre Sainte, et leur parenté en Languedoc," *Cahiers de civilisation médiévale,* VII (1964), 289–311. We do not know in what circumstances Gibelcar passed to Astafort from the Puylaurens line, a descendant of whom returned to the west (Richard, *Comté de Tripoli,* p. 76).

106. *Gestes des Chiprois,* caps. 273, 290–296 (*RHC, Arm.,* II, 744, 748–750). The knights in rebellion refused to submit to the *esgart* of the count's court, and a commission of thirteen had to be set up to settle their dispute with Bohemond VI (Richard, "Le Comté de Tripoli dans les chartes des Porcellet," pp. 353–356). Several of them left the county and entered the service of the lord of the kingdom of Jerusalem.

finally captured and died of starvation.[107] In 1287, another member of the Embriaco family, Bartholomew, led an insurrection against bishop Bartholomew of Tortosa, the representative of countess Sibyl, which ended in the establishment of the commune of Tripoli.[108]

The seriousness of these feudal insurrections which disturbed the county of Tripoli, together with the fact that the king of Jerusalem had been stripped of his authority following the revolt of 1232, marks the period of decline of the Frankish states. The weakened royal authority was held in check by a coalition of the vassals of the kingdom, while in Tripoli the count had to take up arms to subdue his own vassals. This state of affairs marked a distinct break with conditions in the crusader states of the twelfth century.

---

107. Röhricht, *Geschichte,* pp. 972, 974, 982, 984. Bohemond VII first gave his consent to the marriage, then revoked it at the instigation of the bishop of Tortosa, Bartholomew of Antioch, whom the princess-mother Sibyl had made governor of Tripoli, and who wanted to marry the heiress to his own nephew, which the lord of Jubail took no notice of (*Gestes des Chiprois,* caps. 385, 391, in *RHC, Arm.,* II, 780, 781).

108. Bartholomew of Jubail had his own claims which he presented along with those of the commune: to marry his daughter to the young lord of Jubail, Guy II, and his son to Guy's sister (*ibid.,* cap. 470, [II, 801]). Cf. Richard, "Le Comté de Tripoli dans les chartes des Porcellet," pp. 356–358.

C. Monarchical Institutions

In fact, monarchical institutions had revealed considerable strength in the twelfth century, and it took a long development before a feudality which was originally badly organized and lacking cohesion could impose limitations. The primary feature of royal power in Jerusalem was the importance of the royal domain, especially in Judea and Samaria. In Galilee, Godfrey had agreed to a large grant to Tancred, who was charged with conquering the area; but when the principality of Tiberias reverted to Baldwin I, he reduced its importance before enfeoffing it anew.[109] He also avoided fulfilling the promises of his brother, who would have given Jerusalem and Jaffa to the Holy Sepulcher. He reserved for himself Nablus, Acre, and Beirut; Baldwin II added Tyre. Of course, in each city fiefs had been granted to knights; where Italian sailors had helped in the conquest, some quarters had been conceded to them; and the churches also got their share. But what remained to the king was very appreciable, as we can see from the goods and rights that he received from Tyre and the seigneury which surrounded it, listed in an inventory drawn up in 1243 by Marsiglio Zorzi, the bailie of the Venetians, who possessed a third of the seigneury, leaving two thirds to the king.[110]

To these great seigneuries others were added when the king joined to his own domain that of one of his vassals. Thus the county of Jaffa, which had belonged to the king until its infeudation about 1120 to Hugh I of Le Puiset, reverted to the crown in 1132 at the time of the exile of Hugh II of Le Puiset. In 1151 it formed the appanage of the future king Amalric, who joined it to the royal domain in 1163. In 1177 it was assigned to the future queen Sibyl. Later it would go to Aimery of Lusignan. In 1161 Philip of Milly ceded to the king the fief of Maron in exchange for the fief of Transjordan, which had just reverted to the king; Amalric managed to obtain the land of Bei-

109. Cf. Nicholson, *Tancred: A Study of His Career and Work in Their Relation to the First Crusade* (Chicago, 1940).

110. Röhricht, *Regesta,* no. 1114; Prawer, "Étude de quelques problèmes agraires et sociaux d'une seigneurie croisée au XIIIe siècle," *Byzantion,* XXII (1952), 5–61; XXIII (1953), 143–170 (concerning the rural part of the seigneury). The extent of the seigneury of Tyre also resulted from agreements with the Egyptians at the end of the thirteenth century; cf. Richard, "Un Partage de seigneurie," pp. 72–82.

rut in exchange for the small seigneury of Blanchegarde. Humphrey IV of Toron surrendered the great seigneury of Toron and Chastel-Neuf to Baldwin IV. Maron and Chastel-Neuf were almost immediately assigned to the king's uncle, count Joscelin III of Edessa, but it is worth noting that this important concession was made only out of recent acquisitions, without affecting the main part of the royal domain.[111] Even after 1192 the importance of the royal domain, compared to those of the principal vassals of the crown, was notable.

This domain included villages, the casals, and *gastines*. The king collected from them the same revenues as did other lords:[112] a *terragium* (Arabic, *kharāj*) proportional to the harvest; gifts in kind three times a year, the *exenia;* a capitation tax on serfs attached to the casals,[113] forced labor service for the cultivation of the seigneurial reserve, and the banalities of mill, oven, wine-press, and bath. But these incomes were reduced in those places where the king established Frankish or Syrian settlers to repopulate devastated territories.[114]

The towns also certainly availed themselves of charters of franchise, although we know only of those enjoyed by the inhabitants of Jerusalem whom Baldwin II had systematically attracted to the holy city. They were not identical for the Latins, the Syrians living in the city, and the peasants of neighboring villages who frequented the market. Furthermore, the stalls of the Latin merchants were carefully distinguished from those of Syrian merchants.[115] In Acre the separation was completed by prohibiting native Christians from living in the quarters between the market (*funda*) and the port; because of the complete exemption which the Italians enjoyed it was important to prevent the natives from being able to trade directly with the Italians, thus depriving the king of the taxes which he levied on the market.[116]

111. La Monte, "The Rise and Decline of a Frankish Seigneury in Syria in the Time of the Crusades," *Revue historique du sud-est européen,* XV (1938), 301–320; Richard, *Royaume latin,* pp. 71, 74, 81, 85, 135, 136; Nicholson, *Joscelyn III,* pp. 73–79, 97–102, 143–145.

112. Prawer, "Étude de quelques problèmes"; Cahen, "Le Régime rural syrien," pp. 286, 310; cf. chapter VI, below.

113. In the kingdom of Jerusalem the property in serfs was regulated by a custom only recently instituted: proof of the attachment of a serf to one's land had to date back to the year of the arrival of the crusaders before Antioch (1097); cf. Mayer, "Sankt Samuel auf dem Freudenberge und sein Besitz nach einem unbekannten Diplom König Balduins V," *Quellen und Forschungen aus italienischen Archiven und Bibliotheken,* XLIV (1964), 61–62.

114. Prawer, "Colonization Activities in the Latin Kingdom of Jerusalem," *Revue belge de philologie et d'histoire,* XXIX (1951), 1063–1118.

115. Prawer, "The Settlement of the Latins in Jerusalem," *Speculum,* XXVII (1952), 490–503; Richard, "Sur un Passage du 'Pèlerinage de Charlemagne': Le marché de Jérusalem," *Revue belge de philologie et d'histoire,* XLIII (1965), 552–555.

116. Richard, "Colonies marchandes privilégiées et marché seigneurial: La fonde d'Acre

The taxes in question (the "droitures de la fonde," the rates of which have been preserved for Acre) correspond to the western *teloneum*. There were also taxes on the use of weights and measures, on the location of the stalls (*plateaticum*), and tolls levied at gates (*portagium*) and on roads (*peagium*). The caravans crossing the kingdom from Egypt to Syria were made subject in the twelfth century to taxes of this sort. In the ports there was also a tax on entry (*catena*),[117] on anchorage (one silver mark per ship), and a third of the fare paid by pilgrims. One can see how, around 1240, a maritime city like Acre could bring in to the king, its lord, nearly 50,000 pounds.[118] Furthermore, the king possessed houses which paid him an *encensive,* as well as industrial establishments (flour and sugar-cane mills, sugar refineries, etc.). He likewise exploited the natural resources of the kingdom — fishing rights, salt mines, sources of bitumen, and the hunting of migratory birds. Finally, minting was a monopoly of the king, of the counts of Edessa and Tripoli, and of the prince of Antioch, although it seems that some barons began to coin deniers in their own name from the end of the twelfth century on.[119]

The domains and revenues of the prince of Antioch were likewise considerable.[120] The count of Edessa, master of the city of Edessa and Tell Bashir, was no less richly endowed. As for the count of Tripoli, his domain included the rich city of Tripoli, other towns ('Arqah, Rafanīyah), and castles with their appendages (Montferrand, Krak des Chevaliers), as well as a part of Latakia.[121] The importance of the domain that the sovereigns had reserved to themselves, even after the territorial losses at the end of the twelfth century, was a constant factor in the organization of the crusader states.

The domainial administration was usually arranged by farming out the royal revenues (*ad pactum, apaut*), which the *apauteurs* collected,

---

et ses 'droitures'," *Le Moyen-Âge,* LIX (1953), 325–340; see also Prawer, "L'Établissement des coutumes du marché à Saint-Jean d'Acre," *RHDFE,* ser. 4, XXIX (1951), 329–351, and Riley-Smith, "Government in Latin Syria and the Commercial Privileges of Foreign Merchants," in Derek Baker, ed., *Relations between East and West in the Middle Ages* (Edinburgh, 1973), pp. 109–132.

117. This term is met with for the first time in 1164; *funda,* in 1121; cf. Robert B. Patterson, "The Early Existence of the *funda* and *catena* in the Twelfth Century Kingdom of Jerusalem," *Speculum,* XXXIX (1964), 474–477.

118. According to an inquiry conducted by Richard of Cornwall about 1241: Henri Michelant and Gaston Raynaud, ed. and tr., *Itinéraires à Jérusalem et descriptions de la Terre Sainte . . .* (SOL, *SG,* III; Geneva, 1882), p. 137.

119. On royal revenues see Dodu, *Histoire des institutions monarchiques,* pp. 234–250. Cf. Richard, "La Fondation d'une église latine en Orient par Saint Louis: Damiette," *Bibliothèque de l'École des chartes,* CXX (1962), 41–42, 53.

120. Cahen, *Syrie du nord,* pp. 466–467.

121. Richard, *Comté de Tripoli,* pp. 53–57.

an appropriate proportion of which they then paid to a central office. In Antioch, as in Jerusalem, this office was called the *secrète,* after the Byzantine practice. The master of the *secrète* of Antioch, set up in the *mesnil apparent,* ensured the holding of a genuine land survey, the registration of *apauts,* grants of fiefs, and the like.[122] The *secrète* of Jerusalem had local branches, notably in Tyre and Acre, and kept written reports of proceedings dealing with land boundaries (*devises*), the list of horses brought to the army by the vassals, and acts relative to fiefs and rents.[123]

Thanks to this organization, the king of Jerusalem and the other princes of the Latin east were able to use the system of money-fiefs and cash salaries (*soudées*) on a broad scale. The *fiés en besanz* or *assises,* assigned from some royal revenue or other, allowed the king to reward the services of some of his vassals, starting with the great officers,[124] while using *soudées* to reward temporary services.[125]

The domain could likewise be used to reward administrative agents by providing them with hereditary tenures, such as the scribes who received a *scribanagium,* and the interpreters or dragomans, similarly enfeoffed. Scribes and interpreters were usually native Christians.[126] Other scribes were employed in markets and ports, while an *escrivain de la court* kept the records of the viscount's court.[127] The *secrète* received the accounts of all these officials in those cases where the revenues were not farmed out. Included among the officials to whom the king of Jerusalem and the princes entrusted the keeping of their domains were the castellans. They had charge of keeping the fortresses, but with no responsibility other than a military one. In Jerusalem, the king alone could appoint a castellan, or replace him; not even

122. Cahen, *Syrie du nord,* pp. 454, 466.

123. LaMonte, *Feudal Monarchy,* pp. 167 ff. The title "bailli de la secrète" is proved only for the kingdom of Cyprus, despite what Dodu has written in his *Histoire des institutions,* p. 251. See also Charles Kohler, "Chartes de l'abbaye de Josaphat," *ROL,* VII (1899), 180. I have expressed the opinion that the *secrète* of Tyre might have kept the list of services due the king by his vassals before 1187 (Richard, "Les Listes de seigneuries," pp. 563–577).

124. Donation of 10 bezants by Odo of Saint Amand, on the *assisia pincernatus mei* (*AOL,* II-2 [1884], 145; cf. also p. 146, where Humphrey IV of Toron makes a donation from *assisia mea . . . ad fundam Accon*). Cf. John of Ibelin, cap. 144: "Je tel doins à tei et à tes heirs tel ou tels casaus . . . ou tant de besanz assenés en tel leu" (*RHC, Lois,* I, 218).

125. The custom is so common as to occasion surprise at the statement, which Ernoul attributes to the king, that he did not have enough money to pay his soldiers (*Chronique d'Ernoul,* ed. L. de Mas Latrie, pp. 27–29).

126. *Royaume latin,* p. 129; Cahen, "Régime rural," pp. 306–307; Riley-Smith, "Some Lesser Officials in Latin Syria," *English Historical Review,* LXXXVII (1972), 1–26.

127. *Abrégé du Livre des Assises de la Cour des Bourgeois,* cap. 7 (*RHC, Lois,* II, 241); LaMonte, *Feudal Monarchy,* p. 169. The *funda* and *catena* used both Frankish scribes and *escrivains sarrasinois.*

the seneschal of the kingdom could do so.[128] But the castellan had
no administrative or judicial functions. In the kingdom of Jerusalem
and the county of Tripoli, these belonged to a viscount distinct from
the castellan.[129]

In the principality of Antioch there was a viscount in the city itself,
who appears to have been the prince's lieutenant responsible for administration and justice within the city, while bailies had this responsibility in the prince's domains, and "dukes" in Latakia and Jabala.[130]
The viscounts appear always to have been knights, but with some
exceptions[131] they were not provided with hereditary fiefs. Finally,
the ra'ises or *reguli* (village chiefs) exercised administrative functions
of which we know little.[132]

About the judicial functions in these states, however, we know
much more, thanks to the preservation of the collection of *assises*
and of numerous verdicts preserved in ecclesiastical cartularies. The
judicial organization of the crusader states was based on the existence
of parallel institutions in the domains of the king, prince, and two
counts, on the one hand, and in the domains of the lords endowed
with rights of justice, on the other. John of Ibelin includes in his *Livre*
a list of lords who had "court et coins et justise," and the "court de
borgesie et justise" in the towns of their seigneuries. The list, however, is incomplete and inaccurate; it seems to have been drawn up
as a mnemonic recital.[133] It does show, however, that in each seigneury, just as in the royal domain, there was a court which brought
the vassals into the presence of their lord to judge matters having
to do with fiefs and liege men on the model of the high court of the
kingdom.[134] This seigneurial court was distinct from those which met
under the direction of seigneurial officials to judge cases pertaining
to other types of tenure or persons of lower social rank. Doubtless
some cases involving serious offenses might be judged summarily by

128. LaMonte, *Feudal Monarchy,* p. 136; Dodu, *Histoire des institutions,* p. 177; Cahen,
Syrie du nord, p. 461. Some fortresses were conferred on persons of lesser rank, sometimes
even Syrians; see William of Tyre, XXII, 15 (*RHC, Occ.,* I, 1090–1092).

129. LaMonte (*Feudal Monarchy,* p. 136) thought that these functions were combined. But
at Jerusalem, in 1235, Baldwin of Picquigny was castellan, Gerard of Saiges viscount (Röhricht,
Regesta, no. 1065). Peter of Pennedepie, castellan of the Tower of David in 1242, received
an assise of 400 bezants from the revenues of Jerusalem (*ibid.,* no. 1107).

130. Cahen, *Syrie du nord,* pp. 456–457.

131. The viscountship of Nablus was hereditary: LaMonte, "The Viscounts of Naplouse
in the Twelfth Century," *Syria,* XIX (1938), 272–278; so also was that of Tripoli.

132. Cahen, "Régime rural," pp. 306–307; Riley-Smith, "Some Lesser Officials," pp. 1–26.

133. Richard, "Les Listes de seigneuries," pp. 563–577.

134. John of Ibelin, cap. 217 (*RHC, Lois,* I, 345–348).

the king, lord, or seigneurial officials, but a judicial assembly was the usual form.

As for the natives, we know of the court of the *ra'īs,* at least by name. It judged minor matters according to the custom of each community. It had competence when the offense committed carried neither a death sentence nor a sentence of mutilation, or when the case did not involve more than one silver mark.[135] The court of the *ra'īs* does not seem to have existed in the principality of Antioch, but there were persons who had the Byzantine title for judge (κριταί), over whom a *preteur* presided.[136]

The more important cases as well as those involving Latins came under the jurisdiction of the *cour de borgesie,* called, when found in the royal domain, *cour réau* or *cour le roi.* It probably evolved from the high court in the first half of the twelfth century. It was usually made up of twelve Latin jurors who determined the sentence, which was then promulgated by the viscount, who carried it out with the assistance of a *mathésep* (Arabic, *muḥtasib*) and other sergeants.[137] The kingdom alone had some forty courts of this kind in the period of their greatest extent.[138] There were also similar assemblies where there were no viscounts, as for example at Mahomerie (al-Bīrah), where the prior of the Holy Sepulcher held a "full court" bringing together all the Frankish burgesses of the place, and where an inhabitant appeared to renounce his tenure and take it up again under new conditions, as he would have done in the time of the *grands jours* of a western seigneury.[139]

In the county of Tripoli there were courts of the viscount in the city of Tripoli, at 'Arqah, probably at Rafanīyah, and also in the part of Latakia belonging to the count. In Antioch the prince's court had its own peculiarities, including the participation of natives of the Greek rite alongside Latin judges in the running of the court.

The competence of the "court of the burgesses" was very extensive; except where the cases were to be heard in the high court, it included crimes involving death, cases of treason, and matters relative to land ownership (even when having to do with a *borgesie* held by a knight). We know about its jurisdiction thanks to the *Livre des Assises de*

135. *RHC, Lois,* I, 26; II, 171–172; LaMonte, *Feudal Monarchy,* p. 108.

136. Cahen, *Syrie du nord,* pp. 455–456.

137. LaMonte, *Feudal Monarchy,* pp. 106–107; *RHC, Lois,* II, 236, 244.

138. John of Ibelin, cap. 240 (*RHC, Lois,* I, 419–421), lists thirty-seven; there were others at Qāqūn, Qalansuwā, Majdal (Mirabel), and Lajjūn (Richard, *Royaume latin,* p. 119).

139. Rozière, *Cartulaire,* pp. 240–241. The canons of the Holy Sepulcher had full rights of justice in the villages which they had opened to colonization; cf. Prawer, "Colonization Activities," pp. 1063–1118.

la Cour des Bourgeois, written in the thirteenth century. As Joshua Prawer has shown, however, this work has more the form of a learned treatise on law than of a collection of judicial decisions.[140]

There were also some exceptional jurisdictions. The Italian colonies possessed their own courts. From 1105 on, the Genoese had a viscount at Acre, and their consul at Tyre was called the Genoese viscount of Tyre in 1187. The Venetians in 1123 obtained the right for cases concerning Venetians alone to be dealt with by a separate Venetian court. The Pisans were exempted from the jurisdiction of the royal viscount in 1156 and then again in 1168. Similar privileges were granted by the princes of Antioch and the counts of Tripoli.[141] These courts did not in principle have the right to judge major cases or crimes of violence, nor matters having to do with land ownership, but in the thirteenth century they went beyond these limitations and the streets of the merchants would lay claim to a veritable right of asylum.[142]

There were also commercial courts. The bailie of the *catena* presided over a court composed of jurors chosen from among merchants and mariners to settle minor cases relative to the armament of ships, shipwreck, problems between sailors and captains, and so on; it also prepared more important cases to be heard in the viscount's court. It applied the assises issued by king Amalric, which suggests that he was the one who created this court.[143]

The market court of the *funda* was also in origin a commercial court, but it was transformed into a court with mixed jurisdiction to deal with cases involving Franks and Syrians, eliminating the court of the *ra'īs* wherever it was introduced. The bailie of the *funda* presided; of the six jurors, four were Syrians, two Latins. It heard civil cases of minor importance as well as acting as a court of registration for commercial transactions.[144]

In each of the four states the central government was in the hands of the sovereign assisted by major officers, who are also to be found in the service of less important lords.[145] The most complete list of

140. Prawer, "Étude préliminaire sur les sources et la composition du *Livre des assises des bourgeois*," *RHDFE*, ser. 4, XXXII (1954), 198–227, 358–382. On Antiochene law see Cahen, *Syrie du nord,* pp. 446–452.

141. LaMonte, *Feudal Monarchy,* pp. 226–242; Cahen, *Syrie du nord,* pp. 490–500; Richard, *Royaume latin,* pp. 217–227; *idem, Comté de Tripoli,* pp. 84, 85.

142. Cf. the difficulties, about 1260, aroused by the arrest in the Pisan quarter of John Renia (or Orenia), the murderer of bishop Hugh of Famagusta; René Grousset, *Histoire des croisades et du royaume franc de Jérusalem* (3 vols., Paris, 1934–1936), III, 557.

143. LaMonte, *Feudal Monarchy,* p. 109.

144. *Ibid.,* p. 108.

145. John of Ibelin defined the *baronie* by the fact that the baron employed both a constable and a marshal.

these officers is that for the kingdom of Jerusalem; it differs at several points from those of the other states.[146] These great officers were usually chosen by the sovereign at his accession (theoretically ending the powers of the officers of his predecessor, although, in fact, they were frequently renewed), or on the vacancy of an office. Some men consequently made a virtual career in the service of the royal household, occupying successively, as did Aimery of Lusignan, various great offices. Some offices, however, were hereditary in the principality of Antioch and the county of Tripoli. And in Jerusalem the marshal, though named by the king, swore homage to the constable whose lieutenant he was.

The seneschal emerged as the head of the royal household. He played a leading role in the ceremony of the royal coronation and on feast days. He could take the king's place in the high court, although custom did not allow him to hear cases concerning the life, honor, or fief of a knight except when the case had been brought up before the king himself. He took the king's place in the army, commanding the king's "battle" when the king was absent, in which case he received part of the booty due to the king. It was he who represented the king when the latter was prevented from exercising his prerogatives. He also controlled the administration of the royal domain, as well as the fortresses which he maintained and garrisoned. He had charge of the royal treasure, and could preside over the *secrète,* which was answerable to him.

The chamberlain played only a secondary role, guarding the royal treasure, administering the royal residence, and receiving liege homages on behalf of the king. The position of butler seems to have been of little importance.

The constable rivaled the seneschal as an officer of the first rank. He presided over the high court in the king's absence. He dealt with the boundaries of the royal domain and the fiefs of vassals. He commanded the army in the king's absence. He divided the troops into "battles" and personally commanded the vanguard. He reviewed the soldiers and could strike them if they were at fault (he could not strike a knight, but could kill his horse).

---

146. LaMonte, *Feudal Monarchy,* pp. 114–137. The *Livre au roi* defines their competence (caps. 9–12 in *RHC, Lois,* I, 612–614). At Antioch there were two marshals instead of one; the position of seneschal was hereditary (Cahen, *Syrie du nord,* pp. 452–455, 463–464). At Tripoli there seem to have been two constables at the outset; later, the position of constable became hereditary (Richard, *Comté de Tripoli,* pp. 49–50; Röhricht, *Regesta regni Hierosolymitani, Additamentum* [Innsbruck, 1904; repr. New York, 1960], no. 1224a). When the county and the principality were joined, the two sets of officers continued, but one of the two offices of marshal disappeared at Antioch.

The marshal assisted the constable, helping him to organize the men into "battles." He was particularly responsible for the *restor* (the replacement of horses killed in the king's service). He could confiscate the fief or the pay of a soldier insufficiently armed. And he commanded the rear guard of the army.

Both constable and marshal had legal jurisdictions. The constable was the judge of the army, even when there was no campaign, as far as the knights were concerned.[147] However, a *soudoyer* who presented a claim for pay went before the marshal if he was only a squire.

The army did not include only knights who held fiefs. There were those who were not knights, among whom the turcopoles were a group apart. In imitation of the Byzantine *tourkopouloi* they were lightly armed cavalry, mostly converted Moslems, who had been given small fiefs. They formed the vanguard of the army.[148] There were also contingents of sergeants recruited from among the townsmen. Each town, each *bourgade,* as well as prelates and abbeys, had to supply a fixed number of men (totaling altogether 5,025 sergeants and 577 knights). In addition, towns and bourgades having a Frankish population had to provide soldiers for the defense of the walls. In addition, there were Christian Syrians as well as contingents furnished voluntarily by the confraternities which had taken upon themselves the duty of helping in the defense of the Holy Land.

Knights and sergeants who held fiefs had to be ready on the order of the king to go where they were assigned and stay there under the king's orders for a whole year.[149] But there were also recruited men who did not hold fiefs or specialized tenures, especially pilgrims who came to the Holy Land every year, and who often had made a vow to stay there for some period of time in its defense. Some of the knights took them into their service,[150] but the king had wide recourse to this kind of recruitment, offering pay (*soudée*) to knights and sergeants (*soudoyers*). The marshal was in charge of them, getting four bezants for each *soudoyer.* He maintained strict discipline among them. A *soudoyer* leaving the service before the end of an engagement was punished by confiscation of his horse and armor, if he was

---

147. *Livre au roi,* cap. 14: "Li counestables est tenus d'oyr et d'entendre les clains et les tors que l'un chevaler fait à l'autre . . . et par devant le counestable deivent estre jugiés et chastiés les mausfais as chevalers" (*RHC, Lois,* I, 615).

148. Richard, *Royaume latin,* pp. 129–130. The title of *turcopolier* given their leader was known only in the kingdom of Cyprus.

149. John of Ibelin, cap. 217 (*RHC, Lois,* I, 345–348).

150. Thus John of Rheims had to furnish the king one pilgrim knight for his fief (*idem,* cap. 271 [*ibid.,* I, 425]).

a knight or sergeant; if he was in the infantry, his hands were pierced with a red-hot iron.[151]

We know little about the war fleets in the Latin east. The crusader states often had recourse to the Italians. However, in 1161 count Raymond III of Tripoli equipped galleys to devastate Cyprus, as Reginald of Antioch had done in 1156. Baldwin III raised a fleet of fifteen galleys which he in 1153 placed under the command of Gerard of Sidon, who was called *mestre des galiës*. And we know of a fief that the count of Tripoli gave to a vassal on condition that he keep an armed galley in readiness.[152]

The last great office was the chancellery. In each state a chancellor, usually an ecclesiastic, was the head of the palace clerks. He drew up the *privilèges* issued by the king, prince, or count. These acts, drawn up on the model of the *charte,* tell us something of the chancellor's assistants, recruited among the chaplains. The chancellery had no great development; there were other offices responsible for administrative or judicial correspondence in Latin (or French, from the thirteenth century on) as well as in native languages, which were not under the direction of the chancellor.

In the kingdom of Jerusalem we occasionally find representative assemblies, distinct from the high court, which come together for the purpose of deliberating over the affairs of the kingdom. In 1120 a *concilium* met at Nablus, including prelates and barons, to work out solutions for the difficult situation in which the kingdom found itself, and to establish peace; this meeting recalls the peace assemblies then held in the west.[153] In 1152 possibly only the knights met in Nablus to deliberate when a clan of Turcomans sought to take Jerusalem by surprise.[154] But in 1166 it was in the presence of a *curia generalis* in Nablus, at which there were present the patriarch, Amalric of Nesle, the prelates, and the barons and people, that king Amalric discussed the needs of the kingdom.[155] In 1177 an assembly of barons and prelates studied the means necessary to repair the walls of Jerusalem,

151. *Idem,* caps. 134–137 (*ibid.,* I, 209–212).

152. Richard, *Comté de Tripoli,* p. 54; Röhricht, *Regesta,* no. 754.

153. William of Tyre, XII, 13 (*RHC, Occ.,* I, 531–533); Mansi, *Concilia,* XXI, col. 262. On the conditions under which it was held cf. Richard, "Quelques textes sur les premiers temps de l'église latine de Jérusalem," *Recueil de travaux offerts à M. Clovis Brunel,* II (Paris, 1955), 426–430.

154. Grousset, "Sur un Passage obscur de Guillaume de Tyr," *Mélanges syriens offerts à M. René Dussaud* (Bibliothèque archéologique et historique, XXX; Paris, 1939), II, 937–939.

155. William of Tyre, XIX, 13 (*RHC, Occ.,* I, 902–904). In 1171 another assembly met to provide against the danger posed by the unification of Syria and Egypt, but its composition appears to have been more limited ("convocat universi regni principes," according to William of Tyre, XX, 22, *ibid.,* I, 980–983).

and it would be surprising if the residents of the town were not also consulted.[156] Finally, in 1183 a full assembly discussed the means for resisting Saladin.[157] The assemblies of 1166 and 1183, in particular, recall those which in France gave birth to the assemblies of estates, and in England to parliament.

In fact, they too had financial consequences. That of 1166 decided to levy a tax of a tenth on the movable goods of all subjects of the kingdom.[158] In 1183 the assembly reached a decision, the text of which William of Tyre has preserved, to establish a tax of one bezant on all property worth 100 bezants, of two per cent on all incomes other than the *soudées* (taxed at one per cent only), and a hearth tax of one bezant on all households of serfs or of freemen having less than 100 bezants income. The responsibility for collection of these taxes was given to four leading citizens of each diocese; each of three other men held a key to one of the two coffers (of Jerusalem and of Acre) where the money was to be kept, so that the king could not use it for purposes other than the defense of the kingdom.

These assemblies are comparable to those which met to draw up assises, but while the high court rendered judgments which set a precedent, these *ad hoc* meetings effectively made decisions of a legislative nature.[159] John of Ibelin says that the first elements of the law of Jerusalem were brought together by Godfrey of Bouillon during a meeting with the patriarch, princes, and barons present on the crusade, and that later, with each "passage" (that is, at the time of the arrival of pilgrims from the west), the king assembled at Acre the patriarch, barons, knights, and the most qualified clerics or laymen, together with persons of rank from the west who were versed in legal matters, in order to draw up the assises. These texts were later transcribed on parchment, sealed by the king, the patriarch, and the viscount of Jerusalem, and locked up in a coffer in the Holy Sepulcher.[160]

This account has certainly been embellished, but it preserves evidence of the participation of certain pilgrims from the west in juridi-

---

156. *Idem,* XXI, 25 (*ibid.,* I, 1047–1049).

157. *Idem,* XXII, 23 (*ibid.,* I, 1099–1112); Benjamin Z. Kedar, "The General Tax of 1183 in the Crusading Kingdom of Jerusalem," *English Historical Review,* LXXXIX (1974), 339–345.

158. The Latin text says "nemine excepto"; the French translator says that those who participated in the Egyptian campaign would be exempt from the tax; cf. LaMonte, *Feudal Monarchy,* pp. 179–182.

159. LaMonte, "Three Questions Concerning the Assises of Jerusalem," *Byzantina-metabyzantina,* I (1946), 204–208; Maurice Grandclaude, "Liste d'assises remontant au premier royaume de Jérusalem," in *Mélanges Paul Fournier* (Paris, 1929), pp. 329–346.

160. John of Ibelin, prologue (*RHC, Lois,* I, 3–4).

cal decisions.[161] The assemblies which drew up the assises had an im-
provisational character, such as the one which prepared the assise of
Bilbais limiting the participation of knights in sieges. Some included
only knights, such as the one king Amalric held at Tyre to deal with
the participation of vassals in the payment of a ransom for their lord,[162]
or the one which dealt with street-sweeping and was later considered
void because it had been promulgated by the king without the assent
of the people. There was a good deal of uncertainty, therefore, about
these seemingly legislative assemblies. Some assises might be drawn
up in meetings of the high court, more or less enlarged; others ema-
nated directly from the king. Aimery of Lusignan considered having
an edition of a collection of assises made by a commission of the
best jurists of the kingdom.[163] The high court, as LaMonte has shown,
was in origin only an unspecialized *curia regis,* the composition of
which the king might extend or limit according to need, and was competent to make legislative decisions.

From the end of the twelfth century, the weakness of the authority
of the king and the other princes led to the appearance of a very unusual communal movement, marked by the birth of the communes
of Antioch (1193), Acre (1231), and Tripoli (1288).[164] This was not
a bourgeois movement seeking improvement in the status of townsmen or a new administrative or judicial autonomy but, as Prawer
has shown, a means of overcoming the impossibility of making the
normal institutions work in a period of crisis. In Antioch the commune was proclaimed in 1193 or 1194, following the treaty of Baghrās,
which ceded Antioch to the Ṛoupenid prince Leon II, in order to
prevent the Armenians from occupying the city. Prince Bohemond

161. Thus Stephen, count of Sancerre, played a decisive role, in 1171, in resolving the problem of the partition of a fief among three sisters who succeeded Henry le Buffle, the brother
of Philip of Milly.

162. *Gestes des Chiprois,* cap. 202 (*RHC, Arm.,* II, 721); John of Ibelin, cap. 249 (*RHC,
Lois,* I, 398). See above, notes 124 and 132.

163. Philip of Novara, cap. 47 (*RHC, Lois,* I, 522–523).

164. Cf. LaMonte, "The Communal Movement in Syria in the Thirteenth Century," in *Anniversary Essays in Mediaeval History by Students of Charles Homer Haskins,* ed. Charles
H. Taylor (Boston and New York, 1929), pp. 117–131, and especially Prawer, "Estates, Communities and the Constitution of the Latin Kingdom"; the question of the communal movement
has been taken up following Prawer's study: Mayer, "Zwei Kommunen in Akkon?" *Deutsches
Archiv,* XXVI (1970), 434–453; idem, "On the Beginnings of the Communal Movement in the
Holy Land: The Commune of Tyre," *Traditio,* XXIV (1968), 443–457; Riley-Smith, "The *Assise
sur la ligèce* and the Commune of Acre," *Traditio,* XXVII (1971), 179–204; idem, *The Feudal
Nobility;* and Richard, "La Féodalité de l'Orient latin et le mouvement communal: Un état
des questions," in *Structures féodales et féodalisme dans l'Occident méditerranéan (Xe-XIIIe
siècles)* (Collection de l'École française de Rome, 44; Rome, 1980), pp. 651–665.

III and his eldest son Raymond were captives. The new patriarch, Ralph II, took over the leadership of the popular rising which had broken out, and the knights joined in. They all bound themselves together in a communal oath. Greeks and Latins stood shoulder to shoulder. The commune was directed by a mayor and consuls. It had its bell tower to summon everyone. It could impose taxes on all the inhabitants. After driving off the Armenians it continued in existence. Bohemond IV sought its support in 1198 in his claim to succeed to the principality, turning to account his anti-Armenian stance, which was much stronger than that of the court of the barons, which supported Raymond Roupen. In 1206 the patriarch changed sides, and with the help of the knights tried to evict Bohemond's partisans from the commune. His failure allowed Bohemond in turn to use the commune as an instrument of his power. With its aid he evicted the barons, knights, and burgesses who were opposed to him. The Greek element was predominant, which upset Innocent III. But after the end of the war of succession in Antioch the commune vanished, and the normal institutions reappeared.

The communes of Acre and Tripoli were established by using the framework of an earlier institution, that of the confraternities or brotherhoods (*fraries*).[165] The brotherhood was a pious association accepting the patronage of a saint or indulging in some particular devotion to the cult which it sought to promote. The members bound themselves together by obligations of mutual assistance. The statutes of the Italian brotherhood of the Holy Spirit in Acre (1216) looked after the distribution of alms to the sick, the organization of an almshouse, the ransoming of captives, and the relief of the poor. The brotherhood arbitrated disputes among its members, and took the place of absent relatives in the pursuit of justice when one of its members was murdered. It also had a military organization, arming and leading its members grouped under its banner to the defense of the kingdom. Most of these brotherhoods had a national or ethnic character; the Italians, other than those in the maritime towns, belonged to the Holy Spirit, the Spaniards to St. James, the Melkites to St. George and Bethlehem. Even the merchants from Mosul had their brotherhood. But in the thirteenth century another one, that of St. Andrew, accepted members without distinction as to origins.[166]

---

165. On the brotherhoods cf. Richard, *Royaume latin,* pp. 230–231, and "La Confrérie des 'Mosserins' d'Acre et les marchands de Mossoul au XIIIe siècle," *L'Orient syrien,* XI (1966), 451–460. See also Riley-Smith, "A Note on Confraternities in the Latin Kingdom of Jerusalem," *Bulletin of the Institute of Historical Research,* XLIV (1971), 301–308.

166. It seems quite likely that the seal of the *elemosina fraternitatis Acconensis* (in Schlum-

When the barons of John of Ibelin's party sought some means of organizing resistance against Frederick II's representative Richard Filangieri in 1231, they decided to use the brotherhood of St. Andrew; barons, knights, and townsmen joined it with the discreet encouragement of the patriarch. The brethren were therefore able to respond to John of Ibelin's appeal by sending him a contingent of forty-three knights. Then John effected the transformation of the brotherhood into a commune. Each brother took the communal oath; they elected a mayor (John himself), as well as consuls and captains; they had a bell tower to summon the members of the commune. These were normally residents of Acre, but they included the chief barons of the kingdom. Frederick II and Gregory IX sought in vain to procure the dissolution of this commune.[167] It represented, in fact, a compromise between a commune which took over the administration of a town, and a lordship governing a state on the Italian model. It allowed barons, knights, and townsmen to govern themselves in the absence of a regent of the kingdom, capable of summoning the high court and receiving the homage and oaths of fealty. The recognition of queen Alice and her husband Ralph of Nesle (or "of Soissons") as "lords of the kingdom" would render it unnecessary, and seems to have led to its disappearance.[168]

The institutions of the kingdom were just as deeply affected. Acre, with its turbulent townsmen, foreign colonies, fortified houses of religious orders, and households of great barons, was the first city of the kingdom. The representative of the "lord of the kingdom" had difficulty in establishing his authority. Thenceforth one could not avoid dealing with the brotherhoods. For example, a letter of Urban IV in 1264 was addressed to the rectors of the brotherhoods among other high persons of authority in the kingdom.[169] The brotherhoods put themselves under the military orders, influenced by their common religious devotion. That of St. James of the Spaniards was bound by oath to the Hospitallers, and fought by the side of the Genoese against other brotherhoods during the war of Saint Sabas. In 1264

---

berger *et al., Sigillographie de l'Orient latin,* p. 140) belonged to this brotherhood. See also Chandon de Briailles, "Bulles de l'Orient latin," *Syria,* XXVII (1950), 296–297.

167. Prawer, "Estates, Communities, and the Constitution of the Latin Kingdom"; see also *AOL,* I (1881), 401–403; *MGH, Epistolae saeculi XIII,* I, 554, 571. Prawer has shown that this commune served Simon of Montfort as a model for the Provisions of Oxford.

168. Demonstrated by Prawer in his excellent discussion. However, in 1257 there was still a "syndic and proctor of the seigneury of Jerusalem," Stephen of Sauvegny (Röhricht, *Regesta,* no. 1259), whose title is reminiscent of the "syndics" of the commune cited in a letter of Gregory IX in 1235 (Rodenberg, *op. cit.,* p. 554).

169. *Les Registres d'Urbain IV (1261–1264),* ed. Jean Guiraud, II (Paris, 1901), 419 (no. 867).

the brotherhoods participated in the choosing of the bailie of the kingdom. These groups became powers comparable to the religious orders and to the "communes" of the privileged foreigners, within an urban framework which was thenceforth the characteristic feature of the life of the kingdom.[170]

The commune of Tripoli emerged as a provisional expedient also, bringing together barons and townsmen who refused to recognize the authority of princess Sibyl's representative. Here also they adopted a religious patron, Our Lady. They elected various officers and a captain (*chevetaine*). But the commune disappeared very quickly when the Mamluks besieged Tripoli.

The appearance of these institutions born of insurrection accompanied the weakening of the king and the prince of Antioch. The inhabitants of the towns, and above all the barons, succeeded in organizing a government which did without the participation of the sovereign, whose authority was thus limited more and more by the need to gain the assent of vassals and townsmen who were theoretically his subjects.

170. For the evidence see Prawer, "Estates, Communities and the Constitution of the Latin Kingdom," cf. Richard, "La Confrérie des 'Mosserins' d'Acre."

D. The Establishment of the Latin Church

Alongside the political organization of states, the Latin church was established in territories conquered by the crusades.[171] Before this, Christians of the Latin rite had only places devoted to the service of pilgrims in the Holy Land, the Benedictine monastery of St. Mary *Latine* at Latakia, and the Hospital of St. John founded by the Amalfitans in Jerusalem. Latin Christians recognized as their own the church which professed dogmas defined by the Council of Chalcedon and which had at its head the Greek patriarchs of Jerusalem and Antioch. In Palestine, however, the Greek church was weak; other than the patriarch there were only three or four bishops. In Syria it was stronger, thanks to a century of reoccupation by the Byzantines. The hierarchy had suffered during the Turkish invasion, but it had survived. The more recent Greek schism had been accepted without much enthusiasm by the eastern patriarchs, and so the illusion of the church's unity could still be maintained.

It is not surprising that the Latins accepted the Greek patriarch of Antioch, John V the Oxite, whom they found on their arrival. They returned his cathedral to him, and showered it with gifts. At Albara, however, where they found no bishop when they took the town, they selected their own, Peter of Narbonne, and placed him on the episcopal see which had been reëstablished there.[172] In fact it was logical that the Latins, now the dominant social group, would choose from their own ranks the clerics and bishops for the churches they restored, while still recognizing the legitimacy of Greek prelates who in principle belonged to the same church as they did.

171. The fundamental study remains that of Wilhelm Hotzelt, "Kirchliche Organisation und religiöses Leben in Palästina während der Kreuzzugszeit," *Das Heilige Land (Palästinahefte des Deutschen Palästina-Vereins)*, II (1940), 1–106. This was redone in more complete form, including a monograph on each of the patriarchs of Jerusalem, under the title *Kirchengeschichte Palästinas im Zeitalter der Kreuzzüge 1099–1291* (Cologne, 1940). See also Mayer, *Bistümer, Klöster und Stifte im Königreich Jerusalem* (*MGH, Schriften*, XXVI; Stuttgart, 1977). The reconstitution of the Latin church in the crusader states, and its relation to early ecclesiastical geography, have been studied by Giorgio Fedalto, *La Chiesa latina in Oriente*, I (Verona, 1973), 49–134; and Bernard Hamilton, *The Latin Church in the Crusader States: The Secular Church* (London, 1980), with important bibliography.

172. Cahen, *Syrie du nord*, p. 308; Richard, "Note sur l'archidiocèse d'Apamée et les conquêtes de Raymond de Saint-Gilles en Syrie du nord," *Syria*, XXV (1946–1948), 103–108.

But it was a delicate situation. The Greek patriarch followed a pro-Byzantine policy, and did not expressly recognize the primacy of the pope. The differences which arose between Bohemond and Alexius Comnenus made John V's position untenable. From 1099 on, Latin archbishops were enthroned at Tarsus, Mamistra, and Edessa; none of them seem to have been consecrated by John V. In 1100 John left for Constantinople, where he abdicated.[173] The bishop of Artesia ('Artāḥ), Bernard of Valence, was chosen by the Latin clergy to succeed him. He took over the cathedral and the possessions of the patriarchate, surrounding himself with Latin canons. The basileus did not accept this replacement. From 1108 on, by the treaty of Devol, Alexius I claimed the right to appoint to the see of Antioch a Greek patriarch to be chosen from among the clergy of the great church of Constantinople. John Comnenus made the same claim in 1137, and titular patriarchs of the see of Antioch succeeded one another in Constantinople. In 1158 Manuel Comnenus forced prince Reginald to accept a Greek, Sotericus, but he was never installed. Athanasius II was installed in 1165, but died in the earthquake of 1170 and was not succeeded by another Greek. In 1206 or 1207 Bohemond IV installed a Greek, Symeon II, after driving out the Latin patriarch. Under pressure from the Mongols, Bohemond VI did the same in 1260. But these were exceptional cases, arising from external pressure or internal crisis.[174]

The same sort of thing happened in 1158 when the Byzantines drove the Latins out of Cilicia. The Latin archbishops of Tarsus and Mamistra had to withdraw from their sees, which they reoccupied only when the princes of Antioch and then the Armenian barons of the Amanus retook the Cilician plain.[175]

In Jerusalem the Latins found the see vacant. Mistaken tradition had it that the patriarch, Symeon II, driven from the city by the Egyp-

173. His departure was definitely in 1100 (Yewdale, *Bohemond I,* p. 103). His abdication is dated October 1100 (Venance Grumel, "Les Patriarches grecs d'Antioche du nom de Jean," *Échos d'Orient,* XXXII [1933], 295–296. The three archbishops were, respectively, Roger, Bartholomew I, and Benedict.

174. Grumel, "Le Patriarcat et les patriarches d'Antioche sous la domination byzantine," *Échos d'Orient,* XXXIII (1934), 53–55. On the problems caused by the adhesion of the patriarch David to the program of church union proposed by Innocent IV in 1245, because of the simultaneous presence of two hierarchies both in communion with Rome, see Martiniano Roncaglia, "Frère Laurent de Portugal, O.F.M., et sa légation en Orient (1245–1248)," *Bolletino della badia greca di Grottaferrata,* new ser., VII (1953), 33–44; Hamilton, *Latin Church,* pp. 217–221. Symeon II had been elected at Antioch instead of being designated, as was customary, by the emperor and the patriarch of Constantinople (at Nicaea 1204–1261).

175. It was in reaction against his excommunication that Leon II in 1212 replaced a deceased Latin archbishop-elect of Tarsus with a Greek (Cahen, *Syrie du nord,* p. 619).

tians, had taken refuge in Cyprus where he died. In fact, he had gone to Constantinople. The Latins chose a new patriarch from their own ranks. So another succession of Greek titular patriarchs was established in Constantinople, although after the middle of the twelfth century they returned to Jerusalem and resided in a Greek monastery.[176]

Latins, therefore, replaced Greeks in the cathedrals, and took possession of the goods of patriarchates, bishoprics, and some monasteries, above all those of the Holy Sepulcher. But in Jerusalem itself an act of 1173 shows the presence of a group of Greek clerics attached to the Holy Sepulcher, with their *protopapas,* and a certain Meletos had the title of archbishop of the Greeks and Syrians (Melkites) of Gaza and Eleutheropolis (Beth Gibelin). This is an example, undoubtedly, of a Greek prelate installed within the framework of a diocese of the Latin church to govern the clergy and faithful of the Greek rite living in the diocese, one whose election had to be submitted to and approved by the Latin bishop. In order to satisfy the prescriptions of canon law, this arrangement required that the Greek prelate take the name of an episcopal city other than one of which a Latin bishop was the titular; this arrangement seems to have become common.[177]

The difficulties which arose between Latins and Greeks, who thought of themselves as belonging to the same church, and so in principle coming under the same bishop, did not arise between Latins and other kinds of Christians, whom the Latin church looked upon not only as schismatics, but even as heretics. Armenians, Nestorians, and Monophysites regained their churches and, after some difficulty, their property; they intended to keep their traditional hierarchy without being forced to recognize the supremacy of the local Latin clergy, even when they declared their obedience to the church of Rome.[178]

---

176. Hotzelt, "Kirchliche Organisation," pp. 68, 96. It was only after Saladin's death (1193) that the Moslems allowed the Greek patriarchs to return to the Holy Land: Dositheus (1187–1189) and Mark Cataphlorus (1189–1195) never left Constantinople, but Euthymius (1195–1222) died at Sinai (Hamilton, *Latin Church,* pp. 180, 310–312).

177. J. Delaville Le Roulx, "Chartes relatives aux Hospitaliers," *AOL,* I (1881), 413. When, in 1220, the episcopal hierarchy of Cyprus was set up on the same basis, with a Greek bishop in each diocese, but with the title of another city, it was done by evoking the custom of the kingdom of Jerusalem; see Aloysius L. Tăutu, ed., *Acta Honorii III (1216–1227) et Gregorii IX (1227–1241)* (PC, Fontes, ser. 3, vol. III; Vatican City, 1950), no. 108.

178. For example, the Maronites. Likewise, in 1247, the Jacobite patriarch Ignatius II, making an act of obedience to the pope, asked that the prelates and churches under him not come under the jurisdiction of Latin clergy (Hotzelt, "Kirchliche Organisation," pp. 72–73). On the problem of conscience for the Latins, respecting their attitude toward the "heretics" and "schismatics" whom they found on their arrival at Antioch, cf. the letter sent from Antioch by the crusade leaders in 1098: ". . . Turcos et paganos expugnavimus: haereticos autem . . . expugnare nequivimus," they wrote to Urban II, declaring themselves ready on the pope's orders to help him to "eradicate and destroy all heresies" (Fulcher of Chartres, in *RHC, Occ.,* III, 351).

Some of the Orthodox, however, made no difficulty about being placed under the jurisdiction of the Latin patriarchs,[179] but in principle the Latin patriarch's jurisdiction extended only to Latins or to native Christians of the Latin rite. It was because of this that wherever the Moslem reconquest annihilated the Latin population, the Latin church disappeared.

The selection of two patriarchs was a novelty in the Latin church. It illustrates the desire of newcomers to accommodate themselves to the traditional organization of the eastern church. But the act in itself was exceptional: to choose a bishop was usually the affair of the cathedral chapter, and there were as yet no chapters. In Jerusalem the clergy in the ranks of the crusading army designated as patriarch Arnulf "Malecorne" of Chocques, chaplain of duke Robert II of Normandy; Arnulf had been invested with the powers of a legate by Urban II and had to some extent taken the place of Adhémar of Monteil after the latter's death.[180] Did Arnulf actually receive the title of patriarch? Both Raymond of Aguilers and Guibert of Nogent say that he did. Fulcher of Chartres says that he was designated only provisionally subject to papal confirmation, but it is possible that this interpretation was made after the event.[181] Late in 1099 a new papal legate, Daimbert of Pisa, declared the election irregular on the grounds of simony, and he later took Arnulf's place on the patriarchal throne after having been designated in an assembly held in Jerusalem, under pressure from Bohemond and Baldwin of Edessa (December 21, 1100).

Daimbert clashed with king Baldwin I, was accused before a council presided over by the cardinal-legate Maurice of Porto in March 1101, and went into exile at the end of that year, but the prince of Antioch reëstablished him in his see in 1102. A new council judged him and deposed him on grounds of simony, embezzlement, treason against the king, and the shedding of blood (the Pisans whom he had led had

179. A Georgian monastery, for example, was put under the authority of the patriarch Gibelin (Richard, "Quelques textes," pp. 423–426).

180. The fact is reported by Clarius, who got it from Alexander, one-time chaplain of Stephen of Blois who had also been invested with the powers of a legate; cf. Richard, "Quelques textes." On Arnulf, cf. Raymonde Foreville, "Un Chef de la première croisade, Arnoul Malecouronne," *Bulletin historique du Comité des travaux historiques et scientifiques* (1953-1954), pp. 377–390.

181. Cf. Emil Hampel, *Untersuchungen über das lateinische Patriarchat von Jerusalem . . . (1099 bis 1118)* (Breslau, 1899), pp. 8–14. Albert of Aachen, VI, 39 (*RHC, Occ.,* IV, 489), says that he was given the titles of "cancellarius sanctae Ecclesiae Iherusalem, procurator sanctarum reliquiarum et custos eleemosynarum fidelium," but he probably received these titles only after he gave up the patriarchate (on these functions, cf. the text of Clarius cited above, note 180; see also Hansen, *Das Problem eines Kirchenstaates in Jerusalem,* pp. 23, 26, 29).

slain Greek Christians during their crusade). Evremar of Chocques replaced him, but Daimbert appealed to Rome and was about to recover his see when he died in 1105. Arnulf now claimed that the finding in Rome amounted to Evremar's deposition. The pope had to intervene, but Evremar preferred to resign (December 1107) and was replaced by the papal legate Gibelin of Sabran (1108).[182] On Gibelin's death Arnulf was elected patriarch by the canons of the Holy Sepulcher (1112), and, although condemned for simony by a council held at Jerusalem in 1115, he was able to clear himself at Rome and remained patriarch until his death in 1118.[183]

From then on the patriarchs were regularly elected by the canons of the Holy Sepulcher. They proceeded by selecting two candidates whom they presented to the king. He chose one of them and invested him.[184] The patriarchs, however, had to tolerate the activity of papal legates invested with extensive powers and enjoying broad prerogatives.[185] However, in the thirteenth century, the pope ordinarily conferred legatine powers on the patriarch himself within the jurisdiction of his patriarchate.[186]

After 1187 the patriarch did not live in Jerusalem, but in Acre. The reoccupation of the holy city in 1229 did not lead to his renewed residence there except on rare occasions. After 1244 his residence at Acre became the norm. This raised some difficulties for the local bishop. Alexander IV had to exempt the patriarch and his entourage from the jurisdiction of the bishop, and the patriarch James Pantaléon (1253–1261), after he became pope as Urban IV, decided to unite the see of Acre to the patriarchate.[187]

---

182. Hampel, *Untersuchungen über das lateinisches Patriarchat,* pp. 49, 59–62. See also the corresponding notices in Hotzelt, *Kirchengeschichte Palästinas.*

183. William of Tyre echoes traditions hostile to Arnulf, accusing him of imposing the rule of canons regular on the chapter of the Holy Sepulcher in order to monopolize the goods of the canons (1114). But not only was this kind of change very frequent in the west at the time; on this particular occasion it had been necessary to establish some kind of division of goods between the patriarch's *mensa* and that of the chapter. The division is specified in a bull of Celestine III (1195), edited by Rozière (*Cartulaire,* no. 128, pp. 233–238); cf. Hotzelt, "Die Chorherren des heiligen Grabes," *Das heilige Land,* II (1940), 107–136.

184. On the succession of patriarchs cf. Louis de Mas Latrie, "Les Patriarches latins de Jérusalem," *ROL,* I (1893), 16–41, and Hotzelt, *Kirchengeschichte Palästinas.* On the method of election cf. Rudolf Hiestand and H. E. Mayer, "Die Nachfolge des Patriarchen Monachus von Jerusalem," *Basler Zeitschrift für Geschichte,* LXXIV (1974), 109–130.

185. Cf. William of Tyre, XVIII, 29 (on the reception of the cardinal, John, sent by Alexander III in 1161 to obtain his recognition as legitimate pope), in *RHC, Occ.,* I, 870–871.

186. This custom began with the patriarch Ralph of Mérencourt (1223), and was continued by Gerald of Lausanne (1225–1239); cf. Wilhelm Jacobs, *Patriarch Gerold von Jerusalem* (Aachen, 1905).

187. *Les Registres d'Alexandre IV,* ed. Joseph de Loye and Pierre de Cenival, II (Paris,

The patriarchate of Antioch posed a problem. It was the oldest see of St. Peter, and the crusaders wondered if the pope ought not to take it over himself. It was in this sense that they wrote to Urban II.[188] After John the Oxite's departure, however, the Latin prelates dependent on Antioch unanimously chose Bernard of Valence (1100–1135), who had no difficulties either with the prince or with the canons of his cathedral chapter.[189] It may have been Bernard, however, who began to take advantage of the fact that his see was older than that of Rome, in order to establish a certain independence of the papacy.[190] His successor, Ralph of Domfront (1135–1139), elected somewhat irregularly, claimed that he could confer the pallium on himself without having to ask the pope for it, on the grounds of this claim of temporal priority. Threatened with deposition, however, he submitted. He went to Rome in order to get rescinded the sentence which had been imposed on him at the synod of Antioch in November 1139.[191]

He was succeeded by a great churchman, Aimery of Limoges (1139–1193), who had to withdraw from Antioch temporarily in 1165 to give place to the Greek patriarch Athanasius II. He installed himself in the castle of Cursat (Quṣair), which became the preferred residence of the patriarchs thenceforth. Aimery is known above all for his relations with the eastern churches. He obtained from the Jacobite patriarch, Michael the Syrian, the treatise *Against the Manichaeans,* to be used at the Third Lateran Council (1179); and it was at his instigation that the Maronite patriarch Jacob undertook an act of obedience to Rome.[192] Peter of Angoulême, however, who was elected

---

1917), 547–548 (no. 1775); *Registres d'Urbain IV,* ed. Guiraud, II, 65 (no. 168). James Pantaléon designated two vicars to replace him in the administration of the bishopric of Acre and the patriarchate. One of these, Thomas Agni of Lentini, bishop of Bethlehem, took over the legation for almost the entire pontificate (*ibid.,* nos. 191 and 191 bis).

188. They wrote on September 11, 1098, as follows: "Quid igitur in orbe rectius esse videtur, quam ut tu . . . ad urbem principalem et capitalem Christiani nominis venias . . . ? Mandamus igitur . . . ut tu . . . qui beati Petri es vicarius, in cathedra ejus sedeas" (Fulcher of Chartres, in *RHC, Occ.,* III, 351; cf. Heinrich Hagenmeyer, *Epistulae et chartae ad historiam primi belli sacri spectantes* [Innsbruck, 1901], no. xvi).

189. The chapter first had twelve canons; the number went up to twenty in the thirteenth century. There is a list of the bishops of the patriarchate in Cahen, *Syrie du nord,* pp. 319–323; see also Mas Latrie, "Les Patriarches latins d'Antioche," *ROL,* II (1894), 192–205.

190. Such is the hypothesis, with respect to the quarrel over the obedience of the province of Tyre (below, p. 240), of John G. Rowe, "The Papacy and the Ecclesiastical Province of Tyre," *Bulletin of the John Rylands Library,* XLIII (1960), 160–189. It is not convincing.

191. *Ibid.,* pp. 183–184.

192. The Maronite patriarch had made a nominal act of obedience in 1140, but he officially abjured Monotheletism on the eve of the Lateran council; cf. Kamal S. Salibi, "The Maronite Church in the Middle Ages," *Oriens Christianus,* XLII (1958), 92–104. The act of obedience was renewed under Innocent III, but some Maronite elements resisted the union with Rome which a large part of their church had accepted, which necessitated more discussion.

in 1196, supported Leon II of Cilician Armenia against Bohemond IV, and was deposed by the cardinal legate Soffredo on disciplinary grounds. In 1208 the prince threw him into prison, where he died of thirst; Bohemond had already replaced him with a Greek patriarch, Symeon II. The next patriarch was again a Latin, Peter of Locedio (1209–1217). Opizo Fieschi (1247–1268, d. 1292) was also forced by the Mongols to give place to the Greek Euthymius, and withdrew from Antioch to Italy about 1260, leaving behind a vicar, Bartholomew; he soon became bishop of Tortosa, being replaced as vicar in 1263 by the Dominican Christian, who was killed by the Egyptians in 1268.

The establishment of an episcopal hierarchy in each of the patriarchates would raise difficulties. There was a decision attributed to Urban II according to which the conquered territories were to come under sees in the states to which such territories had previously belonged, and a decree attributed to Adhémar of Monteil fixing the river an-Nahr al-Kabīr, in the county of Tripoli, as the boundary between the patriarchates of Antioch and Jerusalem.[193] Both these texts are suspect. The first elevations of episcopal sees seem to have come about at random, where some conquered town seemed important enough to have a bishop, or where it appeared that a surviving church ought to be a cathedral (such as at Lydda). It is worth noting that the patriarch Daimbert of Jerusalem in December 1099 consecrated the bishop of Artesia and the archbishops of Edessa, Tarsus, and Mamistra,[194] while Peter of Albara and Robert of Lydda received the episcopal blessing of the bishops who participated in the crusade, thus allowing Robert to install Daimbert in the patriarchal see.

Very quickly, however, the Latins decided to adopt as episcopal sees those towns which had been such before the Moslem occupation, and to reorganize the ecclesiastical provinces by using the *Notitiae* which had described the divisions of the bishoprics and archbishoprics of each patriarchate. The question gave no difficulty in the principality of Antioch, and archbishop Benedict of Edessa made no trouble about his subjection to the patriarch of Antioch.

The ecclesiastical province of Phoenicia presented a more delicate problem. The metropolitan center, Tyre, remained in Moslem hands until 1124. The bishoprics of Beirut, Sidon, Acre, and Banyas would

---

193. Röhricht, *Regesta*, no. 72. If Urban II really made the decision attributed to him, it was only in the case where there might have been some doubt respecting the connection of an episcopal see to an already existing ecclesiastical province.

194. Ralph of Caen, in *RHC, Occ.*, III, 704 (the Greek patriarch John the Oxite was then established at Antioch).

be conquered by the kings of Jerusalem, while those of Tripoli, Botron, Arca ('Arqah), Orthosias, Byblos (Jubail), Maraclea, and Tortosa were conquered by the counts of Tripoli. Frankish occupation was first undertaken from the county of Tripoli. It has been suggested that Raymond of St. Gilles had unsuccessfully tried to make Tripoli the metropolitan center by appointing an archbishop there.[195] Another hypothesis, however, is that the reason no bishop was nominated at Tortosa and Jubail, but only at Tripoli, was that the patriarch of Antioch was waiting for Tyre to be taken in order to reorganize the province entirely and determine which sees were to be established.[196]

In any case, the fall of Beirut to Baldwin I was followed by the king's nomination of a bishop, also named Baldwin, who acknowledged the authority of the patriarch of Jerusalem (1111–1112). Bernard, the patriarch of Antioch, protested, arguing that Beirut and all of Phoenicia belonged to his see. Rome could not make up its mind, because no one knew at the outset the details of the *Notitia* of Antioch, and because king Baldwin I and patriarch Arnulf of Jerusalem based their claim on the decision attributed to Urban II about the connections of bishoprics to ecclesiastical circumscriptions modeled on the states founded by the crusaders. In 1113 Paschal II decided in favor of the Antiochene view. The episcopate of the county of Tripoli continued to look to Antioch,[197] but Jerusalem retained Beirut. Although the see of Tyre was erected in 1124, it remained vacant for some time; the conflict would break out again when the patriarch of Jerusalem, basing his claim on an earlier decision by Paschal in his favor, got from Honorius II confirmation of this decision and an order to the bishops of the county of Tripoli to recognize the authority of the archbishop of Tyre.[198]

In 1135, however, the new archbishop of Tyre, Fulcher of Angoulême, undertook to restore the unity of his province, and entered into relations with the patriarch of Antioch, to whom he proposed to sub-

195. A text from Languedoc, in fact, mentions an "archbishop" of Tripoli between 1105 and 1107 (Richard, *Comté de Tripoli*, p. 59).

196. Rowe, "The Papacy and the Ecclesiastical Province of Tyre," pp. 163–164. The only support for this lies in the fact that the texts do not mention bishops at Tortosa and Jubail at the beginning of the twelfth century, but acts concerning this province are scarce.

197. Thus in 1125 the church of Tripoli made an agreement with the Hospitallers over the tithes of the diocese of Arcas, with a reservation in the event that the patriarch of Antioch might terminate the union of the sees of Arcas and Tripoli (Delaville Le Roulx, *Cartulaire général,* I, no. 72).

198. Rowe, "The Papacy and the Ecclesiastical Province of Tyre," has connected the raising of the siege of Tortosa, which he puts in 1127, and that of Jubail, which he puts after 1128, with these vicissitudes, and thinks that Honorius II reverted to Paschal II's first decision because his second decision could not be put into effect; all this is uncertain.

ject himself in return for the restoration of the bishoprics of Tripoli. Rome gave its consent, after some hesitation, to the reconstitution of the province of Tyre in 1139, but the patriarch of Jerusalem, William of Messines, would not agree. The archbishop of Tyre had to settle for the obedience of the bishops of old Phoenicia located within the kingdom of Jerusalem, while the three bishoprics in Tripoli continued in their dependence on Antioch.[199]

A similar conflict arose with respect to the old province of Arabia, with Bosra as metropolitan center, when king Amalric of Jerusalem reëstablished an archiepiscopal see at Kerak in 1167. Since Arabia had earlier depended on Antioch, the patriarch Aimery demanded the submission of the new archbishop, Guerricus, when raising the question of Tyre, but without success.[200]

Aside from these problems, which arose because of the refusal of the king of Jerusalem to accept the recognition by any bishop in his kingdom of the authority of any patriarch other than that of Jerusalem, the reconstruction of ecclesiastical provinces under their traditional metropolitans seems to have gone on without hindrance. The old province of II Syria, divided between the principality of Antioch and the county of Tripoli, and pierced by Moslem enclaves, was revived with its metropolitan center at Apamea, to which the bishop of Albara was transferred, with bishoprics at Valania and Rafanīyah.[201]

The desire to revive those churches which had disappeared under Moslem domination did not result in the systematic restoration of all the bishoprics in conquered towns. Some of them were deserted and not worth reviving, although the crusaders gave the title of bishop of Lydda to Robert, conceding to him the great church of St. George and the neighboring town of Ramla;[202] others were much too important. The Latins respected the old ecclesiastical organization, leaving to each diocese its individuality, but they adopted the technique of

199. On all this see Rowe, *op. cit.* Tyre claimed (in error) the obedience of Haifa (Cayphas), which the patriarch of Jerusalem turned down.

200. Cf. Richard, "Évêchés titulaires et missionnaires dans le *Provinciale romanae ecclesiae,*" *Mélanges d'archéologie et d'histoire,* LXI (1949), 228–230; the matter was still pending in 1206 (see below, note 207). William of Tyre, XX, 3 (*RHC, Occ.,* I, 944), calls the archbishop Guerus.

201. Richard, "Note sur l'archidiocèse d'Apamée," pp. 103–108; only in 1263 did Urban IV end the dependence of the diocese of Rafanīyah (reduced by this time to the region of Krak des Chevaliers) on Apamea, by uniting Rafanīyah and Tortosa. We have the text of the profession of obedience of bishop Eustace of Valania to the archbishop, Otto, dated December 6, 1214; Francis Wormald, "The Pontifical of Apamea," *Het Nederlands kunsthistorisch Jaarboek,* V (1954), 271–279.

202. During the crusade (June 3, 1099). Possibly the crusaders wanted to give a bishop the fortress of Ramla, which they had just taken, as they had already done at Albara.

uniting churches on a large scale. This allowed a bishop to administer several dioceses while preserving the possibility of their future separation.[203] Thus Acre, an important town conquered as early as 1104, received its own bishop only about 1130, after its diocese had been administered by the patriarch of Jerusalem.[204] The restoration of dioceses, therefore, was a gradual affair.

On the other hand, some places which had not hitherto been bishoprics, but which had been pilgrim centers, became the residence of a bishop and cathedral chapter, as also did some prominent centers which had been unimportant before the Arab conquest. This was effected by the transference of a bishopric. The establishment of a bishop in Bethlehem (1110), for example, was irregular; it was thought that the see of Bethlehem might replace that of Ascalon.[205] In Galilee the monastery of Mount Tabor seems to have claimed the archiepiscopal title, but backed down before bishop William, who had been legally installed in Nazareth and who became archbishop in 1128 when it was decided to transfer the archiepiscopal see of Scythopolis (Bethsan)[206] to Nazareth. In 1168 the archiepiscopal see of Philadelphia ('Ammān), which the crusaders never occupied, was transferred to Kerak, which was wrongly thought to have been the ancient Petra.[207]

When it was finished, the ecclesiastical organization of the Latin church in the crusader states had the following form. The patriarchate of Antioch comprised six archbishoprics, Apamea (made an archiepiscopal see to which bishop Peter of Albara was transferred after the fall of Albara), Mamistra, Tarsus, Duluk (transferred from Hierapolis, although the archbishop resided in fact at Tell Bashir),

203. See above, note 197; the diocese of Arcas was united to that of Tripoli. In 1168 patriarch Amalric of Jerusalem was confirmed by pope Alexander III in the possession of the tithes and properties of Darum, Jericho, Nablus, and other principal places of dioceses not provided with bishops (Röhricht, *Regesta,* no. 439).

204. At the time of the council of Nablus in 1120, patriarch Gormond appropriated, as coming from *sua diocesis,* the tithes of Jerusalem, Nablus, and Acre (Ptolemais); he also disposed of the tithes of the diocese of Acre in 1129 (Mansi, *Concilia,* XXI, col. 263; Röhricht, *Additamentum,* no. 129a). John, the *primus Latinorum episcopus Tholomaidae,* is cited in 1135 (Röhricht, *Regesta,* no. 155); he was termed "praepositus" in 1129 (*ibid.,* no. 127).

205. This raised difficulties in 1153 when Ascalon was occupied by the Latins, and a bishop named Absalom was appointed; cf. Paul Riant,"Éclaircissements sur . . . l'église de Bethléem-Ascalon,"*ROL,* I (1893), 140. The first Latin bishop of Bethlehem was Aschetimus (1110, d. 1130).

206. The history of this is obscured by the forgery of certain claims of Mount Tabor; cf. Hotzelt, "Kirchliche Organisation," p. 59.

207. William of Tyre, XX, 3 (*RHC, Occ.,* I, 944–945). Some confusion arose; the *Notitia episcopatuum* of Antioch attached the province of Arabia to Antioch, with Bosra as metropolitan center and Philadelphia as one of its suffragans. The *Notitia* of Jerusalem put under Jerusalem a province of Syria, with Bosra as metropolitan center, and a province of Arabia with Rabbath Ammon ('Ammān, Philadelphia) as metropolitan center. This is why Antioch protested against the elevation of Kerak.

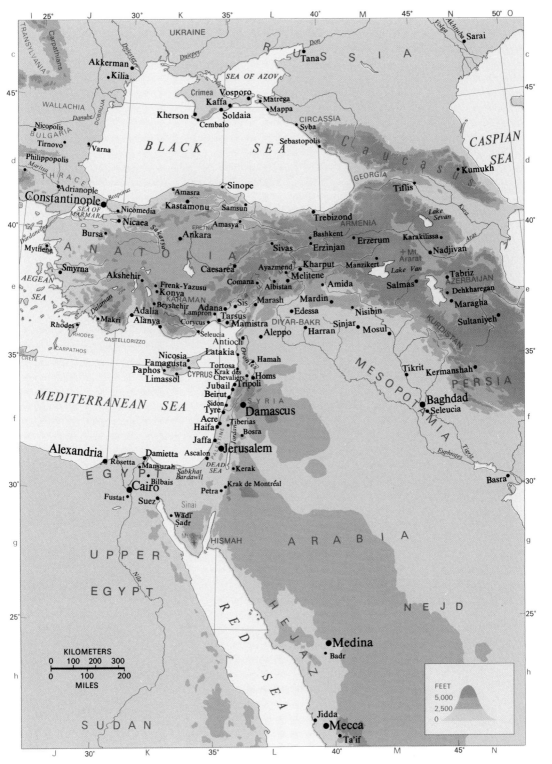

1. The Near East

2. Western Europe

3. Central Europe

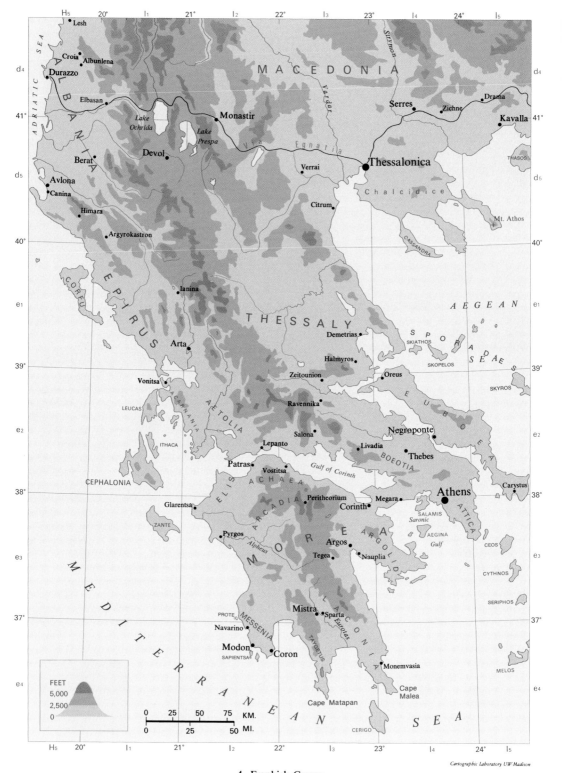

4. Frankish Greece

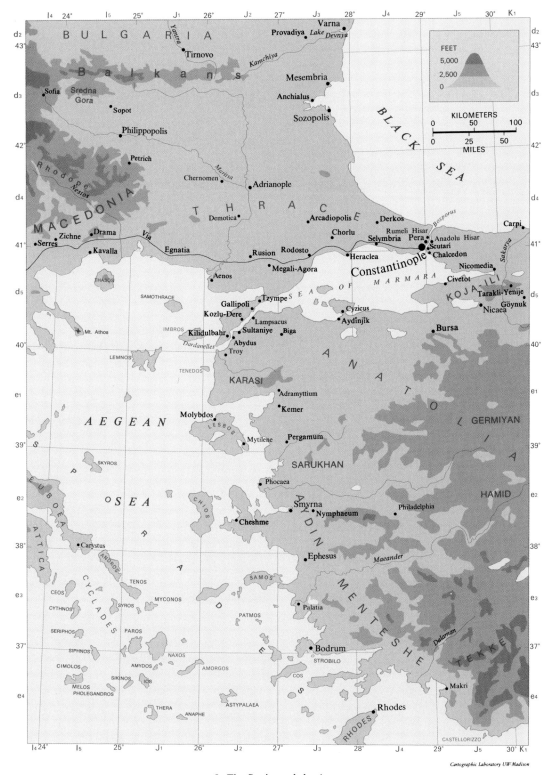

5. The Straits and the Aegean

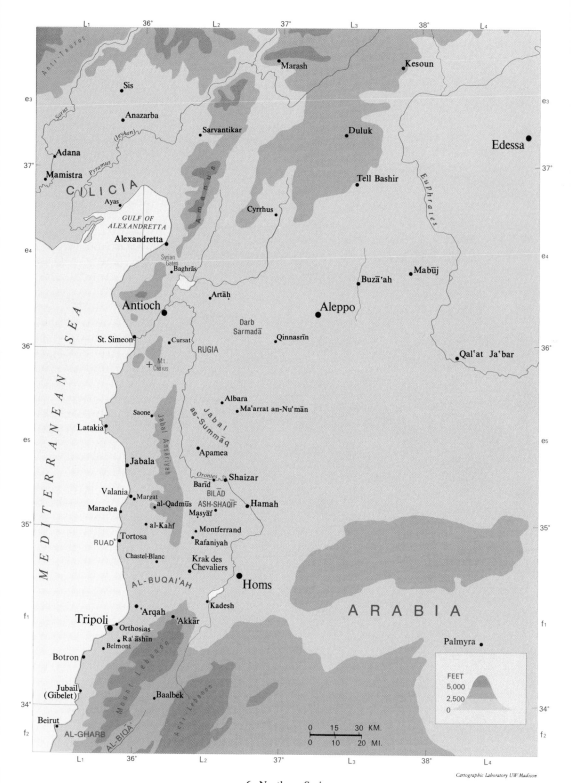

Anti-Taurus

e3

Marash

Kesoun

Sis

Anazarba

Sarus

Adana

(Jeyhan)

Sarvantikar

Duluk

Edessa

Mamistra

Pyramus

C A L I C I A

Tell Bashir

Euphrates

37°

Ayas

Cyrrhus

GULF OF
ALEXANDRETTA

Alexandretta

e4

Buzā'ah

Mabūj

Syrian
Gates

Baghrās

Artāḥ

Antioch

Aleppo

St. Simeon

Cursat

Darb
Sarmadā

Qinnasrīn

Qal'at Ja'bar

36°

M E D I T E R R A N E A N   S E A

Mt.
Casius

RUGIA

Albara

Ma'arrat an-Nu'mān

Saone

Jabal Anṣārīyah

*Jabal
as-Summāq*

Latakia

e5

Apamea

Jabala

Orontes

Shaizar

Barīd

BILĀD

Valania

Margat

al-Qadmūs

ASH-SHAQĪF

Hamah

Maraclea

Maṣyāf

al-Kahf

Montferrand

35°

Tortosa

Rafaniyah

RUAD

Chastel-Blanc

Krak des
Chevaliers

AL-BUQAI'AH

Homs

A R A B I A

'Arqah

Kadesh

Tripoli

'Akkār

Orthosias

f1

Palmyra

Ra'āshīn

Belmont

Botron

Mount Lebanon

Jubail
(Gibelet)

Baalbek

34°

Beirut

Anti Lebanon

AL-GHARB

AL-BIQA

f2

FEET	
5,000	
2,500	
0	

0   15   30 KM.

0   10   20 MI.

Cartographic Laboratory UW-Madison

6. Northern Syria

K₄ 34°   K₅   35°   L₁   36°   L₂

f₁   Nephin   **Tripoli**   f₁
al-Batrūn   Belmont
(Botron)   Besharri
Hadath
Maifūq   Aqūrah
Jubail   Lihfid   al-Munaiṭirah
(Gibelet)   Yānūh   **Baalbek**

34°   **Beirut**   Calamona   34°
AL-GHARB

SCHUF   Sardenay

f₂   Belhacem   *Wādī-*   f₂
al-Auwali   *t-Taim*
Sidon   Tyron
MARJ-ʿUYŪN   **Damascus**

Belfort
Humairah   Banyas
Tyre   Sedinum
Theiretenne   H A U R A N
Chastel-Neuf
Toron

33°   Casal Imbert   **Montfort**   33°
Castellum Regis
Judin
Acre   Muzairib
Haifa   Hattin   *Sea of*
Mount   Tiberias   *Galilee*   Ḥabis Jaldak
Carmel   AS-SAWĀD
GALILEE
Château   **Nazareth**   Mount   **Bosra**
Pèlerin   Tabor
Sarepta   Caymont
al-Lajjun
f₃   Caesarea   ʿAin Jālūt   f₃
Bethsan
Qāqūn
Arthabec   Sebastia
Qalansuwā   ʿAjlūn
S A M A R I A
Arsuf
Nablus
Jaffa   Mirabel
32°   Sinjil   as-Ṣalt   32°
Lydda   G H O R
Ramla   al-Bīrah
Ibelin   Bains   Jericho   ʿAmmān
Hulda   St. George   St. John
Blanche Garde   **Jerusalem**   St. Euthymius
Ascalon   Bethany   St. Theodosius
Bethlehem   St. Sabas
Beth Gibelin   J U D E A   al-Qastal   f₄
St. Chariton
f₄   Gaza   Hebron   *DEAD*
Darum   Engedi   *SEA*

Raffiyah   L A   B E R R I E   **ARABIA**
Kerak
0   15   30 KM.
0   10   20 MI.   Segor

31°   K₄ 34°   K₅   35°   L₁   36°   L₂   31°

Cartographic Laboratory UW-Madison

FEET
5,000
2,500
0

M E D I T E R R A N E A N

S E A

7. Palestine

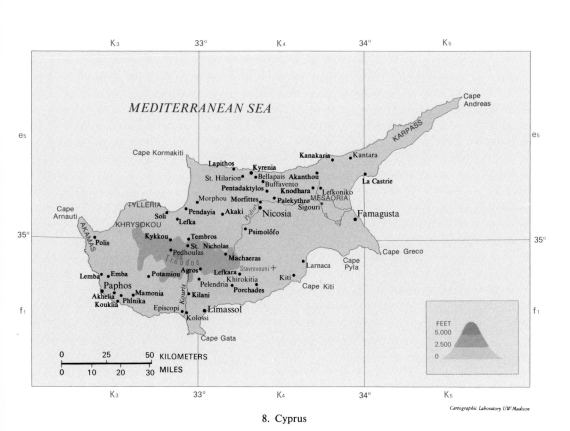

MEDITERRANEAN SEA

Cape
Andreas

KARPASS

e5

Cape Kormakiti

Lapithos   Kanakaria   Kantara
              Kyrenia
St. Hilarion   Bellapais Akanthou   La Castrie
           Buffavento
Pentadaktylos   Knodhara   Lefkoniko
Morphou Morfittes   Palekythro   MESAORIA
          Pendayia Akaki   Nicosia
Cape   Soli   Sigouri   Famagusta
Arnauti   Lefka
TYLLERIA
KHRYSOKOU
35°   35°
        Kykkou   Tembros   Psimolófo
Polis   St. Nicholas
        Pedhoulas   Cape Greco
       Troodos Machaeras   Cape Kiti
Lemba Emba   Agros Lefkara Stavrovouni   Larnaca   Cape
Paphos   Potamiou   Khirokitia   Kiti   Pyla
Akhelia Mamonia   Kilani Pelendria Porchades   Cape Kiti
Kouklia Phinika
      Episcopi   Limassol
         Kolossi

Cape Gata

0   25   50 KILOMETERS
0 10   20   30 MILES

FEET
5,000
2,500
0

8. Cyprus

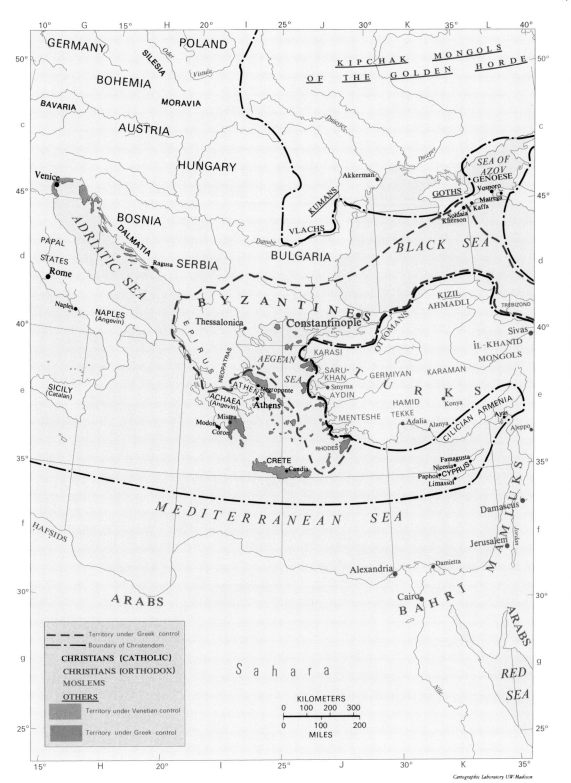

9. Venice and the Levant in 1300

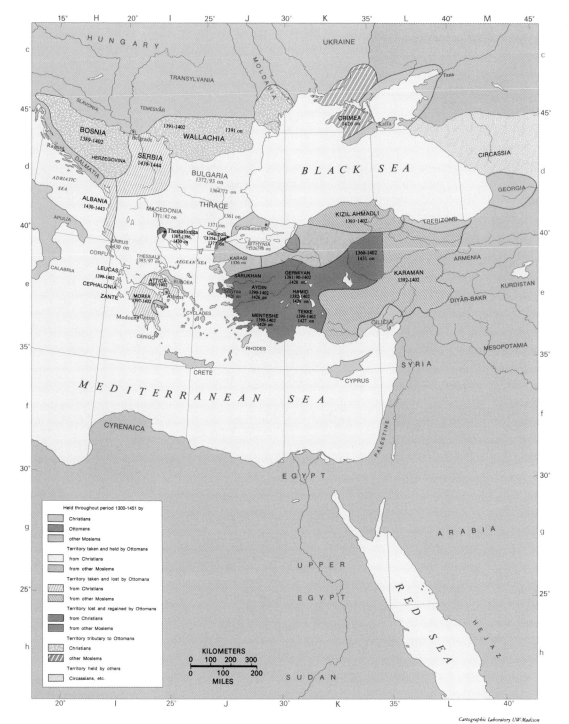

10. The Ottoman Empire 1300–1451

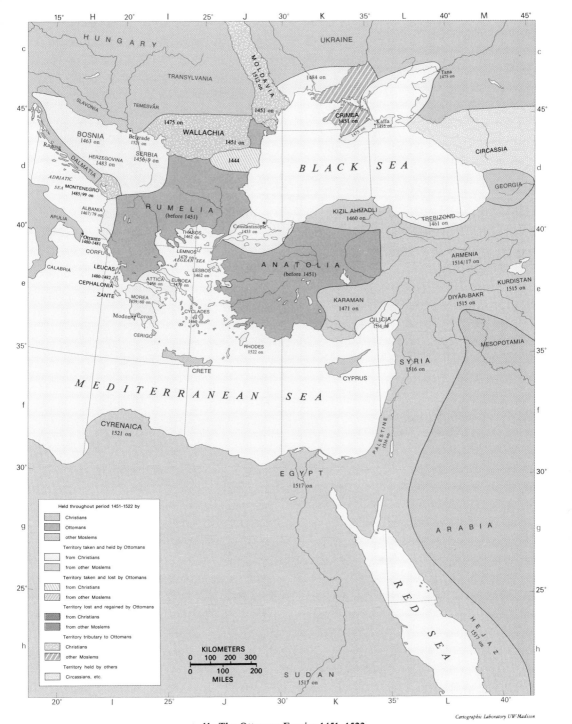

11. The Ottoman Empire 1451–1522

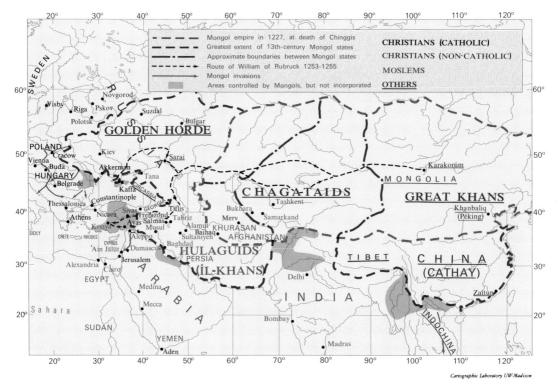

12. Mongols and Missions in the Thirteenth Century

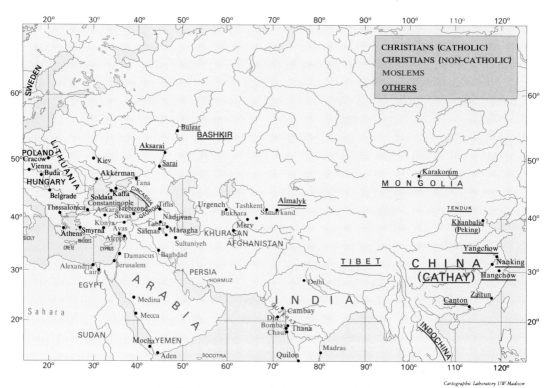

13. Missions and Mongols in the Fourteenth Century

Cyrrhus, and Edessa. The province of Apamea included the sees of Rafanīyah and Valania; Duluk, the sees of Marash and probably Kesoun. The sees of Artāḥ, Jabala, Latakia, Tortosa, Tripoli, and Jubail came directly under the patriarch.[208] In the patriarchate of Jerusalem many of the sees were filled rather late. There were four archbishoprics: Tyre, Caesarea, Nazareth (which had been made an archbishopric in 1128), and "Petra" or Kerak (created in 1168). The archbishop of Caesarea had a suffragan at Sebastia (created about 1145); the archbishop of Tyre had suffragans at Beirut, Sidon, Acre (created about 1130), and Banyas; the archbishop of Nazareth had a suffragan at Tiberias (created about 1130). The bishoprics of Bethlehem, Lydda, and Hebron (created in 1168) fell directly under the patriarch.[209]

However, the Moslem reconquest had already wiped out some of the sees, such as those of the county of Edessa, all of which disappeared about 1150. Many ceased to be provided with bishops, but not all. Some titularies took refuge in villages still in Frankish hands, either within their own dioceses or elsewhere. Thus the bishop of Sidon stayed for some time in Sarepta before Sidon was retaken by the Franks in 1228. Bishop Geoffrey of Tiberias fled to Sidon in 1243.[210] Urban IV sought to reorganize the episcopal hierarchy affected by these dislocations, by uniting the see of Acre to the patriarchate of Jerusalem, and the see of Rafanīyah to that of Tortosa. But bishops and archbishops succeeded one another regularly, despite the loss of their episcopal cities, thus leading to the titular episcopacy of later centuries.

Parish organization in each diocese depended upon the importance of the Latin communities to be served. In the beginning these were not very numerous. A Tripolitan text informs us that the entire seigneury of Nephin, stretching some twelve miles along the coast, formed a single parish.[211] However, Latin parishes became more and more

208. Cahen, *Syrie du nord*, pp. 319–323. Cyrrhus appears in this list as a simple bishopric. Its status as an archbishopric is clear from William of Tyre (XVII, 17, in *RHC, Occ.*, I, 786–789), and from the *Provinciale romanae ecclesiae*, both of which refer to a *Coricensis archiepiscopus*.

209. Hotzelt, "Kirchliche Organisation," pp. 49–51. The see of Ascalon, created in 1153 at the time the town was occupied, had been suppressed, having been transferred to Bethlehem. Alexander III, who had elevated Hebron and "Petra," intended in 1169 to do the same for Jaffa; cf. Hotzelt, "Die Chorherren," p. 121. John of Ibelin, cap. 261 (*RHC, Lois,* I, 415), cites in addition an archbishop of "Bussereth" (Bosra), and gives the archbishop of "Petra" a suffragan in the person of the (Greek) bishop of Pharan, residing at Sinai.

210. *MGH, SS,* XXIII, 899; Röhricht, *Additamentum,* no. 1151b: 1247.

211. In fact, I believe that the "ecclesia parochialis, habens baptisterium, cimiterium, oblationes . . . et cetera omnia que parochiali ecclesie conveniunt," granted by bishop Pons of Tripoli to the Hospitallers in 1119 (Delaville Le Roulx, *Cartulaire,* I, 40, no. 48), is the *ecclesia*

numerous with the creation of new towns settled by Franks and the growth of towns already having a Frankish population.[212]

In the maritime towns, however, there were some difficulties arising from the concession of quarters to Pisans, Venetians, and Genoese, within each of which there was a church endowed with parish rights. Dedicated to the patron saint of the home city (St. Peter of Pisa, St. Mark of Venice, and St. Lawrence of Genoa), these parish churches paid tribute (*census*) to the cathedrals of Pisa and Genoa, and the bishop of Castello. But they also fell under the local bishop. For example, the patriarch of Jerusalem sent the holy chrism to St. Lawrence of Acre, and the chaplain of St. Lawrence of Tyre owed obedience to the archbishop of Tyre.[213] The Venetians, however, claimed exemption from the diocesan bishop for St. Mark of Tyre, founded in the third of the city belonging to Venice; and St. Mark of Acre likewise claimed to be exempt from the bishop of Acre.[214] Furthermore, the churches of the Italian quarters also asserted particular privileges: the Pisans of Acre, for example, married only in their church of St. Peter, even when they lived in the parishes of St. Andrew or St. Michael.[215]

Many parish churches belonged to monastic establishments, such as St. Peter of Jaffa, the property of the Holy Sepulcher, which thereby had the right to select the chaplain who was to serve the church, and to receive a share of its revenues, leaving to the diocesan bishop spiritual jurisdiction and the right to consecrate the *parochialis vicarius*.[216] There was little difference in this respect between Latin

---

de Nephinis that the Hospitallers claimed in 1198 from the bishop on the grounds of a privilege of "pope C," i.e., the privilege of Calixtus II edited in *Cartulaire*, I, 40 (pp. 635-659). This church was in the *terra que fuit Pontii de Medenes,* and it was the Meynes (*de Medenes*) family which held Nephin (Rudt de Collenberg, "Les Raynouard, seigneurs de Nephin," pp. 289-311).

212. There was a *capellanus* at Lajjūn (ecclesia Ligionis), another at the casal of Bains, and one at Ramla (Röhricht, *Regesta,* nos. 239, 333); in the county of Edessa, there was one at "Cesson" (Kesoun; *ibid.,* no. 390, dated 1163 in error). Some Latin parishes were established in 1168 in the new towns founded by the Holy Sepulcher (Rozière, *Cartulaire,* pp. 238-239), in the new *burgus* of Nablus (Röhricht, *Regesta,* no. 444), and at Jaffa (*ibid.,* nos. 440, 456).

213. Röhricht, *Regesta,* nos. 599, 692, 850, 1131, 1132, 1146; *Additamentum,* no. 1214b.

214. Röhricht, *Regesta,* nos. 770, 881, 887, 1114, 1148, 1151, 1171, 1463 for Tyre; *Regesta,* no. 1285, and *Additamentum,* no. 1061b for Acre. In 1216, Honorius III put St. Mark of Tyre under the spiritual direction of the archbishop, Simon of Maugastel, but in 1243 the Venetian bailie Marsiglio Zorzi (Giorgio) insisted that it was exempt. In 1247, a *census* was to be paid to the holy see by St. Mark of Venice for the churches of Tyre and Acre; it was still being paid in 1286, although the pope had conceded to the archbishop of Tyre the *census* due from St. Mark of Tyre. At Acre, the *plebanus* paid a *census* to the bishop as a mark of obedience only for the parish church of St. Demetrius, annexed to the Venetian quarter (1260).

215. Röhricht, *Regesta,* no. 775.

216. Hotzelt, "Chorherren," p. 121; *idem,* "Kirchliche Organisation," pp. 56, 86. According to Mayer, *Bistümer,* when a former see was not restored by the Latins, the abbots who con-

parishes and Greek or Syrian parishes; equally viewed as the property of this or that religious establishment, they had to make payments to these establishments even though they were not subject to the authority of a Latin bishop.[217]

Some priories, communities of monks dependent upon a large abbey, also enjoyed parish rights. The priory of St. Mary *Latine* at Latakia served as a parish church.[218] Gradually, because of this predominance of regular clergy, the parish clergy acquired a new status. The titles of rector or chaplain gave place to that of prior. From 1264 the church of St. Gilles of Acre, held by a nonresident prior who farmed out the goods of the church to the Templars, was called *rectoria seu prioratus secularis;* in the fourteenth century, the clergy of Cyprus in charge of parishes would be generally called *prieurs paroissiens.*[219]

Besides the parish clergy, each diocese also had its cathedral chapter. These sometimes adopted the rule of canons regular which was the vogue in the west at the end of the eleventh and the beginning of the twelfth century. Such was the case of the Holy Sepulcher in Jerusalem,[220] and also St. John of Sebastia, where Usāmah admired the piety of the canons serving the cathedral. The chapter elected the bishop. It had the usual dignitaries, although there was only one archdeacon, since the dioceses, unlike those of France and England, were not subdivided into archdeaconries. Besides their responsibility for liturgical service, of particular importance where the cathedral was a well-known pilgrimage center, the canons played a role in the education of the clergy. There was a school at the Holy Sepulcher, and at Acre a lecturer in theology, although in the thirteenth century the mendicant orders also contributed to clerical education.[221]

A large part of the activity of the chapters had to do with the pilgrims. In particular, they undertook charitable activities which, in

---

trolled the former cathedrals enjoyed episcopal prerogatives. On the difficulties between abbot Guy of Josaphat and archbishop Robert of Nazareth over the designation of a chaplain of Lajjūn, see Röhricht, *Regesta,* no. 239; for the consecration in 1112 of the vicar of Tabor by bishop Bernard of Nazareth, *ibid.,* no. 69.

217. Cf. Richard, "Église latine et églises orientales dans les états des croisés: La destinée d'un prieuré de Josaphat," in *Mélanges offerts à Jean Dauvillier,* ed. Germain Sicard (Toulouse, 1979), pp. 743–752.

218. Röhricht, *Regesta,* no. 331.

219. *Registres d'Urbain IV,* ed. Guiraud, II, 80–81 (no. 193); III, 442–444 (no. 2640); Richard, *Documents chypriotes des archives du Vatican, XIVe et XVe siècles* (Bibliothèque archéologique et historique, LXXIII; Paris, 1962), p. 73.

220. See above, note 183.

221. Hotzelt, "Kirchliche Organisation," p. 55; also "Die Chorherren," describing the life of the canons of the Holy Sepulcher.

the case of some of the chapters, attracted a large number of gifts. The canons of Bethlehem were gradually transformed into a Hospitaller chapter, while those of the Holy Sepulcher transferred the care of pilgrims to Hospitallers who acted under their direction.

Contrary to what Gaston Dodu has written, that the Latin church sought to undermine the foundation and development of the crusader states,[222] one of the most striking features of the history of these states is the collaboration between the church and civil society. It is equally difficult to accept LaMonte's view that Urban II sought through the establishment of Franks in the Holy Land to extend the patrimony of St. Peter, but that his successors gave this plan up in fear of seeing the patriarch of Jerusalem, who claimed supremacy over the royal power, emerge as a rival of the pope.[223]

The drive to establish an ecclesiastical principality, to include the holy city itself as well as the port of Jaffa, came from Daimbert and his successor Stephen of La Ferté (1128–1130), and Godfrey of Bouillon probably looked on it as compatible with his title of "advocate."[224] Daimbert went even further, since he was able to get the homage of Bohemond and Godfrey in 1099, *propter amorem Dei,*[225] and at Easter 1100 to secure from Godfrey the acknowledgment that he was the vassal of the Holy Sepulcher and of the patriarch, which Baldwin I also acknowledged before his coronation.[226] Later, however, there is no evidence of the paying of homage by the king or by the prince of Antioch to the patriarch of Jerusalem. The coronation ceremony included no such obligation. The king of Jerusalem was no more the vassal of the patriarch than of the Holy See.[227]

In Antioch, however, the prince paid homage to the patriarch of Antioch. Possibly the custom was introduced when the patriarch Bernard consecrated Roger in 1112. It is certainly attested to by Raymond

222. "La royauté latine périt, et le royaume latin avec elle, parce que . . . l'Église chrétienne d'Orient resta non seulement une puissance à côté de l'État ou dans l'État, mais contre l'État" (Dodu, *Le Royaume latin de Jérusalem* [Paris, 1914], p. 96).

223. *Feudal Monarchy,* pp. 203–205.

224. See above, p. 197 and note.

225. Fulcher of Chartres (ed. Hagenmeyer, *Fulcherii Carnotensis historia Hierosolymitana* [Heidelberg, 1913], p. 741 [III, 34]) writes: "Dux Godefridus et dominus Boamundus acceperunt terram suam a patriarcha Daiberto propter amorem Dei"; William of Tyre says that they received from Daimbert the *investitura* of their respective dignities. Cf. Hansen, *Das Problem eines Kirchenstaates,* p. 42.

226. Hampel, *Untersuchungen über das lateinisches Patriarchat,* p. 34; see also Hamilton, *Latin Church,* pp. 53–55.

227. Hotzelt, "Kirchliche Organisation," p. 48.

of Poitiers (1136) and by Raymond Roupen (1216).[228] We do not know, however, which fief the prince agreed to hold from the patriarch, and some princes seem not to have paid homage at all. Certainly there were quarrels between patriarchs and princes unknown in Jerusalem. Raymond of Poitiers deposed Ralph of Domfront in 1139. Reginald of Châtillon imprisoned Aimery of Limoges, who had refused him money. Bohemond III was excommunicated when he married Sibyl in 1180 despite the fact that he already had a wife, Theodora Comnena; Antioch was placed under the interdict, while the prince besieged the patriarch Aimery in Cursat. Some patriarchs had to undertake the defense of the principality against Moslems, Byzantines, or Armenians, sometimes despite the prince himself. Finally, the crisis created by the conflict between Bohemond IV and Raymond Roupen forced the patriarch to take sides; Peter I died in prison in 1208. Only in 1239 did Bohemond V cease to be excommunicated.

Both in Jerusalem and in Antioch the ruler controlled the election of the patriarch. Baldwin I got rid of Daimbert and succeeded in appointing Arnulf, and custom would allow the king to choose between candidates designated by the canons. Henry of Champagne later defended this privilege, which had fallen into disuse when Rome began appointing the patriarch directly.[229] The king apparently also claimed the right to appoint certain ecclesiastical dignitaries, as well as to influence episcopal nominations: royal chancellors received bishoprics. William of Tyre reports that on his return to the Holy Land king Amalric would have given him the benefices of which he was the patron if he had not been prevented by those envious of William; later, however, when the opportunity arose, he had the diocesan bishops provide for him.[230] Here again is the kind of development which gave the papacy the opportunity of providing a large number of benefices and dignities, thus diminishing royal influence in the nomination of ecclesiastics.

The independence of the church was well established. It had its own possessions, often considerable; it also had its own jurisdiction. Church courts dealt only with cases concerning the clergy (except when the offense was murder or treason against the lord), heresy, sorcery,

---

228. Cahen, *Syrie du nord*, pp. 312, 502, 621; Joseph Gill, "The Tribulations of the Greek Church in Cyprus, 1196–c. 1280," *Byzantinische Forschungen*, V (1977), 73–93 (repr. in *Church Union, Rome, and Byzantium* [London, 1979], IV).

229. Hotzelt, "Kirchliche Organisation," p. 54; LaMonte, *Feudal Monarchy*, p. 211; *Estoire d'Eracles (RHC, Occ.,* II, 203). For Antioch see Cahen, *Syrie du nord*, pp. 312–313.

230. R. B. C. Huygens, "Guillaume de Tyr étudiant," *Latomus,* XXI (1962), 815–816.

and marriage (including adultery), but left perjury to the civil courts.[231] As for cases having to do with ecclesiastical property, a process of 1140 at Antioch reveals the custom of the principality: a dispute between the Holy Sepulcher and the abbey of St. Paul was transferred from the patriarch's to the prince's court because the property involved had originally been a grant made by a lay authority.[232] Besides the established church courts, papal judge-delegates played an increasingly large role in the thirteenth century, while in the twelfth legates had intervened above all to ensure that councils were summoned where accused prelates had to be judged.[233] Questions of episcopal succession were decided at Rome, which was not peculiar to the Latin east.

Tithes were always one of the great sources of contention between the church and civil authorities. In the west the tithe was primarily agricultural in nature; the clergy levied it directly on the produce of the peasantry. In the east the peasants did not belong to the Latin rite except in those villages settled by Franks, where the ecclesiastical lord collected the tithe according to the western custom.[234] Also, the clergy claimed tithes not from peasants but from the lords themselves[235] who caused much difficulty over their payment. It was only at the assembly of Nablus (1120) that the king of Jerusalem agreed to pay a tithe on his own revenues; but other documents prove that the practice had already been introduced.[236] Bishops were the beneficiaries of the tithe, part of which they allocated to their canons or to religious establishments, which were normally exempt from paying a tithe on their own property.[237]

The agricultural wealth of the churches aroused some restrictive measures designed to limit its growth. The Assises of Jerusalem forbade the sale or the grant of a fief to a church or to a religious order

231. Dodu, *Histoire des institutions,* pp. 325–328.

232. Rozière, *Cartulaire,* pp. 172–173; cf. Cahen, *Syrie du nord,* p. 443.

233. For a case concerning the forging of a papal provision see Röhricht, *Regesta,* no. 1226.

234. Rozière, *Cartulaire,* p. 238, 251.

235. This probably explains the claim of the Latin prelates, if we can believe Ernoul, to tithe Armenian colonists whom prince Toros proposed to settle in the Holy Land. See the interpretation of this episode in Cahen, "Le Régime rural syrien," p. 301.

236. Mansi, *Concilia,* XXI, col. 263; Röhricht, *Regesta,* nos. 36, 67, 69 (concerning the *decima de militia* and the *decima peregrinorum militum* on the booty taken in battle).

237. On the collection and distribution of the tithe see Richard, *Documents chypriotes,* p. 63. Rudt de (von) Collenberg, "Les Cardinaux Hugues et Lancelot de Lusignan et l'autonomie de l'église latine de Chypre, 1378–1467" (to appear in the *Praktika* of the 2nd International Congress of Cypriot Studies, Nicosia, 1982), shows how the Cypriote royal family monopolized the ecclesiastical benefices from the time of the Great Schism on.

incapable of providing the requisite service,[238] since it was impossible for a church to pay homage to the king. In fact, however, some ecclesiastical lordships had obligations similar to those of the vassals. The archbishop of Nazareth sent ten knights to the royal host under the command of his marshal; the bishop of Lydda sent six. Nazareth, Lydda, Apamea, and Cursat were the centers of veritable ecclesiastical seigneuries where the prelates raised their own contingents and undertook the defense of their own fortresses. Most of the religious establishments, however, had to contribute companies of sergeants, sometimes rather important (a thousand from the patriarch of Jerusalem and the Holy Sepulcher, two hundred from the bishop of Lydda). Thus, without counting the military orders, the church of the kingdom made an appreciable contribution to the defense of the territory, although only a few prelates[239] were great feudatories with their own vassals.

Thus the church took its place within the states founded by the crusaders who had responded to the appeal of the Council of Clermont. It left temporal power to the princes and barons. It is in this sense that we may interpret the definition of John of Ibelin according to which the king was the *seignor temporel,* the patriarch, the *seignor espirituel.* The ecclesiastical hierarchy remained for the most part outside the political framework, but took cognizance of it; the interventions of the patriarchs to lead the barons of Antioch or Jerusalem in moments of danger illustrate this, and the coöperation of the churches in the defense of the territory was marked by the importance of their contingents as well as their financial contributions when an assembly decided on a general tax (for example, in 1166 and 1183).

But the catastrophe of 1187 transformed the machinery of the Frankish states. Deprived of their territorial basis, these states could no longer guarantee any institutional continuity. They depended increasingly on outside help which brought in its wake the interference of western powers which viewed the kingdom of Outremer as a colony. From Frederick II on, the monarch was nonresident, further undermining royal authority. The barons closed ranks to oppose a foreign authority who sought to eliminate the customary control of vassals over the acts of their lord, a control which in Jerusalem drew particular force from the predominance of certain great families and

238. John of Ibelin, cap. 143 (*RHC, Lois,* I, 217).
239. Including the abbot of Mount Tabor (Richard, *Royaume latin,* pp. 102–103, 129–130). At Jerusalem the patriarch possessed an extensive domain, with broad seigneurial rights, but he apparently did not furnish a contingent for the royal army; see Prawer, *Crusader Institutions.*

the interpretation which they placed on the *Assise de la ligèce*. The result was an atmosphere of rebellion. The commune of Acre persisted for twelve years, giving way to a simple substitute for monarchical authority in the person of the "lord of the kingdom," a mere representative of the last Hohenstaufens. The restoration of Hugh III of Antioch-Lusignan in 1268 came too late to reëstablish royal authority. Meanwhile the lands belonging to the princes of Antioch were torn apart by the struggle between the princely dynasty and the great families. This weakening of royal and feudal institutions went hand in hand with the gradual collapse of the crusader states, provoked above all by the increasing power of a Moslem state, Egypt of the Aiyūbids and Mamluks.

It was then that the church took on a new role. The patriarchs of Jerusalem, legates in the Holy Land, were the natural intermediaries to transmit the appeals for help and manage the assistance sent from the west at the instigation of the papacy. With the institutions of the monarchy weak, and a feudality incapable of providing the services for which it had been created, it was the church itself, now profoundly transformed, which assured the survival of the Latin states and controlled their temporal as well as their spiritual life during the last years of their existence.[240]

It is more useful, however, to think of the internal organization of the crusader states as it was before this period of decline, characterized by a balance established among the monarchy, the feudality, and the church, with a strict definition of their respective powers. It is precisely this balance which explains the interest which historians have always taken in their institutions.

240. *Ibid.*, pp. 296–302.

VI

AGRICULTURAL CONDITIONS
IN THE CRUSADER STATES

Agriculture played a large role in the life of those states born
of the crusades. This aspect of their history has often been overlooked
—somewhat surprisingly, since in large part the fate of the different
states hinged on their agricultural capacities. We shall try to determine the extent to which each could feed itself, or had to rely on
other countries for essential imports. It is also important to determine which of them had so productive an agriculture as to contribute
to international trade, and thus acquired the wealth which made them
stronger than their neighbors. Agricultural productivity, however, will
not be our only concern. The study of the agrarian regime is closely
bound up with that of agriculture proper, and cannot be ignored.
Finally, to complete our examination of agricultural conditions we
shall consider how the soil was exploited by the crusaders' descendants.

There are two recent studies: Claude Cahen, "Notes sur l'histoire des croisades et de l'Orient
latin, II: Le régime rural syrien au temps de la domination franque," *Bulletin de la Faculté
des lettres de Strasbourg,* XXIX (1950–1951), 286–310, and Joshua Prawer, "Étude de quelques
problèmes agraires et sociaux d'une seigneurie croisée au XIIIe siècle," *Byzantion,* XXII (1952),
5–61; XXIII (1953), 143–170, which refers principally to the *memoriale possessionum* drawn
up in 1243 by Marsiglio Zorzi, the Venetian bailie of Acre, published by Tafel and Thomas,
II, 351–398. Still useful, however, are the following: Helen G. Preston, *Rural Conditions in
the Latin Kingdom of Jerusalem* (Philadelphia, 1903); Hans Prutz, *Kulturgeschichte der Kreuzzüge* (Berlin, 1883; repr. Hildesheim, 1964); Emmanuel G. Rey, *Les Colonies franques de Syrie
aux XIIe et XIIIe siècles* (Paris, 1883). On geographical conditions see André Latron, *La Vie
rurale en Syrie et au Liban* (Mémoires de l'Institut français de Damas; Beirut, 1936), and Félix
M. Abel, *Géographie de la Palestine,* I (Paris, 1933). See also Maurice Gaudefroy-Demombynes,
La Syrie à l'époque des Mamelouks d'après les auteurs arabes (Bibliothèque archéologique et
historique, III; Paris, 1923), and Robert Mantran and Jean Sauvaget, *Règlements fiscaux otto-
mans: Les provinces syriennes* (Institut français de Damas; Paris, 1951). Essentially the sources
comprise the charters to be found for the most part in the *Regesta regni Hierosolymitani* of
Reinhold Röhricht (2 vols., Innsbruck, 1893–1904; repr. New York, 1960). Cf. also Ernst Strehlke,
Tabulae ordinis theutonici (Berlin, 1869; repr. Toronto, 1975), and Eugène de Rozière, *Cartulaire de l'église du Saint-Sépulcre de Jérusalem* (Paris, 1849; repr. in *PL,* 155 [Paris, 1880],
cols. 1105–1262).

Among those who have assisted me in the completion of this work I must thank, above
all, the late Henri Seyrig, then Director of the Institut français d'archéologie in Beirut, who
made it possible for me to study present conditions of rural life in the Levant and in Cyprus
on the spot.

Agriculture and agrarian organization differed in the three major areas occupied by the crusaders—Frankish Syria, Cyprus, and the Latin empire of Constantinople. Each of these areas will be the subject of a separate section, and for each we shall give as complete a picture as possible of rural life during its occupation by the crusaders.

Moslem pilgrims on their way to Mecca. From the collections of the Bibliothèque nationale

A. Agriculture in Frankish Syria

To designate the collection of Frankish colonies established in the territory of the ancient provinces of Syria, Palestine, Phoenicia, and Arabia, the Middle Ages used the generic term *Surie*. The name will serve us to signify the area embracing the kingdom of Jerusalem, the counties of Tripoli and Edessa, and the principality of Antioch. With the exception of Edessa, which did not remain in Frankish hands very long and has left us hardly any documents, this area forms something of a geographic unit because of the two chains of mountains parallel to the coast marching north from the Red Sea up to the edge of the Anatolian plateau. The relatively narrow plain along the shore; the mountains of Lebanon, Jabal Anṣārīyah, and the Amanus range, continuing the hills of Judea and Samaria; an interior valley starting south of the Dead Sea and extending to the valleys of Ghor, al-Biqāʿ, Rugia (ar-Rūj), and the plain of Antioch; and finally the chalk ranges of Transjordan, Anti-Lebanon, and northern Syria—these comprise four separate regions, each of which has quite similar agricultural characteristics from south to north, distinct from those of its neighbors to west or east.

The coastal plain offers a very narrow area for intensive cultivation, which is possible only where a river springs from some gorge cut in the mountains, or where an important water source makes irrigation possible. The mountains of the Lebanese area are carved into terraces which retain cultivable soil while a relatively abundant rainfall assures needed moisture. Elsewhere, as in Judea, the rocky aspect of the mountains and hills gives an impression of barrenness, but how false this is has been shown by travelers like Nāṣir-i-Khusrau and Ludolf of Suchem (Sudheim); provided there is no winter drought, the land there is fertile enough to give a good cereal crop, and to support fruit trees, grapevines, and fig or olive trees.[2] The situation is similar in the Jabal Anṣārīyah, but with a few variations. As for the interior valley, there are excellent facilities for irrigation because of the rivers, the Jordan, Litani (Leontes), and Orontes, running

---

2. Ludolf of Sudheim, *AOL*, II-1 (1884), 363–366; *Sefer nameh: Relation du voyage de Nassiri Khosrau,* ed. and tr. Charles Schefer (Paris, 1881), p. 67.

through it, and it is especially fertile because of its alluvial deposits. To the east, the plateaus of Transjordan provide excellent land for wheat, but as one moves farther north the mountain barrier to the west reduces the moisture in the interior. Nevertheless, the vast chalk range of northern Syria still had important plantations of grapevines and olive trees at the time of the crusades.[3]

Thus natural conditions favored agriculture, at least where there was careful irrigation to develop the fields of the coastal strip and the interior plains. Otherwise, as Moslem authors of the Middle Ages noted, good harvests had to depend on the winter rains, which were only too often unreliable.[4]

The agrarian organization of the Frankish period has been studied by several scholars who have described it in detail.[5] The basic unit was the village, or *casal;* in effect, rural life was communal and isolated homesteads did not exist. The casal comprised a variable number of inhabitants, forming a community the members of which were bound together by the performance of collective services under the direction of chiefs called ra'ises. The casals included waste lands (*gâtines*), an exact description of which is difficult to come by. They were certainly unoccupied, serving as common pasture or as a reserve of cultivable land where new villages could be built. The arable land of the casal was measured in carucates (*carrucatae*), a term which had a double meaning. Some of these carucates corresponded to the *faddān 'arabī,* the area that a pair of oxen could plow in one day (the word *jornata* was also used); others corresponded to the *faddān rūmī,* the amount of land which one team could cultivate in a whole year (these were called *carrucatae grecae,* a term which appears to be synonymous with *carrucatae francesiae:* one assize gave their measure as 24 cords by 16, or about 75 acres).[6] It is in this latter sense that the texts ordinarily use the word carucate, which may be equated with *mansus.* Like the western manse, the carucate was the usual holding of a peasant, although this did not stop some

3. Georges Tchalenko, *Villages antiques de la Syrie du nord* (Bibliothèque archéologique et historique de l'Institut français de Beyrouth, L; 3 vols., Paris, 1953-1958).

4. Gaudefroy-Demombynes, *La Syrie,* p. 24.

5. In particular Helen Preston, Claude Cahen, and Joshua Prawer.

6. Strehlke, *Tabulae,* pp. 26-27; Cahen, "Notes," p. 295. The distinction which Prawer has established between these two kinds of carucates corresponds with that made by Latron, *Vie rurale,* pp. 11-16. The very words *carrucata graeca* appear to be an exact translation of *faddān rūmī* (Mantran and Sauvaget, *Règlements,* p. 4 and note). The team is always composed of oxen; the *caballaria* is the fief of one knight and not the land cultivated by a team of horses. The measure of the carucate, derived from that of the cord, has been established by Rey and by Prawer (who discusses this text in "Étude," pp. 26-30).

of them from farming more than one carucate. The question whether these carucates were always cultivated by the same tenants or were redistributed by the rural community has not received any final answer.

The peasant, cultivating one or more carucates, was bound to the lord of the casal by obligations the details of which have come down to us in the documents.[7] Some of these peasants were free, others not; at least, certain documents distinguish between free and unfree carucates, the latter very likely being held by the *homliges,* who no doubt were serfs. The "free carucates" appear to have been burdened only by a fixed rent of two bezants a year.[8]

We know little about the obligations of the free men. The villeins cited in the texts which have been preserved appear for the most part to have been serfs. These were bound to their holdings under conditions varying from place to place. An act of 1258 specified that in the county of Tripoli those who quit the land of a lord in order to establish themselves on the land of another might be seized on the demand of their first master, but it implies that the customs of Jerusalem, Antioch, and Cyprus might well have been different. In fact, there was at least one casal in the principality of Antioch, Pont-de-Fer, where the lords could not get their runaway villeins restored to them.[9] At Jerusalem, however, the lord's right of pursuit was recognized by the *Assises,* as also the right of *formariage,* which obliged a lord whose male serf married the female serf of another lord to give the latter another female serf.[10]

The payments demanded of these peasants were of two sorts, those proportional to the harvest, and *redditus personales* of fixed amounts. This distinction must have continued after the Frankish period: in Mamluk Syria the proportional *kharāj* and the fixed *dīmūz* were distinct, the latter apparently the descendant of the old Byzantine personal taxes (δημόσιον).[11] Each of these taxes appears to have had a territorial base, the carucate (the old *jugatio*) serving as the

---

7. The casal might have several lords, either dividing among themselves the tenures, or possibly sharing among themselves the entire revenue of the village, as happened in the undivided seigneuries between Franks and Moslems; see Jean Richard, "Un Partage de seigneurie entre Francs et Mamelouks: Les 'casaux de Sur'," *Syria,* XXX, 72–82.

8. Preston, *Rural Conditions,* pp. 39, 40, 44; Tafel and Thomas, p. 370; Strehlke, *Tabulae,* pp. 14–15, 28.

9. Strehlke, *Tabulae,* pp. 101; Röhricht, "Syria sacra," *ZDPV,* X (1887), 4, note 3.

10. Cahen, "Notes," p. 298.

11. *Redditus personales:* Tafel and Thomas, p. 371. Cf. Mantran and Sauvaget, *Règlements,* pp. 5 ff., and Abraham N. Poliak, *Feudalism in Egypt, Syria, Palestine, and the Lebanon, 1250–1900* (London, 1939), *passim.*

fiscal unit. A head tax was levied on the Moslems in the region of Tyre, but we do not know whether it fell on all the serfs. The fixed rents paid on each carucate bore the name of "gifts" (*exenia*). Three times a year—at Christmas, at the beginning of Lent, and at Easter —the lord received a hen, ten eggs, a cheese, and a load of wood (or, in some places, wax and honey), or their equivalent in money.[12]

The rent paid in proportion to the harvest (*kharāj*, sometimes latinized as *carragium*) ordinarily consisted of payments to the lord of a part of the harvest varying from one quarter to one half the produce of the fields, but most often a third.[13] The same proportion applied to grapes and olives. A contract in August 1236, between the Hospitallers of Tripoli and some peasants allowing the latter to plant olives on their lands, fixes the share of the knights at one third.[14] There were other payments as well. In addition to his *partison,* or third of the harvest, the lord might require of the villeins a hogshead of cheese per carucate, and a hen as interest for the seed which he advanced them each year *ut melius terra seminetur.*[15] Finally, we should mention the taxes on livestock, especially that on goats (*computagium*) amounting to one carouble per head, and the tax on bees.[16] The peasants of Syria, however, though heavily burdened, apparently were not forced to perform any very heavy corvées. This suggests that there was practically no seigneurial "reserve," all the lands of the casal being divided among the tenants. Certain plots, however, were reserved for particular purposes, such as the sugar-cane plantations near Tyre cultivated under Venetian control. These plantations were probably worked by tenants fulfilling their corvées as well as by agricultural laborers or even slaves. Joshua Prawer believes that the one day's labor per carucate required from the tenants in this area is one day per week, and so four to six days per month.[17] It is possible that the seigneurial domain was of more importance in some other areas; in the diocese of Acre the Teutonic Knights cultivated lands, vineyards, and olive groves at their own expense.[18]

Besides the lord's arable land, which was not very important in

---

12. Cahen, "Notes," p. 300; Preston, *Rural Conditions,* p. 46.

13. Cahen, *loc. cit.*

14. J. Delaville Le Roulx, "Inventaire de pièces de Terre Sainte de l'ordre de l'Hôpital," *ROL,* III (1895), 84 (no. 249).

15. Strehlke, *Tabulae,* pp. 92–93; Tafel and Thomas, pp. 371, 374.

16. Strehlke, *Tabulae,* p. 28.

17. Preston, *Rural Conditions,* p. 45; Prawer proposes an interpretation which would allow for four to six days corvée a month ("Étude," p. 165). Helen Preston (p. 45) interprets the same quotation as referring to one day's labor per year—a very light burden.

18. Strehlke, *Tabulae,* p. 91.

comparison with the extensive peasant holdings, the seigneurial reserve included a certain number of buildings for economic exploitation. Probably the presses where the grapes or olives were brought
and the ovens in which the bread was baked were directly controlled
by the lord, or else by some intermediary who held them directly of
the lord *en apaut*.[19] The lord also owned the mills. Some of them
were turned by animal power; some, at least from the time of the
Third Crusade, were driven by wind like those at the castle of Safad;[20]
but the most important mills were run by water power. Those which
the Venetians had below Tyre had only one or two millstones, but
the mills which Bohemond IV of Antioch had constructed under the
walls of Antioch had three, and it was possible to add a fourth. In
principle, only the tenants of a lord had the right to use his mill,
except when the lord enjoyed a privilege similar to that which Bohemond IV granted the Teutonic Knights, *tel franchise que tuit cil qui
voudrunt modre a vostre molin par la dreiture payant, . . . que il faire
le poïssent*.[21] These banalities — presses, ovens, and mills — naturally
brought to the lord a *droiture*, just as the use of his measures to sell
the produce of their lands obliged the peasants to pay him a *men-
suragium*. Apparently the owner of the threshing floor on which they
threshed their grain exacted the payment of still another fee (*portagium herbarum ad areas*), and in the casals of the Venetians near Tyre
the straw remaining on the floor belonged to the lord as well.[22]

As in the west, the lord supplanted the village community by taking
under his own control the installations serving the entire community
and charging a fee for their use. We do not know what part he played
in irrigation: a Tripolitan text of 1264 shows that it was up to the
lord to maintain certain canals (perhaps only the main ones) and to
name the *sergent* who had to watch them, and no doubt oversee the
distribution of the water over the fields.[23] The *cysternarius* cited in
another document probably had a similar function.[24]

We know more about other seigneurial officers. Aside from the

---

19. Preston, *Rural Conditions,* pp. 37–38.

20. *De constructione castri Saphet,* cited by Paul Deschamps, *Le Crac des Chevaliers* (Paris,
1934), p. 103. Prutz gives windmills an eastern origin (*op. cit.,* p. 317); but Ambrose writes:
"Et lors firent . . . li Aleman . . . le premerain molin à vent que onques fust feiz en Sulie"
(*L'Estoire de la guerre sainte,* v. 3227, ed. Gaston Paris [Paris, 1897]).

21. Tafel and Thomas, pp. 369–370; Strehlke, *Tabulae,* p. 50. Cf. also Rozière, *Cartulaire,*
p. 222, and the passage concerning the mill of Fierge in the charter of Casal Imbert (Strehlke,
Tabulae, pp. 1 ff.).

22. Strehlke, *Tabulae,* pp. 92–93; Tafel and Thomas, p. 371.

23. I hope to edit the text of 1264; cf. also Tafel and Thomas, p. 368, and Rozière, *Cartulaire,* p. 277.

24. Röhricht, *Regesta,* no. 533.

provost, to be found on Venetian lands in the thirteenth century under the Italian name *gastaldus,* and the *ra'īs,* the head of the community, it was mainly the *escriveins* and *drogmans* who held true "sergeanty tenures," designated by the words *scribanagium* and *drugumanagium.* The purview of these officials might embrace several casals. Usually their fief included the receipt of a tax paid by the inhabitants of these casals toward their compensation.[25] Possibly the *gardagium* cited in a text of 1257 was a tax also, paid by the villagers to reimburse the officers assigned by the lord to watch over their flocks or their fields.[26]

Within this framework of casal and seigneury there was a wide variety of crops. Grain was the most important: wheat, barley, oats, and millet were grown almost everywhere. Even in the south of Judea, around Hebron where wheat was harder to raise, barley was abundant.[27] And the fertility of the soil, a century after the departure of the Franks, could still amaze Ludolf of Suchem, who assures us that a sufficient rain immediately after seeding (which was done in September–October) brought a harvest in March or April sufficient to meet their needs for several years, and that after a good harvest one *gros* could buy as much wheat as a person could eat in a month.[28]

From a careful examination of Venetian texts concerning the seigneury of Tyre, Prawer has been able to throw some light on the problem of field rotation. He has shown that after a grain harvest the land was left fallow for only a few months. In the following autumn, half the arable land continued fallow, and vegetables were planted in the other half, to be harvested the next spring. The land on which they were grown was then left fallow until autumn, while the other half was sown with summer plants (chick-peas, sesame, sorghum). Thus only two years would elapse between two grain harvests from the same soil, and in the interval a vegetable crop would also have been raised. Field rotation was biennial, and half the land of each casal, at least in the region of Tyre, was always planted with the sort of cereals that yielded up to five- or even seven-fold.

Vegetables were planted in the same soil as cereals. Beans, lentils, peas, and plants of lesser importance certainly played a large part in the diet of the natives as well as of the Franks. We know very little about fodder; however, it was bound to be needed for the Frank-

---

25. Strehlke, *Tabulae,* pp. 15–16; Cahen, "Notes," pp. 297, 306–307 (who asserts that the functions of the *drogman* and *escrivein* were given to the same person, about which it is difficult to be certain).

26. Strehlke, *Tabulae,* pp. 92–93.

27. *Sefer nameh,* p. 103.

28. *AOL,* II-1 (1884), 363, 366.

ish cavalry, since the horses would have no fresh grass except in a few favored places.[29]

It seems that the Franks sought, wherever possible, to convert cereal lands into more remunerative plantations. At least, we find the Teutonic Knights thinking about growing sugarcane on lands which had to continue paying the tithe to the bishop of Acre in wheat and barley.[30] Sugarcane could be planted only on irrigated land. There was hardly any land suitable for it except in the interior valleys (particularly in the Ghor near Baisan [Bethsan], and in the neighborhood of Nablus), and on the coastal plain. In 1036 Nāṣir-i-Khusrau had admired the "immense plantations of sugarcane" near Tripoli, which remained a great center of sugar cultivation in the Frankish period, and also at Sidon.[31] We know of such plantations around Tyre and Acre as well. Burchard of Mount Sion carefully observed how these *cannemelle* were cultivated: in the spring the young shoots were planted in moist places; in the following February when they were grown they were cut into pieces half a palm in length. These were taken to the press (*mazara*) to have the juice squeezed into bronze vats in which it was cooked until it acquired the consistency of syrup. This was then left to dry in finely woven straw baskets. As it hardened the *mel zucare* or molasses seeped through.[32] The presses, a seigneurial possession, often appear in the texts, and the great sugar factory at Acre with its huge vats is described by Arab historians in connection with its destruction in 1187.[33]

Sugarcane did not monopolize the lands which were *abeveraiz* (irrigated); there were many gardens.[34] The texts tell us little about what grew in these *orti,* which also served as orchards. Palestinian fruits have always been celebrated. Marino Sanudo tells us that they were exported to Egypt, and James of Vitry and other visitors ecstatically reported their variety. Dates, bananas (called "apples of paradise"), figs, lemons, limes used on meat and fish during summer, oranges, pomegranates, and almonds weighed down the trees of these *jardi-*

---

29. The pasturages noted by Sanudo are the plains of the Krak des Chevaliers, Tortosa, and Arsuf (*Liber secretorum fidelium crucis,* ed. Jacques Bongars, *Gesta Dei per Francos* [Hanau, 1611; repr. Jerusalem, 1972], II, 152, 245).

30. Sanudo, ed. Bongars, II, 93. In this respect we may recall that the tithes were paid to the Latin church only on the revenues of Frankish lords, and not on those of the peasants as in the west.

31. *Sefer nameh,* pp. 40, 46.

32. Burchard of Mount Sion (ed. J. C. M. Laurent, in *Peregrinatores medii aevi quatuor,* 2nd ed. [Leipzig, 1873], p. 87); Strehlke, *Tabulae,* pp. 9, 17; Tafel and Thomas, p. 368.

33. Abū-Shāmah, *Livre des deux jardins* (*RHC, Or.,* IV, 296–297).

34. For a garden irrigated by a spring called Elysium see Sanudo, ed. Bongars, II, 247.

neroies, as Ambrose called them in describing the orchards of Jaffa.[35] Aside from the cooking vegetables known in the west, they grew cucumbers, melons, and gourds, the size of which astounded James of Vitry, who also praised a "sort of thorn" the young shoots of which were edible—asparagus. We also know that the pilgrims besieging Acre in 1189 were saved by locust beans and walnuts.[36]

Other trees were cultivated outside these gardens: balsam, whence came the *opobalsamum,* on the banks of the Jordan and the Dead Sea, at Jericho and Engedi; fig, in the Judean countryside as well as the rich plain of "Boquée" (al-Buqai'ah) at the foot of Krak des Chevaliers; and especially olive trees. Throughout all of coastal Syria occupied by the Franks the olive was the tree par excellence. Palm trees, more characteristic of the interior, could also be found in the southern oases such as Segor (biblical Zoar), or on the coast where we know of the palm grove of Haifa. The olive crop went primarily into the making of oil, and Sanudo tells us that at the beginning of the fourteenth century Egypt imported from Syria not only oil for eating purposes but soap made from the oil of an inferior olive called *souri.*[37]

Besides olives there were grapes, to be found in the same general areas, in particular between Antioch and Latakia, in the region of Tortosa and Tripoli, near Acre and Tyre, in Galilee, near Nablus, and as far as the vicinity of the Dead Sea (Bethlehem, Engedi, Jericho).[38] The vineyards seem to have become more extensive after the crusades began. Indeed, in the region of Nablus there were some *vineae quas Franci coluerunt* which might well have been cultivated by Frankish settlers; there can be no doubt, however, in the case of the extensive arable area converted into vineyards around 1220 in the neighborhood of Tyre.[39] Frankish domination certainly brought with it a considerable increase in wine drinking (Moslems for the most part only ate the grapes or raisins); this wine, which caused deaths among the ill who drank it at the siege of Acre because of their weakened state,[40] was highly enough prized in the west that even after the end of Frank-

35. Sanudo, ed. Bongars, II, 53; James of Vitry, ed. Bongars, *op. cit.,* I, 1099; Ambrose, *op cit.,* v. 3941.

36. Ambrose, *op. cit.,* v. 4361.

37. Sanudo, ed. Bongars, II, 53; Prawer, "Étude," p. 57.

38. Rey, *Colonies franques,* p. 250.

39. Ferdinand Chalandon, "Un Diplôme inédit d'Amaury I, roi de Jérusalem, en faveur . . . du Temple-Notre-Seigneur," *ROL,* VIII (1900–1901), 314; Tafel and Thomas, p. 379. See Richard, "Le Comté de Tripoli dans les chartes du fonds des Porcellet," *Bibliothèque de l'École des chartes,* CXXX (1972), 363, 366.

40. Ambrose, *op. cit.,* vv. 4361 ff.

ish domination we can find cargoes of ten tuns of Tripolitan wine on a single ship.[41]

Plants of importance in the manufacture of textiles appear to have been widely cultivated following the crusades. Cotton was the most important, and in 1140 the cotton of Antioch was being exported to Genoa.[42] Cotton was grown primarily throughout northern Syria (near Cilicia and in the valley of the Orontes), but it could also be found in Palestine. Gilbert of Lannoy saw much cotton around Tyre, although Marsiglio Zorzi's Venetian *memoriale* of 1243 makes no mention of it.[43] Mulberry bushes to raise silkworms were mostly to be found near Tripoli.[44]

We know very little about animal husbandry. In the region of the steppes the beduins continued to herd their camels or sheep without paying any attention to boundaries, except to pay rent to the Frankish lord on whose lands they grazed their herds. Baldwin III's seizure of the herdsmen who had obtained from him the right to pasture their animals (and in particular three excellent horses) in the "forest of Banyas" in 1156 is a well-known incident. It was also in this forest that the Hospitallers proposed to raise herds of cows and sheep.[45] The grazing land in the hills of Judea and Samaria, of Lebanon and the Antioch range lent themselves equally to the raising of cattle, sheep, or goats, but water buffalo were to be found only in the lower regions. Donkeys, mules, and camels served for transportation, but the crusaders appear to have had great difficulty in procuring real warhorses strong enough to bear the weight of a fully equipped knight, and it was probably necessary to import them from the kingdom of Sicily and possibly also from Moslem countries.[46] The cows and the *bestes menues* furnished the milk foods which formed a large part of the diet of peasants and lords alike (taxes could be paid in cheeses), and their hides were used in the tanneries which were to be found throughout the area. There appears to have been an abundance of poultry.

Hans Prutz, who had no admiration for the crusaders, blamed them for bringing about a decline in the cultivation of Syrian lands.[47] This

41. Genoa, Archivio notarile, Antonio Fellone, filza I, fol. 28ᵛ.
42. Cahen, *La Syrie du nord à l'époque des croisades et la principauté franque d'Antioche* (IFD, BO, I; Paris, 1940), p. 476, n. 39.
43. Ghillebert de Lannoy, *Oeuvres* . . ., ed. Charles Potvin (Louvain, 1878), p. 150.
44. Cahen, *La Syrie du nord*, p. 475.
45. Preston, *Rural Conditions*, pp. 28–29, 48; William of Tyre, XVIII, 11–12 (*RHC, Occ.*, I, 836–837).
46. Prutz, *op. cit.*, p. 322.
47. *Ibid.*, p. 329.

is by no means certain. In fact, the texts indicate a great effort in rural colonization. There was colonization by "Syrians" arriving from other areas: around 1120 the Frankish kings drew to their kingdom of Jerusalem a number of Christians from Transjordan. But even in 1115 Ekkehard of Aura was amazed by the revival of agricultural life. A spontaneous movement, no doubt, led the dwellers on the frontiers to establish themselves in the casals under Frankish domination.[48] Be that as it may, new villages were established, for example the "casal d'Aleman, so named after its founder, in the region of Caesarea,"[49] which raises the question whether each of the many casals bearing the name of Frankish landholders did not owe its origin to the initiative of some knight who had attracted settlers to his lands. The movement for the foundation of villages was flourishing in the west at the same time and might have influenced the crusaders in their new domains. Several casals bore the names of townsmen of Jerusalem, some of whom were wealthy enough to have been able to take an active part in the movement.

Christian Syrians, and Moslem prisoners bound to the land of those to whom they had been sold, were not the only ones to settle in the Frankish estates. Latins also came to settle and to work the land in "villes neuves" reminiscent of those of the west because of the charters of freedoms which they were given. The settlers of Casal Imbert, for example, were required to pay only a seventh of their harvest, a quarter of the produce of their gardens and vines, and two thirds of their olives, and to use the lord's oven (one loaf out of fifteen), the mill of Fierge, the exclusive use of which they had for half the time, the wheat measures, and the bath; and they were exempt from taxation on food sold in the market of Acre. The native peasants who supplied Jerusalem had benefitted from a similar privilege because of the difficulties of victualing the holy city in 1121.[50] The twelfth century saw the creation of a moderate number of these free towns, which did not survive the conquest of Saladin and apparently failed to reappear in the thirteenth century.

Would these efforts to found new villages (which indicate how sparse agricultural settlement was before the arrival of the crusaders) assure Frankish colonies the eventual means for self-support? Prutz's reply

48. William of Tyre, XI, 27 (*RHC, Occ.,* I, 500–501; cf. Prawer, "The Settlement of the Latins in Jerusalem," *Speculum,* XXVII [1952], 496); Ekkehard of Aura, *Hierosolymita,* ed. Heinrich Hagenmeyer (Tübingen, 1877), XXXVI.

49. Chalandon, "Un Diplôme inédit," p. 314.

50. Strehlke, *Tabulae,* p. 1; Prawer, "Colonization Activities in the Latin Kingdom of Jerusalem," *Revue belge de philologie et d'histoire,* XXIX (1951), 1063–1118 (esp. pp. 1115–1117).

was that since the only really fertile regions, the coastal plains, were devoted to market gardening and the growing of cotton, grapes, and sugarcane, there was always a shortage of cereals. The matter, however, is not that simple.

In discussing the capture of Ascalon in 1154, William of Tyre described the famine which struck the Holy Land in that year. The price of a hogshead of wheat (nearly five bushels)[51] had risen to four gold bezants, and only the great store of provisions to be found in Ascalon, the frontier place where supplies had been collected for fifty years, kept the *menue gent* from starving to death. But the taking of the town had another result. By getting rid of the danger of Egyptian brigands, it allowed an extended area to be brought under cultivation, land which had lain fallow since the First Crusade and in which the yields were very high.[52] A little later, the construction of the fortress of Darum allowed the area of cultivation to be extended even farther.[53] All danger of famine was thus apparently dispelled. William of Tyre considered the kingdom of Jerusalem practically self-supporting by the middle of the twelfth century.

It had not been so when the Russian Daniel and the Englishman Saewulf visited the Holy Land. The fields lay deserted, the lands barren. Even around 1120 locust plagues, invasions of field mice, and a persistent drought brought on a famine, which was one of the reasons for convoking the council of Nablus.[54]

Except for these early years, the kingdom of Jerusalem throughout the twelfth century was at its greatest extent. Embracing all the highlands of Judea, Samaria, and Galilee, the Ghor, the plateaus of Transjordan and the land of as-Sawād, it benefitted from the possession of large fertile areas together with revenues from districts which, though under the Moslems, nevertheless had to pay not less than half their harvests to the Franks. The county of Tripoli and the principality of Antioch were just as well off. The large towns of these three Frankish states had sufficient wheat fields in their hinterlands to avoid famine in normal times, although Antioch would find itself in trouble after the conquests of Zengi and Nūr-ad-Dīn (1144–1150).

After 1187, however, Frankish possessions were limited to the coast, that is, to several important towns without a sufficient agricultural hinterland. The attempts at reconquest which went on from 1189 to 1248 succeeded for some years in obtaining an extension of territory,

51. Prawer, "Étude," pp. 59–61.
52. William of Tyre, XVIII, 1 (*RHC, Occ.*, I, 816–817).
53. *Idem*, XX, 19 (*ibid.*, I, 973–975).
54. Mansi, *Concilia*, XXI, 262.

but this did not last. The granaries of the kingdom—the plains of Galilee, the area around Hebron and Ascalon— were gone, and with them the rich alluvial land of the Ghor. After 1263 the Mamluk reconquest aggravated the difficulty even more, by reducing Frankish possessions to the coastal towns alone, the "seigneuries" of which had to share their yields with the Moslems; thus the revenues of the hundred casals which depended on Tyre had to be brought to one spot where the representatives of the sultan and those of the lord of Tyre proceeded to divide them equally.[55] The county of Tripoli and the principality of Antioch, which had not been severely affected by the disasters of 1187, now met with a similar fate. The years of scarcity, the *caristie,* reappeared: in 1280, a hogshead of wheat cost six *livres* at the beginning of winter, which would indicate that it might go as high as ten *livres.*[56] But even aside from these years of poor harvests, what remained of Frankish Syria was certainly incapable of supporting itself.

Of course, the Franks could lean on Moslem Syria. When in 1185 the drought, together with Saladin's devastation, aroused fear of a *caristia,* Raymond III of Tripoli obtained a truce during which the Saracens brought so much wheat into Frankish Syria that its price dropped considerably.[57] But Moslem Syria had also known bad times. The last years of the twelfth century and the first years of the thirteenth had been years of perpetual Franco-Moslem warfare; the sultans had evacuated whole areas and razed their fortresses, and it was only in the time of Baybars that Moslem Syria began to be resettled. Even so, the Mongol ravages had been a serious strain. Furthermore, the years of warfare came frequently enough that one could not always count on Moslem supply.

John of Joinville, who spent several years at Acre, tells us how he provided for the welfare of his men. Around October 1 he bought some hogs and sheep, flour and wine, to last the whole winter, since food grew dearer during the winter because of the storms which made the sea more dangerous then than in the summer. In this he was only doing what others did.[58] The essential role of import by sea is confirmed in other sources. There is an allusion in the *Règle de Temple* to the dismissal of the "commander of the *Voute d'Acre*" who had

55. Richard, "Un Partage de seigneurie," p. 75.
56. Thomas Rymer, *Foedera* (Record Commission, London, 1816), I, part II, 188–189.
57. Ernoul, *Chronique,* ed. Louis de Mas Latrie (Société de l'histoire de France; Paris, 1871), p. 124.
58. John of Joinville, *Histoire de Saint Louis,* ed. and tr. Natalis de Wailly (Paris, 1868), pp. 179–180.

failed to check up on the condition of a wheat cargo from overseas, and the complaints of Ambrose on the scarcity of grain which prevailed around Acre until the arrival of the first barge after the winter storms.[59]

At first the Byzantine empire had figured among the principal exporters of wheat to the crusader states. During the First Crusade Genoese, Greek, and English ships carried foodstuffs from Cyprus and the Archipelago, and in 1110 a Greek vessel was captured by the Egyptians off Haifa while carrying merchandise and food *de regno Grecorum*.[60] The role of the Greek empire would lose its importance, however, especially when Cyprus and Cilician Armenia broke away from it. Cyprus and Armenia continued to furnish wheat to Frankish Syria, which came to depend on their shipments in the second half of the thirteenth century.[61]

It was necessary, however, to seek additional imports from the chief wheat producer of the Mediterranean, the kingdom of Sicily. In 1104 a grain ship left Otranto for Antioch (which Byzantium may have refused to supply), and the countess Adelaide of Sicily when she married Baldwin I brought ships loaded with wheat, wine, oil, and salted food.[62] This commerce reappeared with the sharp decrease of grain production in the Holy Land. In 1197–1199 the monastery of St. Mary *Latine* got from the ruler of Sicily permission to send abroad 200 *somma* of wheat; in 1240 Frederick II sent to Tyre a ship carrying 2,000 *somma* for the payment of his knights; in 1280, a famine year, large cargoes of grain, barley, salted food, cheese, beans, and peas left for Acre.[63] These examples could be multiplied.

The importance of the Sicilian role in provisioning must not be underestimated. In 1280 the vicar of patriarch Elias of Jerusalem wrote to king Edward I of England about the disturbing situation of the Latin kingdom: there was a famine in Cyprus and in Cilician Armenia, which had been devastated by locusts, and it was feared that

59. Ambrose, *op. cit.,* vv. 4215, 4347, 4483; *Règle et statuts secrets des Templiers* (ed. Maillard de Chambure, Paris, 1840), p. 471.

60. Albert of Aachen, XI, 27 (*RHC, Occ.,* IV, 675–676); Adolf Schaube, *Handelsgeschichte der romanischen Völker des Mittelmeergebietes* . . . (Munich and Berlin, 1906), p. 124.

61. Rymer, *loc. cit.*

62. Raimondo Morozzo della Rocca and Antonino Lombardo, *Documenti del commercio veneziano nei secoli XI–XIII* (Regesta chartarum Italiae, 28–29; 2 vols., Rome and Turin, 1940), I, 31; William of Tyre, XI, 31 (*RHC, Occ.,* I, 508–509).

63. P. Sinopoli di Giunta, *La Badia regia di S. Maria Latina* (Acireale, 1911); J. L. A. Huillard-Bréholles, ed., *Historia diplomatica Friderici secundi* (6 vols., Paris, 1852–1861), V, 848 (cf. V, 587; VI, 747); Evelyn M. Jamison, "Documents from the Angevin Registers of Naples: Charles I," in *Papers of the British School at Rome,* XVII (1949), 138. The *somma* of Sicily measures about 265 liters; the *somma grossa,* 344.

the king of Sicily, Charles of Anjou, would not allow grain to be exported because of his war with the Byzantines. Some weeks later the treasurer of the Hospitallers expressed the same fears.[64] Thus an administrative act of the king of Sicily would determine whether there would be an abundance or a shortage in Syria, for the Sicilian export system presupposed that the merchants had obtained an import license from the vicar-general of the kingdom of Jerusalem or, for Acre, from the grand master of the Temple.[65] Any Syrian baron who refused to recognize the Angevin king of Sicily as king of Jerusalem had no hope of getting one of these precious import permits.

Before Charles of Anjou, Frederick II was thought capable of influencing the internal politics of the kingdom of Jerusalem by threatening to forbid the shipping of grain. Until 1244 he agreed to allow the imperial ships to carry grain to Acre; after the taking of Tyre by the Guelfs, he established a veritable blockade against Acre and the persons placed under the ban of the empire.[66] Earlier still, the threat of holding up the import of grain coming from the Byzantine empire was a weapon used to keep the counts of Tripoli in subjection to the emperor, as well as a measure against the Normans of Antioch.[67]

Thus, unable to supply its own needs other than in the period 1120–1187, Frankish Syria necessarily fell into political and economic dependence on those countries that could provide supplies.

---

64. Rymer, *loc. cit.*; "Lettre de Joseph de Cancy . . . à Edouard Ier," in *Bulletin de la Société d'histoire de France,* 1-2 (1834), 10. This is translated by William B. Saunders in *PPTS,* V-5 (London, 1896).

65. Georges Yver, *Le Commerce et les marchands dans l'Italie méridionale au XIIIe et au XIVe siècles* (Bibliothèque de l'École française de Rome, LXXXVIII: Paris, 1903), pp. 110 ff.

66. Huillard-Bréholles, *op. cit.,* VI, 466–467.

67. Anna Comnena, *Alexiad (RHC, Grecs,* I, 196) (to force the count to restore the money deposited by the imperial envoys).

B. *Agriculture in the Kingdom of Cyprus*[68]

In contrast to the Frankish colonies on the Syrian coast, the island of Cyprus remained completely under the domination of Latins from 1191 to 1571. Its agriculture therefore was not affected by political events; at most, the Genoese occupation of Famagusta from 1373 to 1464 led to the peasants' abandoning the part of the neighboring plain which was ruined by the wars. In the same period, devastation by pirates, who carried off many villagers into slavery, certainly disrupted agricultural life.

The soil of Cyprus is quite varied and it is best to distinguish among the several regions according to their agricultural capacity. The west is a mountainous region (Akamas, Tylleria, and Troödos) which, because of the extension of the Makheras mountains, stretches north of Larnaca. This highland is cut by deep valleys rich in vegetation

---

68. The principal sources are Mas Latrie, *Histoire de l'île de Chypre sous le règne des princes de la maison de Lusignan,* II, III, *Documents et mémoires* (Paris, 1852-1855) (among the published documents is included the *Livre des remembrances de la Secrète* of 1468, as well as some Venetian statistics); and *idem, Documents nouveaux servant de preuves à l'histoire de l'île de Chypre . . .* (Collection de documents inédits sur l'histoire de France: Mélanges historiques, IV; Paris, 1882), pp. 337-619, and "Nouvelles preuves de l'histoire de Chypre," *Bibliothèque de l'École de chartes,* XXXII (1871), 341-378; XXXIV (1873), 47-87; XXXV (1874), 99-158. For seigneurial accounts, there are those of Knodhara and Morfittes, published by Édouard Poncelet, "Compte du domaine de Gautier de Brienne au royaume de Chypre," *Bulletin de la commission royale d'histoire,* XCVIII (1934), 1-28, and of Psimolófo, on which see Richard, "Le Casal de Psimolofo et la vie rurale en Chypre au XIVe siècle," *Mélanges d'archéologie et d'histoire,* LIX (1947), 121-153. See also *idem,* "Un Évêque d'Orient latin au XIVe siècle: Guy d'Ibelin, O.P., évêque de Limassol, et l'inventaire de ses biens," *Bulletin de correspondance héllénique,* LXXIV (1950), 98-133; and *idem,* "Documents chypriotes des archives du Vatican (XIVe et XVe siècles)," in *Chypre sous les Lusignan,* I (Bibliothèque archéologique et historique, LXXIII; Paris, 1962). There still remain some unpublished documents in the protocols of Genoese notaries. Some of the accounts of travelers are useful, especially that of Denis Poussot, *Le Voyage de Terre Sainte* (ed. Schefer, Recueil de voyages et documents, XI; Paris, 1890) and of Nicholas of Martoni (ed. Léon Le Grand, "Relation du pèlerinage à Jérusalem de Nicolas de Martoni notaire italien [1394-1395]," *ROL,* III [1895], 566-669).

For modern works one need only note Mas Latrie, *L'Île de Chypre: Sa situation présente: Ses souvenirs du moyen-âge* (Paris, 1879), and George Hill, *A History of Cyprus* (Cambridge, 1948), II, 6-11, and *passim.* On measurements, the conclusions of my "Documents chypriotes," pp. 16-21, do not agree with those of Cornelio Desimoni, "Observations sur les monnaies, les poids et les mesures cités dans les actes du notaire gênois Lamberto di Sambuceto," *ROL,* III (1895), 21-25. Elements of this chapter are used in Richard, "Une Économie coloniale? Chypre et ses ressources agricoles au moyen-âge," *Byzantinische Forschungen,* IX (1976), 331-354.

(one of them is called Myrianthoussa, "the land of 10,000 flowers"); to the west the region of Khrysokhou is especially fertile. In general the mountains are well watered; the sides of the valleys can be terraced for cultivation. To the south of this highland is a shore plain cut in two by a mountainous promontory, the Paphos plain and the Limassol plain. In places this plain is very rich, where the streams converge from the mountains; but it terminates in the east, near Larnaca, in a veritable steppe. To the north of the mountains stretches the Mesaoria, a dry plain cut by stream beds which fill only in the winter. It is best suited to the cultivation of cereals, but in places one can get water from wells to irrigate gardens and orchards. Where the rivers end near the sea there are even marshes. To the north of the Mesaoria there is a new chain of mountains which extends eastward to the Karpass peninsula. The northern edge of this chain, falling to the sea, is one of the most fertile and best watered areas on the island.

Natural conditions seem to have been much the same in the Middle Ages as now. Possibly, as Louis de Mas Latrie says, there were more woods. In the fourteenth century the forest still furnished lumber for shipbuilding, and it was possibly under Turkish domination that excessive exploitation and the multiplication of goat herds aggravated deforestation, the plague of the island.[69] There are no traces now of the large forests which have disappeared since that time, and Ṣāliḥ ibn-Yaḥyâ found the region of Cape Kiti, near Larnaca, as desolate in 1425 as it is now.[70] Concern over water has dominated agriculture ever since, drought being an even more terrible calamity than the plagues of the locusts, which could reduce the yield to ten percent of normal.[71] For cereals one depended on the winter rains, but other crops required additional irrigation. Sugarcane, cotton, and the gardens required lands which were *abevreyces,* lands over which water could be directed from the canals or creeks (*condutz* or *flumaires*). The canal water was drawn either from some river or from a spring — what the texts call *aigues courrans et sourdans*. Where there was neither river nor spring, it was necessary to tap sources of ground water. Denis Poussot in 1532 saw the cotton fields near Larnaca watered by means of water wheels (*norias*) turned, as today, by a blindfolded horse or ass.[72]

69. Richard, "Une Économie coloniale," pp. 332–333. There is an account of 1325–1326 on shipbuilding in *idem,* "Documents chypriotes," pp. 33–49.

70. Louis Cheikho, "Un Dernier écho des croisades," *Mélanges de la Faculté orientale,* I (1906), 351.

71. Mas Latrie, *Histoire,* III, 496.

72. Poussot, *Le Voyage de Terre Sainte,* p. 148.

For those who were located along the upper reaches of a stream, it was a great temptation to hold up as much of the water as possible to irrigate their own lands, and the king's court had to adjudicate many conflicts occasioned by a *noveleté d'aigue.* The "turcopolier" James de Nores had redirected the Pedias, in so doing ruining the land of the titular patriarch William of Jerusalem at Psimolófo. The patriarch, unable to get justice from king Peter I, obtained a request from pope Innocent VI to the king to reëstablish the stream in its old course (1360). Between the Corners (Cornaros), Venetian lords of Episcopi, and the Hospitallers of Kolossi, there were several royal decisions regarding the use of the waters of the Kouris, which ran between these villages. We also have the account of a visit made by commissioners appointed by king Janus in 1413 for the purpose of giving satisfaction to the inhabitants of Palekythro, who complained that they no longer received the waters of the spring of Kythrea, which had formerly been used to water their lands and turn their mill. The commissioners followed the course of the stream and forbade the blocking up of the irrigation canals so as not to deprive Palekythro of water. Each village had a *neroforo* (a Greek title which the account of Psimolófo translates *custos aque molendini*); he had to see to it that "chascun ay sa razion par mezure et par ordenement."[73]

If conditions of cultivation do not appear to have changed in Cyprus since the Middle Ages, the number of villages seems to have diminished. The documents of the fourteenth and fifteenth centuries mention villages which no longer exist. The statistics of the fifteenth century give the island a population of something like 150,000 to 180,000 persons living in from 834 to 839 casals and *prastii.*[74] The importance of these villages varied. Psimolófo, with 60 households, was certainly bigger than average. There was a difference between the casals and the *presteries,* which were mere hamlets dependent upon a casal.[75] Some of these *presteries* were undoubtedly inhabited only by the representative of the lord, with some slaves or wage laborers;

73. *RHC, Lois,* II, 378; Mas Latrie, *Histoire,* II, 504; *idem,* in *Bibliothèque de l'École des chartes,* XXXV, 111; Richard, "Le Casal de Psimolofo," p. 125; Bustron, *Chronique,* p. 29 (fountain of Kythrea). See also Jean Darrouzès, "Notes pour servir à l'histoire de Chypre (quatrième article)," Κυπριακαι Σπουδαι, ΚΓ΄ (1959), 47–51.

74. Richard, "Une Économie coloniale," pp. 333–334.

75. Bustron, *Chronique,* p. 462. In the Byzantine empire the nucleated village (χωρίον) and the separate farmstead (κτῆσις) were the two main types of peasant settlement. The προάστεια were large estates run with slaves or small leaseholders (George Ostrogorsky, "Agrarian Conditions in the Byzantine Empire in the Middle Ages," in *Cambridge Economic History of Europe,* 1st ed., I [Cambridge, Eng., 1942], 198, 201). The Cypriote πράστειον would correspond to both the κτῆσις and the προάστεια, the casal to the χωρίον.

others were practically small villages whose inhabitants cultivated their holdings and where the lord might also have lands of his own.

In most of the villages the lord seems to have had his own holdings (*demainne*) next to the lands cultivated by the peasants who owed him dues. Seigneurial exploitation had its center in the "court," which comprised a whole collection of buildings, although a seigneurial manor-house seems to have existed only in the most important places, and even then it was only rarely fortified. There is mention, however, of towers at Kiti and Pyla. In the smaller holdings the lord was often content to live in a tent when he spent any time there.[76]

In each court there were houses for general accommodation, built according to the technique used in 1317 at Psimolófo—stone foundations, walls of unbaked brick, and terraced roofs with lathes and joists held up by "French columns" of wood. There were stables, granaries, and wine cellars. Also in the lord's court were the oven, the bakehouse (*paneteria*), the winepress, and sometimes a sugar mill, or else an olive grinder and press. As for the flour mills, some were run by water (as at Palekythro and Psimolófo), others by animal power. There is mention of a *molin de bestes* at Nicosia in 1367.[77] Finally, many casals had a *canute*, which seems to have been a tavern; presumably it was here that the lord had his wine sold.[78]

To exploit his demesne, the lord—if he did not farm it out to someone to hold *en apaut*—established an intendent, the *bailli*, assisted by an *ecrivain*, a *grenetier*, a *canutier*, some artisans (blacksmith, carpenter, bakers), some wage laborers (*soudoyers*), and often also slaves who were clothed, fed, and lodged at his expense. The number of these people varied according to the importance of the seigneurial reserve. At Psimolófo the lord's portion was one seventh of the arable land. Some of the buildings belonging to the reserve, however, were not used by the lord, but were *apautée*. The mills, for example, were rented out.

The rest of the land of the casal was cultivated by the peasants, who were either serfs (*pariques*) or free men (*elevteres* or *francomates*), each of these categories having clearly defined obligations to the lord. The pariques were attached to the soil, and a periodic census called a *practico* recorded their names and the ages of members of their families.[79] A parique who left his land was considered a fugitive, and

---

76. Richard, "Guy d'Ibelin," p. 124. Cf. Nicholas of Martoni, "Relation," p. 637.

77. The account of the church of Limassol: Richard, "Documents chypriotes," pp. 61–110.

78. Canute (mistakenly read *camete* by Poncelet and *camire* by Mas Latrie, *Histoire,* III, 256, 263, 273) is the Cypriote χανοῦτι.

79. In the documents of the fifteenth century: "en serfz personnez cent dis sept, ce est hom-

royal ordinances—especially that of 1355—established measures to return him to his master and to punish those who kept him on some other land.[80] The marriage of pariques was also regulated. When a female serf of one seigneury married a serf of another seigneury, her new master had to give one of his female serfs to her old lord. To be ordained a priest or to leave a casal, the parique was required to pay a sum of money.[81] Finally, it seems that the transference of his goods to his children was limited. On his death a portion of his cattle (which he had possibly needed for field work) may have reverted to his master.[82]

In the acts of enfranchisement, where the obligations of the pariques were designated by the words *servage, chevage, anguaires, dimois, apaut,*[83] it is probable that the term *servage* applied to these restrictions of personal liberty. *Chevage* was received from all serfs aged fifteen to sixty. Leontius Machaeras identified it with the old head tax, which became the *kapnikon.*[84] Likewise another Byzantine impost had become a seigneurial levy on the serfs alone, the *dimois.*[85] *Anguaires,* also of Byzantine origin, required that serfs work on the lord's land two days a week—possibly three up to the middle of the fourteenth century, if we can believe Philip of Mézières, who says that the villagers were required to present themselves in the market on Sunday in order to be able to work for three days on their own lands, and that religious scruples led the king to reduce the length of these corvées. The lord was required, it seems, to provide meals for the *rustici de angaria.*[86] From the land which they cultivated for

---

mes, femez et enfans mermiaux, ce est des serfs du prahtico dudit lieu" (Richard, "Documents chypriotes," p. 143). Cf. Mas Latrie, *Histoire,* III, 465. Some of the documents specify the age of the children.

80. *RHC, Lois,* II, 373; Mas Latrie, *Histoire,* III, 192.

81. Mas Latrie, *Histoire,* III, 226–227, 234–235.

82. Richard, "Le Casal de Psimolofo," p. 146; Delaville Le Roulx, *Cartulaire,* III, no. 4515 (prohibiting the custom on the serf's death of taking *aratrum et asinos* when his heirs continue to fulfill his obligations "a coustume del vilenage"). Compare this with the custom in the Morea of exempting from seizure the land of the parique, his team of oxen, or his ass, all considered to be the property of the lord.

83. Mas Latrie, *Histoire,* III, 254, 270.

84. Cf. Andreas M. Andreades, "Deux Livres récents sur les finances byzantines," *Byzantinische Zeitschrift,* XXVIII (1928), 312. The *chevage* possibly corresponded to the Byzantine κεφαλητιών.

85. In 1222 queen Alice of Cyprus gave up the *chevagia et dimos que solvebantur regine . . . a rusticis ecclesiarum* (Mas Latrie, *Histoire,* III, 620). The *dimois* (δημόσιον) was possibly the old Byzantine land tax. *Dimois* and *chevage* appear to have been confounded under the name *catepanage.*

86. Richard, "Le Casal de Psimolofo," pp. 134–135; Mas Latrie, *Histoire,* II, 382; III, 125, 520. For a market at Episcopi see *ibid.,* III, 179. A recently discovered text indicates that the villagers of Marethasa owed the king 26 days' corvée in May for gathering sugarcane and 26

themselves, called *stagia,* the pariques owed the lord a third of the
produce (*partizon o tiers*). From the fifteenth century at least they
owed another tenth besides.[87] Finally, the Byzantine impost on herds
was still raised from the pariques, who paid a tenth of their animals
in money or kind.[88]

The number of pariques continually declined. Because of the harshness of their condition they sought to escape by becoming francomates. In 1355 the majority of peasants were serfs, and the francomate had to prove his freedom by producing documentary evidence.
King Peter I sold enfranchisements, which town dwellers especially
took advantage of, but undoubtedly many countrymen did as well;
and we possess the texts of individual acts of enfranchisement by the
king and by lords. In addition, the pariques benefitted from the fact
that every foundling was considered free. They pretended to abandon
their children on the public way and took them back the next day.
In the time of the Venetians the number of francomates was always
greater than that of the pariques, and a Venetian governor had to
require the francomates themselves to give 36 days corvée a year, with
a team of oxen, in return for a salary, all of which provoked revolts.[89]
But in the fourteenth century it had become difficult to have seigneurial reserves cultivated by serfs and slaves alone. The Cistercian
nuns of St. Theodore of Nicosia were obliged in 1338 to convert their
lands of Sterviga to "censives" because of the impossibility of finding
serfs to cultivate them.[90]

The payment of a "cens" was in fact the principal obligation of
the francomates. We have the text of a grant made by William of
Acre in 1468 to three Syrians of Episcopi who agreed to settle in his
casal of Potamía.[91] A house and garden were given them rent-free,
and they received land to cultivate in return for a fifth of its produce
(at Psimolófo in 1421 the cens paid by the francomates was estimated

---

days in August for harvesting crops: Richard, "Une Famille de 'vénitiens blancs' à Chypre au
milieu du XVe siècle: Les Audeth et la seigneurie du Marethasse," *Miscellanea in onore di
Agostino Pertusi* (*Rivista internazionale di studi bizantini e slavi,* I [1981], 89–129).

87. The custom of paying a tenth over and above a third (Mas Latrie, *Histoire,* III, 540)
possibly resulted from the imposition of a royal tenth on the revenues of fiefs at the end of
the fourteenth century. For *stagia* see Rozière, *Cartulaire,* p. 315 (1210).

88. Richard, "Le Casal de Psimolofo," p. 145. Germaine Rouillard is mistaken in thinking
that this tenth fell only on the nomadic shepherds ("La Dîme des bergers valaques sous Alexis
Comnène," *Mélanges offerts à M. Nicolas Iorga* [Paris, 1933], p. 784).

89. Mas Latrie, *Histoire,* III, 457, 551–553. On the proportions of francomates and pariques see *ibid.,* pp. 496, 534, 541.

90. *Benoît XII (1334–1342): Lettres communes et curiales analysées d'après les registres dits
d'Avignon et du Vatican,* ed. Jean M. Vidal (3 vols., Paris, 1903–1911), II, 90 (no. 6196).

91. Mas Latrie, *Histoire,* III, 297.

at a fourth or a fifth of their produce), a site to plant vines on which they would pay a cens and the tenth and where they could plant olives in return for a fifth of the fruit. The lord agreed furthermore to advance them two pairs of oxen and the barley and wheat seed necessary for the first year (the practice of lending seed grain and money to peasants to buy work animals is attested at Psimolófo and Knodhara). The francomate, free to leave the casal,[92] was therefore required, until the introduction of the *fattion francomatica* by the Venetians, only to pay a cens on the vineyards and gardens and a rent corresponding to a fifth of the produce of the other lands. In addition, the lord appears to have enjoyed a right of *marechaussie* on their beasts.[93]

An important part of the rural population was made up of slaves, Moslem or Christian, and freedmen. The latter, called "baties" or "batiees" when they were baptized Moslems, were tied to their master by bonds very like those which governed slaves. We know that 1,500 slaves had been seized between the years 1400 and 1415 from the lands of the Egyptian sultan by the naval forces of king Janus of Cyprus, and that the king refused to return them because they were needed for the sugarcane cultivation. These slaves were clothed and fed by their masters, who used them on their own domains; after being freed, however, they were assimilated to the population of the pariques.[94]

The pariques and the francomates were probably associated in a true village community. No matter what their personal condition, services fell heavily on all the village inhabitants, for example the arrangement for the distribution of water. We know little about the responsibilities of the officials who appear to have lived in the villages. We find a *juré,* who might have been a kind of village mayor; a *catepan,* undoubtedly an old imperial official, now become an officer of the seigneury (the personal taxes which the pariques paid, a survival of the fiscal system of the Byzantine empire, were called *catepanagium*); and various sergeants performed various tasks, overseeing harvests, maintaining canals, collecting dues, rewarded by the lord out of revenues called *sergentagium,* which the villagers paid.

92. *Ibid.,* p. 238.

93. *Ibid.,* pp. 217, 539 (5 bezants a year for 100 sheep or goats, but not known for the other animals).

94. *RHC, Lois,* II, 374–375 (assize of 1355 on fugitive slaves); Richard, "Documents chypriotes," p. 137; Pierre H. Dopp, *Traité d'Emmanuel Piloti sur le passage en Terre-Sainte, 1420* (Paris and Louvain, 1958), pp. 174–175; Richard, "Le Casal de Psimolofo," p. 131. The purchase of slaves to work the land is attested in *Jean XXII (1316–1334): Lettres communes analysées . . .,* ed. Guillaume Mollat and G. de Lesquen (16 vols., Paris, 1904–1947), VII, 44 (no. 43118).

As for the *aguelarchus* or *quisitor* at Psimolófo, he may have had to watch the common flock which the villagers pastured in the woods and on the lord's pasture lands.[95]

Cereals were the principal crop of the island. The soil lent itself to grain nearly everywhere, but especially in the Mesaoria, and a Catalan would write in 1421 from Psimolófo "ço ques fa aldit casal es tant solament blat." The soil was worked before the winter rains by a plow usually drawn by a pair of oxen (undoubtedly one of those wooden plows which can still be seen on the island), and the peasants then sowed the grain advanced to them by the lord. The harvests (*seailles*) began early in April, and were completed by the end of June. They required the gathering together of a considerable number of *seors*, who cut the wheat with a sickle and gathered it in large sheaves tied with rope which they carried to the nearby threshing floors of the village. Denis Poussot saw grain being threshed on these floors as it is still done: boards, weighted with stones and dragged by animals, crushed the ears; the grain was collected into bags, while the chaff was carried to *ostels* unless it was sold "a menu es aires."[96]

The most abundant cereal was barley.[97] Around 1540, in the whole island about 1,600,000 bushels were harvested, while the "white and red" wheat (hard and soft wheat) came to only 1,400,000 bushels. The fertility was such that they could expect a return of 7.5 to 1 when it was not too dry and when the locusts did not descend on the island. In some regions where the harvest was early it was possible to plant cotton right after the harvest and crop it just before seeding time again.[98]

Oats were not so abundant — about 37,000 bushels — because the animals were usually fed with cotton seed, leguminous plants, and barley. Besides the main cereals, therefore, we must look at the leguminous plants. Unfortunately Venetian statistics differ a great deal. Beans (*feves*) were the most important (37,000 to 115,000 bushels). They were grown everywhere and were used, together with wheat and barley, for payments in kind made to cathedral canons as well as to

95. An *aguelarchus* is cited at Psimolófo. There is a discussion on the meaning of this word in Constantine N. Sathas, *Documents inédits relatifs à l'histoire de la Grèce au moyen-âge* (9 vols., Paris, 1880–1890), IV, lii.

96. Poussot, *Le Voyage de Terre Sainte*, p. 150; *RHC, Lois*, II, 373. For the sale of chaff at Knodhara and Morfittes, see Poncelet, *op. cit.*

97. The figures to be given here come from a Venetian report at the end of the fifteenth century (Mas Latrie, *Histoire*, III, 493–498) and from that of Francesco Attar (*ibid.*, pp. 534–536).

98. Richard, "Une Économie coloniale," p. 338.

the workers and sergeants of the casals.[99] The *fasiaus* (*faseoli,* kidney beans) were of equal importance. Lentils and chick peas (*pesiaus*) were hardly less important in the statistics of the sixteenth century. Finally, among the leguminous plants which the climate of the island favored, we must note crops which do not find a place in these summary tables but whose importance is clear from other texts: the *gelbans* or *julbans* (*julbān* in Arabic: vetches) and *cressiniaus* (Arabic *qirṣaʻnah*: ers or black vetches).[100] At Knodhara, there was purchased for the slaves "four hogsheads of lobster seed," a plant which grew wild in the region of the Dead Sea and which the monks of that country ate, leading James of Vitry to think that it was this plant, not locusts (*locustae,* fr. *langoustes*) which nourished John the Baptist in the desert of Jordan.[101]

Cyprus also grew a large quantity of onions, both at Psimolófo in the Mesaoria and at Phínika in the mountains of the diocese of Paphos.[102] Onions remained one of the principal articles of produce and export.

There were other crops for the making of oil. It was certainly for this purpose that they grew sesame, the annual harvest of which amounted to 3,500 to 7,000 bushels in the sixteenth century. Olives could be found all over the island. The eating of olives was undoubtedly less important than the making of olive oil, which was estimated by Francesco Attar at 850 cantars (about 200 tons). A significant proportion of this oil was not for consumption but for the making of soap. The planting of olive trees was the subject of agreements similar to those to be found in the contract between William of Acre and the Syrians of Potamía, who promised to the landlord a fifth of the fruit of the trees they planted.

Among the other fruit-bearing trees the most important were the carob, which, then as now, proliferated in the coastal plains of north and south. The carobs, measured by the bag, had a place in the export trade. But other than the carob tree, most fruit trees were to be found in gardens where they could be properly irrigated. Nicholas of Martoni was amazed by the gardens of Nicosia, and Gabriel Capodilista praised the magnificent gardens of Episcopi where he found

---

99. Cf. Richard, "Le Casal de Psimolofo," pp. 141–143, and the account of the church of Limassol in Richard, "Documents chypriotes," p. 105.

100. George E. Post, *Flora of Syria, Palestine and Sinai,* I (Beirut, 1932), 425, 430. The identification of *gelbani* with galbanum was an error in my "Le Casal de Psimolofo," p. 143.

101. Poncelet, *op. cit.;* James of Vitry, *Historia Hierosolymitana,* LIII (ed. Bongars, I, 1075).

102. Richard, "Le Casal de Psimolofo," p. 128; Mas Latrie, *Histoire,* II, 500.

oranges, citron, carob, and bananas; although not so renowned as these, gardens certainly existed in all the casals and the best of the irrigated lands were used for them. A text of 1458 gives us a complete description of a garden at Nicosia, with its wells, its cistern (*berquil*), its grape arbors, its fruit trees (pomegranates, mulberry, fig, apple, peach, walnut, orange, jujube), and its rose bushes, but without many details of the vegetables grown there.[103]

The vineyards of Cyprus were famous. Besides the arbors for the production of raisins, there were immense vineyards, especially in the south of the island (in the dioceses of Paphos and Limassol) such as the *vinea Engadi,* two miles square — an old vineyard of the Templars, undoubtedly to the northwest of Paphos — where Ludolf of Suchem saw a hundred Moslem slaves working.[104] In the diocese of Limassol, the wines of Pelendria and Kilani appear to have been the most highly prized.

We know a good deal about work in the vineyards. It required a large amount of hard labor, since the ordinance of 1355 forbade that serfs suspected of having abandoned their holdings be seized either during harvest time or at the time of the grape harvest (September–October) and the time of the "labour des vignes," which fell in March and April. The account of the casal of Porchades (Parsata near Lefkara) listed the various steps in this work: "premier fer" and "segond fer" (plowing), "sermenter" (pruning), "saper" and "environner" (cultivating), "nétéer" and "traire les traillies hors" (cutting off the shoots), "paratrohio" (layering the runners), and finally picking the grapes and trampling them.[105] Then they were taken to the presses, and the juice was stored in great vessels of baked earth, the *pitaires.* Some of these held more than 55 gallons; they were kept in the cellars of the casals.[106] To transport the wine they used goat skins, *boutizelles* (the *boutes* themselves were casks holding over 65 gallons).

The reports of pilgrims often mention the wines of Cyprus. Though Nicholas of Martoni said only that they were sweet (*dulce*), Ludolf of Suchem, who tells us that this red wine became white after six

---

103. Nicholas of Martoni, "Relation," p. 635; Mas Latrie, *Histoire,* III, 76, 292. For the export of carobs see Genoa, Archivio notarile, Antonio Fellone, filza I, fol. 32ᵛ (1302).

104. Mas Latrie, *Histoire,* II, 212. There were vines called *herminezes* (*idem,* "Nouvelles preuves," XXXV, 123).

105. Mas Latrie, *Histoire,* III, 303. Professor Roland Martin tells me that on Thera παρατρέχειν was used in the sense of "layering" (*marcotter*).

106. Richard, "Guy d'Ibelin," pp. 117–119; Nicholas of Martoni, "Relation," p. 635. Documents of the fifteenth century list *pitaires* with presses and wine-cellars as indispensable parts of the casal.

to nine years in the *pitaires,* says that it was necessary to cut it with nine parts of water to one of wine, and that if taken straight a large quantity would not intoxicate but would burn one's bowels. No wonder he thought that the Cypriotes were the biggest and best drinkers in the world![107]

Besides foodstuffs they grew textile plants. Cotton was the most important, grown especially on the irrigated lands of the coastal plain in the south (Denis Poussot described vast fields of cotton near Limassol, and other fields near Larnaca, where he saw a waterwheel for the first time), and on the plain of Famagusta. The statistics of the sixteenth century gave inconsistent figures of 1,810 and 4,600 tons. Most of this production was exported to the west; of the remainder, what was not used for seed was used to fatten the cattle. Flax too was grown for its fiber and seed; Venetian estimates refer to it as an important product, more so than the hemp which was also grown on the island.

We must also note the spices and dyes listed in these statistics. Colocynth, safran, sumac, kermes seed, and others, which undoubtedly played only a small part in the produce of the island, caught the attention of the merchants who came there. The Middle Ages also viewed as a spice the most famous of Cyprus crops: sugar. The cultivation of sugarcane required irrigated land, and the problem of water was so vital for the plantations that a royal decision, rendered in favor of the Hospitallers of Kolossi over a question of irrigation, resulted in the loss of all the sugarcane at Episcopi—the Corners, following this disaster, could not find any new plants in Cyprus to rebuild their plantations, and they had to import them from Syria.[108] Sugar was harvested only in the wettest places: Sígouri, in the marsh where the present Kouklia reservoir is (where the kings of Cyprus had a castle built to watch out for the Genoese of Famagusta);[109] Palekythro, where the spring of Kythrea issues forth; Akanthou and Kanakaria, in the eastern part of the northern coastal plain; Lapithos, in the west of the same plain near one of the best springs on the island; and Morphou and Lefka, in the region of Pendayia. The area of Paphos and Limassol had the best plantations; besides some casals in the mountain valleys where sugar took up only narrow sites, as at Mamonia and Phínika, there were extensive plantations near Paphos, at Emba

---

107. Mas Latrie, *Histoire,* II, 214.

108. *Idem, Documents nouveaux,* pp. 396–397 (1368).

109. Poncelet, *op. cit.;* Nicholas of Martoni, "Relation," p. 637 (who calls the castle of Sígouri "Baffa").

and Lemba, Akhelia and Kouklia, and near Limassol, at Episcopi and Kolossi. In this last place there are still ruins of a sugarworks, later repaired in the Turkish period.[110]

All these places were familiar to merchants, for they took care to note from which casal came the cane used to make sugar for sale. Francesco Balducci Pegolotti recommended that one find out the place of production. This custom allowed Venice to force the king to meet his agreements with Venetian merchants by forbidding others from buying sugar in the casals from which their own deliveries had been promised, if these deliveries had not been completed.[111]

The manufacture of sugar took place at two different times. The cane was crushed in mills which were probably situated in the casals themselves, and the juice was collected in the *boutres.* This "cane honey" — molasses — might be exported (to Venice for example) in order to be refined; but it might be refined in Cyprus itself, under conditions described in a contract drawn up between king James II and master Francesco Coupiou, *refineouir de sucre,* who replaced the Syrian refiners. The sugar thus obtained could be sold either as sugarloaf or as loose sugar — and Pegolotti tells us that the best powdered sugar came from Cyprus. It was called *dezamburada,* rid of impurities which accumulate on the top of the sugar loaf, the *zambour.*[112] At the beginning of the sixteenth century it was estimated that Cyprus produced from 345 to 400 tons *"de premiere cuitte,"* 57 to 103 tons of *zambours,* and 57 to 181 tons of molasses.

Denis Poussot, in his *Voyage de Terre Sainte* of 1532, shows Cyprus producing "force sucre et cannelle," and also "force soye que les vers font, force moriers, arbres desquelz lesdictz vers sont nourris." The cultivation of mulberries and the raising of silk worms were probably of long standing in Cyprus, but they got a new impulse in the sixteenth century. A Venetian report says of silk: "si traze per ducati mille e va moltiplicando" at the beginning of the century; about 1540, Francesco Attar valued the silk production at 3,000 ducats, and although his estimates were always much greater than those of the Venetian report, it is still evident that production had increased.[113]

110. Mas Latrie, *Histoire,* II, 500; III, 88, 218-219; *idem,* "Nouvelles preuves," XXXV, 111; Bustron, *Chronique,* p. 29. On the sugar-works of Kolossi see Camille Enlart, *L'Art gothique et de la Renaissance en Chypre,* II (Paris, 1899), 685.

111. Francesco Balducci Pegolotti, *La Pratica della mercatura,* ed. Allan Evans (Mediaeval Academy of America, Publications, XXIV; Cambridge, Mass., 1936), p. 364; Mas Latrie, "Nouvelles preuves," XXXV, 113.

112. Mas Latrie, *Histoire,* III, 88 and note, 219.

113. Poussot, *Le Voyage de Terre Sainte,* p. 139; Mas Latrie, *Histoire,* III, 497-499, 535-536; cf. Richard, "Une Économie coloniale," pp. 341-343.

Turning to animal husbandry, a Venetian report at the beginning of the sixteenth century estimated 22,150 pairs of oxen throughout the island; these are the only animals included in the report. They were the work animals *par excellence;* they drew the cart which Nicholas of Martoni had the misfortune to hire to get from Famagusta to Nicosia; they were used for plowing, and the casal accounts never overlook the number of *bues dou domaine;* the word *charuga* was synonymous with ox-team.[114] A large number of cows were raised; their milk, along with that of the goats and sheep, went into the making of cheese, which was among the principal products of the island (estimated by Attar as 850 cantars, around 200 tons). Horses, asses, and mules appear to have been numerous — at Psimolófo the lord advanced funds to the villagers to buy asses as well as oxen, which indicates the importance of these animals for carting and plowing. There was an indigenous strain of pack horse or draft horse which seems not to have been highly thought of, to judge from the little *ronsin cipriain* which Guy of Ibelin had. Turcoman horses were used, probably imported from Anatolia.[115] Finally, camels were also used to carry loads, at least in the great interior plain, as they still are.[116]

The smaller animals comprised both the flocks of the seigneurial reserve, often watched by slaves, and those of the peasants. Sheep and goats appear to have been very numerous and pigs were raised in great number. Nicholas of Martoni, who suffered so many bitter trials in Cyprus, complained that people used to let animals into their houses, where they introduced a parasite that would not let the unfortunate traveler close his eyes.[117] As in the west, the meat was salted, and a pig was killed at Christmas for the workers on the domain.

During the summer the animals usually grazed abroad — at Psimolófo there was an "animal keeper in the forest." In winter the cattle had to be fed cottonseed or beans. As for fowl, the accounts mention pigeons, geese, hens, and capons, and we know that the villagers were required to give hens to their lords as a form of revenue. Chicken wings were a delicacy mentioned in the *Assises*.[118]

114. Nicholas of Martoni, "Relation," pp. 633–634; Richard, "Le Casal de Psimolofo," p. 131, note; *idem,* "Une Économie coloniale," p. 343, note 47.

115. Richard, "Guy d'Ibelin," p. 121; *idem,* "Le Casal de Psimolofo," pp. 146, 149. The "fauvel de Chypre" which Richard the Lionhearted rode while on the crusade, and whose qualities Ambrose praised, was not necessarily a war horse raised in Cyprus. The king of England had taken it from Isaac Comnenus.

116. *Jean XXII: Lettres communes,* ed. Mollat, VII, 44 (no. 43118).

117. Nicholas of Martoni, "Relation," p. 634; Richard, "Le Casal de Psimolofo," p. 145; *idem,* "Guy d'Ibelin," p. 125.

118. *Assises de la Cour des Bourgeois,* in *RHC, Lois,* II, 193; Richard, "Une Économie coloniale," p. 345.

The *Assises* also refers to bees, in dealing with the case of those who attracted someone else's bees to their own hives (*vaisseaus*) and of bees found in an *arbre sauvage qui n'a point de seignor*. Unlike the custom in the west, in this latter case bees and honey belonged to him who found them, not to the lord of the village. Denis Poussot was astonished that bees were raised in hollows made in the walls of houses rather than in hives. A tax of 16 deniers was paid for each *abeillier*.[119] In the Venetian reports wax and honey are mentioned among the principal products of the island. The honey was estimated at 300 or 400 cantars (70 to 90 tons) a year, and wax at about 18 tons.

Among the natural resources we should also note game and fish. Although nothing is known of fishing in the seas around Cyprus, we do know something about the lagoons on the southern coast. Not only did these pools produce salt, as at Limassol and the "salines" of Larnaca, but there were so many fish caught in the former (mostly giltheads) that Florio Bustron found it worth mentioning.[120] and their sale brought in 5,370 bezants a year to the king, according to the account of the tithes of Limassol (1367). Hunting was the favorite pastime of the Frankish nobility. The animals they hunted have since been so thinned out that they have almost disappeared, at least as regards rabbits and hares; but at the time of the Lusignans they could still hunt wild sheep and roebucks called *agrini*. Travelers have left us accounts of the hunt, the lords often spending a month under canvas in pursuit of the game through the forests and mountains, using trained leopards and hunting dogs. The Venetian statistics mention wild fowl also. They were hunted with falcons. The travelers were scandalized by the luxurious trappings of the chase. Ludolf saw the 500 hunting dogs of Hugh of Ibelin, the titular count of Jaffa, with a huntsman for every two dogs, and he figured that each nobleman had enough falcons to keep a dozen falconers busy (an exaggerated number to judge from the bishop of Limassol, Guy of Ibelin, who had only three). Nicholas of Martoni says that king James I had 24 hunting leopards and 300 falcons.[121] The cost of these animals is suggested by an *assise* of king Hugh IV on May 16, 1355, setting a reward of two bezants for whoever found and returned to the owner an adult groshawk or falcon, one bezant for the *tressiaus* (tercels?), sparrowhawks, and merlins, and two bezants for hunting dogs. A heavy fine

119. *RHC, Lois,* II, 192–193; Poussot, *Le Voyage de Terre Sainte,* p. 147; Richard, "Le Casal de Psimolofo," p. 144.

120. P. 28.

121. Nicholas of Martoni, "Relation," p. 635; Ludolf of Suchem, in Mas Latrie, *Histoire,* II, 215.

was imposed on those who received stolen animals.[122] No wonder that Cyprus was a country in which hunting literature flourished: it was probably in the fourteenth century that the two authors of tracts on falconry lived; one of them, Michelin, had been a falconer to a king of Cyprus, while the other, Molopin, dedicated his *Livre dou Prince* to prince John of Antioch, Peter I's brother.[123]

The census of the produce of Cyprus confirms the impressions of travelers, who were amazed that a country covered with rocky hills could be so fertile. The resources of Cyprus were extremely varied, and a large enough number of people worked on the land so that in the middle of the sixteenth century Francesco Attar figured that nine tenths of the cultivable soil was in production. But was such cultivation designed to feed the populace or to enrich the Frankish lords? In defining the general characteristics of Cypriote agriculture a recent book has insisted on the "colonial" character of the production of the Mediterranean islands in general and of Cyprus in particular. According to the author, Fernand Braudel, everything was sacrificed to the needs of the western cities Genoa and Venice, of which Cyprus had been a protectorate. These cities had forced Cyprus to develop certain crops—cotton, wine, and sugarcane—at the expense of the needs of the inhabitants of the island and for the sole profit of the dominant aristocracy, to such an extent that the Turkish conquest seemed to the islanders an economic liberation raising their standard of living.[124]

That Cyprus was an exporting country of colonial produce was certainly true. Sugar in particular played a large role in the commerce of the island. Although it is possible that sugarcane cultivation was of recent introduction (tenth century?), and although it developed especially when the possibility of the west's getting sugar from Syria declined, it was sufficiently important at the beginning of the fourteenth century for contracts drawn up in Famagusta to preserve evidence of purchases made by Genoese merchants at Episcopi from

---

122. *RHC, Lois,* II, 373–374; Richard, "Une Économie coloniale," p. 345, note 57.

123. These two tracts were used by Jean de Francières to write his well-known *Fauconnerie* at the end of the fifteenth century: Rolf Wistedt, "Le Livre de fauconnerie de Jean de Francières: L'auteur et ses sources," *Filologist Arkiv,* XI (1967).

124. Fernand Braudel, *La Méditerranée et le monde méditerranéen à l'époque de Philippe II* (Paris, 1949), pp. 122–125.

125. Genoa, Archivio notarile, Lamberto di Sambuceto, filza III, fol. 32ᵛ (1307); Pegolotti, ed. Evans, p. 364. Cf. Mas Latrie, "Nouvelles preuves," XXXV, 137, and Sanudo, *op. cit.,* p. 24. The exploitation of Episcopi by the Corner family has been studied by Gino Luzzatto, "Capitalismo coloniale nel Trecento," *Studi di storia economica veneziana* (Padua, 1954), pp. 117–123.

the countess of Jaffa, and for Pegolotti to emphasize the importance of Cyprus sugar.[125] Cotton also appeared in these contracts.[126] Products such as resin and indigo were certainly destined for the western market.[127] Cyprus wine was also known overseas. Bishop Arnulf of Lisieux about 1147 compared the eloquence of another prelate to Cypriote wine, "sweet to the taste, but fatal if unmixed with water"; and the *Bataille des vins* of Henri d'Andeli around the end of the twelfth century ranked Cyprus wine first.[128] In 1307 a boat left Cyprus to take wine to the Hospitallers besieging Rhodes.[129] Its popularity would last throughout the Middle Ages. It was precisely to compete with Cyprus that the Portuguese planted sugarcane and vines imported from Cyprus in the island of Madeira.

The example of Madeira, however, where the exclusive cultivation of sugar and grapes had disastrous effects on forest and soil alike, cannot be applied to Cyprus. There sugar and cotton could be grown in only a small part of the country, which was much drier than the Atlantic island, and vineyards prospered only in a limited area beneath the slopes of the Troödos. The greater part of the island was given over to cereals and other foodstuffs, and the harvests were sufficiently abundant to provide large exports. In the twelfth century Cyprus appears to have victualed the crusaders; in the thirteenth it was the abundance of food there which dictated the use of the island as the base of operations for the crusades. Louis IX's provisioners had been prepared to buy veritable "mountains" of wheat and barley, which Joinville found amazing. Contracts of 1300, 1301, and 1302 reveal cargoes of wheat and barley, beans and vetches destined for Cilician Armenia (possibly for Egypt also, although illegally).[130] In 1347 a cargo of wheat left for Venice, a city which continually had to count on Cyprus for the grain for which it had such pressing need. The *provedditore* Bernard Sagredo complained in 1562 that the Signoria overestimated the capacities of the island in demanding that he send 40,000 *stara* of grain.[131]

126. Genoa, Archivio notarile, Antonio Fellone, filza I, fol. 32ᵛ (1302), and Lamberto di Sambuceto, filza II, fols. 257 and 283ᵛ.

127. *Ibid.,* Antonio Fellone, filza I, fol. 17ᵛ: the purchase by a Genoese of 58 "rotes" of resin.

128. ". . . dicens eum habere naturam Ciprici vini, quod in ore quidem dulce est sed occidit, si non aqua fuerit temperatum" (*Historia pontificalis*, in *MGH, SS,* XX, 535); "Vin de Cypre fit apostoile" (*Oeuvres de Henri d'Andeli*, ed. Alexandre Héron [Paris, 1881], p. 30).

129. Lamberto di Sambuceto, filza III, fols. 37ᵛ, 38ᵛ.

130. Desimoni, "Actes passés à Famabuceto de 1299 à 1301 par devant le notaire gênois Lamberto di Sambuceto," *ROL,* I (1893), 138, 310, 322, 325, 327 (1300); Antonio Fellone, filza I, fol. 8 (1302); Giovanni Bardi, filza IV, fol. 133ᵛ. For the shipping of wheat, barley, and biscuit to Rhodes in 1449 see Mas Latrie, *Histoire,* III, 59–60.

131. Mas Latrie, "Nouvelles preuves," XXXV, 102; *idem, Histoire,* III, 554.

Cyprus, a greater producer of cereals than even of sugar or wine, provided its inhabitants the means of a good life.[132] In a normal year a hogshead of wheat was worth one bezant; a *rote* (5 lbs.) of the whitest bread was never more than 6 deniers, and the same weight of barley bread (*gruau*) which the poorest ate was rarely more than 2 deniers.[133] The daily pay of a carpenter in the shipyards of Famagusta rarely fell below half a bezant (24 deniers, the price of a hen); and two centuries later the francomates required to do forced labor by Venice received one bezant a day. Cyprus therefore had a low cost of living.

Since Cyprus was above all an agricultural country, it can be regarded as a vast exploitative enterprise yielding fat profits to the king and the Frankish aristocracy. The lords' granaries and cellars were the source of their wealth, and the merchants beat a path to their door. It was to the storehouses of John of Ibelin, the titular lord of Arsuf, that a Genoese went to buy 130 jars of "Paralime" wine on October 14, 1300. In 1406 the Bragadin family intended to withhold 7,878 hogsheads of wheat bought from queen Heloise *in magazenum ad casalia*. Despite their precautions in sealing the storehouse door, the queen had it reopened to sell the wheat at a better price a little later.[134] Moreover, the king's financial year was determined by the date he leased out his casals, as well as when he sold his wheat, cotton, and wine; very frequently he made his payments in sugar to be drawn from the harvest of one of the "bailliages" of the royal domain where sugarcane was grown.[135] Not only the king but the entire Frankish nobility of Cyprus lived off the sale to the merchants of Outremer of the products of their lands, like Antilles planters in the eighteenth century.

However, the Cypriote population did not suffer much under their regime. The most striking fact of the history of the peasantry during the Frankish period is the steady improvement in its condition. All

---

132. The importation of wheat is mentioned for the years of famine caused either by the influx of refugees from the Holy Land or by drought — or even by excessive rainfall; *e.g.,* 1296, when it was necessary to fix bread prices and when the drought caused a famine in Egypt, or 1309, when the winter storms and the snow were late: R. de Mas Latrie, ed., *Chroniques de Chypre d'Amadi et de Strambaldi* (2 vols., Paris, 1891–1893), I, 233, 243 note, 292–293. Cf. also Yver, *Le Commerce et les marchands,* pp. 118, note 4, 141.

133. Richard, "L'Ordonnance de décembre 1296 sur le prix du pain à Chypre," Ἐπετηρὶς τοῦ Κέντρου Ἐπιστημονικῶν Ἐρευνῶν, I (Nicosia, 1967–1968), 45–51.

134. Desimoni, "Actes passés à Famagouste," *ROL,* I, 137; Mas Latrie, "Nouvelles preuves," XXXV, 113–114. Wine-cellars and granaries were pillaged by the peasants in 1421 during an uprising the causes of which made it similar to the Jacquerie of 1356. The peasants rebelled less against the harshness of the seigneurial regime than against the inability of their lords to defend them against Moslem invasion.

135. Mas Latrie, "Nouvelles preuves," XXXV, 111 ff.

the charges which continued to burden the pariques had been imposed during the Byzantine regime; the Franks seem not to have introduced any new ones (before instituting the tax to pay tribute, first to Genoa, then to Egypt, and in particular the "mete dou sel").[136] Under the Lusignans emancipations increased, and seigneurial domains were subdivided for the benefit of the francomates who had to pay only the "cens." Attempts to exploit these lands with slaves would fail, especially when the Genoese prompted the slaves to revolt in 1373. With the decline of labor provided by the corvées (as well as a reduction in the number of days of the corvées, if Philip of Mézières is correct), the exploitation of the seigneurial reserves became increasingly difficult; we find great planters like the Corners forced to rely on some 50 francomates, in addition to their slaves and serfs, to harvest the sugarcane at Episcopi in 1396.[137]

The passing of most of the peasants into the free classes and the reduction of their obligations would have unforeseen results. The Venetians, seeking to get as much out of their new colony as possible, tried to keep the pariques in their service by every means at their command, and to get labor for the seigneurial estates by forcing the francomates to perform the corvée. At the same time they tried to develop production of those things particularly necessary to Venetian industry, such as silk. The passing of the island into Venetian hands therefore modified the conditions of agricultural life. Under the Lusignans agriculture guaranteed a livelihood, supported local industry (textiles, soap, and so forth), and provided a surplus for export which enriched the nobility and, by giving the peasants the means to buy their freedom, led to an amelioration of their lives. The misfortunes of the late fourteenth and fifteenth centuries, and the Venetian conquest, converted an economy essentially Cypriote into an economy increasingly colonial.

---

136. Richard, "La Révolution de 1369 dans le royaume de Chypre," *Bibliothèque de l'École des chartes,* CX (1952), 113.

137. *Idem,* "Guy d'Ibelin," p. 121; Mas Latrie, "Documents nouveaux concernant divers pays de l'Orient latin," *Bibliothèque de l'École des chartes,* LVIII (1897), 108-110.

C. Agriculture in the Latin Empire of Constantinople[138]

It is impossible to describe the conditions of rural life in the whole of the Latin empire of Constantinople, because it lasted such a short time and left us so few records. We can, however, get some impression of those conditions from the texts provided by those parts of the empire which remained in Frankish hands a somewhat longer time. Except for the Morea, however, specific studies are lacking, allowing us only a brief sketch.

The parts of the Latin empire which we shall deal with are the principality of the Morea, which was Frankish throughout the thirteenth century but began to slip away during the fourteenth; the Venetian towns of the Morea (Coron, Modon, and their dependencies); and

138. I was able to use an important article by Jean Longnon on "Les Classes rurales dans la Grèce franque," the manuscript of which he has kindly allowed me to examine, and a résumé of which has appeared in his *L'Empire latin de Constantinople et la principauté de Morée* (Paris, 1949), pp. 209–212. Other studies include Peter Topping, "Le Régime agraire dans le Péloponnèse latin au XIVe siècle," *L'Héllénisme contemporain,* ser. 2, X (1956), 255–295; David Jacoby, "Les Archontes grecs et la féodalité en Morée franque," *Centre de recherche d'histoire et civilisation byzantines: Travaux et mémoires,* II (1967), 421–481; and (for the Venetian possessions) Freddy Thiriet, *La Romanie vénitienne au moyen-âge* (Paris, 1959). The sources include legislative texts, accounts of chroniclers, and, above all, the fief descriptions and demesne accounts. These documents, some edited by J. A. C. Buchon, *Nouvelles recherches historiques sur la principauté française de Morée et ses hautes baronnies,* II-1 (Paris, 1843), and by Spyros P. Lampros, Ἔγγραφα ἀναφερόμενα εἰς τὴν μεσαιωνικὴν ἱστορίαν τῶν Ἀθηνῶν (Athens, 1906), following his translation of the work of Gregorovius, are now accessible in Longnon and Topping, *Documents sur le régime des terres dans la principauté de Morée au XIVe siècle* (Paris and The Hague, 1969), with very important comments. Some property titles are edited by Ernst Gerland, *Neue Quellen zur Geschichte des lateinischen Erzbistums Patras* (Bibliotheca graecorum et romanorum Teubneriana, Scriptores sacri et profani, V; Leipzig, 1903). As for the documents in Venetian archives, they have given rise to two important publications: Sathas, *Documents inédits relatifs à l'histoire de la Grèce au moyen-âge* (9 vols., Paris, 1880–1890); and Hippolyte Noiret, *Documents inédits pour servir à l'histoire de la domination vénitienne en Crète de 1380 à 1485* (Bibliothèque des Ècoles françaises d'Athènes et de Rome, LXI; Paris, 1892). A systematic search through the archives of Venice, Genoa (especially for Chios), and Malta (for Rhodes) would certainly turn up a number of new documents; I have given here only a sketch of our present knowledge, which documentary discoveries may in large part modify. On Chios the sixteenth-century work by Hieronimo Giustiniani, *History of Chios* (ed. Philip Argenti, Cambridge, Eng., 1943), is useful. See also Thiriet, "Villes et campagnes en Crète vénitienne aux XIVe–XVe siècles," *Actes du IIe congrès international des études du sud-est européen,* II (Athens, 1972), 447–459.

the Venetian islands (Corfu, Euboea, Tenos, Myconos, and especially Crete). The islands in the hands of independent lords (duchy of Naxos, Zante, Cephalonia) have left hardly any documents.

This spread hardly lends itself to a precise description of the infinitely varied natural conditions of the different countries. There are some well-developed mountain areas as well as fertile alluvial plains such as the valley of the Eurotas, the plains of Messenia and of Elis in the Morea, and the Lelantian plain, which one text calls "the eye and the garden of Negroponte."[139]

The seigneurial regime appears to have been much the same everywhere. It seems to have been a survival of the Byzantine regime, save that in the Morea the lords had replaced the emperor and taken the imperial revenues for themselves. In the Venetian colonies the commune of Venice was able to reserve quite extensive powers for itself and to exact from the nobles, to whom fiefs had been granted, payments in kind. This made the nobles tenants of a special kind, but did not leave them the independence which they would have enjoyed in the principality of the Morea. Most of the peasants were serfs, and we find here the name "pariques" which we have met in Cyprus. These pariques, or *vilani,* subjected to the *vinculum vilanutici* or *servitutis,* were tied to their *stasis,* bound by restrictions concerning marriage and the right to dispose of their goods. The *stasis,* or holding, together with the team of oxen or the ass with which it was worked, was in any case inalienable and was considered the property of the lord.[140]

The peasants paid the *angaria personnalis,* a personal tax like the Cypriote *chevage*—but one which was undoubtedly imposed on the peasant in place of forced labor—which Venice offered to cancel in 1434 in return for the payment of a large lump sum, hoping thus to avoid the high costs of collection.[141] Further, they had to pay a land tax to the lord, the old Byzantine *acrostiche,* and a proportion of their harvest, the *datio, facion* or *terraticum.*[142] As for the Cypriote

139. Sathas, *op. cit.,* III, 455.

140. Longnon and Topping, *Documents,* pp. 265–267; Sathas, *op. cit.,* I, 285; III, 83; IV, 20, 31, 71, 182–183 (granting the inhabitants of Coron and Modon greater freedom to make wills, 1305); Noiret, *op. cit.,* p. 256.

141. Sathas, *op. cit.,* I, 269–270 (in 1473 the lords of Zante wanted to have the refugees from the Morea *contribuire real e personalment* like *i suoi parchi e villani*); II, 24; III, 421; Noiret, *op. cit.,* p. 363. This *angaria personnalis* probably corresponds to the *servitium personale* cited in Buchon, *op. cit.,* p. 55. Cf. Topping, "Régime agraire," pp. 268–272; Longnon and Topping, *Documents,* pp. 271–272.

142. Sathas, *op. cit.,* II, 24; Noiret, *op. cit.,* p. 409. The *facion* possibly corresponds to the *modiaticum* (Longnon and Topping, *Documents,* pp. 268–269), which was paid besides

kapnikon, for which there was no equivalent in Frankish Morea, it existed in Euboea, Tenos, and Myconos under the name *capinicho e vigliatico,* and appears to have been a payment in lieu of military service.[143] The pariques were also required to do forced labor, either on the lord's demesne, or in Venetian territories on public works, or even to take part in the great hunts (such as the annual partridge hunt, the *paganea,* of Chios). Despite their complaints, those who depended on Venice saw the number of their days of corvée increased from one a month to two; then, in spite of the rules, to four.[144] They often demanded the suppression of other customs (delivery of straw and hay to the Venetian governors, gifts to the castellans) without success.[145] Moreover, the custom of making gifts (*exenia*) to the lord existed in Frankish Morea also.[146]

The pariques, however, enjoyed the right to have recourse to the books in which were inscribed their names and the details of their obligations, books which were called *practico* or *catasticos.*[147] These also included the names of those who settled in the casals to work the wastelands. Possibly these were the people (called *vaginiti* in Corfu in 1413) who formed the class of *nicarii* which Longnon noted in the Morea.[148] Then there were the Albanian tribesmen who invaded Greece in the fourteenth and fifteenth centuries. They asked to be allowed to settle in the Venetian territories (Euboea for example), agreeing to pay one ducat per household *pro recognitione servitutis* and to give military service. These seminomadic herdsmen were thus assimilated to the serfs.[149]

We do not know if the Albanians were required, as the pariques were, to pay taxes on their cattle. The tithe on small animals, like that of Cyprus, is cited in the Moreote texts,[150] and there was a tax

---

the *acrosticho.* In Crete these revenues were a third of the harvest, the *terziarie* (Noiret, *op. cit.,* p. 497).

143. Sathas, *op. cit.,* II, 63; III, 127, 221, 311, 363; Topping, "Régime agraire," p. 264; Thiriet, *La Romanie,* p. 225.

144. Sathas, *op. cit.,* III, 2, 70, 197; Noiret, *op. cit.,* pp. 252–253; Giustiniani, ed. Argenti, p. 385.

145. Sathas, *op. cit.,* I, 291–292, 300; III, 68, 163.

146. Buchon, *op. cit.,* pp. 74–75; Longnon and Topping, *Documents,* p. 269.

147. Buchon, *op. cit.,* p. 97; Sathas, *op. cit.,* II, 190, 221; Thiriet, *La Romanie,* p. 223.

148. Sathas, *op. cit.,* III, 38–39 (in Crete the *villani ascripti* and the *villani liberi* were distinct: Noiret, *op. cit.,* p. 474); Longnon, *L'Empire latin,* p. 211; Topping, "Régime agraire," p. 282; Longnon and Topping, *Documents,* p. 263.

149. Sathas, *op. cit.,* I, 176, 178–179, 215.

150. Buchon, *op. cit.,* p. 60; Lampros, *Eggrapha,* pp. 99–100, 102; Topping, "Régime agraire," pp. 277–278.

called *zovaticum* collected on the other animals at the rate of nine hogsheads of cheese per ox, four and a half per cow.[151] On Tenos and Myconos, horse-raising country, a *thimainicho* was levied under the pretext that the lord ought to have a stud banality.[152] Finally, the herds which grazed in the forests overnight gave occasion for the raising of new taxes.[153]

We know even less about the demands made on the freedmen, the *franchis* whose liberty Venice recognized in 1299.[154] Probably they were subjected only to the payment of the cens on their land.[155] It seems that the old free rural Byzantine communities continued to flourish by hanging on to their old privilege of paying their taxes jointly. The pariques sought enfranchisement, and even tried to invoke the thirty-year prescription to escape the servile bond. An enfranchisement granted in 1364 to a Cretan reveals that by not paying either the personal tax or the proportionate levy on the harvest, and by avoiding the corvée, one could prove one's "franchise."[156]

There were not enough pariques to cultivate the land. In Crete the lords employed day laborers or even bought slaves for the job.[157] Besides the lands cultivated *ad acrosticho,* there were others given out on lease (*ad affitto*).[158]

The villages in the Morea and the islands were also called casals, and they had the same officials to be found in Cyprus, although with different titles. In place of *catepans, aguelarchi, jurés,* or *neroforos,* there were *curatori* and *vetrani,* and the apportionment of water in the fields was in the hands of a *potamarcho.*[159]

The seigneuries of the Morea, better known to us than those of

---

151. Sathas, *op. cit.,* II, 24, 25; III, 68, 71, 161; Jacoby, "Un Aspect de la fiscalité vénitienne dans le Péloponnèse aux XIVe et XVe siècles: Le *zovaticum," Centre de recherche d'histoire et civilisation byzantines: Travaux et mémoires,* I (1965), 405–420.

152. Sathas, *op. cit.,* III, 363.

153. *Ibid.,* III, 84.

154. Gerland, *Neue Quellen,* p. 85; *idem, Das Archiv des Herzogs von Kandia im Kgl. Staatsarchiv zu Venedig* (Strasbourg, 1899), pp. 124–125.

155. Sathas, *op. cit.,* I, 269–270; II, 79; Longnon and Topping, *Documents,* pp. 263–264.

156. Noiret, *op. cit.,* pp. 256 and 365 ("liberum et franchum . . . ab omni datio, angaria et tello et quolibet alio vinculo servitutis"—without doubt *angaria* here refers to the corvée, ᾽αγγαρεία, and *tello* to the personal tax τέλος). On this word see Longnon and Topping, *Documents,* p. 269.

157. Noiret, *op. cit.,* pp. 54, 409–410; Thiriet, *La Romanie,* pp. 314–315.

158. Sathas, *op. cit.,* I, 285; IV, 12; Longnon and Topping, *Documents,* pp. 272–273.

159. Sathas, *op. cit.,* I, 293; III, 361, 455; IV, 3, 7; Noiret, *op. cit.,* p. 53. At Chios the "elders" responsible for collecting the taxes, who were elected by the other inhabitants, had the title of *protogero* (Giustiniani, ed. Argenti, p. 385). *Terrae appactatae*: Topping, "Régime agraire," pp. 272–276.

the islands, included a seigneurial reserve of some importance, called the *despotico*. It comprised cultivated fields, lands planted with vines or fruit trees (*ambellonia*), and gardens, and included banalities of mill, olive press (*carpetum*), the *linobrosium* where linen was treated, the tavern for the sale of wine, the silk workshop, and probably also the wine press.[160]

The different areas which made up the Byzantine empire before 1204 did not have the same agricultural capacities, and their produce varied widely. The Morea, the largest of the Frankish colonies, had insufficient wheat fields to feed its population, but it had other resources. Its wines were known in the west; the wines of "Clarence" (Glarentsa) on the northwest coast and the "Malmsey" (Monemvasia) wines of the east coast attained a wide renown. The texts reveal that vines prospered throughout the peninsula. They were grown both on the seigneurial reserves and on the peasant holdings, and the peasants got special privileges for bringing land under cultivation by planting vines. The wines, however, were not all of the same quality; some spoiled quickly and it was necessary to sell them in the taverns of the casals since it was impossible to export them.[161]

Olives were also important in the Morea. The peninsula exported both raisins and olives preserved in salt; primarily, however, olives were used to produce oil.[162] Textile plants were also grown, especially flax. Venice had to forbid its being steeped in the rivers which provided water for its colonies of Coron and Modon.[163] The production of sugar was large enough to warrant the notice of Sanudo;[164] and bees supplied honey and wax in abundance. The raising of silkworms was also important, and Laconia was one of the regions which produced the most raw silk, to be sent off either to Italy or to the weavers of Thebes. Some dyes were produced, above all the scarlet seed of the kermes oak.[165]

The Morea also possessed two resources which most of the Latin east lacked: forests and prairies. Sanudo thought that this region

160. Buchon, *op. cit.,* pp. 61-63, 77; Lampros, *Eggrapha,* pp. 97, 99-100. For a herd of cows on the domain of Lise du Quartier in 1337 see Buchon, *op. cit.,* p. 90. See also Longnon and Topping, *Documents,* p. 275.

161. Lampros, *Eggrapha,* pp. 96, 102-103. For leases of vineyards see Gerland, *Neue Quellen,* pp. 233, 235.

162. Lampros, *Eggrapha,* pp. 99-100 (for legislation against the destruction of olive trees, in 1467, see Sathas, *op. cit.,* IV, 35).

163. Sathas, *op. cit.,* IV, 15.

164. Sanudo, *Liber secretorum* (ed. Bongars, II), p. 24.

165. For all this cf. Longnon, *L'Empire latin,* p. 212; Sathas, *op. cit.,* III, 241.

could provide a crusade with the wood needed for the construction of ships and war machines.[166] The acorns of the Morea provided food for pigs as well as *vallonées* used by the dyers of the west.[167] Pasture lands not only allowed the raising of cattle, but several regions were turned over to horse-raising, especially Elis, Messenia, the plain of Tegea, and the duchy of Athens (the duke of Athens asked the Venetians of Negroponte to look after his stud horses during the threat of a Turkish invasion; no doubt they were usually kept in the plain of Boeotia).[168]

The produce of the Venetian islands showed less variety. Corfu produced cotton, silk, and scarlet seed; Euboea, wood and cotton.[169] But the archipelago lent itself to little more than animal pasturage. Other than the cotton of Thera (Santorin) and the mill wheels of Melos, it was usually for their horses and mules that the islands were known.[170] They tried to develop other resources: in 1432 Venice farmed out Tenos and Myconos to a contractor to bring the uncultivated land into production, to plant vines and fruit trees, and to develop the production of honey, with what success we do not know.[171] Chios was famous for its mastic, produced by a tree of the *lentiscus* family; Rhodes produced sugar.[172] But the small size of these islands did not allow production comparable to that of the Morea or Crete.

Crete was the best example of a colony exploited at the orders and for the needs of the metropolis. It had an unsettled history. The thirteenth century and most of the fourteenth were marked by frequent revolts, and Venice had to keep a close watch over the government of the great island and take measures to prevent any new uprisings. As a result, agriculture was forbidden in some of the most fertile locations, since they happened to be too close to the habitual centers of revolt, to deprive potential rebels of the possibility of obtaining provisions which could sustain their uprising. The plain of Lasithi and the region of Anopolis were therefore empty from 1364 to 1463 because of government orders.[173]

166. Sanudo, ed. Bongars, p. 68.
167. Buchon, *op. cit.,* p. 63; Sathas, *op. cit.,* III, 90.
168. Sathas, *op. cit.,* I, 178–179; this question has been studied especially by Longnon in *Classes rurales.*
169. Sanudo, ed. Bongars, pp. 67–68; Sathas, *op. cit.,* II, 107, 108; III, 90.
170. Sathas, *op. cit.,* II, 119; Noiret, *op. cit.,* pp. 215, 297; Sanudo, ed. Bongars, pp. 67–68.
171. Sathas, *op. cit.,* III, 412.
172. Sanudo, ed. Bongars, p. 24. On the mastic of Chios and the regulation of its export, see Giustiniani, ed. Argenti, pp. 207–209. The island also produced cotton, silk, some reputable wines, and fruits (pp. 205, 82–84, 75–79, 85–86); Giustiniani gives details on the use of rivers and waterwheels for irrigation (pp. 17–19, 75, 80).
173. Noiret, *op. cit.,* pp. 36, 488.

But in the early fourteenth century Venice made Crete its principal supplier of wheat. Marino Sanudo complained about this, suggesting that the Venetian government might better get its wheat from the nearer Apulia (where the wheat was a better grade anyway) and leave the island as a possible supplier for the crusades.[174] By the end of the century, however, everything was subordinated to the production of the wheat needed by Venice. There was a *descriptio bladorum,* an accounting of the harvest, on the basis of which the government decided on the amount of wheat the seigneurs had to deliver to the state granaries and the amount they could dispose of for sale abroad. Even then they could sell only to countries subject to Venice. They got export licenses (*bulletae*), which had to be endorsed by the Venetian authorities at the places of sale. Thus the third of their harvest which the peasants owed their lords came under the disposition of the government.[175]

These irksome measures eventually provoked shortages. The famine of 1455 appears to have been brought on (if we can believe the complaints of the island feudatories) when the government stipulated the quantities of wheat to be exported on the basis of an assessment of land under cultivation rather than of the actual harvest. The harvest was bad, exports drained the island of wheat, and famine was the result. Following the crisis, Venice was asked to send millet seed to introduce this new crop into the island and thus provide a new food source. Venice refused (1462) because of the expense, and the only measure taken to avoid the recurrence of famine, by planting the plain of Lasithi and the other areas where cultivation had been forbidden since 1364, reinforced still more the single wheat crop.[176]

The concentration on wheat was not complete, but the worry about the food supply of Venetian colonies overrode all other concerns. The feudatories always had the greatest difficulty in maintaining the horses which they owed the commune for their military service. The horses of the Archipelago, and with still more reason the mules of the same area, could be used only as draft animals (and it was still necessary to have Venetian authorization to import them). Furthermore, the knights ruined themselves buying riding horses in the west or in Turkey.

---

174. Sanudo, ed. Bongars, p. 67.

175. Noiret, *op. cit.,* pp. 89, 228, 260, 490; Thiriet, *La Romanie,* pp. 232–233, 317–319. The *feudatarii* objected to surrendering the *terziarie* on the grounds that they still had to advance money to their peasants to buy cattle (pp. 472 ff.), and sought to escape the obligation by renting out their land (p. 498). For proceedings against one who had sent grain and *faxoli* to Chios see p. 542; and for unusual licenses for exporting grain to Patmos and Rhodes during years of abundance see pp. 2, 225.

176. Noiret, *op. cit.,* pp. 451, 472, 475, 488, 494, 497; Thiriet, *La Romanie,* p. 413.

In 1462 they asked for permission to turn some of the lands near Candia into pasturage, but Venice granted permission only in 1471, and it was only after that that horses could be raised on Crete.[177] Venice did try to introduce products of particular interest to merchants, such as sugarcane and mastic trees. But the privileges granted to those who were given the task of introducing them appear to have been insufficient to guarantee success, and Crete continued to produce the same old crops.[178]

Crete had some very important cotton plantations, and there was also flax. Scarlet seed was an article of export.[179] Crete also exported cypress wood, which was widely popular, but Venice limited its exploitation in 1412. Since it was used extensively for the construction of boats and houses, the eventual result was that it could be found only on the steep slopes which the mules could not reach without great difficulty. Thenceforth its export was prohibited and its use on the island regulated.[180]

Grapevines prospered throughout the island—too much so, indeed, for the various villages tried to forbid the introduction into their own territory of wine coming from other parts of Crete. They had to import casks, especially from "Romania." These were so cheap as to threaten the ruin of Venetian cask makers, and so their import was taxed. Cretan wine—of the Malmsey type—provided an important item of export. We know that it went not only to Alexandria, but also to London and Flanders; it was necessary to stop smugglers from hiding spices in the wine casks leaving for these countries.[181]

Animal husbandry was based on oxen, which provided a source of labor power. Venice had to take steps to forbid speculators from selling them to peasants at excessive prices.[182] Likewise, there were attempts to stop speculation in sheep (merchants advanced to the peasants the price of their cheeses to allow them to buy animals), but it was necessary to bow to the necessities of cheese-making, one of the foods Crete exported; Egypt in particular bought Cretan cheese.[183] It was also necessary to modify the regulations to allow commerce

---

177. Noiret, *op. cit.*, pp. 54, 89, 177, 215, 252, 272, 481, 515.

178. *Ibid.*, pp. 324, 347, 352, 402; Thiriet, *La Romanie*, pp. 417–418.

179. Noiret, pp. 143, 148, 163, 293, 343, 355, 526.

180. *Ibid.*, pp. 226, 233; Thiriet, *La Romanie*, pp. 322, 416.

181. Noiret, *op. cit.*, pp. 62, 225, 250, 256, 390, 391. Crete produced primarily Malmsey wines; in 1421 a merchant loads *monovasia* for Flanders (Noiret, *op. cit.*, p. 287; cf. Wilhelm Heyd, *Histoire du commerce du Levant*, tr. Furcy Reynaud [2 vols., Leipzig, 1885–1886; repr. Leipzig, 1936, Amsterdam, 1967], I, 279–280).

182. Noiret, *op. cit.*, pp. 251, 343 (Crete exported hides [*pelomina*] to Egypt); Thiriet, *La Romanie*, pp. 320–321, 415.

183. Noiret, *op. cit.*, pp. 55, 59, 225, 230; Thiriet, *La Romanie*, p. 324.

in oxen and sheep destined for the abattoir, so as to supply meat to the Venetian squadrons at Canea,[184] although it was primarily the wheat biscuit which the squadrons bought in Crete.[185]

Despite the existence of these other products, however, Crete was devoted above all to the production of wheat. Probably natural conditions had a hand in this, but the policy of Venice gave to wheat production a preponderant place, to the detriment of a balanced economy in the island. Crete thus offers a particularly noteworthy example of a medieval colony exploited in the exclusive interest of a metropolis. It submitted because the aristocracy living on the island, Venetian or Greek, had been harshly repressed after its revolts,[186] and because it had passed without change from Byzantine domination to Venetian.

Of the other countries of the Latin east, none presents the same characteristics so clearly. Cyprus, a fertile island and not too exposed to danger, had been cultivated for the great benefit of its kings and the Frankish nobles who sold their wine and sugar, but even under the domination of Venice it was not subjected to any agricultural specialization similar to that of Crete. The islands of the archipelago did not provide sufficient resources, although the Morea, incapable of self-sufficiency because of a shortage of wheat, did provide a quantity of foodstuffs which found a good market abroad, bringing in considerable revenues to the nobility living either in the peninsula or in Italy. Unfortunately we know little about the duchy of Athens, but the wealth of its dukes from the thirteenth to the fifteenth century suggests a sufficient agricultural productivity.[187]

The case of Frankish Syria is quite different. It was a crusading territory, exposed to frequent devastation, menaced unceasingly, and obliged to nourish pilgrims and crusaders in addition to the indigenous population. The Frankish nobles could not exploit their domains as the lords of Cyprus and the Morea did theirs. The sale of sugar, cotton, and other products demanded by overseas commerce was offset by the need to import foodstuffs. Outside of a short period (the second half of the twelfth century) agriculture was not an important source of revenue.

In all these areas, agricultural exploitation was carried on within

---

184. Noiret, *op. cit.,* p. 520.

185. *Ibid.,* p. 459.

186. Gerland has noted that the Venetian system of exploitation of the island reached perfection after the repression of the last revolt in 1364: "Kreta als venetianische Kolonie (1204–1669)," *Historisches Jahrbuch des Görresgesellschaft,* XX (1899), 19.

187. Heyd mentions only figs and raisins from Attica (*op. cit.,* I, 273); the plains of Boeotia were certainly covered with cereals, and fed herds of horses, but documents are very scarce for the duchy of Athens.

the framework of the seigneurial regime. This does not appear to have become more severe during the period of the domination by crusaders — the Venetian rule was probably no harsher than the Byzantine which it replaced. The condition of the peasantry in the Holy Land was much as it was in the time of the Moslems, who themselves had retained many traces of old Byzantine institutions. Cyprus preserved the regime which had existed under the Comneni; the Morea and the islands, the Byzantine regime at the time of the Fourth Crusade. Almost everywhere the Frankish aristocracy took the place of the previous public authorities, but the levies which the peasants paid corresponded to the taxes which they had previously paid. And gradually, as the centuries went by, a slow evolution tended to enlarge personal liberty.

VII

THE POPULATION
OF THE CRUSADER STATES

Population pressure was stressed by pope Urban II in his famous
speech at Clermont. Speaking of the condition of France, he is alleged by Robert the Monk to have said: "This land in which you live,
surrounded on one side by the sea and on the other side by mountain
peaks, can scarcely contain so many of you. It does not abound in
wealth; indeed, it scarcely provides enough food for those who cultivate it. Because of this you murder and devour one another, you wage
wars, and you frequently wound and kill one another. . . . Begin the
journey to the Holy Sepulcher; conquer that land. . . . "[1] This overpopulation was hardly true of northern France, whatever the condition of the area near Clermont, but it may have been true of the fighting class from which the crusaders were drawn, although too many
of the others went along. Since each knight was drawn from almost

A short account of medieval population is Josiah C. Russell, "Population in Europe 500-1500,"
Fontana Economic History of Europe, ed. Carlo M. Cipolla, I (London, 1972), pp. 25-70.
A longer account may be found in Russell, *Late Ancient and Medieval Population* (Transac-
tions of the American Philosophical Society, n.s., 48, no. 3; Philadelphia, 1958), and there
is information about the population of 1250-1348 in his *Mediaeval Regions and Their Cities*
(Newton Abbot, 1972).

On Syria a brief account appears in Hans Prutz, *Kulturgeschichte der Kreuzzüge* (Berlin,
1883; repr. Hildesheim, 1964), pp. 91-107; see also Joshua Prawer, *A History of the Latin Kingdom
of Jerusalem* (2 vols., Jerusalem, 1963), I, 459-461 (in Hebrew, for which Professor Prawer
kindly supplied me with a translation). Excellent studies of crusading cities are Jean Sauvaget,
Alep (Paris, 1941) and "Le Plan antique de Damas," *Syria,* XXVI (1949), 314-358. Very good
information is given by Emmanuel G. Rey, especially in his *Les Colonies franques de Syrie
au XIIe et XIIIe siècles* (Paris, 1883). The Palestine Exploration Fund has published valuable
reports on their excavations in their *Quarterly Statements. The Encyclopaedia of Islām* gives
much information about Moslem persons and cities. On conditions of rural settlement see Claude
Cahen, "Le Régime rural syrien au temps de la domination franque," *Bulletin de la Faculté
des lettres de Strasbourg,* XXIX (1950-1951), 286-310. On efforts to bring western colonists
to settle villages see Prawer, "Colonization Activities in the Latin Kingdom of Jerusalem," *Revue
belge de philologie et d'histoire,* XXIX (1951), 1063-1118, and on the economic conditions of
the seignory of Tyre his "Étude de quelques problèmes agraires et sociaux d'une seigneurie
croisée au XIIIe siècle," *Byzantion,* XXII (1952), 5-61; XXIII (1953), 143-170.

1. James A. Brundage, *The Crusades: A Documentary Survey* (Milwaukee, 1962), p. 19.

a thousand persons, a considerable population was required to provide a financial base for the crusading armies and to pay their very heavy expenses. Their opponents had the same problems, but without the extra cost of transportation to the scenes of battle and pilgrimage. This population had a definite bearing on the ultimate results of the ventures. Its analysis helps explain why the Syrian expeditions failed, why the campaigns against Moors, Albigensian heretics, and pagan Slavs in eastern Europe succeeded, and why the political crusades resulted in something like a draw.

Demographically, the crusades occurred at a time of great population increase, the period 1000–1348. The period is somewhat deficient in demographic data, despite the existence of occasional collections such as the Domesday Book in England. Except for a slow but steady increase in total population, conditions were fairly stable and probably much the same throughout the crusading areas east and west.

Usually there were more men than women, except in the cities. In part this was caused by the shorter life of women, but even allowing for this, the numbers of females appear inordinately low, a major demographic mystery. The sex ratio (number of men to 100 women) often was as high as 120. The average length of life of males was about thirty to thirty-five years, while the females lived about five years less. Of course the heavy infant and maternal mortality was responsible for shortening the average length of life. If a man lived to be twenty, he could well hope to make it to forty-five or fifty years of age. If he lived to be sixty he still had about a ten years' expectation. Half of the people were under the age of twenty. On the average, four to five children were born to a family, but the number in a simple family (man-wife-children) at any one time was about three and a half. If the grandparents or other relatives lived with the family, the number in the household was higher. It can be seen that some conditions were quite different from those we know today.[2]

Not much different, however, was the span of life, the approximate number of years attained by those who lived longest. Long before the crusades, the pillar saints (Stylites) of the Holy Land had provided examples of how long men could live under favorable conditions of life isolated from contact with communicable disease. The pillar saints lived on platforms on the tops of pillars, sheltered by a roof above and protected by a railing around the top of the column. They were saved from contagion by their lofty position and their infrequent communication with persons below. They might live close

2. See Russell, "Population in Europe 500–1500," pp. 25–50.

to a hundred years. By the time of the crusades this movement was largely spent.[3] Of secular persons in the east the famous fighter and writer Usāmah Ibn-Munqidh lived until he was ninety-three, while his nurse was alleged to have lived to be nearly a hundred. His uncle, Sulṭān, lived between seventy-two and eighty-five years, but his father Murshid only sixty-nine.[4] No crusader is known to have lived past seventy.[5] In the west, persons occasionally lived a hundred years. Table 1 gives the age at death of those crusaders for whom it is known, while the ages of death of Moslems are from Syria and nearby Islamic countries,[6] derived mostly from the *Encyclopaedia of Islām*. Since they include scholars and other civilians who survived childhood, they are not quite comparable to the western crusader list, but the notable difference in age expectancy can hardly be explained by differences in types of occupations. Shortness of life among the crusaders often led to troublesome minorities, wardships, and short terms for holders of fiefs, preventing consistency of policies. Failure to adjust to the climate must be reckoned among the foremost crusading problems.

The indication of the healthiness of upper-class Moslems is paralleled by some information about the Syrian peasants, although the sample is small. In a few villages near Tyre fourteen family units show ten men who had twenty-one sons.[7] Since three of the children are indicated as being four or five years of age, we may assume that all the children were under twenty. Contemporary English experience

3. Russell, *Late Ancient and Medieval Population,* pp. 33–34.

4. Philip K. Hitti, tr., *An Arab-Syrian Gentleman and Warrior in the Period of the Crusades* (*CURC,* 10; New York, 1929): p. 21 for Usāmah's age; p. 5 for his father; p. 6 for his uncle, who was born before Usāmah's grandfather died in 1082 and after his father's elder brother was born in 1068; p. 218 for Usāmah's nurse Lu'lu'ah, who was alleged to have lived to nearly 100 Moslem lunar years, equivalent to 97 of our years.

5. The one reputed octogenarian associated with the crusades has been reduced in age: James M. Buckley, "The Problematical Octogenarianism of John of Brienne," *Speculum,* XXXII (1957), 315–322.

6. The 35 Christians were (in alphabetical order) Alice of Champagne (1192/7)–1246; Amalric 1136–1174; Baldwin I (1061/6)–1118; Baldwin III 1130–1163; Baldwin IV 1161–1185; Baldwin V 1178–1186; Bohemond II 1108–1130; Bohemond III 1144–1201; Bohemond VI 1237–1275; Fulk of Anjou 1092–1143; Godfrey of Bouillon 1061–1100; Henry I of Cyprus 1217–1253; Henry II 1271–1324; Hugh I of Cyprus 1195–1218; Hugh II 1252–1267; Humphrey II of Toron 1117–1179; Isabel (of Jerusalem) 1172–1205; Isabel of Brienne 1211–1228; Isabel of Lusignan 1219–1264; John I of Cyprus 1267–1285; John I of Ibelin (1176/1180)–1236; Joscelyn III 1134–1200; Mary of Montferrat 1192–1212; Melisend 1110–1161; Philip of Ibelin (1176/1180)–1227; Pons of Tripoli 1098–1137; Raymond of Poitiers (*ca.* 1116)–1149; Raymond of St. Gilles 1043–1105; Raymond II of Tripoli (*ca.* 1117)–1152; Raymond III of Tripoli 1139–1187; Reginald of Châtillon (1124/6)–1187; Sibyl (of Jerusalem) 1159–1190; Tancred 1075–1112; William of Tyre (*ca.* 1130–1187); and an unnamed son of Amalric, less than a year. On the span of life in late medieval England see Russell, *British Medieval Population* (Albuquerque, 1948), pp. 192–193.

7. Data in Tafel and Thomas, II, 351–398.

TABLE 1

Comparison of Ages at Death of Christians and Moslems

Years of Age at Death	Christians in Syria for Whom Age at Death Is Known	Moslems in Syria and Nearby Islamic Countries
0–9	2	1
10–19	3	5
20–29	4	9
30–39	11	9
40–49	3	13
50–59	8	19
60–69	4	28
70–79		29
80–89		11
90–99		3

would suggest that twenty-one sons would normally replace twelve fathers. If the twenty-one here were replacing only the ten men said to be fathers, Syrian conditions were probably healthier. Since English conditions were better than average, this sample of Syrian conditions suggests that they were good enough to increase the population.[8]

The populations of the European areas which provided those active in the crusades may be estimated as follows (in millions):

	A.D. 1000	A.D. 1200
France and Low Countries	6	10
Germany and Scandinavia	4	7
British Isles	1.7	2.8
Italy	5	7.8
Iberia	7	8
	23.7	35.6

This excludes the Byzantine empire and the Balkans, which were largely neutral, although the empire did help the Franks at times. The populations of Islamic territory were roughly as follows (in millions):

	A.D. 1000	A.D. 1200
Anatolia	8	7
Syria	2	2.7
Egypt	1.5	2.5
North Africa	1	1.5
	12.5	13.7

Even here much of Anatolia was either Christian or under Byzantine rule, although areas like that of Mosul and even Baghdad might have

---

8. Assuming that children aged 5–15 were replacing fathers of 30–40; see Russell, *British Medieval Population*, pp. 181–182.

helped to offset the Anatolian situation. The population of Egypt was increasing rapidly in this period;[9] there is no certainty about the size of the North African population. The weight of western population should have led to the conquest of the Near East in 1095, especially since the Islamic world was badly splintered.

Probably the growth in numbers of the fighting class in the west was even greater than that of the population at large. In the first place, there was a change in nursing which saw the growing use of wet nurses, especially in royal and noble families; mothers who nursed their own children gave birth less frequently than those who allowed wet nurses to care for them.[10] This meant a large increase among the upper classes in the number of younger sons, ideal candidates for the crusades. Except for the church, medieval society had few places for younger sons. Later, of course, the increase in royal authority offered openings for the more ambitious among them as mercenaries, officials, and lawyers, while the tremendous increase in the regular clergy in the new orders absorbed thousands.[11] But in 1095 the crusades offered exceptional opportunities, both religious and secular.

Even though the members of the military class in 1095 were numerous and eager, they had some habits and customs which were undesirable in pilgrim-crusaders. They had no inhibitions, as the pope had noted in his Clermont address, against fighting other Christians. The urge to pillage any convenient locality was very strong and, of course, the right to pasture animals at will was assumed. What chance then was there for armies of such men to pass day after day, particularly in a foreign land, without getting into trouble, even in Christian lands? Retaliation from countries as powerful as Hungary, Byzantium, and even the Serbs and Bulgars might be serious.

Furthermore, the northern fighter seldom considered water transit. One exception was the abbot of Cerne, who was said to have bought a ship for himself and his associates. More typical was Joinville, who meditated somewhat fearfully on the perils of the sea: "Soon the wind filled the sails and had taken us out of sight of land, so that we could see nothing but sky and water; and every day the wind took us farther from the homes in which we were born. How foolhardy . . . for when

---

9. The data in the table above are from Russell, *Late Ancient and Medieval Population,* p. 148, except those for Egypt, for which see *idem,* "The Population of Medieval Egypt," *Journal of the American Research Center in Egypt,* V (1966), 74–77.

10. See Russell, "Aspects démographiques des débuts de la féodalité," *Annales: Économies, sociétés, civilisations,* XX (1965), 1118–1127, esp. 1124–1125.

11. The subdivisions of parishes and the increase of schools also opened places for thousands.

you go to sleep at night you do not know whether you may find your-self in the morning at the bottom of the sea."[12] This aversion, if not outright fear, must be taken into account when one tries to explain why crusaders continued to go east by land.

The demographic implications of the crusades as pilgrimages to the east are of importance, particularly with respect to the several countries through which the crusaders passed. Years ago Professor Duncalf showed that the pope had a plan for the First Crusade which included meeting at Constantinople in the spring of 1097. Recently H. E. J. Cowdrey has confirmed that the main objective was Jerusa-lem, whether the plan was primarily for a pilgrimage or for holy war.[13] Since the objective was clear, the meeting at Constantinople meant war against Turkish forces in Anatolia with its demographic problems.

While one may assume a very considerable ignorance by medieval man about geographic conditions even in his own country,[14] the pope must be assumed to have been as well versed in traveling conditions as anyone in his day: he said at Clermont that it was now a two months' journey through the conquered land (of Anatolia presum-ably). His messengers were constantly traversing the ecclesiastical world, especially in the east, since Urban II was on good terms with the emperor and in touch with him. Pilgrims also went to Jerusalem regu-larly in the century before the crusades. In planning for such a great expedition, considerable attention should have been paid to the prob-lems of moving a large army toward the chief objective, Jerusalem. This is of importance because one did not have to pass through Anatolia to reach Jerusalem: there was the alternative, even from Constanti-nople, of going by sea.

It is an axiom of medieval economic history that travel by sea was less expensive and usually faster than by land. Already by 1085 the great cities of Venice, Genoa, and Pisa had sent ships to the east, so that regular patterns of sailing had emerged to take advantage of Mediterranean winds and to avoid fog, rain, and bad weather. Usu-

12. For the abbot of Cerne's purchase of a ship to go to Jerusalem, see H. E. J. Cowdrey, "Pope Urban II's Preaching of the First Crusade," *History,* LV (1970), 183. On the abbot (either Haymon, who was deposed in 1102, or his predecessor) see Anselm of Canterbury, *Opera om-nia,* vol. IV, ed. Francis S. Schmitt (Edinburgh, 1949; repr. Stuttgart, 1968), ep. 195 (pp. 85–86), written in 1095. For Joinville's statement see Brundage, *The Crusades,* p. 234.

13. Frederic Duncalf, "The Pope's Plan for the First Crusade," *The Crusades and Other Historical Essays Presented to Dana C. Munro,* ed. Louis J. Paetow (New York, 1928), pp. 44–56; Cowdrey, *op. cit.,* pp. 177–188; August C. Krey, "Urban's Crusade – Success or Failure," *American Historical Review,* LIII (1948), 235–250.

14. Norman J. G. Pounds and Sue Simons Ball, "Core-Areas and the Development of the European States System," *Annals of the Association of American Geographers,* LIV (1964), 24–40, esp. pp. 24–25.

ally one round trip a year was made to the east. Ships were apt to sail east either in the spring, or—more likely—in the early fall, not to return until the following spring.[15] Later crusades followed similar patterns. In 1239 French crusaders sailed from Marseilles in August and were at Acre in September.[16] Even faster, the next year Richard of Cornwall left England on June 10, 1240, spent three months getting to Marseilles, but sailed from that city in mid-September and landed in Acre October 8.[17] In 1248 Louis IX left Aigues-Mortes about August 25 and was in Cyprus by September 17. Returning a few years later he sailed from Acre on April 24, 1254, and "after a long and dangerous voyage he landed at Hyères in Provence early in July."[18] The great Italian cities all sent fleets which operated successfully within the first decade of the crusading period.

From Venice to Antioch was probably a sea voyage of about sixteen to seventeen hundred miles, from Genoa perhaps a hundred miles more. The trip by sea (which, of course, could be planned ahead) took from three weeks to over two months, to judge from the instances above. These were fair samples, since they involved crusading armies with their horses and weapons. Although Louis IX obviously had the means to prepare very carefully for the journey, the other two expeditions probably would not have been able to prepare as thoroughly. To the time needed for crossing from the Italian seaports to Syria, the march from Paris to Genoa or from Cologne to Venice would add 500 miles. The crusaders probably marched in several groups since they did not need guidance or protection. The march might have taken two months, since the Alps had to be crossed. In short, the journey from the west to Antioch would have been a matter of four months, possibly five to allow for delays at the port of embarkation.

The demographic implications of the sea voyage should not have been very serious. Before embarkation, the crusaders were in their own or friendly countries, presumably in small enough groups so that they had ample market facilities and knew the languages well enough for communication to be simple. At sea there were the usual problems of heavy weather and Moslem corsairs, even though the Italian cities had mastered the Mediterranean quite well. The problem was that they occasionally went ashore and were apparently ready to fight

---

15. In the fourteenth century the compass would allow winter navigation; see Frederic C. Lane, "The Economic Meaning of the Invention of the Compass," *American Historical Review,* LXVIII (1963), 605–617.

16. See volume II of the present work, p. 472.

17. *Ibid.,* II, 483.

18. *Ibid.,* II, 493, 508.

with little reason. Richard I of England took Messina by storm and sacked the city while arranging for winter quarters, and then captured Cyprus the following spring; one division of his fleet aided the Portuguese in capturing Silves as it passed by. His forces thus had considerable practice on the way. Even the saintly Louis IX had difficulty getting to Palestine: he captured Damietta on his first expedition before losing his army in the Nile delta, and died fighting at Tunis on his second expedition. Thus one may wonder whether, had the First and Second Crusades gone by sea, they would have passed between Crete and Cyprus on one side and Egypt on the other without yielding to temptation. Crusaders had great psychological difficulties in getting to the Holy Land without fighting. This made the size and strength of the population, which they could not resist fighting, a matter of considerable importance.

According to Sir Steven Runciman, "land travel was always cheaper than sea travel, and the Byzantine roads through Anatolia down into Syria were excellent."[19] Perhaps for a pilgrim or small groups of pilgrims begging their way it was cheaper, but for any who paid their way this is very doubtful. Consider merely the energy involved. If a man sailed from Venice or Genoa, he sat or slept on the ship for a few weeks, needing a minimum of food. If he went by road he used his own energy or that of a horse. Food for both, as part of a large migrating group, was expensive; many crusaders complained of the high price of food or even of its lack. The very size of the great caravans caused scarcity of which the local people took advantage. If the crusader slept out, he had to carry his shelter, which meant more horses and servants. If he slept in inns, it was often expensive. The reasons for choosing the land rather than the sea route must be sought in medieval habits of traveling and thought rather than in considerations of cost.

The journey by land was quite different from the land-sea voyage from western Europe, even if both went through Italy. The great German pilgrimage of 1064–1065 was probably what the pope and crusaders had in mind as a precedent for the First Crusade. The pilgrims left Regensburg in the middle of November and reached Jerusalem on April 12, a journey of only about five months. Apparently they sailed part of the return journey. One pilgrim, bishop Gunther of Bamberg, died in Pannonia on July 23, a few weeks' journey from Regensburg.[20] From that city to Constantinople must have been a

19. *Ibid.*, I, 73.
20. Einar Joranson, "The Great German Pilgrimage of 1064–1065," *Crusades and Other Historical Essays,* pp. 3–43, esp. pp. 16, 37, 39.

thousand miles, with another six hundred to Antioch, and two hundred more to Jerusalem. If one started from Paris another four hundred miles had to be added. It took at least six months to go the 2,200 miles from Paris to Jerusalem. Those who went by Italy and the Balkans had about the same distance, not counting in some cases the crossing of the Alps. Most pilgrims who set out for Jerusalem were probably veterans whose trip was the culmination of a career of lesser pilgrimages to the shrines of the west. Their experience and traveling ability would hardly be duplicated by a crusade of the feudal lords and lesser folk often setting out for the first time on such a venture.

In the spring of 1097 five crusading armies converged on Constantinople, a city of perhaps 100,000.[21] The population of the Byzantine empire in Europe was probably about four to five million, although this included some Serbians and Bulgarians. In Anatolia the imperial subjects probably numbered a couple of million: Turks held Nicaea, not far from the capital. The population of Anatolia was probably about seven million, of which the Turks, although a minority, were masters of perhaps four million. The crusaders at Constantinople must have numbered at least 2,500 knights as part of a mass of perhaps 20,000 persons of all sorts, even after the initial venture of Peter the Hermit across the Bosporus had been crushed.[22] Granted that the attitude of Byzantium and the crusaders to the Turks was hostile, what was the degree of hostility? Even more interesting, how did the parties to the coming confrontation on the march between Nicaea and Antioch regard their relations: as a holy war to drive the Turks from Anatolia or as the passage by a hostile armed force bent primarily on a pilgrimage? The Byzantine empire probably had many more in Anatolia who were favorable to it even if subject to the Turks.

Subject to more careful study, the demographic connotations would seem to be in favor of the thesis that all three parties viewed the crusading expedition as essentially an armed pilgrimage rather than a holy war, despite the pope's emphasis on helping Byzantium. The Byzantines apparently doubted that a combination of empire and crusaders could destroy the Turkish power; this rather suggests a lower estimate of the size of the crusading army. Still, the Byzantine emperor Alexius Comnenus hoped that the Turks would be so weakened by the crusaders that they would not threaten the empire, while if

21. Russell, *Late Ancient and Medieval Population,* p. 99.

22. Marshall M. Knappen, "Robert II of Flanders in the First Crusade," *Crusades and Other Historical Essays,* pp. 84–85.

the crusaders were hurt badly, the Turks might not blame the empire for helping them. The Turks hoped to damage the crusaders as much as possible, and to avoid being hurt so badly that the empire would profit. The crusaders, in no mood to go all out to restore the Byzantine empire in Anatolia, were not eager to fight the Turks to the finish. In fact, however, the demographic situation would have favored success of a joint crusader-Byzantine venture in 1097, a success that might have prevented the development of the Ottoman power later and given the crusaders a better chance to capture all Syria and hold it a much longer time.

The First Crusade suffered serious losses while crossing Anatolia. The three ventures of 1101 and the two in 1147 all experienced disastrous failures: apparently only the faster mounts escaped, and few fought another day.[23] In 1190 Frederick I, in spite of sending embassies to the Turks, had serious trouble before he drowned near the end of the journey, after which only a small fraction of his army got through. Actually until 1187 the enemies of the crusaders were stronger in Anatolia than in Syria.

Once the armies were in Syria the character of the crusading project changed abruptly from pilgrimage to holy war. It was nearly a year from the time the siege of Antioch began until they captured Jerusalem. Feudal customs and habits of fighting at the end of a short journey no longer handicapped the crusaders; in fact they were almost ideal for the situation in Syria, a land of small Moslem communities each independent and fighting to preserve or to enlarge its own territory. The crusading armies, even after they suffered losses crossing Anatolia, were still probably larger than any later ones, perhaps in the neighborhood of three thousand knights and twenty thousand others, some reinforcements having come directly by sea. The demographic questions now concerned the number and social status of those who came and remained, the number and attitude of the mass of Syrian peasants, and the size and distribution of Moslem armed forces in the country.

Once the crusaders took over an area and were reasonably successful in their fighting, they could apparently count upon the local people to supply the usual payments and services which they were accustomed to pay to any dominant group. There was little danger of disaffection from even the local Moslems unless the crusaders were losing badly. On the other hand they could not count upon the undying support of Armenian or Syrian Christians, who had done well

23. James Lea Cate, "The Crusade of 1101," volume I of the present work, pp. 355–367.

under Moslem rule. The control of the country centered about walled cities and castles or other strongly fortified places; they were local administrative centers as well as military strongholds. Their strength made them difficult to assault, and the custom of avoiding winter fighting made lengthy sieges impractical and unusual. Thus the size and character of the area taken in the First Crusade was vital, since the Moslem forces were caught unprepared and at their weakest while the crusading strength was at its highest. The adjustments made in the first few years would not be easily altered. If we assume that the Syrian population, like that of western Europe, would support about one knight or horseman of first rank to each thousand of the population, its size can be related to the position of the two contending groups.[24]

The population of Syria has been estimated at about 2.7 million.[25] The estimated size of the ten largest cities, shown in table 2, is based on the area within their walls (at 125 people per hectare, except Tripoli), since the constant fighting probably made for relatively little extra-mural building. Hebron was about the size of Acre. Many famous towns are not included in this list; their population is sometimes hard to estimate for the crusading period, since older walls of great extent remain. A quick survey will show how small many of the remaining cities were.

Several places, although experiencing some of their greatest days, were still quite small. One of these was Ascalon. The Byzantine city may have been only ten hectares in area; under the crusaders it probably reached about twenty-four hectares with a population of about three thousand. The chronicler who tells of its siege in 1099 says that of ten thousand killed, two thousand seven hundred were residents of the town. In 1111 it had to pay only 7,000 dinars to a besieging force, a relatively modest sum. William of Tyre tells of its mighty walls and trained defenders, who were said to have been double the number of the crusaders' besieging army in 1153; it is possible that troops poured into the city in time of siege.[26]

24. A good discussion of this appears in Raymond C. Smail, *Crusading Warfare (1097–1193)* (Cambridge, Eng., 1956), pp. 40–63.

25. Russell, *Late Ancient and Medieval Population,* p. 148.

26. *Encyclopaedia of Islām,* I (Leyden, 1908), *s.v.* "Askalan"; Palestine Exploration Fund, *Quarterly Statement* (1921), p. 72a, and (1913), p. 20a. Plans exist in both Émile Isambert, *Itinéraire descriptif, historique et archéologique de l'Orient* (Paris, 1882), III, 215, and Rey, *Étude sur les monuments de l'architecture militaire des croisés en Syrie* (Paris, 1871), pl. xix. Cf. Ibn-al-Qalānisī, *Damascus Chronicle of the Crusades,* tr. H. A. R. Gibb (London, 1932), pp. 48–49. For the year 1111 see Sibṭ Ibn-al-Jauzī, in *RHC, Or.,* III, 541. For 1153 see William of Tyre, tr. Emily A. Babcock and Krey (*CURC,* 35; 2 vols., New York, 1943), II, 220.

TABLE 2
Estimated Size of the Largest Syrian Cities about A.D. 1200*

Rank	City	Hectares	Population
1	Antioch	325	40,625
2	Edessa	192	24,000
3	Damascus	120	15,000
4	Aleppo	112	14,000
5	Jerusalem	80	10,000
6	Tripoli	80	8,000
7	Homs	56	7,000
8	Hamah	54	6,750
9	Gaza	49	6,125
10	Acre	45	5,625

*From Russell, *Mediaeval Regions and their Cities*, pp. 201–205. The density of Tripoli is assumed to be only 100 (instead of 125) persons per hectare, because the move from the old city to the new must have thinned the density.

Three other cities besides Homs which had served as provincial capitals under the Fāṭimids were quite small in this period: Qinnasrīn, Ramla, and Tiberias. Qinnasrīn had become very small, although its exact area is not known. Ramla was the capital of Moslem Filistīn and, al-Idrīsī said in 1154, was the largest city in Filistīn after Jerusalem, perhaps 160 hectares in area. It had been wrecked in 1133 by an earthquake, which apparently destroyed a third of it. Saladin is said to have destroyed it anew in 1187.[27] Tiberias was a long narrow city beside the Sea of Galilee; although once capital of the province of Jordan, it enclosed only about eighteen hectares. The mighty fortress, Krak des Chevaliers, covered only thirty-five hectares.[28]

Other cities were small in the crusading period although they had been famous at an earlier date. Sidon comprised about fifteen to twenty-five hectares in this period, but Caesarea only about ten. Yāqūt said in the thirteenth century that Caesarea was only a village although it had once been a fine city. Jaffa had a walled area (probably medieval) of about the same size. More is known about Tyre, which had perhaps three thousand inhabitants.[29] Four inland places which had been

27. *Encyclopaedia of Islām,* II (Leyden, 1927), *s.v.* "Kinnasrīn," and III (Leyden, 1936), *s.v.* "al-Ramla." Al-Idrīsī is quoted by Johann N. Sepp, *Jerusalem und das heilige Land* (Schaffhausen, 1863), I, 32; cf. Prawer, "Colonization Activities," pp. 1077–1095.

28. Tiberias: Palestine Exploration Fund, *Quarterly Statement* (1887), p. 88; Krak: Rey, *Les Colonies franques,* p. 19; *idem, Étude sur les monuments,* pl. xiv.

29. Sidon: Carston Niebuhr, *Reisebeschreibung nach Arabien und andern umliegenden Ländern* (Hamburg, 1837), III, 72a; Isambert, *Itinéraire,* III, 575; Caesarea: Palestine Exploration Fund, *Quarterly Statement* (1888), p. 135; Rey, *Étude sur les monuments,* pl. xxii; Isambert, *Itinéraire,* III, 423; Prutz, *Kulturgeschichte,* pp. 98–124; Guy Le Strange, *Palestine under the Moslems* (London, 1890; repr. Beirut, 1965), p. 474; Jaffa: Isambert, *Itinéraire,* III, 230;

better known earlier were also quite small during the time of the crusades. Baalbek was a small Arab village scattered among the four-
hundred-hectare remains of the city. Jericho, if its medieval walls were
no more extensive than the ancient walls, comprised about thirty-six
hectares. Bosra, although a rather important desert center, covered
only about twenty-two hectares, while Palmyra, well out in the desert, probably had comprised about twenty.[30] In general the border
areas next to the desert seem to have been drier during the period
of the crusades than earlier.

The areas of some of the other places may also be estimated. Beirut, to judge from the obviously medieval area of the modern city,
may have comprised about thirty-five hectares, but some of this area
may have dated from the later medieval period. Gezer (Mont Gisard)
had perhaps twenty-seven hectares.[31] Jubail (Byblos) seems to have
covered only five to seven hectares. Nablus was a fair-sized city of
perhaps thirty-six hectares, again judging from the medieval appearance of a section of a modern map, while Tortosa enclosed about
fifteen to nineteen hectares.[32] As can be seen, information is usually
accidental for the smaller places: there were many places for the size
of which no information seems to remain. In the north, particularly
in the Edessa-Aleppo area, even larger places existed about which
little data remain.

The size of the inhabited area of Syria is hard to estimate because
of the desert next to it and the mountainous character of the land
itself. Perhaps it included about 100,000–110,000 square kilometers.
If we divide the largest estimate for the village units (12 square km)
into the smallest estimate of habitable land (100,000 square km), this
gives about 8,300 villages. Dividing 110,000 square km by 7 square
km gives about 16,000 villages. The range between these is thus quite
large. The average population of the villages has been estimated as

---

Palestine Exploration Fund, *Quarterly Statement* (1898), p. 244a; Tyre: Russell, *Mediaeval Regions
and Their Cities,* pp. 200–201.

30. Michel M. Alouf, *History of Baalbek* (Beirut, 1890), pp. 4, 7 (tr. L. Mooyaart, 1898);
Jericho: Palestine Exploration Fund, *Quarterly Statement* (1931), p. 196b. The modern inhabited
area of Bosra is about twelve hectares but the earlier area apparently was larger; see Isambert,
Itinéraire, III, 529; Palmyra (Tadmor): Theodor Wiegand *et al., Palmyra* (Berlin, 1932), I,
15; Isambert, *Itinéraire,* III, 653.

31. Karl Baedeker, *Palestine and Syria* (Leipzig, 1876), plan of Beirut on p. 436; Isambert,
Itinéraire, III, 585.

32. Isambert, *Itinéraire,* III, 595 (Jubail), 395 (Nablus), 695 (Tortosa); Rey, *Étude,* pl. xxi
(Tortosa); Rey, *Les Colonies franques,* p. 441 (Jubail), p. 131 (Tortosa). For Jubail see also
Maurice Dunand, *Fouilles de Byblos,* I (Paris, 1937), pl. cciv, an estimate of the medieval por-
tion of the city.

about 200–210 persons.[33] At this size the total village population would vary from a low of about 1.7 million to perhaps double that. Given the mountainous character of the land, an estimate of about 2.3 million for the total village population of Syria would seem reasonable, if very approximate, living in perhaps 11,000 villages. This would mean a horseman to each four or five villages (much like the support of a knight in the west) and two foot-soldiers to a village, assuming about seven foot-soldiers to each knight.

The assumption then is that table 3 gives a fair model of the Syrian population. The military establishment is estimated at 2,500 horsemen, a little higher than the ratio of one to a thousand despite the mountainous character of the land. It is assumed that each horseman would have about four retainers and the footmen one apiece. The top ten cities would have about 137,000 and the next sixty-five or so (those above a population of a thousand) about 130,000.

TABLE 3
Estimate of the Population of Syria about A.D. 1100, by Social Group

Group	No. of Units	Total in Group
Horsemen	2,500	10,000
Their retainers	10,000	40,000
Foot-soldiers	20,000	80,000
Their retainers	20,000	80,000
First 10 cities		137,000
Next 65 cities		130,000
Villagers		2,300,000
		2,777,000

In the first years of the initial crusade the crusaders took six of the ten largest cities, which probably represented about the same proportion of the land. The estimated population of the cities held by the two sides was (in thousands):

Crusader		Moslem	
Antioch	40.6	Damascus	15
Edessa	24	Aleppo	14
Jerusalem	10	Homs	7
Tripoli	8	Hamah	6.8
Gaza	6.1		42.8
Hebron	5.6		
	94.3		

The crusaders thus held about 68 percent. If one estimates a total knight service for all Syria at about 2,500, this proportion would sug-

33. Russell, *Mediaeval Regions and Their Cities*, p. 206.

gest 1,700 crusader knights, and about 800 for their enemies. In fact, the crusaders set up a system of military service approximately as follows (in number of horsemen):[34]

Kingdom of Jerusalem	647–675
Tripoli	100
Antioch & Edessa	700
Temple & Hospital	300
	1,747–1,775

The coincidence is reasonably close: a part of the support of the Temple and Hospital came from the west.

The situation was complicated because both crusading and Moslem groups were divided among principalities which sometimes fought intra-faith battles. Aleppo was in a notably weak position and might well have been captured by the crusaders if the three crusades of 1101 had not all broken up fighting in Anatolia. The disastrous effect of crossing Anatolia was never worse, for from that date the crusaders were, in general, on the defensive. The struggle in the north saw outside forces from Mardin, Mosul, and even Baghdad intervening and offsetting the inherent initial advantage of the crusaders within Syria. The metropolis was Mosul, a great commercial center of Iraq in the ancient Assyrian part, a city probably the size of Antioch. Eventually the combination of Mosul and Aleppo under Zengi was too much for the crusaders, who lost the large city of Edessa to him in 1144. Even within the crusading states this now produced an approximate equality of lands supporting horsemen. Still, the distance of Mosul and even Edessa from Antioch and Palestine made it difficult for the Moslem forces to take over all of Syria; Kerbogha's army from Mosul arrived too late to prevent the Frankish conquest of Antioch.

The great growth of the Egyptian population made the eventual conquest of the crusading states inevitable. Unlike Syria, which seems to have grown only slowly during the period of the crusades, Egypt grew very rapidly by medieval standards: this seems clear from surveys of land taxes then, which suggest a population of about a million and a half at the time of the First Crusade.[35] Egypt was very weak both demographically and militarily; despite its later growth in population, the low opinion which the crusaders had of it never changed. By the time of Saladin its population had reached about two and a

___

34. For horsemen see Smail, *Crusading Warfare,* pp. 89–90, 89 note 3, 96 note 8. The range of estimates varies about these figures: see volume I of the present work, pp. 351, 375, 381, 402, 424, 520, 565, 585, 608–609, and especially 599. This is about Prawer's estimate, *History of the Latin Kingdom,* I, 459–461.

35. Russell, "The Population of Medieval Egypt," pp. 75–76.

half million, in part because of a great expansion along the west border
of the delta and up the Nile river. By the end of the thirteenth century,
surveys indicate that the population had reached four million. The
Egyptian population grew only as fast as its commerce, so the large
population had a strong economic base. Saladin's use of the power
of both Egypt and the Moslem parts of Syria was obviously too much
for the crusaders: only his death and the subsequent difficulties of
his successors postponed the end. The victory by the Mamluks under
Baybars in 1260 over the Mongol hordes, a victory no other force
between Japan and central Europe could match, indicates the great
strength of the Egyptian-Syrian army. Even if the crusaders had possessed all of Syria, their defeat would merely have been postponed.
The attempts of the crusaders after the two captures of Damietta to
go on to Cairo must be classed as gross miscalculations.

   Most of the holy wars proclaimed outside the Holy Land dealt only
with enemies within the country or within relatively easy journeys.
Chief among these were the Reconquista of Iberia from the Moors,
the war against the Albigensian heretics of southern France, and the
conquests of the pagans in Prussia and the Baltic region by the Teutonic Knights and their associates. The reduction of the enemies of
the church was rewarded by granting much the same privileges to
these expeditions as the eastern crusaders received. For the governments in each of these cases there were secular rewards in making
the conquests parts of the kingdoms and in some cases taking the
actual possessions of the defeated. The losers had to join the church
and pay the tithe, the heaviest regularly collected tax in the west. The
shortness of the journeys, the extent of the rewards, and the religious
advantages made these crusades much more attractive than the adventures in the east, except as pilgrimages to the holiest of Christian shrines.
   The demographic picture of the Iberian peninsula during the Reconquista is quite complicated except at the beginning and the end
of the Middle Ages. At first and occasionally thereafter for three centuries the population of a single state, the emirate and caliphate of
Cordova, was pitted against a group of small states in the north. At
the end, for more than two centuries, the kingdoms of Aragon, Castile, and Portugal dominated the emirate of Granada. At each of these
times the demographic picture is rather simple. In between, the problem is complicated not only by the confusion of many states within
the peninsula but by the appearance of help or aggression from outside
— the Berbers, such as the Murābiṭs (Almoravids) and the Muwaḥḥids
(Almohads), of North Africa and the French and other crusaders from

northern Europe. Both sides were occasionally willing to accept help from outside, but generally neither side was particularly happy to have massive invasion: the invaders too frequently stayed as rulers.

Islam was always a religious and cultural minority, although many Christians (*renegados*) were converted to Islam or accepted its presence and coexisted with it. On the other hand the connections of Spanish and Portuguese Christianity with other parts of the Latin church were a matter of no small importance.

Demographically, two developments influenced the situation. The first was the more rapid growth of population in the northern half beginning in the tenth century, a growth evident throughout Europe.[36] The second was the Christian colonization of lands taken from the Moslem governments, which accelerated the momentum of the drive southward. This included an extensive substitution of conquerors for conquered, as in parts of the Balearic islands and some of the cities: Valencia, Seville, and others. In addition, villages and surrounding farm lands were distributed by land charters which designated the area and the types of colonists permitted. This probably gave the Spanish the experience which made them such successful colonists in the New World.

Europe in the Middle Ages was primarily an area of regions with metropolitan cities as the driving forces. The history of late medieval Iberia reflects such a pattern, with the regions of Barcelona, Toledo, and Lisbon impinging upon and gradually taking over the region of Cordova. Even this development was helpful to the Christians, since the division, as mentioned above, left the Moors with only one great center in the peninsula. Furthermore, the demographic developments of outside forces were in favor of the Christians: France, England, and Germany were all rapidly increasing in population while North Africa seems not to have changed much. Certainly the latter after 1200 showed little tendency toward territorial expansion.

In the Iberian peninsula the institutionalization of crusading zeal led to the creation of several military orders which eventually acquired great stretches of land and vast wealth. The leaders of the orders were among the great and influential men of the realms. From the standpoint of social classes the result of the crusading effort, so long and so successful in Iberia, was to raise in prestige the religious-military values at the expense of those of the commercial classes. We know who acquired the holdings in and around Seville, for instance,[37] but

---

36. Russell, *Mediaeval Regions and Their Cities,* pp. 176–177.
37. Julio Gonzalez, *Repartimiento de Sevilla* (Madrid, 1951).

not who lost the holdings, although they were probably men of commercial interests. The military, non-commercial character of the new men is evident. The great decline of seventeenth-century Spain was certainly exacerbated by the deterioration of the commercial classes in the peninsula.

The reduction of the Albigensians was, of course, on a much smaller scale both chronologically and demographically than the Reconquista. It occurred in the south of France, while the crusade came largely from the north, especially from the regions of Paris and Dijon.[38] The north of France, like that of Iberia, grew much more rapidly from 1000 to 1348 than did the south. By 1200 the region of Paris was one of the most thickly settled areas of northern Europe. The problem of crushing the relatively weak Albigensians and their local protectors was difficult only before Peter II was killed at Muret in 1213. It hardly needed a crusade, but the expeditions provided advantages for the crusaders. The people of Carcassonne left the city "taking with them nothing but their sins": obviously many in the army of the crusaders received more than absolution for their sins.[39] Probably Béziers was the object of similar exploitation. The demographic factor was a minor one: other factors easily explain its quick success.

The order of the Teutonic Knights began their campaign to convert and conquer Prussia at just about the time of the conclusion of the Albigensian Crusade, although earlier German groups had had permission to lead crusades east. Here the conquered were largely pagan in religion and Slavic in race. The paganism of the conquered made the conquest a virtuous act and the thinly settled character of Slavic culture made it a relatively easy matter. The crusade was, indeed, merely a continuation of the *Drang nach Osten,* much like the work of the Iberian military orders in southern Spain. In fact, one could compile a single account of the military orders as a whole: there were many common developments inspired by the success of the earlier orders. The Prussian military groups descended from the Teutonic Knights functioned in German history much like the Iberian military orders in Spanish and Portuguese history. But of these, the Teutonic Knights were the most successful in that they became the ruling class of a great area south and east of the Baltic. Demographically, the thinly settled character of their lands allowed the order to rule until the rapid increase in the population of neighboring Poland and Lithu-

---

38. "No useful estimate of the size of the army can be made; in their report to the pope the legates describe it as the greatest army ever assembled in Christendom" (Austin P. Evans, in volume II of the present work, p. 287, from *PL,* 216, cols. 138–139).

39. Evans, *ibid.,* p. 289.

ania enabled those nations to crush the order in the battle of Tannenberg of 1410.

The political crusades of the thirteenth century, declared by the
popes against Hohenstaufen and Aragonese leaders who seemed to
threaten the papal states in Italy by enveloping them, do have interesting implications. By 1239 it was clear that the regions of Venice,
Milan, and Florence included a very powerful group of cities in an
area with a total population of perhaps four million.[40] Even as early
as 1176 a group of them known as the Lombard League had defeated
Frederick Barbarossa and his powerful German army. In the thirteenth century these cities were stronger while the German imperial
government was much weaker and, indeed, sent little help to Frederick II. In his kingdom of Sicily, which included southern Italy, Frederick II ruled a population of perhaps 2.5 million. In energy and in
strength, even in warfare, the south was no match for any important
combination of northern Italian cities. Parma, alone, a city of perhaps twenty thousand, practically wrecked the imperial expedition
in 1248 by a single sally. Under the circumstances it is difficult to
believe that the papacy was really threatened by the emperor's attempt to conquer Italy. The attempt to exterminate the Hohenstaufens was an irrational, vindictive policy which blinded the curia to
the danger of its side effects.

From an Italian standpoint the imposition of a French prince, Charles
of Anjou, as king of Naples and Sicily and defender of the papacy
was unfortunate. The region of Paris was, as mentioned earlier, a
thickly settled area with a population of probably over five million.
To it the crown had already added much of the regions of Toulouse
and Montpellier and even part of the region of Dijon.[41] The population of the kingdom of France in the second half of the thirteenth
century must have been well over ten million. This made it twice as
large as any other political unit in western Europe except Germany,
which at the time was chaotic politically. France had an aggressive
policy; Louis IX tried first to conquer Egypt and then Tunisia, and
was active in the extension of royal power in France. Shortly after
entering Italy as king of Sicily, Charles of Anjou achieved a dominant
position in the peninsula, threatening the papacy there and the Byzantine empire across the Adriatic. He was thwarted only by a series of

40. Russell, *Mediaeval Regions and Their Cities,* pp. 47, 71.
41. Pounds, "Overpopulation in France and the Low Countries in the Later Middle Ages,"
Journal of Social History, III (1969–1970), 237–238; for a smaller estimate, but still large, see
Russell, *Mediaeval Regions and Their Cities,* p. 152; for the regions of Toulouse, p. 159; Montpellier, p. 165; Dijon, p. 90.

accidents. French influence inevitably increased within the church, especially during the seventy years that the papacy was in Avignon and during the schism which followed. In the long run the papacy escaped from France only because of the incredible inefficency of the French army, which was tied up by England, one-third the size of France.

With the exception of the papal crusade against the Hohenstaufens, the crusades in western Europe were sound demographically. They were undertaken by populations in France and Germany with both weight of numbers and momentum in their favor. Neither the Albigensian heretic, the Moor, nor the pagan Slav could offset that disadvantage. These thirteenth-century armies were much better disciplined than the more purely feudal forces of the preceding centuries.

Demographically, the crusades provide an interesting study. The great superiority of western Europe, particularly of feudal families, made it possible for the First Crusade to draw at least three thousand knights and perhaps seven times as many others to Constantinople in 1097. The combination of those armies with the Byzantine should have succeeded, as Urban II had planned, in clearing Turkish rule from Anatolia. Whatever the failure, it was not demographic. The armies which reached Syria, supplemented by men and supplies brought by the Italian cities, should have been enough to conquer all Syria: they failed to take Aleppo, Homs, Hamah, and Damascus, or to colonize the conquered countryside. Later expeditions, from 1101 to 1189, did not take account of the military strength of the Turks based on the large population of Anatolia; the same armies carried by sea would have reached Palestine in a few weeks with relatively little danger. They attacked Egypt just when it was increasing rapidly in population and in military strength. Even when they captured Damietta and could probably have traded it for Jerusalem, they twice tried to go on to Cairo and foundered in the Delta. The crusades failed in the east, not from lack of manpower, but from failure to take into consideration demographic realities, notably in Anatolia and Egypt.

VIII

THE TEUTONIC KNIGHTS
IN THE CRUSADER STATES

A. Foundation and Organization of the Order

The two oldest military religious orders—the order of the Temple and the order of the Hospital of St. John—came into existence after the successful First Crusade. The former evolved from a handful of devout Frankish knights in Jerusalem who had vowed to defend with the sword the Christian pilgrims and pilgrim routes to the holy places

The basic source for the founding of the Teutonic order is an anonymous contemporary account, *Narracio de primordiis ordinis theutonici;* the best editions of the text are by Max Töppen in *Scriptores rerum prussicarum: Die Geschichtsquellen der preussischen Vorzeit bis zum Untergange der Ordensherrschaft* (5 vols., Leipzig, 1861–1874), I, 220–225; Max Perlbach, *Die Statuten des Deutschen Ordens* (Halle, 1890), pp. 159–160; and Walther Hubatsch, *Quellen zur Geschichte des Deutschen Ordens* (Quellensammlung zur Kulturgeschichte, V; Göttingen, 1954), pp. 26–30. The authoritative source for the organization and internal life of the Teutonic Knights is the statutes of the order, ed. Perlbach (see above); tr. Indrikis Sterns, *The Statutes of the Teutonic Knights: A Study of Religious Chivalry* (diss., University of Pennsylvania, 1969). The principal collection of original documents relative to the compilation of the statutes, the order's possessions in the crusader states, its economic policy, and its disputes with the Hospitallers and Templars is edited by Ernst Strehlke, *Tabulae ordinis theutonici ex tabularii regii Berolinensis codice* (Berlin, 1869; repr. Toronto, 1975).

There is no single collection of sources for the deeds of the Teutonic Knights; their participation in crusade warfare is only occasionally mentioned in various medieval chronicles. The chief works are Oliver (Saxo), *Historia Damiatina,* ed. Hermann Hoogeweg, *Die Schriften des Kölner Domscholasters, späteren Bischofs von Paderborn und Kardinal-Bischofs von S.* [*sic,* error] *Sabina Oliverus,* in *Bibliothek des litterarischen Vereins in Stuttgart,* CCII (Tübingen, 1894), 159–282; tr. John J. Gavigan, *The Capture of Damietta by Oliver of Paderborn* (Philadelphia, 1948); Matthew Paris, *Chronica majora,* ed. Henry R. Luard (Rolls Series, 57; 7 vols., 1872–1883); tr. John A. Giles, *Matthew Paris's English History from the Year 1235 to 1273* (3 vols., London, 1852–1854); Roger of Wendover, *Flores historiarum,* ed. Henry G. Hewlett (Rolls Series, 84; 3 vols., 1886–1889); tr. Giles, *Flowers of History: The History of England from the Descent of the Saxons to A.D. 1235* (2 vols., London, 1849); *L'Estoire de Eracles empereur et la conquest de la terre d'Outremer: La continuation de l'Estoire de Guillaume arcevesque de Sur (RHC, Occ.,* II, 1–481); *Continuation de Guillaume de Tyr, de 1229 à 1261, dite du manuscrit de Rothelin (RHC, Occ.,* II, 483–639); Philip of Novara, *Mémoires,* in *Les Gestes des Chiprois,* ed. Gaston Raynaud (SOL, *SH,* V; Geneva, 1887), pp. 25–138; also in *RHC, Arm.,* II, 651–736; portion ed. Charles Kohler (Les Classiques français du moyen-âge, X; Paris, 1913); tr. John L. LaMonte and Merton J. Hubert, *The Wars of Frederick II*

in Palestine. The latter arose from an Amalfitan hospital brotherhood in Jerusalem, whose members cared for the sick, the old, and the poor. Only gradually did the brethren of these two foundations assume the duty of defending the crusader states, but once they began to participate in skirmishes and wars against the Saracens, their reputation as zealous Christian knights grew rapidly, and their possessions and wealth increased accordingly.

The third of the great military religious orders, the order of the German Hospital of St. Mary of Jerusalem, commonly known as the Teutonic order or the Teutonic Knights, was not established until al-

---

against the Ibelins in Syria and Cyprus (*CURC,* 25; New York, 1936); the "Templar of Tyre," *Chronique,* in *Les Gestes des Chiprois,* ed. Raynaud, pp. 139–334; also in *RHC, Arm.,* II, 737–872. On the participation of the Teutonic Knights in the defense of Acre in 1291 the most detailed accounts are by Ludolph of "Suchem" (Sudheim), *De itinere Terrae Sanctae,* ed. Ferdinand Deycks, in *Bibliothek des literarischen Vereins in Stuttgart,* XXV (Stuttgart, 1851), 1–104; also a German version, *Reise ins Heilige Land,* ed. Ivar von Stapelmohr (Lunder germanistische Forschungen, VI; Lund, 1937), pp. 93–158; tr. Aubrey Stewart, *Description of the Holy Land and of the Way Thither* (*PPTS,* XII-3 [1895], 1–142); and by Ottokar of Styria, *Österreichische Reimchronik,* ed. Joseph Seemüller (*MGH, Scriptores qui vernacula lingua usi sunt,* V, 1890–1893). For the short-lived enterprise of the Teutonic Knights in Transylvania the main collection of sources is *Urkundenbuch zur Geschichte des Deutschen in Siebenbürgen,* ed. Franz Zimmermann and Carl Werner (Hermannstadt, 1892).

About the deeds of the individual masters only those of the fourth master Hermann of Salza are widely reflected in contemporary sources. The indispensable work about Hermann and his relations with emperor Frederick II is the calendar of Frederick compiled by Johann F. Böhmer, *Regesta imperii,* vol. V, *Die Regesten des Kaiserreichs unter Philipp, Otto IV., Friedrich II., Heinrich (VII.), Conrad IV., Heinrich Raspe, Wilhelm und Richard, 1198–1272, . . .,* ed. Julius Ficker and Eduard Winkelmann (3 vols. in 5, Innsbruck, 1881–1901). The basic collection of primary sources about Hermann under Frederick II is edited by J. L. A. Huillard-Bréholles, *Historia diplomatica Friderici Secundi* (7 vols. in 12, Paris, 1852–1861); many of the documents also appear in *MGH, Epistolae saeculi XIII e regestis pontificum romanorum,* ed. Georg H. Pertz and Carl Rodenberg (3 vols., 1883–1894), and *MGH, Legum,* sect. IV: *Constitutiones et acta publica imperatorum et regum,* II (Hanover, 1896), ed. Ludwig Weiland. The most important contemporary narrative in which Hermann is mentioned was written by Richard of San Germano, *Chronica 1189–1243,* ed. Pertz (*MGH, SS.,* XIX [1866], 321–384). About Hermann's role in the incorporation of the Swordbearers of Livonia into the Teutonic order the most explicit contemporary account is written by the eleventh master, Hartmann of Heldrungen, "Bericht über die Vereinigung des Schwertbrüderordens mit dem Deutschen Orden und über die Erwerbung Livlands durch den Letztern," ed. Theodor Hirsch (*SSRP,* V, 168–172). Short remarks about the anniversaries of the masters are collected by Perlbach, "Deutsch-Ordens Necrologe," in *Forschungen zur deutschen Geschichte,* XVII (Göttingen, 1877), 357–371.

About the official residence of the master in the Holy Land, Montfort, and its destruction, the scanty information comes from Arabic sources: ad-Dimashqī (Muḥammad ibn-Ibrāhīm), "Nukhbat ad-dahr fī 'ajā'ib al-barr wa-l-bahr," in August F. Mehren, *Cosmosgraphie de Chems-ed-Din Abou Abdallah Mohammed ed-Dimichqui* (St. Petersburg, 1866); the text relative to Montfort tr. Guy Le Strange, *Palestine under the Moslems* (Boston, 1890; repr. Beirut, 1965), p. 495; Ibn-al-Furāt, *Ta'rikh ad-duwal wa-l-mulūk,* Arabic MS. Cod. Vind. (Vienna, AF 814), the text relative to Montfort tr. Kurt Forstreuter, *Der Deutsche Orden am Mittelmeer* (Quellen und Studien zur Geschichte des Deutschen Ordens, II; Bonn, 1967), 232–233. Archaeological evidence about Montfort is described and evaluated by Bashford Dean, *A Crusader's Fortress*

most eighty years later, after the disastrous German failure in the Third Crusade. It was founded by a few German clerics and knights from the remnants of the scattered crusader army of emperor Frederick I Barbarossa, who had drowned in Anatolia. Though the deeds, achievements, and significance of the Teutonic Knights differ from those of the Knights Templar and Knights Hospitaller, their history is closely related to that of the other two military religious orders.

Tradition links the Teutonic order with German hospitals in Jerusalem and Acre. There is no official document extant about the founding of the Teutonic order, but the clearest references to a German hospi-

---

in Palestine: A Report of Explorations Made by the Museum, 1926 (The Bulletin of the Metropolitan Museum of Art, XXII-2, New York, September 1927).

The sole source about medical work among the Teutonic Knights is their statutes (see above). The general advance of medicine in the west during the crusades is well depicted in The School of Salernum: Regimen sanitatis Salernitanum (Latin text with Engl. tr. of 1609 by John Harington; a recent ed. by Paul B. Hoeber, New York, 1920). For Moslem knowledge of medicine in the Near East, see Usāmah Ibn-Munqidh, An Arab-Syrian Gentleman and Warrior in the Period of the Crusades: Memoirs of Usāmah ibn-Munqidh, tr. Philip K. Hitti (CURC, 10; New York, 1929), and as-Samarqandī, The Medical Formulary of Al-Samarqandi, tr. Martin Levey and Noury Al-Khaledy (Philadelphia, 1967).

Among the principal secondary works, mention must be made first of Reinhold Röhricht, Geschichte des Königreichs Jerusalem (Innsbruck, 1898); LaMonte, Feudal Monarchy in the Latin Kingdom of Jerusalem 1100 to 1291 (Cambridge, Mass., 1932); Steven Runciman, A History of the Crusades (3 vols., Cambridge, Eng., 1951-1954); Hans Prutz, Die geistlichen Ritterorden: Ihre Stellung zur kirchlichen, politischen, gesellschaftlichen und wirtschaftlichen Entwicklung des Mittelalters (Berlin, 1908); and Josef Fleckenstein and Manfred Hellman, eds., Die Geistlichen Ritterorden Europas (Konstanzer Arbeitskreis für mittelalterliche Geschichte, Vorträger und Forschungen, XVI; Sigmaringen, 1980). Of more specific character are Marian Tumler, Der Deutsche Orden im Werden, Wachsen und Wirken bis 1400 mit einem Abriss der Geschichte des Ordens von 1400 bis zur neuesten Zeit (Montreal, 1955); Ernst Hering, Der Deutsche Orden (Leipzig, 1934); and Forstreuter, Der Deutsche Orden am Mittelmeer (cited above).

Among the specialized monographs, the most valuable are Prutz, Die Besitzungen des Deutschen Ordens im Heiligen Lande (Leipzig, 1877); Hubatsch, "Montfort und die Bildung des Deutschordensstaates im Heiligen Lande," Nachrichten der Akademie der Wissenschaften in Göttingen, philologisch-historische Klasse (Göttingen, 1966), pp. 161-199; Meron Benvenisti, The Crusaders in the Holy Land (Jerusalem, 1970), pp. 331-337; and Perlbach, "Der Deutsche Orden in Siebenbürgen," Mitteilungen des Instituts für österreichische Geschichtsforschung, XXVI (1905), 415-430. About Hermann of Salza the most authoritative studies are by Erich Caspar, Hermann von Salza und die Gründung des Deutschordensstaats in Preussen (Tübingen, 1924); Andreas Lorck, Hermann von Salza: Sein Itinerar (diss., University of Kiel, 1880); and Hermann Heimpel, "Hermann von Salza," Die grossen Deutschen: Eine Biographie (5 vols., Berlin, 1956-1957), I, 171-186. A good biographical and genealogical study of all the masters is Ottomar Schreiber's dissertation (University of Königsberg), "Die Personal- und Amtsdaten der Hochmeister des Deutschen Ritterordens von seiner Gründung bis zum Jahre 1525," Oberländische Geschichtsblätter, III (Königsberg, 1909-1913), 615-762; brief modern biographies of the masters are found in Altpreussische Biographie, ed. Christian Krollmann, Kurt Forstreuter, and Fritz Gause (2 vols., Königsberg and Marburg, 1941-1967), sub nominibus. Crusader coins are briefly discussed by Henri Lavoix, Monnaies à légendes arabes frappées en Syrie par les croisés (Paris, 1877), and Georg Wegemann, Die Münzen der Kreuzfahrerstaaten (Halle, 1934). A comprehensive bibliography may be found in Rudolf ten Haaf, Kurze Bibliographie zur Geschichte des Deutschen Ordens 1198-1561 (Göttingen, 1949).

tal in Jerusalem are those of James of Vitry, bishop of Acre (1216–1228), and John of Ypres, abbot of St. Bertin (d. 1383).[1] James of Vitry has left us an account of German pilgrimages to Jerusalem in the early twelfth century, in which he states that after the conquest of Jerusalem in 1099 by the crusaders, many Germans went thither as pilgrims, but that only a few of them knew Latin or Arabic. Therefore a German couple who lived in the city built at their own expense a hospital for the care and housing of poor and sick Germans, as well as a chapel dedicated to the Virgin Mary. This account is very similar to the tale of the Amalfitans and their hospital a century before. The German couple seem to have maintained the establishment from their own wealth and from alms, for many Germans gave money in order to support the hospital, and some even forsook worldly occupations in order to care for the sick.[2]

John of Ypres gives a similar account. He then goes on to describe the development of the German house in Jerusalem in a somewhat confused passage: "With the increase of devotion increased also the number of brothers there serving the Lord, and they subjected themselves to the order or rule of St. Augustine, wearing white mantles (*mantellos albos deferentes*). In the following years, like the Hospitallers, they were virtually forced to take up arms, and they devoted themselves to God and the rule of St. Augustine in defense of their lands and the fatherland,[3] and added black crosses to their white vestments as well as to their banners . . . in the year 1127. This order is the German order and the order of St. Mary of the Teutons."[4] Such were the vague traditions about the early years of the German hospital in Jerusalem which John, writing over two centuries later in Flanders, had picked up. Possibly about that time the German hospital in Jerusalem established some relation with the Hospital of St. John.

Some time in the early twelfth century the German hospital in Jerusalem was, for some unknown reason, on bad terms with the Hospitallers, who brought charges against the German hospital before the papal curia. On December 9, 1143, pope Celestine II wrote to the master of the Hospitallers, Raymond of Le Puy, that the German

---

1. James of Vitry, *Historia orientalis seu Iherosolimitana*, ed. Jacques Bongars, in *Gesta Dei per Francos* (2 vols., Hanau, 1611), I, 1047–1145; abr. tr. Stewart, "The History of Jerusalem," *PPTS*, XI-2, 1–128. John of Ypres, *Chronicon . . . Sancti Bertini*, in *Thesaurus novus anecdotorum*, ed. Edmond Martène and Ursin Durand (5 vols., Paris, 1717), III, 442–776; see especially pp. 443–446 and 625–626.

2. James of Vitry, ed. Bongars, I, 1085; John of Ypres, *Chronicon,* III, 626.

3. That is, the kingdom of Jerusalem.

4. John of Ypres, *loc. cit.*

hospital had stirred up dissensions and scandals. In order to avoid further discord the pope placed the German hospital under the supervision of the Hospital of St. John, though allowing the Germans to retain their own prior, servants, and the German language.[5] There is no evidence in the sources that Conrad III had any relations with the German hospital during his stay in Jerusalem in 1148.

In the sixties or seventies of the twelfth century a priest, John of Würzburg, visited Jerusalem and later wrote a *Description of the Holy Land*,[6] in which there is a short passage on the German hospital: "In the same street which leads to the house of the Temple lies a hospital with a chapel which is being rebuilt anew in honor of St. Mary, and which is called the German house (*Domus Alemannorum*). Few other than German-speaking people contribute anything to its support."[7] At that time, seemingly, the German hospital in Jerusalem was of little significance.

In 1172 Henry the Lion, duke of Saxony and Bavaria, made a pilgrimage to Jerusalem. In an extended account of the journey, Arnold of Lübeck describes how Henry was met outside the gates of the holy city by the Knights Templar and Knights Hospitaller. Arnold goes on to relate how Henry gave arms and a thousand marks to each order and how the Templars accompanied him to Bethlehem and Nazareth and bade farewell to him at Antioch. But Arnold writes not a single word about the German hospital in Jerusalem.[8] Some four years later Sophia, countess of Holland, died on her third pilgrimage to Jerusalem and was buried in the German hospital.[9]

On the origin and development of the German hospital in Acre and its transformation into a military religious order we are better informed. The most explicit source is the anonymous contemporary account called *A Narrative on the Origin of the Teutonic Order*.[10]

---

5. J. Delaville Le Roulx, ed., *Cartulaire général de l'ordre des Hospitaliers de S. Jean de Jérusalem (1100–1310)* (4 vols., Paris, 1894–1906), nos. 154 and 155.

6. John of Würzburg, *Descriptio Terrae Sanctae*, in *PL*, 155, cols. 1053–1090; abr. tr. Stewart, "Description of the Holy Land," *PPTS*, V-2, 1–72. Stewart (p. x) assumes that John visited the Holy Land between 1160 and 1170; Prutz, *Besitzungen*, p. 11, says 1165; Runciman, *op. cit.*, II, 294, suggests about 1175.

7. John of Würzburg, in *PL*, 155, col. 1086.

8. Arnold of Lübeck, who accompanied Henry the Lion to Jerusalem (and who continued, to 1209, Helmold's "Chronicle of the Slavs"), *Chronica*, ed. Johann M. Lappenberg (*MGH, SS.*, XXI), p. 121.

9. *Annales Egmundani*, ed. Pertz (*MGH, SS.*, XVI), p. 468. For this chronicle of the monastery of Egmund in Frisia, written from the twelfth to thirteenth centuries by several writers, see Introduction, *ibid.*, pp. 442–445.

10. Perlbach, *Statuten*, p. xliii, assumes that the *Narracio* was written about 1211, after the hospital was transformed into an order; Hubatsch, *Quellen*, p. 26, between 1204 and 1211. Cf. *Narracio*, I, 220–225.

According to it, on September 1, 1190, a contingent of German crusaders in fifty-five ships arrived in the port of Acre and prepared to help Guy of Lusignan, king of Jerusalem, in the siege of the city. Among them were citizens from Bremen and Lübeck who, under the leadership of a certain Sibrand, set up near the cemetery of St. Nicholas a hospital to care for the wounded, using the sail of a ship for shelter. For over a month they carried on their work as good Samaritans until the arrival of Frederick, duke of Swabia and Alsace, and son of the late Frederick I Barbarossa, to take command of the remnants of his father's army. Soon afterward the crusaders from Bremen and Lübeck left for Germany, but before departing, on the insistence of duke Frederick and other noblemen of the German army, they handed the hospital over to Frederick's chaplain Conrad and his chamberlain Burkhard. This, the only hospital for the German forces, seems to have been well endowed with alms for its work in caring for the sick and wounded. Conrad and Burkhard renounced the world and devoted themselves to the hospital. Like the German hospital in Jerusalem this new hospital was dedicated to the Virgin Mary, probably in the hope that after the reconquest of the Holy Land it might be moved to Jerusalem and made the principal house.[11]

From the *Narrative* it is clear that the German hospital outside the walls of Acre was a new establishment independent of the German hospital in Jerusalem; but the German hospital of St. Mary in Jerusalem was still remembered, and it was clearly the intention of the German crusaders to revive it in Jerusalem, which, even if it had not been destroyed, was in the hands of the Saracens. The *Narrative* goes on to relate that duke Frederick sent messengers with letters to his brother (later the emperor Henry VI) asking him to obtain papal recognition for the hospital at Acre. In his letter of December 21, 1196, to the German hospital in Jerusalem, Celestine III listed the hospital at Acre among its possessions, probably repeating an acknowledgment by Clement III some five years earlier.[12]

In the meantime, before the fall of Acre, some crusaders joined the German hospital. After the capture of the city on July 12, 1191, the brethren bought a garden inside the walls at the gate of St. Nicholas where they built a church, a hospital, and other buildings. In the church the remains of duke Frederick, who had died on January 20,

---

11. *Ibid.,* I, 220–221, and note 1 on p. 221.

12. Strehlke, *Tabulae,* no. 296: bull of Celestine III, December 21, 1196, taking the order under his protection; identical to no. 295: bull of Clement III, February 6, 1191, which is regarded by Strehlke as probably a forgery. There are, however, many instances in papal correspondence of this kind of repetitive reissue.

1191, were buried, and in the hospital, run by clerics, the sick and the poor were cared for.[13] When, in 1196, Celestine III took the hospital of Jerusalem and its dependencies under his protection and exempted it from papal tithes, he placed the brethren under the ecclesiastical supervision of the local bishop, if he was a Catholic approved by the apostolic see, and granted them the right to elect their own master.

Emperor Henry VI had assembled a great army in Palestine, but died on September 28, 1197, before taking command. After news of the emperor's death reached them, a number of the German princes and magnates decided to "donate" to the German hospital in Acre the "rule of the Knights Templar." To carry out this decision the German ecclesiastical and temporal princes met in the house of the Templars and invited the prelates and barons of Palestine to the parley.[14] All present unanimously decided that the German hospital should be modeled on the hospital of St. John of Jerusalem, in the care of the poor and sick, but that religious, knightly, and other activities should be modeled after those of the Knights Templar.

Then, says the *Narrative,* the brothers of the German hospital who were present elected one of the knights, Hermann,[15] called Walpot, as master, and to him the master of the Templars, Gilbert Horal, handed a copy of the rule of the Knights Templar. A knight named Hermann of Kirchheim entered the German order, and to him Horal gave the white mantle of the Templars. Then the German princes and prelates present at the meeting sent master Hermann Walpot, accompanied by bishop Wolfger of Passau, to the Roman curia, with letters to pope

13. *Narracio,* I, 222.

14. *Ibid.,* I, 223: "hospitali prelibato ordo milicie templi donaretur." The *Narracio* dates the gathering March 1195, but Töppen gives evidence to show that 1198 would be more logical.

15. *Narracio,* I, 225, says "quondam fratrem Hermannum nomine." Peter of Dusburg, in dedicating in 1326 his major work *Chronicon terrae Prussiae* (ed. Töppen in *SSRP,* I, 21–219) to the master Werner of Orseln, states that his chronicle is an official history of the deeds of the order, and he begins with the story of the founding of the order in the Holy Land, basing it on the *Narracio,* but naming (p. 29) the first master Henry (instead of Hermann) Walpot. For Peter of Dusburg see *Altpreussische Biographie, sub nomine;* see also Helmut Bauer, "Peter von Dusburg und die Geschichtsschreibung des Deutschen Ordens im 14. Jahrhundert in Preussen," *Historische Studien,* CCLXXII (1935), 7–56. Since the brothers of the Teutonic order did not understand Latin, the master Luther of Brunswick (1331–1335) ordered a member of the order, Nicholas of Jeroschin (about 1290 to 1345), to translate the Latin chronicle of Peter of Dusburg into German verse; this task was completed sometime after 1335. For Nicholas see *Altpreussische Biographie, sub nomine,* and Bauer, *op. cit.,* pp. 56–59. Nicholas's work *Di Kronike von Pruzinlant* is edited by Strehlke in *SSRP,* I, 303–624. Nicholas, like his source Peter, calls the first master Henry (p. 313). The older generation of German historians, such as Töppen, favor Hermann Walpot, the younger generation, Henry Walpot; see Hubatsch, *Quellen,* pp. 28–29, and Schreiber, *op. cit.,* pp. 647–648.

Innocent III asking for confirmation of the new order.[16] Thus by 1198 the Germans were observing the rule of the Templars and wearing the white mantle in accordance with that rule.

By a bull of February 19, 1199, Innocent III confirmed the order of the hospital "quod Theutonicum appelatur," and specified that it should model itself on the Templars as far as priests and knights were concerned, and on the Hospitallers in caring for the sick and the poor.[17] The order was variously called, but the usual appellation was either *hospitale sancte Marie Theutonicorum Jerosolimitanum* or *der orden des Dûschen hûses.*[18]

A sharp distinction must be made between the German hospital in Jerusalem and the hospital in Acre: the former was founded by German merchants, the latter by German crusaders; the former was established for the care of sick and poor pilgrims, the latter for the care of sick or wounded crusaders. There is no evidence that the members of the hospital in Jerusalem ever undertook military duties, but the hospital in Acre within eight years was turned into a military brotherhood, like the Templars, with the additional duty of caring for the sick and the poor, like the Hospitallers. Why the change? While there is no evidence apart from the statement in the *Narrative* that the German princes insisted on a reorganization, it seems plausible that the German hospital was turned into an order with the hope of keeping permanently in Palestine some of the Germans eager to go home. This view is supported by the fact that at the gathering in 1198 where the change was decided upon, all the principal ecclesiastical and secular magnates of the kingdom of Jerusalem were present, along with important German princes of the dispersing army of Henry VI.[19]

16. *Narracio,* I, 225.

17. Strehlke, *Tabulae,* no. 297: "Specialiter autem ordinationem factam in ecclesia vestra iuxta modum Templariorum in clericis et militibus et ad exemplum Hospitalariorum in pauperibus et infirmis, sicut provide facta est et a vobis recepta et hactenus observata, devotioni vestre auctoritate apostolica confirmamus et presentis scripti pagina communimus"; see also *Die Register Innocenz' III,* I, *Pontifikatsjahr 1198/99, Texte,* ed. Othmar Hageneder and Anton Haidacher (Publikationen der Abteilung für historische Studien des Österreichischen Kulturinstituts in Rom, Abt. II, Reihe I, Bd. I; Graz and Cologne, 1964), no. 564. For a critical analysis of the sources dealing with the founding of the Teutonic order, and a somewhat different interpretation of the sequence of events involved in the elevation of the German hospital to an order, see Marie Louise Favreau, *Studien zur Frühgeschichte des Deutschen Ordens* (Kieler historische Studien, 21; Stuttgart, 1974).

18. Strehlke, *Tabulae,* no. 304: bull of Honorius III, December 19, 1216; Perlbach, *Statuten,* p. 22; German version of the prologue of the statutes. See also Strehlke, *Tabulae,* nos. 299, 301: bulls of Innocent III, August 27, 1210, and July 28, 1211: "hospitale Theutonicorum Acconense" and "hospitale sancte Marie Theutonicorum in Accon."

19. *Narracio,* I, 223, names as present: Aymar "the Monk," the patriarch of Jerusalem; Henry (error for Aimery), ruler of Jerusalem; the archbishops Nicholas (?) of Nazareth, Joscius

In this connection a passage in the chronicle of James of Vitry is pertinent: "They [the Teutonic Knights] . . . are humbly obedient to the Lord Patriarch and to the other prelates. They render tithes of all they possess, according to the existing law and divine institution, not molesting the prelates."[20] Perhaps, too, some of the German knights wished to stay in Palestine, but did not wish to enter any of the existing non-German military orders.

The Teutonic Knights did not for some time have a distinct rule of their own. Innocent III as late as 1209 referred only to the customs (*consuetudines*) which had been observed by the order since its foundation. These customs included the privilege of wearing the white habit of the Knights Templar. However, in 1210 the Templars complained to Innocent about this practice,[21] and the pope forbade the Germans to wear the white habit. In the following year, however, after the patriarch of Jerusalem had negotiated a compromise between the Teutonic Knights and the Templars, Innocent restored the privilege of wearing the white habit to the Teutonic Knights. When the Templars continued to complain to Rome, pope Honorius III tried on January 9, 1221, to end the dispute by declaring that the Teutonic Knights were allowed to wear the white mantles and other vestments "according to their statutes."[22] Thus it appears that by 1221 one can already speak of some form of "statutes" of the Teutonic Knights. But the Templars still objected, and the controversy dragged on until 1230, when pope Gregory IX forbade the Templars to molest the Teutonic Knights any longer on the question of the white mantles.[23] About this time, too, the Hospitallers again began pressing their claims to jurisdiction over the Teutonic Knights.

---

of Tyre, and Bartholomew (?) of Caesarea; bishops Peter of Bethlehem and Theobald of Acre; the masters of the Knights Templar (Gilbert Horal) and Knights Hospitaller (Geoffrey of Le Donjon); Ralph, titular lord of Tiberias, and his brother Hugh; Reginald Grenier, lord of Sidon; Aymar, lord of Caesarea, and John I of Ibelin, lord of Beirut and constable of Jerusalem; also Conrad, archbishop of Mainz; Conrad, bishop of Würzburg and imperial chancellor; Wolfger, bishop of Passau, later patriarch of Aquileia; bishops Gardolph of Halberstadt and Berthold of Naumburg and Zeitz; Henry, count-palatine of the Rhine and duke of Brunswick; Frederick, duke of Austria; Henry, duke of Brabant, the commander of the army; the count-palatine and landgrave Hermann I of Thuringia; Conrad, margrave of Landsberg; Dietrich, margrave of Meissen; Albert, brother of margrave Otto of Brandenburg; and Henry of Kalden, the imperial marshal.

20. James of Vitry, ed. Bongars, I, 1085.

21. Strehlke, *Tabulae,* nos. 299, 300: bulls to the Teutonic Knights and the patriarch of Jerusalem, August 27, 1210.

22. Strehlke, *Tabulae,* nos. 301, 308: bulls to the Teutonic Knights, July 28, 1211, and January 9, 1221.

23. Strehlke, *Tabulae,* nos. 368, 449: bulls to the Teutonic Knights, April 17, 1222, and September 15, 1230.

Whatever the claims of the Templars and Hospitallers — and as late as the treaty of 1258 among the three military orders the Hospitallers continued to claim authority over the Germans — the Teutonic Knights after 1240 succeeded in gaining effective autonomy. Some time before February 9, 1244, when Innocent IV replied to their petition, the Teutonic Knights asked permission to discard certain paragraphs of their rule, still based on the rule of the Templars. The pope granted the order's petition, declaring, "We allow you . . . with the approval of your chapter or the greater and wiser part of it, to alter the afore-mentioned and other paragraphs of your rule, in the observation of which neither spiritual usefulness nor knightly honor is served."[24] From the pope's words it appears that the reason given by the Teu-tonic Knights for the desired change was that the brothers were not observing those parts of the rule which seemed useless to them. This may have been true, but it was probably the hidden intent of the Ger-mans to get their own rule, and make themselves independent of both Hospitallers and Templars.

There is no direct evidence as to what action was taken by the Teu-tonic Knights immediately after 1244 to adapt the rule of the Tem-plars to their own needs. The oldest extant copy of the statutes of the Teutonic Knights dates from 1264; it contains, besides the rule, the calendar, the laws, the customs, the vigils, and the genuflections. Thus in the twenty years following the papal authorization of 1244 the Teutonic Knights not only changed certain paragraphs of the rule of the Templars, but also compiled new, or codified old, regulations for their order.

The chief source shedding some light on the final composition of the statutes is an undated letter containing regulations for the Prus-sian branch of the order, issued in Prussia by the vicemaster Eberhard of Sayn.[25] In this letter Eberhard refers to the rule (*ordo*), the cus-toms (*consuetudines*), and the laws (*iudicia*) of the Teutonic Knights, so by dating Eberhard's letter we may approximately date the time

---

24. Strehlke, *Tabulae*, no. 470: bull to the Teutonic Knights, February 9, 1244. Perlbach, *Statuten*, pp. xlvi–xlvii, has shown that these pertain to the rule of the Templars; see Henri de Curzon, ed., *La Règle du Temple* (Paris, 1886), pars. 12, 25, 26, 27, 53.

25. Eberhard of Sayn was grand commander of the order in the Holy Land before his depar-ture for Prussia; see Strehlke, *Tabulae*, no. 100: letter of sale of John l'Aleman, lord of Caesa-rea, April 30, 1249. Apparently Eberhard was sent by the master to Prussia and Livonia to visit and to reorganize and supervise the order's affairs in its northern provinces. After his arrival in Prussia he issued regulations for the Prussian branch of the order in which he calls himself "Frater E. de Seyne vicem magistri . . . gerens in Prussia"; for this document see Perl-bach, *Statuten*, pp. 161–162, and Ernst Hennig, ed., *Die Statuten des Deutschen Ordens* (Königs-berg, 1806), pp. 221–224.

when these were already in existence. It is clear that Eberhard visited Prussia in 1249 after master Henry of Hohenlohe's death, for on January 1, 1250, he renewed for the Prussian branch the order's charter of privileges, which had been burned;[26] by 1252 he was active in Livonia. Thus it seems that by 1250 the rule, the customs, and at least a part of the laws were already in existence, and that the revision of the rule of the Templars for use by the Teutonic Knights had been undertaken during the years 1244–1249, while Henry of Hohenlohe was master and before Eberhard of Sayn arrived in Prussia. Eberhard must have taken with him a copy of these recently revised statutes, for paragraph fourteen of Eberhard's regulations states: "Every Sunday during the chapter meeting a section of the rule, of the customs, and of the laws shall be recited before the brothers."[27]

The statutes, as drawn up by 1264, comprise the calendar, the Easter tables, a prologue, the titles of the rule, the rule, the laws, the customs, the vigils, and the genuflections.[28] Thus the term "statutes" means a complex of statutory regulations for the use and observance of the brethren of the Teutonic order. They themselves called this collection the *Ordenbûch* — the "Book of the Order." It contains no indication of papal approval, nor is there any known evidence of such confirmation in the surviving fragments of the order's archives from the Holy Land or in the records of the papal chancery.[29] Moreover,

26. Erich Joachim and Walther Hubatsch, eds., *Regesta historico-diplomatica Ordinis S. Mariae Theutonicorum 1198–1525* (2 vols. in 3, Göttingen, 1948–1950), II, no. 107.

27. There is no certainty as to who undertook the revision of the rule of the Templars for the use of the Teutonic Knights. Perlbach conjectures (*Statuten*, p. xlvii) that the revision was done by cardinal-bishop William of Sabina, who had for many years dealt with the affairs of the Teutonic Knights in Prussia and Livonia. Even so, the reviser did not necessarily compile the customs and the laws, for the prologue refers explicitly only to the rule (*regula*). The rest of the statutes may have been compiled at Acre by a priest or priests of the order who knew which regulations and rules taken over from other statute books were observed by the Teutonic Knights. Likewise, certain resolutions and decisions of the chapter of the order at Acre were incorporated in the laws. Since no complete record of these decisions is extant, it is difficult to determine exactly how many were worked into the statutes. For William of Sabina see Gustav A. Donner, *Kardinal Wilhelm von Sabina, Bischof von Modena 1222–1234, päpstlicher Legat in den nordischen Ländern (d. 1251)* (Societas scientiarum Fennica, Commentationes humanarum litterarum, II, sect. 5; Helsingfors, 1929), and Agostino Paravicini Bagliani, *Cardinali di curia e 'familiae' cardinalizie dal 1227 al 1254* (Padua, 1972), I, 186–197.

28. Perlbach, *Statuten*, pp. xv–xvi. For the genuflexions (Latin, *veniae;* German, *Venien*) see *The Monastic Constitutions of Lanfranc*, tr. Dom David Knowles (Medieval Classics, London, 1951), p. 24, note 2: "The phrase *veniam petere, accipere*, etc., originally used of the act of 'doing penance', came to bear the entirely neutral sense of 'genuflect'."

29. The question of the original language of the official version of the *Ordenbûch* is discussed at some length by Perlbach (*Statuten*, pp. xxix–xxx, xlvi–xlix), who believes that the prologue and the rule of the statutes were compiled in Latin. Even so, there must have existed contemporary translations into German, for chapters of the rule were to be read before the brethren of the order.

prior to the 1442 revision of the statutes there are only four known copies of the statutes in Latin, whereas from the same period there are at least twenty-five extant manuscripts in German.

The medieval chroniclers and the members of the papal court regarded the Teutonic Knights as a German order, and the express reason for founding a German hospital in Jerusalem was the German pilgrims' ignorance of languages other than German. There is no reason to believe that the German crusaders in the thirteenth century were more fluent in other tongues than the pilgrims of the twelfth century. The statutes themselves offer some insight into the literacy of the Teutonic Knights. A candidate for admission into the order was required to learn, within six months of his admission, only the Lord's Prayer, the Hail Mary, and the Creed, evidently in Latin; if he had not learned them in the first half year, he was given another six months to do so. If he had not learned them in a year, he was to leave the order, unless the master and the brethren allowed him to remain. Even this minimal requirement was too high for some brothers, for master Werner of Orseln (1324–1330) repeated this regulation in his laws, with the addition: "If the brother does not understand Latin, let him recite the Lord's Prayer, the Hail Mary, and the Creed in German."[30]

The Teutonic Knights regarded the statutes, as preserved in the copy of 1264, as unchangeable, for later additions to the statutes were never organically incorporated into the existing regulations, but were added as supplements, as new laws, by the ruling master, leaving unchanged the original "Book of the Order."

The more than thirty extant German manuscripts are in various dialects, for every commandery had to have its own copy of the Ordenbûch. Naturally, as more and more copies were made, they began to differ not only in language but also in accuracy, and various supplements were made. Therefore in 1442 the chapter of the order decided to revise the "Book of the Order" and make three master copies, one to be kept in the main house in Marienburg, another in the German master's residence in Horneck, and a third in the Livonian branch in Riga. All further copies were to be made only from these three master copies.[31] Thus the German version was made the official version of the statutes of the Teutonic Knights. There is again no evidence that approval was sought from the pope.

To analyze the structure and organization of the order and the functions of its various office-holders in the crusader states, the basic source

---

30. Perlbach, *Statuten,* p. 147.

31. For the extant manuscripts see Perlbach, *Statuten,* pp. x–xxx, lix; also Hennig, *Statuten,* pp. 29–30.

of information is the 1264 version of the "Book of the Order," as supplemented by chapter decrees before the transfer of the headquarters of the order in 1309 to Marienburg in Prussia.

In organization the closest models for the Teutonic order were the two other religious military orders, the Templars and the Hospitallers. Like the other two, the Teutonic Knights based their rule on the rule of St. Benedict. In administration, however, the Germans followed neither the more rigorously centralized Dominicans nor the loosely organized Franciscans, but the federated organization of the Cistercians. It cannot be proved that Bernard of Clairvaux introduced into the rule of the Templars the administrative pattern of the Cistercians, for no version of that rule contains such organizational details as are found in the *Carta caritatis* of the Cistercians. However, in later statutes the Templars adopted many institutions concerning organization from the Cistercians, and in turn the Teutonic Knights took over these organizational patterns from the Templars, though the organization of the Teutonic Knights was later modified by the canons of the Fourth Lateran Council. Thus the Teutonic order had, in its structural pattern, the characteristics of the religious life—the three monastic vows, the living in community, the religious exercises, the chapter and chapter meetings, and an official hierarchy—combined with other worldly knightly features.

The head of the Teutonic order was the elected master, who was "over all the others" (rule, par. 34), for "all the honor of the order and the salvation of souls and the virtue of life, and the way of justice, and the protection of discipline depend on a good shepherd and on the head of an order" (customs, par. 4). The master not only was to "rule over the house and the order" (customs, par. 6), but was also the highest judge among the brothers (rule, par. 37). Furthermore, the master was the commander-in-chief (customs, par. 24), entitled to four horses, and an extra one in war. His household was made up of a chaplain and his assistant, an Arabic scribe, a cook, and three Turcopoles, of whom one was his shield-bearer, one his messenger, and one his chamberlain, and in the field he had an extra Turcopole. On long journeys, if needed, his retinue was increased by two brother knights as companions and one brother sergeant as steward; when in the field, by two sergeants. The master was expected to reside in the Holy Land (customs, par. 12). By 1244 his headquarters was the castle of Montfort (Starkenberg); after the fall of Montfort in 1271, it was shifted to Acre.

The master was elected for life by an electoral college made up of thirteen brothers of the order. Though not specifically stated, the master had to be a knight, and no one who was of illegitimate birth or who had been convicted of unchastity or theft could be master (customs, par. 4). The symbols of his office were the master's ring and the order's seal (customs, par. 6). He had his own standard, and special insignia on shield and surcoat (customs, par. 32).

The two greatest officials below the master, sometimes deputizing for him, were the grand commander and the marshal, each acting in his strictly prescribed field (customs, pars. 21, 22, 30). The marshal's status is clearly defined in the customs: "All the brothers who are given arms are subject to the marshal and shall be obedient to him after the master." To the marshal's office belonged everything pertaining to arms: horses, mules, weapons, tents, the saddlery, and the forge (customs, par. 19). He was the order's minister of war and the commanding general of the order's army in the absence of the master (customs, par. 24).

The marshal's counterpart in matters of administration, finance, and supply was the grand commander, originally the commander of the house at Acre. "To the office of the grand commander pertain the treasury and the grain supply, and the ships, and all the brother clerics and lay brothers and their domestics who live in the house, and the camels, pack-animals, wagons, slaves, craftsmen, the armory and all the other workshops save those under the marshal" (customs, par. 28). But "if the marshal is sent out of the province, the grand commander shall take his place in looking after the horses and all things pertaining to arms" (customs, par. 21). Furthermore, "the marshal shall have precedence, when on campaign, and shall hold the chapter if the master himself is not present or his deputy. But if the marshal is not present, then the commander shall hold the chapter." But "when they are home, then the commander by right has precedence and holds the chapter. But if the commander is not present, then the marshal shall hold it" (customs, par. 22). In short, both officials "shall take pains to be in harmony and to bear each other's burdens, so that, when one of them is not there, the other shall take his place and carry out his duties" (customs, par. 30). These regulations clearly demonstrate how well the central administration of the order was organized.

The master's most essential or intrinsic duty was representation of the order. The customs (par. 32) make this clear: "The brother who deputizes for the master may raise his standard and have carpets and the great tent and the things which he needs to do the honors for guests whom he may receive in the master's place. He shall, however, not use the master's shield and coat of mail; also he shall not take his place at table or in church." The master's second prerogative was doing justice: "If the master or his deputy has imposed a penance on any brother, he may not be relieved . . . either by the commander or by the marshal or by any other brother without the permission of the master or his deputy" (laws, III, 4). Yet the rule (par. 35) and the laws (III, pars. 35, 36) make clear that the chapter was the actual body that decided on the punishment of a brother, and that the master administered the chapter's decision.

Like the master, the marshal and the grand commander each had his own entourage: both were chosen, and could be dismissed, jointly by the master and the chapter of the main house of Acre; thus their offices, strictly speaking, were not for life.

Various brothers might deputize for the master, but the commander and marshal had permanent deputies: the vice-commander, or "little commander," and the vice-marshal, or "under-marshal." The former was in charge of the workshops and the servants in the workshops, and of the gardens. He had to provide "camels and wagons, slaves, carpenters, masons, and other workmen, whom he shall put to work and supply with whatever they need." He had likewise to see to the proper disposal of grain and cloth arriving by ship (customs, par. 35). The exact nature of the duties of the vice-marshal or "under-marshal" (customs, par. 19) are not given, but he may have been the same person as the "master of the esquires," in charge of allocating the esquires to the brothers and of paying those serving for wages (customs, par. 39). He also gave out fodder, curry-combs, and other supplies for the horses.

To complete the central administration of the order, the master jointly with the chapter chose four more high office-holders: the hospitaller (in charge of charity), the drapier (responsible for armor and clothing), the treasurer, and the castellan of the fortress of Starkenberg (customs, par. 8). The treasury was guarded with three locks and three keys, "of which one shall be in the master's hands, another in the grand commander's hands, and the third in the treasurer's hands, so that no one of them alone may have separate access" (customs, par. 9).

The marshal had two subordinate supply officers, the brother in charge of the saddlery (customs, par. 40) and the brother in charge of the small forge. The latter repaired bits, stirrups, and spurs, and handed out the rings for hose, belly-bands, surcingles, and pack straps (customs, par. 41). The saddlery supplied all kinds of belts and straps for the brothers' arms and for harnessing the horses (customs, par. 40).

The grand commander likewise had two important subordinate supply officers, the master of victuals (customs, pars. 55 and 59) and the brother in charge of the armory (customs, par. 30). The armory (*snithûs*) was probably a shop and storeroom where crossbows, bows (customs, par. 29) and arrows, and similar weapons of wood were made and repaired. The master of victuals was in charge of food supply and distribution to the brothers (customs, pars. 55 and 59). These four supply officers of lesser rank were chosen by the master with the advice of the most discreet brothers, and had to render their accounts not to the chapter, but to the master and their respective superiors (customs, pars. 7a and 8).

This analysis of the order's hierarchy in the Holy Land shows how well the order was organized and administered, and prepared for military operations. In addition to all the regulations for horses, supplies, and equipment, we find in the customs detailed regulations for military expeditions, the chain of command, the order of battle, and other matters (customs, pars. 44, 46–51, 53–54, 61, 63).

The organization of the branches or provinces elsewhere seemingly was modeled on the main organization in the Holy Land. The head of the province was the provincial commander or master, who was appointed by the grand master with the approval of the chapter (customs, par. 8). Thus it appears that a provincial master was lower in rank than the six high office-holders in the Holy Land who were chosen jointly by the master and the chapter—the grand commander, the marshal, the hospitaller, the treasurer, the drapier, and the castellan of Starkenberg—but higher than all the rest of the office-holders in the Holy Land, who were chosen by the master with the counsel of the most discreet brothers. Once installed, the provincial master was almost independent and removable only for the gravest crimes. The master could visit a province in person (customs, par. 14), or send others as visitors (laws, II, b), but he could remove a provincial master only for grave misconduct, or, as the customs put it, if he found "any commander so infamous and vicious that he cannot be tolerated or excused." As long as a provincial commander was kept in office, the master could put no one over him (customs, par. 15).

Provincial masters were given a free hand in military activities, for the main branch in the Holy Land could neither organize nor support operations in a distant province. The rule allowed the superior, with the counsel of the wisest brothers, to decide all things in the land where the war was fought, "since the customs of the enemy in fighting and in other matters differ in different lands, and therefore it is necessary to oppose the enemy in different ways" (rule, par. 22).

This would obviously apply to provinces like Prussia and Livonia where the order had conquered much territory and was in constant combat defending it. As in the main branch, provincial office-holders were chosen by the provincial chapters and had to give account of their offices in the annual chapters (laws, II, b; customs, par. 7a).

The basic unit of the order, however, was the individual house. A major house had a convent, that is, twelve brothers, in accord with the number of Christ's disciples, and a commander (rule, par. 13). A house which did not have a convent was a minor house. According to Eberhard of Sayn's instructions of 1250, the commanders of individual houses were to be installed and dismissed with the advice of the provincial chapter (par. 4); the provincial commanders and chapters could admit new brothers to the order (par. 13); and provincial masters should have their own seals (par. 1).

An important aspect of the organization of the order is the chapter and its role in giving counsel. Many statutes emphasize that the master and the higher officers had constantly to seek the advice of the wisest brothers, singly or in chapter. The general rule was simple: in very important matters advice and consent was to be obtained from the chapter, where the opinion of the wiser part was to prevail; in less important matters, from the wisest brothers at hand; on minor matters, no advice was needed (rule, par. 27). The rule states: "Which is the wiser part in case of disagreement shall be left to the judgment of the master or his deputies; and, furthermore, piety, discretion, knowledge, and good repute shall have more weight than a mere plurality of the brothers" (par. 27).

Matters on which counsel had to be sought from the entire chapter were numerous. They included admitting new members to the order (rule, pars. 27, 29, 30; admission ritual), alienation of property (rule, par. 27; customs, par. 17), loans or gifts of 500 bezants or more (customs, par. 10), absence of the master from the Holy Land (customs, par. 12), imposition and termination of penances (laws, III, pars. 36–44), and revocation of customs (laws, III, par. 31).

Three kinds of chapters may be distinguished. First, there was a weekly chapter on Sundays (laws, II, introduction and par. f). Here the brothers in each house gathered together to listen to the reading of portions of the statutes, and some brothers were disciplined (laws, III, pars. 25, 38). Whether this chapter also discussed the business of the house, or whether this was done at another time, is not stated in the statutes. Second, there was the annual general chapter, held on September 14 in the main house and in all the provinces (customs, par. 18). By this chapter the higher office-holders in the Holy Land

and in the provinces were chosen each year, and in this chapter they surrendered their offices and rendered their accounts to the brothers (customs, pars. 7a, 18). In the annual chapter in Acre were discussed all the important matters referring to the order; each provincial chapter discussed business regarding its province. The third kind of chapter was the electoral chapter which was convened after the master's death to elect a new master (customs, pars. 2a–6).

The members of the electoral college were coöpted until thirteen were chosen — one priest, eight knights, and four other brothers. "Care shall be taken to avoid having a majority from one province." Therefore to the electoral chapter were summoned the commanders of the provinces of Prussia, the German lands, Austria, Apulia, Romania, Cilician Armenia, and Livonia, to join with the convent of the main house in the electoral proceedings and, as representatives of the new master, to carry the news home to their subordinates (customs, pars. 2a–6).

Thus the order was organized on representative principles, but "democratic" representation was not typical of the Middle Ages. A superior, seeking advice from the chapter or from the wisest brothers, in theory obtained the consent of the entire community of the brothers of a house, a province, or the brotherhood in the Holy Land. A superior's decree or a chapter's decision was binding on everyone; appeal outside the order against the laws of the order warranted a one-year penance (laws, II, d). It was the master and his council, in fact, who, as an oligarchy, ruled the order in the Holy Land.

In many respects, however, the provinces were independent. They held their own annual chapters where they elected and dismissed their own office-holders, and also elected the commanders of the individual houses. The provincial commanders and chapters admitted new members and carried out visitations of individual houses. The provincial commanders, though appointed by the master, could be dismissed only for the gravest offenses. Since conditions varied in the different provinces, the provincial commanders were given a wide discretion in conducting military operations. Unlike the Hospitallers, the provinces did not have to contribute financially to the support of the main house. But the provinces had to send an annual report to the main house (Eberhard of Sayn, par. 18), and every second or third year each province had to send a representative to the Holy Land to report on the province (Eberhard, par. 18). Every new brother admitted by the provincial chapters had to swear allegiance to the master and obedience to the chapter in the Holy Land (Eberhard, par. 13). Finally, new laws decreed by the provincial commander, with the consent of the provincial chapter, had to be confirmed by the master and the chapter in the Holy Land (Eberhard, par. 16). Thus the Teutonic order, in the mid-thirteenth century at least, displayed certain characteristics of a centralized state, and certain aspects of a federation. In the early days, with provinces spread from Livonia to Armenia, the federative aspects probably predominated, but with the move to Marienburg in 1309, the possibilities for centralization increased.

The order's professed brothers included knights, priests and clerics, and a group of lay brothers serving in military or other capacities. Orbiting around this nucleus was a large group comprising military auxiliaries such as mercenary knights and Turcopoles, esquires, domestic servants, *halpswesteren,* and slaves. We know that the order of the Teutonic Knights was the smallest of the three military orders in the Holy Land. How many Teutonic Knights there were we do not know, but we can get some idea of the relative strength and importance of the three classes of professed brothers from the composition of the electoral college, which was made up of eight knights, one priest, and four other brothers.

Though "this order had a hospital before it had knights" (rule, par. 4), yet the brother knights dominated the order, which was "specially founded for knights fighting the enemies of the Cross and of the faith" (rule, par. 22). The order was the "Holy Knightly Order of the Hospital of Saint Mary of the German House" (prologue, par. 4). The brother knights were the actual electors of the master; most of the highest office-holders of the order were knights. Since the brother clerics were subordinate to the grand commander, himself a knight, the knights in the order controlled the religious life of the order, though, of course, they did not celebrate divine service.

A knight who decided to join the order had to secure a sponsor among the brothers to recommend his admission (rule, par. 29). Admission took place in full chapter, where the candidate was questioned on his marital, legal, and religious status, his health, and his financial liabilities. If no impediments to his entering the order were found, the candidate was asked to promise to care for the sick, to defend the Holy Land and the lands pertaining to it, to keep the counsel of the chapter and the master, not to leave the order without permission, and to observe the rule, the laws, and the customs. After making these promises, the candidate might choose either to enter after a one-year probation period or to be received at once. In the latter case he took the three vows of poverty, chastity, and obedience, vow-

ing to be obedient to the master until death, and then was clothed
with the habit of the order and, on the same day, participated in the
sacrament of the mass (admission ritual). This was the ritual for all
who entered the order, but the prospective brother knight, as a sign
of his religious knighthood, was clothed in the white mantle with the
cross, which had been blessed and asperged with holy water (rule,
par. 29).

The distinctive features of the knight's clothing were the white mantle and the surcoat (rule, par. 11). Otherwise his clothing, as well as
bedding, did not differ from that of the older brothers. Clothing consisted of linen shirts, drawers, hose, cape with the cross, and, for
the knights, one or two mantles and surcoat, all with the cross. In
cold climates the brothers also wore fur coats (rule, par. 11). Each
slept on a bed of straw, with one sheet, coverlet, rug, and pillow (customs, par. 34). The military outfit of a knight consisted of the customary accoutrement of any secular knight, including horses, of which
he might have four (customs, par. 42). However, his arms and the
trappings of his horses, in contrast to those of secular knights, were
not to be ornamented (rule, par. 22). Brother knights were not allowed to participate in tournaments and other knightly games, or attend worldly festivities (rule, par. 28). The chase was permitted for
food and clothing (furs), but hunting with hounds and hawks was
prohibited (rule, par. 23). All kissing and converse with women was
strictly forbidden (rule, par. 28; laws, III, par. 36, no. 2). These latter
regulations applied as well to other brothers in the order.

When the knights were commanded to prepare for combat, they
had to do everything according to order: they could neither don their
armor nor saddle their horses until told to do so, nor could they
mount their steeds or ride out of the convent of their own accord
(customs, pars. 46 and 60). Every pace of the knights' progress on
the road was regulated. They had to ride in rank and file, surrounded
by their esquires and trailed by the caravan of spare horses and pack-
animals. While proceeding in battle array, they were not allowed to
ride about or talk to each other except in an emergency; even water-
ing of horses was restricted (customs, pars. 46–48). In the field they
were under discipline as rigorous as in the convent. They had to pitch
their tents, usually in a ring, to protect the horses, the arms, and
the "chapel"; attend divine service day and night (customs, pars. 50–
52), and continue their penances, if they were doing any (customs,
par. 65). They were not even allowed to take off their armor at will
(customs, par. 60), or to graze their horses, or to go far from camp
without special permission (customs, pars. 52–53).

Their greatest hour came "whenever the marshal or he who carries the standard attacks the enemy" (customs, par. 61). Then the brother knights advanced to battle while their attendants (esquires) gathered round a standard, carried by a brother sergeant-at-arms, with the spare horses and spare weapons, and prayed "until God send their lords back again" (customs, par. 61). No brother knight could attack "before he who carries the standard [of the order] has attacked." After the knight joined in the attack, his next steps were left to God's dictates "in his heart," but when it seemed "opportune," he might return to the standard (customs, para. 61). The Knights Templar had detailed instructions on conduct in battle; the Teutonic Knight had only to remember: "If a brother in cowardice flees from the standard or from the army," or "goes over from the Christians to the heathen," he was committing the most serious sin, for which there was no pardon or redress; he lost the order forever (laws, III, par. 39, nos. 4, 5, and end). As a matter of fact, when a religious knight met the enemy of the faith in battle, he had only one choice, so gallantly portrayed by the poet Hartmann of Aue:

> Nû zinsent, ritter, iuwer leben
> und ouch den muot
> durch in der in dâ hât gegeben
> lîp unde guot.
> . . . .
> Wan swem daz ist beschert
> daz er dâ wol gevert,
> daz giltet beidiu teil,
> der werlte lop, der sêle heil.[32]

Pope Urban II promised no more to his crusaders when he proclaimed at Clermont: "Enpurpled with your own blood, you will gain everlasting glory."

If a sick or aging brother were lucky, he could leave the Holy Land, not to go "at his own pleasure here and there, where he wishes," but to spend his last days in a convent of the order in Europe, where he could expect tender treatment (customs, par. 13). Those who, because of wounds or for other reasons, had to spend their days in the infirmary in the Holy Land were to be honored and cared for with patience (rule, par. 25). When the brave brother knight's last hour

---

32. "Now, oh knights, pay your tribute with your life and your courage to him who has sacrificed for you both his body and his riches. . . . For he on whom the lot has fallen to depart thither, will be rewarded two-fold: with the world's acclaim and the soul's salvation." See Hartman of Aue (d. *c.* 1220), "Dem kriuze zimt wol reiner mout," in Karl Bartsch and Wolfgang Golther, eds., *Deutsche Liederdichter des zwölften bis vierzehnten Jahrhunderts: Eine Auswahl,* 4th ed. (Berlin, 1910), pp. 86–87.

had come, he confessed and received the eucharist and extreme unction (laws, III, par. 10). If a brother died before vespers, he was to be buried at once, his body covered with a white cloth with the black cross; if he died after vespers, he was to be buried the next day after prime (rule, par. 6; laws, III, par. 20). The clothes of the deceased brother were distributed to the poor, as were the food and drink to which he was entitled, for forty days, "since alms liberate from death and shorten the punishment of the soul who has departed in grace" (rule, par. 10).

A brother knight was not, however, only a warrior; he was also a religious who, like the canons regular, had to take the three religious vows (admission ritual), live in a convent (rule, *passim*), attend mass and the canonical hours, and receive the sacrament (rule, pars. 8, 9; customs, par. 63). He was tonsured (rule, par. 12), and communications with the world outside, sending and receiving letters, and receiving visitors and gifts were restricted (rule, par. 19; laws, III, 37, no. 2; customs, pars. 38, 56, 57). His meals, if the rule was rigorously observed, were meager (rule, par. 13), his bodily strength was weakened by regular fasting (rule, par. 15), and his religious maturity was promoted, to some extent, by learning the Lord's Prayer, the Hail Mary, and the Creed (laws, II, f, e). If the lay brothers (and these included the knights) were sufficiently literate they might, with the permission of the superior, "recite with the priests the canonical hours or the hours of Our Lady with the psalms and the other things pertaining to the priestly office" (rule, par. 8).

A penal code, not the most severe but certainly the most systematic of all penal codes of the military orders in the Holy Land, was drawn up, and if rigorously applied, beyond doubt could not only have brought any sturdy knight to his knees, but also have broken his body and his devotion to the religious life. However, one may doubt whether a one-year penance was often enforced upon a brother knight who fought against the "infidels," for the Holy Land was more in need of bold, though turbulent, warriors than of religious and emaciated penitents. Even the Roman pontiffs prescribed fighting against the heathen as a penance.

"Among the members are also priests who play a worthy and useful role, for in time of peace they shine in the midst of the lay brothers, urge them to observe the rules strictly, celebrate for them divine service, and administer to them the sacraments . . . [and in war] strengthen the brothers for battle and admonish them to remember how God also suffered death for them on the Cross," states the prologue (par. 5). The clerics were not numerous and possibly possessed little weight in running the order's business; their role was spiritual rather than administrative. "The other brothers shall honor the brother priests and provide for their needs before all others, because of the dignity of their order and office, for God is honored in them; and moreover [the brothers] shall honor them the more diligently, since they are lovers of the order and of the religious life and are gladly furthering the religious life" (laws, III, par. 2).

The role of the brother priests and clerics was to provide for and guide the religious life of the lay brothers. They officiated at the canonical hours, celebrated mass, administered the eucharist to the brothers seven times a year, and also the other sacraments (rule, par. 9), prayed for the brothers, servants, and benefactors of the order, living and dead (rule, par. 10), said grace at meals (rule, par. 13), and conducted worship in the hospital for the sick poor and in the infirmary for the brothers (rule, pars. 5 and 24; laws, III, par. 12). Moreover, the brother clerics probably taught the lay brothers the Creed, the Lord's Prayer, and the Hail Mary (laws, II, e), heard their confessions (laws, III, par. 21), read the rule and the laws to the brothers, and acted as scribes (laws, III, par. 27). The Teutonic order had a special penal code for the brother priests and brother clerics, but in general a sinful cleric was treated like a lay brother: he was tried in the chapter and received the same punishment as the lay brothers.

Like the other military orders, the membership of the Teutonic order included, besides knights and priests and clerics, "other brothers," mentioned occasionally as sergeants, or serving brothers: sergeants at arms, at office, at service, or at labor. While the three highest office-holders (customs, par. 8) and the castellan were certainly knights, and the hospitaller (rule, pars. 5, 6; customs, pars. 21, 31) and treasurer (customs, pars. 9, 16, 31, 36) probably were, the drapier may possibly have been a brother sergeant at service (customs, pars. 35, 38), as may also have been the brothers in charge of the saddlery, forge, and other workshops, and the master of victuals (customs, pars. 40, 41, 35, 55, 56). Tacked on to the admission ritual was a statement that "brothers who do not wish to practise their trade shall be kept on bread and water until they do it cheerfully." All these "other brothers" had their place in the chapter, but probably had little or no voice in the affairs of the order, though some were members of the master's council (customs, par. 9).

Assisting the professed brothers of the order was a host of individuals ranging from auxiliary knights to "slaves, if there are any in the house" (laws, III, par. 38). Highest in rank were the knights who served the order for charity; they were probably crusaders of knightly birth.

Another category of fighting men was the Turcopoles, who initially were mercenaries of Turkish origin in the Byzantine imperial army, and now and then are mentioned in crusader chronicles. William of Tyre calls them light-armed knights or cavalry,[33] and Raymond of Aguilers says that "Turcopoles were so named because they were either reared with Turks or were the offspring of a Christian mother and of a Turkish father."[34] Turcopoles fought in Alexius I Comnenus's army against the Turks and the Latins and were used also by later Byzantine emperors.[35]

In the crusader states separate fighting units called Turcopoles were in the employ of the military religious orders, and seemingly were recruited locally either from indigenous converts or from mixed native and Latin stock who served the crusader cause as soldiers. The statutes of the Knights Templar and Knights Hospitaller clearly indicate that they were second-class members of the orders, inferior to the brother knights but higher in rank than the servants.[36] They comprised the orders' light cavalry, and under their own commander participated in the defense of the crusader states.[37] The Teutonic Knights, adapting much of their organizational pattern from the two older orders, also took over the idea of such a native auxiliary force. They

33. William of Tyre, *Historia rerum in partibus transmarinis gestarum*, in *RHC, Occ.*, I; tr. Emily A. Babcock and August C. Krey, *A History of Deeds Done Beyond the Sea* (*CURC*, 35; 2 vols., New York, 1943), XIX, 25, and XXII, 17.

34. Raymond of Aguilers, *Historia Francorum qui ceperunt Iherusalem* (*RHC, Occ.*, III, 231–309); tr. John Hugh Hill and Laurita L. Hill, *Raymond d'Aguilers: Historia Francorum qui ceperunt Iherusalem* (Memoirs of the American Philosophical Society, LXXI; Philadelphia, 1968), cap. 4; Albert of Aachen, *Liber Christianae expeditionis pro ereptione, emundatione, restitutione sanctae Hierosolymitanae ecclesiae* (*RHC, Occ.*, IV, 265–713), V, 3, calls them "an impious breed, said to be Christians only by name, not deed, born of a Turkish father and a Greek mother."

35. Nicephorus Gregoras, *Byzantina historia,* ed. Ludwig Schopen and Immanuel Bekker (*CSHB*, XIX; 3 vols., Bonn, 1829–1855), VII, 4; Fulcher of Chartres, *Historia Hierosolymitana 1095–1127,* ed. Heinrich Hagenmeyer (Heidelberg, 1913); tr. Frances R. Ryan, *A History of the Expedition to Jerusalem 1095–1127,* ed. Harold S. Fink (Knoxville, Tenn., 1969), I, 8; Baldric of Dol, *Historia Jerosolimitana* (*RHC, Occ.*, IV, 1–111), cap. 14; Albert of Aachen, *op. cit.,* II, 12, IV, 40, V, 3; VIII, 7, 15, 22, 46; Raymond of Aguilers, *op. cit.,* cap. 4; [Anonymi] *Gesta Francorum at aliorum Hierosolimitanorum,* ed. and tr. Rosalind Hill, *The Deeds of the Franks and the Other Pilgrims to Jerusalem* (Medieval Texts; London, 1962), pp. 6, 9, 16; Ambrose, "The History of the Holy War," in *Three Old French Chronicles of the Crusades,* tr. Edward N. Stone (University of Washington Publications in the Social Sciences, X; Seattle, 1939), caps. 10, 55.

36. Two brother knights were entitled to as much meat as three Turcopoles, and two Turcopoles to as much as three servants (Curzon, *La Règle du Temple,* par. 153; see also pars. 370 and 375); the Turcopoles did not eat together with brother knights, but sat at their own table; only those brother knights had to sit with the Turcopoles who were doing penance in full garment (*ibid.,* par. 271; Delaville Le Roulx, *Cartulaire,* no. 1193, par. 10).

37. Curzon, *La Règle,* pars. 169–171; Delaville Le Roulx, *Cartulaire,* no. 4612, par. 5.

were organized into a special unit with its own commander, the turcopolier, who in turn was under the command of the marshal; he was
also the commander of the brother sergeants-at-arms, with his own
standard. Turcopoles were assigned to the master's household: one
as shield-bearer, another as messenger, and a third as chamberlain;
and on campaign, a fourth (customs, par. 11); the marshal's standard-
bearer also was a Turcopole (customs, par. 19). The grand commander
likewise had one Turcopole at home and a second in the field (customs, par. 29).

As light-armed soldiers the Turcopoles and the sergeants-at-arms
in battle array rode either in the van or in the rear. There is no information as to the number or deeds of the Turcopoles who were in the
service of the Teutonic Knights. After the expulsion from Acre in
1291 the order temporarily established its headquarters in Venice. In
1292 a general chapter was held in Frankfurt, where the master, Conrad of Feuchtwangen, decreed supplemental laws about Turcopoles
and sergeants-at-arms.[38] However, by then the institution of Turcopoles in the Teutonic order had lost its meaning, for in the conquered
territories of Prussia and Livonia the Teutonic Knights did not admit
the natives to the ranks of the order. In these countries, in case of
war, the order's light cavalry was supplied by the order's German vassals, and the conquered native peasantry gradually became serfs and
were often forced to accompany the order's army as footsoldiers and
in the supply train. The term "Turcopoles" disappears from documents after the fourteenth century.

Another segment of the order's membership was the squires. Like
secular knights, each of the brother knights had attendants (*knehte*)
(rule, par. 22) or squires, who were under the master of the squires
(*meister der schiltknehte*), who received them into service, allocated
them to the brother knights, and determined their pay, if they were
not serving for charity; once a week he held a chapter with these attendants (customs, par. 39). When the brother knights rode in battle
array, these attendants naturally accompanied them (customs, par.
46), but ordinarily did not participate in battle; instead they rallied
round the standard behind the lines, and were expected to pray for
the safe return of their lords (customs, par. 61). Since the same word,
knehte, is used in the "Book of the Order" for squires and for domestic servants, it is sometimes hard to determine which are referred to.

The *halpswesteren* or sister-aids provided for in the rule certainly
were domestics. They were "not admitted in full service and fellow-

---

38. Perlbach, *Statuten,* pp. 141–143.

ship" but were introduced because there were "some services for the sick . . . and also for livestock which are better performed by women than by men" (rule, par. 31); they may also have worked in the laundry (customs, par. 34). They lived in separate quarters from the men. By the latter half of the thirteenth century, there were also *halpbrûdern*,[39] who were used to graze and tend the cattle, to cultivate and till the fields, and to do other kinds of work according to the commander's wishes and the needs of the house. They received food and clothes from the order. Their outer garment was a short mantle (*schaprun*) "of religious hue" with wide arms, but without the full cross. Their shoes were three or four finger-widths higher than those of the brother knights, and they were required to cut their beards and hair in line with their ears. They had to learn the Creed and to fast like the professed brothers, but their punishments for offenses in certain cases were lighter. When they applied for admission to the order, they were asked the same questions as the full brothers, but they were not asked to do a year's probation. Both the *halpbrûderen* and the *halpswesteren* had to take the vows of chastity, poverty, and obedience (laws of Burkhard, par. 1; supplementary laws, 1264–1269, first collection, par. 5).

The order also received lay people, married or single, as domestics, "who submit their bodies and property to the direction of the brothers." If one of the married domestics died, half of the estate fell to the order, the other half "to the survivor until his death; and after his death the entire estate falls to the use of the order." Married or single, they had to lead an honest life and were not to pursue illicit trade. They also, like the *halpbrûderen* and *halpswesteren,* wore garments "of religious hue, and without the full cross" (rule, par. 34).

In addition to all these servants, whether called *halpbrûderen, halpswesteren, heimliche, knehte, gesinde,* or *pflegere* (in the hospitals and infirmaries), there were other servants: artisans and laborers who worked for charity or for wages. Gardeners, carpenters, masons, and other workmen were under the command of the vice-commander (customs, par. 35).

At the bottom of the scale were the people perpetually bound to the order, the serfs and the slaves. The rule (par. 2) allowed the order to "possess in perpetual right people, men and women, serfs, male and female." These serfs, probably donated along with lands to the order, may have worked directly for the brothers. Slaves were prob-

---

39. See later supplements to the "Book of the Order": two collections of laws from the Holy Land (decreed between 1264 and 1269), and the laws of Burkhard of Schwanden (1289), ed. Perlbach, *Statuten,* pp. 136–139.

ably to be distinguished from them. The laws (III, par. 38) decree that a brother doing a one-year penance "shall remain with the slaves, if there are any in the house." The slaves "pertained" to the office of the grand commander, and the vice-commander had to provide the slaves (customs, pars. 28, 35). The statutes do not describe more closely this group of unfree people, nor state how they were acquired. In Prussia and Livonia slaves were the heathen prisoners-of-war or persons who had committed crimes and, unable to pay heavy compensation, had to pawn their own bodies to save their lives.

The measure of drink is an index to the relative rank of these people in or serving the order. A brother was entitled to two quarts of drink a day, a Turcopole to a quart and a half, and a *knehte* to a quart (customs, par. 58).

The statutes of the order also regulated the care of the sick brothers. They were entitled to special attention in the infirmary according to their needs and the resources of the house; they had to be treated honorably and with patience (rule, par. 24; customs, par. 55); they were allowed to go barefoot (laws, I, par. a) and sleep on featherbeds, mattresses, or felt (laws, I, par. p). Whenever a brother, even a high office-holder, except the master, became sick, he was allowed to have three meals daily in his bed; but no meat, eggs, cheese, fish, or wine (laws, III, par. 10).

During the first half of the thirteenth century, when the statutes of the Teutonic Knights were compiled, the most celebrated center of medical learning in the west was the medical school of Salerno in southern Italy. There is no question that the fame of its physicians was well known to the Teutonic Knights, for their most renowned master, Hermann of Salza, sought a cure for his illness in Salerno in 1238. It is likely that medical knowledge among the crusaders and in the military religious orders in the Holy Land was based mainly on the teachings and practice at the medical school there.

Our best information about the application of medical learning at Salerno is derived from the *Regimen sanitatis Salernitanum,* an anonymous twelfth-century verse compendium, probably by several authors,[40] on diet, hygiene, treatment of diseases, and medical practices. To supplement our scanty knowledge about the curing of the sick by the Teutonic Knights, on the assumption that they followed the medical practices of the west,[41] one can compare the various pro-

40. For the authorship of the *Regimen* see George Sarton, *Introduction to the History of Science* (3 vols. in 5, Baltimore, 1927–1948), II-1, 434; II-2, 894.

41. A late-fourteenth-century MS. of 152 folios which among other texts contains a Latin

visions of the statutes of the Teutonic Knights with the *Regimen*. The *Regimen* gives the following advice on meals for the sick: "All pears and apples, peaches, milk and cheese, salt meats, red deer, hare, beef, and goat, all these are foods that breed ill blood and melancholy; if sick you be, to feed on them were folly" (p. 80).[42] About cheese it adds: "For healthy men cheese may be wholesome food, but for the weak and sickly it is not good" (p. 97). However, eggs, fish, and wine were recommended for the healthy, and not forbidden to the sick.

If a brother knight's illness worsened, he had to go to the infirmary which was set up at every house of the order and was looked after by a warden. In the infirmary the sick first confessed and received the eucharist and, in case of emergency, extreme unction (laws, III, par. 10). The grand commander was in charge of supplies for the infirmary, including the provision of a physician, if one could conveniently be secured (rule, par. 24; laws, III, par. 11). The physician was admonished to pay equal attention to all brothers in the infirmary.

No direct information about drugs and medical treatment in the infirmary has survived, but it seems that, besides improved food and blood-letting, spicy herbs, syrups, and electuaries were the basic cures. The use of syrups (sticky liquids of fruit and vegetable juices cooked with sugar), electuaries (pasty masses of honey or sugar and drugs), and spices was forbidden to the brothers without permission, as these remedies were reserved, as was common in the Middle Ages, for the sick. Wine, mixed with spices, was regarded as good medicine for all ills, and its use was recommended in the *Regimen,* particularly during the winter (p. 130). To the Teutonic Knights, as to religious in general, the making[43] and consuming of spiced wine (German *lütertrank,* Latin *pigmentum*)[44] was forbidden (laws, I, par. o). Sugar for making syrups certainly was used by the Teutonic Knights, for al-

---

version of the statutes from 1398 also includes two treatises, one entitled *Regimen sanitatis,* and another on diet; see A. J. H. Steffenhagen, ed., *Catalogus codicum manuscriptorum bibliothecae regiae et universitatis Regimontanae* (Königsberg, 1867–1872), II, no. 284. This MS. was written in Prussia, and is in the possession of the University Library, Toruń, Poland. For the order's medical work in Prussia see Christian Probst, *Der Deutsche Orden und sein Medizinalwesen in Preussen* (Quellen und Studien zur Geschichte des Deutschen Ordens, XXIX; Bad Godesberg, 1969).

42. Quotations from the 1609 tr. of Sir John Harington, *The School of Salernum,* ed. Hoeber; the spelling is modernized.

43. Probably to such practices could be traced the origins of liqueur-making by the religious houses.

44. Charles du Fresne Du Cange, *Glossarium mediae et infimae latinitatis,* ed. G. A. L. Henschel (7 vols., Paris, 1840–1850), *sub verbis* "pigmentum" and "species"; and Matthias Lexer, *Mittelhochdeutsches Taschenwörterbuch,* 24th ed. (Leipzig, 1944): *s.v.* "lutertranc—über kräuter und gewürze abgeklärter rotwein."

ready in February 1198 (before the German hospital in Acre was transformed into an order) the hospital received sugar for the needs of the sick.[45] Comparing the described spices, syrups, and electuaries with corresponding medicine used by Moslem physicians in the late twelfth and early thirteenth centuries, as described in *The Medical Formulary of as-Samarqandī* (d. 1222/3), one notices a close similarity between the drugs administered at Salerno and by Arab physicians.[46] Likewise vinegar was a common remedy among Arab physicians.

Another way of improving the health of a sick brother of the Teutonic Knights was bathing: only the sick in the infirmary were allowed to bathe;[47] all others had to obtain the permission of their superior (laws, III, par. 11). The Salernitan *Regimen* recommends bathing in the spring, advises one to keep warm after a bath, and adds: "Wine, women, bath, by art or nature warm, used or abused do much good or harm" (p. 84; cf. p. 124). As-Samarqandī's *Formulary* contains a brief chapter on aromatic bathing, recommending it as a therapeutic exercise.

The statutes of the Teutonic Knights contain long and detailed regulations about fasting.[48] Although the idea of fasting was based on biblical rules, it was undoubtedly also regarded as a form of dieting, to keep the human body in good health. The *Regimen* is very explicit about the benefits of diet and fasting: "To keep good diet, you should never eat until you find your stomach clean and void" (p. 80). Fasting was recommended in every season, but particularly in the summer: it keeps the body dry, and is a remedy for vomiting and dysentery (p. 128). For the sick in the infirmary the statutes of the Teutonic Knights ordered improved food according to the means of the house, but at least one dish more than for the brothers at the convent table. However, beef, salt meat, salt fish, salt cheese, lentils, unpeeled beans, and other "unhealthy" foods were not allowed in the infirmary (laws, III, par. 8). About the use of salt the *Regimen* says: "Salt makes unsavory viands edible; to drive some poisons out, salt has ability, yet things too salt are never recommendable: they hurt the sight, in nature cause debility, the scab and itch on them are ever breeding, the which on meats too salt are often feeding" (p. 107). Beans and lentils,

45. Strehlke, *Tabulae,* no. 34: letter of sale of Aimery, king of Jerusalem, February 8, 1198.
46. *Op. cit., passim;* particularly chap. 1, "Syrups and robs," and chap. 2, "Stomachic confections and electuaries." For a general survey of Arab influence on European medicine see Heinrich Schipperger, *Die Assimilation der arabischen Medizin durch das lateinische Mittelalter* (Sudhoffs Archiv für Geschichte der Medizin und der Naturwissenschaften, Beiheft 3; Wiesbaden, 1964).
47. Perlbach, *Statuten,* p. 134: "Capitelbeschlüsse vor 1264," I, par. 4.
48. Perlbach, *Statuten,* "Die Regel," pars. 13 and 15.

according to the *Regimen,* spoil eyesight (p. 124); about peas the *Regimen* comments: "In peas good qualities and bad are tried, to take them with the skin that grows aloft, they windy be, but good without the hide" (p. 96).

Those members of the Teutonic order who were wounded, or who had contracted dysentery or some other illness which might disturb the comfort of the brothers, slept apart from others in the infirmary (laws, III, par. 13), and brothers suffering from quartan fever (malaria) were, with the master's permission, given meat three days a week during the fast period before Advent and Christmas; they were also exempt from attending divine service (laws, III, par. 14). To those who suffered from dysentery the *Regimen* advised fasting and goose meat (p. 48; cf. p. 98); of malaria, called ague, the Salerno physicians said that it is bred by long sleep after noon, and recommended as a cure butter (but not milk) (p. 97), white pepper, purging, and blood-letting (pp. 97, 122, 130). For fever as-Samarqandī recommended cress powder and lohochs, syrups, and lozenges, "but the keynote in treating fevers is the opening of blockages which cause putrefaction of humor." For this process violets, plums, apricots, tamarisks, jujubes, the root and seed of endive, rhubarb, agrimony, and cuscuta could be used.[49]

Blood-letting (phlebotomy) was recommended by the Salerno doctors as a cure for malaria. It was also practised by the Teutonic Knights, for the laws clearly state that blood-letting can be administered to the sick in the infirmary only with the permission of the head of the infirmary (laws, III, par. 12). Blood-letting was considered a universal remedy for all maladies, and the *Regimen* offers detailed information about its alleged salutary effect; a person's age and strength, the quantity of blood let (venesected), and the season of the year were to be taken into consideration. Neither drunkards nor persons recovering from long sickness nor the too young or too old were fit for venesection (p. 150). The incision for bleeding should be made neither too long nor too deep, so that sinews were not touched but there was a sufficient cut for speedy escape of the blood (p. 154). In the spring and summer one should be bled in the right arm, in fall and winter in the left arm; in the spring blood can be let twice as much as in the fall (p. 155). For six hours after bleeding sleep and exposure to moist and unwholesome air had to be avoided; consumption of cold meats, spirits, milk, and meals made with milk had to be postponed for a similar period (p. 154). Moderate food of light meats was recommended, as well as gentle physical exercise (p. 153).

---

49. As-Samarqandī, *op. cit.,* p. 93.

The presumed benefits of blood-letting were many: the pensive were cheered; "the raging furies bred by burning love" were removed (p. 153); the spirit and senses were renewed; the brain was cleansed; the eyes were relieved; appetite was improved; sleep was restored; voice, touch, smell, taste, and hearing were mended; the marrow was given heat (p. 148); and to the spleen, breast, and entrails exceeding help was lent (p. 156). Spring and summer bleeding mended the heart and liver; fall and winter venesection, the hand and the foot (p. 156). The Moslem Syrian memoirist Usāmah says that blood-letting was widely practised by Moslem physicians to cure sickness, and Usāmah himself recommended phlebotomy even after heavy bleeding from wounds.[50] He also believed that bleeding in the forehead could cure inflamation of the eye.

Surgery, if one believes Usāmah, was more advanced among the Moslems than among their western contemporaries,[51] though considered to be on a lower level than medicine among both the Latins and the Arabs, and surgeons were regarded as less respectable medical practitioners than physicians. In fact, surgery was approved neither by the Moslem nor by the Christian faith, because of the prohibition in the Koran and the Bible against spilling human blood, and because of the insult to the human body, which was created by God in his own likeness.[52] Moreover, Innocent III in the Fourth Lateran Council had forbidden subdeacons, deacons, and priests to participate in surgery if cutting and burning were performed.[53]

The Teutonic Knights cared not only for their sick brothers but also for the laity. The rule of the order contains regulations for establishing, operating, and financing hospitals. "Because this order," the rule states (par. 4), "had a hospital before it had knights, as appears clearly from its name, for it is called the hospital, so we decree that in the main house, or where the master with the counsel of the chapter decides, there will be a hospital at all times, but elsewhere, if someone wishes to give an established hospital with funds to the house, the provincial commander with the counsel of the wisest brothers may accept or refuse. In other houses of this order, where there is no hospital, none shall be established without special command of the master with the counsel of the wiser brothers." Thus hospitals were estab-

---

50. Usāmah Ibn-Munqidh, tr. Hitti, p. 59.

51. *Ibid.,* pp. 162, 193.

52. Benjamin L. Gordon, *Medieval and Renaissance Medicine* (New York, 1959), *passim;* particularly chap. 21, "The Chirurgeon and the Barber Surgeon."

53. Canon XVIII of the decrees of the Fourth Lateran Council, in Mansi, *Concilia,* XXII, col. 1007: *nec illam chirurgiae partem subdiaconus, diaconus, vel sacerdos exerceant, quae ad ustionem vel incisionem inducit.*

lished for the care of sick lay people; the sick brothers of the order were admitted to the infirmary.

Admission to the hospital was very similar to admission to the infirmary. After a sick layman had arrived at the hospital, but before he was put to bed, he had to confess and receive the eucharist, and he had to hand his possessions (if he had brought any with him) over to the brother in charge of the hospital in exchange for a written receipt (rule, par. 5). The hospitaller then decided about the needs of the sick person and entrusted the patient to the care of the warden, the actual administrator of the hospital, and of physicians and attendants. Again, emphasis was put on loving care, improved food, and spiritual needs: on Sundays the epistles and the gospels were read, the sick were asperged with holy water, and the healthy brothers had to walk in procession before the sick; at night a light had to be kept burning in the hospital (rule, par. 6).

The compiler of the rule of the Teutonic Knights was zealous in following the decrees of Innocent III.[54] The sick in the hospital were given food in charity before the brothers of the order had had their meal, and every care was to be taken to supply all the necessities for the welfare of the sick (rule, par. 6).

The hospital was not only a place where the sick were given medical treatment and spiritual care, but also an asylum for the aged and the infirm. About the organization and the medical care in the hospital the statutes of the Teutonic Knights are silent, but it can be assumed that treatment in the hospital was similar to the care of the sick brothers in the infirmary. The rule provided for the admission of sister-aids as members of the order, "since there are some services for the sick in the hospital . . . which are better performed by women than by men." However, "they shall be received only with the permission of the provincial commander, and, after they are received, they shall be housed apart from the quarters of the brothers, for the chastity of professed brothers, who dwell with women, although a light is kept on, still is not safe, and may not last long without scandal" (rule, par. 31).

Some light may be shed on the German medical work in the crusader states by the regulations of the Hospitallers, for the Teutonic Knights followed the rule of the Knights Hospitaller in regard to the care of the sick. In 1181 the hospital of St. John in Jerusalem was ordered to employ four physicians who knew how to examine urine,

54. *Ibid.,* cols. 1010, 1011.

diagnose disease, and administer appropriate remedies. Provisioning was organized by fixing the deliveries from the subordinate houses: 200 cotton sheets to be sent to Jerusalem yearly, 4,000 ells of fustian, 2,000 ells of cotton cloth for coverlets, and 4 quintals of sugar for making syrups and medicine for the sick. The sick were to be given fresh meat, pork, mutton, or chicken three days a week, also comfortable beds, long enough and wide enough, each with its own sheets, and also each was to have a fur cloak and boots for going to the latrines; abandoned children were to be received and fed in the hospital, and cradles were to be made for babies born to women pilgrims; the almoner was to give twelve pennies to prisoners when they were released from jail, and the convent was to feed thirty poor persons every day at the convent table. The rule of the Teutonic Knights (pars. 4–7) includes regulations for the hospital, evidently taken over from the Hospitallers, but the laws and the customs include no further regulations. Thus, though the German house started as a foundation to care for the sick poor, by about 1244 such care seemingly played a decreasing role in the activities of the Teutonic Knights.

John of Würzburg, who visited Jerusalem about 1170, has left a brief description of the hospital of the order of St. John. The hospital was annexed to their church of John the Baptist; it occupied several rooms, and there were housed about two thousand people, both men and women, who were "tended and restored to health daily at a very great expense." John also admits that the mortality in the hospital was rather high: "in the course of one day and night more than fifty are carried out dead, while many other fresh ones keep continually arriving." The Hospitallers also supported with victuals many more poor people who did not live in the hospital.[55] Another traveler from Germany, Theoderic, who visited Jerusalem at about the same time as John, or perhaps a few years later, mentioned that the hospital of the Knights of St. John was a beautiful building abundantly "supplied with rooms and beds and other material for the use of poor and sick people"; according to his estimate there were more than one

55. John of Würzburg, tr. Stewart, in *PPTS,* V-2, 44. For a general account of the hospitals of the Knights Hospitaller see Edgar E. Hume, *Medical Work of the Knights Hospitallers of Saint John of Jerusalem* (Baltimore, 1940), and Jesko von Steynitz, *Mittelalterliche Hospitäler der Orden und Städte als Einrichtungen des sozialen Sicherung* (Sozialpolitische Schriften, XXVI: Berlin, 1970).

thousand beds in the hospital.[56] Naturally, the hospitals of the Teutonic Knights at Acre and at Montfort were much smaller; there is also no evidence that the provinces of the Teutonic order had to deliver supplies to the hospitals in the Holy Land.

The most famous of Moslem hospitals in the thirteenth century, called the great hospital of al-Manṣūr (Kalavun), was founded in Cairo in 1284. It was open to all the sick, rich as well as poor; it contained wards for both men and women; and the sick were cared for by male and female attendants, like the sick in the hospital of the Teutonic Knights. The Cairo hospital had four different wards: one for bloodletting, one for surgery, another for sufferers from fevers (probably malaria), and the fourth ward for dysentery and kindred ailments.[57] There was thus some resemblance to the arrangement in the infirmary and hospital of the Teutonic Knights.

For running hospitals, supporting their own members, and defending the Holy Land, the Teutonic Knights certainly needed material wealth: funds, bequests, and regular income. To support their work, the Teutonic order in Acre was richly endowed with alms of all kinds. As early as the siege of Acre in September 1190, soon after the founding of the German field hospital, the king of Jerusalem, Guy of Lusignan, donated to the hospital a house within the walls of the city, at the gate of St. Nicholas, and another place for building a permanent hospital, as well as four acres (*carrucatae*) of land near Acre.[58] After the capture of the city in July 1191, the brothers of the hospital bought a garden adjacent to the house, and built there their residence, a hospital, and a chapel;[59] in February 1192 king Guy confirmed an earlier donation and the new acquisitions and buildings. The hospital already housed the sick.[60] In 1193 Henry II, the ruler of the kingdom of Jerusalem and count-palatine of Troyes, donated to the brotherhood of the German hospital a manor (*casale*), Cafresi, in the district of Acre, and a rampart (*barbacana*) at the gate of St. Nicholas, together with towers and walls, a moat, and a vault at the town wall,

---

56. Theoderic, "Theoderich's Description of the Holy Places," tr. Stewart (in *PPTS,* V-4), p. 22.

57. Edward G. Brown, *Arabian Medicine* (Cambridge, Eng., 1921), pp. 101–102; Edward T. Wittington, *Medical History from the Earliest Times: A Popular History of the Healing Art* (London, 1964), p. 166.

58. Strehlke, *Tabulae,* no. 25: letter of grant to the German hospital outside Acre, mid-September, 1190.

59. *Narracio,* I, 222.

60. Strehlke, *Tabulae,* no. 27: letter of grant of king Guy to the German hospital in Acre, February 10, 1192.

on condition that the brothers repair the rampart as required for the defense of the city,[61] so with this bequest the brothers of the German hospital in Acre were entrusted with their first military task.

In April 1195 Henry II presented to the hospital a house in Tyre and two acres of land at Sedinum, north of Tyre.[62] In the following year Henry II gave as a present to the hospital land in Jaffa and a vineyard outside the city.[63] All these possessions were confirmed to the hospital on December 21, 1196, by pope Celestine III.[64] In February 1198 Aimery of Lusignan, king of Jerusalem and Cyprus, sold to the German hospital a manor called Aguille in the district of Acre, together with its *villani* and *gastini*.[65] Thus the German hospital in Acre possessed landed property in and around the city before it was transformed into a military religious order.

Acre, the main crusader city after the loss of Jerusalem in 1187, also remained the headquarters and the center of activities of the Teutonic Knights. Acquisitions of new possessions continued after the official founding of the order in 1198: more houses, gardens, plots of land, and other buildings were acquired, mostly by purchase, in Acre and in the nearby towns north of Acre,[66] and in Tyre,[67] Sidon,[68] Tripoli,[69] and Antioch,[70] as well as south of Acre in Caesarea,[71] Jaffa,[72] Ramla,[73] and Ascalon,[74] and in many other locations, for the most part unidentifiable.[75] In April 1229, after Frederick II had negotiated

61. *Ibid.,* nos. 28, 29: letters of grant of Henry II, count-palatine of Troyes, to the German hospital in Acre, 1193; cf. no. 128, pp. 121–122: a register of the possessions of the Teutonic Knights in the Holy Land.

62. *Ibid.,* no. 31: same. Prutz, *Besitzungen,* p. 16, identifies Sedinum with "Shadinah," northeast of Tyre.

63. Strehlke, *Tabulae,* no. 32: same, March 1196.

64. *Ibid.,* no. 296.

65. *Ibid.,* no. 34: letter of grant to the German hospital in Acre.

66. *Ibid.,* nos. 41, 42, 50, 53, 65, 70, 76, 92, 104, 113: letters of various lords to the Teutonic Knights, dating from 1206 to 1257; cf. no. 128, pp. 123–126.

67. *Ibid.,* nos. 36, 45, 56, 57: same, from 1200 to 1222; cf. no. 128, pp. 123–124.

68. *Ibid.,* no. 62: letter of grant of Balian, lord of Sidon, to the Teutonic Knights, February 11, 1228; cf. no. 128, p. 126.

69. *Ibid.,* no. 44: letter of grant of Bohemond IV, prince of Antioch, September 4, 1209; cf. no. 128, p. 126.

70. *Ibid.,* no. 61: same, January 1228; cf. no. 128, p. 126.

71. *Ibid.,* no. 40: letter of grant of Juliana, wife of Aymar of Lairon, lord of Caesarea, to the Teutonic Knights, February 1206; cf. no. 128, p. 123.

72. *Ibid.,* no. 128, p. 122.

73. *Ibid.,* no. 303, p. 272: bull of Honorius III, December 8, 1216.

74. *Ibid.*

75. *Ibid.,* no. 128, pp. 120–121.

the transfer of Jerusalem to the Christians, he gave to the Teutonic order the former house of the Germans in Jerusalem. In addition, he gave them a house which once had belonged to king Baldwin, located in the Armenian Street near the church of St. Thomas, as well as a garden and six acres of land.[76] However, the Teutonic Knights did not move their seat from Acre to Jerusalem, as they seemingly had wished to do in 1198; they retained their headquarters in Acre, but built a new residence for the master at Montfort. After the Moslem recapture of Jerusalem in 1244, the Teutonic Knights again lost their possessions in the holy city, never to regain them.

It seems, however, that economically more important and profitable to the Teutonic Knights than their possessions in cities were the landed estates in the country, because from these holdings the order not only obtained part of the victuals and income for the support of the brothers, but frequently also established there convents or houses, and eventually built fortresses, thus contributing their share to the defense of the crusader states.

The first landed estates were obtained by Germans before the official founding of the order. Further donations and purchases of estates were for the most part located in three districts: around Acre, near Tyre, and between Sidon and Beirut. These last possessions, northeast of Sidon, were acquired by the order partly as donations, partly as purchases between 1257 and 1261 from the lord of Sidon, Julian Grenier, and were made up of a large land complex, called Souf or Schuf, which contained about one hundred manors; as part payment the order gave Julian of Sidon 23,000 crusader bezants.[77] In 1258 the order bought a manor from John de la Tour, the constable of Sidon, and from John of Schuf two more manors. In 1261 the order bought from Andrew of Schuf a fief called Schuf, which was made up of several manors;[78] all these possessions were located between Sidon and Beirut. In addition to all this, Julian Grenier of Sidon in 1257 donated to the order a fortress called the Cave of Tyron,[79] located about twelve miles east of Sidon. However, all these possessions were

76. *Ibid.*, no. 69: letter of confirmation of rights of Frederick II, April 1229. Prutz, *Die Besitzungen,* says that the king was Baldwin I.

77. *Ibid.*, nos. 108, 109, 111: letters of grant from January 1257; and no. 117: letter of grant from March 1261.

78. *Ibid.*, nos. 114, 115, 118: letters of confirmation of rights of Julian, lord of Sidon, March 20 and June 11, 1258, and March 1261.

79. *Ibid.*, no. 110: letter of grant of Julian, January 4, 1257.

lost to the Moslems in May 1263 after the victory of Baybars at Sidon. In the vicinity of Tyre the order held two acres of land at Sedinum from 1195 on, and later acquired more land and a house outside Tyre.

The order, however, possessed by far its greatest complex of landed estates in the region of Acre. It inherited from the German hospital in Acre two manors and two acres of land. Then, again partly from donations, partly by purchase, the order in 1200 acquired cultivated and unoccupied land, such as two manors north of Acre,[80] and in 1220 a complex of fiefs, again north of Acre, made up of forty-six manors.[81] In 1228 the order acquired another complex of fiefs, made up of fifteen manors and two parcels of wasteland; this complex of lands also included an old fortress called Montfort.[82] Northeast of this, in the vicinity of Toron and Chastel-Neuf, eight more manors were restored to the order in 1229.[83] The acquisition of land continued until 1261, when the order obtained from John II of Ibelin, lord of Beirut, three more manors north of Acre.[84] It seems that after this acquisition in 1261, the order acquired no more rural land; the last traceable acquisition was a house in Acre in 1273.[85] Besides all these mentioned localities, the order possessed many unspecified and, for the most part, unidentifiable parcels of land; it also possessed property in Cilician Armenia and Cyprus.[86] Of great significance were the order's possessions in Europe,[87] especially after the fall of Acre in 1291.

Little is known about the nature and exploitation of the order's landed estates, but a manor (*casale*) normally contained cultivated and unoccupied land (*gastina*), peasant families, mountains, valleys, plains, woods, waters, and pastures.[88] The manor was worked and

---

80. *Ibid.,* no. 38: letter of sale of Aimery, king of Jerusalem, October 1200.

81. *Ibid.,* nos. 53, 54, 58: letters of confirmation of rights of John of Brienne, regent of Jerusalem, Honorius III, and Frederick II, May and October 1220, and January 1226.

82. *Ibid.,* no. 63: letter of exchange of land of James of Amigdala, April 20, 1228; and no. 65: the emperor's confirmation of the exchange, April 1229.

83. *Ibid.,* no. 66: letter of restitution of rights, April 1229.

84. *Ibid.,* nos. 73, 77, 78, 79, 81, 82, 84, 87, 90, 100, 119, 121: letters of various lords to the Teutonic Knights, October 1230 to November 1261; cf. no. 128.

85. *Ibid.,* no. 126: agreement between the Teutonic Knights and the Dominicans in Acre, August 11, 1273.

86. *Ibid.,* nos. 46, 71, 83: letters of the kings of Armenia and Cyprus to the Teutonic Knights, April 1212, June 1229, and January 1236; cf. no. 128, pp. 126–127.

87. *Ibid.,* no. 128, pp. 127–128.

88. *Ibid.,* no. 77: letter of sale of Isabel of Bethsan and her husband Bertrand Porcelet, 1234; and no. 78: confirmation of the sale by Richard Filangieri, imperial bailie at Tyre. The description of the appurtenances of this manor is very similar to the usual description of manors in feudal charters.

tilled by local native peasants who were obliged to deliver to the order as dues in kind part of their produce: wheat, barley, oats, buckwheat, millet, chickpeas, lentils, beans, peas, figs, fruit from orchards, wine, oil, sugar, salt, honey, wax, cattle, sheep, goats, hens, eggs, cheese, and vegetables.[89] All these victuals are mentioned in the statutes of the order as needed for their table and in the infirmary (rule, par. 13; laws, III, par. 8). The order also could make use of its wooded hills to provide its own firewood and stakes.[90] Thus the Teutonic order in the Holy Land was not only a fighting force and a charitable organization but also a landlord, deeply involved in the economic exploitation of its landed possessions.

Moreover, besides being exempted from paying tolls, dues, and taxes and from offering obedience,[91] the order was allowed to levy its own dues, such as gate toll, chancery dues, measure dues,[92] the tithe,[93] and alms collection.[94] Raymond Roupen, lord of Antioch, in March 1219 granted the Teutonic Knights the right of free commerce in his principality,[95] and Bohemond IV, who succeeded Raymond in June 1228, donated to the order one hundred crusader bezants of income yearly from his share of the tolls at Acre.[96] Emperor Frederick II in April 1229 conceded to the Teutonic Knights 6,400 crusader bezants of annual income from the tolls at Acre,[97] and in July 1244

89. *Ibid.*, no. 112, pp. 92–93: agreement between the Teutonic Knights and Florent, archbishop of Acre, September 1257.

90. *Ibid.*, p. 93.

91. *Ibid.*, no. 30: in 1194 Henry II of Champagne exempted the German hospital at Acre, like the Knights Hospitaller and Knights Templar, from paying tolls in his kingdom on all victuals and garments purchased for their own use. The Teutonic Knights interpreted this privilege as a free trade license in the kingdom of Jerusalem; see no. 128; p. 125: "De libertate vendendi et emendi." No. 303, p. 273: in 1216 Honorius III forbade secular and ecclesiastical lords to request from the Teutonic Knights any oath of allegiance, homage, or oath of obedience, as well as other assurances demanded from secular persons. No. 305: in 1218 Honorius III reserved to himself the right to excommunicate the Teutonic order; see also no. 405. No. 306, pp. 277–278: in 1220 Honorius exempted the Teutonic Knights from episcopal jurisdiction. No. 319: in 1221 Honorius forbade the extortion of the tithe from those possessions of the Teutonic Knights which they themselves cultivated.

92. *Ibid.*, no. 112, p. 92.

93. *Ibid.*, no. 306, p. 277.

94. *Ibid.*, nos. 312, 314, 315, 331, 341, 367: bulls of Honorius III to the Teutonic Knights, January 15, 1221, to February 20, 1222.

95. *Ibid.*, no. 51: privilege to the Teutonic Knights.

96. *Ibid.*, no. 64: letter of grant; cf. no. 128, p. 125.

97. *Ibid.*, no. 68: privilege to the Teutonic Knights; cf. no. 128, p. 125. This amount of money was spent on the purchase of the complex of fiefs called Trefile, which included the fortress Montfort.

from James of Amigdala the order received 7,000 crusader bezants of yearly income from the harbor of Acre;[98] thus the order's income from tolls at Acre alone totaled some 13,400 crusader bezants yearly. Counting four grams of gold to a bezant, it comes to nearly 54 kilograms or 118 pounds of gold as annual income.[99]

Because of lack of information no one will ever know the economic value of the order's possessions and enterprises in the crusader states. However, the German historian Hans Prutz has imaginatively interpreted very limited information about the tithe the order paid to the bishops of Acre from the income of its lands and possessions in the diocese of Acre, which was under the order's own management.[100] According to the order's own estimate the tithe, for an uncertain period of time, was 24,000 crusader bezants.[101] Thus the full value of the income from the villages, manors, and properties and economic enterprises from the diocese of Acre alone was about 240,000 crusader bezants, or 960 kilograms or 2,112 pounds of gold. It should be kept in mind, however, that a large part of the order's possessions was cultivated by the native peasants, whose labor represented an additional income now impossible to estimate.

The legal base of the order's economic undertakings may be found in the second paragraph of the rule: "The brothers, on account of the great expenses arising from the needs of so many people and hospitals and of the knights and the sick and the poor, may possess, to be held in common in the name of the order and their chapters, movables and inheritances, land and fields, vineyards, mills, fortresses, villages, parishes, chapels, tithes, and such things as are granted in their privileges. They may also possess in perpetual right people, men and women, serfs, male and female."

The order's wealth and landed estates provided the financial and economic basis for the supplies to its army and fortifications. We know nothing more of its headquarters in Acre than the bare fact that it had there a church, a hospital, part of the city wall with the

---

98. *Ibid.*, no. 98: agreement between the Teutonic Knights and James of Amigdala, July 7, 1244; cf. no. 128, p. 125.

99. On crusader coins see Lavoix, *op. cit.*, Wegemann, *op. cit.*, and Friedrich von Schrötter, ed., *Wörterbuch der Münzkunde* (Berlin, 1930), *sub verbis* "bézant," "dinar," "saracenatus."

100. Prutz, *Besitzungen*, p. 66.

101. Strehlke, *Tabulae*, no. 112, p. 92.

adjoining rampart, and the conventual lodging.[102] To contribute their share to the defense system of the crusader states the Teutonic Knights acquired and rebuilt several strongholds in the vicinity of Acre, such as Judin, Castellum Regis,[103] and Montfort, which the Germans renamed Starkenberg. All three fortresses were located northeast of Acre, in a mountainous region.[104] About Judin we know nothing besides its name and location some three miles south of Montfort.[105] Castellum Regis, together with its appurtenances, the order bought in May 1220 from count Otto of Henneberg for 7,000 marks silver and 2,000 crusader bezants;[106] about the castle itself nothing is known. When the chronicler Burchard of Mount Sion visited the Holy Land after Baybars' attacks and his devastation of the district of Acre, he found Castellum Regis in the hands of the Saracens and castle Judin in ruins.[107]

Montfort lies about seven miles northeast of Acre in a mountainous region called Trefile, and was purchased by the Teutonic Knights on April 20, 1228, from James of Amigdala, together with the entire complex of fiefs, for 6,400 crusader bezants (25.6 kilograms or 56.3 pounds of gold), which were given to the order by emperor Frederick II from his income from the tolls in the harbor of Acre. This purchase was confirmed by the emperor in April 1229 at his palace at Acre.[108] The Teutonic Knights called Montfort the new castle, indicating that there was already an old castle of which the Teutonic Knights took possession in 1229, immediately beginning its reconstruction and expansion. The rebuilding of Montfort was permitted by the peace treaty between Frederick II and sultan al-Kāmil, concluded on February 18, 1229.

The fortress was halfway between Acre and Tyre, on a wooded hill between the branches of the brook Wādī Kurn; being some six

---

102. Burchard of Mount Sion, tr. Stewart (*PPTS*, XII-1), p. 9; Ludolph of Suchem, tr. Stewart, p. 53. For Ludolph see Wolfgang Stammler and Karl Langosch, eds., *Die Deutsche Literatur des Mittelalters: Verfasserlexicon* (5 vols., Berlin and Leipzig, 1933-1955), III, 85-86.

103. Burchard of Mount Sion, *op. cit.,* p. 26; Marino Sanudo, *Secrets for True Crusaders to Help Them to Recover the Holy Land,* part XIV of book III, tr. Stewart (*PPTS,* XII-2), p. 24.

104. Marino Sanudo, tr. Stewart, p. 35.

105. Hubatsch, "Montfort," p. 197.

106. Strehlke, *Tabulae,* nos. 53, 54: letters of confirmation of sale of John of Brienne and Honorius III, May and October 1220; nos. 58, 59: letters of confirmation of possession of the Teutonic Knights by Frederick II and his wife Isabel, January 1226.

107. Burchard of Mount Sion, tr. Stewart, p. 26.

108. Strehlke, *Tabulae,* nos. 63, 65: letter of exchange of land of James of Amigdala, April 20, 1228, and the emperor's confirmation of it, April 1229; cf. no. 128, p. 125.

hundred feet above the brook level, it was difficult of access. Located close to Saracen territory, it was regarded by the knights, the papacy, and the westerners as a good stronghold against Moslem invasion of Christian territory. To obtain funds for rebuilding and fortifying the old castle the master, Hermann of Salza, asked the pope for financial support, and in July 1230 Gregory IX published an indulgence for ten years of a yearly remission of the seventh part of penitence to Christians who contributed money for rebuilding Montfort.[109] By 1240 the castle was already occupied and had a castellan, and by 1244 the reconstruction of the fortress was far enough advanced to permit the moving of the seat of the master to Montfort.[110] (Master Gerard of Malberg resigned his office at Montfort in 1244.)[111] To complete the rebuilding of Montfort pope Innocent IV in September 1245 granted a new indulgence of forty days to all Christians who contributed funds for this purpose.[112] As early as 1266 Montfort was attacked by sultan Baybars, but the fortress was not taken.[113]

In 1271 Baybars renewed his offensive against Christian possessions in the crusader states; after capturing the Templar castle Chastel-Blanc in February and the mighty Hospitaller fortresses Krak des Chevaliers and 'Akkār in May, he marched southward and in early June laid siege to Montfort. On June 11 Baybars took the suburb and on June 18 the bastion, and then the Saracen soldiers began to make breaches in the wall of the fortress. Baybars promised 1,000 dirhems for each stone the soldiers removed from the wall. As the battle for the fortress advanced, messengers appeared from the castle, sent by the Teutonic Knights to negotiate terms of surrender. The sultan allowed the garrison of Montfort a safe conduct to Acre, but the knights were not allowed to take with them any possessions or arms. After the German withdrawal the sultan's standard was raised on the fortress. Later Baybars ordered the destruction of Montfort; its demolition was completed by July 4, 1271.[114] Such was the inglorious end of the mightiest German fortress in the Holy Land. Since Baybars' destruction the castle has never been occupied or rebuilt. Burchard

109. *Ibid.*, no. 72: encyclical of Gregory IX, July 10, 1230.

110. *Ibid.*, no. 89: agreement between the Teutonic Knights and the Knights Hospitaller about the income from the manor Arabia, 1240; and no. 99: letter of grant of James of Amigdala, July 7, 1244.

111. *Ibid.*, no. 486: bull of Innocent IV, January 16, 1245.

112. Ibn-al-Furāt, *Ta'rīkh,* tr. Forstreuter, p. 232.

113. Röhricht, *Geschichte,* p. 930; *L'Estoire de Eracles (RHC, Occ.,* II), p. 454, note f.

114. Ibn-al-Furāt, *Ta'rīkh,* as quoted in Forstreuter, pp. 232–233.

of Mount Sion, who saw the fortress after its destruction, could only sadly testify to its utter ruin.[115]

Western travelers and scholars of later centuries have visited Montfort and left several descriptions of the ruins of the fortress. According to the most reliable of these descriptions,[116] Montfort lies 590 feet above sea level at the confluence of two streams on a rather narrow ridge, which restricted the shape of the castle's layout. The stone castle was about 350 feet long, 80 feet wide, and probably three stories or approximately 90 feet high, with a large convent hall, a chapel, dormitories, rooms for the household, and a partial basement. The castle was surrounded by a wall about 1,500 feet long, with an independent detached donjon within the walls. Water was supplied to the castle from cisterns. At the bottom of the hill lay the ruins of another building complex, which have been variously identified as a mill, as a church, and as an infirmary or hospital.[117]

115. Burchard of Mount Sion, tr. Stewart, p. 21. The Moslem geographer ad-Dimashqī (1256–1327) visited Montfort about 1300 and wrote a brief description of it in his cosmography, cited in the bibliographical note, above. The paragraph relative to Montfort (tr. Le Strange, p. 495): "A fine castle on a hill and well fortified. In its lands is Al Kurain (Montfort), an impregnable castle lying between the two hills, and this was a frontier fortress of the Franks. It was taken by Sultan Baybars. There lies near it a valley most pleasant and celebrated among all the valleys, for its musk-pears, the like of which are found nowhere else for exquisiteness of perfume and excellence of flavour. There are also grown here citrons of such a size that a single fruit weighs 6 Damascus Ratls (or about 18 lbs.)."

116. Bashford Dean, op. cit., passim; Hubatsch, "Montfort," pp. 186–199.

117. Hubatsch, "Montfort," pp. 188–196; Forstreuter, Deutsche Orden, p. 44.

B. Deeds of the Order and its Masters

About the first three masters of the Teutonic Knights nothing definite is known. We are not even sure of their correct names, as some sources call the first master Hermann Walpot, others Henry. Walpot died on November 5, before 1208, for by September 1208 the master was Otto of Kerpen; he died on February 7, 1209. In 1209 the new master was a certain Bart, who, like Walpot, is called "Henry" in some sources, "Hermann" in others; he died on June 3, presumably in 1210.[118]

The fourth master was Hermann of Salza (1210?–March 20, 1239). It is not known when he was born nor when he was elected master, but it was probably in 1210, for in October of that year a master Hermann was present in Acre, with other dignitaries of the crusader states, at the coronation of John of Brienne as king of Jerusalem.[119] In contemporary documents Hermann is mentioned as the master for the first time on February 14, 1211.[120] Hermann was a son of a family of the lower gentry whose members served the landgraves of Thuringia. Because of his devotion, energy, and talent, Hermann became not only the most famous master of the Teutonic Knights, but also a confidant, counselor, and agent of emperor Frederick II. He was a gifted diplomat and the founder of the order's state in Prussia.[121] His early years as the master, until 1215, were probably spent in the Near East.[122]

In 1211 the Teutonic Knights made their first appearance in Transyl-

---

118. On the first three masters see Perlbach, "Necrologe," *passim;* Peter of Dusburg, in *SSRP,* I, 29–30. For a fourteenth-century list of the masters see *Canonici Sambiensis annales,* ed. Wilhelm F. Arndt (*MGH, SS.,* XIX), pp. 701–702. For modern accounts of the masters see Schreiber, *op. cit.,* pp. 647–651, and Tumler, *op. cit.,* pp. 30–33.

119. *Estoire de Eracles,* XXXI, 1; a brother Hermann, master of the Teutonic Knights, is mentioned in 1209 (*ibid.,* XXX, 16), but it is impossible to establish whether this was Hermann Bart or Hermann of Salza; see Perlbach, "Necrologe," *passim;* Peter of Dusburg, *SSRP,* I, 30–32; Schreiber, *op. cit.,* pp. 651–653.

120. Strehlke, *Tabulae,* no. 45: patriarch Albert of Jerusalem's letter of arbitration between Martin Rozia and Hermann of Salza, February 14, 1211.

121. Heimpel, "Hermann von Salza," *Die grossen Deutschen,* I, 171–186; Tumler, *op. cit.,* pp. 33–42; Hubatsch, "Montfort," pp. 177–184; *Altpreussische Biographie, sub nomine.*

122. Strehlke, *Tabulae,* no. 45 (see above, note 120) and no. 48; Böhmer, *Regesta imperii,* no. 15047: Matilda of Schwarzenberg's letter to the Teutonic Knights, April 9, 1215.

vania; they were called in by king Andrew II of Hungary to fight the Kumans there, and received from the king as their base a district called Burzenland, a stretch of land between Transylvania and Wallachia.[123] In the next two years the order obtained from Andrew the privilege of using its own coinage in Transylvania and also received the castle of Kreuzburg.[124]

In 1216 Hermann of Salza appeared in the west: in December, he was in Nuremberg at the court of Frederick II; because of Hermann's piety and honesty, the emperor bestowed upon the Teutonic Knights a house and other income in Brindisi in southern Italy.[125] It is not known under what circumstances these two men first met, or how Hermann attracted Frederick's attention, but once their mutual trust was established they remained friends for life. From this time on Hermann was a member of the emperor's court; he accompanied Frederick on his journeys, and traveled as his emissary throughout the Hohenstaufen empire.[126] Only seldom and on special occasions did he return to the Holy Land.

In 1217 Hermann returned from Germany to Palestine to lead his order in the Fifth Crusade. In October Hermann, together with the brothers Peter and Garin of Montaigu, masters respectively of the Knights Templar and Knights Hospitaller, and other dignitaries and leaders of the crusade, took part in a council of war in Acre, over which Andrew II, the king of Hungary, presided.[127] The leaders of the crusade had selected the Templar castle Château Pèlerin as their place of assembly. Therefore in the spring of 1218 the Templars, aided by the Teutonic Knights, fortified that castle.[128]

In May 1218 Hermann and his knights arrived at Château Pèlerin to embark for Egypt; they landed off Damietta on May 30.[129] They participated in the siege of Damietta, and in February 1219 they occupied the abandoned Moslem camp on the west bank of the Nile.[130] On July 31 the Teutonic Knights went to the rescue of the Templar

123. Zimmermann and Werner, *Urkundenbuch*, no. 19, and Strehlke, *Tabulae*, no. 158: feudal charter of Andrew II to the Teutonic Knights, May 1211; Peter of Dusburg, *SSRP*, I, 31.

124. Zimmermann and Werner, *Urkundenbuch*, no. 22, and Strehlke, *Tabulae*, nos. 159, 160: feudal charters of Andrew II, 1212.

125. Böhmer, *Regesta*, nos. 887, 888: feudal charters of Frederick II, December 1216.

126. Lorck, *Hermann von Salza, passim*.

127. *Estoire de Eracles*, XXXI, 10; Böhmer, *Regesta imperii*, V, no. 15049a.

128. *Estoire de Eracles*, XXXI, 13; Matthew Paris, *Chronica majora*, ed. Luard, III, 14; Oliver, ed. Hoogeweg, cap. 11.

129. *Estoire de Eracles*, XXXI, 13; Matthew Paris, *Chronica majora*, III, 35; Oliver, ed. Hoogeweg, cap. 10.

130. Böhmer, *Regesta imperii*, V, no. 10824: letter to Frederick II, June 15, 1218; and *MGH, Epistolae saeculi XIII*, I, no. 77: papal transcript of this letter; *Estoire de Eracles*, XXXII, 8.

camp, which was being heavily attacked by the Saracens. On August 29 they participated in a battle against the Moslems and, like the other two military religious orders, suffered heavy losses: the Teutonic order lost thirty knights.[131] Sultan al-Kāmil then offered the Christians the return of Moslem-occupied territory in the kingdom of Jerusalem, and the return of the Holy Cross and the Christian captives who were in his hands, in exchange for a complete Christian withdrawal from Egypt. To consider this proposal the Christian leaders at Damietta convened in a council; the Teutonic Knights, John of Brienne, the regent of Jerusalem, and some of the prelates were in favor of accepting this proposal, whereas the Knights Templar, the Knights Hospitaller, the Italians, and many other prelates successfully opposed it.[132] After the Egyptian garrison abandoned Damietta on November 5, 1219, Hermann, together with other dignitaries, on November 11 sent to pope Honorius III a report on the capture of Damietta by the crusaders and on the planned advance toward Cairo.[133] Hermann also wrote a letter to Leo, cardinal-priest of Santa Croce, complaining about the plundering and pillaging of the captured city by the Christians.[134] In March 1220 the Teutonic Knights were forced to turn over to John of Brienne half of the order's spoils taken at Damietta.[135] By May 30 Hermann was back in Acre, leaving his knights in Damietta, where they were attacked by the Saracens and lost a ship with a supply of barley.[136]

Meanwhile Hermann himself had proceeded from the Holy Land to Italy, where in October he was acting as Frederick II's messenger to the pope, and on November 25 we find the master in the emperor's entourage, near Rome.[137] Since that was only three days after the coronation of the emperor by Honorius III, one must assume that Hermann was present at the ceremony.[138] He had probably conveyed

131. Oliver, ed. Hoogeweg, caps. 27, 29; Matthew Paris, *Chronica majora,* III, 48–50.

132. *Estoire de Eracles,* XXXII, 11.

133. Böhmer, *Regesta imperii,* V, no. 10845; Röhricht, *Regesta,* no. 925.

134. Böhmer, *Regesta imperii,* V, no. 10848; Röhricht, *Regesta,* no. 926; for the pillaging of Damietta see Oliver, ed. Hoogeweg, cap. 48.

135. Böhmer, *Regesta imperii,* V, no. 10856, and Röhricht, *Regesta,* no. 930: open letter of John of Brienne, March 1220.

136. Strehlke, *Tabulae,* no. 52: letter of sale of Otto, count of Henneberg, May 30, 1220; Oliver, ed. Hoogeweg, caps. 48–49.

137. *Estoire de Eracles,* XXXII, 17, and Böhmer, *Regesta imperii,* V, no. 1180: letter of Frederick II to Honorius III, October 4, 1220; nos. 1224, 1228: Frederick II's proclamations, November 25, 1220.

138. Some indirect indication of Hermann's presence at the coronation can be traced to Frederick's letter of confirmation of privileges to the Teutonic Knights, December 1221, in Huillard-Bréholles, *Historia,* II, 224–225.

a message to the pope in October regarding the proposed crowning. In April 1221 at Taranto Hermann secured from Frederick II several privileges for the Teutonic Knights, the most important being the right to voyage freely between Calabria and Sicily, exemption from taxes and customs, free use of waters, pastures, and woods, the right to receive fiefs within the empire, and the donation of a hospital at Palermo.[139]

Hermann was not only a crusader and a friend of the emperor; he was also the head of the Teutonic order, and he never missed an opportunity to secure from the Roman curia new privileges for his brothers. While on crusade he had asked the emperor to intercede with the pope to help him to obtain for his order the same status that the two other military religious orders, the Knights Templar and the Knights Hospitaller, enjoyed, as well as papal permission to wear the white mantle. On his coronation day Frederick II approached Honorius III on this matter and received a sympathetic hearing.[140] On January 9, 1221, the pope in two separate bulls granted Hermann and his brothers the right to wear, as the Templars did, the white mantle, and also granted the Teutonic Knights the same immunity as the Knights Templar and Knights Hospitaller had.[141] In order to provide means for the Teutonic Knights to procure white mantles, the emperor in December 1221 provided the order with 200 ounces of gold in yearly income from the town of Brindisi.[142]

Hermann, once having won the goodwill of Honorius III, continued to strike while the iron was hot: during his month-long sojourn at the papal court in the Lateran palace from January 9 until February 9 Hermann secured from the Roman pontiff no less than fifty-four separate bulls confirming existing privileges and granting new exemptions to the Teutonic order.[143] Hermann had secured the benevolence and protection of the two most powerful men in western Christendom. He remained a trusted friend and a valued servant both to the emperor and to the papacy for the rest of his life.

In July 1221 Hermann was back in Egypt,[144] where he participated in the negotiations between the Christians and the Moslems for the return of Damietta to al-Kāmil, and was delivered, together with the masters of the Templars and Hospitallers, as a hostage to the sultan

139. *Ibid.,* II, 156–166: letters of Frederick II to the Teutonic Knights, April 1221; and 226–228: Frederick's confirmation of privileges to the same, December 1221.
140. *Ibid.,* II, 224.
141. Strehlke, *Tabulae,* nos. 308–309: bulls of Honorius III, January 9, 1221.
142. Huillard-Bréholles, *loc. cit.*
143. Strehlke, *Tabulae,* nos. 308–362.
144. Oliver, ed. Hoogeweg, cap. 57.

to ensure the surrender of Damietta to the Moslems according to the provisions of the treaty.[145] On September 8, 1221, Hermann and the master of the Templars, as representatives of the Christian army in Egypt, surrendered Damietta to the Saracens.[146]

By February 5, 1222, Hermann was back in Italy to report directly to the pope and the emperor on the failure of the Fifth Crusade. On the same day he obtained from Frederick II for the order the church of St. Thomas at Barletta,[147] where seventeen years later his body was buried in the order's chapel; today no trace of his tomb is to be found.

By 1222 the order had made good headway in Transylvania: it had built several strong stone castles, had gained more land, and had begun to colonize the acquired territory with settlers from Germany. Thus the order had begun to build its own state in Transylvania, in territory which was part of the Hungarian kingdom, presumably with the consent of Andrew II.[148] But the Teutonic Knights in that country not only increased their power and grip on their possessions; they also began to treat the Hungarian nobility and clergy with indignity. There is no evidence of the part Hermann played in shaping the order's local policy in Transylvania, but anti-Teutonic sentiment in Hungary was increasing. When pope Honorius III in 1224 issued a bull which informed the Hungarian bishops that he was taking the order's possessions in Transylvania under papal protection and was exempting the order's lands from local episcopal jurisdiction,[149] it was evident that the publication of the bull was the result of Hermann's diplomacy. This bull also revealed the political goals of the Teutonic Knights in Transylvania: with papal support the master wanted to establish a German mission state, independent of the king of Hungary, between the Hungarians and their eastern neighbors, the Kumans, thus converting the Transylvanian branch of his order into a state of the order.

In the winter of 1224–1225 the resentful Hungarian nobility, led by king Andrew II, attacked the Teutonic Knights and expelled them from Transylvania. Hermann returned to Italy in the early spring of 1225, and probably approached Honorius III with a complaint about

---

145. *Ibid.,* cap. 79.

146. *Ibid.,* cap. 81; Huillard-Bréholles, *Historia,* III, 41: Frederick II's open letter, December 8, 1227.

147. *Estoire de Eracles,* XXXII, 29; Böhmer, *Regesta imperii,* V, no. 1372: feudal charter of Frederick II.

148. Zimmermann and Werner, *Urkundenbuch,* no. 31, and Strehlke, *Tabulae,* no. 163: feudal charter to the Teutonic Knights, 1222.

149. Zimmermann and Werner, *Urkundenbuch,* nos. 40–41, and Strehlke, *Tabulae,* nos. 164–165: bulls of Honorius III, April 30, 1224.

the expulsion, for in June the pope asked Andrew for the restitution of the possessions and privileges of the Teutonic Knights in Transylvania. The Hungarians paid no heed:[150] Transylvania was lost to the Teutonic Knights forever.

Late in 1225 Frederick II married Isabel of Brienne, princess of Jerusalem, and became regent of the kingdom; Hermann of Salza was present at the wedding ceremony.[151] Hermann used this occasion to obtain new favors for his order from the newlyweds: in January 1226 Frederick, because of Hermann's faithful service, took under his special protection the order, its brethren, and all their possessions in the kingdom of Jerusalem; Isabel in a separate document affirmed that the emperor had acted with her consent.[152]

The loss of Transylvania by the Teutonic Knights in 1225 was compensated for by an offer in the same year from Conrad, the Polish duke of Masovia, who sent a delegation to the master in Italy asking the order to undertake a crusade against the pagan Prussians. During the pontificate of Innocent III, a Cistercian monk named Christian had been appointed bishop to the Prussians, and energetically begun to spread the word of God among the Prussian tribes. In 1221 Christian even organized a crusade against the Prussians in which several Polish dukes and bishops participated. But in 1224 the Prussians destroyed Christian's mission, attacked their eastern Polish neighbors, and devastated the borderland between Prussian and Polish territory. In order to check Prussian attacks and save his own land from further destruction, Conrad of Masovia solicited the aid of the Teutonic Knights. Whether there was any connection between the expulsion of the German knights from Transylvania and their invitation to Prussia is difficult to establish, but such a request suited Hermann's goals. He neither refused it nor accepted it outright, but, being a shrewd politician and farsighted diplomat, sought the emperor's support and protection for such an intervention.

Consequently, Frederick II in March 1226 at Rimini issued one of the most important imperial edicts concerning the Teutonic Knights: this edict, usually called the Golden Bull of Rimini, not only opened the door for German colonization of Prussia, but also legalized the founding of the order's state in the conquered territory. From this

---

150. Zimmermann and Werner, *Urkundenbuch,* nos. 44–49, 51, 53–55, 59, 61, 68: papal bulls, June 10, 1225, to October 11, 1234.

151. *Estoire de Eracles,* XXXII, 20.

152. Strehlke, *Tabulae,* nos. 58, 59, and Böhmer, *Regesta imperii,* V, nos. 1590, 1591: imperial privileges to the Teutonic Knights.

edict we also learn that in return for the requested help, Conrad was compelled to cede to the Teutonic Knights a border district between Prussia and Masovia called Kulm, and another unnamed territory. Furthermore, Hermann secured from Conrad his consent in advance for the Teutonic Knights to keep any territory they conquered from the Prussians; it was easy for Conrad to give away territory that was not part of his domain. To confirm the agreement, Frederick in his edict solemnly announced: "We concede and confirm to this master, his successors, and his house in perpetuity the above-mentioned land [Kulm] which he will receive, as promised by the aforenamed duke, and in addition, land that may be given to him [in the future], as well as the whole of territory which he, with God's help, will conquer in Prussia."[153] Hermann did not depart for Prussia but sent one of his knights, Conrad of Landsberg, to Masovia to investigate conditions there; Hermann was needed at the court of Frederick II to help him to prepare for the long-delayed crusade.

Honorius III died on March 18, 1227, while Hermann was still in Germany, and the new pope, Gregory IX, in April supported Hermann's mission in Germany by repeating his predecessor's plea to the Germans.[154] In June Hermann was back in Italy and was sent by the emperor to Gregory,[155] probably to introduce himself to the new pope and to discuss matters relative to the crusade. Finally, in August 1227, the main body of the crusade of Frederick II sailed from Brindisi to the Holy Land, and the emperor followed on September 8, accompanied by the leader of the German contingent, landgrave Louis of Thuringia. But the landgrave, stricken by plague, died shortly after leaving Brindisi, and the emperor, also ill, on the advice of his companions disembarked at Otranto to recover from his illness. However, the emperor's flotilla of twenty ships, under the command of duke Henry of Limburg, Gerald, patriarch of Jerusalem, and Hermann of Salza, in mid-September continued its voyage to the east.[156] From Otranto Frederick sent envoys to Gregory at Anagni to inform him of the new delay, but the pope, placing no credence in Frederick's story, excommunicated him on September 29.

After stopping at Cyprus the flotilla, with Hermann aboard, arrived in the Holy Land, probably in October 1227.[157] Frederick, still

153. Hubatsch, *Quellen,* no. 5: privilege to the Teutonic Knights, March 1226.
154. *MGH, Epistolae saeculi XIII,* I, nos. 351–354, and Böhmer, *Regesta imperii,* V, no. 6685: papal letters to the emperor and various German princes, April 16, 1227.
155. Richard of San Germano, *Chronica,* p. 347.
156. Huillard-Bréholles, *Historia,* III, 44: open letter of Frederick II, December 8, 1227.
157. Matthew Paris, *Chronica majora,* III, 128.

under papal excommunication, landed at Acre on September 7, 1228, a year after his first embarkation at Brindisi. In Acre the emperor was met by many local dignitaries, including the masters of the Templars, the Hospitallers, and the Teutonic Knights. However, it soon became apparent that because of the papal ban, many of the leaders hesitated to support Frederick and his plans for the crusader states; only the Teutonic Knights, the Genoese, and the Pisans stood by the emperor.[158]

Hermann of Salza met Frederick at Acre and accompanied him during his stay in the Holy Land, acting as his counselor and emissary. When the emperor moved to Jaffa in mid-November, Hermann was with him and remained with him until he left the city in mid-March 1229. During this time Frederick conducted negotiations with sultan al-Kāmil for the return of the holy city to the Christians, and though it appears that Hermann had no active role in the negotiations, his opinion was sought by the emperor. Hermann, together with the masters of the other two orders (Peter of Montaigu and Bertrand of Thessy) and the English bishops, advised the emperor to obtain consent for such a treaty from the patriarch of Jerusalem, Gerald, an unyielding supporter of Gregory IX and the leader of the anti-imperial party in the Holy Land, but Frederick disdained the advice. The agreement between the emperor and the sultan was concluded on February 18, and Hermann, with Thomas, count of Acerra, and Balian, lord of Sidon, was dispatched by Frederick to al-Kāmil to secure his oath to the treaty. After receiving al-Kāmil's oath, the latter two departed for the court of an-Nāṣir Dā'ūd, the ruler of Damascus, to obtain his support for the treaty, while Hermann was sent to patriarch Gerald to procure his consent, as well as to ask the patriarch to participate in Frederick's solemn entry into the holy city. Hermann's eloquence failed to persuade the patriarch, and consequently Frederick decided to effect his entrance into Jerusalem without Gerald.

On March 17, 1229, Frederick entered the holy city, and the master of the Teutonic Knights and many of the crusaders accompanied the emperor. The Knights Templar and the Knights Hospitaller, however, obeyed the ban by the patriarch against associating with the emperor as an excommunicate and outlaw of the Roman church.[159] Next day in the church of the Holy Sepulcher Frederick—Hermann again being present—crowned himself king of Jerusalem, and afterward read to the congregation, probably in Italian, a manifesto about his cru-

158. *Ibid.,* III, 160; Böhmer, *Regesta imperii,* V, no. 1732x: description of Frederick II's landing at Acre, September 7, 1228.
159. *Estoire de Eracles,* XXXIII, 5–7.

sade, which the master of the Teutonic Knights was asked to render in Latin and German.[160] After the coronation ceremonies, Hermann advised the emperor to request Templar and Hospitaller support for the rebuilding of the fortifications of Jerusalem; on behalf of the emperor Hermann then made such requests to the masters of the two orders. But they hesitated to promise their support, and Frederick, angered by their reluctance, departed the following day for Jaffa; on March 22 the emperor, accompanied by the Teutonic Knights, entered Acre. Frederick rewarded the service of Hermann and his knights rather generously: he granted the order 6,400 crusader bezants in yearly income from the revenues of the harbor of Acre, for a period of four years.

The Teutonic Knights served Frederick well, not only in the Holy Land, but also at home in Italy. On March 7, 1229, a Teutonic Knight named Leonard had brought to the emperor at Jaffa news from Italy about the invasion of Apulia by papal troops. Perhaps he had also brought Frederick the letter from Thomas, the count of Acerra, warning him of the dangers of papal animosity and describing the speedy progress of the army led by John of Brienne in southern Italy.[161] On May 1, 1229, Frederick left Acre for Italy, accompanied by Hermann of Salza. After stopping at Cyprus, Frederick landed in Brindisi on June 10, and shortly afterward sent Hermann, together with other members of the order, as emissaries to Gregory IX to negotiate peace.[162] The negotiations progressed rather slowly, and Hermann had to make several missions to the curia; during these peace overtures Hermann was the chief negotiator, though he was always accompanied by ecclesiastical and lay dignitaries, including cardinals, archbishops, and a delegation of German princes.

Finally on July 23 at San Germano the emperor took an oath to atone for all matters over which he had been excommunicated. On August 28, 1230, he was absolved by two papal emissaries, John Halgrin, cardinal-bishop of Sabina, and Thomas of Capua, cardinal-priest of St. Sabina.[163] On September 1 the emperor was received with great pomp by Gregory in Anagni, where the former adversaries had a long

---

160. Huillard-Bréholles, *Historia,* III, 100; according to Hermann of Salza's account: "verba sua ipsis latine et theutonice exponeremus"; according to patriarch Gerald's account (*ibid.,* III, 109): "primo in theutonico et postea in gallico ad nobiles et populum inchoavit."

161. Böhmer, *Regesta imperii,* V, no. 1736a; Huillard-Bréholles, *Historia,* III, 110–112: Thomas of Capua's letter, February or March 1229.

162. Böhmer, *Regesta imperii,* V, nos. 1753a, 1755b; Richard of San Germano, *Chronica,* pp. 353, 355.

163. Richard of San Germano, *Chronica,* pp. 359–362; see also Böhmer, *Regesta imperii,* V, no. 6805b; Huillard-Bréholles, *Historia,* III, 227: Frederick II's encyclical, September 1230.

private conversation in the papal chamber, with only the master of the Teutonic Knights present. The next day Frederick returned to his camp outside Anagni, and Hermann went with him.[164]

Hermann, while striving after peace, did not forget the interests of his own order: in May 1230 the emperor confirmed a gift to the Teutonic Knights of several possessions in Apulia, while Gregory on January 18, at Hermann's request, confirmed to the order those grants of castles and territories which had been made by Conrad, duke of Masovia in 1228, and urged the Teutonic Knights to undertake a crusade against the heathen Prussians. On August 27, 1230, the pope repeated this confirmation.[165] But Hermann's role in rehabilitating the emperor was not over yet. Frederick had crowned himself king of Jerusalem, but Gregory had not recognized his title. Hermann continued to carry on negotiations between the pope and the emperor until the pope finally recognized Frederick's title in August 1231.[166] The grateful emperor in September granted the Teutonic Knights more possessions in Italy: "In view of the unfailing faithfulness and praiseworthy devotion of brother Hermann, the venerable master of the German House of the Hospital of St. Mary, and of his convent, our faithful supporters . . . and in view of the service offered and received, which the master and convent have fully rendered to our Majesty, both in the kingdom [of Sicily] and overseas, unstintingly render now, and . . . may render in the future, out of our natural generosity, and in gratitude, by which we are used to provide for our good servants and followers, we grant and concede [certain specified pieces of land] . . ."[167]

In 1233, upon the insistence of the people of the kingdom of Jerusalem, Hermann was sent to the Holy Land by the emperor as his representative to negotiate a reconciliation between the imperial and the papal parties in Acre. In 1234 an agreement was reached and the pope and the emperor approved it and urged the barons and the bishops in the Holy Land to respect it. In July 1234 Hermann was back in Italy and remained with the imperial entourage.[168]

---

164. Richard of San Germano, *Chronica*, p. 362.

165. Huillard-Bréholles, *Historia*, III, 195–196: Frederick II's letter to the Teutonic Knights, May 1230; *MGH, Epistolae saeculi XIII*, I, no. 411, and Böhmer, *Regesta imperii*, V, no. 6801: bull of Gregory IX, January 1230; Joachim and Hubatsch, *Regesta*, II, no. 49: bull of Gregory IX to the Teutonic Knights, August 27, 1230.

166. Huillard-Bréholles, *Historia*, III, 298–299: letter of Gregory IX to Frederick II, August 12, 1231.

167. *Ibid.*, III, 303: letter of Frederick II to the Teutonic Knights, September 1231.

168. *Estoire de Eracles*, XXXIII, 40; Huillard-Bréholles, *Historia*, IV, 481–483; *MGH, Epistulae saeculi XIII*, I, nos. 578, 594; and Böhmer, *Regesta imperii*, V, nos. 7017, 7036: letters

Frederick's second wife, Isabel of Brienne, had died in 1228 after giving birth to a son, Conrad (IV). In 1235 Frederick was contemplating his third marriage, this time to Isabel Plantagenet, daughter of king John and sister to Henry III of England. According to Matthew Paris, Frederick sent two Teutonic Knights with an entourage to Henry with a letter requesting Isabel's hand. The messengers arrived at Westminster on February 23; four days later they were given Henry's favorable reply. What Hermann's role in the marriage arrangements were, we do not know, but the king of England in late April asked the master to intervene on his behalf at the papal and imperial courts.[169] Meanwhile Frederick was preoccupied with another problem, the independent polity of his son Henry (VII) in Germany. To bring him to obedience and to celebrate his wedding with Isabel, Frederick left Italy for Germany. Hermann accompanied him, and persuaded Henry to submit to his father. Frederick took his son captive at Worms on July 4,[170] and on July 15 in the same old imperial city married Isabel Plantagenet.

At Viterbo, while vainly awaiting Lombard negotiators, Hermann in the presence of the pope succeeded early in 1236 in concluding an agreement with the representatives of the citizens of Acre which restored to Frederick and Conrad, his son by Isabel of Brienne, all their rights and privileges in the Holy Land.[171]

Hartmann of Heldrungen, a Teutonic Knight and future master of the order, reports[172] that for six years the master of the order of the Swordbearers, Volquin, had been asking Hermann of Salza to agree to the incorporation of the Swordbearers into the Teutonic Knights. After long hesitation, Hermann finally in 1235 dispatched two brothers to Livonia to investigate conditions there. They returned to Germany in 1236, when Hermann was in Italy. Hermann's deputy in Germany, Louis of Öttingen, convoked a chapter of seventy brothers at Marburg to whom the emissaries reported their conclusions

---

of Gregory IX to the prelates and barons of the kingdom of Jerusalem, March 22 and August 8, 1234; Huillard-Bréholles, *Historia,* IV, 479–481, and Böhmer, *Regesta imperii,* V, no. 2051: letter of Frederick II to the same, August 1234; *ibid.,* V, no. 14722: letter of confirmation of Frederick II, July 1234.

169. Matthew Paris, *Chronica majora,* III, 318; Böhmer, *Regesta imperii,* V, no. 11157: letter of Henry III of England to Frederick II, April 27, 1235.

170. Böhmer, *Regesta imperii,* V, nos. 2090, 2092, 2096–2097: letters of Frederick II to various lords, May to June 22, 1235; nos. 4383a, 4383b: reports in contemporary chronicles on the proceedings at Worms, June 1235; Richard of San Germano, *Chronica,* p. 373.

171. *MGH, Epistolae saeculi XIII,* I, no. 674, and Böhmer, *Regesta imperii,* V, no. 7123: letter of Gregory IX to Frederick II, February 21, 1236; see also *MGH, op. cit.,* I, no. 673: letter of Gregory IX to the Teutonic Knights in Acre, February 19, 1236.

172. "Hartmanns von Heldrungen Bericht," ed. Hirsch, *SSRP,* V, 168–172.

about conditions in Livonia. Since the chapter could not reach a consensus, it decided to refer the matter to the master, and Hermann, after returning from Italy, received in Vienna, perhaps in January 1237, a delegation which included Hartmann and Louis. After consultation with this delegation, Hermann decided to receive the brethren of the order of the Swordbearers into the Teutonic order.

To obtain papal sanction for his decision, Hermann "himself rode to the Roman curia," evidently in March 1237, accompanied by Hartmann and a representative of the order of the Swordbearers. They found the pope at Viterbo, but while the delegation was awaiting the papal decision, another messenger from the Swordbearers arrived to inform the pope that the master of the Swordbearers had been killed in a battle with the heathen natives, together with sixty members of that order; thus the order was practically annihilated. The pope again was pressed for his consent to the incorporation of the Swordbearers into the Teutonic order, and finally on May 12, 1237, Gregory agreed to this.[173] The act of incorporation was solemnly performed in the presence of the pope: the representatives of the Swordbearers knelt before Gregory; he addressed them, and they then took off their white mantles with the red sword and star of the Swordbearers and put on white mantles with the black cross of the Teutonic Knights; a brother of the Teutonic Knights, Conrad of Strassburg, served as papal marshal. After the act of incorporation, Hermann asked his companions in their quarters: "Tell me, brothers, what have we gained in castles and land?" and Hartmann responded that Livonia was a rich country.

Hermann's decision about the Swordbearers in Livonia became the cornerstone on which was founded the expansion of the Teutonic order in that remote northeastern corner of Europe. Later, after the loss of Acre and the expulsion of the Teutonic order from the Holy Land in 1291, both of Hermann's decisions—to participate in the conquest of Prussia in 1226 and to incorporate the Swordbearers in Livonia into the order in 1237—proved so wise and advantageous that the possession of these two countries not only justified the continued existence of the Teutonic Knights, but also made the order a mighty territorial lord and a German and Catholic bulwark against Russian and Greek Orthodox expansion in the Baltic region. Therefore all German historians consider Hermann of Salza the founder of the *Deutschordensstaat*. His decision to seek papal approval instead of

---

173. Friedrich G. Bunge *et al.*, eds., *Liv-, Est- und Kurländisches Urkundenbuch* (15 vols., Reval *et alibi*, 1853–1914), I, no. 149, and Strehlke, *Tabulae*, no. 244: bull of Gregory IX on the incorporation of the Swordbearers into the Teutonic order, May 12, 1237.

imperial sanction, as he did in 1226 about Prussia, probably reflected the fact that the Swordbearers were subject to papal authority, not to the emperor. Moreover, by this move of Hermann, Livonia was formally exempted from the jurisdiction of the emperor.

In August 1238 Hermann departed for Salerno to seek a cure for his illness from the famous physicians there.[174] However, their skill could not heal the ailing master: he died in Salerno, probably on March 20, 1239.[175] On the same day, Gregory IX again excommunicated emperor Frederick II, and on June 11 he threatened to revoke all the privileges of the order if they supported the emperor against the papacy.[176]

Theobald IV, count of Champagne and king of Navarre, landed with his French crusaders at Acre in September 1239 and soon afterward held a council of war with the local barons; among the participants was the recently elected master of the Teutonic Knights, Conrad of Thuringia,[177] the youngest son of landgrave Hermann I. At this meeting it was decided to attack Ascalon, but on November 13 the Saracens defeated the main Christian army near Gaza; many were taken prisoner. When this news reached Theobald, he hurried with the Teutonic Knights to the aid of the Christians, but the Germans arrived too late to rescue the captives.[178]

The Knights Hospitaller, taking advantage of the rift between Gregory IX and Frederick II and of Hermann of Salza's death, had asked the Roman curia to subject the Teutonic order to the jurisdiction of the Hospitallers. On January 12, 1240, Gregory ordered the Teutonic Knights to send their representative to Rome to answer the Hospitallers' demands. Consequently the new master, Conrad of Thuringia, departed for Rome in April to defend his order. Many German princes urged Gregory IX to use the good offices of the master to negotiate a reconciliation with the emperor; however, Conrad died on July 24, 1240, soon after his arrival in Rome. In 1241 at Acre a former marshal of the Teutonic Knights, Gerard of Malberg, was chosen the new master of the order.[179]

174. Richard of San Germano, *Chronica*, p. 376: "Magister domus Alamannorum Salernum se confert pro sanitate recuperanda."

175. Perlbach, "Necrologe," *passim*.

176. *MGH, Epistolae saeculi XIII*, I, no. 749: letter of Gregory IX to the Teutonic Knights, June 11, 1239.

177. *Manuscrit de Rothelin (RHC, Occ.,* II, 483–639), cap. 22.

178. *Ibid.,* cap. 29.

179. Strehlke, *Tabulae*, no. 468: letter of Gregory IX to the Teutonic Knights, January 12, 1240; *MGH, Epistolae saeculi XIII*, I, no. 768: a summary of letters of various German princes

In the meantime, on October 11, 1240, the brother of the king of England, Richard, earl of Cornwall, had landed in Acre with his crusaders, and the crusader barons with the support of the Templars and the Teutonic Knights attempted to persuade the earl to respect the peace treaty which had been concluded between Theobald of Champagne and the Aiyūbids earlier in 1240.[180] In the Holy Land relations between the various Christian lords were not much better than those in Italy between the papacy and the emperor. By 1241 the Hospitallers were engaged in open hostilities with the Templars, who also had attacked the Teutonic Knights at Acre and driven the main body of their convent out of the city, for the Teutonic Knights were known as staunch supporters of the Templars' enemy, Frederick II.[181] In February 1242 the master of the Teutonic Knights, Gerard of Malberg, departed for Italy, perhaps to complain to Frederick about the Templars, and to take up again with the papal curia the Hospitallers' request for the subordination of the Teutonic Knights to the Knights Hospitaller. Frederick II took advantage of the master's appearance at his court to send him as his emissary to the papal curia to pursue negotiations in the Lombard quarrel.[182] Thus Frederick continued his policy of using the master of the Teutonic Knights as his advisor on and mediator with the papacy.

When on June 25, 1243, Innocent IV was elected pope, Frederick immediately notified him of Gerard's official status as his emissary.[183] The new pope received the master sympathetically: Gerard offered the pope his oath of fidelity, and Innocent, in turn, renewed the order's rights over Prussia, and granted the order certain concessions in regard to its statutes.[184] With this, Gerard's mission to Italy was completed, and he returned to the Holy Land. It appears that at Acre —during the feud between the Templars and the Teutonic Knights, which lasted well into 1243—a strong opposition to the master had grown among his own brethren; in fact, internal strife had developed between two factions within the order. As a result of these quarrels, of which we know nothing, Gerard with his adherents resigned from

---

to Gregory IX, April 4 to May 11, 1240. For Gerard of Malberg see Richard of San Germano, *Chronica,* p. 382, where he mentions that in February 1242 a recently elected master has arrived at the papal court; the exact election date of Gerard is not known.

180. Philip of Novara, "Mémoires," ed. Raynaud, p. 123.
181. Matthew Paris, *Chronica majora,* IV, 167–168.
182. Richard of San Germano, *Chronica,* p. 382.
183. *MGH, Legum: Constitutiones,* II, no. 239: letter of Frederick II to Innocent IV, June 26, 1243.
184. Strehlke, *Tabulae,* no. 470: bull of February 9, 1244.

the order at some time before July 1244, at Montfort. In January 1245 Innocent IV granted Gerard the right to enter the Knights Templar,[185] but he never did so. From Innocent's privilege, it is apparent that work at Montfort had advanced far enough to allow its use as the master's official residence.

After Gerard's resignation, the Teutonic Knights elected as their new master Henry of Hohenlohe, who is first mentioned as master on July 7, 1244. The first engagement in which Henry might have participated as master of the Teutonic Knights took place in October 1244 near Gaza, where the Egyptians and the Khwarizmians annihilated the combined Christian and Syrian army. According to Matthew Paris and the Continuator of William of Tyre, only three Teutonic Knights escaped captivity or death;[186] if these accounts are correct, then Henry was not present at the battle. After this disastrous defeat Henry departed for the imperial court in Italy. From there Frederick II in April 1245 sent the master to the Council of Lyons to negotiate peace between the emperor and the papacy,[187] but his efforts brought no positive results. In the following year Henry went to Prussia to lead in person the order's campaigns against the duke of Pomerelia, Svantopelk. After the conclusion of a peace treaty with Svantopelk in 1248, Henry of Hohenlohe returned to Germany, where he died on July 15, 1249.[188]

In 1250 Gunther of Willersleben was elected as the next master;[189] there is no information about his deeds. However, before Gunther's election Louis IX, the king of France, had landed with his crusaders in Egypt, and on June 6, 1249, captured the city of Damietta and allocated certain houses in the city to the Templars, the Hospitallers, and the Teutonic Knights, who had fought with the crusader army. The great defeat of the Christians came on February 8, 1250, at Mansurah, where the vanguard of the crusader army, led by the king's brother, count Robert of Artois, was completely destroyed. According to the Continuator of William of Tyre, only four Teutonic Knights

185. Matthew Paris, *Chronica majora,* IV, 256; Strehlke, *Tabulae,* no. 483: letter to the Teutonic Knights; *MGH, Epistolae saeculi XIII,* I, nos. 83–84, January 16, 1245, and no. 127, August 5, 1245: letters of Innocent IV to the Teutonic Knights.

186. Matthew Paris, *Chronica majora,* IV, 302, 339, 342; Huillard-Bréholles, *Historia,* VI, 254–259: Frederick II's letter to Richard, earl of Cornwall, February 27, 1245; *Manuscrit de Rothelin,* cap. 41.

187. Matthew Paris, *Chronica majora,* IV, 538–544: encyclical of Frederick II, July 31, 1246.

188. Joachim and Hubatsch, *Regesta,* II, nos. 93, 95; Tumler, *op. cit.,* p. 47; Perlbach, "Necrologe," pp. 359, 362.

189. Schreiber, *op. cit.,* p. 662.

were lost; however, Matthew Paris records that only three Teutonic Knights escaped.[190] Then, on April 6, Louis was taken captive with the rest of the French contingent. Negotiations for ransoming the king and the release of the prisoners were begun immediately, and after Louis had agreed to deliver the city of Damietta to the Saracens and pay a substantial amount of money, he was released from captivity together with William of Châteauneuf, the master of the Hospitallers, twenty-five knights of that order, fifteen Templars, ten Teutonic Knights, and seven hundred other captives.[191] Whether Gunther of Willersleben had any part in the crusade of Louis IX is not known. Gunther died on May 3 or 4, 1252.[192]

Poppo of Osterna was elected in 1252 to succeed Gunther; about his deeds as master nothing is known. In 1256 in Rome, where he held a general chapter, Poppo resigned his office.[193] This same chapter elected as his successor Anno (abbreviation of Johannes?) of Sangerhausen, who is first mentioned in documents as master on January 4, 1257.[194] Before his election Anno was the master of the Teutonic Knights in Livonia; during his long tenure many important events in the order's life took place in the Holy Land. According to the Continuator of William of Tyre, the Teutonic Knights, together with the Templars and the local barons, in 1257 acknowledged Henry II de Lusignan as the legal king of Jerusalem.[195] He was opposed by the Hohenstaufen Conradin, the son of Conrad IV (who died in 1254) and grandson of emperor Frederick II (who died in 1250). If the author of the *Eracles* is correct, this was a shift in the traditional policy of the Teutonic Knights from support of the Hohenstaufens and their claims to the throne of the kingdom of Jerusalem.

In 1256 the frequent and enduring disputes between the Venetian and Genoese merchants in Acre had led to open hostilities, nicknamed the war of St. Sabas (1256–1261), over the possession of the monastery of St. Sabas on the mound of Montjoie, which overlooked the city. The military religious orders became involved in this conflict, with the Knights Hospitaller supporting the Genoese, while the Teu-

---

190. *Manuscrit de Rothelin,* caps. 62, 63; Matthew Paris, *Chronica majora,* V, 158.

191. *Manuscrit de Rothelin,* cap. 71.

192. Perlbach, "Necrologe," pp. 359, 364.

193. Schreiber, *op. cit.,* pp. 664–665; Strehlke, *Tabulae,* no. 104: agreement between the Teutonic Knights and Bartholomew, bishop of Hebron, September 26, 1253; *ibid.,* no. 249: Poppo's letter to the Livonian branch of the order, September 13, 1254; *ibid.,* no. 567: letter of Alexander IV to the Teutonic Knights, August 9, 1257; Peter of Dusburg, *SSRP,* I, 200; *Livländische Reimchronik,* ed. Leo Meyer (Paderborn, 1876), lines 4309–4358.

194. Strehlke, *Tabulae,* no. 108: grant of land to the Teutonic Knights by Julian of Sidon.

195. *Manuscrit de Rothelin,* cap. 79.

tonic Knights and the Templars sided with the Venetians. The Teutonic Knights strove for a peaceful settlement of the conflict, but to no avail.[196]

During the war of St. Sabas the masters of the three orders—Thomas Berard of the Knights Templar, Hugh Revel of the Knights Hospitaller, and Anno of Sangerhausen of the Teutonic Knights—met on October 9, 1253, in the church of the Holy Sepulcher in Acre to sign an agreement to end their mutual feud and conclude a "permanent peace and pleasing harmony."[197] To stress the importance of this reconciliation the great dignitaries in the Holy Land assembled to witness the signing of the treaty: the papal legate to the kingdom of Jerusalem, patriarch James of Jerusalem; John of Ibelin, lord of Arsuf and constable and bailie of Jerusalem; Geoffrey of Sargines, seneschal of Jerusalem; and many others. More significant than the witnesses, however, were the solemn pledges undertaken by the three orders to respect the reconciliation: the text of the agreement was to be recited and sworn to every year by the present masters and by every newly elected master in the general chapter of his order in the presence of twelve brethren from the other two orders; likewise all brothers of the three orders were bidden to observe the agreement inviolably. Furthermore, as soon as they were elected, all commanders, castellans, and their subordinates in the crusader states and in Cyprus had to take an oath similar to that of the masters to respect this agreement. In case of breach of the agreement, in part or completely, the offending order was obliged to compensate the other two orders with one thousand marks in silver; the orders' movable and landed possessions were offered as surety. Finally, to give the agreement a greater effect, it was sworn to upon the Holy Gospel and was accompanied by renunciation of all privileges and immunities of the three orders that would contradict this agreement.

Subject to this agreement were all questions and quarrels among the three masters and the brothers of their orders in the kingdoms of Jerusalem, Cyprus, and Cilician Armenia, the principality of Antioch, and the county of Tripoli. Exempted, however, were disagreements over castles, manors, and hamlets; such disputes were to be brought before ecclesiastical or secular courts.

The brothers of the three orders agreed to support each other with counsel, aid, and assistance in their wars against the enemies of the faith, and each order had to offer aid at its own expense to the other

196. Templar of Tyre, *Chronique,* ed. Raynaud, caps. 270–271.
197. Strehlke, *Tabulae,* no. 116: agreement among the Teutonic Knights, the Knights Templar, and the Knights Hospitaller, October 9, 1258.

two if war should be waged in the kingdom of Jerusalem, Cilician Armenia, the county of Tripoli, or the principality of Antioch. However, if the Teutonic Knights went to the aid of the Knights Templar and Knights Hospitaller in Tripoli and Antioch, their expenses for victuals, forage, and men were to be met by the order to whose aid the Teutonic Knights were called. There was a further stipulation that in joint operations within the kingdom of Jerusalem the Teutonic Knights had to support themselves only for one month, and only west of the Jordan. If the hostilities continued beyond a month, then the order which had asked for help from the Teutonic Knights had to supply victuals and fodder for the German troops for three months. On the other hand, if the Knights Templar and the Knights Hospitaller went to the aid of the Teutonic Knights against the enemies of the faith, it was their obligation to support themselves anywhere in the crusader states (*citra mare*), though not in Europe. This restriction entailed the exclusion of the Templars and Hospitallers from participation in the wars of the Teutonic Knights in Prussia and Livonia. This stipulation was as convenient to the Templars and Hospitallers as to the Teutonic Knights: the former two were not committed to participate in the wars of the Teutons outside the Holy Land, while the Teutonic Knights kept the other two orders out of territories which the Germans claimed as their own.

The concluding paragraphs of the agreement regulated administrative matters and the jurisdiction of the orders: brethren of the three orders could not bear arms against each other; if a master of one order left the crusader states, presumably for Europe, before his departure he had to make arrangements with the other two masters and their brethren for the support and defense of his order during his absence. This regulation was inserted probably because of the frequent and prolonged absences of the master of the Teutonic Knights from the Holy Land. The final statement, beyond doubt, was included at the request of the Teutonic Knights: "We order that, in case the master or the convent of the Hospital of St. John raise the question of obedience of the master and brethren of the German hospital of St. Mary, the independence of the orders in question has to be preserved according to the present agreement." This agreement would receive papal confirmation only some seventeen years later, on March 13, 1275, by Gregory X, and then upon the express request of the Knights Hospitaller.[198] One result, nevertheless, appears certain: the Hospitallers never again tried to exercise jurisdiction over the Teutonic Knights.

198. *Ibid.,* no. 127: bull of Gregory X.

Whether the decision by the chapter of the Teutonic order after 1264,[199] which states that no master should leave the Holy Land without the chapter's consent, was the immediate result of the 1258 agreement, it is impossible to determine. However, the document clearly indicates the growing resentment by the brothers of the order against the established tradition of the long absence of the masters from the Holy Land.

During the tenure of Anno of Sangerhausen, in 1260, while a war was being waged between the Mamluks and the Mongols, the Teutonic Knights jointly with the Hospitallers and the Templars fortified the cities of Acre and Tyre.[200] After the Mamluk general Baybars seized the throne of Egypt and Syria in 1260, he became increasingly active against the Christians; in the summer of 1266 he even attempted to take the city of Acre. To oppose Baybars, Hugh II of Lusignan hurried from Cyprus to the Holy Land in October 1266 and led a combined army of his knights, Templars, Hospitallers, and Teutonic Knights against the Mamluks. The Saracens killed some five hundred of the Christians, but failed to take the city. In 1269 Baybars again appeared before Acre, the knights of the three military religious orders again fought side by side in defense of the city, and Baybars had to retreat without taking Acre.[201]

However, Baybars' pressure on the Christians continued: after capturing the Hospitaller stronghold Krak des Chevaliers and the Templar fortress Chastel Blanc, Baybars on June 5, 1271, appeared before the seat of the master of the Teutonic Knights, Starkenberg (Montfort), and after a week's siege, took the castle on June 12, and destroyed its fortifications.[202] On June 15, 1271, Anno concluded an agreement with the Armenian lord Constantine of Sarvantikar, who allowed the Teutonic Knights to erect a customshouse, probably in the city of Sarvantikar.

The skirmishes between the Christians and the Saracens continued; on November 23 the three military religious orders, aided by the king of Cyprus and the crusaders, departed to the district of Caesarea to capture the tower of Caco (Qaqūn).[203] Unfortunately for the Christians, no real unity prevailed in their ranks: when in 1272 a quarrel arose between the king of Cyprus and Jerusalem, Hugh III and his

---

199. Perlbach, *Statuten* ("Capitelbeschlüsse vor 1289"), III, par. 1 (p. 135); see also "Gewohnheiten," par. 12.

200. *Manuscrit de Rothelin*, cap. 80.

201. *Estoire de Eracles*, XXXIV, 9; Templar of Tyre, ed. Raynaud, cap. 349.

202. Templar of Tyre, ed. Raynaud, cap. 378; *Estoire de Eracles*, XXXIV, cap. 14.

203. *Estoire de Eracles*, *loc. cit.*

barons, the master of the Templars, the marshal of the Hospitallers, and the grand commander of the Teutonic Knights sailed for Cyprus to patch up their differences; they returned to Acre without achieving anything.[204] Not until a year later was a compromise reached. Even then the coöperation among Hugh, the barons, and the three orders did not improve: in 1276 Hugh III went to Acre by a ship which belonged to the Teutonic Knights[205] but, enraged by the hostility of the Templars and the commune of Acre, he departed for Tyre, intending to return to Cyprus. The Templars and the Venetians now openly displayed their hostility toward Hugh, whereas the Hospitallers, the Teutonic Knights, the Pisans, the Genoese, the prelates, and the commune of Acre realized the danger of the Christian discord in the Holy Land and asked Hugh to appoint a bailie for the kingdom of Jerusalem.[206]

In the meantime master Anno of Sangerhausen had died on July 6, 1273;[207] he was succeeded by Hartmann of Heldrungen. There is no information about the Teutonic Knights in the Holy Land during the tenure of Hartmann. He was succeeded in 1283 by Burkhard of Schwanden, the last master elected in the Holy Land.[208] The bitter strife between the Lusignan king of Cyprus and Jerusalem and his subjects at Acre continued during the tenure of Burkhard: in June 1286 Henry, the infant king of Jerusalem, arrived at Tyre to be crowned king, but the three masters of the military religious orders were hesitant to welcome him; only after learning of the popular enthusiasm which greeted Henry did they change their attitude toward the young king. Even as late as 1288 discord was raging among the potentates of the Holy Land, though the masters of the three orders now held to a common line in the internal disputes.[209]

Finally in the year 1290 a Mamluk army from Egypt under sultan Kalavun began the last assaults on the Christians in Acre. In this year Burkhard returned to the Holy Land after a recruiting mission in Europe, bringing with him forty brothers and some four hundred crusaders. Shortly after his return Burkhard, for undisclosed reasons, suddenly resigned his office and joined the Hospitallers.[210] The com-

204. *Ibid.,* cap. 16.
205. Templar of Tyre, ed. Raynaud, cap. 388.
206. *Estoire de Eracles,* XXXIV, 28.
207. Perlbach, "Necrologe," pp. 358–359, 362.
208. Schreiber, *op. cit.,* p. 672.
209. Templar of Tyre, ed. Raynaud, caps. 438, 467–468.
210. Peter of Dusburg, *SSRP,* I, 205; Ottokar of Styria, *Österreichische Reimchronik,* ed. Seemüller, lines 48210–48220, gives the number of the recruited crusaders as seven hundred. For Ottokar see Stammler and Langosch, *Die Deutsche Literatur,* V, cols. 834–842.

mand of the Teutonic Knights in the Holy Land was taken over by Henry of Bolanden, who because of the siege and the critical situation in Acre was never officially elected master. The Teutonic Knights under his command, together with the royal troops, defended the most vulnerable part of the town wall, the triangle at the Accursed Tower. Henry of Bolanden fell in the final assault on the city, on May 18, 1291.[211] Thaddeus of Naples, though giving no specific facts, praises the bravery of the Teutonic Knights during the siege,[212] and Ludolph of Suchem (Sudheim) relates the last days of the Teutonic Knights in Acre: "the masters and brethren of the orders alone defended themselves, and fought unceasingly against the Saracens, until they were nearly all slain; indeed, the master [Henry of Bolanden] and brethren of the house of the Teutonic order, together with their followers and friends, all fell dead at one and the same time."[213]

Upon Henry of Bolanden's death the master of Germany, Conrad of Feuchtwangen, who had accompanied Burkhard of Schwanden,[214] being the highest surviving commander among the Teutonic Knights, was chosen, again without regular election, by the brother knights in Acre as their new master. Conrad, seeing the crusader cause lost and wishing to return to his own province of Germany, followed the example of the Hospitallers and with the surviving German knights battled his way through the enemy to the ships. Ottokar of Styria, who between 1301 and 1319 completed his "Austrian Chronicle" in verse, tells his readers that the knights had requested Conrad to stay and fight on and share the fate of the rest of the defenders of Acre. However, Conrad had told the Teutonic Knights that it would be a mistake to allow the sultan to kill the knights "without guilt and without need."[215] Ottokar also made Conrad promise to avenge the slaughter of the knights in Acre with the destruction of heathens in Prussia and Livonia.[216] Conrad of Feuchtwangen with some Teutonic Knights and the surviving Hospitallers and Templars escaped by sea to Cyprus, and Ottokar of Styria, combining melancholy and sarcasm, continues his story of the crusader tragedy at Acre: "Now, on the high seas, gathered the small army who called themselves Christians."[217]

---

211. Perlbach, "Necrologe," p. 364; Templar of Tyre, ed. Raynaud, cap. 485.

212. Thaddeus of Naples, *Hystoria de desolacione et conculcacione civitatis Acconensis et tocius Terre Sancte in A.D. MCCXCI*, ed. Paul Riant (Geneva, 1873), pp. 23–24.

213. Ludolph of Suchem, tr. Stewart, p. 57.

214. Ottokar of Styria, *op. cit.*, lines 48215–48220; Schreiber, *op. cit.*, pp. 684–685.

215. Ottokar of Styria, *op. cit.*, lines 51773–51804.

216. *Ibid.*, lines 51808–51817.

217. *Ibid.*, lines 51965–51967.

Conrad of Feuchtwangen and his knights did not settle in Cyprus, but took sail to Venice, which remained the official seat of the master until 1309, when it was permanently moved to Marienburg in Prussia.[218] With that move their second and greater epoch began.[219]

218. Walter Raddatz, *Die Uebersiedlung des Deutschen Ordens von Palästina nach Venedig und Marienburg, 1291–1309* (diss., University of Halle, Wittenberg; Halle, 1914); Perlbach, "Das Haus des Deutschen Ordens zu Venedig," in *Altpreussische Monatsschrift,* XVII (1880), 270–272.

219. See Edgar N. Johnson, "The German Crusade on the Baltic," in volume III of the present work, chapter XVI.

IX

VENICE AND THE CRUSADES

The growth of Venice depended upon the profits to be gained from sailing the seas. Aware of its dependence upon Byzantium, Venice at first extended its seaborne trade under the protective mantle of the Greek navy. Beginning in the eleventh century, however, Venetian maritime strength became great enough to assist, to challenge, and finally to supplant the Greeks in the waters of the eastern Mediterranean. Venice gradually gained marketing privileges from local rulers, next received small enclaves in these cities, then took possession of entire towns, and finally conquered the hinterland of several of these ports. Venetian trade and colonies were concentrated in Romania, those lands bordering the Aegean Sea and the approaches to Constantinople which were under Byzantine political control before 1204. To trade successfully in Romania, Venice had to protect its shipping on outbound and homeward voyages on the Adriatic and Ionian seas.

Since the emphasis in this chapter is on Venice, this bibliography will be limited to significant works relating to Venetian affairs. The early narrative sources include John the Deacon, *Chronicon venetum et gradense (MGH, SS.,* VII, 1–47); Geoffroi de Villehardouin, *La Conquête de Constantinople,* ed. and tr. Edmond Faral, 2nd ed. (Les Classiques de l'histoire de France au moyen-âge; 2 vols., Paris, 1961); *Chronicon venetum quod vulgo dicunt Altinate (MGH, SS.,* XIV, 1–97); Andrea Dandolo, *Chronica,* ed. Ester Pastorello (*RISS,* XII-1, new ed., Bologna, 1938–1958); and Martin da Canal, *Les Estoires de Venise,* ed. and tr. Alberto Limentani (Fondazione Cini, Civiltà veneziana, fonti e testi, XII; Florence, 1972). This excellent new edition supplants the older *La Cronique des Venéciens de Maistre Martin da Canal,* ed. Filippo L. Polidori, *Archivio storico italiano,* VIII (1845), 229–798. The greatest collection of documents is the old and accurate *Urkunden zur älteren Handels- und Staatsgeschichte der Republik Venedig mit besonderer Beziehung auf Byzanz und die Levante,* ed. Gottlieb L. F. Tafel and Georg M. Thomas (Fontes rerum austriacarum, Diplomataria et acta, XII–XIV; 3 vols., Vienna, 1856–1857; repr. Amsterdam, 1964).

Venetian law codes from this period include *Gli Statuti veneziani di Jacopo Tiepolo del 1242 e le loro glosse,* ed. Roberto Cessi (Memorie del R. Istituto di scienze, lettere ed arti, XXX-2; Venice, 1938); and *Gli Statuti marittimi veneziani fino al 1255,* ed. Riccardo Predelli and Adolfo Sacerdoti (Venice, 1903).

For commercial documents see *Documenti del commercio veneziano nei secoli XI–XIII,* ed. Raimondo Morozzo della Rocca and Antonino Lombardo (Documenti e studi per la storia del commercio e del diritto commerciale italiano, XIX, XX; 2 vols., Rome and Turin, 1940); *Nuovi documenti del commercio veneto dei sec. XI–XIII,* ed. Lombardo and Morozzo della Rocca (Monumenti storici: Deputazione di storia patria per le Venezie, n.s., VII; Venice, 1953).

During the crusading centuries two additional trading areas attracted Venetians: the shores of Syria and Palestine, where the crusaders established Latin states at the beginning of the twelfth century, and Moslem Egypt. Other Italian seafaring peoples — the Pisans, the Genoese, the men of Amalfi and Gaeta — similarly extended their influence into the eastern Mediterranean during the Middle Ages. The military expeditions of the crusades provided a stimulus for these developments. This chapter is a summary of the Venetian commercial colonization in Romania, in Syria-Palestine, and in Egypt during the eleventh, twelfth, and thirteenth centuries.

For several centuries after its founding, Venice recognized the political superiority of the Byzantine emperors and gave constant but distant allegiance to the Greek world, rather than to the Latin world in the Italian peninsula. As part of the Greek world, Venetian seafarers

---

Of particular significance for this chapter are the following volumes of private notarial documents: *S. Giorgio Maggiore,* II, III, ed. Luigi Lanfranchi (Fonti per la storia di Venezia, II; Archivi ecclesiastici: Diocesi Castellana; Venice, 1968); *Famiglia Zusto,* ed. Lanfranchi (Fonti per la storia di Venezia, IV; Archivi privati; Venice, 1955); *S. Lorenzo di Ammiana,* ed. Lanfranchi (Fonti per la storia di Venezia, II; Archivi ecclesiastici: Diocesi Torcellana; Venice, 1947; repr. 1969). Also very significant is the oldest collection of documents issuing from the Venetian Council, but the published edition should be used with caution: *Deliberazioni del Maggior Consiglio di Venezia,* I, *Liber communis qui vulgo nuncupatur Plegiorum,* ed. Cessi (Accademia dei Lincei: Atti delle Assemblee costituzionale italiane; Bologna, 1950).

For modern studies of general relevance see Jean J. M. Armingaud, "Venise et le bas-empire," *Archives des missions scientifiques et littéraires,* ser. 2, IV (1867), 299-443; Guido Astuti, "L'Organizzazione giuridica del sistema coloniale e della navigazione mercantile delle città italiane nel medio evo," *Mediterraneo e Oceano Indiano: Atti del VI colloquio di storia marittima* (Fondazione G. Cini, Civiltà veneziana, studi, XXIII; Florence, 1970), pp. 57-90; Horatio F. Brown, *The Venetian Republic* (London, 1902); *idem,* "The Venetians and the Venetian Quarter in Constantinople to the Close of the Twelfth Century," *Journal of Hellenic Studies,* XL (1920), 68-88; Rinaldo Caddeo, M. Nani Mocenigo, *et al., Storia marittima dell' Italia dall' evo antico ai nostri giorni,* I (Milan, 1942), to be used with discretion; Cessi, *Le Colonie medioevali italiane in Oriente,* I, *La Conquista* (Bologna, 1942); Giorgio Cracco, *Società e stato nel medioevo veneziano* (Florence, 1967); René Grousset, *Histoire des croisades,* vols. I, II (Paris, 1934-1935); Michael F. Hendy, "Byzantium, 1081-1204: An Economic Reappraisal," *Transactions of the Royal Historical Society,* ser. 5, XX (1970), 31-52; Wilhelm Heyd, *Histoire du commerce du Levant au moyen-âge,* tr. Furcy Raynaud (2 vols., Leipzig, 1885-1886; repr. Leipzig, 1936, and Amsterdam, 1967); Heinrich Kretschmayr, *Geschichte von Venedig* (3 vols., Gotha, 1905-1934; repr. Stuttgart, 1964); Frederic C. Lane, *Venice, a Maritime Republic* (Baltimore, 1973); *idem, Venice and History* (Baltimore, 1966); Archibald Lewis, *Naval Power and Trade in the Mediterranean, A.D. 500-1100* (Princeton, 1951); Jean Longnon, *L'Empire latin de Constantinople et la principauté de Morée* (Paris, 1949); Camillo Manfroni, *I Colonizzatori italiani durante il medio evo e il rinascimento,* vols. I, II, (Rome, 1933), to be used with caution; *idem, Storia della marina italiana dalle invasioni barbariche al trattato di Ninfeo* (Leghorn, 1899); Joshua Prawer, *The Latin Kingdom of Jerusalem: European Colonialism in The Middle Ages* (London, 1972, publ. in New York, 1972, as *The Crusaders' Kingdom*); *idem,* "Étude de quelques problèmes agraires et sociaux d'une seigneurie croisée au XIIIe siècle," *Byzantion,* XXII (1952), 5-61; *idem, Histoire du royaume latin de Jérusalem* (2 vols., Paris, 1969-1970); Louise Buenger Robbert, "The Venetian Money Market, 1150-1229," *Studi veneziani,* XIII (1971), 1-94; Samuele Romanin, *Storia documentata di Venezia,* 2nd ed. (Venice, 1912; repr. 1925); Adolf Schaube,

accepted the protection of the Byzantine fleet and of Byzantine laws, and Venice grew increasingly strong as a western Byzantine outpost. When Byzantium was no longer able to protect the Adriatic, the growing Venetian navy gradually assumed the defense of these waters. The Greeks, hoping to continue their domination there, relied more and more upon Venetian assistance against the Saracens and, later, the Norman kings of Sicily.

Venice, like the other Italian sea republics of Amalfi, Pisa, and Genoa, fought against Saracen sea power two centuries before the crusading epoch. In the ninth century Pisa and Genoa fought independently against Moslem sea powers in the western Mediterranean and the Tyrrhenian Sea, while Venetian fleets in collaboration with the Byzantines fought against Saracen encroachments in the Adriatic. Expeditions are recorded for the years 827, 829, 840, 842, and

---

Handelsgeschichte der romanischen Völker des Mittelmeergebiets bis zum Ende der Kreuzzüge (Munich and Berlin, 1906); Vsevolod Slessarev, "*Ecclesiae mercatorum* and the Rise of Merchant Colonies," *Business History Review,* XLI (1967), 181-197; Freddy Thiriet, *La Romanie vénitienne au moyen-âge* (Paris, 1959); and *idem,* "Les Chroniques vénitiennes de la Marcianne," *Mélanges d'archéologie et d'histoire,* LXXIV (1954), 241-292.

Studies which illustrate the growth and organization of Venetian colonial enterprise to 1200 are Enrico Besta, "La Cattura dei Veneziani in Oriente per ordine dell' imperatore Emmanuele Comneno," *Antologia veneta,* I (1900), 35-46, 111-123; Charles M. Brand, *Byzantium Confronts the West 1180-1204* (Cambridge, Mass., 1968); Cessi, "Politica, Economica, Religione," *Storia di Venezia,* II (Venice, 1958), 67-476; *idem, Venezia ducale,* II-1: *Commune venetiarum* (Deputazione di storia patria per le Venezie; Venice, 1965); John Danstrip, "Manual I's Coup against Genoa and Venice in the Light of Byzantine Commercial Policy," *Classica et Mediaevalia,* X (1948), 204-212, to be used cautiously; Carlo Errara, "I Crociati veneziani in Terra Santa," *Archivio veneto,* XXXVIII (1889), 237-277; Philip Grierson, "From Solidus to Hyperperon: The Names of Byzantine Gold Coins," *Spink & Son Ltd.: The Numismatic Circular,* LXXIV, 5 (May 1966), 123-124; Reinhard Heynen, *Zur Entstehung des Kapitalismus in Venedig* (Stuttgart, 1905; repr. New York, 1971); Lane, "Investment and Usury," *Venice and History* (Baltimore, 1966), pp. 56-68; Robert S. Lopez, *The Commercial Revolution of the Middle Ages* (Englewood Cliffs, N.J., 1971); Lopez and Irving W. Raymond, *Medieval Trade in the Mediterranean World* (London, 1955); Lopez, "The Trade of Medieval Europe: The South," *The Cambridge Economic History of Europe,* ed. Moisi Postan and Edwin E. Rich, II (Cambridge, Eng., 1952), 257-354; Gino Luzzatto, *Studi di storia economica veneziana* (Padua, 1954); *idem, Storia economica di Venezia dall' XI al XVI secolo* (Venice, 1961); Margarete Merores, "Der venezianische Adel," *Vierteljahrschrift für Sozial- und Wirtschaftsgeschichte,* XIX (1926), 193-237; *I Prestiti della Repubblica di Venezia (Secoli XIII-XV): Introduzione storica e documenti,* ed. Luzzatto, *Documenti finanziari della Repubblica di Venezia,* ser. 3, vol. I-1 (Padua, 1929); John H. Pryor, "The Origins of the *Commenda* Contract," *Speculum,* LII (1977), 5-37; Paolo Sarpi, *Il Dominio de Mare Adriatico,* ed. with introduction by Cessi (Padua, 1945); Giorgio Zordan, "I Vari aspetti della Comunione familiare di Beni nella Venezia dei secoli XI-XIII," *Studi veneziani,* VIII (1966), 127-194.

Studies which refer particularly to the Venetian colonial empire during and after the Fourth Crusade include Silvano Borsari, "Il Commercio veneziano nell' impero bizantino nel XII secolo," *Rivista storica italiana,* LXXVI (1964), 982-1011; *idem, Il Dominio veneziano a Creta nel XIII secolo* (Naples, 1963); *idem,* "Per la Storia del commercio veneziano col mondo bizantino nel XII secolo," *Rivista storica italiana,* LXXXVIII (1976), 104-126; *idem, Studi sulle colonie veneziane in Romanía nel XIII secolo* (Naples, 1966); John B. Bury, "The Lombards and

846.[1] A powerful Venetian fleet of sixty ships was destroyed in 840 as it attempted to drive the Saracens from Taranto. Consequently, Moslems operated farther north in the Adriatic. Although Venice won a naval victory over the Saracens based on Taranto in 871, Saracen corsairs continued to raid Adriatic shipping.

During these early centuries of its existence, Venice tried to regulate its commerce in conformity with Byzantine law. In 876 and 960 Venetian doges promulgated decrees prohibiting their citizens from engaging in the slave trade.[2] The Byzantine emperor Leo V (813–820) prohibited his subjects from visiting Moslem ports, and, in response to an official request presented by legates of the Greek emperor, doge

---

Venetians in Euboia," *Journal of Hellenic Studies,* VII (1886), 309–352; VIII (1887), 194–213; IX (1888), 91–117; Antonio Carile, "Partitio terrarum imperii Romania," *Studi veneziani,* VII (1965), 125–305; Cessi, "Venezia e la Quarta Crociata," *Archivio veneto,* ser. 5, XLVIII–XLIX (1915), 1–52; Julian Chrysostomides, "Venetian Commercial Privileges under the Palaeologi," *Studi veneziani,* XII (1970), 267–356; John K. Fotheringham, *Marco Sanudo, Conqueror of the Archipelago* (Oxford, 1915); Deno J. Geanakoplos, *Emperor Michael Palaeologus and the West* (Cambridge, Mass., 1959); Ernst Gerland, *Histoire de la noblesse crétoise au moyen-âge* (Paris, 1907); David Jacoby, "The Encounter of Two Societies: Western Conquerors and Byzantines in the Peloponnesus after the Fourth Crusade," *American Historical Review,* LXXVIII (1973), 873–906; idem, *La Féodalité en Grèce médiévale: Les "Assises de Romanie": sources, application et diffusion* (Paris, 1971); idem, "Mémoires et documents: Les quartiers juifs de Constantinople à l'époque byzantine," *Byzantion,* XXXVII (1967), 167–227; Donald E. Queller, ed., *The Latin Conquest of Constantinople* (New York, 1971); Raymond J. Loenertz, *Byzantina et Franco-Graeca* (Rome, 1970); idem, "Généalogie des Ghisi, dynastes vénitiens dans l'Archipel, 1207–1390," *Orientalia Christiana periodica,* XXVIII (1962), 121–172, 322–335; idem, "Les Seigneurs terciers de Négropont de 1205 à 1280," *Byzantion,* XXXV (1965), 235–276; Stephen B. Luce, "Modon—a Venetian Station in Medieval Greece," *Classical and Mediaeval Studies in Honor of Edward K. Rand,* ed. Leslie W. Jones (New York, 1938), pp. 195–208; Manfroni, "Relazioni di Genova con Venezia dal 1270 al 1290," *Giornale storico e letterario della Liguria,* II (1901), 361–401; Louis de Mas Latrie, "Les Ducs de l'Archipel ou des Cyclades," *Monumenti storici* (Miscellanea della Deputazione di storia patria per le Venezie; Venice, 1887), pp. 4–15; William Miller, *Essays on the Latin Orient* (Cambridge, Eng., 1921; repr. Chicago, 1967); idem, *The Latins in the Levant* (London, 1908; repr. 1964); *Nel VII Centenario della nascità di Marco Polo* (Istituto veneto di scienze, lettere, ed arti; Venice, 1955); Queller, "L'Évolution du rôle de l'ambassadeur: Les pleins pouvoirs et le traité de 1201 entre les croisés et les Vénitiens," *Le Moyen-âge,* XVI (1961), 479–501; Queller, Thomas K. Compton, and Donald A. Campbell, "The Fourth Crusade: The Neglected Majority," *Speculum,* XLIX (1974), 441–465; Queller and Joseph Gill, "Franks, Venetians and Pope Innocent III," *Studi veneziani,* XII (1970), 85–105; Kenneth M. Setton, "The Latins in Greece and the Aegean," *Cambridge Medieval History,* 2nd ed., IV-1 (Cambridge, Eng., 1966), 389–430; *Venezia e il levante fino al secolo XV,* ed. Agostino Pertusi, vol. I (Civiltà veneziana, Studi, 27; Florence, 1973); Robert L. Wolff, "Mortgage and Redemption of an Emperor's Son: Castile and the Latin Empire of Constantinople," *Speculum,* XXIX (1954), 45–84; idem, "The Oath of the Venetian Podestà: A New Document from the Period of the Latin Empire of Constantinople," *Annuaire de l'Institut de philologie et d'histoire orientales et slaves,* XII (1952; *Mélanges Henri Grégoire,* IV), 539–573; and idem, "Politics in the Latin Patriarchate of Constantinople, 1204–1261," *Dumbarton Oaks Papers,* VIII (1954), 225–303.

1. Cessi, "Politica, Economica, Religione," pp. 152–155; John the Deacon, in *MGH, SS.,* VII, 16–19.

2. Andrea Dandolo, *Chronica,* pp. 158–159; Tafel and Thomas, I, 17–25.

Peter IV Candiano in 971 decreed that Venetians should not take lumber or weapons to Saracen lands — Barbary, Egypt, Crete, parts of Anatolia, and Sicily.[3]

With the decline of Byzantine maritime strength, Venice, for its own protection, began to force the seaports on the Adriatic to submit to its authority. The Venetian doges Peter II Candiano (932–939) and Peter III Candiano (942–959) reduced the upper Adriatic (Ravenna to Pola on the Istrian peninsula) to dependence on Venice. Their navies destroyed Comacchio and defeated the Istrian cities by enforcing an economic blockade. However, pirates in the middle Adriatic successfully challenged the Venetian navy before 1000, indicating the weakening of Byzantine naval power.

At the end of the tenth century, the Byzantine emperors Basil II and Constantine VIII asked Venice to supply transport ships to carry a Byzantine military force to southern Italy. In return for this assistance, the emperors in this bull of March 992 granted special commercial favors to their Venetian subjects.[4] These included a reduction to 2 solidi in the taxes paid at Abydus by each Venetian ship bringing cargo to Byzantium and a reduction to 15 solidi for each departing Venetian ship, the difference being because the Venetian ships brought cargoes of low value to the east and took away cargoes of high value. Ships of other nationalities paid more. The Venetian merchants were expected to abide by Byzantine law and were placed under the jurisdiction of a Byzantine official, the *logothete de dromo*.

The recipient of these privileges from the Greeks, doge Peter II Orseolo (992–1009), also received an extension of Venetian commercial rights and privileges on the mainland of Italy from the German kings Otto III, in July 992, and Henry II, in November 1002.

Having gained international recognition, Peter prepared to wage what would be his most successful campaign against the Dalmatian pirates, especially those from the Narenta river and nearby on the Dalmatian islands of Curzola and Lagosta. His victory won for Venice the undisputed dominance over the area and for himself the title duke of Dalmatia.[5] Thus by 1000 Venice had reduced the Dalmatian pirates and had begun to police the Adriatic.

Peter also led the Venetians in a successful military venture against the Saracens. The Apulian city of Bari, nominally under Byzantine

3. Tafel and Thomas, I, 25–30; Thiriet, *La Romanie,* p. 34.

4. Tafel and Thomas, I, 36–39: the text is corrupt; consult Brown, "The Venetians and the Venetian Quarter," pp. 68–70; Thiriet, *La Romanie,* p. 34, note 2; Cessi, *Venezia ducale,* II, 158–172; cf. Andrea Dandolo, *Chronica,* p. 193.

5. Brown, "The Venetians and the Venetian Quarter," p. 70. Both the eastern emperors and the Salian emperor Henry II recognized Venetian rights there.

control, was besieged by the Moslems. A fleet from Venice, probably acting on behalf of Constantinople, assisted the local Christians and saved not only the city but the surrounding countryside from the Moslems in 1002–1003. The mouth of the Adriatic Sea, Venice's threshold, was again freed. The Byzantine emperor Basil II, in gratitude for these Venetian naval victories, betrothed his niece Maria to John, the son of the doge.

During the eleventh century the Venetians assumed further control of the Adriatic by pacts with the German emperors, with the Dalmatian cities, and with Slavic princes, and by tacit recognition from the Croats. Later eleventh-century Venetian treaties with the port towns along the Adriatic coast of Italy, especially Fano, show a nominal respect by Venice for the sovereignty of these cities, but their terms, which included heavy military duties and an oath of *fidelitas,* indicate that Venice was the actual sovereign.

That the Venetians were coöperating with the Greek emperors in policing the Adriatic is further attested by their naval activity against the Normans. Venice sent ships to assist the Byzantines against Robert Guiscard's invasion of the Balkans from 1081 to 1085. Venetian fleets were especially active in the siege of Durazzo from 1081 to 1082 and in curtailing the Norman advances in the lower Adriatic in 1083 and 1084. After Robert Guiscard's death, his Balkan conquests reverted to Byzantine rule, and the entire Dalmatian coast north of Durazzo entered the Venetian sphere of dominance.

As a direct result of this Venetian naval assistance against the Normans, emperor Alexius I Comnenus granted Venice more commercial privileges. These privileges, enumerated in the chrysobull of May 1082,[6] included freedom for Venetians to trade in the Byzantine empire without paying any duties whatsoever. The Greeks also granted annual revenues to the Venetian churches, revenues to Domenico Cervoni, the patriarch of Grado, and a title[7] and revenues to the Venetian doge,

---

6. Tafel and Thomas, I, 50–54; Brown, "The Venetians and the Venetian Quarter," pp. 70–72; Kretschmayr, *Geschichte,* I, 178–179. For another description of the Venetian quarter see *S. Giorgio Maggiore,* ed. Lanfranchi, II, no. 69. Recently Chrysostomides, "Venetian Commercial Privileges under the Palaeologi," p. 268, defined the Venetian commercial privileges thus: "Venetians were given the right to buy and sell, import and export any commodity and to arrive by land or by sea with or without merchandise without paying any of the customary taxes, such as the *teloneum, diabaticum, commercium* or *scalaticum.*" Exceptions were prohibitions of the export of home-grown wheat and the requirement to report goods belonging to non-Venetians on Venetian ships. These privileges were renewed in 1124, 1148, later under the Angeli, and also in 1268 and 1277.

7. The title was either *protoproedus* or *protosebastos* or *dux Dalmacie et Chroacie:* Tafel and Thomas, I, 52; Andrea Dandolo, *Chronica,* p. 217; Besta, "La Cattura," p. 35, note 5; Cessi, *Venezia ducale,* II, 120, note 1.

Domenico Selvo. In addition, the citizens of Amalfi in the empire were required to pay annual tribute to Venice. The emperor also awarded Venice a quarter in Constantinople itself, on the west bank of the Golden Horn between the Gate of Vigla and the Porta Peramatis; it was about one third of a mile long and averaged one hundred seventy yards in width. Drungary Street ran the length of the Venetian quarter and was flanked by houses on each side. Crossroads led down to three wharves. The great Venetian warehouse and market stood just inside the Porta Peramatis. According to the text of 1082, the quarter included the church of St. Akindynos, rededicated by the Venetians to St. Mark, its adjacent bakery ovens, the church of St. Mary of the Latins that had formerly belonged to Amalfi, and the monastery of St. George. There was another religious establishment dedicated to St. Nicholas.[8]

In addition to gaining a quarter in the Byzantine capital, the Venetians obtained the right to trade freely at the following Byzantine ports and inland cities: Latakia, Antioch, Mamistra, Adana, Tarsus, Adalia, Strobilo, Ephesus (Theologo), Phocaea, Abydus, Scutari, Selymbria, Heraclea, Rodosto, Apros, Adrianople, Peritheorium, Thessalonica, Demetrias, Negroponte, Thebes, Athens, Nauplia, Coron, Modon, Corinth, Vonitsa, Corfu, Avlona, and Durazzo. The only Aegean island open to them was Chios.[9] The Black Sea was closed to them, but on the Adriatic the Byzantine emperor ceded to the Venetians, as his faithful subjects, the church of St. Andrew in Durazzo and its revenues. Neither the other Italian merchants nor the Greeks had such privileges as the free trade and the annual Byzantine subsidies. The city of Amalfi lost its privileges in Constantinople because it had become part of the Norman kingdom.

Venice applied in 1119 to Alexius's successor, John II Comnenus, for a renewal of these privileges,[10] but they were not renewed until 1126, and then only after it made warning attacks on the Byzantine islands of Corfu in the Ionian Sea, on Samos, Lesbos, and Rhodes in the Aegean, on Cyprus and Cephalonia, and on the Byzantine port of Modon in the Morea. Obviously the Greeks could not defend their outlying possessions against the Venetians, so John renewed the Venetian subsidies and titles. Venice's other commercial privileges were renewed and the special privileges of the Venetian quarter in Constantinople were reconfirmed; a later act of John

8. Tafel and Thomas, I, 55–63; Raymond Janin, *La Géographie ecclésiastique,* 2nd ed. (Paris, 1969), p. 573.
9. Tafel and Thomas, I, 52–53.
10. Andrea Dandolo, *Chronica,* p. 232; Tafel and Thomas, I, 78.

Comnenus extended the Venetian trading privileges to include Cyprus and Crete.[11]

Not only were the Greeks unable to defend their empire from attacks, such as the Venetians had made in 1124–1125, but they were unable to protect their citizens against attempts by the Sicilian Normans to conquer them. The Byzantine empire continued to need Venetian naval assistance. During the Second Crusade, while the fleets of Genoa and Pisa were supporting the crusade in Spain, the Norman king Roger II, like his father sixty-five years earlier, seized the opportunity to expand his growing kingdom into the Adriatic at Byzantine expense. While the Norman fleet raided the Morea and Attica, the Venetian ambassadors in Constantinople, in return for more privileges, promised naval aid to the Greeks. In a chrysobull of March 1148 emperor Manuel I Comnenus defined in great detail the boundaries of the Venetian quarter in Constantinople.[12] In October 1148 the emperor issued a second bull which permitted the Venetians to trade freely, for the first time, in Rhodes. For his part, doge Peter Polani prohibited all commercial voyages for that season, called Venetian ships home, and organized an armada to assist the Greeks. It was an uneasy alliance, marked by growing tension and quarrels. When, however, the Norman fleet under George of Antioch demonstrated against the Byzantines by threatening the city of Constantinople and its commerce, the Venetians once more coöperated with the Byzantines. The Venetian fleet defeated the returning Normans off the coast of the Morea in 1149.[13]

By mid-century the Venetians had gained the most liberal commercial privileges of any group of merchants in Byzantine waters, and Venetian commerce flourished. They now had complete freedom to trade in the Byzantine empire and complete exemption from all tolls, even those paid by the Greeks themselves. However, Venetian galleys still served in the Byzantine navy; there were thirteen in Byzantine service in 1150.[14] The Greeks had also granted similar, but not as extensive, privileges to the Pisans in 1111 and to the Genoese in 1155. No Italians were permitted to trade on the Black Sea. Byzantine ships probably continued to carry cargoes between ports within the empire.[15]

11. Tafel and Thomas, I, 95–98, 124; Brown, "The Venetians and the Venetian Quarter," p. 73; Borsari, "Il Commercio veneziano," p. 997.

12. Tafel and Thomas, I, 109–113.

13. Andrea Dandolo, *Chronica,* p. 243; *Historia ducum veneticorum,* in *MGH, SS.,* XIV, 75; cf. Manfroni, *Colonizzatori,* I, 150–152.

14. *S. Giorgio Maggiore,* II, no. 240. On flourishing commerce under doge Domenico Morosini (1148–1154) see Martin da Canal, *Les Estoires de Venise,* I, 26 (pp. 38–39).

15. Hendy, "Byzantium, 1081–1204," pp. 40–41.

In addition to the Venetian secular interest in the Greek east, Venetian churches possessed certain areas in Constantinople. As early as 1090 the Venetian doge Vitale Falier donated all the ducal properties in the Venetian quarter of Constantinople to the great Venetian Benedictine monastery of San Giorgio Maggiore. Seventeen years later another Venetian doge, Ordelafo Falier, gave St. Mark (the former St. Akindynos), the main Venetian church in Constantinople, to John Gradenigo, patriarch of Grado, the principal ecclesiastical official in Venice.[16] This church and its possessions, including treasury, ovens, taverns, weights, and measures, were given to repay a debt Venice had incurred under the previous doge, Domenico Selvo. It is possible that these eleventh-century doges donated these state properties to the church in return for money to finance their government, as did their successor, doge Enrico Dandolo, one hundred years later.[17]

Venetian ecclesiastical authorities also owned property on the Byzantine island of Lemnos, in Byzantine Rodosto on the north shore of the Sea of Marmara, and at Halmyros, the Byzantine port in Thessaly. These three ports often served Venetian merchants in the twelfth century. In July 1136 Peter, prior of the Venetian monastery of St. Mark in Constantinople, subject to the monastery of San Giorgio Maggiore, received the oratory of St. Blasius on Lemnos, with its dependencies, from Michael, Orthodox archbishop of Lemnos.[18] In return, the Venetians promised to build a church in honor of St. George the Martyr and to give oil annually to the Greek archbishop.

In 1145 doge Peter Polani granted jurisdiction over the Venetian church of St. Mary in Rodosto to the Venetian monastery of San Giorgio Maggiore. In 1151 San Giorgio's control over St. Mary in Rodosto was declared sovereign, as neither patriarch nor doge nor the commune of Venice had the right to intervene. These privileges in Rodosto were the subject of a special embassy sent in 1147 by Venice to the emperor Manuel. The jurisdiction of San Giorgio Maggiore in Rodosto was further defined in October 1157, when Hugo, the abbot of St. Mary in Adrianople, granted to San Giorgio Maggiore the church of St. Mary in Rodosto, together with "its buildings, hospital, gardens, and all charters new and old, Greek and Latin."[19]

---

16. Tafel and Thomas, I, 55–63; S. *Giorgio Maggiore*, II, no. 69. For St. Akindynos, now St. Mark, see Tafel and Thomas, I, 67–74.

17. Lombardo and Morozzo della Rocca, *Nuovi documenti*, no. 46. Doge Enrico Dandolo in 1198 received 2,871 Venetian pounds from the Opera ecclesiae B. Marci *in oportunitatibus nostri comuni.*

18. Tafel and Thomas, I, 98–101; S. *Giorgio Maggiore*, II, no. 181.

19. On Rodosto see Tafel and Thomas, I, 103–105, 107–109, 137–139; Lombardo and Morozzo della Rocca, *Nuovi documenti*, no. 12.

The Venetian monastery of St. Mark in Constantinople, dependent on San Giorgio Maggiore in Venice, also acquired land with buildings in Halmyros, some of which had belonged to a private Venetian citizen who had pledged it to the monastery as security for a loan. When the sum was not repaid, he ceded his property to the monastery with the privilege of living there for life.[20]

Thus during the first crusading century the Venetians accumulated trading privileges in the Byzantine empire, achieved freedom from Byzantine taxation, acquired a quarter in Constantinople and property on Lemnos and in Rodosto and Halmyros. Numbers of Venetians came to reside in the Greek world, where they made their living as merchants. It is clear from the documents that control of the real estate was passing into the hands of the Venetian church. The great Venetian Benedictine monastery of San Giorgio Maggiore had the most responsibility, exercised through its representative, the monk who was also prior of St. Mark's in Constantinople. In addition to the Latin title of prior, he also bore the Greek title of "most precious."[21] Also important were the holdings of the patriarch of Grado. In his church of St. Mark (St. Akindynos) in Constantinople were kept the weights and measures of Venice. All surviving legal documents of the Venetians in Constantinople are connected to these two Venetian ecclesiastical institutions—the monastery of San Giorgio Maggiore and the partriarchate of Grado. Their representatives in the Greek east controlled the transfer of real estate, the registration and drawing up of notarial contracts, and the regulation of standards of measurement. This control by ecclesiastical officials would not have seemed at all unusual to the Greeks. A secular agent of the doge assumed charge of Venetian affairs in Romania only on those rare occasions when the doge sent special legates to Constantinople.[22]

It would seem that, at least until 1187, Venetians in the Greek world were considered Greek subjects under Greek law, and that their affairs in Constantinople were directed by church officials.[23] Apparently any legal disputes between Venetians and Greeks were settled

20. Tafel and Thomas, I, 125–133, 136–137; *S. Giorgio Maggiore,* II, nos. 231, 232, 233, 271.

21. *S. Giorgio Maggiore,* II, no. 240.

22. See also Slessarev, "*Ecclesiae mercatorum* and the Rise of Merchant Colonies." Names of the known legates are listed in Morozzo della Rocca and Lombardo, *Documenti,* I, no. 35; cf. Lombardo and Morozzo della Rocca, *Nuovi documenti,* no. 8; Tafel and Thomas, I, 107–109; Morozzo della Rocca and Lombardo, *Documenti,* I, no. 95.

23. Wolff, "The Oath of the Venetian Podestà," p. 540; Thiriet, *La Romanie,* p. 46; Heyd, tr. Raynaud, *Histoire du commerce,* I, 255–258; Brand, *Byzantium Confronts the West,* pp. 202–203; Tafel and Thomas, I, 273–278; Lombardo and Morozzo della Rocca, *Nuovi documenti,* nos. 33–35.

in the Byzantine courts. Cases in civil law concerning Venetians only were settled before the Venetian elders in Constantinople.[24] Not until the chrysobull of 1187 did the Byzantine state recognize Venice as independent and equal. Only after the chrysobull of 1198 issued by Alexius III Angelus were Venetians in Constantinople governed by a legate sent from the Venetian doge. This legate could apply Venetian civil law in his court when the defendant was a Venetian. If the defendant was a Greek, the crime or dispute was adjudicated according to Byzantine law. But this Byzantine recognition of Venetian law came barely five years before the fall of Constantinople to the Latins.

The position of Venetian merchants in Syria and Palestine was considerably different. In these lands the Genoese and the Pisans assisted the crusading effort several years before the Venetians, and these western Italian maritime republics gained greater rights and colonial privileges than did the Venetians. Certain cities in the crusader principalities such as Antioch, Jubail, Tyre, and Acre came to be the center of the Genoese colonial empire. The Pisan strength lay in Tyre and Jaffa, with some grants also in Sidon, Acre, and Caesarea. The Venetian colonies in the crusader states were never as large or as profitable as their counterparts in the Byzantine empire. The Venetians, however, like the Genoese and the Pisans, profited from the dependency of the Latin inhabitants of the crusader states upon Italian sea power. Venetian colonies in Syria and Palestine were centers of Venetian law and custom, unlike the Byzantine areas where Venetians were subject not to their own but to Byzantine law. The Venetians in the Holy Land, like the citizens of other Italian cities, gained fractions of ports and also parts of the adjacent countryside.

Whereas during the First Crusade Genoa transported the crusaders to the Levant and assisted them in their battles, and Pisa sent its archbishop, Daimbert, and a powerful fleet, Venice participated only later and unofficially. A private Venetian fleet of only thirty ships commanded by John Michiel, the son of doge Vitale I Michiel, sailed from Venice in July 1099. It stopped at Zara and along the Dalmatian coast, wintered at Rhodes from October 28, 1099, to May 27, 1100, where it defeated a numerically superior Pisan fleet, and finally arrived in Jaffa on the coast of Palestine. In July 1100 the Venetians in Palestine

---

24. Borsari, "Il Commercio veneziano," p. 997 and note 57, draws a distinction between Venetians resident in Constantinople outside the Venetian quarter and those who tarried in Constantinople for brief periods in the Venetian quarter, the former being subject to Byzantine law and obligations, the latter enjoying all the privileges granted to Venetians. It is difficult to accept such a distinction.

received from Godfrey of Bouillon generous promises of privileges in the kingdom of Jerusalem; after his death, they supported the Christian forces besieging Haifa in the fall of 1100 before returning home.

Godfrey's promises included special rights in all cities, inland and coastal, to be conquered by the Franks, comprising in each city a church and a marketplace and exemption from all tribute. The Venetians were to have all rights of recovery in case of shipwreck, especially near Jaffa and Haifa. However, these generous promises were probably not implemented with specific grants in particular cities.[25] The general rights were renewed by Baldwin I, king of Jerusalem, sometime between 1101 and 1104.[26] Evidence of specific Venetian territorial and commercial grants appears later. The Venetians gained a street in Acre as reward for their help in the conquest of Sidon, where they had sent a large force of 100 vessels in 1110.[27]

A decade elapsed before the Venetians participated again in the crusades or received any additional territorial grants in the Latin kingdom of Jerusalem. At the request of legates sent in 1119 by king Baldwin II, doge Domenico Michiel sent a Venetian fleet to Syria.[28] This fleet won a great battle with the Egyptian fleet off Ascalon in 1123 and assisted the Frankish knights in the siege of Tyre until its capitulation July 7, 1124. Venetian money also assisted the crusaders at Tyre; 100,000 bezants were lent to the patriarch and the king.

The specific Venetian privileges promised before these battles are described in detail in a document issued to the Venetians by Gormond ("Warmundus"), patriarch of Jerusalem, the actual ruler of the kingdom while Baldwin II was held captive by Belek, lord of Aleppo.[29] This grant, known as the *pactum Warmundi,* promised Venice one third of the still-to-be-conquered cities of Tyre and Ascalon. Also the Venetians received as much real estate on the Piazza San Marco in Jerusalem as the king had. With their land in Acre they received a mill, an oven, a bath, exemption from tribute, and, unless buying from non-Venetians, the right to use their own weights and measures. In other cities of the kingdom which had been mentioned in earlier

---

25. Tafel and Thomas, I, 64–65; Andrea Dandolo, *Chronica,* pp. 221–223. See also Errara, "I Crociati veneziani," p. 266; Cessi, *Storia di Venezia,* II, 338–342; Schaube, *Handelsgeschichte,* pp. 124–125; Heyd, tr. Raynaud, *Histoire du commerce,* I, 148.

26. Tafel and Thomas, I, 66.

27. Errara, "I Crociati veneziani," pp. 271–275; Schaube, *Handelsgeschichte,* p. 130.

28. Tafel and Thomas, I, 78. Variant MS. readings give the fleet at 200 galleys and warships, or at 4 heavily armed *navi* carrying pilgrims, knights, and horses, along with 40 galleys.

29. *Ibid.,* I, 79–81. See also Prawer, "I Veneziani e le colonie veneziane nel regno latino di Gerusalemme," *Venezia e il levante,* ed. Pertusi, I-2, 633–636.

treaties, the *pactum Warmundi* again promised them a street, a bath, an oven, and full right of personal inheritance, even if the Venetian died intestate. The Venetians were given their own law courts for suits between themselves or whenever a Venetian was sued or accused by a non-Venetian. If, however, a Venetian sued a non-Venetian the case was to be tried in the royal courts. The property of a deceased Venetian would remain in Venetian hands. The Venetian loan to the crusaders at Tyre was to be repaid to Venice by a grant each June of 300 "Saracen bezants" (dinars) from the revenues of Tyre. These privileges, when considered as a whole, signified that Venetians in Acre and Tyre were to enjoy complete extraterritorial rights. In addition to these extraordinary legal rights, the Venetians in the Latin kingdom of Jerusalem, as in the Byzantine empire, had astonishing tax exemptions. They needed to pay no taxes or tributes, in contrast to other local inhabitants, Latin or native. These grants to the Venetians were confirmed by Baldwin II after his release in May 1125. In return, for the future defense of Tyre, Baldwin II forced the Venetians to agree to furnish defenders in proportion to their one-third share of the city. These grants and special privileges were confirmed even in the thirteenth century.

These basic grants of the *pactum Warmundi* were made to the doge Domenico Michiel, to his successors, and to the people of Venice. Tyre became the principal Venetian port in the kingdom of Jerusalem, and the cathedral of St. Mark in Tyre, subject to St. Mark in Venice, became the principal Venetian church in Syria. The doge continued to enjoy these revenues from property in the Latin kingdom of Jerusalem until 1164 when another Michiel doge, Vitale II, needed money to finance his state. He mortgaged his revenues in the Latin kingdom to the *Opera Sancti Marci,* the quasi-public institution in Venice which directed work on the construction of the basilica of St. Mark, and whose chief officer, appointed by the doge in the twelfth century, was called the Procurator of St. Mark. The Tyrian property which the doge thus alienated from his private purse comprised the street in Tyre and the Venetian wharf, the cathedral of St. Mark in Tyre, and the revenue of 300 bezants collected from the customs at the port of Acre. In the spring of 1165 he also alienated title to a street and an oven in Tripoli.[30] The next doge, Sebastian Ziani, in 1176 mortgaged the ducal revenues in Tyre to the Opera Sancti Marci for five years in order to repay Romano Mairano the 600 pounds

---

30. Tafel and Thomas, I, 140–147.

of Venetian pennies he had spent in 1172 to rescue Venetians from Constantinople.[31] Nevertheless, the Venetian citizens in Tyre and Acre continued to enjoy the protection of Venetian law, although after 1164 it was administered not by civil magistrates but by the procurator of the cathedral church of St. Mark in Tyre.

An example of Venetian law functioning in Tyre occurs in a document dated April 1157, after a Venetian citizen, Vitale Pantaleone Malvicinus, died in Tyre. When his nephew John Pantaleone arrived from Romania to claim the inheritance, he called together all the Venetians living in Tyre to meet in the church of St. Mark. There, after much discussion, it was unanimously decided that John should inherit his uncle's house and goods, as well as the case (*saccatellum*) containing the certificate of fief and deeds of land which he had owned. However, Peter Morosini, rector of St. Mark in Tyre, disputed the award, since he had possession of the *saccatellum* and claimed that the deceased had bequeathed the deeds to him.[32] This example of Venetian justice in Tyre illustrates the unusual judicial freedom granted the Venetians in the *pactum Warmundi*. It also illustrates the strength of the great noble land-holding Venetian family of Pantaleone in twelfth-century Tyre.

During the Third Crusade, after the Venetians had sent a fleet to assist the crusaders in the siege of Acre, the Venetian privileges in the Holy Land were reconfirmed in May 1190 by Conrad of Montferrat on behalf of king Philip Augustus. The Venetians also received papal guarantees that their church of St. Mark in Tyre would continue to enjoy its special privileges.

The Venetian state, in separate treaties with the Latin princes of Antioch and Tripoli, had its particular privileges in these principalities confirmed. The first surviving treaty with Antioch is dated May 1140, but a treaty of 1153 refers to grants made by the Antiochene princes to Venice at the beginning of the century. The Venetian privileges granted in May 1140 by Raymond of Poitiers included the right to enter, to depart, and to remain in Antioch. In Seleucia two sacks in each camel-load of merchandise were to be free from tax. The Venetians also gained freedom of the seas and the right to recover ships and merchandise in case of shipwreck, as well as the right to be judged by their own laws in their own courts and the grant of a *fondaco,* a garden, and a house.[33]

---

31. *Ibid.,* I, 167–171.

32. Morozzo della Rocca and Lombardo, *Documenti,* I, no. 126. For the Pantaleoni see Prawer, "Étude de quelques problèmes agraires," pp. 14–15.

33. Tafel and Thomas, I, 102–103. The addition of Seleucia to this treaty suggests that Ray-

These Venetian privileges in Antioch were again detailed in 1153 by Reginald of Châtillon, his wife Constance, and her son Bohemond (III). This enumeration, however, appears to be merely a repetition of the grants made by earlier princes of Antioch, Bohemond I (1099–1111), Tancred (regent 1104–1112), and Bohemond II (1126–1130). It was witnessed by all of Reginald's vassals in the principality of Antioch. By the terms of the grant, the Venetians could come and go freely and, subject to certain taxes, could trade throughout the principality. The Venetians were to pay a sales tax at a lower rate than that paid by other merchants. For transactions in silk and linen cloth the rate was reduced from five percent to four percent, and for other transactions, from seven percent to five percent. The departure tax was also reduced, from 1 bezant 8 denarii to 1 bezant for each ass-load of merchandise, and from 2½ bezants to 2 bezants for each camel-load. They were granted the right to recover their ships and goods should they be shipwrecked on the coasts of the principality of Antioch or of its dependencies. They were also permitted to hold a court in their *fondaco* in Antioch, where Venetian law and legal procedure would prevail, including the right of appeal to Venice itself.[34] Although these princely grants did not mention any Venetian lands in the principality of Antioch, other documents do. Pons, count of Tripoli (1127–1137), gave the usufruct of a house in Tripoli to the church of St. Mark in Venice.[35] In 1167, the Venetian legate to the court of the prince of Antioch received exemption for Venice of one half the commercial tribute, and later Bohemond II exempted Venice from all tribute except a one percent sales tax.[36]

The Venetian privileges in Tyre, Antioch, and Tripoli also were included in the mortgage executed by Vitale II Michiel to the *Opera Sancti Marci* in 1164, and confirmed in a bull of pope Alexander III in the spring of 1165, and renewed in 1176.[37]

This catalogue of privileges enjoyed by Venetians living in the Latin kingdom of Jerusalem and in the principalities of Antioch and Tripoli demonstrates a continuing Venetian mercantile interest in these ports. Here the Venetians could live under Venetian law, which they could not do in the Byzantine empire. As long as Christian Latin rulers held control of the coastal cities in Syria and Palestine

---

mond of Antioch claimed the seaport of the disappearing kingdom of Cilician Armenia. See volume II of the present work, pp. 635–637, 650.

34. Tafel and Thomas, I, 133–135; Schaube, *Handelsgeschichte,* pp. 125, 137.

35. Tafel and Thomas, I, 76–77.

36. *Ibid.,* I, 148–150, 175–177; Schaube, *Handelsgeschichte,* p. 138.

37. Tafel and Thomas, I, 145–147.

in the twelfth century, the Venetians sought to maintain their interests there.

The conditions of Venetian trade with Moslem Egypt were different, because from time to time both popes and Byzantine emperors prohibited Christians from trading with Moslems. Since traces of this trade survive from the earliest years of Venetian overseas commerce, however, Venetians must have found it quite profitable.

The Venetians began commercial relations with Saracen Egypt at an early date, but their commercial and legal privileges there are not well documented until the thirteenth century. In the seventh century, Venetians were already feuding in Egypt with the Byzantine family of Prasini. During the reign of doge Giustiniano Partecipazio (827–829) two Venetian merchants, Bonus, tribune of Malamocco, and Rusticus of Torcello, sailed to Alexandria with ten merchant vessels. The voyage was illegal, because doge Angelo Partecipazio had agreed in 819 to support emperor Leo's prohibition of all trade with Egypt and Syria. When they arrived in Alexandria, Greek monks, who were custodians of the shrine of St. Mark and feared the Moslem Egyptian rulers, assisted the two Venetians in removing the body of St. Mark from its accustomed place and hiding it in a barrel of pickled pork. Here the relic would be safe from search by Egyptian port officials because pork was an abomination to Moslems. After they carried the barrel with its sacred relic on board a Venetian vessel, it was stored directly under the mast. They returned safely to Venice, protected from storms or Egyptian attack by the relics of the saint, or so the chronicles relate.[38] Such clandestine voyages to Egypt continued.

During the century before the crusades, the Venetian fleet was more powerful than the Byzantine navy and operated independently of it. In the marketplaces of Egypt, Venetians exchanged Dalmatian slaves, ship lumber, and weapons for luxury products. The great Venetian doge between 991 and 1009, Peter II Orseolo, legitimized the Venetian trade with Egypt by concluding a commercial treaty with the Fāṭimid imams.[39]

During the later eleventh and twelfth centuries Venetians voyaged to Alexandria in every generation, but with varying frequency. Products carried to the Egyptian ports included oil, horsehair, lumber, and

---

38. For the Prasini affair see Andrea Dandolo, *Chronica,* p. 89. For the episode of the relic of St. Mark see *ibid.,* pp. 146–147; John the Deacon, in *MGH, SS.,* VII, 16; Martin da Canal, *Les Estoires,* ed. Limentani, pp. 18–23; cf. Manfroni, *I Colonizzatori,* I, 7; Kretschmayr, *Geschichte,* I, 61.

39. Kretschmayr, *Geschichte,* I, 76, 139, 177.

copper. Goods brought out of Egypt by Venetians included pepper, alum, and linen.[40] Venetian legal business while in Alexandria was handled by Venetian priests and notaries, who apparently traveled with the ships.[41] No evidence suggests that Venice had any permanent commercial settlements in Egypt before the thirteenth century.

The intermittent nature of these ventures can be explained by Venice's occasional naval assistance to the Latin kingdom of Jerusalem. A Venetian war fleet in Palestine always resulted in a rupture with Egypt, because Moslem Egypt attempted to dominate these waters with its fleet. Early in the twelfth century, when the crusaders were trying to conquer the seaports of Palestine from Egypt and Damascus, the king of Jerusalem and the pope requested Venetian naval assistance. Doge Domenico Michiel led a large Venetian fleet to Palestine and, on May 30, 1123, won a great victory over the Egyptian fleet near the port of Ascalon. The Venetian chronicler reports that so much Saracen blood stained the sea that more blood than water could be seen.[42] After the victory the Venetian ships captured ten Egyptian vessels loaded with rich spices, silks, tapestries, and precious stones. Thereafter, the Venetian fleet participated in the conquest of Tyre. These victories secured for the Venetians important commercial rights in Palestine, as noted above, but Venetian trade with Egypt is not documented again until 1135.

Venetians engaged in vigorous trade with the Egyptian ports of Alexandria and Damietta between 1135 and 1147 and again between 1161 and 1168. The greatest number of Venetian voyages to Egypt cluster in those years when Venetian trade to Constantinople was unsafe or prohibited.[43] Venetian commercial voyages to Egypt abruptly ceased

40. Morozzo della Rocca and Lombardo, *Documenti,* I, nos. 11, 65, 149, 248, 345, 368. The cargo of one Venetian ship in 1182 included linen cloth, armor, soap, wax, raisins, almonds, grain, and olives: *ibid.,* no. 331.

41. The priest and notary Peter Mayrano, possibly related to the Venetian merchant Romano Mairano, figured prominently as the notary who drew up most Venetian commercial contracts in Alexandria. He did not live there, however, but traveled with the Venetian fleet. He also drew up contracts at Zara and Acre. Morozzo della Rocca and Lombardo, *Documenti,* I, nos. 248–262, 291, 293, 309, 310, 312, 322, 323, 331.

42. *Historia ducum veneticorum,* in *MGH, SS., XIV,* 74. See also Kretschmayr, *Geschichte,* I, 225–226; Grousset, *Histoire,* I, 603.

43. For voyages to Egypt before the Byzantine renewal of Venetian trading privileges in 1148 see Morozzo della Rocca and Lombardo, *Documenti,* I, nos. 65 and 74, and *Zusto,* ed. Lanfranchi, pp. 16, 19. For voyages to Egypt again when Venice prohibited trade with Byzantium in 1167–1168 after Greek violence against Latin merchants, see Morozzo della Rocca and Lombardo, *Documenti,* I, nos. 179, 183, 187, 191, 193–198, 201, 203, 207. For voyages to Egypt from 1173 to 1184, when Venetians were expelled from the Venetian quarter in Constantinople, see Morozzo della Rocca and Lombardo, *Documenti,* I, nos. 247, 248, 258, 345, 347, 351, and *Zusto,* ed. Lanfranchi, no. 27.

in March 1168, when the winter voyages between Constantinople and Alexandria of that year were paid off. Because Byzantine and Pisan ships in 1168 and 1169 supported the invasion of Egypt by king Amalric of Jerusalem,[44] it was not safe for any Latin merchants, including the Venetians, in Moslem Egypt.

Between 1173 and 1184 Venetian commercial voyages to Egypt greatly increased. The only twelfth-century evidence of Venetian trade with the North African cities of Ceuta and Bugia comes in these years also. An official peace treaty was drawn up between the government of Saladin in Egypt and doge Sebastian Ziani of Venice about 1175. By its terms Venetians could buy and sell their wares and also travel in safety in Egypt. Simultaneously Venice made peace with the Moslem rulers of Tunisia.[45] These treaties were negotiated to compensate the Venetian merchants for their loss of trading rights in Constantinople after the great Byzantine raid on the Venetian quarter in 1171.

In the last quarter of the century, the Egyptian destination seems to have been an alternative or extra port-of-call for Venetian merchants. In 1182 a Venetian fleet sailing to Constantinople was met by another Venetian fleet fleeing from the Greek attack on the Latins in Constantinople. Warned by their compatriots, the outgoing Venetian fleet redirected its voyage to Egypt.[46] For the next two years, prudent Venetian merchants scheduled their voyages either to Constantinople or to Alexandria.[47] After the Venetians returned to their quarter in Constantinople in 1183, Venetian voyages were often planned to both Constantinople and Alexandria.[48] In 1183 a Christian war fleet, including Venetian ships, sailed against Saladin in Egypt.[49] Nonetheless, Venetian voyages of trade to Egypt continued until 1188, when doge Orio Mastropiero stopped all overseas voyages in response to Venice's preparation for the Third Crusade. A large Venetian war fleet challenged Egyptian naval supremacy in 1189 by landing in Tyre and assisting Richard I of England in recovering Acre.[50] Venetians hesitated to trade in Egypt in the last decade of the century. These rup-

44. Andrea Dandolo, *Chronica,* p. 249; Grousset, *Histoire,* II, 514–531, 542–551.

45. Kretschmayr, *Geschichte,* I, 219; Grousset, *Histoire,* I, 81.

46. "Dixerunt nobis: Quid statis hic, si non fugitis omnes mortui estis, quia nos et omnes Latini de Constantinopoli sunt discomissi." Morozzo della Rocca and Lombardo, *Documenti,* I, no. 331.

47. *Ibid.,* I, nos. 345, 347; *Zusto,* ed. Lanfranchi, no. 27.

48. For such contracts between 1161 and 1168 see Morozzo della Rocca and Lombardo, *Documenti,* I, nos. 148, 149, 155, 159, 179, 183, 187–191, 193–207. From 1183 to 1190 see *ibid.,* I, nos. 345, 347, 368, 375; and *Zusto,* ed. Lanfranchi, no. 29.

49. Kretschmayr, *Geschichte,* I, 219.

50. *Annales venetici breves,* in *MGH, SS.,* XIV, 72; Andrea Dandolo, *Chronica,* p. 270.

tures explain the intermittent character of Venetian commercial contracts with Egypt, in comparison with Byzantium or the crusader states.

In summary, Venetian privileges in the Near East during the first century of the crusades consisted of the right to trade freely in specific ports, to exercise special customs privileges, and to have *fondachi* in certain major centers. These rights were different in the Byzantine empire, in the crusader states, and in Moslem Egypt. The Greek emperors carefully designated which ports were open to Venetian merchants, excluding the Black Sea and most of the islands of the Aegean Sea. They allowed the Venetians to pay lower duties than Byzantine or other Latin merchants, and allowed them their own quarter in Constantinople.

In the Frankish principalities in Syria, Venice received grants even more generous. The absolute dependence by the Latin kings of Jerusalem upon Venetian, Genoese, and Pisan sea power forced them to promise larger trading areas in their seaports than Venice held in Byzantine ports. Often these promises were made even before the Christians had conquered these ports. In addition, the crusader princes regarded Venice as an independent state, permitted it to exercise its own law and justice, and exempted it from most or all taxes in the Syrian and Palestinian cities. Venetians also had the right of recovery in case of shipwreck. Their envoys received these grants not only from the Latin kings of Jerusalem but also from certain princes of Antioch and from Pons, count of Tripoli.

Venetian commercial arrangements with the rulers of Egypt before the Fourth Crusade are not well documented, but certainly such agreements existed as early as the year 1000. When such treaties were in force, Venetian merchants in Egypt could freely buy and sell, come and go. They probably did not settle permanently in Egypt. They sent their vessels to Egypt at irregular intervals, depending on the political situation, the safety of the seas, and the availability of other markets.

We may now turn from the privileges which Venetians enjoyed to the manner in which they profited from trade in the Near East. The city of Constantinople was the most frequently recorded destination of Venetian voyages. For the period 1150 to 1183, there survive sixty-seven contracts to go to Constantinople, forty-three to go to Romania. In contrast there are only twenty-five for the crusader states, of which eighteen specify Acre. There also survive twenty contracts for voyages to Egypt, nineteen for Alexandria and one for Damietta.

As the political situation in the eastern Mediterranean became increasingly muddied after 1183, these proportions changed. Constantinople remained the destination in forty-two of the surviving contracts dated between 1184 and 1205. Other parts of Romania are mentioned in eighteen.[51] In contrast, Venetian trade with the crusader states during the same period slackened; we have records of only twenty-two contracts. Trade with Egypt also diminished, with only ten contracts surviving, nine of these to Alexandria. As the above numbers suggest, Venice carried on more trade with areas under Byzantine control than with other distant ports in the half century before the fall of Constantinople.

The Genoese trade with the Levant, at least during the period 1154–1164, was divided differently, to judge from the cartularies of the notary John Scriba. During this decade, he records fifty-eight commercial agreements concerning Alexandria, thirty-four Syria, and twenty Byzantium. The Genoese sent 9,031 Genoese pounds to Alexandria, 10,075 to Syria, but only 2,007 to Byzantium.[52] Later in the century, Genoa's major trading interest lay in the crusading states; when comparisons can be made, only one-fourth of the annual Genoese investments in Levantine trade had to do with Byzantium. Pisan commercial interests centered on Egypt.[53]

The strength of the Venetian commercial interests in the Byzantine empire in the twelfth century was the result of political ties. Venice had been subject to Byzantium since its founding. Even though the Venetians considered themselves an independent and autonomous state, the emperor Alexius I Comnenus treated them as his own subjects in the chrysobull of 1082. This helps explain why they received such extraordinary commercial privileges in Constantinople and certain other ports, assuring them of the largest share of the carrying trade in the Aegean. Genoa and Pisa, not being subject to Constantinople, received no such commercial privileges at that time. It is significant that most of the surviving Venetian commercial contracts specify Constantinople as a destination. Few documents bear witness to Venetian trade between one Aegean port and another, excluding the capital, or between Venice and an Aegean port only.[54] Perhaps the lack of

51. Other seaports and towns in the Byzantine empire named in commercial contracts from 1150 to 1204 include Abydus, Anido (Anydros), Armiro (Halmyros), Arta, Catodica, Corfu, Corinth, Cotrone, Crete, Kitro (Citrum), LoDromiti (Adramyttium), Smyrna, Sparta, Thebes, and Thessalonica.

52. Prawer, *The Crusaders' Kingdom*, p. 399.

53. Cessi, *Le Colonie medioevali*, I, 61–64. The author is indebted to the late Vsevolod Slessarev for precise information on Genoese trade.

54. For example, Venice to Thebes: Morozzo della Rocca and Lombardo, *Documenti*, I, no. 418; Venice to Corinth: *ibid.*, no. 369; Venice to Thebes, Catodica, and the Morea: *ibid.*,

evidence of commerce between the Aegean ports results from the accident that many of the surviving documents were drawn up in Venice rather than in the Aegean ports. Later thirteenth-century documents from Crete suggest that Venetians engaged in a flourishing Aegean carrying trade. The Genoese also pursued the carrying trade between various points in the Greek empire, as revealed by lists of Genoese losses in Byzantine waters.

The monies used by the Venetians in the Byzantine east were the gold hyperperon of the old weight (*perperi auri veteres pensantes* or the *perperi auri paleoskenurgios bonos pensantes*) and occasionally the good gold hyperperon of the new weight (*perperi auri boni novi pensantes*). After 1184 the Venetians also found their own pounds of Venetian pennies (*libra denariorum venetialium*) increasingly acceptable in Byzantine ports.[55]

During the fifty years before the Fourth Crusade Venetian commercial interest in the crusader states remained at a constant level. They regularly sent trading expeditions to Acre and to Tyre, and less frequently to Antioch, Beirut, and Jaffa. Often investments in voyages to the crusader states specified that the business should be carried on in more than one Syrian port, and several contracts mention as a destination Tyre or Acre and Constantinople, or a Syrian port and Alexandria. The money in circulation in Acre and Tyre was called, by the Venetians, gold Saracen bezants (*bicanci auri saracenates*) or Saracen bezants of the new weight (*bicanci saracenati novi pensantes*). Occasionally the documents added the identifying clause "of the coins of the king of Jerusalem" (*de moneta regis Ierusalem*).[56]

Venetian trade with Egypt took third place among distant areas specified in destinations for overseas investment in the twelfth century. As the century drew to a close, the Venetian contracts for commercial investment in Alexandria stipulated that business investments were to be made not only in Egypt but also in Romania or in the ports of Messina, Acre, Constantinople, or Crete. The money in circulation in Alexandria was called old Saracen gold bezants (*bicanci auri saracenates veteres*).

To these markets on the eastern shores of the Mediterranean Venetian ships brought western goods, including copper, lumber, iron, inexpensive textiles, and some gold. Slaves had also been an important commodity for the Venetian economy for centuries. In the eighth cen-

---

no. 235; Venice to Thebes, Catodica, the Morea, Thessalonica, Corinth, and Constantinople: *ibid.,* no. 353; Venice to Durazzo, Corfu, and Thessalonica: *ibid.,* no. 400.

55. Robbert, "The Venetian Money Market," pp. 13–14, 19, 65–66, 76–78, 85–88.

56. *Ibid.,* p. 81.

tury pope Zacharias (741–752), pope Hadrian I (772–795), and Charlemagne prohibited Venetian or other Italian slavers from going to Moslem lands and placed severe penalties upon such traffic.[57] Several ninth- and tenth-century Venetian doges prohibited, under severe penalties, the sale of Christian slaves, yet Venice continued to be a market for slaves in these pre-crusading centuries. In the ninth century slaves from Bulgaria were sold in Venice by Jewish merchants.[58] Venetian merchants during the twelfth and thirteenth century owned and traded in pagan slaves. For example, in Tyre in 1192–1194, three Venetians and a citizen of Acre shared in the profit from owning a Saracen slave named Cotoble, whom they had obtained through a loan from Conrad of Montferrat.[59] In 1199 a slave from Slavonia was sold in Venice to bishop Dominic of Chioggia, a fishing village near Venice.[60]

Household slaves were often freed by their Venetian owners in their wills.[61] In two of these, freedom was conditioned on serving the testator's children until they reached maturity. A Croatian slave named Dobramiro took his master's surname Sten (Stagnario) and traveled as a merchant for over a decade from Venice to Sparta, Corinth, Constantinople, and Alexandria. His son Pancrazio and grandsons Giovanni, Domenico, and Zaccaria followed in his footsteps with increasing profit.[62] Zaccaria held office as councillor of the Venetian podestà in Constantinople in 1207. Five household slaves of the chaplain-priest of the basilica of St. Mark in Venice were freed and given personal possessions by his will, dated 1151.[63] The trade in human merchandise thus must have continued during the crusading centuries, but recent studies of the Venetian slave trade have concerned the fourteenth and fifteenth centuries, beyond the scope of this chapter.[64]

Other articles of trade which the Italian merchants exported from Italy to the Levant are revealed by the Genoese cartularies.[65] In the

57. Andrea Dandolo, *Chronica,* p. 175.

58. Lopez, in *Cambridge Economic History,* II, 287.

59. Morozzo della Rocca and Lombardo, *Documenti,* I, nos. 441, 412, 425.

60. *Ibid.,* I, no. 442.

61. *Ibid.,* I, nos. 49, 133, 246; II, nos. 535, 661; Lombardo and Morozzo della Rocca, *Nuovi documenti,* nos. 79, 92; Archivio di Stato di Venezia, San Zaccaria, B. 24, 1168, Sept.

62. Borsari, "Il Commercio veneziano," pp. 992–995.

63. Morozzo della Rocca and Lombardo, *Documenti,* I, no. 100.

64. Luzzatto, *Storia economica di Venezia,* pp. 63–64, 148, 176, 184. Charles Verlinden, "Venezia e il commercio degli schiavi provenienti dalle coste orientali del Mediterraneo," *Venezia e il levante,* ed. Pertusi, I-2, 911–929.

65. The late Vsevolod Slessarev, unable to complete his study on Genoa and the crusades for this volume, graciously permitted me to draw on his unpublished results. The following two paragraphs are in part taken from his manuscript.

second half of the twelfth century, the exports "from Genoa to Constantinople . . . consisted mainly of textiles, hauberks, and occasionally of quicksilver and slaves." In the thirteenth century, cargoes from Genoa "consisted mostly of manufactured goods made locally or transshipped from France, the Low Countries, or Lombardy. Textiles of various kinds were most prominent; also, gold thread, silver vases, wooden bowls, and goblets. Iron implements and armor made up the rest of the cargoes; only rarely do the documents mention precious metals. Virtually every branch of Genoa's artisan class took the opportunity to export its wares to Syria. To give but one example, a surprising number of swords, shields, hauberks, daggers, and crossbows found their way to the land of almost perpetual war."

In Syria and Romania, the Venetians and Genoese merchants purchased precious goods and grain. Certain of their purchases were produced locally and others came to Levantine ports from collecting points farther east. Arab sailors on the Indian Ocean brought galingale, nutmeg, camphor, and cloves to Aden. From there, these goods were sent by camel caravans through Arabia to the seaports of Syria. By another route, the silks from China reached the Levant by way of the Indian Ocean and the Persian Gulf. Baghdad, one of the principal inland markets of western Asia, collected merchandise coming overland from the Far East, as well as musk and rhubarb from Central Asia and muslins from Mosul. Baghdad was also a principal market for pearls from the Persian Gulf. Aleppo was the great silk market. Damascus, another terminus of caravan routes from Asia, itself produced silks, gold brocades, fine light cloths, and lamé. The goods purchased in these inland markets were brought by camel and donkey caravan routes directly to the Syrian seaports controlled by the Christians of the Latin kingdom of Jerusalem. Italian merchants did not go to the interior until the next century. In the twelfth century, Genoa imported silk garments, dyestuffs, and grain from Constantinople. In the next century, return shipments to Genoa from the Levant did not consist exclusively of spices and colorants, but included such raw products as cotton and wood.

The crusader states were not oblivious to the profits to be gained from taxing the caravans which criss-crossed their lands. Linen carried from Egypt to Damascus and Baghdad was among the products so taxed. The Assises of Jerusalem reveal that in Acre a merchant could buy rhubarb from the Far East, musk from Tibet, pepper, cinnamon, nutmeg, cloves, aloes, camphor, and other eastern products. There he might also find ivory from India and Africa, or incense and dates from Arabia. Beirut, another port along the Syrian coast frequented by the Genoese but not by Venetians, contained shops selling incense, indigo, brazilwood, and pearls, all from Central Asia.

In addition to purchasing luxury items such as drugs, spices, dyes, and silk in the ports of Syria, Italian merchants also acquired local foods and textiles for export. The land of Syria-Palestine was extremely fertile and produced lemons, oranges, figs, almonds, grapes to be made into fine wine, and olives from which oil could be extracted. The country estates held by the Venetians around the city of Tyre in 1243 included fields, orchards, and vineyards. These were cultivated by native agricultural workers, organized under their own leaders. But a portion of their crops went to their Venetian landlords, including also rents or manorial dues paid in chickens, eggs, and cheese. Of these local products, sugarcane, unknown to Europeans until the First Crusade, was both cultivated and refined for export from Syria during the years of the Latin kingdom of Jerusalem. In addition to the linen and silk products brought to the Syrian ports from Egypt and from the Moslem cities inland, Syria itself also produced cotton and silk for sale to western merchants either as raw fiber, as unfinished cloth, or as fine fabric. Another fine finished textile produced in Syria was camels'-hair cloth. Syrian fabrics received special acclaim in western Europe because they were fabulously dyed in shades of indigo, Tyrian purple, and red. All these dyestuffs likewise were produced in Syria. Very fine, transparent glass from Tyre was also in great demand.

From the lands under Byzantine control the Venetians exported many products. They found grain at Rodosto on the Sea of Marmara, a port where they had special privileges, and furs and salt fish in Thessalonica. They purchased much fine silk at Thebes, other fine woven goods in Boeotia, and silks from Negroponte. Cheese and cotton came from Thebes and Corinth. From Chios they acquired a resin from the mastic tree that was used in tanning and in varnishes. Halmyros, the port of Thessaly, exported grain. In the markets of Sparta and Modon in the Morea (Peloponnesus) the Venetians purchased oil.[66]

To organize these business ventures, Venetian merchants employed several types of business contracts: loans, the *colleganza,* the unilateral *commenda,* and the fraternal company.[67] The loan contract had

---

66. Brand, *Byzantium Confronts the West,* p. 204; Borsari, "Commercio veneziano," p. 996.

67. See Luzzatto, "Capitale e lavoro nel commercio veneziano dei secoli XI e XII," in *Studi di storia,* pp. 99–108; *idem,* "La Commenda nella vita economico dei secoli XII e XIV con particolaro riguardo a Venezia," *ibid.,* pp. 59–79; see also Astuti, *Origine e svolgimento storico della commenda fino al secolo XIII* (Documenti e studi per la storia del commercio e del diritto

two variations—the sea loan and the simple loan. The sea loan (*nauticum foenus*), the most common twelfth-century commercial contract in Venice, would be initiated by a man who was departing on a trading voyage. He borrowed from another more affluent merchant, agreeing to repay a specified sum (which included fixed interest) only after returning to the home port or some other specified destination, and only twenty or thirty days after docking. The traveling business man assumed all the expenses of his voyage. This contract did not limit the borrower in his commercial ventures in any way except to specify the place and time of repayment. In these contracts, the risk of the sea voyage and of piracy was born by the lender. Because the risk was stated, these interest-bearing contracts could avoid the charge of usury. For extremely dangerous voyages, the borrower paid high interest rates, sometimes up to fifty percent.[68]

A second type of sea loan (*cambio marittimo)* connected the loan with the exchange of one money for another. It was drawn up in one city and repayable in another, after the voyage, in another type of money. The amount of interest was disguised in the exchange rate. A variation of this sea-loan-exchange contract, called "dry" exchange, contained another clause in which the borrower was allowed to repay in the city of origin at a designated exchange rate. It was a "dry" exchange, because when the borrower exercised this option no sea voyage took place. The contract was a fiction used to avoid the charge of usury.

Simple business loans (*mutuo*) were repayable in the city of origin. Sometimes these loans were repaid in the same money as was borrowed, sometimes the loan involved an exchange rate. In either case the customary Venetian interest rate was twenty percent (de quinque sex per annum).

The second category of business contract used by the medieval Venetian merchants was the partnership or *commenda*. The subject of much scholarly controversy,[69] it appeared in two forms in twelfth- and thirteenth-century Venice. Essentially the partnership agreement was a legal contract between two parties, and their investment is de-

commerciale italiano, III; Casale Monferrato, 1933); Alfred E. Lieber, "Eastern Business Practices and Medieval European Commerce," *Economic History Review,* ser. 2, XXI (1968), 230–243; Lopez, *The Commercial Revolution,* pp. 73–77; and John H. Pryor, "The Origins of the *Commenda* Contract," pp. 5–37.

68. Morozzo della Rocca and Lombardo, *Documenti,* I, nos. 183, 223, 228, etc.

69. See above, note 67, and Lane, "Investment and Usury," pp. 58–68; his *Venice, a Maritime Republic,* pp. 52–53, 138–140; Lopez and Raymond, *Medieval Trade,* pp. 174–184. Examples of this *colleganza* are in Morozzo della Rocca and Lombardo, *Documenti,* I, nos. 141, 142, 207, 234, 236, 239, 334, 380, 404, 405, 409, 410, 413.

fined as an enterprise or business venture. One of the parties was the sedentary investor (*commendator*) and the other was the traveling partner (*tractator*) whose voyage and destination were sometimes stated. The profits were divided at the termination of the voyage. In the earliest form of Venetian partnership, known in Venice as *colleganza,* in Genoa as the *societas maris,* and termed the bilateral *commenda* in modern scholarship,[70] both parties invested capital. The investor contributed twice as much capital as the traveling partner. At the safe and successful completion of the business venture, usually a voyage, the two agreed to divide the profits in half. With three exceptions,[71] it is the only variety of partnership known to have been used by the Venetians before the Fourth Crusade.

Beginning in 1205, however, the Venetians, like other Italian merchants, began using another type of partnership known as the unilateral *commenda.* According to its terms, the sedentary investor contributed all the capital and assumed all the risk, while the other partner did the traveling for the business venture. They agreed that, at the conclusion of the voyage, three fourths of the profits should accrue to the sedentary investor and one fourth to the traveling partner. In these Venetian unilateral *commenda* contracts (with the exception of two quittances given by Oderico Belli in 1243 and 1253)[72] the notary did not identify the type of contract, as he commonly did in the first form of partnership, the bilateral *commenda.* The feature which distinguishes the *colleganza* (bilateral *commenda*) from the unilateral *commenda* is the shared risk; only the sedentary investor assumed the risk in the unilateral *commenda.* It has been observed that the sedentary investor received the same return on his investment in the unilateral *commenda* as he received when he contributed two thirds of the capital and received one half of the profit. The unilateral *commenda* appeared for the first time among Venetian commercial documents in August 1199, and then not again until 1205. After 1205 it completely replaced the older bilateral *commenda,* becoming even more common than the sea loan.[73] A useful, flexible business agreement, it continued to be used by Venetian merchants as late as the four-

70. The Venetian spelling is *colleganza* or *collegancia.* For examples see Morozzo della Rocca and Lombardo, *Documenti,* I, nos. 141, 234, 334, 337, 424. For the bilateral *commenda* see Pryor, "The Origins of the *Commenda* Contract," pp. 7–13.

71. Morozzo della Rocca and Lombardo, *Documenti,* I, nos. 343, 353, 444.

72. *Ibid.,* II, nos. 757, 816. The documents record repayment of a partnership, but the text uses the term *collegantia.* Compare Oderico Belli's earlier unilateral *commenda* with different partners in which he does not use the term *colleganza, ibid.,* nos. 749, 750.

73. The disappearance of the *colleganza* (bilateral *commenda*) in 1205 resulted from a legal ban against it, found in the statutes issued by Renier Dandolo, vice-doge for his father, Enrico

teenth century for trading ventures where the risk was great and where the Venetians did not regularly use their agents as resident employees in foreign ports.[74]

Venetians in the twelfth century also used a third type of contract, called the *compagnia* (the fraternal company contract). Originally used for apportioning the expense of ship construction between brothers, it developed into a widely used and very flexible type of business agreement. The partners, related by blood ties, combined their resources, of which each partner stated his share, then agreed to work for their common interest, to travel together to named or unnamed destinations, and to divide the profits in proportion to their respective investments. Liability of all partners was joint and unlimited. This agreement, originally made for a single voyage, could be prolonged with the consent of both parties and was used primarily where the investments of a deceased father were continued jointly by his heirs.[75]

These types of business contracts, the loans (especially the sea loan), the *colleganza* or bilateral *commenda,* the unilateral *commenda,* and the fraternal company, formed the bases for profitable investment by the Venetians in the Levant. A Venetian investor in foreign commerce, to minimize the risks, usually concluded several contracts in a single shipping season.

The often-discussed career of Romano Mairano demonstrates these elements of Venetian commerce.[76] Mairano actively participated first in commercial voyages to Halmyros in Thessaly and to Citrum (Kitro) near Thessalonica, but later and more often to Constantinople, to Alexandria, and to Acre. One year he went to Ceuta and Bugia in North Africa. Not only did his credibility and reliability as well as his good fortune rise, but the sums entrusted to him also increased steadily in value from an average of slightly over 30 perperi per contract before 1158 until 1167 when he took 1,106 perperi auri in eight sea loans to Alexandria. He usually sailed in his own ships, whose construction in Venice he had supervised and whose raw materials he had bought. He financed the shipbuilding by selling shares in the ships. Mairano, who frequently was mate (*nauclerius*) of his own ship,

---

Dandolo, absent from Venice on the Fourth Crusade: Pryor, "The Origins of the *Commenda* Contract," p. 13, note 28.

74. For examples after 1205 see Morozzo della Rocca and Lombardo, *Documenti,* II, nos. 467, 468, 469, 475, 478, 479, 483, 494, 495, etc.

75. *Ibid.,* I, nos. 70, 74, 96, 131, 156, 181, 253, 254, 271. See also Lopez and Raymond, *Medieval Trade,* p. 74, and Giorgio Zordan, "I Vari aspetti della Comunione familiare di Beni," pp. 127–194.

76. Heynen, *Zur Entstehung des Kapitalismus,* pp. 86–120; Luzzatto, "Capitale e lavoro," pp. 108–116.

not only purchased pepper and alum from Alexandria for his Venetian partners, but also sold iron, copper, and lumber at distant ports for other partners. His success was so phenomenal that the wealthiest citizen of Venice, Sebastian Ziani, even before he became doge in 1172, entrusted sums to Mairano for commercial voyages. The patriarch of Grado, Enrico Dandolo (uncle of the doge of the same name) appointed Mairano as his agent to collect the revenues from all the patriarchal possessions in Constantinople and granted him the privilege of enjoying there the special rights of the patriarchate. In return for these business opportunities, Mairano was to bring back to the patriarch each year 50 pounds of Venetian pennies in the best ship of the first annual convoy. For this responsibility in 1171 he carried a cargo of copper and a number of sea loans (including two from Sebastian Ziani) to Constantinople in a large new ship. This time he did not have his usual good fortune. A quarrel between the Venetians and the Greeks in Constantinople led to a major Byzantine raid upon the Venetian quarter. Greek hatred for the Venetians had been building up ever since the Venetians had disturbed the peace of the capital city in 1162 by ravaging the Genoese quarter. Aggravated by commercial jealousy and religious rivalry, and not in the least calmed by a succession of embassies between Venice and Constantinople, this hatred led the imperial government in 1171 to imprison the Venetians and confiscate all Venetian assets in Constantinople.

At the time of the raid Romano Mairano succeeded in carrying a number of Venetians to safety in Acre. His own losses, however, were so considerable that twelve years later he had still not repaid all his debts. In June 1175 doge Sebastian Ziani directed the procurator of St. Mark to pay Mairano 600 Venetian pounds from the revenues of the Venetian quarter in Tyre (which Mairano mortgaged to the procurator) because he had expended money amounting to 1,500 bezants in negotiating the escape of Venetian citizens.[77] A month later doge Sebastian Ziani, judge Peter Foscarini, and Romano Mairano's brother Samuel declared that Mairano had repaid the investments they had placed in his hands in 1170. In August of that year, the Mairano brothers, Romano and Samuel, had formed a fraternal company to build a ship for a voyage to Acre. According to its terms, Samuel was to pay off his indebtedness for the ship in Acre with 1500 Saracen bezants and after one year whatever profit they made was to be divided between them.

Even before being repaid through the revenues of the Venetian quar-

---

77. Tafel and Thomas, I, 167–171.

ter in Tyre, Mairano made a considerable profit from a voyage to Alexandria in 1173. Another of his business ventures was a voyage in 1177–1179 to the Barbary coast of Africa, the only recorded Venetian twelfth-century voyage into these Genoese and Pisan waters of the western Mediterranean. Although the expedition was profitable, Venetian commercial voyages to the west were not repeated until 1245.[78] Mairano continued his commercial activity for many years, traveling as mate on his own ships to Alexandria, Romania, and Tyre, with stops at Abydus and Citrum. Later, in 1192 and again in 1199, when Mairano must have been over sixty, his son carried the business investments for him to Apulia and Alexandria.

During the last quarter of the twelfth century, events occurred in the Byzantine empire, in the crusader states, and in Venice itself which anticipated the Fourth Crusade and the changing Venetian commercial interests in the Levant. The Byzantine empire declined in the second half of the twelfth century. Hatred and jealousy had been growing between the Greeks and the Latin merchants for a century or more, and this resulted in several outbursts of violence in Constantinople.[79] In 1162 the Pisans, assisted by the Venetians and the Greeks, attacked and sacked the Genoese merchant colony in Constantinople, causing the Genoese to flee the city. The Byzantines then exiled the Pisans from the capital city, leaving only the Venetians undisturbed. But Venetian relations with Constantinople soon deteriorated. The emperor Manuel, who wished to strengthen his hold on the Dalmatian provinces against king Stephen III of Hungary and against the Norman king William of Sicily, induced the Dalmatian cities of Spalato, Traù, and Ragusa to recognize Byzantine sovereignty once again. The pro-Greek sentiments of Ancona, the principal twelfth-century port on the Adriatic coast of Apulia, were encouraged when Byzantium, in 1167, gave commercial privileges to the Anconitans. The Venetian doge, Vitale II Michiel, in retaliation for these Byzantine acts, reassumed his title of *dux Dalmatiae* and refused to furnish military assistance to Byzantium against the Normans. The Greeks might have considered both the assumption of the title and the refusal of naval aid as acts of war by the Venetians. Possibly the Venetian doge placed an embargo on Venetian shipping to Constantinople about 1167–1170,

78. Morozzo della Rocca and Lombardo, *Documenti,* I, nos. 284, 285, 293, 294, 297; II, nos. 776, 777.

79. Andrea Dandolo, *Chronica,* pp. 249–251; *Historia ducum veneticorum,* in *MGH, SS.,* XIV, 77–78. See also Besta, "La Cattura," pp. 38–41, Brown, "The Venetians and the Venetian Quarter," pp. 83–86, and Brand, *Byzantium Confronts the West,* pp. 195–206.

but commercial documents continue to stipulate Venetian voyages into Greek waters.

Byzantine leaders, however, needed the commerce of the Italian cities. Late in 1169 Genoa began negotiations for renewal of its privileges in Constantinople, which were reëstablished by a treaty of May 1170. Similarly, the Pisan quarter in Constantinople was reëstablished by July 1170. Later that year a Venetian raid on the Genoese colony in Constantinople irritated the emperor Manuel. To alleviate relations with the emperor, Venice sent a strong embassy composed of two of its richest citizens, Sebastian Ziani and Orio Mastropiero, both of whom would later be doges. A promise of renewal of Venetian privileges seems to have been made, and Venetian merchants again began to send their merchant fleets to Constantinople, among them the ship of Romano Mairano. More than twenty thousand Venetians arrived in Constantinople carrying cash for purchases—arms and other merchandise. Hearing rumors of the emperor's bad faith, the doge sent Orio Mastropiero again and Enrico Dandolo, the future doge, to the Byzantine court to receive assurances that no harm was intended. Although the Venetians saw with alarm the concentration of Greek troops pouring into Constantinople, the emperor Manuel assured them of his good intentions. Then, suddenly, on March 12, 1171, the Greeks struck. Ten thousand Venetians in Constantinople were arrested and held in prisons or monasteries and their goods confiscated. Some were fortunate enough to escape, including those who boarded the great ship of Romano Mairano. Possibly this was the *Totus Mundus,* the largest ship ever seen by the Greeks, protected from their flaming projectiles by hides soaked in vinegar. "This was the greatest disaster to the city and so universal that there was not a single family in Venice that did not suffer some loss."[80]

The Venetian colony in Constantinople did not recover from this attack for more than a decade. In contrast, the Genoese and the Pisan colonies there began to prosper until the death of the pro-Latin emperor Manuel in 1180. His youthful son Alexius II Comnenus was deposed three years later by a distant relative, Andronicus Comnenus, whose partisans hated the Latin supporters of the unfortunate young emperor. Just before Andronicus entered Constantinople, he permitted the city mob to attack the Latin colonies. The bloody outrages, known as the Latin massacre, were directed mainly against the Pisans and the Genoese. As a result these colonies became extinct, and Pisan

---

80. Translated from the sixteenth-century chronicle of Daniel Barbaro, as quoted by Thiriet, "Les Chroniques vénitiennes de la Marcianne," p. 248.

and Genoese corsairs plagued the eastern seas until after the Fourth Crusade. Venetian sources make no mention of anti-Latin violence in 1182 because the Venetians had not yet returned to the city after the violence of 1171.[81] Similarly, the Genoese sources do not mention the anti-Venetian actions in Constantinople of 1171 because in that year no Genoese were there.

While the new emperor Andronicus was completing his assumption of power, he perceived his need for maritime allies. Hopes began to rise in Venice where, as early as February 1182, peace with the new emperor was expected.[82] After Andronicus's coronation in September 1183 a peace treaty was signed in which he promised to release the remaining Venetian captives and to reimburse the Venetians for some of their losses of 1171. By 1184 the Venetians again were sending merchant ships to Constantinople. Enrico Dandolo and other prominent Venetians represented the Venetian state in Constantinople in 1184 and 1185, during the brief reign of Andronicus Comnenus, when property lines were redrawn and correct title to real estate was established in the Venetian quarter.[83]

After the Normans of Sicily in 1185 attacked and sacked Thessalonica, the second city of the Byzantine empire, the Greeks in Constantinople rose up and killed Andronicus, the last Comnenus emperor. The new emperor, Isaac II Angelus, did not at first readmit the Genoese and Pisans to Constantinople, but did restore the full Venetian rights and privileges in return for their naval support. After receiving the three Venetian legates of doge Orio Mastropiero, Isaac in February 1187 granted three chrysobulls to the Venetians, who were formerly his subjects, but whom he now called his allies and friends.[84] By reissuing the chrysobulls of 1126 and 1148, he restored to the Venetians their quarter, their exemptions from tolls, and freedom of trade. In addition, the Greeks concluded a defensive alliance with Venice, whereby Venice promised on six months' notice in wartime to furnish between forty and one hundred war galleys under Venetian commanders. The Venetians were exempted from fighting Venice's allies, the German emperor or the Normans in Sicily.[85] Byzantium needed naval assistance because of the Turkish advances after the decisive Byzan-

81. See especially the quotation from the chronicle (1366) of Nicholas Trevisan, *ibid.,* p. 261.

82. Just before his death in 1179, Manuel released some Venetians, and certain Venetian credits in Constantinople were made available about the same time: Morozzo della Rocca and Lombardo, *Documenti,* I, nos. 313, 308, 311, 315, 316, 319, 348.

83. *Ibid.,* I, nos. 344, 345, 347, 348, 349, 351, etc.; Tafel and Thomas, I, 175, 177-178.

84. Brown, "The Venetians and the Venetian Quarter," p. 87; Tafel and Thomas, I, 179-203; Brand, *Byzantium Confronts the West,* pp. 197-199.

85. Tafel and Thomas, I, 179-189, 195-203.

tine defeat at Myriokephalon in 1176, because of the threats from the Norman kings of Sicily and their Hohenstaufen heirs, and because of the menace of the newly formed Second Bulgarian kingdom. In addition to the three chrysobulls of 1187, the Venetians also demanded restitution of damages from the raid of 1171. Finally, after two years of negotiations, and threatened by Frederick Barbarossa's preparations for the Third Crusade, Isaac promised Venice an annual subsidy and a token restitution of about one and one-half percent.[86]

These newly reconfirmed Venetian privileges and possessions in Constantinople were again jeopardized after 1195 when Alexius Angelus deposed and blinded his brother Isaac and assumed the imperial title as Alexius III. The new emperor at first distrusted the Venetians and favored their rivals, Genoa and Pisa, who had returned to Constantinople with privileges granted them by Isaac II in 1192. After Alexius III was threatened in 1196 by a Venetian fleet in Abydus, he renewed the Venetian commercial privileges in a chrysobull of November 1198, regranting the Venetian quarter in Constantinople, confirming Venetian commercial privileges, and renewing the naval alliance with Venice.[87] However, he granted no subsidies and no reimbursement to Venice during his reign (1195–1203), and in addition taxed Venetian property.

In summary, Venetian-Byzantine relations during the first century of the crusades reflected two needs. First, Venetian merchants needed legal confirmation from the Greeks of their right to trade and reside in the Byzantine empire. Whenever these privileges were jeopardized the Venetians made haste to negotiate a new agreement, as in 1148, in 1187, and in 1198. When peaceful negotiations had no result, Venice attacked Byzantine lands (1119–1126) or threatened to do so (1196). Second, the Byzantines needed Italian naval power and commercial experience. The Venetians provided these in a satisfactory manner until about 1150, when the Greek emperor Manuel began to play Genoa, Pisa, and Venice against each other. When one Italian state was privileged, the others were excluded. For example, in 1162 the Greeks exiled the Pisans and the Genoese. The Venetians remained until the destruction of their quarter in 1171. In 1169 the Greeks began negotiations with the Pisans and the Genoese, who shortly returned. Ten years later rioting and revolution destroyed the Genoese and Pisan

---

86. *Ibid.,* I, 206–211; Morozzo della Rocca and Lombardo, *Documenti,* I, nos. 369, 378, 379, 380, 396, 403–418.

87. Tafel and Thomas, I, 246–280. See also *Archivio di Stato di Venezia,* Arch. Proc. di S. Marco di Supra, Sal. Ducale B. VI, c.7, 1198, Sept. Rialto. The author is indebted to Prof. Luigi Lanfranchi for correcting the date of the published document.

colonies, after which the new emperor, Andronicus, permitted the Venetians to return about 1183. The Venetians remained the favored Latin merchants to the end of the century, although the Genoese and Pisans returned in 1192. From 1199 to the Fourth Crusade, Pisa was the most favored Italian city in Byzantium. Neither the Greeks nor the Latin cities could do without each other.

The Latin kingdom of Jerusalem experienced dramatic reverses in the last quarter of the twelfth century. As these developments have received extended treatment elsewhere in these volumes, only brief mention will be made here.[88]

The fall of Jerusalem to Saladin in 1187 shocked western Europe, where Richard the Lionhearted, Philip Augustus of France, and Frederick Barbarossa started to prepare the Third Crusade. With crusading fervor the Venetian doge, Orio Mastropiero, in November 1188 organized a Venetian fleet to provision the crusaders and to transport the crusading army, among whom was a contingent from Bologna. Leaving Venice immediately after Easter 1189, this fleet sailed first to Tyre and then, in September 1189, to the siege of Acre.[89] Through intrigue, battle, and negotiation, the crusaders did reconquer Acre from Saladin, while Richard arranged privileges for the Christians in the principalities of Saladin. The churches and other real estate held by Venice in Acre since 1124 were reconfirmed to it by Conrad of Montferrat, king-elect of Jerusalem. From April to July 1190 the Venetian fleet sailed from Tyre via Abydus to Constantinople. Some Venetians remained in Tyre, however, as two documents of November 1192 attest.[90]

Later in the decade, the Venetian state organized another fleet to go to Syria. In 1197 one large sailing ship was constructed in the northern lagoons near Aquileia and its knightly, non-Venetian shareholders contracted with the great men of Venice, doge Enrico Dandolo and Sebastian Ziani of Caorle, son of the late doge. In April 1198 it was agreed that this ship and other Venetian vessels would go to Syria.[91] Perhaps this fleet should be identified with the ships which, one chron-

---

88. See volume I of the present work, chapters XVIII, XIX, and volume II, chapters II, XV.

89. Andrea Dandolo, *Chronica,* p. 272; Tafel and Thomas, I, 204–206; Morozzo della Rocca and Lombardo, *Documenti,* I, nos. 381, 383–386, 425; Prawer, *Histoire du royaume latin,* II, 33 ff.

90. Morozzo della Rocca and Lombardo, *Documenti,* I, nos. 411, 412. The Venetians are not mentioned in chronicles of the Holy Land in this decade: Prawer, *Histoire du royaume latin,* II, 110, note 13.

91. The author is indebted to Prof. Luigi Lanfranchi for calling her attention to these documents: *Civico Museo Correr,* MSS. Cicogna 2835/2 (1198, Sept., Rialto), and Archivio

icler records, carried French crusaders inspired by Fulk of Neuilly from Venice to an ineffective military venture in the Holy Land.[92]

Between the Third and the Fourth Crusades piracy increased on the Mediterranean. Not only did the Venetians prey on the ships of Ancona and of Pisa, but the Genoese, Moslems, Normans, and Byzantines joined in corsair activity. The most formidable Venetian rivals were the Pisans.[93] Perhaps the general maritime insecurity in March 1196 persuaded the noblemen of a large Venetian fleet in Abydus to agree to remain on the Sea of Marmara notwithstanding the fatigue of the men.[94] Everyone contributed to pay for the continuation of the expedition. At least two other Venetian fleets are recorded for the decade; both set out to fight the Pisans. In 1195 Venice defeated its Pisan commercial rivals at Modon and in 1199 destroyed the Pisan naval base of Brindisi.[95]

After the Third Crusade crusaders still held several seaports on the Palestinian coast, the city and environs of Antioch, and the island of Cyprus. Pisa had the greatest privileges in the remaining cities of the Latin kingdom of Jerusalem; Genoa profited most in the northern Antiochene principalities. Because Venetian privileges remained in Tyre, Acre, Antioch, and Tripoli, Venetians continued to trade there. They dealt with local merchants, content to leave to others the transport and collection of goods from the interior.

These changes in the last quarter of the century in the Byzantine empire and the Latin kingdom of Jerusalem stimulated political change in Venice itself. The great loss of Venetian business and prestige in the 1171 raid on the Venetian quarter in Constantinople aroused the Venetians to send a punitive expedition under doge Vitale II Michiel. When this unsuccessful fleet, wasted by pestilence and storms in the Aegean Sea, returned home in 1172, the maddened starving mob murdered the doge near the ducal palace. Venetians of the old families and those enriched by business took steps to pacify the city and to institute political changes which would prevent a repetition of such domestic violence. They created a new electoral college to name the doge; no longer would the assembled citizenry elect their doge in pub-

di Stato di Venezia, Cancelleria Inferiore, B.I. Notai più antichi diversi (1198, April 3, Aquileia). See also Morozzo della Rocca and Lombardo, *Documenti,* II, no. 436, and their *Nuovi documenti,* no. 45.

92. Andrea Dandolo, *Chronica,* p. 275.

93. Andrea Dandolo, *Chronica,* pp. 272–276; Cessi, *Le Colonie medioevali,* I, 83–85.

94. Tafel and Thomas, I, 217–225.

95. Andrea Dandolo, *Chronica,* pp. 273, 276, 367; *Historia ducum veneticorum,* in *MGH, SS.,* XIV, 91–92; *Annales venetici breves,* in *MGH, SS.,* XIV, 72.

lic meeting. Because the newly elected doge, Sebastian Ziani, was the wealthiest man in Venice and thus a member of the oligarchy, he ruled Venice as a leader coöperating with other leaders, rather than in absolute and solitary splendor. Ziani administered Venice with the assistance of ducal councillors and a larger council whose members were drawn from the Venetian aristocracy. He established a system of price controls and market regulations to ameliorate the problem of food shortages, and encouraged a convoy system for Venetian merchant fleets. He also stabilized the coinage by issuing a new penny designed to be exactly equal to 1/240 of the Venetian pound. In 1177 he helped to negotiate peace between the warring factions of Guelfs and Ghibellines in Italy. This Peace of Venice reconciled the German emperor, Frederick Barbarossa, and pope Alexander III and was sealed with the traditional kiss of peace in the narthex of the basilica of St. Mark.

Ziani's immediate successor, Orio Mastropiero (1178–1192), also possessed great personal wealth. He and the next doge, Enrico Dandolo (1192–1205), governed Venice with the assistance of the Venetian oligarchy and with the intent to increase Venetian commercial and political strength. They made treaties to extend Venetian maritime control on the upper Adriatic, and to restore Venetian commercial privileges and reimbursement in Constantinople. Each of these last three doges of the twelfth century, Sebastian Ziani, Orio Mastropiero, and Enrico Dandolo, had represented Venice as a special envoy to Constantinople at least once between 1169 and 1185.

These changes in the Venetian government and its strong, dynamic solutions to its problems prepared the city for the challenges of the Fourth Crusade. The capture of Constantinople during the Fourth Crusade was the culmination of Venetian commercial interests there; it was also the apogee of Venetian participation in the crusading movement.

The Fourth Crusade provided a unique opportunity for Venice to expand its commerce and colonial establishments in the eastern Mediterranean. The details of the Latin conquest of Constantinople have been given elsewhere in these volumes; others have studied its political, religious, diplomatic, and feudal aspects, as well as the long-argued question of the diversion of the Crusade.[96] Here it will be sufficient to point out that the businessmen of Venice organized the

---

96. See Edgar H. McNeal and Robert L. Wolff, "The Fourth Crusade," in volume II of the present work, pp. 153–186, and its extensive bibliography, pp. 153–154. For the diversion of the crusade, see *ibid.*, pp. 168–176; also Queller, *The Latin Conquest of Constantinople*, and Queller and Gill, "Franks, Venetians and Pope Innocent III," pp. 85–105.

affair as carefully as possible. They prepared the enterprise—its ships, its provisions, its route, its contractual safeguards, and its men—so that it might achieve the greatest possible measure of success given the known risks and the unknown opportunities. Since the magnitude of the enterprise surpassed any previous Venetian venture, it was fortunate for Venice that it was a success.

In the spring of 1201 the Venetians received a proposal from envoys of the north French crusaders, that Venice provide sea transportation, warships, and provisions for the crusaders. Doge Enrico Dandolo offered a typical Venetian partnership for the crusading enterprise.[97] The Frankish crusaders would furnish the land forces, and the Venetians, fifty war galleys. The contract was drawn up for one year, to begin in June 1202, and, at its conclusion, any profits were to be divided in half. In addition, the crusader land forces would be transported and provisioned by the Venetians for a fee of 94,000 marks. Although the precise destination was not stated, as in many Venetian commercial partnership contracts of this era, it was decided to direct the crusade to Egypt. The Frankish envoys accepted the contract after bargaining to reduce the transportation bill from 94,000 to 85,000 marks.[98] The Venetian ratification was accomplished by the doge, who confirmed it with his Council of Forty, with his Great Council, and finally with the Venetian citizenry as a whole, 10,000 strong, before the basilica of St. Mark. These agreements of 1201 were respected, renewed, and amplified in later contracts between the Venetians and the Frankish crusaders until, after the conquest of Constantinople in 1204, the transportation bill was paid from the spoils, and the remaining profits were divided in half.

The Frankish crusaders in the summer of 1202 could not fulfill their promise to prepay part of the transportation bill, although the Venetians scrupulously carried out their part of the agreement.[99] The latter, not wishing to jeopardize the enterprise with such an unhappy beginning, suggested that the crusaders might postpone payment and meanwhile assist them to subdue the upper Dalmatian coast.[100] After

97. Only the clause assigning the risk, which was legally necessary to identify a *commenda,* was absent from the proposal reported by Villehardouin; otherwise this would be a model bilateral *commenda.*

98. Andrea Dandolo, *Chronica,* p. 276; Villehardouin, ed. Faral, I, 27. Cf. Queller, "Évolution du rôle," pp. 490–491, nos. 28, 29, and Cessi, "Quarta Crociata," pp. 10–11.

99. Baldwin of Flanders, one of the French leaders, borrowed 118 marks and 3 ounces from Venetians in October 1202, promising to repay at the Fairs of Champagne: Morozzo della Rocca and Lombardo, *Documenti,* I, no. 462.

100. For 200 years Venice had attempted to control the upper Dalmatian coast. Zara, its principal seaport, had rebelled against Venice five times since 1045. The latest rebellion began

considerable controversy, the crusaders agreed. At this point, and
not before, doge Enrico Dandolo and many Venetians also took the
cross.[101] The fleet sailed October 1, 1202.

After the north Adriatic coast near Venice was subdued by a dem-
onstration of the fleet near Pola and Muggia in the Istrian peninsula,
and by the capture of Zara, the crusading host and the Venetians
wintered in Zara.

During the winter a new opportunity was placed before the crusaders by envoys from the young Alexius, pretender to the Byzantine
throne, and from Philip of Swabia, his brother-in-law. If the Frankish crusaders and the Venetians would proceed to Constantinople to
enthrone Alexius, the Greek claimant offered to pay them 200,000
silver marks and assist their crusading expedition to Egypt for one
year by provisioning the entire host and increasing it, at his own expense, by an additional 10,000 men. This sudden offer to strengthen
the expedition was hotly argued by the Frankish crusaders and the
Venetians. Finally, a new contract was made whereby Alexius's offer
was accepted. The text has not survived, but narrative sources report
its contents.[102] New business opportunities had required that the original compact signed in Venice be thus renegotiated.

The expedition left Zara early in April 1203, the time of the usual
Venetian spring voyages to Constantinople. They traveled the usual
Venetian route, via Durazzo and Corfu, around the Morea, past Negroponte, Andros, and finally Abydus on the Asiatic shore of the
Dardanelles. They arrived before Constantinople on June 24, and took
the city of Constantinople, unseated the usurper, and named Alexius
IV and his imprisoned father, Isaac Angelus, coemperors.[103] However, when Greek hatred for Latins excluded the crusaders from the
city, sparked a civil war, and toppled Isaac Angelus and Alexius from
the throne, the enterprise seemed on the verge of collapse.

By March 1204 the entire crusading venture had to be reëvaluated.
The original contract for Frankish and Venetian coöperation for one
year had expired. Its renewal with the additional participation of the

---

in 1193 when the Venetian-Hungarian treaty expired and Zara accepted the lordship of king
Emeric I of Hungary: Andrea Dandolo, *Chronica,* pp. 211, 228, 230, 250, 267–271, 273.

101. It may be inferred that these Venetians formed a local association under the leadership
of the doge, which remained together until after the conquest of Constantinople: Wolff, "The
Oath of the Venetian Podestà," pp. 540–541, 546. For parallel Venetian expeditions see Tafel
and Thomas, I, 216–225; Fotheringham, *Marco Sanudo,* pp. 51–55; Merores, "Der venezianische
Adel," pp. 234–235.

102. Villehardouin, ed. Faral, I, 92–95; Tafel and Thomas, I, 304–305, 407; Andrea Dandolo, *Chronica,* p. 277; volume II of the present work, p. 174.

103. See McNeal and Wolff, in volume II of the present work, pp. 178–179.

pretender Alexius had been nullified with his death. Now the Venetians and the Franks put into writing a third contract to govern their venture.[104] They agreed to coöperate for one year to recapture the city of Constantinople and to establish their rule over it. The Franks' debt for transportation would be considered paid when the Venetians received three quarters of the spoils, while the remaining booty was to be divided equally. A new emperor would be chosen by six Venetian and six Frankish electors, and he was to possess the imperial palaces of Blachernae and Boukoleon and one fourth of the empire. The patriarchate of Constantinople, with the great church of Hagia Sophia, would be awarded to that party, Frankish or Venetian, which lost the imperial election. All rights which either party had possessed previously under the Byzantines would be respected, which meant earlier Venetian commercial property and both Venetian and Montferratine privileges in the Byzantine empire. The remaining three fourths of the empire was to be divided equally between Franks and Venetians by a twenty-four-man commission, twelve from each party. Thus, one fourth of the empire was allotted to the new emperor, three eighths to the Franks, and three eighths to the Venetians.[105] Everyone holding a fief or honor in the empire, except the doge of Venice, was to do feudal homage to the new emperor. This contract ratified by the Franks and Venetians in 1204 before the second capture of Constantinople repeated the original terms of the agreement of 1201. The Venetians would be reimbursed for transporting the Frankish crusaders and the remainder of their conquests would be divided in half — movable property as well as real estate, civil as well as ecclesiastical power. This contract continued to be couched in the form of a Venetian partnership agreement for a commercial enterprise.

Following this agreement, the Latin forces besieged and took the city on April 13, 1204, and put it to sack for three days. The horrors of the sack, its barbarity and cruelty to the Greeks, and the enormous theft and destruction of property have been described elsewhere.[106] The vengeful Venetian chronicler comments, "the wretched sinful deeds of the emperor Manuel against the Venetians were now punished in full."[107]

The victors then divided their conquests. First, the booty was col-

---

104. Tafel and Thomas, I, 444–452; Andrea Dandolo, *Chronica,* p. 279; Villehardouin, ed. Faral, II, 34–37. Recent discussions of the third contract include Carile, "Partitio terrarum imperii Romania," and Borsari, *Studi sulle colonie veneziane,* pp. 15–21.
105. Or, in the language of 1204, one fourth and one half to each party.
106. See McNeal and Wolff, in volume II of the present work, pp. 184–185.
107. Andrea Dandolo, *Chronica,* p. 279.

lected and, as agreed, three fourths was given to the Venetians. In the city of Constantinople, marquis Boniface of Montferrat, the leader of the crusade, occupied the royal palace of Boukoleon; Henry of Flanders, the future Latin emperor, took the palace of Blachernae, and doge Enrico Dandolo, another palace. The rank and file of Franks took lodging in the conquered city, and the Venetians returned to their quarter.

Twelve electors proceeded, according to the third contract of March 1204, to elect a Latin emperor for Constantinople. They met in Dandolo's palace and, on the second ballot, chose Baldwin, count of Flanders and Hainault, who began his difficult reign May 16, 1204.[108] According to contract, the Venetians then nominated the clerics for the cathedral chapter of Hagia Sophia, who chose the Venetian Thomas Morosini as Latin patriarch of Constantinople. When he heard of this, pope Innocent III criticized their uncanonical act; nevertheless, he confirmed Morosini. Notwithstanding papal interference in succeeding patriarchal elections, Venetians continued to occupy the office and thus dominate the Latin church to 1261.[109]

The division of the spoils of the sack, of the urban real estate, and of political and religious titles between Franks and Venetians was thus accomplished. Considerably more difficult was the division of the Byzantine lands outside Constantinople. As stipulated in the third contract, a commission of twelve Venetians and twelve Franks began to allocate these vast Byzantine territories according to the agreed formula: one fourth to the emperor Baldwin I, three eighths to the Franks, and three eighths to the Venetians. The commission divided up all the territory in the former Byzantine empire excepting Thessalonica and Crete, claimed as his rightful property by Boniface of Montferrat, and Constantinople, divided previously. During the commission's deliberations, most of the lands to be divided were still in the hands of the Greeks (or the Bulgarians). Basing their conclusions on Byzantine tax returns, the commission reached agreement in September and issued the Treaty of Partition in October 1204.[110] It must

108. See Wolff, "The Latin Empire of Constantinople," in volume II of the present work, pp. 187-233. A fourteenth-century Venetian chronicler, Nicholas Trevisan, states that Enrico Dandolo did not win the election because certain Venetian electors, among them Octavian Querini, believed that if Dandolo were elected emperor, the Frankish crusaders would leave Constantinople and the Latin empire would collapse: Thiriet, "Les Chroniques vénitiennes de la Marcianne," p. 265.

109. For a full discussion see Wolff, "Politics in the Latin Patriarchate of Constantinople," and McNeal and Wolff, in volume II of the present work, pp. 195-199.

110. Tafel and Thomas, I, 452-501; volume II of the present work, pp. 190-193, 235-238;

be emphasized that the Treaty of Partition only named the territories promised to each party—the emperor, the Venetians, or the Franks. The lands remained to be conquered. Never did the Latins conquer all the former Byzantine territory from the Greeks. Nor did the Venetians or the Franks ever establish themselves over all the lands awarded them by the commissioners. The Treaty of Partition was a working list, and many localities in the Aegean experienced a development different from that proposed in the Treaty of Partition.

Although details of the Treaty of Partition are given in an earlier chapter,[111] the list of lands promised Venice will be repeated here. Most of the areas promised Venice were coastal, such as would give them control of the sea routes. Close to Constantinople, Venice was promised the Thracian coast, including the seaports of Rodosto and Heraclea near Gallipoli. Also it was to receive inland Thrace as far as Adrianople. Among the Aegean islands, Venice was promised Andros, Aegina, Salamis, and the two extremities of Negroponte (Euboea). On the Greek mainland, the Treaty of Partition awarded Venice the entire Morea except the Argolid and Corinth. To give Venice domination over the Adriatic and Ionian seas, the commissioners promised it the Dalmatian coast and its islands, the Ionian islands, and interior territories of central Greece in Epirus and Albania. Of these vast paper grants, the Republic ultimately conquered and ruled only a few. On the other hand, the island of Crete and the port city of Negroponte were not granted to Venice by the Treaty of Partition, and yet these became two key points of the thirteenth-century Venetian empire.

Venice and Venetian citizens acquired control over parts of the Greek east after the Fourth Crusade in several different ways.[112] In some cases, territory was acquired when official expeditions of conquest were sent out by the government. Other acquisitions were made when the Venetian state purchased rights to lands. In other cases, wealthy Venetians outfitted their own private expeditions to acquire personal real estate. For these latter the Venetian rulers, while remaining citizens of Venice on the lagoons, became feudal vassals of the Latin empire of Constantinople for their Aegean lands. In still other cases, private Venetian citizens acquired former Greek territory through marriage to a Frankish heir. The definition of ultimate sovereignty over

Borsari, *Studi sulle colonie,* pp. 22–25; Carile, "Partitio," pp. 125–305; Fotheringham, *Marco Sanudo,* pp. 36–38; Longnon, *L'Empire latin,* pp. 61–62.

111. More scholarly debate has centered on which Aegean islands were promised the Venetians than on any other clause in the Treaty of Partition; see McNeal and Wolff, in volume II of the present work, pp. 191–192.

112. Loenertz, "Marino Sanudo, seigneur d'Andros," *Byzantina et Franco-Graeca,* pp. 400–402.

former Greek lands remained fluid and ill-defined, a typically medieval situation. However sovereignty was defined, the Venetian control of Greek lands endured longer than any other result of the Fourth Crusade.

In the first of these acquisitions, Venice purchased a free hand in Crete and rights in Thessalonica and Negroponte from Boniface of Montferrat, who was paid 1,000 marks of silver, by the Treaty of Adrianople, August 12, 1204.[113] They concluded the treaty two months before the Treaty of Partition because Boniface claimed that he and his family had held these lands before the fall of Constantinople. He claimed that the emperor Manuel had granted Thessalonica in fief to his father, William III of Montferrat, and that he, Boniface, had inherited it. Boniface also claimed that the young Alexius had granted him Crete in 1202. When Boniface of Montferrat needed cash and Venetian support in the summer of 1204, he sold them Crete and all other Montferratine holdings in the empire; the Treaty of Adrianople records this sale. This meant that Boniface would hold Thessalonica and its dependency Negroponte in fief from the Venetians. In addition, he would protect all Venetian rights on the mainland of the empire, while Venice would protect the Montferrat holdings with its sea power. The agreements concerning Thessalonica were never implemented, but this treaty gave Venice the legal right to intervene in Negroponte and to occupy Crete.

The Treaty of Partition signed in October promised Venice control over the northernmost and the southernmost cities of Negroponte, Oreus and Carystus. Since it assigned the principal and central city of Negroponte to Boniface of Montferrat, he occupied the island in the spring of 1205, by alleged right of inheritance and of the treaty. He established his vassal James II of Avesnes on Negroponte until his disappearance in August. Then Boniface divided the island into three fiefs, giving them to the "terciers," the three gentlemen of Verona, Ravano dalle Carceri, Gilberto of Verona, and Pecoraro da Mercanuovo.[114] Boniface of Montferrat died in 1207, and of the terciers only Ravano dalle Carceri, who had represented Venice at the Treaty of Adrianople in 1204, remained as sole lord in Negroponte.

113. Tafel and Thomas, I, 512–515; Borsari, *Creta,* pp. 11–13, 21; Fotheringham, *Marco Sanudo,* pp. 33–34, 48. See also McNeal and Wolff, in volume II of the present work, pp. 190–191.

114. The recent authoritative work of Loenertz, "Les Seigneurs terciers de Négropont de 1205 à 1280," corrects many mistakes in the earlier work of Karl Hopf, *Geschichte Griechenlands vom Beginne des Mittelalters bis auf unsere Zeit,* in J. S. Ersch and J. G. Gruber, eds., *Allgemeine Encyklopädie der Wissenschaften und Künste,* LXXXV, 67–465; LXXXVI, 1–190 (Leipzig, 1867–1868).

In 1211 he gained the protection of Venice for himself and his heirs by swearing homage to the doge and by granting Venice certain rights and privileges.[115] It gained a church and *fondaco* in the capital city of Negroponte and in the other episcopal cities, and its citizens were granted extraterritorial rights in Negroponte. Venetians received the promise of security and the rights of free trade on the island. Both Latin and Greek magnates on Negroponte, under Ravano dalle Carceri, would continue to have the legal status they held previously and would also be loyal to Venice. Ravano would pay to Venice an annual tribute of 2,100 gold pieces and two pieces of cloth of gold. By these terms the Venetians gained economic and judicial privileges from which they profited. A Venetian bailie represented its interests in Negroponte.

But while Venice and the dalle Carceri were negotiating this treaty, Henry, now the Latin emperor of Constantinople, was taking steps to strengthen his authority over the Latin lords of former Greek territory. He held a parliament at Ravennika in Thessaly, and received homage from many Latin lords. Ravano dalle Carceri did not swear liege homage to him until the emperor Henry demonstrated his military power at the siege of Thebes in May 1209. The lord of Negroponte thenceforth owed allegiance both to the Latin emperor and to the doge of Venice, which provoked no trouble as long as the interests of emperor and doge were parallel. Liege homage was given to the emperor. Notwithstanding the claims of the Latin emperor and his successors, the Venetian position on Negroponte continued to grow stronger.

At the death of both Ravano dalle Carceri and the Latin emperor Henry in 1216, the heirs of the terciers turned to the Venetian bailie Peter Barbo to adjudicate between their conflicting claims. Venice, as feudal overlord, awarded the three parts of the island to the several heirs of the terciers. In so doing, the Venetian bailie extended his jurisdiction from the city of Negroponte to the entire island, and also guaranteed to Venice its property in Negroponte—houses and churches, fields, a wine cellar, and land. The 1216 agreement also stated that Venetian weights and measures should prevail on the island.[116]

The Venetian influence over the terciers on Negroponte appears

---

115. Tafel and Thomas, II, 89–96; "Les Seigneurs terciers," pp. 239–241; Jacoby, *La Féodalité en Grèce médiévale,* pp. 185–189. This treaty was negotiated in Italy two years earlier by doge Peter Ziani and Ravano's Veronese brothers, bishop Henry of Mantua and Redondollo dalle Carceri.

116. Loenertz, "Les Seigneurs terciers," pp. 243–244, no. 23; Tafel and Thomas, II, 175–184; Miller, *Latins in the Levant,* pp. 77–78; Borsari, *Studi,* pp. 52–55; Bury, "Lombards and Venetians in Euboia," pp. 319–320.

more understandable when one considers the increasing Venetian influence over Verona, homeland of the dalle Carceri. This family played a leading role in Veronese affairs. Redondolo dalle Carceri was podestà of Verona in 1210, Pecoraro de' Pecorari da Mercanuovo was podestà in 1215 and 1223. Leon dalle Carceri, podestà, *capitano del popolo,* and head of the Guelf party, led the city in 1225 against the Veronese Ghibellines, whose champion was Ezzelino III of Romano. The Venetian Renier Zeno, a future doge, was Veronese podestà in 1229 and 1230. Later in the century, three other Venetians held office as podestà in Verona: Andrew Zeno in 1261, Marco Zeno in 1262, and Philip Belegno in 1263. Ezzelino da Romano executed the Venetian Peter Gallo in Verona in 1246.[117]

The Veronese terciers on Negroponte began to experience difficulty when their liege lord, the emperor Baldwin II of Constantinople, transferred his sovereignty over the islands of the Archipelago (including Negroponte) in the 1240's to William II of Villehardouin, prince of Achaea, who in the next decade attempted to enforce his authority as feudal sovereign over the terciers. This brought war to Negroponte. Venice assisted the terciers against Villehardouin, and the terciers once more accepted Venetian sovereignty in an agreement of 1256, renewed in 1258. All the earlier Venetian privileges were repeated, the extraterritoriality, the cloth of gold, the weights and measures, the Venetian real estate. This agreement, in addition, granted the Venetians two quarters in the capital city of Negroponte and all the revenue from the import and export taxes (*commercium maris*) instead of the amount fixed previously. These augmented privileges for the Venetians on Negroponte were confirmed by Villehardouin himself in 1262, after the war on Negroponte had come to an end.[118]

By that time the political power of the Latin crusader principalities had so declined that the entire balance of power in the Aegean shifted. In July 1259 the combined Latin forces under William of Villehardouin, deserted by their Greek ally, despot Michael II Ducas of Epirus, had been decisively defeated on the plain of Pelagonia by John Palaeologus, brother of emperor Michael of Nicaea. William of Villehardouin himself was taken prisoner and, in return for his release, granted the Greeks a foothold in the Morea. In 1261 Michael Palaeologus, aided by the Genoese, took Constantinople. The Latin empire, through which Venetian commerce had flourished, was ended.

---

117. Pier Zagata, *Cronica della città di Verona,* ed. Giambattista Biancolini (Verona, 1745), I, 22, 26, 50, 52–60.

118. Loenertz, "Les Seigneurs terciers," pp. 246, 249–256, nos. 34, 45–67; Tafel and Thomas, III, 13–16.

With the Greeks triumphant over William of Villehardouin and once again dominant in Constantinople, the war of Negroponte came to an end. Venice, the terciers, and Villehardouin drew up a peace treaty at Thebes in May 1262.[119] It guaranteed continued Venetian economic domination on Euboea through recognition of Venetian weights and measures on the island and through the payment of all customs revenues to Venice. It restored to the Venetians all property and business rights held earlier and enlarged the Venetian quarter in the capital city of Negroponte. On the other hand, the terciers recognized William of Villehardouin, not Venice, as their feudal overlord, and continued to live in the capital city. The castle of Negroponte, ceded to the Venetians in 1256, was demolished.

The peace did not last long. Licario of Carystus attempted by force of arms to control the island from 1264 to 1280, encouraged by the Greek emperor, Michael VIII Palaeologus. The Greeks wished thus to extend their holdings, and Negroponte like Crete became an arena for Greek and Latin combat. The Venetians assisted the terciers very little in their struggle with Licario.

During the century after Licario's death, Venetian political influence and economic penetration of Negroponte gradually increased. The Villehardouin rights weakened and were inherited by the Angevins of Naples. By 1390 Venice gained full possession of the island, which became its most important commercial and maritime possession in the Aegean. It was not until 1470 that Venice lost Negroponte to the Ottoman Turks.

In addition to rights in Negroponte, Venice purchased the entire island of Crete from Boniface of Montferrat by the Treaty of Adrianople, in August 1204. The geographical position of Crete, the largest of the Greek islands, made its possession extremely important for Venetian commerce.[120] Fleets from Venice stopped at Canea and Candia on the north coast. From there they sailed to Egypt, Syria, the upper Aegean, or Constantinople. Winds, currents, and the need for supplies made this stop an essential one. The inhabitants of Crete eagerly purchased from the Venetians the products of their workshops and lumber from the Adriatic. They sold to the Venetians merchandise from the eastern Mediterranean; pepper and slaves, for example, in addition to the products of local agriculture: wheat, cheese, wool,

119. Tafel and Thomas, III, 46–55.
120. Manoussos I. Manoussacas, "L'Isola di Creta sotto il domino veneziano: Problemi e ricerche," *Venezia e il levante,* ed. Pertusi, I-2, 473–513.

skins, horn from wild Cretan goats, wine, firewood, barley, and salt.[121] A flourishing market in grain futures existed in Crete, providing Venetian merchants, Venetian colonists on Crete, and native merchants with a source for speculative gain. Cretan grain fed not only Venice and other Aegean islands, but also the great Greek monasteries of St. Catherine on Mount Sinai and St. John on Patmos, with dependent monasteries on Crete.

After purchasing title to Crete, Venice gained possession by driving out the Genoese under Henry Pescatore, count of Malta, and by subduing the Greek land-owning noblemen, known as *archontes*. During these campaigns the Venetian general and vice-doge, Renier Dandolo, was captured and died in a Genoese prison on Crete. Jacopo Tiepolo, the first Venetian duke of Crete, finally subdued Pescatore, and effective Venetian control of the island dates from 1211.

The problem of gaining the allegiance and coöperation of the Greek nobility, clergy, and commoners on Crete remained. The Greeks on Crete, organized for centuries under their *archontes,* rebelled against the Venetians just as they had opposed the Byzantine emperors. The Venetian military occupation force on Crete was led by a Venetian duke (or "rector") who was sent from Venice every two years. From his special responsibilities in the capital city, he was often known as the duke of Candia.[122] Venice also systematically organized its own citizens to go to Crete as military colonists. The island was divided into six areas, corresponding to the Byzantine administrative subdivisions and also corresponding to the six sectors of Venice itself. Each sector of the home city was expected to send Venetian nobles and other colonists to the corresponding area in Crete. The first group of colonists from Venice set out in 1211. Other Venetian military colonists were added during the succeeding centuries of Venetian domination of Crete. Exempted from this military partition of Cretan lands was the capital city of Candia, ruled by the Venetian duke of Crete. Also separate were the lands held by the church. With the assistance of this force, Venice kept control over the island, fought the numerous Cretan revolts, and protected the island from invasions by other Greeks, other Italians, and Moslems.[123]

Yet Venice could not hold the island without the coöperation of

---

121. *Liber Plegiorum,* ed. Cessi, p. 117; Borsari, *Creta,* pp. 71–72, 94–95; Setton, "The Latins in Greece," p. 428.

122. These governors are listed for the thirteenth century in Borsari, *Creta,* appendix I, pp. 127–131.

123. Tafel and Thomas, II, 129–142; see also Miller, *Essays,* pp. 178–180, and Borsari, *Creta,* pp. 28–29.

at least some of the native leaders who held the allegiance of the mass
of free and semi-free Greeks. Major revolts against Venetian authority broke out in 1219–1222 and 1282–1299. Some Venetian colonists
with knight's fiefs turned native, joined the Orthodox church, and,
pushed by the same economic and social interests as were the Greeks,
joined the Greeks in revolt against Venice itself. Some freemen owed
allegiance to the feudal lords on Crete, and a small group of free
merchants lived in Cretan cities, but the mass of the Cretans were
serfs. A large majority of the residents of Crete were engaged in agriculture. Even the Venetian military colonists, for the most part, gave
up their interest in trade and became more concerned with the products of the soil and life on a country estate.

The crusading effort did profit from the Venetian possession of
Crete because Crete was a stopping place for military forces en route
to the Holy Land. Before the Venetian occupation, Richard the Lion-
hearted had stopped on Crete in 1191. The Frisian crusaders in 1218
rested in Candia on the way to Acre. The emperor Frederick II sailed
by Crete in 1228 on his way to Cyprus; and king Louis IX considered
stopping in Crete in 1248 en route to Egypt.

Venice would eventually lose the island to the Turks in the war of
Candia, 1645–1669. The last Venetian strongholds fell to the Turks
in 1691, after which the Treaty of Passarovitz of 1718 confirmed Turkish sovereignty over the island. For five centuries Crete was the most
important Venetian acquisition from the Fourth Crusade, because its
material resources and its location contributed so greatly to the strength
of the maritime republic.

While gaining rights on Negroponte and Crete from Boniface of
Montferrat and establishing a long-lived hegemony over these islands,
the government of Venice after the Fourth Crusade also sent embassies and organized expeditions to establish control over the eastern
coast of the Adriatic and the Ionian seas. These coastal areas formed
part of the Venetian grant in the Treaty of Partition in October 1204.
The Republic had fought since the tenth century to make these waters
safe for its shipping, and in 1202 the crusading fleet had confirmed
Venetian possession of the Istrian coast and Zara. The treaty allowed
a continuation of that domination which the Byzantine empire had
permitted earlier.

The first official Venetian expedition of conquest after the Fourth
Crusade took Ragusa and Durazzo on the Dalmatian coast, and the
strategic island fortress of Corfu in the Ionian Sea. The same fleet

continued east and brought Thomas Morosini, the Latin patriarch-elect, to Constantinople in the summer of 1205. When they arrived in Constantinople, they learned that doge Enrico Dandolo had died and that the Venetians in Constantinople had chosen Marino Zeno as their podestà. The question briefly remained open whether Ragusa, Durazzo, and Corfu would fall under his jurisdiction, but the Venetian doge Peter Ziani, elected in August 1205, soon forced the Venetians in Constantinople to recognize that Durazzo and Avlona, former Byzantine territories in the Adriatic, would come under the home government.[124] Thus with the aid of the Venetian crusader fleet of 1202 and the Venetian patriarchal fleet of 1205, Venice reasserted its control over several important seaports on the Adriatic: the Istrian peninsula, Zara, Ragusa, Avlona, and Durazzo, and over the Ionian Sea island of Corfu.

The most important of these acquisitions was Ragusa.[125] Even before the Fourth Crusade, the Ragusans had often accepted a Venetian as count; from 1205 to 1358 the count was named biennially as the doge's representative. Venetian citizens received preferential treatment in Ragusa and its hinterland, but Ragusan merchants in Venice were subjected to restrictions imposed by treaties in 1232, 1236, and 1252. The Ragusans promised Venice annual tribute, ships and sailors for its war fleets, and coöperation against its maritime rivals. They also agreed to accept from the Venetians an archbishop who would be subject to the patriarch of Grado.[126] In return the Venetians protected the sea lanes outside Ragusa from pirates, and encouraged the growth of Ragusa as an entrepôt of trade and center of communication between Italy and the Balkans.

Ragusa provided an outlet for products from the Balkan hinterland such as skins, wool, furs, wax, honey, forest products, rough textiles, and slaves. Silver also became an important export from Ragusa to Venice, especially from 1250 to 1350. About 1300 output from the Serbian silver mines increased greatly. The Ragusans possessed the right to exploit these mines in the Serbian kingdom, but kept only a small part of the silver for their own coinage. Venetian merchants took the rest to Venice, where Serbian silver became an increasingly

124. Tafel and Thomas, I, 569–571.

125. Bariša Krekić, "Contributions of Foreigners to Dubrovnik's Economic Growth in the Late Middle Ages," *Viator,* IX (1978), 375–394.

126. Andrea Dandolo, *Chronica,* p. 293; on Ragusa (Dubrovnik) see also Krekić, "Le Relazione fra Venezia, Ragusa e le popolazioni Serbo-Croate," *Venezia e il levante,* ed. Pertusi, I-1, 390–401; and Francis W. Carter, *Dubrovnik (Ragusa)* (London, 1972), pp. 88–89.

important source of silver for the Venetian mints. Serbian mines also produced some gold, lead, copper, iron, and cinnabar.[127] Venice monopolized the shipping between the Rialto and Ragusa, except for four Ragusan ships each year. Venetian ships sailing down the Adriatic usually stopped at Ragusa for food and water, for final outfitting, and often to recruit ships' crews. From Ragusa south, both Venetian and Ragusan ships carried merchandise back and forth across the Adriatic, to the Aegean Sea area, Constantinople, Syria, and Egypt.[128] Ragusans developed their own merchant marine during the century and a half of Venetian protection and, aided by the Venetians, maintained their freedom from the kings of Serbia, from Dalmatian pirates, and from the Genoese war fleets. In 1358 the Angevin king Louis I of Hungary, after a two-year war with Venice, succeeded in wresting Ragusa and the entire Dalmatian coast from Venetian control. With this event Ragusa, unhampered by its nominal ties to Balkan sovereigns, began two centuries of independent commercial growth, now in competition with Venice.

Durazzo, also conquered in 1205, had been an important Greek city on the Adriatic. Venetian fleets had helped protect the city against Robert Guiscard in 1082. Now the Venetians appointed a strong resident duke of Durazzo, the Venetian nobleman Marino Vallaresso. A Latin bishop of Durazzo presided over the Latin church there after 1205 and inherited certain possessions and revenues from his Greek predecessor. But the Venetian hold on Durazzo lasted only until 1213, when Michael I Ducas, ruler of Epirus, conquered the city. With the Epirote conquest Durazzo lost its importance as a seaport and Ragusa served the Venetian fleets instead as a depot for trade with the Balkans.[129]

The island of Corfu guarded the mouth of the Adriatic, and the Venetian state sent expeditions immediately after the Fourth Crusade to establish its power there also. During this crusade Corfu had been conquered by a Genoese pirate, Leone Vetrane. In response the Venetian patriarchal fleet that had taken Ragusa in the spring of 1205 also occupied Corfu briefly, but the Genoese pirate returned. Venice sent

127. Desank Kovàcevic, "Dans la Serbie et le Bosnie médiévales: Les mines d'or et d'argent," *Annales: Économies, sociétés, civilisations,* XV (1960), 249–252, 254–258.

128. For examples of shipping out of Ragusa see Morozzo della Rocca and Lombardo, *Documenti,* II, nos. 519, 624, 629, 711, 777; Andrea Dandolo, *Chronica,* pp. 281, 299 n., 305, 312–314; and Martin da Canal, *Les Estoires,* ed. Limentani, II, LXXXI, LXXXVI, XCIII.

129. Borsari, *Studi,* pp. 26, 27, 44, 45, 48–50, 94, 102–103, 124. The first known Latin bishop of Durazzo was Manfred in 1209.

a second expedition of thirty-one galleys in 1206 and another expedition in 1207 led by ten noble Venetians, who brought their own military force and the right to conquer Corfu and hold it and its castle for Venice. They were to protect the church and the state as it had existed under the Byzantines, allow Venetians freedom of commerce, and pay annual tribute to Venice.[130] This 1207 expedition successfully conquered and held Corfu until 1214, when the despot of Epirus seized it too.

To protect Venetian interests in the southern Adriatic and the Ionian Sea after the Fourth Crusade, the Republic needed to make agreements with the new rulers of the bordering lands. Both Michael I Ducas, Greek despot of Epirus, and the count palatine of Cephalonia, Maio Orsini, acknowledged Venetian superiority. Michael of Epirus did homage to Venice in 1210 as had the count of Cephalonia in 1209.[131] Each lord swore to hold his lands from Venice, to be its vassal, to pay it feudal dues, to support and protect Venetian commerce in his domains, and to treat the enemies of Venice as his enemies. On parchment, at least, these agreements guaranteed Venetian sovereignty over much former Byzantine territory in the west. But in reality, each vassal of Venice honored these promises only so long as it was personally advantageous. Michael of Epirus demonstrated his independence in 1213 and 1214 by taking both Durazzo and Corfu. Orsini disregarded his oath to Venice when he placed himself directly under pope Innocent III in 1213. Venice had no authority over either the island of Cephalonia or the coast of the despotate of Epirus during the remainder of the thirteenth century. This meant that Venice did not control any Dalmatian seaports south of Ragusa during these years, although it did dominate the northern Adriatic and did influence the commercial and naval operations of Italian ports on the Adriatic.

Venetian shipping around Greece should have benefitted from the Treaty of Partition, which promised Venice the Morea, excepting the fortress of Corinth and the Argolid. But in 1204 William of Champlitte and Geoffrey of Villehardouin, nephew of the chronicler-marshal of Champagne, landed at the protected harbor of Modon on the southwest corner of the Morea. They took the entire Morea with the

---

130. Tafel and Thomas, II, 54–59; Borsari, *Studi,* pp. 26–28, 49–50, 95–96, and Jacoby, *La Féodalité en Grèce médiévale,* p. 253.

131. For Michael Ducas see Tafel and Thomas, II, 119–123; Borsari, *Studi,* pp. 43–45. The text of the treaty with the count of Cephalonia has not survived. See, however, Andrea Dandolo, *Chronica,* p. 284.

assistance of Frankish land forces and the encouragement of Boniface of Montferrat.[132] Notwithstanding this Frankish occupation, pirates seem to have returned to Modon and the nearby seaport of Coron. The Venetian expedition under Renier Dandolo which conquered Corfu from Genoese pirates in 1207 went on to besiege and take Modon and Coron. Shortly after, in 1209, Venice made peace with Geoffrey of Villehardouin, who succeeded William of Champlitte as prince of Achaea. Venice secured its authority over Modon and Coron by means of the Treaty of Sapientsa, by which Villehardouin, like the despot of Epirus and the count of Cephalonia, swore feudal homage to Venice, promising to be its vassal, to recognize its rights in the Morea, to protect Venetian commerce, and to treat Venetian enemies as his own. He also agreed that Venice should retain complete possession of the Morean seaports Modon and Coron.[133] He and his heirs respected Venetian control over these two seaports, as did their successors, the Angevins of Naples. Venice did not control any other part of mainland Greece in the thirteenth century.

Venice held Modon and Coron for almost three hundred years. Renier Dandolo personally governed them until his death on Crete. Thereafter the Venetian doge sent two castellans biennially to Modon and Coron to administer the ports. In the later thirteenth century, the administrators appointed from Venice increased in number. Venice strengthened the fortifications of Coron from 1269 and of Modon from 1293. These two harbors, naturally protected from the interior by rocky hills, also marketed the agricultural products of southern Greece, especially grain, wax, and silk, and provisioned the Venetian fleets which sailed between the Adriatic and the Aegean.[134]

Venetian territorial gains following the Fourth Crusade confirmed the Republic's control over the strategic seaports on the sea-lanes from Venice to Constantinople. To control the Aegean Sea, Venice needed more ports on the Aegean islands. Instead of sending out more expeditions of conquest, it encouraged its citizens to organize private forces at their own expense to conquer additional Greek islands. These private Venetian conquerors retained their Venetian citizenship and

132. See volume II of the present work, p. 236.
133. Tafel and Thomas, II, 96–100; Borsari, *Studi,* p. 46; Andrea Dandolo, *Chronica,* p. 284. Only once, during the war of Negroponte, did a Villehardouin attempt to take Coron, but his siege was unsuccessful.
134. *Liber Plegiorum,* ed. Cessi, pp. 195–196; *Bilanci generali della repubblica di Venezia* (R. Commissione per la pubblicazione dei documenti finanziari della repubblica di Venezia, ser. 2, vol. I, t. I; Venice, 1912), no. 27; Morozzo della Rocca and Lombardo, *Documenti,* II, no. 816; Borsari, *Studi,* pp. 96–98, 124–125; Luce, "Modon," pp. 195–208.

loyalty, even when they became vassals of the Latin emperor for their new lands.[135] Should they wish to dispose of their conquests, they were to be sold or bequeathed only to Venetians.

The most spectacular such private conquest was made by Marco Sanudo, nephew of doge Enrico Dandolo. He had already distinguished himself as a member of the Venetian crusading expedition of 1202–1204, as Dandolo's private envoy to Boniface of Montferrat for the negotiations leading to the Treaty of Adrianople, and as a judge in the Venetian quarter of Constantinople. Marco Sanudo set out from Constantinople in 1207 to conquer the Cyclades with a privately financed expedition of eight galleys manned by Venetian and Italian adventurers.[136] After landing at Potamides in southwest Naxos, Sanudo burnt his galleys behind him to encourage his followers to victory. He had to face Genoese corsairs under Henry Pescatore, count of Malta, who surrendered after a five-week siege. With a second expedition equipped in Venice, he completed the conquest of the other islands in the Cyclades: Paros, Antiparos, Cimolos, Melos, Amorgos, Ios, Cythnos, Sikinos, Siphnos, Syros, and Pholegandros.[137] He awarded Andros as a fief to Marino Dandolo, his cousin, another nephew of the late doge.

By whose authority did Marco Sanudo hold these islands? According to a Venetian decree, any Venetian citizen at his own expense was encouraged to conquer lands promised to Venice in the Treaty of Partition, on condition that the conquests should be bequeathed or sold only to other Venetians. On the other hand, the Treaty of Partition awarded the Cyclades to the Frankish crusaders as fiefs of the Latin emperor. Marco Sanudo, a Venetian nobleman, apparently did homage to the Latin emperor for these islands. He ruled his duchy of Naxos (sometimes called the duchy of the Archipelago) as a powerful, independent feudal lord who coöperated with the doge of Venice only when it suited him. If the Venetians in Crete needed his military assistance, he might sometimes provide it.[138] He built a harbor on Naxos and a unique castle where he lived and under the walls of which he installed the Latin clergy and encouraged a colony of Venetians.[139]

---

135. Jacoby, *La Féodalité*, p. 272; Borsari, *Studi*, p. 39; Fotheringham, *Marco Sanudo*, pp. 48–51, 60–61; Loenertz, "Marino Dandolo," *Byzantina et Franco-Graeca*, pp. 400–401.

136. Fotheringham, *Marco Sanudo*, ch. v; Borsari, *Studi*, pp. 38–40. These authors have organized the confusing evidence given in the sources.

137. Setton, "Latins in Greece," p. 425; Borsari, *Studi*, pp. 38–40; Fotheringham, *Marco Sanudo*, pp. 68–69.

138. Marco Sanudo helped in the conquest of Crete, but he fell out with the Venetian duke of Crete, Jacopo Tiepolo, and withdrew: Fotheringham, *Marco Sanudo*, ch. v.

139. *Ibid.*, pp. 70–75.

His dynasty brought peace and prosperity to the island, and removed the danger of piracy. Greeks and Latins lived amicably side by side under the Sanudo dukes. Marco's heirs gravitated closer to Venice, as its naval protection was essential to the peace of the islands. The Sanudo dynasty died out in 1371 and was succeeded by another Italian family of the Latin east, the Crispi, who ruled Naxos until 1566. Venice continued to influence and protect the islands until 1718 when the last of them, Tenos, was ceded to the Turks in the Treaty of Passarovitz.[140]

Marino Dandolo, residing in Constantinople,[141] held Andros, the second largest of the Cyclades, in fief from his cousin Marco Sanudo, having accompanied him on the expedition of 1207. Marino established the Latin church on the island and built a castle there for his personal residence. He also carried on a long conflict with John, the Latin bishop of Andros, who was forced into exile, appealed to pope Gregory IX, and obtained Marino's excommunication in 1233, all without any result. Between 1238 and 1243 Jeremiah Ghisi and his brother Andrew, Venetian rulers of other Aegean islands, took Andros from Marino Dandolo and sent him into exile, where he died. Dandolo's sister Maria Doro and his widow Felisa, who married Jacopo Querini, appealed to Venice for justice against the Ghisi usurpation. Doge Jacopo Tiepolo upheld their rights, declared confiscated the goods of the Ghisi in Venice, and threatened Jeremiah Ghisi with exile if he would not comply. Nevertheless, the Ghisi held the island for decades. In 1282 doge John Dandolo and the council of Venice, upon the petition of the heirs of Marino Dandolo, declared that Andros should revert back to the possession of its feudal overlord, Marco II Sanudo, duke of Naxos.[142]

The Ghisi of Venice also made independent conquests. The brothers Andrew and Jeremiah Ghisi organized an expedition in 1207; Andrew occupied and held Tenos and Myconos in the Cyclades, and Jeremiah became lord of Skyros, Skiathos, and Skopelos in the northern Sporades.[143] In addition to creating their principality in the Cy-

---

140. Miller, *Essays,* p. 68; *idem, Latins in the Levant,* pp. 591–610. The Marino Dandolo of Andros is not the same as his namesake who was podestà of Constantinople and of Treviso, contender for the ducal office in Venice, and murdered in 1233: Loenertz, "Marino Dandolo," *Byzantina et Franco-Graeca,* pp. 402–403.

141. Lombardo and Morozzo della Rocca, *Nuovi documenti,* no. 43.

142. Loenertz, "Marino Dandolo," *Byzantina et Franco-Graeca,* pp. 399–419; Andrea Dandolo, *Chronica,* p. 282; Fotheringham, *Marco Sanudo,* p. 59; Borsari, *Studi,* p. 40; Miller, *Latins in the Levant,* pp. 44, 578–580.

143. Loenertz, "Marino Dandolo," *Byzantina et Franco-Graeca,* pp. 400, 405; Borsari, *Studi,* p. 41; Fotheringham, *Marco Sanudo,* pp. 56–70.

clades and northern Sporades, the Ghisi made numerous commercial investments and international loans.[144] Another brother, John, and his son Natalis lent a huge sum to king Andrew II of Hungary. In 1224 Andrew sent 201 silver marks to Venice, where doge Peter Ziani and his councillors accepted this pledge for the Ghisi. Andrew Ghisi, lord of Tenos and Myconos, in 1239 lent 400 gold perperi to Angelo Sanudo, duke of Naxos, and was repaid in 1245. The brothers Jeremiah, Marino, and Andrew Ghisi had a fraternal company, which indicates that the family resources existed, in part, as an indissoluble common fund. Their investments were placed in *colleganza* contracts, and three such Ghisi contracts for the decade 1251–1261 have survived. Not all their affairs prospered; in 1252 they were placed under the ban of Venice for having seized Andros. Another misfortune occurred when Andrew Ghisi was victimized by pirates in 1259. He appealed to the doge for relief and the doge lifted the ban against him. Before 1261 members of the family participated in the Great Council of Venice and held office as ducal councillors and as inspector of public works. These details suggest that the Ghisi held their islands, not only by political acumen and by right of conquest, but also by means of financial strength and business ability. They were related by marriage to other Venetian and Frankish lords of the Aegean, and the Ghisi line continued to hold Aegean islands until 1390, when the family became extinct.

Lemnos (called Stalimene by the Latins), where a Latin church dependent upon the Venetian monastery of San Giorgio Maggiore existed in the twelfth century, was assigned to the Latin emperor by the Treaty of Partition. However Filocalo Navigaioso, a Venetian and a member of the Constantinopolitan community, took possession of Lemnos at least as early as 1206, holding it as a fief of the Latin emperor.[145] He held the Byzantine title megaduke, which customarily conferred high naval command. The Navigaioso family held this island for generations.

The tiny islands of Cerigo (Cythera) and Cerigotto (Anticythera), which lie like stepping stones between the Morea and Crete, also became the property of Venetian families. Marco Venier set out from Crete to conquer Cerigo, and James Viaro to conquer Cerigotto. They also assisted the Venetian military effort to subdue Crete. Viaro had

---

144. Loenertz, "Généalogie des Ghisi," pp. 144–148; *Liber Plegiorum,* ed. Cessi, pp. 70–71; Morozzo della Rocca and Lombardo, *Nuovi documenti,* nos. 95, 96; and their *Documenti,* II, no. 774.

145. Morozzo della Rocca and Lombardo, *Documenti,* II, no. 519; Andrea Dandolo, *Chronica,* p. 282; Fotheringham, *Marco Sanudo,* p. 59.

assisted Marco Dandolo previously in the Venetian conquest of Gallipoli. When their families were abruptly dislodged by Licario about
1278, Venetian rule on Cerigo and Cerigotto ended until the fourteenth century.[146]

Another Venetian nobleman, Lorenzo Tiepolo, held territory in the
Aegean. He was the son of doge Jacopo Tiepolo, who had been the
first Venetian duke of Crete, and he too would rule Venice as doge
from 1268 to 1275. Possibly through his second wife, Agnes Ghisi,
he became lord of the islands of Skyros and Skopelos. Lorenzo Tiepolo also held a fief from the Villehardouin princes of Achaea.[147]
The sources do not record who held these islands in the last part of
the century; possibly they reverted back to the Ghisi.

Among the Aegean islands conquered and held privately by Venetians, only the above-noted principalities of the Navigaiosi, Marco
Sanudo, Lorenzo Tiepolo, the Ghisi brothers, Marino Dandolo, the
Veniers, and the Viari were established in the early thirteenth century.
Recent scholarship has refuted the claims of nineteenth-century historians that many other Venetians established feudal principalities on
the Aegean islands at the same time. Not until the end of the thirteenth century did other Venetian families gain possession of Aegean
islands. The evidence[148] suggests that only in the fifteenth century
did the Querini come to Astypalaea (Stampalia); and in the fourteenth
century the Barozzi came to Thera (Santorin) and Therasia, the Fos-
coli to Anaphe (Namfio), and the Ghisi to Chios and Seriphos. These
acquisitions belong to the Venetian holdings of the Renaissance rather
than the crusading epoch.

Of all the islands and the seaports of the Near East, the most important for Venetian commerce had always been Constantinople. The
Venetian quarter in Constantinople had formed the principal center
for its foreign commerce since 1082, and Venetian efforts to maintain
this position against Italian and Byzantine competition had preceded
the Fourth Crusade by over a generation. The establishment of the

146. Borsari, *Studi,* p. 38; Miller, *Latins in the Levant,* pp. 138, 564–568; Fotheringham,
Marco Sanudo, p. 58.

147. Jacoby, *La Féodalité,* p. 195; Loenertz, "Marino Dandolo," *Byzantina et Franco-Graeca,*
p. 409, note 5. Lorenzo Tiepolo's first wife, Agnes, was either a Brienne or the daughter of
a Balkan prince.

148. Borsari, *Studi,* pp. 38–43; Fotheringham, *Marco Sanudo,* pp. 56–70; Loenertz, "Les
Querini, comtes d'Astypalée, 1413–1537," *Byzantina et Franco-Graeca,* pp. 503–536. Loenertz,
"De Quelques îles grecques et de leurs seigneurs vénitiens du XIVe et XVe siècles," *Studi veneziani,* XIV (1972), 9, suggests the possibility of a Venetian lord over Astypalaea in the thirteenth
century, but states that no surviving source documents this possibility.

Latin empire in Constantinople in 1204 jointly by the Venetians and the Frankish crusaders gave the citizens of Venice a greater security in Constantinople than they had ever known.

When the Latin empire was established,[149] the Venetians acted as a unit under their doge to gain economic and ecclesiastical supremacy in Romania. The Fourth Crusade returned all previously held commercial privileges and monopolies to Venice. The well-disciplined coherence of the Venetians in Constantinople is attested by the continuance of their corporate activity in the summer of 1205, after the death of Enrico Dandolo. They elected Marino Zeno to be their podestà in Constantinople, and he surrounded himself with a group of magistrates bearing the same titles as ducal councillors at home—judges of the commune, councillors, treasurer, and advocate. The military and commercial responsibilities of the Venetians in Constantinople necessitated a continuity of leadership. Zeno at first used Enrico Dandolo's title, *dominator quartae partis et dimidie Imperii Romanie.* He remained in office until 1207 but had to acknowledge the leadership of the doge in Venice. In September 1205 he notified doge Peter Ziani of his election as podestà, and promised that the Venetians in Constantinople would in the future accept as their podestà only a man sent from Venice and that the fiefs gained by the Venetians in Romania would not be sold or bequeathed to foreigners. One month later, he acknowledged the doge's sovereignty over all former Byzantine possessions in the Adriatic and Ionian seas granted to Venice by the Treaty of Partition. He also confirmed the obligations and the treaties made in 1204 between the French crusaders and the Venetians under doge Enrico Dandolo.[150] This confirmation was signed in the imperial red ink by Henry, brother of the captured emperor Baldwin I, and by Zeno. According to this confirmation, the Latin emperor could act only with the advice and consent of his council, composed half of Venetians and half of Franks. In addition, the defense of the empire depended during the campaign season upon military contingents from both Franks and Venetians. The Venetians were confirmed in all rights and privileges they had ever held in Constantinople under the Greeks. Venetian strength in Romania also rested on control of its Latin church, whose head, the patriarch of Constantinople, according to arrangements in 1204, was always a Venetian.[151]

The Venetian Civil Law promulgated in 1242 by doge Jacopo Tiepolo testifies to the position of Constantinople as the second city in

---

149. See chapter VI of volume II of the present work.
150. Tafel and Thomas, I, 566–574; Wolff, "The Oath of the Venetian Podestà," pp. 544–551.
151. See McNeal and Wolff, in volume II of the present work, pp. 195–199.

the Venetian dominions. This law restricted the drawing up of *breviaria,* notarized documents, to Venice and Constantinople only. Furthermore, documents notarized in Constantinople had to be drawn up in the presence of the podestà, his agent, or one of the councillors of the doge.[152] The law code further states that private contracts for loans could not be paid off in any city other than that specified, except Venice itself or Constantinople.[153] These laws further demonstrate that the Venetian colony in Constantinople, led by the podestà, had more independent authority and more power than any other Venetian colony.

The colony's strength is further attested by the story, which appears only in the Renaissance chronicle of Daniele Barbaro, that the Venetians debated at length whether or not they ought to transfer the seat of their government to Constantinople. The conservatives won, and the doge remained in Italy. Every Venetian podestà in Constantinople except the first was nominated by the home government, not by the Venetian community in Constantinople. All Marino Zeno's successors took an oath to follow the directives of the home government, and to administer justice for the profit and honor of Venice and for the safety of Romania. They also swore that they would not act in fiscal or financial matters or in foreign affairs without the consent of their councillors.[154] Each was assisted by two councillors, six judges, and a treasurer.

Venice chose some of its most outstanding men to be podestà in Constantinople.[155] Marino Dandolo, probably related to doge Enrico Dandolo, held office as podestà sometime between 1209 and 1221. Later, in Venice, he served as ducal councillor in 1223, and as vice-doge in 1224. Still later, in 1229, he tied with Jacopo Tiepolo for election to the ducal office itself. He never held the office, but became podestà of the nearby city of Treviso and was assassinated in 1233.[156] The noble Venetian family of Michiel, which contributed three doges to Venice in the eleventh and twelfth centuries, gave two podestà to

---

152. *Gli Statuti veneziani di Jacopo Tiepolo del 1242,* ed. Cessi, I, xxvii, 62. *Breviaria* meant any documents drawn up by a notary; *ibid.,* I, xxxvi, 67, esp. gloss 205. Another Venetian gloss from the second half of the thirteenth century (*ibid.,* I, xxvii, 62) extended the right to authenticate such *breviaria* to any Venetian governor be he bailie, podestà, rector, the duke of Crete, or one of their agents. The date of this extension, after 1261, demonstrates that other legal provisions had to be made for authenticating such *breviaria* after the fall of the Latin empire.

153. *Ibid.,* V, viii, 22.

154. Wolff, "The Oath," pp. 552–557; Lombardo and Morozzo della Rocca, *Nuovi documenti,* no. 52; Luzzatto, *Storia economica di Venezia,* p. 62.

155. Wolff, "The Oath," pp. 559–564.

156. See above, note 140.

Constantinople, Marino Michiel in March 1221 and John Michiel in 1240-1241. Marino Storlato, podestà in 1222 and 1223, served the Venetian state at home as judge in 1195, as examiner in 1210, and as councillor in 1219, and represented Venice in Rome as witness to the oath of John of Brienne in April 1231. Teofilo Zeno, one of the wealthiest Venetians, was podestà of Constantinople sometime between 1224 and 1228, and again about 1235-1238. He also served Venice as judge in 1219, and as ducal councillor in 1228 and 1229. Jacob Dolfin, podestà in 1256, also served Venice at home as judge of the commune in 1241. Marco Gradenigo, the last Venetian podestà before the fall of Constantinople to the Greeks in 1261, also served Venice as captain of the Venetian army in Romania before 1256, and as bailie in Negroponte.

The most important podestà of Constantinople was Jacopo Tiepolo. As a young man before the Fourth Crusade he was active in commercial voyages, going to Messina and to Constantinople in 1190.[157] Before becoming podestà he had held the offices of bailie of Negroponte and duke of Crete; he held the chief office in Constantinople in 1219-1221, and again about 1224. In Constantinople Tiepolo carried out a policy designed to bring more commercial advantages to Venice, despite the weakening of the Latin empire.[158] In 1219 he reaffirmed the Venetian responsibilities to the Latin empire in a convention signed with the regent, Conon of Béthune. In the same year he increased Venetian business opportunities by making treaties, on his own authority as podestà, with foreign sovereigns in Anatolia. According to his commercial agreement with Theodore I Lascaris, Greek emperor of Nicaea, Venetians could trade in the empire of Nicaea without paying customs dues. In 1220 Tiepolo made a commercial treaty with Kai-Kobād I, the Turkish sultan of Konya. In 1224, acting as agent for the doge, he settled a dispute with the Latin emperor Robert of Courtenay whereby three eighths of certain fields near Constantinople would be assigned to the Venetians, according to the earlier Franco-Venetian treaties. A document also survives from the years of Tiepolo's leadership wherein the Venetians controlling the seaport of Lampsacus on the Dardanelles agreed to pay annually 1,000 gold perperi to the Venetian podestà in Constantinople.[159] He brought his extensive commercial, political, and administrative experience back to Venice in 1229 upon his election as doge.

---

157. Morozzo della Rocca and Lombardo, *Documenti,* I, nos. 377, 388, 389.
158. See Wolff, "The Latin Empire of Constantinople, 1204-1261," in volume II of the present work, pp. 220-233.
159. Tafel and Thomas, II, 205-210, 214-225, 255.

During his twenty years in that office, Jacopo Tiepolo continued his policy of protecting Venetian commercial advantages in the Near East.[160] His amicable relations with the Greeks at Nicaea ceased when John III (Ducas) Vatatzes ruled Nicaea from 1222 to 1254. On the other hand, as doge he concluded commercial treaties with the Aiyūbid lord of Aleppo, with king Béla IV of Hungary, with king Heṭoum I of Cilician Armenia at Ayas (Lajazzo), with the Aiyūbid sultans al-'Ādil II and aṣ-Ṣāliḥ of Egypt, and with the Hafṣid lord of Tunis, Yaḥyâ I. His commercial agreement with and support of Leo Gabalas, Greek ruler of Rhodes, came to nothing when John Vatatzes of Nicaea took Rhodes. He also carried out the first complete surviving codification of the Venetian civil and maritime laws. His policy, like that of other doges of this era, was economic domination in Romania.

The power of the Venetian podestà continued to be only as strong as Venetian influence in Constantinople and surrounding territories. Of the lands near Constantinople promised to Venice in the Treaty of Partition, not all came under Venetian jurisdiction. Although the Venetians were granted Thrace as far as Adrianople by the Treaty, the Bulgarian king Ioannitsa conquered most of it in 1204–1205. Ioannitsa captured the Latin emperor Baldwin I in April 1205, when he attempted to retake Adrianople. After the siege, doge Enrico Dandolo moved south with his forces to Rodosto on the Sea of Marmara, where he left a Venetian garrison.[161] Rodosto had seen resident Venetian churchmen and traveling Venetian merchants often in the twelfth century. But the Venetians did not hold Rodosto long in 1205. Ioannitsa led the Bulgars south after taking Adrianople, and, after his victory at Rusion in January 31, 1206, took Arcadiopolis, Rodosto, Heraclea, and other places on the Thracian coast. Rodosto must have been regained by the Venetians because they sent a castellan there in 1224. West of Rodosto, at the mouth of the Dardanelles, the seaport of Gallipoli became firmly Venetian when Marco Dandolo and Jacob Viadro conquered it in 1205. Gallipoli too received a Venetian castellan in 1224. Venice held Gallipoli until 1235, when it was taken and sacked by the Greek ruler John Vatatzes.[162] The Venetians also held Lampsacus on the Asiatic shore of the Dardanelles.

Control of seaports was more important to Venice than ephemeral sovereignty over the inland regions of Thrace. At Adrianople the Greeks

---

160. *Ibid.*, II, 274–307.

161. Ivan Dujčev, "Rapporti fra Venezia e Bulgaria nel Medioevo," *Venezia e il levante,* ed. Pertusi, I-1, 246.

162. Andrea Dandolo, *Chronica,* pp. 282, 295; Wolff, in volume II of the present work, p. 219; Fotheringham, *Marco Sanudo,* pp. 50–51; Thiriet, *La Romanie vénitienne,* pp. 85, 92.

soon despaired of Ioannitsa's leadership and secretly arranged to surrender the city to the Greek leader Theodore Branas in Constantinople. By an agreement in 1206, the Venetians in Constantinople gave up their rights in Adrianople to Branas. He entered into actual possession only after the second Latin emperor, Henry, and his army retook the area from the Bulgars in late August 1206.[163] Through these seaports on the Dardanelles and the Sea of Marmara, the Venetian colony in Constantinople not only controlled the approaches to Constantinople but also profited from the renewal of the ancient Venetian commercial privileges there. In return, Venice contributed to the defense of the European possessions of the Latin empire.

Italians, who had not been welcome in the Black Sea until 1204, soon afterward began their eastward voyages in search of markets and grain. Venetian voyages into the Black Sea are known as early as 1206, when one was made to Soldaia in the Crimea.[164] By mid-century Venetian merchants had explored the Black Sea and established commercial contacts, like the Polo agency in Soldaia, which dated from 1250. The Black Sea trade must have yielded mainly grain, timber, and salt fish to the Venetian merchants before the Mongol conquests in the second quarter of the thirteenth century. The unstable and fragmented pre-Mongol governments of the Black Sea littoral would not have attracted the long-distance Asiatic caravans which later, during the *Pax Mongolica,* were to bring precious goods from the Far East.

Venetians were to learn more about the conquests of Genghis Khan and his successors than most Europeans.[165] Mongol horsemen had invaded western Europe, in the 1240's reaching Udine, only about eighty miles from Venice. The Mongols pushed the Hungarians and the central Balkan peoples, who, in turn, put pressure on the Venetian-dominated Dalmatian coast. Renier Zeno, a future doge, represented Venice in 1245 at the First Council of Lyons, where pope Innocent IV discussed the defense of Europe against the Mongols. Before the Greeks returned to Constantinople in 1261 and temporarily prohib-

---

163. Villehardouin, ed. Faral, II, 234–237, 246–247; Tafel and Thomas, II, 17–19; Cessi, *Le Colonie medioevali,* I, 105; Dujčev, *loc. cit.* (note 161, above).

164. Marie Nystazopoulou Pélékidis, "Venise et la Mer Noire," *Venezia e il levante,* ed. Pertusi, I-2, 545–548, believes that the Genoese were allowed to trade in the Black Sea by the Byzantines, in 1169 and 1192, when the Byzantines granted privileges to the Genoese to counteract Venetian predominance; cf. Morozzo della Rocca and Lombardo, *Documenti,* II, nos. 478–479.

165. See Roberto Almagia, "Marco Polo," *Nel VII Centenario della nascità di Marco Polo,* pp. 12–24; Rodolfo Gallo, "Marco Polo, la sua famiglia e il suo libro," *ibid.,* pp. 63–77; Leonardo Olschki, "1254: Venezia, l'Europa, e i Tartari," *ibid.,* pp. 302–308.

ited Venetians from going to the Black Sea, Venetian merchants had
already established themselves in Mongol lands. Jacob Venier and
Nicholas Pisani, two Venetian merchants resident in Kiev, which was
controlled by the Golden Horde, met John of Pian del Carpine, the
official ambassador of pope Innocent IV, about 1244, on his return
from the Mongol empire.

The father and uncles of Marco Polo set out from their agency
in Soldaia, in 1260, on their first long journey into Mongol lands.
They traveled much farther into Mongol domains than other known
Venetians. On their first journey they visited the Ukraine, Bukhara
in Turkestan, and also China, and returned by land in 1269–1270 to
Ayas in Cilician Armenia, and thence by sea to Acre, Negroponte,
and home. The Polo brothers did not return via the Black Sea because, while in Asia, they must have received information that the
Greeks had reconquered Constantinople and had closed the Black
Sea to all but their allies, the Genoese and the Pisans. The Venetians,
however, negotiated a treaty in 1268 with the Greek emperor, Michael
VIII Palaeologus, whereby they could resume trade within the empire
and in the Black Sea. Consequently the Venetians sent a consul to
Soldaia in 1287 with authority over all the Crimean area. They could
now take advantage of the opportunity to purchase precious stones,
metals, luxury textiles from the Far East, furs, pelts, wax, and honey
from Russia, and timber, salt, and salt fish from the regions near
the Crimea. Matthew and Nicholas Polo began their second journey
in 1271, the year after a Venetian truce with Genoa, and took seventeen-
year-old Marco with them. Marco Polo's famous book recounts his
overland journey to the court of Kubilai Khan in Cathay, his long
service under Kubilai Khan, and his return, mainly by sea, reaching
Constantinople and finally Venice in 1295. His travels have become
the best-known Venetian venture of the thirteenth century and demonstrate the unlimited opportunity opened up to Venice by commercial colonization during the crusades.

Syria and Palestine continued to attract Venetian commerce after
1204, despite the beginning of armed conflict between the Italian communes there in the second quarter of the thirteenth century.[166] When
Frederick II became king of Jerusalem, fortified the coastal cities,
and regained Jerusalem on his bloodless crusade,[167] the Venetian position seemed strong. Following Frederick's departure, however, open

166. Cessi, *Le Colonie medioevali,* I, 118–126; volume II of the present work, pp. 546–569.
167. See Thomas C. Van Cleve, "The Crusade of Frederick II," in volume II of the present
work, chapter XII.

warfare broke out among the Latins in the kingdom of Jerusalem. The Hohenstaufen or imperial party, led by the imperial bailie Richard Filangieri and his brothers, included the Teutonic Knights, some local barons, and the Pisans. The Lombard party, led by the Ibelins, included many barons of Jerusalem and the Genoese. At first the Templars, the Hospitallers, and the Venetians held aloof, but later the Venetians joined the Lombard party against the Ghibellines. The fighting attempted to settle whether the local Christian barons or the absent Hohenstaufen king of Jerusalem should rule, and also which Italian sea power should be supreme on the Palestinian and Syrian coast. Until 1243 the Pisans enjoyed the strength which came from their support of the imperial cause. The Pisan strength declined with the decline of the imperial power and their loss of Tyre in July 1243. From this date to the fall of Acre in 1291, the kingdom of Jerusalem was governed loosely by the barons.

The Italian communes formed the strongest and richest elements in the port cities of Antioch, Tripoli, Tyre, Acre, and Jaffa. No harmony existed between them after the common enemy, the Hohenstaufen party, was gone. Every irritation erupted into armed conflict, interrupted only briefly by Louis IX's visit to the Latin kingdom during his first crusade. First Genoa sided with Pisa against Venice. From 1257 on Venice and Genoa fought a long series of wars which lasted over a century. Pisa, gradually weakened through conflict with Genoa at home, sided with Venice in the first war, known as the War of the Communes or the War of St. Sabas because conflict broke out over possession of a house belonging to the abbey of St. Sabas in Acre. After several bloody land and sea battles, the Venetians decisively defeated the Genoese in June 1258 at sea off Acre. Lorenzo Tiepolo, son of doge Jacopo Tiepolo and a future doge himself, commanded the Venetians. After the naval victory the Venetians razed the Genoese quarter in Acre, and Tiepolo carried some of the stones of Acre home in triumph to Venice. Genoa then left Acre, which had formerly been its strongest point, for other coastal cities. The Venetian power appeared in 1258 to be at its height in the Latin kingdom of Jerusalem.

The Venetians in thirteenth-century Tyre retained their commercial privileges, which had first been granted them in the *pactum Warmundi* of 1123. Tyre continued to be their chief center. According to the *pactum Warmundi* the Venetians were to receive one third of the city, and the Latin kingdom two thirds. As they were recorded in the inventory of Venetian holdings in Tyre made in 1243 by the Venetian bailie, Marsiglio Zorzi, Venetian holdings included land and streets along the eastern shore of the harbor, bordering on the holdings of the Genoese, the order of the Hospital of St. John of Jerusalem, and others.[168] The largest structure there, the grand palace of the Venetian *fondaco,* provided substantial rents to Venice. The church of St. Demetrius and the chapel of St. Mark, the arsenal, and many other structures in the area belonged to the Venetians. Venetian law prevailed there. Venetian noblemen resided in this section for years at a time while retaining their property and privileges at home.[169] Other Venetian noblemen and commoners lived in Tyre only for a few months, between the arrival of the fall fleet from Venice and its spring departure. Apparently native Syrians and other Latins also lived in the Venetian section.

One third of the countryside surrounding Tyre also belonged to Venice, and two thirds to the kingdom of Jerusalem. The Venetian share included, according to a recent study, about twenty-one small villages and their surrounding cultivated land. Wheat and barley fields, crops of legumes, and orchards planted on these lands supplied the Tyrians with their food. In other irrigated areas, the Venetians maintained sugar plantations, and sugar presses near Tyre produced a local product for export.[170] Near the Venetian agricultural villages there were 2,000 olive groves worked by compulsory labor. The famous glass-blowers of Tyre also produced exports for Venetian merchants. Some of them emigrated to Venice in the mid-twelfth century to found the Venetian glass industry. In addition to these local products, the Venetians also exported from Tyre other products of the region. Most important were the textiles: cotton cloth and cotton thread, linen, camel's-hair cloth, buckram or canvas, and wool for caps.[171] Other thirteenth-century Venetian exports from the Holy Land included spices, pigments, medicines, and lead.[172]

While the Genoese colonies in Syria and Palestine continued to be exploited mainly by independent Genoese citizens, some of them feudal lords like the Embriachi in Jubail and others on Aegean islands, the Venetian colonies in Palestine were more closely controlled by

168. Tafel and Thomas, II, 351–398; Prawer, "Étude de quelques problèmes," pp. 10–58; *idem,* "Veneziani e colonie veneziane," *Venezia e il levante,* ed. Pertusi, I-2, 637, 643–651.

169. *Ibid.,* pp. 655, 638–642.

170. *Gli Statuti marittimi veneziani fino al 1255,* ed. Predelli and Sacerdoti, p. 73; see also above, pp. 257–259.

171. *Bonbace, bambace filum, filum, zambelloti, boccarani, lana de berretis, Gli Statuti marittimi,* p. 73.

172. *Piper, incensum, endegum, zinzibar, zeroata, mirra, lacca, bomarabica, aloes, nuces muscate, gariofoli, gardamomum, melegete, canfora, auresi, sandalo, mirobalani, galenga, simoniacum, cubebe, piper longum, aurum pigmentum, armoniacum, cera, alumen, vitreum, vitriolum, smerilium, requiricia, spigum, canella, cominum, maci, anisi, zambelloti, ibid.* Prawer has given a translation of this list, *Crusaders' Kingdom,* p. 400.

the Venetian state. The home city regularly sent out its representatives, known as bailies, to the chief colonial city in Palestine. The first known bailie was Teofilo Zeno in 1117. In the thirteenth century the bailie held office for one year and was chosen by the doge of Venice from among those Venetians familiar with conditions in the Latin kingdom. Venetians residing in Palestine, among them the chronicler Martin da Canal, contributed greatly to Venetian life when they returned home. The coastal city of Tyre served as the headquarters for Venice in Palestine throughout most of the thirteenth century, except from 1262 to 1270 when the Genoese forced them to concentrate in Acre. After the conquest of the remainder of the Latin kingdom of Jerusalem by the Mamluks in 1291, the Venetians had to make their peace with the new rulers.

Although Venice had traded with Egypt at least since the tenth century, only thirteenth-century sources present many details. Sometime between 1205 and 1217 Venice stabilized its position in Egypt by negotiating a series of six commercial agreements with the Aiyūbid sultan, al-'Ādil.[173] These agreements outlined the position of Christian merchants in Moslem Egypt and probably reflect the terms of earlier arrangements. The sultan agreed to honor and protect all Venetians and their Christian agents in his domains. He also promised to protect the pilgrims whom they might transport to the Holy Sepulcher. Venetian merchants were to pay no more than the regular customs duties in Egypt. They were granted a *fondaco* in the chicken market in Alexandria where they might live, and the right to come and go freely in Egypt. They were also given freedom to buy and sell any merchandise anywhere in Egypt without restraint. They were to be judged in their own courts. The sultan agreed to respect their customs provided that they were observed within the Venetian *fondaco,* such as the drinking of wine with meals and the taking of usury, both of which were prohibited to Moslems. The Venetians agreed on their part to follow the regulations of the Egyptian customs officers.

These arrangements must have broken down in 1217–1218 during the Fifth Crusade. King Andrew II of Hungary had assumed leadership of the crusading army in 1216, and secured the assistance of Venetian shipping by granting Venice perpetual sovereignty over Zara and various commercial privileges in his realm. Venice was to provide ten

---

173. Although the treaty used to be dated 1202 and given as a cause for the diversion of the Fourth Crusade, the treaty now is dated later; Gabriel Hanotaux, "Les Vénitiens ont-ils trahi la Chrétienté en 1202?" *Revue historique,* IV (1877), 87–100; *The Latin Conquest of Constantinople,* ed. Queller, pp. 24–43; Kretschmayr, *Geschichte,* I, 482. For the text, see Tafel and Thomas, II, 184–193.

large ships, at a rental of 550 Venetian silver marks each, and numerous smaller vessels.[174] The crusaders assembled in Spalato the following summer in such numbers that not enough ships were ready. Eventually transportation for all was secured; and the crusaders proceeded to Acre. There is no evidence of Venetian participation in the Palestinian military phase of the Fifth Crusade, and the Venetians did not assist the Hungarian crusaders to return home. Sick and weakened, king Andrew returned home by land, leading his army through Syria, Cilician Armenia, the Latin empire of Constantinople, and Bulgaria. The Fifth Crusade proceeded without him during 1218, embarking from Acre to attack Damietta in Egypt. Possibly Venetian ships transported the crusaders to Egypt, since Venetian troops and ships were present at Damietta at the time of the military disaster at Mansurah. The Fifth Crusade was the last such venture for the commune of Venice. Except to further its quarrel with Genoa, Venice did not participate in any other thirteenth-century crusade. Some Venetians resided in Acre and assisted in the defense of the city until its fall in April 1291 to the Mamluks. Of all the crusading expeditions before 1291, Venice had participated most fully and gained most from the Fourth Crusade.

After the Fifth Crusade Venice, like the papacy, prohibited any of its citizens or ships from trading with Egypt. Trade in lumber, iron, and ship tackle was specifically prohibited. Evidence of these prohibitions exists for the years 1224 to 1228.[175] Doge Peter Ziani sent a decree to the duke of Crete in 1226 prohibiting Venetian ships from trading with Egypt. Bonds were to be posted to insure compliance and violators of the decree were to suffer confiscation of their goods and fines.[176] But the ships did not stop sailing to Venice from Alexandria. In 1226 the doge fined certain Lombard merchants and confiscated their cargo of dates and seven great elephant tusks brought from Egypt. Venetians were also issued permits for organized piracy against Egyptian shipping in 1226.[177] Venetian trade with Egypt seems to have continued from Constantinople, where the Venetian patriarch had the right to absolve the sins of those who carried on illicit trade with Moslems contrary to papal decree.[178]

Venice resumed its regular trade with Egypt when Jacopo Tiepolo

---

174. Van Cleve, "The Fifth Crusade," in volume II of the present work, pp. 388–389; Andrea Dandolo, *Chronica,* pp. 286–287.

175. *Liber Plegiorum,* ed. Cessi, pp. 17, 19, 28, 29, 31, 33, 94, 95, 98.

176. Tafel and Thomas, II, 260–264. The duke in 1226 was Marino Soranzo.

177. *Liber Plegiorum,* ed. Cessi, pp. 96, 140–142, 144.

178. Wolff, "Politics in the Latin Patriarchate," p. 277.

was doge. The sultan of Egypt, al-Kāmil, in 1238 gave the doge's agents, Romeo Querini and Jacopo Barozzi, knights, a renewal of Venetian privileges.[179] In addition, he promised Venice an additional *fondaco* where its laws might prevail and money, gold, and silver might be exchanged under supervision. The treaty also stated that neither Egyptians nor Venetians should commit acts of piracy against each other. Six years later the Egyptian sultan aṣ-Ṣāliḥ Aiyūb again guaranteed the safety of Venetians and their goods in his domains.[180]

The crusade of Louis IX to Egypt and the end of the Aiyūbid line must have ended the effectiveness of these treaties, for in 1254 Venice negotiated a new pact with the first Mamluk sultan of Egypt, Aybeg, shortly after he assumed power. This pact detailed the customary rights and privileges of the Venetians in Egypt much more clearly and precisely than any earlier pact had.[181] It is not known whether these Venetian privileges in Egypt continued after 1257 when Aybeg was murdered, but Venetian trade continued with Egypt during the remainder of the century.

Tunisia was another area where Venetian merchant diplomats negotiated treaties before the end of the Latin empire. With Pisan merchants already firmly established, the Venetian doge Jacopo Tiepolo in 1231 made a formal compact with the rulers of Tunis to ensure the safety of Venetians, their merchandise, and their shipping.[182] Although the treaty was to run for forty years, the Venetians and the Ḥafṣid rulers of Tunisia renewed it in 1251, probably because Louis's crusading expedition to Egypt had disrupted trade along the North African coast. The treaty of 1251 repeated the usual safeguards to Venetian commerce, and added that, when famine threatened Venice, the Venetians were permitted to export grain from Tunisia if its price did not exceed a certain figure.[183] These arrangements to purchase grain in Tunisia were particularly significant because they were made the same year Venice went to war with Genoa.

The crusades provided Venice with many opportunities for overseas expansion. Not only did the Fourth Crusade give Venice a monopoly of trade in Constantinople, but Venetian merchants enjoyed unusual commercial advantages and protection in the Frankish states of the former Byzantine empire. Pirate nests in Ragusa, Corfu, Mo-

179. Tafel and Thomas, II, 336–341.
180. *Ibid.*, 416–418.
181. *Ibid.*, 483–492.
182. *Ibid.*, 303–307.
183. *Ibid.*, 450–456.

don and Coron, Crete, and Naxos were destroyed by Venetian ships
before 1212, and Venetian colonies in Romania served as bases from
which later Venetian squadrons policed the seas.

Emboldened by greater commercial security, thirteenth-century Venetian merchants sought new markets. They explored the Black Sea and
established commercial colonies from Soldaia in the Crimea eastward
to the Sea of Azov and Tana on the river Don, and southward to
Greek Trebizond. From these distant stations Venetians regularly did
business with the Mongols and met the caravans from the Far East.
In the next century Venetians penetrated deeply into Mongol lands.
Similarly, in the western Mediterranean Venetians frequented the ports
of Moslem Tunisia and the rival Christian ports: Pisa, Genoa, Marseilles, Barcelona, and Palma di Mallorca. Shortly after 1300 Venetian ships would sail past the Strait of Gibraltar north to England
and Flanders.

Certain established markets became more precarious for Venetian
merchants during the thirteenth century. Palestine was convulsed with
wars between the Franks, and by mid-century the hinterland felt the
pressure of the advancing Mongols.

The Genoese and the Greeks repeatedly challenged the Venetian
commercial monopoly of the eastern seas. Open warfare commenced
with the devastating War of St. Sabas in Palestine, which ended in
1258 with the Genoese expulsion from Acre. Then Genoa turned to
Michael VIII Palaeologus, who was consolidating his holdings in Europe and Asia. This Greek emperor of Nicaea allied with Genoa in
the Treaty of Nymphaeum, took Constantinople from the Latins in
1261, and expelled the Venetians. Genoa, replacing Venice in Constantinople, established a permanent commercial colony at Pera, across
the Golden Horn. Although Michael VIII restored Venetian commercial privileges in 1268 and restored the Venetian quarter in Constantinople in 1277, his reconquest had effectively destroyed the Venetian
trade monopoly in Constantinople.

Greeks and Genoese also challenged the large and strategic Venetian islands of Negroponte and Crete. War was endemic on Negroponte in the last half of the century when Licario, supported by the
Palaeologi and the Genoese, led uprisings against the Lombard terciers supported by the Venetians.[184] On Crete, Alexius Callerges, similarly, led revolts against Venice. On both islands, however, the Venetians finally prevailed.

184. Borsari, *Studi,* pp. 98–99; Miller, *Latins in the Levant,* pp. 102–104, 136–141, 208–210;
Loenertz, "Les Seigneurs terciers de Négropont," pp. 249–276.

The century closed with Venice's Second Genoese War, although the two cities had been encouraged to make a truce in 1270 by the French king, Louis IX, in preparation for his last crusade. Hostilities between Venice and Genoa began again in 1294 and involved the Palaeologi the next year, when the Venetian-Byzantine treaties expired. Venice made peace with Genoa in 1299 only after suffering defeat at the disastrous battle of Curzola. Peace was not renewed with Byzantium until the winter of 1302–1303.

In response to these challenges, Venice sought alternate markets in Anatolia, in Greek, Moslem, and Armenian lands. By 1300 Ayas in Cilician Armenia and Alexandria in Egypt had become the foreign ports most often frequented by Venetian merchants.

Despite the failure of Venetian attempts at commercial monopoly of the eastern Mediterranean and Aegean after the fall of the Latin empire, Venetian commercial power and wealth probably grew throughout the century,[185] though precise documentation is not possible. There are, however, a number of Genoese notarial cartularies, largely unpublished, from which Vsevolod Slessarev has drawn figures illustrating the growth of Genoese overseas trade in the thirteenth century.[186] "The minutes of a single notary out of some twenty-nine active in Genoa . . . indicate a flurry of investment to Ultramare (Syria and Palestine) between August 21 and September 24, 1191. The value of goods and cash destined for the Levant amounted to 8,570 Genoese pounds, which suggests [an annual] total of perhaps 80,000 pounds, a staggering sum for that time, partly explainable by the complete absence of investments [in trade with] Alexandria. Seven years later, according to a very fragmentary source, two ships left Genoa for Ultramare and four for Alexandria, indicating thus a return to peacetime commerce."[187] After the Fourth Crusade and the growth of Venetian colonies in Romania, the Genoese trade continued to increase. "Occasional references to customs dues *ad valorem* and the amounts for which they were farmed permit us to calculate the overall growth of the trade. In 1214 the minimum of anticipated turnover, [both] export from and import to Genoa, amounts to 380,520 Genoese pounds; in 1274 to 720,000; and in 1341 to 1,403,400. The share of Ultramare in these sums cannot be ascertained. If a routine survey of many unpublished notarial cartularies can be regarded as evidence, one would

185. Luzzatto, *Storia economica di Venezia,* pp. 45–47.
186. Unable to bring his study of Genoa to completion, the late Vsevolod Slessarev urged me to add his conclusions to this chapter. The following comments on Genoese commerce during the crusades are taken from his unfinished study.
187. For the volume of Genoese trade, cf. Prawer, *Crusaders' Kingdom,* pp. 399–400, 402.

have to concede that of all areas to which the Genoese ships sailed, Syria was able to draw the biggest clusters of investments. For example, between September 17 and 27, 1227, a single notary registered commercial ventures to Ultramare to the impressive total of 21,347 Genoese pounds. Such figures, however, should be viewed with caution, for, as it seems, the preceding year was singularly unfavorable to overseas trade. Another factor . . . was the repeated prohibitions of trade with Alexandria. Judging by the . . . notaries Giovanni di Guiberto and Lanfranco, the Genoese refrained from trading with Egypt in 1205, 1216, and 1226."

In the case of Venice, evidence for the extension and growth of Venetian commerce in the thirteenth century can be found in the wider circulation of Venetian coinage. Venice embarked upon the Fourth Crusade with a monetary system based on silver, which endured until 1282. The grosso, its strongest and most widely recognized coin, appeared in 1194 early in the reign of doge Enrico Dandolo. It maintained the same weight and fineness until 1379. Merchants used these coins for payments of large sums at home and abroad. The coin for petty transactions was the denaro or piccolo, smaller in size and much less pure silver than the grosso. A quarter denaro (first struck to pay shipyard workers for the Fourth Crusade) and a half denaro also circulated. The grosso and piccolo circulated at a ratio of 1:26, but by 1290 the ratio had increased to 1:32. For the measurement of sums and the calculation of accounts, Venetian merchants used two monies of account, the lira di piccoli, which equaled 240 piccoli, and the lira di grossi, which equaled 240 grossi. Because gold coins were often demanded in the Levantine trade, the Byzantine gold coin, the hyperperon, continued in use, although it no longer was issued in quantity by the mints of Constantinople and rival hyperperi were struck by the Greek and Latin successor states in the Aegean. Venetian grossi and silver bullion were exported to the east because the Venetians seem to have needed to supplement their export of western commodities with an export of coinage and bullion. The value of Levantine products brought west to Venice seems to have exceeded that of the European commodities shipped east.[188] Probably the good Venetian silver grosso was more in demand in the eastern Mediterranean because men recognized its constant silver content and the commercial strength of Venice behind it. Historians have long assumed that the Venetian grosso became the principal silver coin of the eastern Medi-

---

188. Luzzatto, *Storia economica di Venezia,* pp. 45–47; Lopez, "Il Problema della bilancia dei pagamenti nel commercio di Levante," *Venezia e il levante,* ed. Pertusi, I-1, 431–451.

terranean in the thirteenth century, which presupposes a tremendous production and export of Venetian silver coin in this century.

The Venetians did not need a gold coin yet, but by 1252 Genoa and Florence began to mint gold coins. The genovino and the florin were struck at the same weight and fineness as the old good standard full-weight Byzantine hyperperon. Probably the growing scarcity of good hyperperi and the increased availability of gold bullion brought about this action. Venice did not take this step for another generation. Apparently its output of silver grossi, fueled by increasing imports of silver bullion from Germany and Hungary, and the use of Levantine gold hyperperi, satisfied its needs. The restored Palaeologi in Constantinople struck a silver coin to rival the grosso but containing less silver. At this challenge Venice in 1282 struck its first gold ducat, later known as *zecchino*. It had the same weight and fineness as the florin, the genovino, and the old good full-weight hyperperon. Venice minted this gold coin for five hundred years, with only two tiny debasements in the sixteenth century. Venice did not strike as many gold ducats in the thirteenth century as in later centuries. It was not recognized or used nearly so extensively in the eastern trade at this time as were the Venetian silver grosso or the Florentine gold florin, both of which were accepted from one end of the Mediterranean to the other in 1300.

In addition to the spread and acceptance of Venetian coin throughout the Mediterranean, the thirteenth century also gives evidence of Venice's position as chief creditor of the Latin east. Already, in 1124, Venice had financed the patriarch of Jerusalem and the Latin knights at the siege of Tyre, and Venetian credit, of course, also financed the Fourth Crusade.[189] The division of the spoils in Constantinople as well as the Treaty of Partition were repayment to Venice for its financial and naval assistance. Individual Venetians during the Latin empire financed impecunious rulers. For example, the Ghisi lent money both to the king of Hungary and to the Venetian duke of Naxos. Only the Venetians could assemble the vast sums necessary to finance the later Latin emperors in Constantinople. In 1238 they advanced 13,134 gold hyperperi to the Frankish barons in Constantinople in return for the pledge of the Crown of Thorns, which was later redeemed by Louis IX of France. Again, between 1248 and 1258, the Ferro brothers, Venetian merchants in Constantinople, advanced a huge sum of money to the last Latin emperor, Baldwin II, in security for which he gave the Venetians the custody of his only son and heir, Philip.

---

189. For example, see Morozzo della Rocca and Lombardo, *Documenti,* I, no. 462.

Philip's mother, the empress Mary of Brienne, finally received the money to redeem her son from Alfonso X of Castile, and the young man was free by 1261.[190] These examples suggest that the Venetians in these decades possessed the greatest financial resources in the eastern Mediterranean.

Money is one Venetian commodity which circulated more widely and in greater quantities in the thirteenth century, and documents suggest other commodities which similarly increased in thirteenth-century Venetian commerce. More references appear to the production and export of agricultural products from Venetian colonies in this century than survive from earlier centuries. Grain, olive oil, wine, and cheese came from Crete, wine from the Moreote ports of Coron and Modon, grain and olive oil from Negroponte. Tyre sent cotton, sugar, dyestuffs, and glass. At the end of the century the Crimea sent wheat, as well as furs and slaves. Venetian shipping seems to have completely supplanted the earlier Greek intercoastal trade in the Aegean. The peoples in the eastern Mediterranean demanded more Italian and Flemish textiles, and European merchants brought them to Venice by way of the river systems of north Italy or the Alpine passes. The Venetians then exported more of these textiles to the east. These commodities and probably others added to the volume of earlier Venetian trade and supplemented the luxury goods from the east and the raw materials from Europe which had been the basis of twelfth-century trade and which were discussed earlier.

Technological changes in shipping also gave the Venetians greater ability to expand their seaborne commerce in the thirteenth century. These changes have been called the nautical and commercial revolution.[191] Portolani, early marine charts with drawings of land forms, became more common and the compass came into regular use. New types of vessels appeared. Triremes began to replace biremes, heralding the fourteenth-century development of the great galleys with their greater capacity and crews. Soon after 1300 the great round sailing ships of the Mediterranean were also transformed. During the thirteenth century trading voyages from Italy to the Levant took on a regular rhythm. Previously the Venetian voyages to Syria had probably not been regularly scheduled, although armed convoys regularly sailed the Adriatic in the twelfth century. The Venetian *muda* system seems to have been organized about 1230. Then Venetian convoys

---

190. Wolff, "Mortgage and Redemption of an Emperor's Son," pp. 45–84.
191. Lane, *Venice, a Maritime Republic*, pp. 119–152.

began to travel from Venice to Constantinople, to Cyprus-Armenia-Syria, and to Alexandria. According to the Venetian maritime statutes of 1233, Venetian vessels in the spring *muda,* which had carried pilgrims to the Levant, were advised to leave Syria for the return voyage on May 8; vessels in the fall *muda* had to depart for Venice on October 8. Venetian vessels setting out from Venice for voyages on the summer *muda* to Cape Malea on the Morea had to prepare to leave Venice by mid-August.[192]

Similarly, in the early thirteenth century the Genoese changed their sailing schedule. Earlier the Genoese dispatched their fleets to the Levant in late September and early October. In 1205, however, the vessels left Genoa shortly after May 20. This was probably dictated by the severe losses of ships in their home port on October 11, 1204, just before their departure for Ultramare, Ceuta, and other markets. "A spring *muda* was certainly foreshadowed, and the Genoese were about to bring their overseas and overland trade with the fairs of Champagne into better harmony."[193]

The growth of Venetian commerce and wealth was paralleled by the growth of Venetian population.[194] The city of Venice itself welcomed newcomers. In the thirteenth century they arrived from the Italian mainland nearby, from Treviso, Padua, Ferrara, Verona, Vicenza, and Istria. Men also immigrated to Venice from other regions of northern Italy, especially from Milan, Florence, and Lucca and their environs. The men whom the Venetians called Germans came from Austria, Germany, Bohemia, and Hungary. In the thirteenth century they were organized as a German colony in Venice in the *Fondaco dei Tedeschi.* Seafaring men also came to Venice from the Adriatic coasts of Apulia and Dalmatia. Jews, Greeks, and Franks also appear as permanent residents. This varying multitude, drawn to Venice by the economic opportunity of the great port city, was assimilated into the Venetian population. Some even gained Venetian citizenship. The thirteenth-century records show no attempt to limit immigration into Venice, nor to deny these men the rights of Venetian citizenship after a certain term of residence.

Not only did foreigners come into Venice, but the Venetians themselves left Venice to take up residence in the east. Every Venetian col-

---

192. Hans E. Mayer, *The Crusades,* tr. John Gillingham (Oxford, 1972), p. 220; Luzzatto, "Navigazione di linea e navigazione libera," *Studi di storia,* p. 54; Lane, "Fleets and Fairs," *Venice and History,* pp. 128–129; *Gli Statuti marittimi veneziani,* ed. Predelli and Sacerdoti, pp. 69–70, 74–75.

193. Slessarev, see above, note 186.

194. Luzzatto, *Storia economica di Venezia,* pp. 38–41, 58–61.

ony records the presence of resident Italians who maintained their Venetian citizenship and yet lived with wives and children in one of the far-flung outposts of the Venetian colonial empire. After years or even generations in residence in an overseas colony, these citizens could return to the home city and be accepted as Venetians. Some indigenous inhabitants of the Venetian overseas colonies also could claim Venetian citizenship in certain cases. To be a Venetian entitled one to the protection of the Republic at home and abroad, and also to the special commercial privileges of Venice.

It has been suggested that the number of inhabitants in the city of Venice in 1300 was about 100,000, which would place Venice among the three largest cities of western Europe, the others being Paris and Naples. The total number of people who called themselves Venetians must have been much greater, if one includes the Venetian residents of all the seaports and islands of the Mediterranean. The Venetians could also draw from an even greater manpower pool to fill their war fleets, since subject and allied cities were expected to contribute ships and men.

Alongside the Venetian growth in numbers and wealth during the years of colonial expansion after the Fourth Crusade, the rich merchant princes of Venice continued to strengthen the Venetian government. These wealthy old noble families had controlled the Venetian state since they had put down the insurrection in 1171 and chosen the businessmen doges of the late twelfth century. The thirteenth-century Venetian governmental regulations were not nearly so restrictive as the rules of later centuries.[195] Since only Venetians could engage in the profitable overseas trade, and since Venice, unlike Florence, did not organize guilds for overseas commerce, navigation, and banking, these occupations were scarcely restricted until the end of the thirteenth century. Foreign businessmen in Venice were much more closely regulated. The artisans of Venice, the small shopkeepers, and the service professions were organized into guilds with written statutes, corporate identity, and ceremonial distinction. The reign of doge Lorenzo Tiepolo (1268–1275) produced the first significant number of these guild statutes. The councils and chief magistrates of the city had their functions and membership more narrowly defined, while the number of public offices proliferated.

The oligarchy further limited the doge with the rewriting of each ducal oath of office. They attempted to limit factional strife by de-

---

195. Lane, *Venice, a Maritime Republic; idem,* "The Enlargement of the Great Council of Venice," *Florilegium historiale* (Toronto, 1971), pp. 236–274.

veloping a complex system for ducal elections and by defining the membership in the Great Council. The Great Council in this century became the chief Venetian legislative body and also the body which elected men to the growing number of public offices. The Great Council defined and enlarged itself in 1297; this was the "closing of the Great Council" (*Serrata del Maggior Consiglio*). These domestic responses to external change were recorded in the laws of Venice, and in the records of its councils and magistrates. These public records survive from the thirteenth century, after the fire in the Venetian public archives of 1223. Written laws and governmental regulations assisted the oligarchy to maintain its control of Venice.

Throughout these centuries Venice had vigorously expanded its trade, its colonies, its population, and its wealth. In the twelfth century Venetian businessmen had exercised their privileges in the Byzantine empire, lived under their own laws in the Latin kingdom of Jerusalem, and sent trading voyages to Moslem Egypt. After the Fourth Crusade, Venetians had greater rights in Romania and ruled many islands of the Aegean. In the thirteenth century Venice obtained commercial privileges in Egypt, Tunis, Cilician Armenia, Konya, and the Black Sea coasts. During these crusading centuries, Venice became in fact the "queen of the Adriatic" and the ruler of the richest commercial empire in the Mediterranean.

X

MISSIONS TO THE EAST
IN THE THIRTEENTH
AND FOURTEENTH CENTURIES

A. Missions in the Thirteenth Century

The organized movement to evangelize oriental peoples which had its origins in the early thirteenth century opened a new period in the missionary history of the church. In earlier centuries missionaries had penetrated the northern and eastern areas of Europe. More recently Peter the Venerable had suggested a missionary approach to the Moslems of Spain, and the establishment of the crusader states early in the twelfth century had made possible occasional rapprochements with oriental Christians. But there had been no sustained effort to convert to Christianity Moslems or other non-Christians of the Near or Far East.

This chapter is concerned with western missions to the Orient during the thirteenth and fourteenth centuries. Papal relations with the Byzantine church have been excluded, as have missions to North Africa.

There are a few important collections of sources for mission history. *BOF* is a compilation of selections with biographical comment by the editor. It also contains considerable material relevant to Dominican missions. The standard Latin edition of the sources for the Central Asia and China journeys and missions of the Franciscans is Anastasius van den Wyngaert, O.F.M., *Sinica franciscana*, I, *Itinera et relationes Fratrum Minorum saeculi XIII et XIV* (Quaracchi, 1929). English translations of some of these can also be found in the publications of the Hakluyt Society, especially Henry Yule, *Cathay and the Way Thither*, revised by Henri Cordier (4 vols., London, 1925–1930), and the editions of John of Pian del Carpine and William of Rubruck by Charles R. Beazley and William W. Rockhill (1900–1903). Arthur C. Moule, *Christians in China before 1550* (London, 1930), includes translations of a number of significant selections. See also Manuel Komroff, ed., *Contemporaries of Marco Polo* (New York, 1928), and Christopher Dawson, ed., *The Mongol Mission* (New York, 1955), each containing extensive translations of sources.

Other primary sources for the history of medieval missions are widely scattered throughout the chronicles, letters, treatises, and documents of the mendicant orders, a few of which have been individually edited or translated, the chronicles and other literature of the crusade period, western and oriental, and the registers of papal correspondence. Relevant papal documents can be found in *Bullarium franciscanum*, ed. Johannes H. Sbaralea (Rome, 1759 ff., cited

452

Effective promotion of oriental missions had to await the appearance of that *vir catholicus et totus apostolicus,* Francis of Assisi, and his contemporary Dominic Guzmán. The impact of these two men and their followers on the civilization of Europe is too well known to require elaboration here, but no discussion of thirteenth-century missions can fail to emphasize two points. First, the type of organization adopted by the Franciscans and Dominicans was admirably suited to the furthering of distant ventures. Second, as the friars injected into the religious life of western Europe a new spirit and vitality, so they gave to a movement as old as Christianity, though languishing in the central Middle Ages, a new élan and direction.

This chapter is not, however, merely an account of missionaries traveling to distant lands, for the history of medieval missions to the Orient must be viewed in relation to a number of contemporary developments. One favorable factor was the remarkable growth of European-Asiatic commerce. In many instances the *fondachi* of the Italian merchants whose spiritual needs the friars served were the bases for missions either in the immediate area or beyond. Paradoxically, the merchants could also be a hindrance to religious propaganda, for there were Italians who engaged in the slave trade and continually flouted papal prohibitions against trade with Moslems.

In certain other respects the period was not propitious for missionary undertakings. European conditions throughout the thirteenth and fourteenth centuries were far from stable, and the western church faced a series of crises. The popes who were to give important direc-

---

as *BF*); *Bullarium ordinis praedicatorum,* ed. Thomas Ripoll (Rome, 1727 ff., cited as *BOP*); August Potthast, ed., *Regesta pontificum Romanorum* (Berlin, 1874–1875), the calendars published by the École française de Rome, on which see Leonard E. Boyle, *A Survey of the Vatican Archives and of Its Medieval Holdings* (Toronto, 1972), pp. 125–127; and *BOF,* cited above.

In addition to Marcellino da Civezza, O.F.M., *Storia universale delle missioni francescane,* vols. I–IV (Rome, 1857–1860), Franciscan mission history has been treated more recently in Leonhard Lemmens, *Geschichte der Franziskanermissionen* (Münster, 1929); Martiniano Roncaglia, O.F.M., *I Francescani in Oriente durante le crociate (secolo XIII) (BOF,* ser. 4: *Studi,* vol. I, *Storia della provincia di Terra Santa,* 1; Cairo, 1954); François de Sessevalle, *Histoire générale de l'ordre de Saint François,* part 1, *Le Moyen-âge, 1209–1517,* vol. II, *Les Missions franciscaines à l'étranger* (Le Puy-en-Velay, 1937); Noè Simonut, *Il Metodo d'evangelizzazione dei Francescani tra Musulmani e Mongoli nei secoli XIII e XIV* (Milan, 1947); Odulphus van der Vat, *Die Anfänge der Franziskanermissionen und ihre Weiterentwicklung im Nahen Orient und in der mohammedanischen Ländern während des 13. Jahrhunderts* (Missionswissenschaftliche Studien, n.s., VI; Werl, 1934).

The most important works on Dominican missions are Berthold Altaner, *Die Dominikanermissionen des 13. Jahrhunderts* (Breslauer Studien zur historischen Theologie, III; Habelschwerdt, 1924); Raymond J. Loenertz, O.P., "Les Missions dominicaines en Orient au quatorzieme siècle et la Société des Frères pérégrinants . . . ," *AFP,* II (1932), 1–83; III (1933), 1–55; IV (1934), 1–47; and *La Société des Frères pérégrinants* (Institutum historicum Fratrum Praedicatorum, Dissertationes historicae, fasc. VII; Rome, 1937).

tion to the missions were deeply involved in European political struggles. Heresy too was a major preoccupation.

Asiatic developments were equally disturbing. As previous chapters have indicated, the Moslems of Egypt, Syria, and Persia were divided politically in the mid-thirteenth century and hence not disposed to wage a *jihād* against the crusader states. Yet Islam as a faith retained considerable vitality. Moreover, the temporary Christian occupation of Jerusalem (1229–1244), made possible by Frederick II's treaty with al-Kāmil, was followed later in the century by the northward advance of the Mamluks and the eventual loss of the missionary bases in the crusader states.

After their first terrifying incursions into eastern Europe in the first half of the thirteenth century and their subsequent withdrawal and concentration in the Near and Far East, the Mongols occasionally permitted visits and even residence by the friars. This was especially true of those Mongols who had pushed southward and overrun the Baghdad caliphate in 1258. The il-khanate of Persia which they established was halted in its westward advance and continually thereafter threatened by the Mamluks of Egypt. More often than not the apparently receptive attitude of the Mongols was politically motivated, though this was rarely understood. It is not surprising that the west remained bewildered by Mongol diplomacy.[1]

The conversion to Catholicism of oriental Christians, both Orthodox and heretical, was one of the major objectives of the missionary friars. These peoples constituted a considerable proportion of the pop-

---

Diplomatic and missionary journeys to the Mongol areas are treated in Paul Pelliot, "Les Mongoles et la papauté," *ROC,* XXIII (1923), 3–30, XXIV (1924), 225–335; XXVIII (1931–1932), 3–84; Jean Richard, "Les Missions chez les Mongoles aux XIIIe et XIVe siècles," *Histoire universelle des missions catholiques,* I, *Les Missions des origines au XVIe siècle* (Paris, 1956); Giovanni Soranzo, *Il Papato, l'Europa cristiana e i Tartari* (Pubblicazioni della Università Cattolica del Sacro Cuore, ser. 5, vol. XII; Milan, 1930); Christian W. Troll, S.J., "Die Chinamission im Mittelalter," *Franziskanische Studien,* XLVIII (1966), 109–150; XLIX (1967), 22–79.

Bishoprics in Mongol lands are discussed in Conrad Eubel, "Die während des 14. Jahrhunderts im Missionsgebiet der Dominikaner und Franziskaner errichteten Bisthümer," in Stephan Ehses, ed., *Festschrift zum elfhundertjährigen Jubiläum des deutschen Campo Santo in Rom* (Freiburg, 1897), pp. 170–195.

The following general works may also be cited: Aziz S. Atiya, *A History of Eastern Christianity* (London and Notre Dame, 1968); Beazley, *The Dawn of Modern Geography* (3 vols., London, 1897–1906); Louis Bréhier, *L'Église et l'Orient au moyen-âge* (Paris, 1919); Richard Hennig, *Terrae incognitae,* vol. III (Leyden, 1938); Kenneth S. Latourette, *A History of the Expansion of Christianity,* vol. II (New York, 1938); Horace K. Mann, *The Lives of the Popes in the Middle Ages,* vols. XII–XVII (London, 1925–1932); and Guillaume Mollat, *Les Papes d'Avignon,* 10th ed. (Paris, 1965); 9th ed., tr. Janet Love (New York, 1963).

1. On the Mongols and the crusades see also Claude Cahen, "The Mongols and the Near East," in volume II of the present work, chapter XXI, and Denis Sinor, "The Mongols and Western Europe," *ibid.,* volume III, chapter XV.

ulation of the coastal cities of the Levant, the kingdoms of Georgia and Cilician Armenia, the turbulent areas of greater Armenia, and the vast reaches of the Mongol domains.[2] The Georgians were traditionally Orthodox, as were the Greeks of Antioch and northern Syria and the Melkites farther south. But the Armenians were predominantly Monophysite, as were most of the Christians of Syria, Egypt, and Ethiopia. Nestorians were few in numbers, but often influential in Persia and regions farther east.

Among certain sectors of oriental Christianity there appeared at this period a disposition to some sort of union with the west. The motives, however, were rarely purely religious. Oriental Christians commonly enjoyed reasonable freedom under Moslem rule, and cultural and linguistic ties prompted rapport with their Moslem masters rather than rapprochement with the west. Before the major Mongol incursions into the Near East shortly after the middle of the century, such pro-western leanings as can be discerned seem to have resulted, in part at least, from rivalries among the oriental Christians themselves. Accustomed to seeking support from Moslem rulers, they tended to shift their policies with the diplomatic vicissitudes of the Moslem states. After the middle of the century, as the Mongol menace increased, those earliest endangered often displayed pro-western sympathies, though this was far from being a consistent attitude. Accordingly, although oriental Christians were often in a position to act as intermediaries between the western church and the worlds of Islam and Tartary, they too were caught in the confusion of local politics.

Inevitably, therefore, missions tended to become involved with diplomacy, and official Europe continued to think, however vainly, in terms of the crusade or of the conversion of important rulers and dignitaries. Most missionaries, particularly at the outset, shared the hopes, fears, and illusions of their time. But they were to learn much and to add significantly to western Europe's knowledge of Asian peoples; this is by no means the least important of their achievements.

EARLY MISSIONARY ORGANIZATION

Francis of Assisi was the first to state clearly the ideal of missions to Moslems, and it is a striking coincidence that this occurred precisely at the time of the ill-fated Fifth Crusade. As early as 1217 it had been decided at the first general chapter of the order, held at

---

2. On oriental Christianity during this period see Atiya, *A History of Eastern Christianity*.

Assisi, that Elias of Cortona should be sent to Syria, where in 1218 he laid the foundations for a Franciscan overseas province ("Ultramare"). After earlier failures to reach the Holy Land and Spain Francis himself journeyed to the Orient in 1219 accompanied by Peter de' Cattani, and was accorded an interview with the Egyptian sultan al-Kāmil. Under a safe conduct granted by the sultan he later visited Syria, and presumably the holy places in Palestine, and returned to Italy with Elias.[3]

In 1221 the so-called "First" Franciscan rule specifically included as an objective the conversion of "Saracens and other unbelievers." To enter upon this task the prospective missionary had to seek the permission of the provincial minister, who was strictly enjoined to grant this only to those he deemed suitable. A much shorter version of the mission chapter, shorn of the scriptural citations which had characterized the first, was included in the official *Regula secunda* of 1223.

During the course of the thirteenth century Franciscan ministers-general, Bonaventura and others, elaborated on the nature of the mission undertaking and the qualities a missionary should possess. Such statements, though by no means uniform in emphasis, form a sort of commentary on the mission chapters in the rule. The missionary's life is viewed, especially in the earlier writings, as one of sacrifice as a witness for Christ by word and example, with martyrdom, the crowning achievement and supreme evidence of religious devotion, always a possibility. In short, the early Franciscan missionary effort was highly idealistic. There was as yet no systematic preparation and no adequate knowledge of the areas to be evangelized.[4]

To some extent such inadequacies were remedied by the establishment of permanent convents in the east. Doubtless profiting from such favorable political factors as the temporary truce (1229–1244) which permitted Latin occupation of Jerusalem, the overseas province of the Franciscans prospered, with convents at Acre, Antioch, and Tripoli. It is possible that a cloister was founded early at Jerusalem. In the course of time, probably before 1263, the province of "Terra Sancta" came to be separate from another early establishment, the province of Greece ("Romania"). With the founding of these convents the first phase of Franciscan missions with its naive fervor came to an end. Convents served the needs of resident Latin Christians,

---

3. For a discussion of Francis's mission purposes and his journey to Egypt see Roncaglia, *I Francescani in Oriente,* pp. 13–17, 21–26; van der Vat, *Die Anfänge,* pp. 1–25, 39–59, 244–255; and volume II of the present work, pp. 378 (bibliographical note), 415–416.

4. On Franciscan missionary policies and ideals see Simonut, *Il Metodo,* pp. 15–38.

but they also made possible a more systematic approach to missions. Very possibly, too, the influence of contemporary Dominican establishments was an important factor, especially in the greater emphasis on training preachers.

Dominicans had from their foundation been dedicated to preaching, and Dominic, despite his preoccupation with Albigensian heretics in Languedoc, had given much thought to the possibility of missions to the east. Successive Dominican masters-general, notably Jordan of Saxony, Raymond of Peñaforte, and Humbert of Romans, were also concerned about promoting missions, and their efforts were seconded by general and provincial chapters. These efforts, however, seem to have been largely designed to serve the areas of Spain and North Africa; preparation directed specifically toward the east is less easily traced. But like the Minorites, the Friars-Preachers established convents in the east. A Dominican province of the Holy Land was independent some time after 1228 and included cloisters at Acre and Tripoli.[5] There was a Dominican community in Jerusalem during the period of truce with the Moslems of Egypt.

During the early decades of the thirteenth century there was also noticeable a more formal direction of missionary activity by Rome. Papal interest is most clearly manifest in the many letters sent to the authorities of the two orders and to prospective missionaries. Such letters are general in nature, but they echo the policies stated in the Franciscan rule that only suitable candidates be accepted and that permission be given by the provincial ministers. As time went on there is more emphasis on adequate religious training. Further, the popes also sent messages to oriental rulers requesting protection for the friars or urging that the recipient embrace the Christian faith.

The first papal letters to missionaries were little more than lists of instructions. Gradually such documents were expanded into detailed directives in which all peoples the missionaries might be expected to encounter and all faculties necessary in any possible missionary situation were specifically enumerated. Toward the middle of the thirteenth century a formula was evolved which combined the faculties for work among Moslems, other non-Christians, and oriental Christians. This new formula first appeared in Gregory IX's bull *Cum hora undecima,* on February 15, 1235, as instructions to the Dominican William of Montferrat. It appeared again in the bulls issued by Innocent IV in 1245 to the first envoys to the Mongols. By about

---

5. The establishments of the mendicant foundations in Syria are discussed in van der Vat, *Die Anfänge,* pp. 60–87; Roncaglia, *I Francescani in Oriente,* pp. 29 ff.; Altaner, *Die Dominikanermissionen,* pp. 1–9, chap. III.

1253 it had become a stereotyped formula of mission instructions. Though not the only form of mission letter used, the *Cum hora undecima* was often repeated in subsequent decades.[6]

The bull first enumerates the peoples whom the friars were expected to visit. Since the curia was not yet well informed regarding orientals, these are lumped together in a list which is comprehensive religiously, ethnically, and geographically, but is otherwise rather indiscriminate and fails to distinguish clearly between the diverse eastern religious groups. The ecclesiastical directives are much clearer. The friars were permitted to baptize converts, confer minor orders, absolve from excommunication, and reinstall separated clergy who desired to return to the Catholic church. They were also permitted to dispense the latter from certain irregularities (defect of birth, age, jurisdiction, and so forth) in the reception of orders, *salva disciplina ordinis*. Even those who contracted matrimony after the reception of orders were not to be disturbed. All who returned to the unity of the Catholic faith were to be permitted to live among their own people and enjoy clerical privileges provided they publicly proclaimed their obedience to the Apostolic See. The friars were also permitted to judge matrimonial cases and rectify situations with ecclesiastical censure if necessary. There were also various instructions regarding the proper celebration of all offices and sacraments, the reception of Holy Orders and similar matters. Portable altars were allowed, and priests among the friars might bless them in cases where Catholic bishops were unavailable. Finally, the friars were to do whatever seemed necessary to the successful furtherance of their mission.

The phraseology of the bull indicates that considerable care was taken in formulating the faculties necessary for reconciling separated Christians. This complicated problem was being squarely faced by the western church for the first time. Until then oriental Christians had, with one or two exceptions, been in direct contact with Byzantium, not Rome. Therefore, though the curia was not well informed about Asiatic peoples, it was evidently attempting in systematic fashion to foresee all contingencies of order, jurisdiction, and ecclesiastical discipline which the missionary friars might face. Moreover, as the contents of *Cum hora undecima* indicate and as further examina-

---

6. Examples of these early mission bulls are cited and discussed fully in van der Vat, *Die Anfänge,* pp. 137–146, 186–189. See also Altaner, *Die Dominikanermissionen,* pp. 44–49, 73–74; Troll, "Die Chinamission," pp. 22–24. The bull of February 15, 1235, can be found in *BOP,* I, 73. For the bulls of 1245 see below, notes 27–29. An example of a typical later bull (1253) is in *BOP,* I, 237. For a discussion of papal mission policies see Simonut, *Il Metodo,* pp. 39–67.

tion of papal policy will reveal, Rome in the mid-thirteenth century was gradually acquiring some flexibility in its attitude toward oriental liturgies and usages. Nevertheless, although the lawyer-popes of that age were willing to tolerate differences in language and rite, they required strict adherence to precise formulas in the administration of sacraments and full acceptance of Roman primacy. Moreover, occasional letters urging adherence to Roman usages indicate that the curial attitude was not without hesitations and inconsistencies. Missionaries and missionary theorists were less hesitant.

Since the baptizing of non-Christians raised few questions of jurisdiction or order, the apostolate among Moslems is less emphasized in these papal letters. And although we must beware of judging policies merely by the number of words allotted in papal bulls to each subject, one complicated, the other comparatively simple, it does appear that the interest of the Holy See in the separated Christians predominated over its solicitude for the Moslem missions. The reasons for this will appear when we examine the missions themselves.

THIRTEENTH-CENTURY MISSIONS TO MOSLEMS

The story of missions to Moslems in the thirteenth century includes examples of dedication and heroism, but is otherwise one of frustration and disappointment. In the first place, the information available to westerners about Islam was insufficient and often inaccurate, and much of it came from Spain.[7] Various mistaken notions persisted into the thirteenth century. It was generally held, for example, that Islam was a heresy, and it was also believed to be on the point of collapse. Toward the end of the century such optimistic views and at least some of the ignorance had been dispelled. But though the attitude of the adherents of each faith to the followers of the other did not preclude many demonstrations of mutual respect, no real understanding of the opposing religious beliefs was reached by either side.

The missionary experiences of the first friars, in North Africa as well as in the east, reveal the inadequacies of their preparation and the extreme difficulties they faced. Presumably they spoke through interpreters, since few if any knew the native tongues at that period. Audiences were apparently not unsympathetic at first and the reli-

7. For western views of Islam see Norman A. Daniel, *Islam and the West* (Edinburgh, 1960); Richard W. Southern, *Western Views of Islam in the Middle Ages* (Cambridge, Mass., 1962); Ugo Monneret de Villard, *Lo Studio dell' Islam in Europa nel XII e nel XIII secolo* (Studi e testi, CX; Vatican City, 1944). Cf. also Simonut, *Il Metodo,* pp. 77–87.

gious dedication evident in the friars' lives made a deep impression. But the friars seem all too often to have spoiled the favorable atmosphere by proceeding immediately to a denunciation of the Islamic religion. Thus they soon discovered that an initial obstacle confronting every Christian missionary to Moslem lands was the legal prohibition of any anti-Moslem propaganda. This was widely supported by public opinion, and any disparagement of Mohammed would invariably place the speaker in danger. Moreover, apostasy from Islam was legally punishable by death. In short, conditions which made Christian instruction feasible could rarely be found except in areas such as the crusaders' states where Moslems lived under Christian rule.

It is not, therefore, surprising that while few missionaries or missionary theorists would have defended the propriety of forcing individuals to accept the Christian faith, almost without exception all agreed that the conquest of a territory was justifiable as a means of promoting missions or, at least, of preventing "infidels" from injuring the faith of Christians. In short, toward the end of the thirteenth century the earlier optimism was turned by actual missionary experience, as well as by Islam's advances in the whole Near East, into a general attitude of pessimism. To most men the crusade still seemed a more effective way of dealing with the Moslem problem than missions. Neither point of view was conducive to that sympathetic understanding requisite to true missionary undertaking.

Records of actual missionary efforts on the part of Franciscan or Dominican friars during the first half of the thirteenth century are extremely scanty. James of Vitry, bishop of Acre, describes how Moslems cordially received the Franciscans, even giving them provisions, and willingly listened to them until they began to denounce Mohammed. At that point, he adds, they were set upon and driven out of town, and doubtless would have been killed but for the "miraculous protection of God." Where these incidents took place the bishop does not say; perhaps in the crusaders' territory and possibly even before Francis's own visit to the Levant.[8]

Somewhat later, papal letters add some, though still very limited, information. Moreover, it must be remembered that papal policy had manifold objectives. In fact, certain missionary undertakings were launched by the Holy See in connection with letters to oriental rulers which not only bespoke conversion to Christianity and a favorable reception for the friars who were being sent, but also attempted to

---

8. Van der Vat, *Die Anfänge,* pp. 56–57; Roncaglia, *I Francescani in Oriente,* p. 84; Simonut, *Il Metodo,* pp. 87–103.

promote political relations. Such, for example, appears to have been the purpose of Gregory IX's letters of 1233. At a time when the oriental world, Moslem and Christian alike, was facing new dangers resulting from the depredations of the Khwarizmian Turks and especially from the early southward drives of the Mongols, the pope addressed the rulers of Damascus, Aleppo, and Konya and the caliph at Baghdad. In the same months the pope also directed several bulls to Franciscan friars traveling or resident in the Orient, conceding faculties not only for the care of the souls of Latin Christians, but also for baptizing non-Christians and for reconciling separated Christians. Existing good relations with Moslem rulers evidently permitted the friars to enter and live in Moslem territory. Accordingly, although precise information is lacking, the possibility of missionary activity cannot be ruled out.[9]

Papal bulls similar to those directed to Franciscans seem to indicate that Dominican friars were also working among Moslems at this time. Somewhat more specific, but still indefinite as to place, is a statement in the report of the Dominican provincial of the Holy Land, friar Philip, in 1237 that several of his brethren had studied Arabic and were preaching in that tongue. These friars could, of course, have been preaching to Arabic-speaking Christians. Indeed, the context so implies. But again there is at least the possibility of an apostolate among Moslems. Moreover, in a bull of March 4, 1238, Gregory IX insisted that the conversion of the infidel was no less acceptable to God than opposing him with arms—a striking illustration of the contemporary attitude—and granted both Dominican and Franciscan friars the customary crusaders' indulgence. Subsequent papal bulls which conceded faculties for the reception of Moslems (1238, 1239, 1244) also indicate at least the possibility of missionary activity.[10]

In 1245, the year following the Khwarizmian sack of Jerusalem which ended the peace of 1229, and in the same months in which he was inaugurating the Mongol missions, Innocent IV also dispatched letters to various Moslem rulers in Syria and Egypt. Although in this case the original papal letters are not extant, some indication of the pope's purposes can be ascertained from the replies dated 1245–1246, which found their way into the papal registers. Communications were received from aṣ-Ṣāliḥ Ismāʿīl, formerly of Damascus, then ruling Baalbek and the Hauran, from al-Manṣūr Ibrāhīm of Homs, who answered in the name of the sultan of Egypt as well as for himself,

9. *MGH, Epistolae saeculi XIII,* I, 410–413; *BF,* I, 93; *BOF,* I, 163; II, 295 ff.

10. *Ibid.,* I, 180; II, 301–305, 370–371; van der Vat, *Die Anfänge,* pp. 127–146, 190–191; Altaner, *Die Dominikanermissionen,* pp. 73–74. On friar Philip's report see below, note 20.

from as-Ṣāliḥ Aiyūb, the sultan of Egypt, and from an-Nāṣir Dā'ūd, the prince of Kerak, or possibly an Egyptian military commander in southern Palestine.[11]

These replies reveal little regarding missionary activity. The Moslem rulers were courteous and disposed to grant safe conduct to friars, presumably for the religious needs of resident Latin Christians. As before, therefore, although the possibility of missions cannot be ruled out, there is no positive evidence thereof. Moreover, one letter which complained that the friars' ignorance of Arabic precluded fruitful conversations indicates that, despite friar Philip's report of progress in language study, much remained to be done in the way of missionary preparation.

Among the missionaries to Moslems in the late thirteenth century two stand out, William of Tripoli and Ricoldo of Monte Croce, both Dominicans. William of Tripoli was born in the east of Christian parents. He had acquired some familiarity with Arabic and an unusually extensive knowledge of the Moslem religion. According to his own account he baptized more than a thousand Saracens. It seems likely that he carried on his work within the crusader states, for only there could he have been able to preach without hindrance. Doubtless many of his converts were captives or slaves. He was, however, at one time an emissary to al-Manṣūr Muḥammad, the ruler of Hamah, and in 1271 he accompanied the Polo brothers as far as Cilicia.

In the same year he dedicated a treatise which he later reëdited (1273), the *De statu Saracenorum et de Mahomete pseudopropheta*

---

11. There are six documents in all: a letter from the former ruler of Damascus, dated at Baalbek (November 20, 1245), a letter from the ruler of Homs (December 30, 1245), two safe-conducts given at Homs (December 1245), a letter from the prince of Kerak (August 6–15, 1246), and one of the same date from Egypt (or from a military commander in Palestine). Perhaps because they all had to be translated (by a cardinal, according to Matthew Paris, *Chronica majora,* ed. Henry R. Luard [Rolls Series, 57], IV, 566 ff.), they were all filed together with five letters from oriental prelates under the third and fourth years of Innocent IV's pontificate (June 1245–June 1247, *BOF,* II, 327 ff.). There has been considerable discussion of these letters; the following are now the most important studies: Altaner, *Die Dominikanermissionen,* pp. 74–81; Pelliot, "Les Mongoles et la papauté," *ROC,* XXIV (1924), 225 ff., XXVIII (1931–1932), 6 ff.; Eugène Tisserant, "La Légation en Orient du Franciscain, Dominique d'Aragon (1245–47)," *ROC,* XXIV (1924), 336–355, and correspondence with Pelliot, *ibid.,* XXVIII (1931–1932), 8; van der Vat, *Die Anfänge,* pp. 155–157, 190–194. See also Reinhold Röhricht, "Zur Korrespondenz der Päpste mit den Sultanen und Mongolkanen des Morgenlandes im Zeitalter der Kreuzzüge," *Theologischen Studien und Kritiken,* LXIX (1891), 357–369.

In view of their previous activities there is a strong presumption in favor of the Minorites as the papal envoys. But the phrase "Fratres Praedicatores" in two of the letters indicates that Dominicans were also sent. It is probable that one of the latter, perhaps the principal one, was Andrew of Longjumeau.

On the Moslem states during this period see H. A. R. Gibb, "The Aiyūbids," in volume II of the present work, pp. 709–710.

et eorum lege et fide, to the papal legate in the east, Tebaldo Visconti, the future Gregory X. This work, which he tells us he based on Arabic texts, contains an account of the career of Mohammed and the expansion of Islam and an analysis of the Islamic religion. In its general tone it differs markedly from most Christian writing on Islam of the period. Probably because his contacts with Moslems were within the protected areas of the Latin east he remained optimistic. He did not compose a crusade tract; rather his purpose was to understand and explain. For William seems to have felt that many Moslems were not far from Christian fundamentals and that more converts might be made once they understood that "the whole and perfect faith is contained in the teaching of Christ. . . . And so through the pure word of God, without philosophical arguments, without the arms of soldiers, as simple sheep they seek the baptism of Christ and cross over into the sheepfold of God." [12]

Some years later Ricoldo of Monte Croce, already an accomplished missionary with some knowledge of Greek, Hebrew, and Syriac, commenced what proved to be a remarkable journey into the Asiatic hinterland. [13] As will be clear later, his most successful work was with oriental Christians. He also, however, made some significant contacts with Moslems. He left Acre, probably in March 1289, and traveled through Cilician Armenia and Konya. Not far from Sivas (Sebastia), where Genoese had established themselves and both Dominicans and Franciscans maintained missions, he entered country under Mongol rule. At Tabriz, then the capital of the Persian il-khanate and an important Jacobite center, he spent six months preaching through an interpreter since he had not yet mastered Arabic. Venetians and Genoese had established themselves there, and Franciscans and Dominicans were using a church in common. From Tabriz Ricoldo journeyed

12. On William of Tripoli, in addition to Southern, *Western Views of Islam,* pp. 62–63, and Daniel, *Islam and the West, passim,* see Altaner, *Dominikanermissionen,* pp. 85–88; and Palmer A. Throop, *Criticism of the Crusade* (Amsterdam, 1940), chap. v. For the text of William's treatise see Hans Prutz, *Kulturgeschichte der Kreuzzüge* (Berlin, 1883; repr. Hildesheim, 1964), pp. 575–598. Monneret de Villard, *Lo Studio dell' Islam,* pp. 70–73, has noted the inadequacy of this edition, which is based on three Parisian manuscripts, and raises the question whether the errors in Arabic terms are the result of William's imperfect knowledge or the faulty transcriptions of later copiers.

13. The most important works on Ricoldo of Monte Croce are those of Monneret de Villard: "La Vita, le opere, e i viaggi di Frate Ricoldo da Montecroce, O.P.," *Orientalia Christiana periodica,* X (1944), 227–274; *Il Libro della peregrinazione nelle parti d'Oriente di Frate Ricoldo da Montecroce* (Dissertationes historicae, fasc. xiii, Institutum historicum Fratrum praedicatorum; Rome, 1948). See also Altaner, *Dominikanermissionen,* pp. 82–84; Pierre F. Mandonnet, O.P., "Fra Ricolde de Montecroce," *Revue biblique,* II (1893), 44–61, 182–202, 584–607; Röhricht, "Lettres de Ricolde de Montecroce," *AOL,* II-2 (1884), 258–296; Southern, *Western Views of Islam,* pp. 68–70; and Daniel, *Islam and the West, passim.*

via Maragha, an important Nestorian and Jacobite center, through Kurdish country to Mosul, where he found a thriving Jewish community and was able to hold public disputations in their synagogue. Finally he reached Baghdad, where the brethren of his own order joyously received him and where also he was greeted by the Nestorian patriarch, Mār Yabhalāhā III, who himself had recently been in communication with the west.

Although Ricoldo spoke of preaching in Arabic at Mosul, it was at Baghdad that he began the serious study of the language as well as of Moslem religion and law. His relations with Moslem scholars were extremely cordial. He attended their schools and was received in their homes. He found them interested in what he said "concerning God and Christ," but he reported no conversions. Apparently he commenced work on a translation of the Koran but later abandoned it.

While he was at Baghdad Ricoldo heard the news of the fall of Acre (1291) and witnessed the miserable plight of Christian prisoners, among whom were a number of Dominicans. He saw more at Mosul, where he took refuge for a time. He may have come back to Baghdad before returning to Europe in the early years of the fourteenth century.

In his *Itinerarium* Ricoldo not only left a detailed account of his journey, but he added many observations about the various peoples he encountered—Mongols, Buddhists, Kurds, and others. His comments on Moslem religious customs are especially important. For, although he was not always well informed and it can scarcely be said that he acquired a profound understanding, he was the first western European to penetrate deeply into eastern Islamic territory and bring back first-hand information. Formerly most of what had been known had come from Spain. Evidently he was favorably impressed and admitted that in many respects, in religious devotion, in regularity of prayer, in almsgiving and charity, Moslems sometimes excelled Christians.

Ricoldo had a high regard for the work of William of Tripoli and after his return to Europe, probably at Florence, he elaborated further some of the material of the *Itinerarium* in a treatise, the *Improbatio Alchorani* or *Tractatus contra legem Saracenorum*. It has been demonstrated that Ricoldo worked entirely from Arabic texts and apparently did not know of the translation of the Koran by Robert of Chester.[14] Indeed, he would have found in early fourteenth-century Florence no such tradition of oriental scholarship as existed in Spain. Moreover, Ricoldo's purpose was different; he remained the mission-

14. Monneret de Villard, *Il Libro della peregrinazione,* pp. 93–118. The title of Ricoldo's work also appears as *Confutatio Alchorani, Tractatus contra legem Mahometi* and *Propugnaculum fidei.*

ary propagandist rather than the detached scholar. Moslem legal precepts he found confused, dark, and irrational. If, as we have mentioned, he respected the religious devotion of Moslems, he expressed surprise that "such works of perfection could exist in such a perfidious law." Perhaps because of his experiences following the fall of Acre he, unlike William of Tripoli, shared the growing pessimism about the future relations of Christendom and Islam.

It is evident that, with the exception of William of Tripoli, medieval missionaries to the Moslems of the east were rarely successful. Many, perhaps most, were insufficiently prepared. But the persistent opposition of Moslem authorities everywhere was unquestionably a major factor. And this opposition, usually backed by popular opinion, was doubtless strengthened later as Rome attempted to win Tatar support against Islam and anti-Moslem crusade propaganda became the order of the day. Gregory X, who received William of Tripoli's treatise, desperately tried to promote a new crusade, and the Council of Lyons in 1274 solicited from Fidenzio of Padua, the Franciscan provincial of the Holy Land, who was exceptionally well informed concerning Islam, a crusade plan, the *De recuperatione Terrae Sanctae,* which, however, he did not complete until 1291. The loss of the last crusaders' states in the same year added to Europe's discouragement and increased its fears. Even so ardent a missionary and missionary propagandist as Raymond Lull composed a crusade tract.

Under such circumstances any exchange of views which might lead to mutual understanding was all but impossible. Attempts to convert Moslems were not abandoned, but were regularly included in reissues of the mission bull, *Cum hora undecima.* But missions to Moslems were in fact feasible only in areas which fell under Mongol control, where the authorities permitted Christian propaganda. After 1291 the friars who resided in the Levantine lands under Moslem rule were concerned principally with the spiritual care of resident Latin Christians, the winning over of separated oriental Christians, or with such special tasks as the care of the holy places in Palestine.[15]

CONTACTS WITH ORIENTAL CHRISTIANS
IN THE FIRST HALF OF THE THIRTEENTH CENTURY

The establishment of the crusaders' states brought western authorities, ecclesiastical and lay, into regular contact with oriental Chris-

15. On the establishment of the Franciscan *custodia* in the Holy Land see Roncaglia, "The

tianity for the first time in centuries. By the early decades of the thirteenth century considerable progress had been made in understanding the different native communities. This is evident in the *Assises de Jérusalem* and in the writings of contemporary chroniclers, notably James of Vitry, who are able to distinguish the diverse groups and no longer—as was formerly the case—lump them all together under the single category of "Syrians."[16] Misinformation, and especially optimistic illusions regarding the possibility of large-scale conversions, persisted. Nevertheless, the early friars were able to make use of a respectable fund of valid information.

The naming of a Latin patriarch of Jerusalem following the First Crusade had placed the Orthodox Christians in the kingdom in an ambiguous position of divided loyalties. Most of these in the south were Arabic in culture and were known as Melkites. As is evident in the papal bulls, Melkites became a concern of the popes in the middle years of the thirteenth century.[17] In 1246 a distinguished Franciscan, Lawrence of Portugal, papal penitentiary and originally destined for the Mongol mission, was sent instead to various places in Anatolia and Syria with instructions to visit, among others, Jacobites, Maronites, and Nestorians. His principal dealings, however, were with the Latin and Greek (or Melkite) hierarchies of Syria, concerning which he and they received letters from Innocent IV.[18]

After the final retreat of the Latins from Jerusalem in 1244 the Syrian Melkite clergy seem for the most part to have turned to patriarch Athanasius II of Jerusalem, who in 1247 was negotiating with Rome through friar Lawrence. Innocent IV supported Athanasius against Robert, the Latin patriarch of Jerusalem, now not resident there, and reserved to Rome the immediate obedience of all bishops

---

Sons of St. Francis in the Holy Land: Official Entrance of the Franciscans as Custodians of the Basilica of the Nativity in Bethlehem," *Franciscan Studies,* X (1950), 257–285; Lemmens, *Franziskanermissionen,* pp. 61–75; and *idem,* "Die Franziskaner im Heiligen Lande, I: Die Franziskaner auf dem Sion (1336–1551)," *Franziskanische Studien,* Beiheft IV, 2nd ed. (Münster, 1925).

Apparently some conversions were made as a consequence of the visit of Louis IX, mostly, it would seem, from among ransomed slaves. On an attempt by friars to refute Islamic doctrines by public argumentation in 1392 which resulted in their death, see Simonut, *Il Metodo,* p. 97.

16. Cf. Enrico Cerulli, *Etiopi in Palestina* (Collezione scientifica e documentaria a cura del Ministero dell' Africa italiana, XII, vol. I; Rome, 1943), 82 ff., and docs. 3, 7.

17. On the term "Mossolini" (Moscelini, Mosoliti) as representing Melkites, see van der Vat, *Die Anfänge,* p. 144, note 38; Altaner, *Die Dominikanermissionen,* p. 48, note 40.

18. *BOF,* II, 319–324; Roncaglia, *Les Frères mineurs et l'église grecque-orthodoxe au XIIIe siècle (1231–1274) (BOF,* ser. 4, vol. II; Cairo, 1954), pp. 92–99; van der Vat, *Die Anfänge,* pp. 152–161; George Every, "Syrian Christians in Palestine, 1183–1283," *Eastern Churches Quarterly,* VII (1947), 49–53; Steven Runciman, *The Eastern Schism* (Oxford, 1955), chap. IV; René Grousset, *Histoire des croisades et du royaume franc de Jérusalem* (Paris, 1936), III, 512–513.

who, or whose predecessors, had not actually submitted to Latin authorities. Somewhat later, Athanasius III of Alexandria was also in communion with Rome at the time of his death in 1308 at the hands of the Moslems. He had, it seems, accepted the provisions of union enunciated at the Council of Lyons in 1274. Thus the Palestinian branch of eastern Christianity, presumably largely Melkite, was in those years in communion with Rome.

The situation in Antioch was somewhat different. There the Orthodox church was ethnically Greek and constituted a strong element in the population. Although less evidently so in the thirteenth century with the decline of Byzantine power, the problem of the patriarchate had always been confused with political issues. Toward 1245 the Greek patriarch, David, seems to have accepted Rome's jurisdiction and been permitted to install himself alongside the Latin patriarch Albert Rezzato, but his successor Euthymius was excommunicated by his Latin colleague Opizo Fieschi, only to be reinstated in 1260 by Bohemond VI acting under extreme pressure from Hulagu. Thereafter most of the Latin patriarchs remained *in absentia* and administered their province through vicars.

Innocent IV was most anxious to protect the uniate Melkites and Greeks of Jerusalem and Antioch against opposition on the part of the Latin patriarchs. In addition to the obvious motives of ecclesiastical policy, the pope was deeply concerned to preserve the unity of eastern Christianity against the Mongol menace. At the same time, he and his legates were aware that the newly reunited Greek clergy, particularly of Antioch, occasionally presumed on papal protection, thereby giving just grievance to the Latins. Apparently Lawrence of Portugal carried out a delicate mission with considerable success. But the union with Rome remained tenuous and presumably was largely lost with the destruction of the crusaders' states at the end of the century.

In 1237 the Jacobite patriarch of Antioch, Ignatius II (1222–1252), made an official visit to Jerusalem, where according to an old tradition the Jacobites had been given a section in the city and where they maintained the convent of St. Mary Magdalen.[19] Jacobites, Monophysite in faith and fairly numerous, were divided into several ethnic or national communities in Syria, Egypt, Nubia, and Ethiopia, under the jurisdiction of patriarchs at Antioch and Alexandria. James of Vitry had distinguished the Jacobites from the Syrian Melkites, and the Latins had become aware that Nubia and Ethiopia lay beyond

19. Cerulli, *Etiopi in Palestina*, pp. 62–73.

the confines of Moslem Egypt. They seem also to have understood something of the difficulties between the two Jacobite patriarchates.

Ignatius, in retaliation for the naming of a metropolitan for Jerusalem by the Coptic patriarch of Alexandria, Cyril III, proceeded to appoint a metropolitan for Ethiopia. This was done against the advice of the Dominicans of Jerusalem, who immediately protested strongly and were joined by the Templars and Hospitallers. Presumably they were afraid of offending the Egyptian government and thereby endangering the truce which permitted the Latin occupation of Jerusalem. Ultimately the matter was smoothed over, partly through the good offices of the friars.

More significant to the present discussion is the report of Ignatius's 1237 visit by friar Philip, Dominican provincial of the Holy Land.[20] On Palm Sunday, Philip reported, Ignatius made a profession of faith in Chaldean (Syriac) and Arabic, proclaiming his allegiance to Rome, and put on the habit of the Friars-Preachers. Similar declarations were made by two archbishops, one a Jacobite from Egypt, probably the Copt recently named metropolitan of Jerusalem, and the other a Nestorian whose jurisdiction included Syria. Philip then mentioned that letters received from William of Montferrat, for whom, it will be recalled, the papal bull of 1235 had been issued, indicated that he and two other Dominicans conversant with the language had spent some time with the Nestorian catholicus ("iakelinus"), Sabarjesus V, whose jurisdiction extended eastward to include the domains of Prester John, and found him disposed to return to the Catholic church.

To the Coptic patriarch of Alexandria, who had also, according to Philip, expressed a desire to return to ecclesiastical unity, he sent friars. Among the Egyptians, Philip went on to explain, Saracen influences apparently cause more deviations in custom than among other oriental Christians. But he adds significantly that Libya (presumably Nubia) and Ethiopia were not subject to Moslem rule. There is no further information about the friars Philip sent. But if perchance

---

20. Altaner, *Die Dominikanermissionen,* pp. 45 ff. Philip's report can be found in Matthew Paris, *Chronica majora,* III, 396 ff., and *MGH, SS.,* XXIII, 941–942. Jean B. Chabot, "Échos des croisades," *Comptes rendus de l'Académie des inscriptions et belles lettres* (1938), pp. 448–453, questions Ignatius's conversion and notes that Bar Hebraeus in describing the patriarch's visit does not mention it (*Chronicon ecclesiasticum,* ed. Jean B. Abbeloos and Thomas J. Lamy, I [Louvain, 1872], 653–654; also cited in Cerulli, *Etiopi in Palestina,* pp. 74–76). But Cahen, *La Syrie du nord à l'époque des croisades et la principauté franque d'Antioche* (IFD, BO, I; Paris, 1940), pp. 681–682, accounts for this omission on the basis of Bar Hebraeus's hostility to the Latins. Apparently Ignatius, who resided several years at Antioch, aroused considerable opposition among other Jacobites. Cf. also Richard, "Les Premiers missionnaires latins en Éthiopie (XIIIe–XIVe siècles)," *Studi Etiopi* (Accademia nazionale dei Lincei), CCCLVII (1959), 324, on the relations between Dominicans and the Ethiopian hierarchy.

they went beyond Egypt into Nubia or Ethiopia they would have been the first known to have done so.

Philip also mentioned that the Maronites of the Lebanon, long since returned to obedience, were persevering in their faith, and added that oriental Christians in general were listening to the friars. Only the Greeks remained hostile. Philip concluded his report with the information about language study, particularly Arabic, by himself and his fellow friars which was discussed above in connection with the possibility of missions to Moslems.

It seems clear that Philip's report was overly optimistic. As he remarked, Ignatius's jurisdiction included lands already devastated by Mongol incursions. The same would have been true of the Nestorian catholicus farther east, and both may have been concerned about possible western aid. Nevertheless, the report made an impression in Rome, and pope Gregory IX immediately sent a cordial letter to Ignatius and the other prelates.[21]

As has already been mentioned, a majority of Armenians were Monophysite. But the relations between the Cilician kingdom of Armenia and the crusader states had been close, and successive rulers and *catholicoi* had sought to bring the Armenian church out of what seemed to them a position of isolation. As a consequence, the king, the catholicus, and at least a part of the church of Cilician Armenia might be said to have been in formal union with Rome in the first decades of the thirteenth century.[22]

Such moves apparently made possible some western missionary activity. In his report Philip mentioned that at the urging of king and nobles he had sent four friars to Cilicia to learn the Armenian language. Some further indications of western contacts appear as a consequence of the expeditions and letters sent by Innocent IV in 1245 which will be discussed presently. The papal envoy, Dominic of Aragon, traveled extensively in the Levant and visited Cilicia, and it was perhaps owing to his efforts that the catholicus Constantine I, then

21. Aloysius L. Tăutu, ed., *Acta Honorii III et Gregorii IX* (PC, Fontes, ser. 3, III; Vatican City, 1950), pp. 303–305 (no. 227). In the following year the pope granted permission to Templars captured by Saracens to receive absolution from Jacobite priests (*ibid.,* p. 318, no. 239).

22. Henry F. Tournebize, *Histoire politique et religieuse de l'Arménie . . .* (Paris, 1910), pp. 235–284; Cahen, *La Syrie du nord,* pp. 588 ff.; Sirarpie Der Nersessian, "The Kingdom of Cilician Armenia," volume II of the present work, pp. 647 ff.; Bertold Spuler, ed., *Handbuch der Orientalistik,* 1, *Die Nahe und der Mittlere Osten,* VIII-2, *Religionsgeschichte des Orients in der Zeit der Weltreligionen* (Leyden and Cologne, 1961), pp. 254–257; Atiya, *A History of Eastern Christianity,* pp. 332–334. It should be noted that both Gregory IX and Innocent IV supported the Armenian patriarch against interference from the Latin patriarch of Antioch.

residing at Sis, presented an exposition of the Armenian faith. Later in the thirteenth century Franciscans were active in Cilicia, and some time after 1270 mission stations were established at Tarsus and Sis, and at Sivas in northeastern Anatolia.

Despite these evidences of rapport, it seems clear that many Armenians in the kingdom and probably most in the diaspora, then under Moslem rule, were still unwilling to recognize either the decrees of the Council of Chalcedon or Roman primacy. Moreover, even for those who did, primacy usually meant a vague, distant suzerainty, not an active jurisdiction.

The kingdom of Georgia, during this period, was Orthodox and perhaps in a technical sense still in union with Rome. Although the kingdom's exposed position vis-à-vis the Mongols may have prompted the rulers to regard the west favorably, remoteness and a clergy not particularly well disposed toward Rome made the union scarcely a reality. In 1233 Gregory IX sent a cordial letter to the ruler. This was to be delivered by Jacob of Russano, who with other Franciscans had been in Georgia. Moreover, general instructions to friars traveling to the Orient now included Georgians among the peoples named. Nothing is known of Jacob's mission except that he reached Constantinople.

The mission letters of the next few years (1233–1240) do not mention Georgians, but some time in the third decade of the century a Dominican convent was established at Tiflis. In 1240 the pope again wrote to the queen-regent Rusudan and her son David IV requesting her to receive a deputation of Friars-Preachers. In 1254 Innocent IV wrote to the Georgian bishops and clergy bespeaking a favorable reception for the Dominican friars en route eastward and in a tone implying normal ecclesiastical relations with the Holy See.[23]

THE MONGOL INVASIONS AND THE MISSIONS

The course of the mission effort in the thirteenth century was profoundly affected by the incursions of the Mongols into eastern Europe and the Levant. Europeans were terrified, and Innocent IV placed

23. Van der Vat, *Die Anfänge*, pp. 142–143; Altaner, *Die Dominikanermissionen*, pp. 68–70; Cahen, *La Syrie du nord*, p. 686. The papal letters are in *BOF*, I, 165, II, 299–301. It is not clear why in 1233 the pope addressed the king and not the queen-regent, Rusudan, who was then ruling for her son David. In the bull *Cum messis multa (ibid.,* II, 301), to friars "in terras Georgianum, Sarracenorum et aliorum paganorum profiscentibus," the pope included faculties for dealing with Latins and mentioned friars who were priests. Presumably this letter was directed to friars then established in the Orient (April 8, 1233).

the Mongol problem on the agenda of the Council of Lyons in 1245. As other chapters have indicated, the first attacks were followed by the stabilization of the Mongol empire, the subsequent reorientation of Mongol expansion eastward toward China and southward into the Levant, and its eventual division into smaller khanates. This, in turn, made possible communication between Europe and Asia and opened the way to diplomatic negotiations and eventually to missions.

A persistent difficulty confronting western authorities throughout this period was the lack of trustworthy information. Various legends, such as those concerning Prester John or a Christian king David, continued to find western acceptance. Moreover, the actual existence of Nestorian Christianity in Asia and the exaggerated, if not deliberately falsified, accounts of the extent of Asian Christianity which occasionally reached the west tended to perpetuate an overly optimistic attitude regarding mission possibilities. And the Mongols, it may be added, seem to have been equally ignorant of the west. Nevertheless, some misunderstandings were cleared up, and among the objects of papal diplomacy the acquisition of reliable information held an important place.[24]

Even before 1245 Innocent IV had received reports from Hungary concerning the first Mongol incursions toward the west. King Béla IV (1235–1270), representative of a people immediately endangered, had already promoted more than one exploratory mission before the Mongols actually attacked his own kingdom. The best known of these early ventures was that of the Dominican friar Julian, who in 1236–1237 traveled via Constantinople, Matrega, and the Alan country and thence northward into the region of the Volga or the Don. Julian reported his experiences in a letter to the papal legate in Hungary, bishop Salvius of Perugia. It seems that Béla forwarded this letter to the patriarch of Aquileia, Berthold of Andechs, a prelate later present at Innocent IV's curia and presumably one of the experts on Mongol affairs. A Russian bishop named Peter also appeared at the Council of Lyons with further information.[25]

---

24. There is a considerable literature on the Prester John problem. Recent studies include José M. Prou y Marti, O.F.M., "La Leyenda del Preste Juan entre los Franciscanos de la Edad Media," *Antonianum*, XX (1945), 65–96; Charles E. Nowell, "The Historical Prester John," *Speculum*, XXVIII (1953), 435–445 (who identifies him as Yeh-lü Ta-shih [1087–1143], gur-khan of the Kara-Khitai); Richard, "L'Extrême-Orient légendaire au moyen-âge: Roi David et Prêtre Jean," *Annales d'Éthiopie*, II (1957), 225–242; Vsevolod Slessarev, *Prester John: The Letter and the Legend* (Minneapolis, 1959).

25. Sinor, "Un Voyageur du treizième siècle: Le Dominicain, Julien de Hongrie," *London University, School of Oriental and African Studies, Bulletin*, XIV (1952), 589–602. Sinor differs from previous writers in holding that Julian made only one journey and did not reach "greater

Whatever the extent of his information at the time of the Council of Lyons in 1245, Innocent's decision to attempt negotiations with Mongol rulers was a new and bold step and was taken in connection with several important contemporary developments, European, Moslem, and Mongol. The coincidence of such events as the death of khan Ögödei (1242), the ultimatum to prince Bohemond IV of Antioch in 1244, the fall of Jerusalem to the Khwarizmian Turks and the launching of a new crusade by Louis IX of France in the same year should be noted. Moreover, at the time the pope was not undisputed master in his own house, for it was at the same council that he solemnly excommunicated emperor Frederick II and authorized a crusade against him.

In the spring and early summer of 1245 three missions penetrated deeply into Mongol territory.[26] Whether each of these resulted from specific papal commissions given to the friars at Lyons is not always clear, since such commissions do not exist in every case. At any rate, in March, even before the opening of the council (June 28, 1245), the pope had drawn up two letters addressed to the "king and people of the Tatars." The first of these (March 5) was religious in tenor and invited the khan to embrace Christianity. It was originally entrusted to the Franciscan friar Lawrence of Portugal, but this commission, it seems, was subsequently withdrawn, for it was in the following year that Lawrence visited instead the Greek and Melkite clergy of the Levant.

About the same time a commission was given to the Franciscan Dominic of Aragon, possibly that originally intended for Lawrence. Dominic's actual journey, however, was confined to the Levant, with perhaps some penetration of the Moslem hinterland. He visited, as we have mentioned, Cilicia and possibly Moslem Syria and Egypt.

Hungary." The view that the friar traveled eastward twice (1234–1235, 1237) and reached "greater Hungary" on the first trip has again been proposed by Heinrich A. Dörrie, *Drei Texte zur Geschichte der Ungarn und Mongolen* (Akademie der Wissenschaft in Göttingen, Philologische-historische Klasse, *Nachrichten*, 1956, no. 6), pp. 125–202. Dörrie also mentions the appearance at the Lyons council of the Russian bishop Peter.

26. These missions are discussed at length in Altaner, *Die Dominikanermissionen*, pp. 53–63, 120–138; Pelliot, "Les Mongoles et la papauté," *ROC*, XXIII (1922–1923), 3–30 (on John of Pian del Carpine); XXIV (1924), 225–335 (on Ascelin and Andrew); XXVIII (1931–1932), 3–84 (on Andrew); van der Vat, *Die Anfänge*, pp. 150–160; Soranzo, *Il Papato*, pp. 92 ff. Pelliot's second installment (1924) and Altaner's study appeared in the same year and were written independently. Pelliot, however, was able to procure a copy of Altaner's work while his own was in press and added a few references in his notes. Precisely the same thing occurred with Pelliot's third installment (1931–1932) and Soranzo, *Il Papato*. For general discussions see also Sinor, "Les Relations entre les Mongoles et l'Europe jusqu'à la mort d'Arghoun et de Béla IV," *Cahiers d'histoire mondiale*, III (1956), 39–62; Leonardo Olschki, *L'Asia di Marco Polo* (Biblioteca storica Sansona, n.s., XXX; Florence, 1957), chap. II; Troll, "Die Chinamission," pp. 118–123.

He returned in the summer of 1247 after a protracted stay at Constantinople, where his good offices in pacifying various dissident factions were gratefully recognized by the authorities. Apparently, therefore, the first papal commission to Franciscan friars directed specifically to the Mongols was not carried out.[27]

The second papal letter to the "king and people of the Tatars" (March 13) was primarily, though not exclusively, diplomatic and was designed among other things to moderate the ravages in eastern Europe. This letter was carried to the court of the great khan by the Franciscan John of Pian del Carpine, who returned to the curia in November 1247 bringing a haughty reply from the newly elected khan Güyük rejecting any cessation of hostilities and demanding total submission of all Christian rulers. Despite its pessimism the record of John's journey, the *Historia Mongalorum,* is a precious document, Europe's first real view into inner Asia.[28]

In addition to these specific commissions to Franciscans the pope added more general instructions and grants of faculties to friars journeying to the Orient in the general bull *Cum hora undecima* (March 21), which included the now customary long list of peoples, Moslem, pagan, and separated Christian. And on March 25 a letter was sent to schismatic prelates inviting them to return *ad unitatem ecclesiae* and recommending the Franciscan friars.[29]

27. Tisserant, "La Légation en Orient du Franciscain, Dominique d'Aragon (1245–47)," pp. 336 ff.; Roncaglia, *Les Frères mineurs,* pp. 87–88, 92–99; van der Vat, *Die Anfänge,* pp. 152–154, 158–160. Although no papal letter to Dominic exists, the pope wrote on March 10 to the Hospitallers and apparently also the Templars urging them to give the friar and his companions all possible help. On March 21 the Latin ecclesiastical authorities were similarly informed. While the direction of these letters would seem to imply the crusader states, the second letter specifically mentions non-Christians. It has, therefore, been suggested that the papal commission withdrawn from Lawrence of Portugal was herewith given to Dominic of Aragon. The papal letters mentioned are cited in *BOF,* II, 321 (*BF,* I, 354), 324–325 (*BF,* I, 771 ff.).

28. *BF,* I, 353 ff. A translation of John of Pian del Carpine's account can be found in Dawson, ed., *Mission to Asia* (London, 1955), pp. 3–86. Pelliot, *ROC,* XXIII (1922–1923), 8–9, suggests, on the basis of a passage in Güyük's reply which seems to indicate an invitation to conversion, that perhaps John took the letter intended for Lawrence of Portugal; cf. van der Vat, *Die Anfänge,* p. 152. It is worth noting that Innocent IV was also in communication with various princes and prelates, Latin, Greek, and Slavonic, in eastern Europe, cf. Soranzo, *Il Papato,* pp. 88 ff. The role of Benedict the Pole, John's companion, in negotiations with the church in Ruthenia is discussed by Bolesław Szczesniak, "Benoît le Polonais, dit le Vratislavien, et son rôle dans l'union de la Ruthénie de Halicz avec Rome en 1246," *Antemurale,* I (1954), 39–50.

29. *BOF,* II, 316; *BF,* I, 357, 360, 362; Theodosius T. Haluščynskyj and Meletius M. Wugnar, eds., *Acta Innocentii papae IV* (Rome, 1962), pp. 36–39 (no. 19), 43–46 (no. 20). Van der Vat, *Die Anfänge,* p. 145, thinks that the general papal bulls were intended for John of Pian del Carpine only. But Pelliot, *ROC,* XXIV (1924), 329, suggests that one of the prelates interviewed by the Dominicans may have seen the letter addressed to the oriental prelates.

Two expeditions of Dominican friars also set out in 1245. The first was headed by friar Ascelino, probably a Lombard, who left Lyons perhaps as early as March and was later joined at the Dominican convent of Acre by three other Dominican friars.[30] Another friar, Guiscard of Cremona, joined them at Tiflis. Although a copy of Ascelino's commission does not exist, it is possible that it resembled that of John of Pian del Carpine in purpose. Because of a considerable delay in reaching his destination, his journey took a longer time—considerably over three years—than any of the others. Not until May 24, 1247, did Ascelino and his companions reach the camp of the Mongol general Baiju, probably somewhere in the mountains of Transcaucasia east of Lake Sevan. Despite threats against his life, Ascelino persisted in his refusal to prostrate himself before the Mongol dignitaries, even though one of his more experienced companions pointed out that no idolatry was implied. Since he also resisted demands that he travel to the court of the great khan Güyük, the friars' letters had to be translated and sent on. Finally, toward the end of July 1247, after the arrival of an envoy from the khan, the general Eljigidei, they were permitted to leave, accompanied by two Mongol envoys. They reached Acre in September and the curia sometime early in the following summer (1248). Baiju's reply, which they delivered to the pope, was strikingly similar in tone to that of Güyük. On the way home, presumably at Tabriz, they visited a Nestorian prelate named Simeon Rabban Ata, who, as we shall see, had been interviewed by the other Dominican envoy of 1245, the Frenchman Andrew of Longjumeau.

The record of Andrew's instructions has also been lost, but his journey had considerable religious as well as diplomatic significance.[31] It was he and one companion, it will be remembered, who may have

---

30. Pelliot has reconstructed Ascelino's journey; see above, note 26. He feels that Ascelino may have occupied himself for some time with oriental Christians. On the analogy of the two types of commission, one diplomatic, the other missionary, and one each to the great khan and to some lesser dignitary, Altaner, *Die Dominikanermissionen*, pp. 122 ff., holds that Ascelino's commission probably resembled that given to John of Pian del Carpine while that given to Andrew of Longjumeau was similar to the one intended for Lawrence of Portugal. This "symmetrical" interpretation has been rejected by Tisserant and van der Vat. Although there has been discussion regarding the validity of the principal source for Ascelino's journey, Simon of Saint Quentin (e.g., Soranzo, *Il Papato*, pp. 114-119), the matter seems now to have been settled definitively by the new edition of Richard, *Simon de Saint-Quentin: Histoire des Tartares* (Documents relatifs à l'histoire des croisades, VIII; Paris, 1965); for the passages relevant here see pp. 94-117. Cf. also Olschki, *Marco Polo's Precursors* (Baltimore, 1946), pp. 48 ff.

31. Andrew's commission and journey have been examined at length by Pelliot and Altaner (see above, note 26). Cf. also Soranzo, *Il Papato*, pp. 119 ff.

been the bearers of one of the pope's letters to and replies from Moslem princes of Syria. More pertinent to the present discussion are his communications with oriental prelates. For it is principally as a consequence of Andrew's achievements and the five letters from oriental prelates which he brought back that we have some insight into papal dealings with oriental Christianity during this period.

Andrew traveled from Syria to Mosul, where the Jacobite maphrian John XV (1232–1253) made an Orthodox profession of faith. Some seventeen days journey beyond Mosul, presumably near Tabriz, Andrew met a detachment of Mongol troops. To the commanders of this contingent, which was very likely an advance guard of Baiju's army, he delivered the pope's letters. It is probable that it was also at Tabriz that he talked with Simeon Rabban Ata, a representative of the Nestorian catholicus, who styled himself *vicarius orientis*. Probably a Syrian, he was, it seems, patriarchal visitor to the Nestorian communities of central and eastern Asia, and apparently had won the respect of the Mongols. Expressing himself as extremely grateful for the pope's embassy, Simeon urged the pope to make peace with emperor Frederick II, and apparently he wrote the emperor in the same vein. To Andrew he presented to be delivered to the pope a *libellus* on matters of faith which he had brought from China. This has not been preserved, but the papal archives do contain professions from the archbishop of Nisibis, Išoyahb bar Malkhon, and five other prelates including Simeon.[32] He requested the pope to insure proper treatment of Nestorians in the crusader states, especially at Antioch, Tripoli, and Acre, and he made intercession for his friend the archbishop of Jerusalem. The friars remained with Simeon for twenty days and were given a costly ivory staff for the pope.

It is worth noting that these contacts were made with a representative of the Nestorian hierarchy of upper Mesopotamia, Persia, and greater Armenia, by envoys sent expressly to Mongols. Although there is no reason to suppose that the catholicus was hostile to what Simeon was doing, it is true that he then resided at Seleucia (near Ctesiphon) in the territory of the Baghdad caliphate, not yet occupied by the Mongols. Presumably he feared them. For some unexplained reason Simeon did not remain well disposed toward the western church. When Ascelino and his associates stayed with him on their return

---

32. *BOF,* II, 356, cites the documents, but, following Tournebize, *Histoire de l'Arménie,* p. 289, wrongly identifies Simeon Rabban Ata as Armenian and Andrew as Franciscan. Pelliot, *ROC,* XXIV (1924), 230–235, points out that the use of the word "catholicus" here as applied to Simeon is probably the result of an error on the part of a papal scribe.

trip from Baiju's headquarters they found him in an entirely different mood. While they were awaiting a reply to a papal letter, possibly one delivered by Andrew, he died.[33]

Meanwhile, on his return journey Andrew met at Antioch the Jacobite patriarch Ignatius II, who, it will be recalled, had made a profession of faith in Jerusalem some years earlier.[34] He had subsequently received letters from Gregory IX and now, it would appear, Innocent IV was following up his predecessor's moves and perhaps requiring a more precise definition of the terms of union. At any rate, Ignatius presented another profession to Andrew and added a number of significant requests which reveal something of the often difficult relations between eastern and western Christians. He asked that there be free election of the patriarch by the archbishops, independence of the Jacobite hierarchy from the jurisdiction of Latin bishops, and freedom of all Jacobites and of their establishments in Latin territory from any financial exactions. Finally, baptized Jacobites should not be required when marrying Latins to be rebaptized. The patriarch assured the pope of his coöperation, especially in the freeing of slaves and prisoners. Andrew returned to the curia in the spring or early summer of 1247 and delivered the replies to the pope's communications of 1245 to oriental prelates and perhaps also replies from Moslem princes. His own report was overly optimistic about the position and future of Christianity in Asia.

Andrew of Longjumeau is next encountered at Cyprus, where Louis IX was completing preparations for his attack on Egypt and where on December 19, 1248, there arrived two envoys sent by the Mongol general Eljigidei, then in command of armies in northern Mesopotamia, probably near Tabriz. Very possibly he was already meditating an attack on Baghdad. The envoys were Nestorians and the principal one, David, was known to Andrew, whom he had probably met in 1246. It was Andrew who translated Eljigidei's letter to the king from the original Persian into Latin. Although the letter was far more cordial in tone than the earlier reply of Güyük, it is possible that it was designed to create a deceptively favorable impression. This would enable the Mongols to avoid a confrontation with Louis's crusading armies if they moved against Baghdad.[35]

---

33. It is not clear whether Ascelino presented to Simeon a new letter or whether this refers to a previous communication delivered by Andrew. Pelliot suggests that it was probably the letter sent by the pope to dissident prelates on March 25, 1245 (*ibid.*, p. 329); cf. above, note 29.

34. According to Cahen, *La Syrie du nord,* pp. 681–682, and Altaner, *Die Dominikanermissionen,* p. 53, Andrew met Ignatius at Mardin, northwest of Nisibin.

35. Pelliot, *ROC,* XXVIII (1931–1932), 19–20, 26, 37, 66–67, contends, against certain older

At any rate Eljigidei's communication seems to have strengthened the impression already created by Andrew, at least as far as mission possibilities were concerned. For after discussing the matter in council and with the papal legate, cardinal Odo of Tusculum, the king decided to respond by sending a legation of which certain members would return after delivering letters to Eljigidei while others would proceed further to the court of the great khan Güyük, the news of whose death in the spring of 1248 had evidently not yet reached the west. Andrew of Longjumeau was chosen to head the embassy and was accompanied by two other Dominicans, one of them being his brother, William, who also spoke Arabic, two seculars, two royal officers, and the two Mongol envoys. Another cleric of Acre, named Theodulf, accompanied them in a private capacity into Persia. He eventually left the group and was found later by William of Rubruck in Karakorum.

The details of the journey are of no concern here. Suffice it to say that the entire party, including perhaps even the Mongols' envoy David, after reporting from some point en route, continued on to the Mongol imperial court, then presided over by the queen-mother and regent, Oghul Kaimish, and probably situated in the valley of the river Imil east of Lake Balkhash. The ambassadors were courteously received, and returned to report to the king at Caesarea in the spring or early summer of 1251. But neither was the cause of Christianity furthered nor were closer diplomatic ties promoted.

Thus Andrew of Longjumeau returned once again from Asia. Although perhaps too much influenced by oriental propaganda after his first trip, he was nevertheless an accomplished missionary and ambassador. Moreover, in the course of his travels he had mastered Arabic and Persian and perhaps understood Greek. He had also seen Christians in lands under Mongol and Moslem dominion. As a consequence, his experience was recognized and his advice sought. When, for example, he urged that some missionary friars be raised to the episcopate, king Louis wrote to the pope in this vein. By the bull of February 20, 1253, Innocent gave his legate in the Orient, Odo of Tusculum, powers to proceed with the consecrations. Although not then carried out, this plan, inspired by the advice of Andrew,

authors, including Beazley, *The Dawn of Modern Geography,* II, 278, 645, that the envoys were not impostors and that the letter was not a fabrication. Cf. Richard, "The Mongols and the Franks," *Journal of Asian History,* III (1969), 50–51. It should also be noted that western optimism regarding the extent of Christianity in Asia was further strengthened by the receipt of a letter which the Armenian constable Sempad wrote to his brother-in-law, king Henry I of Cyprus. It was written from Samarkand en route to the Mongol court: Altaner, *Die Dominikanermissionen,* p. 132; Grousset, *Histoire des croisades,* III, 526–527; Soranzo, *Il Papato,* p. 157.

foreshadowed the establishment of a Latin hierarchy in the Orient in the following century. Andrew's influence may also perhaps be observed in the preparations made by William of Rubruck, the Franciscan missionary, whom he met in Syria in 1252.[36]

Meanwhile the kingdom of Cilician Armenia had also established contact with the Mongols, whom they found to be a welcome counterpoise to the Turks of Konya. The constable Sempad, brother of Heṭoum I, journeyed into Mongol territory and from Samarkand wrote in 1248 to his brother-in-law, Henry I of Cyprus. From these varied sources came further indications of Christianity in Asia, among them the report that Sartak, son of Batu, khan of the Kipchak Golden Horde and ruler of a territory west of the Volga, was a Christian. It was this especially which prompted king Louis, then at Acre, to authorize the journey of William of Rubruck.[37]

William, a Franciscan friar at the convent at Acre, set out with the original purpose of establishing a mission center in Sartak's kingdom. He did, it is true, carry letters of recommendation from king Louis to Sartak, to his father, Batu, and to the great khan Möngke. As a consequence, he occasionally had to protest his unofficial capacity. But he also took with him religious books, vestments, and articles suitable to his evangelical intentions, and insisted that he desired only to fulfil the missionary ideals of his order. Thus, unlike John of Pian del Carpine and the Dominicans, and despite some misunderstanding among the Mongols, William was exclusively a missionary.

Friar William set out from Acre early in 1253 with friar Bartholomew and two others and an interpreter. He first stopped at Constantinople and then traveled north and east and reached Sartak's camp at the end of July 1253. About Sartak's Christianity William expressed some doubts. Moreover, he and his companions were told that it was necessary for them to proceed to Batu's camp. Accordingly, they left

---

36. The definitive account of Andrew's journey can be found in Pelliot, *ROC*, XXVIII (1931-1932), 37-82. Cf. also Altaner, *Die Dominikanermissionen*, pp. 134-137; Soranzo, *Il Papato*, pp. 128 ff. For Innocent IV's bull see *Acta Innocentii papae IV*, p. 148 (no. 86).

37. There have been many studies on William of Rubruck. The principal ones are listed in Soranzo, *Il Papato*, p. 144, note 1; Olschki, *Marco Polo's Precursors*, pp. 49 ff., and *idem*, *Guillaume Boucher* (Baltimore, 1946), pp. 18 ff. See Chrysologus Schollmeyer, O.F.M., "Die missionarische Sendung des Frater Wilhelm von Rubruk," *Ostkirchliche Studien*, IV (1955), 138-146, and "Die Missionsfahrt Bruder Wilhelms von Rubruk," *ZMR*, XL (1956), 200-205; Jean Dauvillier, "Guillaume de Rubrouck et les communautés chaldéennes d'Asie centrale au moyen-âge," *Annuaire de l'École des législations religieuses* (1951-1952), II, 36-42; Troll, "Die Chinamission," pp. 124-125. Cf. also Southern, *Western Views of Islam*, pp. 47-52. On the influence of Andrew of Longjumeau see Pelliot, *ROC*, XXVIII (1931-1932), 77. For translations of William's account see Rockhill, *The Journey of William Rubruk to Eastern Parts of the World, 1253-55* (Hakluyt Society, London, 1900), and Dawson, *Mission to Asia*, pp. 87-220.

with Sartak their books and vestments, save a Bible and book of Sentences which William managed to keep with him, and journeyed to Batu's headquarters on the east bank of the Volga, only to find that he in turn insisted that they travel to the court of the great khan Möngke at Karakorum. They reached the court on December 27, 1253.

At the imperial court William lost no opportunity to exercise his ministry. He was especially welcome to the many European Christians, mostly captives or technicians resident at the khan's headquarters. He was able to establish friendly relations with Nestorians although he was highly critical of their practices, and he participated with them and with Moslems and *tuins,* a term he used to describe Asiatic pagans in general, in a public debate before the great khan. According to king Heṭoum of Armenia, who visited the Mongol court shortly afterward, William offended the khan by the intemperance of his preaching, but to judge from his own straightforward account he seems to have acquitted himself well.[38] His evident skill in debate impressed the Moslems. As might be expected of a man who was appointed lector at the convent at Acre on his return, he had a thorough knowledge of scripture and a capacity to organize and present an argument. Of his success as a missionary it is difficult to judge. He mentions only a few converts of his own and describes the baptism of some sixty persons by Nestorians.

In August 1254 William took his leave, parting with great sadness from his colleague Bartholomew, whose illness precluded any such journey at that time. It was not until May 1255 that William again saw the Mediterranean. Since he was ordered to remain at Acre, he was not able to report to king Louis in person, for the king had returned to France. Somewhat later, through the influence of the king, he did return to Paris; there he met Roger Bacon, who was greatly impressed by what he had to say. Meanwhile he composed a written account of his journey (*Itinerarium*) which still stands as one of the most significant travel reports of the Middle Ages. As far as missions are concerned, William's experiences prompted him to suggest that instead of humble friars the pope should send a bishop in order to make a suitable impression. Significantly, too, he emphasized the necessity of adequate interpreters.

Thus all the early politico-missionary expeditions to the Mongols failed to achieve fruitful results, and attempts to establish diplomatic

---

38. Van der Vat, *Die Anfänge,* p. 80, note 90; Soranzo, *Il Papato,* p. 155, note 2; de Sessevalle, *Histoire générale de l'ordre de Saint François,* II, 622. Southern (*Western Views of Islam,* pp. 47–52) identifies William's pagan opponents as Buddhists; he also comments on William's influence on Roger Bacon. See also Simonut, *Il Metodo,* pp. 135–137.

relations ceased for some years as Europe awaited or feared renewed Mongol attacks. The few contacts with oriental prelates seemed more promising, but it must be observed that although such dignitaries as made professions of faith gave evidence of a desire to live in harmony with Rome, there was no assurance that they fully understood the primacy of jurisdiction. This may, for example, explain Innocent IV's seeking through Andrew of Longjumeau a second profession from Ignatius II. Further, there is little doubt that hope of western aid was a powerful motive in certain cases, and the conversion of individual prelates was usually not followed by corporate movements of the faithful. It has been pointed out that Ignatius II spoke for only a section of the Jacobite church. After his death in 1252, his successor John VI (the maphrian John XV) maintained a precarious union for a short time, but the majority of Jacobites followed a rival, Dionysius VII, who was traditionally Monophysite and anti-Latin.[39]

THE SECOND HALF OF THE THIRTEENTH CENTURY

During the 1260's changes in the political balance of the Levantine world opened up new opportunities for missionaries. In 1261 the Byzantine empire was restored with the assistance of the Genoese, who subsequently established themselves in the Black Sea area. The northern coast of the Black Sea lay within the jurisdiction of the khanate of the Kipchak Golden Horde, which also comprised the territory stretching from southern Russia to the Caspian. A variety of peoples inhabited the region, Goths, Alans, Circassians, Abkhasians, Georgians, as well as Russians and Greeks, all in the main Christian, in addition to Khazars, Turks, Kumans, and Mongols. A large Armenian colony had settled in Kaffa, the principal city and port of the Crimea.

Although Islam steadily gained adherents in the Kipchak khanate, diplomatic and commercial interests, especially rivalry with the Mongol rulers of Persia and a long frontier with western Christendom in Poland and Hungary, prompted the khans to grant protection to merchants and missionaries and to maintain formally cordial rela-

---

39. Runciman, *A History of the Crusades* (3 vols., Cambridge, Eng., 1951–1954), III, 232; Cahen, *La Syrie du nord,* pp. 681–684. Chabot, "Échos des croisades," p. 453, has pointed out that since the professions of faith made by oriental prelates are extant only in the Latin form and may have been drawn up under missionary direction, they may not represent the real views of the signers. See also Altaner, "Sprachkenntnisse und Dolmetscherwesen im missionarischen und diplomatischen Verkehr zwischen Abendland (päpstliche Kurie) und Orient im 13. und 14. Jahrhundert," *Zeitschrift für Kirchengeschichte,* LV (1936), 83–126.

tions with Rome. Thus the Genoese obtained from the Mongol authorities the right to establish a colony at Kaffa. Their rivals, the Venetians, at first excluded, came on the scene somewhat later with a consul at Soldaia, and the Pisans began to exploit the Azov region.

Meanwhile the Byzantine emperor Michael VIII Palaeologus and his son Andronicus, while attempting to maintain correct relations with Rome after accepting a formula of reunion at the Council of Lyons in 1274, but menaced from the west by Charles of Anjou and from the north by the Bulgars, were disposed to remain on terms of virtual alliance with the Kipchak khanate. In such a situation, and especially in view of the growing predominance of Islam in the entire region, missions depended on a policy of toleration dictated by a diplomacy which could easily change. Nevertheless, it was in this area that both mendicant orders established missionary organizations and bases which were also important to their work farther east and south.

In the thirteenth century the Franciscans took the lead. The minister-general Bonagratia (1279–1283) was especially active in promoting missions and dispatching friars to what chroniclers began to call the vicariate of the north (*vicaria aquilonis*). A somewhat overly optimistic report of friar Ladislas (1287), *custos* of Gazaria (the Crimea), indicates that within the vicariate of the north there were two *custodiae,* one in the Crimea with its principal center at Kaffa, the other centering at Sarai (old Sarai on the Akhtuba), the Kipchak capital.[40]

Meanwhile the Dominicans were also entering this area. The preaching friars had been in Constantinople during the thirteenth century, but with the Byzantine recovery in 1261 and the Venetian sack of Pera in 1296 their residences had been lost. In the last years of the thirteenth century, however, new convents were established at Pera and at Kaffa. The missionaries who set out from these stations to more distant residences came to be known as *peregrinantes,* religious outside the established convents. It was evidently to regularize their position and to maintain discipline that the Dominican authorities between 1300 and 1304 appointed a vicar, probably Franco of Perugia, over the friars in the Black Sea region. This proved to be the first move in the formation of a new missionary organization, the *Societas fratrum peregrinantium propter Christum,* which was to play a major mission role during the fourteenth century.

Equally significant for the missionary effort farther south was the halting of the Mongol southwestward advance by the Moslems of

---

40. *BOF,* II, 266, 443. On the origin of the Franciscan vicariates see van der Vat, *Die Anfänge,* pp. 131 ff.

Egypt. After encompassing the fall of the Baghdad caliphate in 1258, the Mongols were stopped at 'Ain Jālūt in Syria (1260). Thereafter, a resurgent Islam, led by the Egyptian Mamluks, increased the danger to the kingdom of Cilician Armenia and the crusader states. The new balance of power did, however, offer certain advantages. The il-khanate of Persia, also menaced from Egypt and insecure in its relations with other Mongol khanates, was disposed to solicit western aid. As the situation in the Latin Levant steadily worsened the attitude of Rome and the Latin Christians, previously hostile to the Mongols, underwent a change. Beginning around 1264, when the curia was informed that the il-khan Hulagu was disposed to become a Christian, there was considerable diplomatic activity designed to establish some sort of Christian-Mongol coöperation against Islam.[41]

Commercial relations also improved during this period. Italians maintained stations in several places within the il-khanate as well as farther north. Tabriz, the Mongol capital, was an important depot. Trebizond on the Black Sea prospered as a port of entry, especially after the loss of the crusader states in 1291. The Genoese were established in Sivas on the routes which linked Persia with the Black Sea and the Mediterranean. As in other areas, the presence of western Christians was often the initial reason for the establishment by the friars of a station which might also serve the missions.

Late thirteenth-century Franciscan lists of stations mention Tabriz, "Salamastrum" (Salmas), Sivas, and Arzenga (Erzinjan).[42] At Tabriz the friars maintained a second station at the principal church in the city, which they served alternately with the Dominicans. Within this territory, which was included in the Franciscan vicariate of the east, the Minorites continued, at least occasionally, their efforts to convert Moslems. Two friars were martyred in Persia about 1284, and other martyrdoms were reported early in the fourteenth century. But to judge from subsequent developments native Christians were the principal objects of missionary attention.

Dominicans were also moving into Persia in the later years of the thirteenth century. Ricoldo of Monte Croce, whose contacts with the Moslems have already been described, was equally active among ori-

---

41. Richard, "Le Début des relations entre la papauté et les Mongoles de Perse," *Journal asiatique,* CCXXXVII (1949), 291–297, in discussing the papal reply to Hulagu, formerly dated 1260 (Alexander IV), places this shortly before October 2, 1264, the death of Urban IV. The change in attitude may, therefore, be placed at this time. For further discussion on this and the contrast in papal policy as recently as 1260 see the same author's "The Mongols and the Franks," *Journal of Asian History,* III (1969), 55 ff.

42. *BOF,* II, 265.

ental Christians.[43] At Tabriz, it will be recalled, he preached first through an interpreter. But in Mosul he preached openly in Arabic to the Jacobite clergy and people. At the convent of St. Matthew outside Mosul, the seat of the Jacobite maphrian, he held public conversations and the maphrian Gregory III was one of the converts. Later, at Tikrit, he received a profession of faith from an archbishop and a number of formerly Monothelite Maronites. In the account of his travels Ricoldo also mentions meeting other Dominican friars whom he found residing at Sivas and Maragha. Finally, he recalls the warm welcome he received from his confreres at Baghdad, where he first heard the news of the disasters of 1291.

At Baghdad Ricoldo was at first cordially treated by the Nestorians. Then when he attacked their beliefs he was driven from the church they had granted him. The catholicus Mār Yabhalāhā III, who had been sent a profession of faith in 1288 by pope Nicholas IV, intervened and directed, against the will of many of his clergy, that Ricoldo be allowed to preach freely. He also received the friar at his pontifical throne. Apparently many converts were made.

Mār Yabhalāhā III had been involved in one of the most important missions sent to the west by the Mongol government of Persia. In 1287–1288 his chief deputy, Rabban (Mār) Ṣaumā, a remarkable Nestorian bishop of Uighur parentage and a native of Peking (Khanbaliq), visited Rome and the west bearing letters from the patriarch and the il-khan Arghun.[44] When he and his associates arrived at Rome, probably in April 1287, pope Honorius IV had just died. During the ten-month interval before the election of a new pope the envoys traveled through Italy to the court of Philip IV at Paris, thence to an interview with Edward I of England in Gascony. Finally, on their return to Rome they presented to the newly elected Nicholas IV (1288–1292), the former Jerome Masci of Ascoli, minister-general of the Franciscans, the gifts and letters of Arghun.

The cordial, even enthusiastic welcome everywhere accorded the en-

43. For the literature on Ricoldo see above, note 13. On the Dominican residences see Loenertz, *Frères pérégrinants,* pp. 152–153, 160–161.

44. Chabot, *Histoire de Mar Jabalaha III et du moine Rabban Çauma* (Paris, 1895), also in *ROL,* I (1893), 567–610; II (1894), 73–142, 235–304, 630–638, 641–643; James A. Montgomery, *The History of Yaballaha III, Nestorian Patriarch* (New York, 1927); Moule, *Christians in China,* ch. IV; E. A. Wallis Budge, ed. and tr., *The Monks of Kûblâi Khân, Emperor of China* (London, 1928); Richard, "La Mission en Europe de Rabban Çauma et l'union des églises," *Oriente ed Occidente nel medio evo* (Accademia dei Lincei, XIIo Convegno Volta; Rome, 1957), pp. 162–167; Franz Altheim and Ruth Stiehl, "Rabban Sauma's Reise nach dem Westen, 1287–1288," *Geschichte der Hunnen,* vol. III (Berlin, 1961), 190–217; *BOF,* II, 433–437; Soranzo, *Il Papato,* pp. 260 ff.

voys seemed evidence that a formidable crusade was to be launched. Such, of course, was not to be the case, even though the pope, despite involvement in Italian and Sicilian diplomatic problems, attempted to organize military assistance to the beleaguered east both before and after the fall of Acre in 1291.

More relevant to the progress of missions are the religious discussions with Rabban Ṣaumā at the curia. Possibly owing to mistakes made by inexpert interpreters, Nicholas IV and the cardinals apparently either misunderstood or overlooked the envoy's Nestorianism and confused his faith with that of the Greek schismatics. At any rate he was questioned about the procession of the Holy Spirit. He received communion at the hands of the pope and among the letters entrusted to him on his return was one to Mār Yabhalāhā which exhorted him to persevere and which contained the profession mentioned above, identical to that sent by Clement IV to Michael Palaeologus in 1267. To Arghun the pope wrote expressing his gratitude for his favors and protection to Christians. But he rejected the idea that the khan, who had apparently expressed a desire to become a Christian, should await the capture of Jerusalem before receiving the sacrament of baptism. The papal letters to the queen-mother Maria (Palaeologina, called Despoina Mugulion) and other Mongol dignitaries also remained on the same purely religious plane.[45]

Other letters consigned to Rabban Ṣaumā on his return journey give the same impression. These included a communication to nine Latin Christian interpreters of the Mongol ruler praising their zeal and urging them to aid even more the work of the missionaries. Since their names all appear to be Italian, it is probable that they were resident merchants who had perhaps offered their services. A letter to all the Franciscan friars confirming and enlarging their faculties for the missionary apostolate was also included, as was also a gracious letter to the Jacobite bishop Dionysius of Tabriz, who had apparently been won over by the Minorites. He was sent a profession of faith and urged to further the work of the missionaries.

In the following summer (1289) another important batch of letters was entrusted to the Franciscan John of Monte Corvino.[46] John, who

45. For a discussion of Nicholas IV's correspondence and his religious and diplomatic aims, including citations from his principal letters, see Soranzo, *Il Papato*, pp. 266 ff.; *BOF,* II, 437–442. For a summary of thirteenth-century papal mission policy with special emphasis on Nicholas IV see Mann, *The Lives of the Popes in the Middle Ages*, XVII, 14–141. According to the *History of Yaballaha*, p. 72, Yabhalāhā was given patriarchal authority over all oriental Christians and Rabban Ṣaumā power of visitation. No such concessions appear in papal documents. Cf. Soranzo, *Il Papato*, pp. 265–266.

46. *BOF,* II, 440–442; Soranzo, *Il Papato,* pp. 273 ff. How many of these letters were de-

was to become perhaps the most celebrated of medieval missionaries to the east, was already a friar of considerable oriental experience and something of a linguist. He had been in Persia and had brought to the pope letters from Arghun and from Heṭoum II of Armenia, whose envoy he was. Cilician Armenia was then hard pressed by the Egyptian advance northward. Moreover, Heṭoum was personally well disposed toward the western church. What is important here is that Nicholas IV was evidently much impressed by friar John's reports and disposed to place considerable confidence in his experience.

Among the persons to whom John was directly to carry papal letters were Arghun, king Heṭoum II of Armenia, and various dignitaries, lay and ecclesiastical, including a number of distinguished Jacobite, Nestorian, Armenian, and Georgian prelates whose "good works" he had reported and who were urged either to profess or to continue in conformity with the faith of the Roman church. Finally, John was given missionary commissions well beyond the area of the Persian khanate. He was directed to send a communication to the emperor (Solomon I, 1285–1294), archbishops, bishops, and people of Ethiopia bespeaking observance of Catholic teaching, and to khan Kaidu of Turkestan urging his conversion and requesting liberty for missionaries. Then John was to continue on to the court of the great khan Kubilai at Khanbaliq.

While these communications show Nicholas's energy in promoting missions, it also seems clear that hopes for coöperation against Islam were not far from his mind and reflect the attitude of many in the curia. Moreover, in August 1290 and again a year later, following receipt of news of the fall of Acre, the pope addressed a large number of letters to eastern rulers and prelates. Many of these were religious in content and urged perseverence in the faith or, as in the case of the letter to Arghun's third son, who had been baptized and taken the name of Nicholas, included a profession of faith. Yet to Arghun the pope addressed two letters, one religious in character, the other political, as though the two subjects, being of a different order of importance, were to be treated separately.[47]

Nicholas IV's pontificate was critical in the history of papal dealings with the Orient, much as that of Innocent IV had been. Though

---

livered is not known. Since John traveled to India and China by sea, he could not have delivered the letter to khan Kaidu of Turkestan personally. Presumably he also forwarded the letter intended for Ethiopia.

47. Ernest Langlois, ed., *Les Registres de Nicolas IV* (2 vols., Paris, 1886–1905), pp. 894–895 (no. 6722), 904 (no. 6814); *BOF*, II, 473 ff., where Golubovich points out that the envoys could have learned of Arghun's death (July 22, 1291) at Trebizond or Constantinople, but would nevertheless have fulfilled their mission. Cf. also Soranzo, *Il Papato*, pp. 290–291.

missions were inevitably involved with diplomacy both before and after the events of 1291, the pope, a former Franciscan minister-general, tried to keep the two distinct, and it is possible to discern the greater emphasis on religious matters. Most of the pope's letters, it is true, were sent to lay or ecclesiastical dignitaries, for Rome still attached great importance to the conversion of such persons. But such a tactic did not exclude missions to peoples. Nicholas issued mission bulls, sent out friars, solicited from rulers protection for missionaries, and called for reports of the entire eastern situation.

Nicholas's hopes were not to be fulfilled. Arghun died in March 1291 without having formally embraced the Christian faith, and no coalition against Egypt materialized. In fact Ghazan, who came to the throne of the il-khanate in 1295, renounced the religious policies of earlier Mongol rulers and became a Moslem. Nicholas himself died in April 1292. A two-year interregnum was followed first by the pontificate of Celestine V and then by that of Boniface VIII and by continuing European diplomatic crises. In the east the Egyptian advance which overran the crusader states subjected Cilician Armenia to repeated marauding and threatened its very existence. A number of residences maintained by the friars were destroyed or abandoned, and an entirely new orientation had to be found in the succeeding decades. Oriental prelates who persevered in union with Rome did so increasingly at their peril. Mār Yabhalāhā, for example, remained well disposed toward the western church, and in 1304 the Dominican friar James of Arles translated and brought to Rome a second profession of faith from the patriarch which, it should be noted, clarified those points, particularly concerning the Virgin Mary as the mother of God, which had not been emphasized in the document originally sent in 1288. But it has also been noted that Mār Yabhalāhā's letter, though exclusively religious in content, was sent at a critical moment in east and west. Benedict XI had just succeeded Boniface VIII. Ghazan's successor was Arghun's third son, "Nicholas," now called Öljeitu, or Khodābanda Muḥammad, who had renounced his Christian religion and, it was feared, might be even less disposed than his predecessor to seek rapport with the west.[48]

Mission methods and policies will be discussed more fully at the end of this chapter, but it may be well to summarize briefly what had been done during the thirteenth century.[49] Rome, much preoccu-

48. Soranzo, *Il Papato*, pp. 341–344; Chabot, *Histoire de Mar Jabalaha III*, pp. 250–256. In this case the original text in Turco-Uighur is extant. Moule, *Christians in China*, pp. 132–134, doubts Yabhalāhā's submission to Rome.

49. The most important recent work on this subject is Simonut, *Il Metodo*. An excellent

pied with European crises and deeply concerned with the protection of Christendom's frontiers, had given its sanction and support to an entirely new mission venture. Curial policy remained closely associated with diplomacy and the promotion of the crusade, but with the pontificate of Nicholas IV religious and political objectives tended to become more distinct. The curia had acquired considerable information about the Orient, but its knowledge of actual conditions still left much to be desired.

Organization of the mission effort was the responsibility of the two mendicant orders, and while the almost naive fervor of the early Franciscan days had not entirely disappeared, experience had pointed the way to somewhat more rational procedures. For example, Franciscan general chapters in 1263 and 1292 addressed themselves to the problem of recruiting. Evidently, therefore, the eastern missions were regarded as a responsibility of the entire order and not merely of the provinces immediately concerned. Toward the end of the century each order had laid the foundations for a mission organization: the Franciscan vicariate and the Dominican *Societas fratrum peregrinantium*.

Consideration had been given to the problem of missionary preparation. Later commentaries on the Franciscan rule add practical suggestions regarding training and conduct. No one was to be constrained to undertake a mission against his will nor was any friar to enter upon the task lightly or simply to escape discipline. Martyrdom was not to be sought for its own sake; indeed, under certain circumstances it was to be avoided. Significantly, too, in addition to Mos-

---

brief treatment is Mathias Braun, "Missionary Problems in the Thirteenth Century," *Catholic Historical Review,* XXV (1939–1940), 146–159. Particularly important are the many studies by Altaner; in addition to the references in his *Die Dominikanermissionen,* the following are the most important articles: "Sprachstudien und Sprachkenntnisse im Dienste der Mission des 13. und 14. Jahrhunderts," *ZMR,* XXI (1931), 113–135; "Raymundus Lullus und der Sprachkanon des Konzils von Vienne (1312)," *Historisches Jahrbuch der Görresgesellschaft,* LIII (1933), 190–219; "Die Durchführung des vienner Konzilbeschlusses über die Errichtung von Lehrstuhlen für orientalische Sprachen," *Zeitschrift für Kirchengeschichte,* LII (1933), 226–236; "Die fremdsprachliche Ausbildung der Dominikanermissionäre während des 13. und 14. Jahrhunderts," *ZMR,* XXIII (1933), 233–241; "Sprachkenntnisse und Dolmetscherwesen," pp. 83–126; "Zur Geschichte der antiislamischen Polemik während des 13. und 14. Jahrhunderts," *Historisches Jahrbuch,* LIV (1936), 227–233; "Zur Geschichte des Unterrichts und der Wissenschaft in der spätmittelalterlichen Mission," *ZMR,* XXVI (1936), 165–171; "Zur Kenntnis der Arabischen im 13. und 14. Jahrhundert," *Orientalia Christiana periodica,* II (1937), 427–452.

See also Martin Grabmann, O.P., "Die Missionsidee bei den Dominikanertheologen des 13. Jahrhunderts," *ZMR,* I (1911), 137–146; Fritz Heintke, *Humbert von Romans* (Historische Studien, no. 122; Berlin, 1933); Throop, *Criticism of the Crusade* (Amsterdam, 1940), chapter XXI in volume II of the present work; Cahen, *Die Anfänge,* pp. 11–17, 29–36, 206; de Sessevalle, *Histoire générale de l'ordre de Saint François,* II, 610–612; Monneret de Villard, *Lo Studio dell' Islam,* pp. 35–51; and Joshua Prawer, *Histoire du royaume latin de Jérusalem,* II (Paris, 1970), ch. III.

lems and infidels specifically mentioned in the rule, schismatics and heretics were also included. There is also greater emphasis on preaching and training for it. Indeed, in both orders the thirteenth-century missionary approach was the sermon. Doubtless intimate individual work followed, but the accent seems always to have been on public disputation.

Among Dominican writers Humbert of Romans and Ricoldo of Monte Croce stand out, and both urged a tolerant and flexible attitude toward eastern ecclesiastical usages. Ricoldo, of course, spoke from personal experience. In dealing with oriental Christians, he maintained, the missionary should distinguish the fundamental matters of faith from those of ecclesiastical discipline or liturgy. He should be conversant with the culture and speech of the country. A solid knowledge of scripture was indispensable, and in discussion the missionary should commence with the less complicated problems. Above all, he should avoid overbearing and impolite behavior and always strive to conduct himself humbly and respectfully. Like most men of his day Ricoldo felt that it was important to win over the leaders of a given community first. Others would then be more likely to follow.

A conspicuous weakness in thirteenth-century missionary preparation was the absence of adequate language preparation. Successive Dominican masters-general attacked this problem, and their efforts were seconded by the acts of general and provincial chapters. But these efforts seem to have been largely designed to serve the area of Spain and North Africa, and linguistic preparation directed specifically toward the east is less easily traced. Humbert of Romans in a circular letter of 1256 urged the study of Arabic, Hebrew, Greek and the language of the "barbarians," and directed that instruction be provided by convents in the east. Nothing, however, is known of the results. Information regarding similar action by the Franciscans is lacking, despite the fact that Roger Bacon, who spoke with William of Rubruck on his return from Asia, publicized the necessity for better language preparation.

The principal effort of Rome to promote language study came in 1311 at the Council of Vienne and was inspired by the Franciscan tertiary Raymond Lull. Lull, who met his death while preaching to Moors in North Africa (1315/6) spent most of his life promoting missions. He learned Arabic and in his voluminous writings repeatedly harped on the importance of training not only in that language but also in other oriental languages. He understood the diplomatic significance of the Mongol conquests and the importance of knowing their speech and also the languages spoken by the separated Christians within their domains. His efforts to enlist the support of the curia were rewarded when the Council of Vienne in Canon 11 decreed the establishment of schools for the teaching of Arabic, Hebrew, Syriac, and Greek at the curia and at the universities of Bologna, Paris, Oxford, and Salamanca.

This ambitious program was not, however, destined to be realized, and scattered references indicate language teachers only temporarily at Paris. It would seem, therefore, that the medieval academic community — not unlike its twentieth century counterpart — was interested in procuring translations of essential scientific and philosophical material, not in oriental languages as a means of communication. Presumably, therefore, those friars who mastered oriental speech did so in the mission field, and there is at least one record of formal training in the Orient. The report of the Dominican provincial of the Holy Land, friar Philip, in 1237, which was mentioned above, states that four friars had been sent to Armenia to study the language. More important, Philip indicates that he had directed that native languages be studied in each convent. No further reference to any such schools can be found and apparently only a few friars became adept.

Popes were also aware of the advisability of training a native clergy. This appears to have been the purpose of Innocent IV's attempt to establish an oriental study center at Paris. References from the chancery of Alexander IV and Honorius IV indicate its continued existence for a time, but give no further details.

In an age still convinced of the necessity for the crusade it is significant that some ecclesiastical writers were becoming more aware of the antithesis between war and peaceful persuasion. The Franciscan Adam Marsh, in a memorandum to the pope (about 1250), while not repudiating the crusade, urged most eloquently the promotion of propaganda by preaching. As we have seen, the Dominican William of Tripoli pleaded for a contact "without arms." Thirteenth-century theology would have condemned attempts to convert unbelievers by force, force being justified only to avert danger to the Christian faith. But there is no evidence of any tendency toward the modern concept of the "salus infidelium."

Despite all these shortcomings and the frustrations and disappointments it would be incorrect to characterize thirteenth-century missions as a failure. If nothing else, a great deal of experience had been gained which was of incalculable importance to any future planning. Above all, the vast size of the world and the relative insignificance of the Christian population as compared with the adherents of other faiths was beginning to dawn on the consciousness of western Christendom.

B. Missions in the Fourteenth Century

NEW ORGANIZATION

The pontificate of Clement V and the subsequent papal residence at Avignon did not materially change the diplomacy of the Holy See with regard to the Orient. Clement and his successors were as eager to promote new expeditions to recover the Holy Land as their predecessors and they were aware of the precarious position of the kingdom of Cilician Armenia. European politics precluded any major crusade effort, however, especially when the outbreak of the Hundred Years' War removed the possibility of French or English participation. Finally, whatever hopes remained were dashed by the ravages of the Black Death in the middle of the century.

The various Mongol khanates, particularly after the death of Kubilai Khan (1294), generally pursued diverse and often opposing diplomatic policies.[50] The Persian il-khanate, though its rulers were Moslem, was still concerned about the power of Egypt and continued for a time to seek accord with the papacy and the west. But when it became evident that no western military expedition was to be expected, the rulers, beginning with Abū Saʻīd (d. 1335), perforce turned to a *modus vivendi* with Egypt. The death of Abū Saʻīd was followed by the political disintegration of both Persia and formerly Selchükid Anatolia. Cilician Armenia continued to be a prey to Egyptian attacks and was finally overrun in 1375.

Fourteenth-century missions in the Kipchak khanate were, as in earlier years, dependent partly on the goodwill of the Mongol rulers and partly on the assistance of Italian merchants. A few Tatar princes and princesses were Christian, but the khans themselves remained cold to papal entreaties. For as Islam gained ground in the Kipchak khanate and in Central Asia Moslem influence at the court increased. Some, it is true, have held that Toktai (1291–1312) became a Christian, but this remains doubtful. Certainly he was outraged by the slave trade, which victimized Tatars among others; he expelled the Genoese from Sarai in 1307 and took over Kaffa in the following year.

---

50. For the politics of the Near East in this period see Mustafa M. Ziada, "The Mamluk Sultans, 1291–1517," volume III of the present work, chapter XIV, Sinor, *ibid.,* chapter XV, and Soranzo, *Il Papato,* chaps. XII, XIII.

Uzbeg (1312–1342), his successor, permitted the restoration of the Genoese colony in Kaffa. Though Moslem influence remained strong and relations with Egypt close, Uzbeg seems to have limited his opposition to Christians to forbidding them to ring their church bells. Moreover, he maintained a cordial correspondence with both John XXII and Benedict XII.

Under Janibeg (1342–1356) sporadic violence again endangered Christian settlements. But, following an accord with Venice which assured the independence of their colony at Tana from the control of Genoa, Janibeg too returned, doubtless for political and economic reasons, to a general policy of toleration.

The presence and support of Italian merchants remained essential to the friars. But they could also be a hindrance and embarrassment. The Dominican William Adam, among others, scathingly denounced the Genoese slave traffic, although he was careful to point out that many opposed it. All in all, no less than in the thirteenth century, missions were beset with persistent difficulties.

The missionary organizations which the mendicant orders launched in the later years of the thirteenth century were carried further in the early years of the fourteenth. The Franciscan vicariate of the north included, it will be recalled, two *custodiae,* Gazaria (the Crimea) and Sarai. An important document dating probably somewhat before 1318, the *De locis fratrum minorum et predicatorum in Tartaria,* lists the stations maintained by the friars around that date.[51] In addition to a large establishment at Sarai, the capital of the Kipchak khanate, there were two convents at Kaffa and fourteen other residences of which Soldaia, Cembalo (Balaclava), Tana (Azov), and Kherson were probably convents, the rest smaller stations. Most of these, it will be observed, were in the Black Sea region, an important area of Italian trade.

The Franciscan vicariate of the east by the early fourteenth century was divided into three *custodiae;* Trebizond, comprising all but the extreme western part of Anatolia; Tabriz, which included greater Armenia, Azerbaijan, southern Georgia, and Mesopotamia; and Constantinople, which included western Anatolia. Despite losses, by around 1318 the number of stations had grown to eleven. Not all were of equal importance, but at least Constantinople, Trebizond, and Tabriz supported convents.[52]

While the Franciscans were establishing the vicariate as a basis for

---

51. Golubovich (*BOF,* II, 72) dates the *De locis* around 1320. Loenertz (*Frères pérégrinants,* p. 3, and *AFP,* II [1932], 72–74) dates it sometime before 1318.

52. Golubovich (*BOF,* II, 265 ff.) designates practically all mission stations as convents. De Sessevalle, *Histoire générale de l'ordre de Saint François,* II, 527–528, follows Golubovich.

missionary organization, the Dominicans were developing their own characteristic missionary society. In the first years of the fourteenth century, as has been noted, the *peregrinantes,* or friars not connected with regular convents, were placed under the obedience of a vicar, Franco of Perugia. By the year 1312 the term *fratres peregrinantes inter gentes* was used.

Since this new congregation, the *Societas fratrum peregrinantium propter Christum* as it came to be called, had no geographical unity, it was not organized into a province. It was, in fact, a "society," a word whose meaning excluded territorial limitations. Although it did possess the right to bestow the habit if vocations were forthcoming, it was, like its missionary predecessor the province of the Holy Land, composed largely of religious from other provinces. Gradually the office of vicar-general developed from a simple delegation of authority by the master-general into a position of considerable importance resembling that of a provincial.[53] The society flourished in the first half of the fourteenth century, but suffered grievously as a consequence of the Black Death. In 1363 the convents of Pera, Kaffa, and Trebizond were incorporated into the province of Greece. The society, restored in 1375, was suppressed after the capture of Constantinople in 1453 and again restored in 1464.

The missionary jurisdiction of the *fratres peregrinantes* included parts of Greece, Egypt, and Nubia, and all Asia except Palestine, Syria, and Cilician Armenia. This vast area was divided into sections

---

The *De locis* uses the terms "monasteria immobilia" or "loca," as do most of the Franciscan documents. Cf., e.g., *BOF,* I, 301–355, II, 265 ff. It seems advisable to designate as convents only those stations where there is record of a "guardian" (*custos*) or where there is evidence of a considerable number of friars. For the vicariate of the east only Trebizond and Tabriz, the residences of the *custodes,* satisfy these requirements. Golubovich (*BOF,* II, 131, 568; III, 437) repeatedly refers to two convents at Tabriz, but since the second station, or at least its church, was served alternately by Franciscans and Dominicans, and since the latter claimed no convent at Tabriz, it seems unlikely that there were two "large convents" of Minorites there. Presumably most of the other stations were occupied by only a few friars, although comparable evidence is lacking. They were Sultaniyeh, Salamastrum (Salmas), Karachisia (Karakilissa) between Erzerum and Mt. Ararat, Erzerum, and Tiflis, all in the *custodia* of Tabriz. Porsico, Summiso (Samsun), and Carpi (Kerpe), on the southern shore of the Black Sea, were in the *custodia* of Trebizond. Loenertz, *Frères pérégrinants,* pp. 189–190, notes 46–50, places both Carpi and Porsico (identified with Pisanith) in the region of Erzerum and Tiflis, but identifies Karachisia with the Armenian monastery of St. Thaddeus of Karakilissa or Sisian, not with Karaköse in the province of Erzerum.

53. The standard work on the *Societas fratrum peregrinantium* is Loenertz, *La Société des Frères pérégrinants.* See also Altaner, "Zur Geschichte der Societas fratrum peregrinantium propter Christum," *ZMR,* XII (1922), 116–118. Loenertz has pointed out that the society included principally Italians, a number of French, a few English, and occasional Spanish, German, Hungarian, and Polish friars. Novices from mission territory included Latins from the Orient, Greeks, and Armenians.

(*contratae*) which may conveniently be called "missions." The principal missions were Greece (Romania), the Black Sea region (Gazaria or Tartaria aquilonaris), and the territories of greater Armenia, Georgia, and Persia (Tartaria orientalis). Within these areas were two kinds of establishment, the convent and the more modest residence.

In the Black Sea region the *De locis* lists two Dominican residences, Kaffa and Tana, and three in "Tartaria orientalis," Tabriz, Maragha, and Dekharegan. Apparently a convent was also founded at Trebizond not long after 1315. In addition, the report of the Franciscan bishop of Kaffa, Jerome Catalani, in 1323, and the presence of Dominican bishops later would seem to indicate the possibility of perhaps temporary Dominican stations in Vosporo (Kerch), Kherson, Soldaia, Cembalo, and Sebastopolis. Tana, it seems, was abandoned in 1343.[54]

The next step in the organization of missionary activity in the early fourteenth century was taken by the papal curia when the suggestion made by mid-thirteenth-century missionaries that missionary bishops be provided was finally carried out. The immediate cause of this important move was the receipt of letters from the Franciscan John of Monte Corvino, perhaps the most celebrated of all medieval missionaries. It will be recalled that among the letters which Nicholas IV entrusted to friar John in 1289 was one addressed to the great khan Kubilai.

Doubtless the pope, as had his predecessors, sought contact with the chief Mongol ruler for the usual diplomatic reasons. But this, the most distant of medieval missions, was the least involved with diplomacy. In fact, the domains of the great khan contained at that time considerable numbers of Christians. Most of the Turkic peoples who had inhabited the border lands of the Chinese kingdom and who had in large numbers moved west with the Mongol conquests were Nestorians, as were many non-Chinese inhabitants of large cities. In addition, a large body of Greek Orthodox Alans from the Black Sea region had been brought to China by the Mongol conquerors.

Before he left Tabriz in 1291, friar John had already had considerable experience as a missionary and ambassador. He was familiar with Armenian and Persian and, either then or soon thereafter, learned the speech, probably Uighur Turkish, common in Tartary. Accompanied by a Dominican friar, Nicholas of Pistoia, and Peter Lucalongo, an Italian merchant, he took the sea journey to India, where Nicholas died and where John remained a year preaching and baptizing

---

54. For the statement of Jerome Catalani see *BOF,* III, 48 ff.

some hundred converts. Sometime in 1294 John reached Khanbaliq and was courteously received by Kubilai's successor, Temür Öljeitu (Ch'êng Tsung).[55]

The full story of John of Monte Corvino's extraordinary mission lies beyond the scope of this chapter. What does concern us is the impact on papal mission policy. In 1305 and 1306 John was able to dispatch two letters to the west. The first, dated January 8, 1305, was entrusted to Venetian merchants who handed it on, along with a tablet from the great khan, to a Dominican missionary. He, in turn, gave it to some Dominican and Franciscan friars farther west and added the interesting information that a number of Dominicans, acquainted with the Mongol speech, had set out for China, but were forced to turn back after reaching the Crimea. The second letter, dated February 13, 1306, was brought to the curia, then at Poitiers, in the early summer of 1307 by Thomas of Tolentino, a Franciscan missionary in Tartary. It was addressed, moreover, to the vicars-general and friars of both mendicant orders then in Persia. Apparently friar John, who had originally set out with a Dominican friar, hoped for a collaboration of the two orders in the Asia mission. Together, the letters constitute one of the most remarkable of missionary reports and it is not difficult to understand why they made such a profound impression on the curia and the pope.[56]

Clement V, despite poor health and persistent difficulties with king Philip IV, did not neglect the east. Naturally overjoyed by friar John's communications, he issued the bull of July 23, 1307, in which the intrepid missionary was named archbishop and primate of the church in Tartary and patriarch of the Orient with jurisdiction from the Pacific to the borders of eastern Europe.[57] Suffragan bishops chosen by the minister-general of the Franciscans were consecrated by the pope and instructed to consecrate John. These suffragans, it should be added, were not assigned sees by the pope; clearly the new metropolitan was to exercise his own judgement in this matter. The suffragans also car-

---

55. The sources for the China mission are listed above in the bibliographical note. See also van den Wyngaert, *Jean de Mont Corvin, O.F.M., premier évêque de Khanbaliq (1247–1328)* (Lille, 1924). Two studies which summarize present knowledge are Richard, "Essor et déclin de l'église catholique de Chine au XIVe siècle," *Bulletin de la Société des missions étrangères de Paris,* ser. 2, no. 134 (1960), 285–295, and Troll, "Die Chinamission im Mittelalter," with full bibliography of earlier works. See also the chapter by Fortunato Margiotti, "China 13–14 Jahrhundert," in *Historia missionum Fratrum Minorum: Asia-centro-orientalis* (Secretarius missionum, O.F.M.; I, 1967).

56. For the letters of John of Monte Corvino see Golubovich, *op. cit.,* III, 87–93. There is an English translation in Dawson, *Mission to Asia,* pp. 224–231. Loenertz, *Frères pérégrinants,* pp. 183–184, emphasizes the role of the Dominicans.

57. *BOF,* III, 93–95.

ried letters to the great khan announcing Monte Corvino's promotion and bespeaking favors for Christians and missionaries.

Of the seven bishops named only three survived the dangers and hardships of the long journey. With a number of other friars they arrived in Khanbaliq, probably sometime in 1308, and there consecrated John archbishop. Two of them, Andrew of Perugia and Peregrine of Castello, were retained at the capital while other friars were sent to found new missions elsewhere. Later reports would indicate that these were at Yangiu (Yangchow), Quinsai (Hangchow), and possibly Nanking. Bishop Gerard Albuini took up residence at Zaitun (Chüanchow, Tsinkiang) where a wealthy Armenian woman built what became the cathedral church. Thus Zaitun, one of the great ports of the Far East, became the second see of China. In 1311 Clement V named three more suffragans for the China mission, doubtless to replace those who had died, but only one, Peter of Florence, actually completed the journey.

A further step in the formation of an oriental hierarchy was taken by John XXII in April 1318 when he withdrew a large section from the original Franciscan province of Khanbaliq and created for the Dominicans a second Asiatic province with its archiepiscopal seat at Sultaniyeh (Kangurlan) in Persia, then the residence of the il-khan Abū-Saʿīd. The pope was probably influenced by the Dominican William Adam, a celebrated and much-traveled missionary, who had been in Persia in the years preceding and who was then at Avignon, where he composed his crusade treatise, *De modo Saracenis extirpandi.*[58]

Since Franciscans not unnaturally protested the proposed infringement on their original jurisdiction, the boundaries between the two were the result of an agreement between the two orders. It is likely that the Franciscan Jerome Catalani, a distinguished missionary, one of the suffragans named in 1311, and in February 1318 named bishop of Kaffa, was active in the negotiations. At any rate, he was present at Avignon in 1318.

Thus it seems clear that the pope's move was, at least in part, a consequence of rivalries between the two orders and that he was seeking to rectify the imbalance in oriental missions by bringing the Dominicans more prominently into the picture. Most rivalries resulted

58. *Ibid.,* III, 197–207; Soranzo, *Il Papato,* pp. 514–521; Loenertz, *Frères pérégrinants,* pp. 137–140. A second bull of May 1 assigned suffragans, and a third of August 8 conferred the pallium on Franco of Perugia. On William Adam see Charles Kohler in *RHC, Arm.,* II, introduction; "Documents relatifs à Guillaume Adam, archevêque de Sultanieh, puis d'Antivari, et son entourage, 1318–46," *ROL,* X, (1903–1904), 38–48; and Henri A. Omont, "Guillaume Adam, missionnaire," *Histoire littéraire de la France,* XXV (1921), 277–283.

from a rather natural desire of one order to maintain exclusive operations in a given area. But in the early and middle years of the fourteenth century they were accentuated by the fact that among the
Franciscan missionaries were a number of adherents of a controver-
sial doctrine concerning the poverty of Jesus and his apostles which
John XXII condemned in 1323.

It is difficult to determine precisely the dividing line between the
two provinces. It may have run along the northern and eastern shores
of the Black Sea to a point not far from the Crimea, or have passed
south of the coast to Mount Ararat. Thence it extended east to the
Caspian coast and followed the line of demarcation between the Kipchak khanate and the Mongol domains east of the Caspian. Owing
to the difficulty of determining the exact boundaries of the central
Asiatic kingdoms of "Doha and Chaydo" mentioned in the bull, the
eastern limits of the province of Sultaniyeh are not clear. But apparently the northern jurisdiction consigned to the Franciscans included
the Kipchak khanate, the eastern part of the Central Asiatic khanate
of Chagatai, and the eastern empire of the great khan. The Dominican jurisdiction comprised Anatolia, the Persian khanate, including
Tiflis in Georgia, and Transoxiana with the diocese of Samarkand,
India, and "Ethiopia."[59]

The curia was also at some pains to regularize the relations between
the missionary bishops of the new dioceses and the superiors of their
respective orders. The friars, or their native affiliates, were normally
the clergy of the missionary dioceses, and each order had stations
in the province of the other. Accordingly, while it was provided that
the province of Khanbaliq should in general be the responsibility of
the Franciscans and Sultaniyeh that of the Dominicans, it was also
stipulated that the archbishops and their successors should obey their

59. According to Soranzo, *Il Papato*, p. 515, note 1, the "Mons Barrius" mentioned in the
bull was probably somewhere in the western chain of the Caucasus near the Black Sea and
was not Mt. Ararat, as Golubovich and others have suggested. This would explain the inclusion
of Sebastopolis on the eastern shore of the Black Sea in the province of Sultaniyeh, as well
as all (not part) of Anatolia. The problem of the northeastern boundary of the province of
Sultaniyeh is complicated by the fact that the kingdoms of "Chaydo and Doha" have been
identified (e.g., by William Adam) as equivalent to the *medium imperium*. Evidently, however,
eastern Turkestan and the diocese of Almalyk were included in the province of Khanbaliq.
Soranzo also maintains, against Golubovich, that the Ethiopia mentioned in the bull signified
the kingdom in Africa, not lower India.

Loenertz, *Frères pérégrinants*, pp. 137–140, follows Golubovich in placing the southern boundary of the Khanbaliq province south of the Black Sea shore and so drawn as to exclude Smyrna,
Sivas, and Sebastopolis from the province of Sultaniyeh. It is worth noting that the see of
Smyrna, then in Turkish hands, was transferred to Tiflis (Dominican) in 1329. It was revived
after 1358 for the Franciscans. Cf. *BOF,* V, 70 ff.; de Sessevalle, *Histoire générale de l'ordre
de Saint François,* II, 535–555; Troll, "Die Chinamission," pp. 34–36.

respective masters-general (or their vicars) as vicars of the Holy See in missionary areas; the power of removal, however, was specifically excluded. Further, suffragans were to be subject to their respective provincials saving the authority of the Holy See in all things. On the death of a provincial the Dominican (or Franciscan) prior was to administer the archdiocese, and the friars of the archiepiscopal see were to convoke the suffragans as electors.

Thus, although Franciscan suffragans who might be chosen in Dominican territory were to remain and be subject to the Dominican archbishop and vice versa, the masters-general of the two orders were given considerable authority. As in the case of Khanbaliq in 1307, the archbishop of Sultaniyeh might designate sees and provide them with incumbents.

The dioceses of the Orient bore only a slight resemblance to those of Europe. Bishops had no regular revenues from their sees and no cathedrals. Their pastorate consisted of the small commercial communities of Latin Christians, the resident friars, and converts, and strict adherence to the rule of residence was neither practicable nor desirable. Jurisdictional lines were not always observed, and as conditions changed new sees were instituted and old ones transferred or suppressed. In certain areas where considerable numbers of oriental Christians were brought into contact with the western church bishops were a necessity. It was the policy of the Holy See to reordain conditionally all formerly dissident clerics about whose ordinations there was any doubt.

In addition to providing missionary bishops the curia demonstrated its solicitude for the missions in other ways. Letters were sent frequently to Latin and uniate clergy and to oriental rulers, for the Avignon papacy attempted, insofar as it was possible, to impose on eastern clergies the same authority it was so efficiently implementing in the west. Papal correspondence reveals repeated efforts to enforce the Roman primacy of jurisdiction. Eastern liturgies were, it is true, not forbidden, but a Latinizing tendency persisted, for the papacy, fearful that doctrinal error might be associated with divergence of rite, held to the ideal of uniformity in all matters. Thus the impression was conveyed that oriental liturgies were tolerated only by papal concession. Such policies inevitably met resistance from eastern churches accustomed to a centuries-old tradition of autonomy, and could scarcely have reassured prospective converts.[60]

All these procedures were especially evident during the pontificate

---

60. On the mission policies of the Avignon popes see Wilhelm de Vries, S.J., "Die Päpste

of John XXII (1316–1334). His mission bulls followed a form similar to those already described. Certain additional clauses reflect the controversy over poverty within the Franciscan order, others, particularly the reservation to Rome of absolution from the sin of shipping contraband to Moslems, his hopes, however vain, for the crusade. In the provision of prospective missionaries John urged the selection of well-trained experienced men, and he was concerned over their material support. In one or two instances he provided a subvention. Letters were written to oriental rulers and prelates bespeaking protection for missionaries, and under his auspices several departures took place. Certain letters, such as instructions given Dominican missionaries in 1333 concerning conditional rebaptism and reordination in cases of doubt, reveal that solicitude for uniformity so characteristic of the Avignon popes.[61]

John XXII stands out as a pope concerned over missions, but his predecessors had pointed the way and his successors continued his policies. Furthermore, what was done was accomplished in the face of mounting obstacles at home. The difficulties which had become apparent during the pontificate of John XXII grew worse. The war between France and England became a reality. The situation in the papal states and Italy remained unstable. The Black Death was a disaster which affected everybody, and, finally, the papal schism which began in 1378 enormously complicated all ecclesiastical activities.

MISSIONS IN THE PROVINCE OF KHANBALIQ

The Franciscan China mission continued well past the middle of the century and was in some respects the most flourishing of the medieval missions, perhaps embracing as many as 30,000 souls. Sometime around 1322 Odoric Mattiuzzi of Pordenone, one of the best-known Franciscan travelers, visited China after extensive journeys in Asia. He brought the remains of four Minorites martyred at Thana

---

von Avignon und der christliche Osten," *Orientalia Christiana periodica*, XXX (1964), 85–128. See also Jules Gay, *Le Pape Clément VI et les affaires d'Orient (1342–52)* (Paris, 1904); Francesco Giunta, "Sulla Politica orientale di Clemente VI," *Studi di storia in onore de Roberto Cessi* (Rome, 1958), pp. 149–162; and "Sulla Politica orientale di Innocenzo VI," *Miscellanea in onore de Roberto Cessi* (Rome, 1958), I, 305–320.

61. For typical bulls of John XXII see *BOP*, II, 136–137, 153–155, 182–186; *BOF*, III, 214–218 (1321), 350–359 (1329), 404 ff. The instructions regarding conditional rebaptizing and reordaining were repeated by Urban V and Gregory XI; see de Vries, "Die Päpste von Avignon," p. 112; Soranzo, *Il Papato*, pp. 521–523.

in India to Zaitun where he deposited them in one of the two Franciscan residences he found there. Odoric also described the mission at Quinsai and added to our knowledge of the mission in the Mongol capital.[62]

There are, however, a number of indications that after John of Monte Corvino's death (about 1328) regular communication between the China mission and the Holy See was not successfully maintained. There was, for example, considerable delay in naming John's successor. Not until 1333 was Nicholas of Botras, professor of theology at Paris, designated, and he appears not to have reached his post. In 1336 khan Toghan Temür sent an embassy, guided by a Genoese merchant, Andalo of Savignone, to Benedict XII urging more regular contacts and conveying a significant request from five Alan chieftains. These men asked for the pope's blessing and, recalling the ministrations of John of Monte Corvino, complained that they had been long without a shepherd. Apparently it was not known at Avignon that bishops Peter and Andrew, the last of the suffragans, had died. John de' Marignoli, a Franciscan who set out in 1339 as papal nuncio accompanied by some fifty friars, made an impressive appearance before the khan (1342), and remained four years, was sent back with a similar request. The khan asked that he or some higher representative of the pope, preferably a cardinal and a bishop, should return as soon as possible. Marignoli's account of his visit pictured an otherwise flourishing Christian community.[63]

Although Marignoli's report prompted pope Innocent VI to urge renewed efforts on the Franciscans, there appears to have been little or no response. And, so far as is known, no episcopal nominees reached their posts in China. Meanwhile the Black Death had taken its toll of active and prospective missionaries, and the spread of Islam throughout the Near East and Central Asia added to the difficulties of communication. And when in 1368 the tolerant Mongol Yüan dynasty was replaced by the Mings the mission experienced added difficulties. No doubt, too, the popes' return to Rome from Avignon and the subsequent schism hampered papal initiative. It would seem, therefore, that the final decline can be attributed largely to the breakdown of regular contact combined with the failure of what had apparently

62. *BOF,* III, 375–393; de Sessevalle, *Histoire générale de l'ordre de Saint François,* II, 575–578.

63. *BOF,* IV, 257–309. On his return John de' Marignoli was designated bishop of Bisignano in Calabria (May 12, 1354) and consecrated later the same year. See Moule, *Christians in China,* pp. 196, 254; Robert S. Lopez, "European Merchants in the Medieval Indies," *Journal of Economic History,* III (1943), 181, and *idem,* "Nuovi luci sugli italiani in estremo Oriente prima di Colombo," *Studi Colombiani,* III (1951), 387, 397–398.

been the pope's plan for a relatively autonomous province capable of existing on its own resources.[64]

John de' Marignoli's name is also associated with a kind of by-product of the China mission which lasted for a short time in the Central Asiatic khanate of Chagatai. As we have seen, Nicholas of Botras, named in 1333 to succeed John of Monte Corvino, apparently never reached Khanbaliq, but he did find a cordial reception at Almalyk in 1334. Some of the twenty-six friars who had accompanied him remained there with Richard of Burgundy as bishop. Two Christian courtiers of khan Buzan, probably Alans, donated a place in the city and built a church for one of the friars. Friar Francis of Alessandria, who had cured the khan of illness, became the tutor of his son, whom he later baptized. During a brief period of Moslem ascendancy the bishop, several friars, two lay brothers, a tertiary who acted as interpreter, and a Genoese merchant suffered martyrdom (1340). Among them was friar Paschal of Vittoria, a remarkable missionary who had come alone to Almalyk and had foreseen the danger consequent on the accession in 1338 of a new khan, Yosün Temür.

When John de' Marignoli stopped at Almalyk in the following year on the way to China, he was able to preach freely. In fact, he built a new church and baptized a number of converts. These conditions were, however, destined to be of short duration. The latest report from the region dates from 1362 when James of Florence, named bishop of Zaitun, was put to death by Saracens. Two other friars were imprisoned and starved by Nestorians. These events presumably took place in Almalyk.[65]

What were the actual accomplishments of the Franciscan mission

---

64. The problem of a hierarchy is discussed by Richard, "Essor et déclin de l'église catholique de Chine au XIVe siècle." There were requests for the appointment of an archbishop, notably from the Alans. Nicholas of Botras, professor of theology at Paris, was designated in 1333 and apparently reached Almalyk in Central Asia. News of this had reached the curia by 1338, and one of the letters entrusted to John de' Marignoli was addressed to Nicholas as archbishop. Although there is no evidence that Nicholas reached Khanbaliq, the curia evidently so assumed. Marignoli, as indicated, returned with another request for an archbishop. Apparently the news of the fall of the Mongol dynasty had not reached Avignon by 1370, for in that year Urban V sent out friar William of Prato as archbishop (*BOF,* V, 149–154). De Sessevalle, *Histoire générale,* II, 645, maintains that Nicholas reached Khanbaliq and lived until 1369. Loenertz, *AFP,* II (1932), 50, notes that Dominicans were recommended to the emperor in 1333 along with archbishop Nicholas; the curia may have supposed that there were Dominicans in China. A letter of king John I of Aragon, dated 1391, mentions a Franciscan who had just returned from a mission of many years at the court of "Prester John" (*BOF,* V, 281). This might indicate that some Franciscans were still in the Far East, possibly in Tenduk. Cf. also Troll, "Die Chinamission," pp. 145–150.

65. *BOF,* IV, 248, 273, 297, 310; V, 92; V. Rondelez, "Un Évêché en Asie centrale au XIVe siècle," *Neue Zietschrift fur Missionswissenschaft,* VI (1951), 1–17.

to the Far East? John of Monte Corvino mentions figures of around six thousand converts. The Alans were said to number fifteen thousand. Perhaps the total number reached thirty thousand. Apparently the friars were free to preach to anyone. Peregrine even mentions preaching in Moslem mosques and John de' Marignoli speaks of disputations with Jews and adherents of other faiths. There remains the difficult question whether many of the converts were Chinese. None of the missionaries mentions learning Chinese. In fact, Monte Corvino tells how he "had six pictures made of the Old and New Testaments for the instruction of the ignorant, and they have inscriptions in Latin, Turkish, and Persian." Of course, the friars may have used interpreters, and a Latin gravestone recently discovered at Yangchow shows unmistakable evidence of having been done by a Chinese artist. On the other hand the presence of numerous non-Chinese in the cities is well known. The Nestorian communities, for example, were probably largely non-Chinese. Moreover, after 1318 Monte Corvino devoted his labors to a church of the Armenian rite.

John did, however, report that he "had an adequate knowledge of the Tatar language and script," and in a temporarily successful mission established in the domains of the Ongut prince George of Tenduk along the frontier of the Chinese empire, he tells how he "had translated into that language and script the whole of the New Testament and the Psalter," and says that while the prince lived, "mass was celebrated . . . according to the Latin rite in their own script and language, both the words of the canon and the preface."[66]

On the whole, therefore, it would seem correct to conclude that Chinese converts were few in number and that the medieval Chinese mission, oriental though it certainly was, ministered principally to foreigners living among the Chinese.

Meanwhile the Franciscans were continuing their work in the vicariate of the north, which lay largely within the domains of the khanate of the Kipchak Golden Horde. The episcopal sees of this area had formally been under the jurisdiction of the metropolitan of Khanbaliq, but the distances involved, combined with the fact that after

---

66. See especially Richard, "Essor et déclin," and Troll, "Die Chinamission," pp. 68–69. See also the discussion by Pasquale M. d'Elia in *Fonti Ricciane,* I, *Storia dell' introduzione del Cristianismo in Cina* (Rome, 1942), pp. lxxv ff. D'Elia accepts the view of Moule, *Christians in China,* p. 150, note 7, and "The Primitive Failure of Christianity in China,"*International Review of Missions,* XX (1931), 459, that the bulk of the converts were non-Chinese. Van den Wyngaert, *Sinica franciscana,* I, ciii ff., contends, however, that the non-Nestorian converts were Chinese. The quotations are from the translation of John's letters in Dawson, *Mission to Asia,* pp. 227–228.

John of Monte Corvino's death no replacement seems to have reached the Mongol capital, meant that any effective direction was impossible.

The most important see of the Black Sea region was Kaffa, which, it will be recalled, had been established in February of 1318 by John XXII with the Franciscan Jerome Catalani named as the first incumbent. Since Kaffa was a center of Dominican as well as of Franciscan missions, there were occasional Dominican bishops. The same was true of other sees—Sebastopolis, Soldaia (Sudak), Tana (Azov), Cembalo (Balaclava), Surgat (Solgat), and a short-lived archdiocese of Vosporo (Kerch), with a suffragan see at Kherson.

Sarai, the Mongol capital and the seat of a bishop from around 1319, was raised to an archdiocese sometime after the middle of the century, and a papal document of 1363 mentions an archdiocese of Matrega with suffragan sees of Mappa (Anapa), Syba, and Lucuk. Apparently these archdioceses were also ephemeral and presumably reflect the practical acceptance of the nonexistence of any effective jurisdiction from Khanbaliq. They are also, however, evidence of Franciscan mission expansion north and east of the Black Sea.[67]

The continued expansion of Franciscan missions is evident in other ways. Among the letters sent back to the authorities in the west two are especially significant: one addressed by friar Iohanca, a Hungarian, and his associates to Michael of Cesena, the Franciscan minister-general, and dated 1320 at Bashkir (Bascardia) in "greater Hungary," and the second sent from the friars at Kaffa to the general chapter of the order at Toulouse in 1323.[68] Both letters report considerable success in conversions and in ministering to the many Christian captives among the Tatars despite constant harassment by Moslems. In fact, they estimate that a large proportion (one-third to one-half) of the population was Christian. Each letter appeals urgently for more friars to assist in this important work and, since those who do not know the language give instruction through interpreters, it is suggested that English, German, or Hungarian friars be sent because they seem to learn the language of the area more easily than others.

Friar Iohanca reported that he had been at Bashkir for six years,

67. For the episcopal sees see *BOF,* III, 205; IV, 310; V, 40-47, 92-94, 109-110, 233. Aksarai (Zarew, New Sarai) was founded sometime around 1331 (*ibid.,* II, 541); according to Golubovich, this became the seat of the bishop, but the evidence does not seem clear (*ibid.,* II, 564; III, 205, 223-224; IV, 233, 252; V, 69, 92-94). In 1396 Surgat was raised to an archdiocese (*ibid.,* V, 314).

68. Michael Bihl, O.F.M. and A. C. Moule, eds., "Tria nova documenta de missionibus Fratrum Minorum Tartariae Aquilonaris annorum 1314-22," *AFP,* XVII (1924), 55-71; "De duabus epistolis Fratrum Minorum Tartariae Aquilonaris an. 1323," *ibid.,* XVI (1923), 89-112; Simonut, *Il Metodo,* pp. 120 ff., *passim.*

but he was constantly on the move following the camps of the Mongol armies. Friars in the convents in the towns could not leave to assist him without neglecting their own charges. Saracens, about whose doctrines he seems singularly well informed, strove to subvert the converts. When he tried to demonstrate the falsity of their beliefs "in every way possible," they threw him into prison and tortured him. Only their fear of the Mongol authorities prevented his death. While he was in Bashkir Iohanca received a request from Sibur (Siberia) for four Latin priests. A Ruthenian "schismatic," he tells us, had made many converts. Once again, the scarcity of missionaries available prevented any response to the request.

The friars at Kaffa described how they were able to redeem a number of captives with the alms given them and how they had trained some of the young boys to be friars. Since they were fluent in the native speech they could teach others and made excellent missionaries. Although the Kaffa letter refers to pope John XXII's having received joyfully some news of their work, there seems to have been no effective response from the west at that time. Perhaps the contentions within the Franciscan order were partly responsible for the failure, for it was in the same year 1323 that John XXII condemned the teachings of the Franciscan extremists.

Missions in the Kipchak khanate did, however, continue though with increasing difficulty after the death of Uzbeg (1342). Friar Elias of Hungary seems to have been *persona grata* at Uzbeg's court and useful as an envoy both to and from the curia. A letter of friar Paschal of Vittoria (1338) reports that Sarai had remained a center for language study, for he stopped there to study the *lingua Cumanica et lettera Vingurica*. Thence he traveled to Urgench, a remote Franciscan station south of the Aral Sea, and finally on to the Franciscan residence at Almalyk, where, as we have seen, he was martyred in the Moslem reaction of 1340. En route he had preached the Christian faith to Saracens and was severely maltreated as a consequence.[69]

The Black Death took its toll of actual and prospective missionaries, but in later years the Minorites continued to push eastward and northward. Although the lists of stations for the years up to 1390 show some losses near the Black Sea, there were gains farther afield. Uzbeg permitted an establishment in New Sarai (Aksarai), the new capital on the Akhtuba some miles south of the old. Apparently even after the Black Death reinforcements kept coming from Europe, though probably not in sufficient numbers. In 1370 Urban V sent a Fran-

---

69. On Paschal of Vittoria see *BOF*, III, 18; IV, 244 ff.

ciscan bishop and twenty-five friars to "Georgia and other parts."
More friars were commissioned the following year after a visit to Avignon by Francis of Podio (Le Puy), the vicar of the north, and, along
with Dominicans, again in 1375.

Some time before 1389 a diocese was established at Kumukh in the
Caspian region, and in 1392 two Franciscans whom the northern vicar
sent to Avignon for recruiting purposes spoke of the urgent need for
more missionaries in this remote area. With what seems some exaggeration, readily understandable under the circumstances, they maintained that "more than ten thousand converts there . . . and many
multitudes elsewhere" stood in dire need of priests to prevent them
from falling back into schism or embracing Islam. A letter of Boniface
IX which mentions the mission stations along or near the Caspian
coast is additionally significant because it mentions a Franciscan *Societas peregrinantium*. This is one of the earliest references to the Franciscan counterpart of the Dominican *fratres peregrinantes*.[70]

Dominican missions in the Black Sea region were, as has been pointed
out, less extensive, and with the exception of Kaffa little is known
about them. Franco of Perugia could preach in the Tatar language
and translate documents. It will be recalled that the Dominican missionaries bound for China in 1308, but forced to remain in the Crimea, apparently knew the language. There are other such references,
and in 1333 the Dominican general chapter at Dijon directed that a
language school be set up in Kaffa.

Meanwhile Armenian communities in the Crimea and elsewhere
were proving to be an important factor in the missions. Around 1335
a young Armenian named Nicholas was converted at Kaffa, journeyed to Florence, and returned as a Dominican missionary. The Armenian Dominican Thaddeus, who translated part of the Dominican breviary into Armenian, was Latin bishop of Kaffa from 1334 to about
1357. Especially after the middle of the fourteenth century, when western missions suffered irreparable losses as a consequence of the Black
Death, Armenian communities remained important points of contact
with western Christianity.

Another community with which the preaching friars seem to have
made fruitful contacts was the Alan element in the city of Vosporo
(Kerch). They were active there around 1333 when John XXII designated the city a metropolitan see.[71]

---

70. For the missions of the later years of the century see *BOF,* V, 144 ff., 149 ff., 159–160,
213, 301, 314, 320, 330–333, and II, 266, 272. For the Franciscan *Societas fratrum peregrinantium* see Autbert Groeteken, "Eine mittelalterliche Missionsgesellschaft," *ZMR,* II (1912), 1–13.
71. Loenertz, *Frères pérégrinants,* pp. 89–134.

Evidence concerning the actual accomplishments of the missionaries is, as is so often the case, not clear. Papal letters and missionary reports indicating "numerous" or "thousands" of converts from "schismatics and unbelievers" reveal progress but little specific information. Presumably, separated Christians constituted the bulk of the conversions, though one or two reports specify Mongol magnates and their families. Presumably too, the peak of missionary achievement was reached by the mid-fourteenth century before the ravages of the plague. Certainly by the end of the century on the eve of the invasions of Timur (Tamerlane), the mission situation had deteriorated. By the early years of the fifteenth century the Franciscan vicariate of the north had shrunk to the *custodia* of the Crimea, then called the vicariate of the Crimea. Dominican missions in the Black Sea area were by that time largely the responsibility of the Armenian *fratres unitores,* an organization which had become an affiliate of the Dominican order.

MISSIONS IN THE PROVINCE OF SULTANIYEH

When John XXII created the province of Sultaniyeh for the preaching friars, he provided that six suffragan sees should be designated and their incumbents installed by the new metropolitan. Since both pastoral and missionary work was the responsibility of the *fratres peregrinantes,* it was appropriate that the first archbishop of Sultaniyeh was Franco of Perugia, vicar-general and one of the founders of the Dominican missionary organization. A month after the original bull six suffragans were named and duly established by Franco at Smyrna, Sivas, Sebastopolis, Tabriz, Dehkharegan, and Maragha.[72]

The first three of these sees were situated at some distance north and west of the centers of Dominican activity in Azerbaijan, and they proved to be of short duration. Smyrna was taken by the Turks and no successor was named for William Adam when he was transferred to Sultaniyeh as Franco's successor in 1322. When the city was recovered in 1344 there began a new series of bishops, none of whom was a Dominican. Meanwhile in 1329 the pope had transferred the Dominican see to Tiflis; its designation as an episcopal see indicates at least the possibility of renewed mission activity in Georgia. The original Dominican residence there, abandoned toward the end of

---

72. *Ibid.,* pp. 137–141; Loenertz notes that three sees were outside the frontiers of the province. But see above, note 59, for a discussion of the boundaries between the two Asiatic provinces.

the thirteenth century, had been restored by the *peregrinantes,* but little else is known.[73]

Apparently Sivas too had been abandoned toward the end of the thirteenth century. But since a suffragan, Bernard of Piacenza, was named in 1318 it can be assumed that the friars had returned. Bernard is, however, the only incumbent who is known to have taken up residence. It is clear, therefore, that soon after the bull of 1318 the problem of staffing the missionary dioceses had become extremely difficult. In fact, it was necessary in 1329 to appoint new bishops for Sultaniyeh, Tabriz, and Dehkharegan.

Sebastopolis, in ancient Colchis, on the eastern shore of the Black Sea, was in a part of Georgia not then under Mongol domination. The inhabitants were largely Abkhasians, related to the Circassians, who like the Georgians followed the Byzantine rite. The ruler at the time was favorably disposed to missionaries. The city was, however, a prominent slave mart, and in 1330 the second bishop, Peter Geraldi, sent to the bishops of England a remarkable letter in which he described his ineffectual efforts to curtail the shameful traffic as well as many other difficulties which confronted a missionary bishop living among separated Christians, not all of whom were well disposed, and hostile Moslems. Doubtless it was such frustrations which prompted him to plead for military aid from the west. There are no records of any successors.

There was, however, a growing awareness that the principal Dominican sphere of activity was to be in greater Armenia. Whether this area ever constituted an official *contrata* of the *peregrinantes* is doubtful. Nevertheless, it is here that the Dominicans achieved their greatest successes, and it is significant that some time between 1333 and 1356 Nadjivan (Nakhchevan) was added as a suffragan see of Sultaniyeh.[74]

In this same Armenian region the Franciscans had already labored with considerable success. Since this proved to be one of the rare instances where a natural rivalry between the two orders degenerated into serious tension, it will be wise to describe the Franciscan activities first.

Traditionally, the "dispersed" churches of greater Armenia were dependent on the metropolitan see of Sis in the kingdom of Cilician Armenia, long in close political and religious association with the west,

---

73. *Ibid.,* pp. 172–175.

74. *Ibid.,* pp. 135–172, for a discussion of all the suffragan sees of Sultaniyeh. Loenertz doubts that Persia can with any certainty be classified as a *contrata* under a vicar. A French translation of Peter Geraldus's letter is given *ibid.,* pp. 133–134.

and where formal union had been ratified by synods at Sis (1307) and Adana (1316). Union with the western church was, however, never popular with the bulk of the clergy and faithful, especially in the areas of greater Armenia not under the political dominion of the Cilician kingdom. Accordingly, the Holy See, and notably John XXII, gave the entire Armenian problem considerable attention. This meant diplomatic communications with rulers and attempts to launch a crusade as well as frequent letters to bishops in both the Cilician kingdom and the wider area to the north and west.

This region lay within the Franciscan *custodia* of Tabriz, where fourteenth-century lists mention two establishments in the city of Tabriz, one shared with the Dominicans, and stations at Sultaniyeh, Salmas, and Erzerum. The most successful mission was maintained at the monastery of St. Thaddeus at Karakalissa near Maku. Around 1321 bishop Zacharias, who made his headquarters at St. Thaddeus, accepted union with the Holy See and speedily became a bulwark of the native Armeno-Catholic community and protector of both mendicant orders.[75]

Prominent among a group of Franciscans who left Europe for the east and greater Armenia was William Saurati, a man of considerable learning. Saurati finally established himself at the monastery of St. Thaddeus, where he mastered Armenian and translated books from Latin into the native tongue. He then proceeded to give public lectures on holy scripture in Armenian, and his discourses were attended by native monks as well as by archbishop Zacharias. Another Minorite associated with St. Thaddeus was friar Ponzio, who also mastered the Armenian tongue and while at Avignon in 1344 completed an Armenian version of the Roman missal. In 1345, after Clement VI had named him titular archbishop of Seleucia in Cilicia, he returned to his charges in Persia.[76]

During these years Dominican missions had also been growing in the same area. In 1323 William Adam, whom John XXII had named to succeed Franco of Perugia, was especially urged to promote missions among the Armenians of Persia. The pope also wrote to the catholicus Constantine IV, in union with Rome, informing him of this mission and asking for his assistance. William was metropolitan of Sultaniyeh only two years, and we know nothing of his missionary accomplishments there. But some information comes from the re-

75. *BOF,* III, 215–218, 370–373. On John XXII's letters see also above, note 61, and Tournebize, *Histoire politique et religieuse de l'Arménie,* pp. 317 ff.

76. *BOF,* III, 407–413; IV, 381–388; de Sessevalle, *Histoire générale de l'ordre de Saint François,* II, 556 ff.

ports of Jordan Catalani of Sévérac, a Dominican who had acquired considerable experience and a thorough command of the native tongue in Persia. In 1328 he returned to Europe after several years in India. Jordan reported that the church of Sultaniyeh had a congregation of some five hundred and that a thousand converts had been made from dissident Christians at both Tabriz and Maragha.[77]

It can readily be understood that the appearance of Dominicans in a region where Franciscans had already been successful might occasion some resentment. In Tabriz, for example, where a single church was served, probably in alternate weeks, by both Franciscans and Dominicans, the Dominican bishop had only limited rights over what would normally have been his own church. In 1332 the Franciscans refused to recognize the bishop, William of Cigiis, and went so far as to celebrate a second mass on Holy Thursday, a procedure contrary to the liturgical usage of that period.[78]

As the Dominicans apparently had considerable success in promoting the doctrines of Thomas Aquinas, recently canonized (1323), among certain communities of Armenian clergy, this, too, created tension, and Saurati, among other Franciscans, expressed opposition to the intrusion of such teachings.

Evidently, therefore, the situation had passed beyond the stage of natural rivalry. The root of the matter seems to lie in the rift within the Franciscan order following John XXII's condemnation in 1323 of the extreme doctrine regarding the poverty of Jesus and his apostles. Many adherents of the faction of "Spirituals" had left Europe and a number appeared in the Franciscan community at Tabriz. Finally, faced with rebellion on a doctrinal matter, William of Cigiis held an inquest in which he was assisted by the local Dominican vicar and the vicar of Persia. Although Saurati was probably not an adherent of extreme Spiritual teachings, apparently he was on good terms with those who were and who eagerly sought his advice. At any rate, his correspondence constituted part of the dossier of evidence along with other letters and the depositions of local Italian merchants. The friars named were not given a hearing. In 1334 the report was forwarded to Avignon, where bishop William appeared in person later in the same year.

The outcome of this matter is not known, but twelve Franciscans, suspected of adherence to the extreme doctrines, were expelled from Persia sometime after the death of John XXII (1334). In 1344–1345

---

77. Loenertz, *Frères pérégrinants,* pp. 153, 162, 165.
78. *Ibid.,* pp. 154–155.

Clement VI published a bull against the Spirituals in Asia and instructed the archbishop of Sultaniyeh to investigate rumors that friar Ponzio had embraced this heresy. No record of any inquest has survived. Undoubtedly this whole affair seriously damaged the Franciscan missions in Persia, and most of the evidence of continued effort comes from Dominican sources.[79]

Sometime around 1328 Bartholomew, Dominican bishop of Maragha, was visited by a Basilian monk, John of Qrna, superior of the convent of St. Mary, mother of God. Completely won over to the cause of union with the western church, he asked Bartholomew to accompany him northward to Qrna. This the bishop did in 1329, and before his death in 1330 he and John had laid the foundation for a new Armeno-Catholic community.

John had originally hoped to transfer his community bodily into the Dominican order, but finding this impracticable, he set out to reform his monks along Dominican lines. Assisted by the Friars-Preachers, they studied Latin and western theology. The Dominicans, in turn, applied themselves to the Armenian language. From this combined effort came translations of theological works, principally those of Aquinas, the constitutions of the Dominican order, and the Dominican breviary and missal.

Meanwhile John of Qrna had visited Avignon and returned to organize what was in effect a new religious congregation where several houses were grouped under one "governor." Sometime after 1333 John of Florence, recently instituted bishop of Tiflis (1330) and Bartholomew's successor in the direction of the enterprise, formally received the vows of John of Qrna and his associates. Thus was established what became known as the *fratres unitores* (of St. Gregory the Illuminator), an Armenian branch of the Dominican order. In 1356 Innocent VI gave his official approbation and decreed that the Dominican master-general should have the right of visitation, a measure which resulted in occasional friction between the *unitores* and the *peregrinantes*.[80]

It has been pointed out that the popes repeatedly gave instructions regarding conditional rebaptism and reordination, and that the "repe-

79. *BOF*, III, 424-452; IV, 378-379, 381-383; de Sessevalle, *Histoire générale de l'ordre de Saint François*, pp. 556-559; Loenertz, *Frères pérégrinants*, pp. 157, 169.

80. For the Dominican missions in general and the *fratres unitores* see Loenertz, *Frères pérégrinants*, pp. 135-175, 188-198; "Les Missions dominicaines . . . ," *AFP*, II (1932), 33-45; and "Évêques dominicains des deux Arménies," *AFP*, V (1940), 258-291. There are also several studies by Marcus A. van den Oudenrijn, O.P., of which the latest and most comprehensive is "Uniteurs et Dominicains d'Arménie," *Oriens Christianus*, XL (1956), 94-112; XLII (1958), 110-133; and XLIII (1959), 110-119.

tition" of sacraments, as the Armenians viewed it, continued to arouse hostility. Apparently the *unitores* were inclined to be over-zealous in such matters. Some of them, including it seems John of Qrna, in a desire to promote uniformity, overemphasized minor matters of usage rather than significant differences of doctrines. An extreme example was the list of 117 errors presented to the curia by the *unitor* Nerses Balientz. It was an Armenian Franciscan, Daniel of Tabriz, who took it upon himself to defend his Armenian coreligionists. In 1341 he presented at Avignon a detailed refutation of the charges. After the Council of Sis in 1345, where the matter was further discussed, Daniel visited the curia once again and returned after Clement VI had named him bishop of Bosra in Syria.[81] The ultimate effect of such controversies on Armenian Christianity is not clear, but it does seem evident that the *unitores* were commonly regarded as "Latinizers" and were far from popular, especially in the areas where Monophysitism remained strong.

When the Black Death took its toll of the *fratres peregrinantes* after 1348, the *unitores* proved to be the bulwark of Catholicism in the Near East. At one time there were no bishops in Persia and only three friars. Finally the curia and the Dominican authorities in Europe heeded the pleas of the Armenians and in 1356 named Thomas of Tabriz to the see of Nadjivan. Thomas was an Armenian bishop and probably a member of the *unitores*.

By 1363 the situation had so deteriorated that what was left of the *fratres peregrinantes* was temporarily placed under the jurisdiction of the Dominican province of Greece. In 1365 the *unitores* were accorded the same privileges formerly enjoyed by the *peregrinantes*. A decade later, largely owing to the pleadings of the *unitores,* the Holy See revoked the earlier decisions of the Dominican authorities and reëstablished the *fratres peregrinantes*. Constitutionally, it was much the same as the congregation founded by Franco of Perugia, but times had changed. Islam was advancing rapidly, and virtually the only surviving Catholic communities were in the Crimea and in greater Armenia. In fact, the friars who went out in the later years of the fourteenth century formed a sort of mission of assistance to their Armenian brethren and, as a rule, resided in their houses.

During the fifteenth century, after Cilician Armenia had been conquered by Egypt, and then, along with greater Armenia, had been overrun by Timur in 1394, the Crimean communities of the *unitores*

---

81. *BOF,* IV, 333–362. Cf. also the chronicle hostile to Armenians written around 1322 and presented to king Philip V of France by a Dominican (*ibid.,* III, 404–407).

took on added importance. But after the fall of Kaffa in 1475 contacts between the *peregrinantes* and the *unitores* were broken once again. The latter, however, persisted in regarding themselves as Dominicans. Finally, in the sixteenth century, the Dominican authorities legalized what had already transpired by designating Nadjivan a province of the order.[82]

The tradition of the residence and martyrdom of St. Thomas the Apostle in India had remained strong during the Middle Ages, though much confused with legend. Moreover, although scholars have debated the exact locations, Christian communities existed in India from early times.[83] The evangelization of India in the Middle Ages first developed as an outgrowth of journeys to China. As we have mentioned, John of Monte Corvino visited the east and west coasts and baptized some one hundred persons. He reported that he had spent thirteen months "in the church of St. Thomas the Apostle." Somewhat later William Adam traveled as far as Thana, Cambay, and Quilon, and preached in various places.

The most important missionary to India in the fourteenth century was the Dominican Jordan Catalani of Sévérac.[84] Friar Jordan had acquired considerable experience and a thorough command of the native tongue in Persia. In 1320 he and two Genoese merchants joined Thomas of Tolentino and three other Franciscans bound for China. Thomas was a missionary of some standing who, it will be recalled, had delivered John of Monte Corvino's letter to the curia. The party took the sea route, intending to stop first at Quilon on the southern Malabar coast in order to visit the church of St. Thomas the Apostle. They were forced to disembark on the island of Salsette near the modern site of Bombay. At the nearby town of Thana they were received by some Nestorians (March 1231). Jordan was then persuaded to visit the community of Sofale some miles up the coast, where he found a church built on the ruins of an older edifice attributed to St. Thomas and where he baptized some twenty persons.

Meanwhile Thomas of Tolentino and his companions had been ar-

82. Loenertz, *Frères pérégrinants,* p. 150.

83. On Indian Christianity see Atiya, *A History of Eastern Christianity,* pp. 359 ff.; Slessarev, *Prester John: The Letter and the Legend,* pp. 7 ff.

84. In addition to the works of Loenertz: *Frères pérégrinants,* pp. 175–182, and "Missions dominicaines," *AFP,* II (1932), 50–55, see Moule, "Brother Jordan of Sévérac," *Journal of the Royal Asiatic Society* (1928), 348–376; Charles V. Langlois, "Jourdain Catala, missionnaire," *Histoire littéraire de la France,* XXXV (1921), 260–267; Beazley, *Dawn of Modern Geography,* III, 231 ff.; and Cordier, *Les Merveilles de l'Asie par le père Jourdain Catalani de Sévérac* (Paris, 1935).

rested by the Moslem governor at Thana. As Jordan returned to assist them he learned news of their martyrdom. Apparently the death of the Franciscans made such a profound impression that even several Moslems requested baptism. But the vigilance of the authorities forced Jordan to abstain from all propaganda. He did, however, after a long delay obtain permission to bury the martyrs.

Returning to Sofale with some of the relics of the martyrs Jordan resumed his mission among the Christians of the region. At length (October 12, 1321), while he was at Ghogah on the Kathiawar peninsula, he was able to entrust a report to one of the Genoese, who took it to the Dominican and Franciscan headquarters at Tabriz.[85] By this time Jordan had baptized some one hundred and twenty converts.

Although the Dominican Nicholas of Rome left Tabriz shortly after the receipt of Jordan's letter, the latter was again at Thana in 1323, for in January of that year he wrote another letter far less hopeful in tone. Difficulties were mounting and only ten more converts had been made. Two other letters and relics of the Thana martyrs were sent to Dominicans in Persia. Jordan also spoke of Ethiopia, which he hoped to visit, and pleaded that ships be equipped in the Indian Ocean for a new crusade against Egypt. Not for some years did other friars arrive and enable Jordan to return to Europe. The precise date is not known, but he was in Avignon in 1329.

In Avignon Jordan was named bishop of Quilon (Coilum) in southern India and entrusted with letters from the pope to various Christian communities in India, to a number of Indian princes, and to the king of Ethiopia, 'Amda Seyon. Apparently Jordan was still in Avignon in 1330, but that is the last that is heard of him and virtually the last of the medieval Indian mission. Sixteen years later the Franciscan John de' Marignoli, who spent a year in Quilon on his return from China, mentioned a Latin church of St. George and some "friars," but told practically nothing of the western Christian community in India.

While at Avignon Jordan met Thomas Mancasola, who had brought to the curia a report of Dominican activities in the western section of the khanate of Chagatai, which according to the demarcation of 1318 was included in the province of Sultaniyeh. Mancasola, it seems, had been sent to Avignon by khan Eljigidei, and his favorable report prompted the pope to reply and to appoint the Dominican friar the first bishop of Samarkand. He was to have left for the Orient with Jordan, which raises the question whether in fact he departed. If he

85. *BOF,* II, 69–71, 113.

did, he had returned to Avignon by 1342, and no other bishops of Samarkand are mentioned.[86]

Although the Egyptian government permitted the friars to maintain a caretaker establishment in Jerusalem and to serve the spiritual needs of Latin Christians resident in their domains, they were hostile to missionary effort and suspicious of any dealings between westerners and the Christians of Ethiopia and Nubia. Nevertheless, there is some evidence which indicates the possibility of contacts with the Christians of Ethiopia during the thirteenth century. It was mentioned above that the friars sent about 1237 to "the Jacobite patriarch of the Egyptians" by Philip, the Dominican provincial of the Holy Land, might have gone beyond the Egyptian frontier. Moreover, from the time of Innocent IV the rulers and people of Ethiopia and Nubia were regularly included in the papal missionary letters. A letter of Clement IV asking the master-general of the Dominicans to send friars to various lands including Ethiopia is somewhat more specific in that it mentions that they were to be accompanied by a certain friar Vasinpace who had been there. And it will also be recalled that among the commissions entrusted to John of Monte Corvino was a letter to the archbishop of Ethiopia. Moreover, John later mentioned that he had received a delegation from Ethiopia requesting missionaries. Evidently, therefore, the curia was aware of the existence of an Ethiopian hierarchy. Further evidence of missionary journeys is lacking.[87]

William Adam, the Dominican whose activities in Persia and India have been mentioned, stayed some time on the island of Socotra awaiting a chance to enter Abyssinia. Not only did he desire to evangelize the Ethiopians, but he considered Socotra a possible base for crusaders. As we have seen, Jordan Catalani had similar ideas. Such references may have contributed to the growing belief that Prester John's empire was to be located in the southern continent.

There are reports of considerable missionary activity on the part of the Dominicans in the fourteenth century, but they appear to be of late origin and not substantiated by contemporary documents. It must, therefore, be concluded that the possibility, even the probability, of missions in east Africa during the thirteenth and fourteenth centuries may be admitted, but that conclusive evidence of actual journeys or accomplishments is lacking.

86. Loenertz, *Frères pérégrinants*, pp. 168–169, 176.

87. On fourteenth-century missions to Ethiopia, in addition to the material cited above in notes 19 and 20, see Richard, "L'Extrême-Orient légendaire," pp. 225–242. Cf. also Carlo Conti Rossini, "Sulle Missioni dominicane in Etiopia nel secolo XIV," *Reale Accademia d'Italia, Rendiconti della classe di scienze morali e storiche*, ser. 7, I (1940), 71–98.

MISSIONARY METHODS
IN THE FOURTEENTH CENTURY: CONCLUSION

The principal innovation in the policy of the western church toward the east during the fourteenth century was the establishment of an oriental hierarchy.[88] This, together with the formation of the *fratres peregrinantes* and the expansion of the Franciscan vicariates, enabled the popes and the mendicant orders to proceed in a somewhat more systematic fashion. This is evident in a number of ways. Papal letters and the official pronouncements of the orders indicate, for example, an insistence that the missions be served by adequately trained men and that those unfit be removed. With regard to such matters as religious training and theological competence there is evidence that friars, even on the longest journeys, carried books. Books are mentioned in mission reports, in instructions to missionaries, and in financial provisions by the curia. Primarily, as might be expected, these are liturgical books. But Dominicans, it will be recalled, taught Aquinas in Armenia and translated some of his works into the native language. Friar Iohanca cited Peter Lombard, albeit incorrectly, in refuting the doctrines of the Ruthenian "schismatics." Since Iohanca seems in other ways to have been a well-educated person, his mistake may well have resulted from the lack of books in his remote station.[89]

Scarcity of material precludes any detailed analysis of the methods of the missionaries themselves, but some tentative conclusions can be drawn. In order to facilitate the friars' adjustment to varied surroundings — "accommodation" as it is called in modern times — the curia granted privileges regarding dress, beards, and such matters not enjoyed by their confrères in Europe. Although results are difficult to estimate, some modest attempts were made to train native clergies, a policy suggested, it will be remembered, as early as the pontificate of Innocent IV. We have already referred to the ruler of Tenduk on whom John of Monte Corvino conferred minor orders and his report that he was training forty native boys and had taught them to chant in Latin, as well as to the 1323 report of the Franciscans of the Kipchak khanate that they were training converts to become friars. A later notice of the year 1364 emphasized the teaching of Latin, and

---

88. In addition to the works cited above in note 49 see the following studies by van den Oudenrijn on the Armenian mission: *Das Officium des heiligen Dominicus des Bekenners im Brevier der "Fratres Unitores" von Ostarmenien* (Rome, 1955); "Eine armenische Übersetzung der Summa Theologica des Hl. Thomas im 14. Jahrhundert," *Divus Thomas,* VIII (1930), 245–278; "Oratiuncula S. Thomas Aquinatis in Armenica lingua," *Angelicum,* VI (1929), 77–82. On papal policy see de Vries, "Die Päpste von Avignon," pp. 85–128.

89. Cf. Bihl and Moule, "Tria nova documenta," p. 69, note 4.

in 1370 Franciscan official instructions to missionary vicars directed that no new members be received without careful testing of their orthodoxy.[90] From such scattered references as these it can be assumed that at last a beginning had been made and that the problem was being faced. Further, these same sources indicate that, despite the emphasis on preaching and disputation which persisted into the fourteenth century, some progress was made toward promoting more intimate work with individuals.

One intensely practical concern of the missionary friars was that of material support. In China, and perhaps in other Mongol countries, the khan provided a special subsidy for the Franciscan friars. Apparently it was the custom for the Mongol rulers thus to provide for ambassadors and envoys of foreign rulers. On certain occasions the papacy furnished travel expenses and money for books. Both Dominicans and Franciscans were permitted to make use of ill-gotten goods which might be turned over to them provided those to whom restitution was due could not be found. The Dominican authorities allowed the missionary friars to use money and permitted solicitation everywhere regardless of conventual or provincial regulations. At least one master-general, Berengar of Landorre, recommended the *fratres peregrinantes* to the good offices of all priors and ordered that when in Europe they be given hospitality and provided with liturgical books. The expenses of the vicar of the *peregrinantes* were defrayed by a subvention levied on all convents of the order.

The principal means of support were the merchants whose spiritual needs the missionaries served. In fact, it must be evident from the preceding pages that many friars were chaplains to merchant establishments first and missionaries second. Apparently a certain amount of papal pressure was sometimes necessary. Gregory IX, for example, specifically requested merchants to defray certain expenses for the first installations of the Dominicans.[91] Moreover, there were occasions, as for example when they opposed the slave traffic or trade with the Moslems, when friars incurred the enmity of merchants.

Although accurate figures are not available, it seems clear that the

90. Altaner, "Zur Geschichte des Unterrichts," p. 167. For the report of 1323 see above, pp. 502–503, and note 68. Van der Vat cites the 1370 directive in his review of Simonut, *Il Metodo,* in *Neue Zeitschrift für Missionswissenschaft,* IV (1948), 154. He also points out the difficulty of determining the ethnic origin of converts and the possibility that some may have been repurchased slaves; see his "Expensae camerae apostolicae pro missionibus Fratrum Minorum inter Tartaros ann. 1318–53," *AFP,* XXXI (1938), 538–540.

91. On expenses, concessions regarding dress, and so on see de Sessevalle, *Histoire générale de l'ordre de Saint François,* II, 610–612; van der Vat, *Die Anfänge,* note 87; *BOF,* V, 112–113, 148. Gregory's bull is cited in Potthast, *Regesta,* no. 9846; cf. Tăutu, *Acta Honorii III et*

Franciscans, the larger of the two mendicant orders, sent out more missionaries and maintained a larger number of permanent stations. Doubtless there was rivalry, for even after the delimitation of the two oriental provinces in 1318 members of each order could be found in most of the territories of the other. But the most spectacular cases of friction were a byproduct of the controversy within the Franciscan order over poverty. Certainly in Persia this must have interfered seriously with the work both orders were promoting.

There is also, however, ample evidence of coöperation. The houses of both orders were open to missionaries en route. John of Monte Corvino set out for China in company with a Dominican, addressed one of his letters to the authorities of both orders, and apparently hoped that both might be established in China. The Dominican Jordan Catalani traveled with Franciscans to India, cared for the relics of the Franciscan martyrs, and reported to the authorities of both orders in Persia. Other examples could be cited.

If such developments may be regarded as positive achievements, it must also be added that in the entire mission picture there remained many inadequacies. The overall impression left by the scanty sources is one of experiment, of trial and error, of a beginning only in the confrontation of an enormous task. It has already been pointed out, for example, that the projected plans for systematic language training in Europe did not materialize. Only Paris, apparently, and only for a short time, carried out the directives of the Council of Vienne. Something of the discouragement as well as the strangely provincial attitude prevailing in the west, even at the curia, may be seen in John XXII's suggestion to the king of Cilician Armenia that to facilitate the work of the friars his subjects should devote themselves to the study of Latin. Thus, while it is true that a considerable number of missionaries learned one or more oriental languages—an impressive achievement, and an improvement over the preceding decades—the use of intepreters continued. Further, it has been pointed out that the curia was less well equipped with interpreters than were the courts of eastern magnates.[92]

Somewhat similar observations can be made about the west's knowledge of oriental civilization and religion. Something has already been said of the lack of any real understanding of Islam. Understanding of oriental Christianity, though it did improve in the fourteenth century, was still insufficient. The Holy See continued to be overly optimistic

---

Gregorii IX, pp. 286–287 (no. 210). On the merchants in Asia see Lopez, "European Merchants in Asia," p. 131, and "Nuovi luci," pp. 337–398.

92. Altaner, "Sprachstudien und Sprachkenntnisse," pp. 129–131.

about the possibility of large-scale conversions, and it still attached too much importance to the conversion of magnates, ecclesiastical or secular. Moreover, though the plan for an oriental hierarchy may have been bold and imaginative, it proved difficult to implement. Viewed in retrospect, it seems too ambitious, perhaps revealing more zeal and energy than comprehension of Asiatic conditions.

In a work dedicated to the history of the crusades, it would seem appropriate to add some observations about the relation between mission and crusade. What has been presented here points inescapably to the conclusion that missions were more often than not associated with diplomacy. While the appearance of the Mongols first posed a new danger and then raised hopes of coöperation, Europe's constant concern remained Islam. This was, after all, still the age of the crusades, though becoming increasingly theoretical in the fourteenth century. The twentieth-century west has only to consult its own fears of communism to understand how deeply the expansion of Islam must have affected the mentality of the thirteenth and fourteenth centuries. There is no doubt that many, perhaps most, of the missionaries shared the feelings of their contemporaries and accepted the war with Islam as an unavoidable necessity. Moreover, in an age when religious and political affairs were not so compartmentalized as they are today it could scarcely have been otherwise.

From the standpoint of numbers converted the medieval missionary achievement in the Orient was not brilliant. Moreover, as is evident in so many mission reports, the total number of missionaries sent out was hardly sufficient. Such observations must not, however, be permitted to obscure certain very real accomplishments. Mission stations in widely separated and distant lands had been maintained for decades. Contacts had been renewed with oriental Christians, some of which, at least, proved to be permanent. Europeans had finally gained some first-hand knowledge of Asia and its peoples.

It must again be emphasized that European conditions were adverse, while after the middle of the thirteenth century in the east the triumph of Islam in Central Asia and the overthrow of the Mongol dynasty in China were followed by the rise of the Ottoman Turks in Anatolia. Meanwhile the Black Death took its toll of active and prospective missionaries. As a consequence of all these things, much that had been started could not be carried forward.

In short, medieval missions to the Orient were in a real sense only a beginning. In many areas, where centuries were to pass before missionaries were able to take up again the work begun by the friars of the high Middle Ages, they represent a beginning without a sequel.

The most impressive feature of the entire mission story is the extraordinary dedication of the friars themselves. Many of them faced incredible obstacles. Oriental Christians were often jealous and Moslems hostile. Martyrdoms were not infrequent. Travel in the thirteenth and fourteenth centuries was always difficult and usually dangerous. The trip to the Levant had become fairly routine, but the overland journey into central and eastern Asia commonly required many months to complete, and the endurance of hunger, thirst, intense heat, and severe cold. Food was scarce and often unpalatable to westerners. Moreover, the ships which plied the Indian Ocean were not designed to reassure the faint-hearted. A considerable number of friars never reached their destinations. Those men who braved all the hazards which confronted the medieval missionary to the Orient deserve to be numbered among the great pioneers of history.

GAZETTEER
AND NOTE ON MAPS

This gazetteer has been prepared to fill a variety of functions. Every relevant place-name found in the text or on the maps is here alphabetized and identified, variant spellings and equivalent names in other languages are supplied, and the map location is indicated. Thus it not only serves as an index to the maps and a supplement to them, but is itself a source for reference on matters of historical geography and changing nomenclature.

In the gazetteer, alphabetization is by the first capital letter of the form used in maps and text, disregarding such lower-case prefixes as *al-* and such geographical words as Cape, Gulf, Lake, Mount, and the like. The designation "classical" may mean Greek, Latin, biblical, or other ancient usage, and the designation "medieval" generally means that the name in question was in common use among speakers of various languages during the crusades, or appears in contemporary sources.

On the maps may be found nearly every place name occurring in the text of this volume or of volume VI, since the same maps appear in both volumes. Exceptions include a few places whose exact locations are unknown, a few outside the regions mapped, several in areas overcrowded with names, and some of minimal importance or common knowledge. Maps 1–8 are revised versions of those appearing in earlier volumes of this work; maps 9 and 12 are completely revised from maps in volume III, and maps 10, 11, and 13 are new.

All maps for this volume have been designed and prepared in the University of Wisconsin Cartographic Laboratory under the direction of Onno Brouwer, assisted by Kenneth Parsons. Base information was compiled from U.S.A.F. Jet Navigation Charts at a scale of 1:2,000,000. Historical data have been supplied by Dr. Harry W. Hazard (who also compiled the gazetteer) from such standard works as Sprüner-Menke, Stieler, Andree, and Baedeker for Europe, Lévi-Provençal for Moslem Spain, Rubió i Lluch and Bon for Frankish Greece, and Honigmann, Dussaud, Deschamps, Cahen, and LeStrange for the Near East. Additional information was found in *The Encyclopaedia of Islām* (old and new editions) and *İslâm Ansiklopedisi,* in Yāqūt and other Arabic

519

sources, in *The Columbia Lippincott Gazetteer of the World,* on Michelin and Hallweg road maps, and of course in the text of this volume.

Aachen (German), Aix-la-Chapelle (French): city—F2b5: 2, 3.
Ablasṭa: town—see Albistan.
Abydus (Latin), Abydos (Greek): town, now abandoned—J2d5: 3, 5.
Abyssinia: region—see Ethiopia.
Acerra (Italian): town 8 miles NNE of Naples (G5d5: 3).
Achaea (Latin), Achaïa (classical Greek), Akhaïa (modern Greek): district of northern Morea—I2e2: 4.
Acre; Ptolemaïs (classical), Saint Jean d'Acre (medieval), 'Akkā (Arabic), 'Akko (Israeli): city, port—L1f3: 1, 7.
Adalia or Satalia (medieval), Attalia (classical), Antalya (Turkish): port—K1e4: 1, 3.
Adana (classical, Armenian, Turkish): city—L1e3: 1, 6.
Aden; 'Adan (Arabic): port—N1j3: 12, 13.
Adramyttium (Latin), Lo Dromiti (medieval), Edremit (Turkish): town—J3e1: 3, 5.
Adrianople; Hadrianopolis (classical), Edirne (Turkish): city—J2d4: 1, 3, 5.
Adriatic Sea; Hadria or Mare Hadriaticum (Latin)—GHd: 2, 3, 4.
Aegean Sea; Aigaion Pelagos (Greek), Mare Aegaeum (Latin), Ege Denizi (Turkish)—IJe: 1, 3, 4, 5.
Aegina (Latin), Engia (medieval Italian), Ekine (Turkish), Aíyina (modern Greek): island—I4e3: 4.
Aenos or Aenus (Latin), Enos or Menas (medieval), Enez (Turkish): town—J2d5: 3, 5.
Aetolia (Latin), Aitōlia (classical Greek), Aitolía (modern Greek): district of central Greece—I2e2: 4.
Afghanistan: region, now a nation, east of northern Persia—QRSef: 12, 13.
Ager sanguinis: battlefield—see Darb Sarmadā.
Agros (Greek): Greek Orthodox monastery—K4f1: 8.
Aguilers (medieval), Aighuile or Aiguilhe (French): village just north of Le Puy (E4c5: 2).
Aguille (medieval): manor near Acre (L1f3: 7).
Aigaion Pelagos—see Aegean Sea.
Aigues-Mortes (French): port—E5d2: 2.
'Ain Jālūt (Arabic: well of Goliath), Geluth or Well of Harod (medieval), 'En Ḥarod (Israeli): village—L1f3: 7.
Aire-sur-l'Adour (French): town—D5d2: 2.
Aix-la-Chapelle: city—see Aachen.
'Ajlūn (Arabic): town—L1f3: 7.
Akaki (Greek): village—K4e5: 8.
Akamas (Greek): district SE of Cape Arnauti—K3e5: 8.
Akanthou (Greek): village—K4e5: 8.
Akhelia (Greek): village—K3f1: 8.
Akhtuba (Russian): river—N3c3: 1.
'Akkā, 'Akko: city, port—see Acre.
'Akkār, (Arabic), Gibelcar (medieval): fortress—L2f1: 6.
Akkerman (medieval), Belgorod Dnestrovski (Russian): port—K1c4: 1.
Aksarai or Sarai-Berke (Tatar): town, now unimportant—N2c2: 13.
Akshehir; Akşehir (Turkish: white city), Philomelium (Latin), Philomēlion (medieval Greek): town—K2e2: 1, 3.
Alamut; Alamūt (Persian, Arabic): fortress—O1e4: 12.

Alanya (Turkish), Scandelore or Candeloro (medieval), 'Ala'īyah or 'Alāyā (Arabic): port—K2e4: 1, 3.

Alba Julia (Latin), Weissenburg (German), Gyulafehérvár (Hungarian), Alba Iulia (Rumanian): town—I4c4: 3.

Albania (medieval), Shqipni or Shqipri (Albanian): region NW of Epirus, now a nation—Hd: 3, 4.

Albano Laziale (Italian): town 14 miles SE of Rome (G3d4: 2, 3,).

Albara (medieval), al-Bārah (Arabic): village—L2e5: 6.

Albistan (medieval), Arabissus (Latin), Ablasṭa (Armenian), Elbistan (Turkish): town—L3e2: 1.

Albunlena (medieval): battlefield—H5d4: 4.

Aleman (medieval): casal near Caesarea (K5f3: 7).

Aleppo (Italian), Beroea or Chalybon (classical), Ḥalab (Arabic), Haleb (Turkish): city—L3e4: 1, 6.

Alessandria (Italian): town 17 miles SE of Montferrat (F4c5: 3).

Alexandretta (medieval), İskenderun (Turkish): port—L2e4: 6.

Alexandretta, Gulf of; Sinus Issicus (Latin), İskenderun Körfezi (Turkish)—L1e4: 6.

Alexandria (classical), al-Iskandarīyah (Arabic): city, port—J5f4: 1, 3.

Alignan-du-Vent (French): village 25 miles west of Montpellier (E4d2: 2).

Almalyk (Turkish), Armalech (medieval): town—R5d5: 13.

Alpheus (Latin), Alpheios (classical Greek), Charbon (medieval), Alfíos (modern Greek): river—I2e3: 4.

Alps: mountain range—FGc: 2, 3.

Alsace (French), Alsatia (Latin), Elsass (German): region west of the upper Rhine—Fc: 2, 3.

Altoluogo: town—see Ephesus.

Amalfi (Italian): port—G5d5: 3.

Amanus (Latin), Gavur, Alma, or Elma Dağı (Turkish): mountain range—L2e4: 6.

Amasra (Turkish), Amastris (classical): port—K3d4: 1, 3.

Amasya (Turkish), Amasia (classical): town—L1d5: 1.

Amida (classical), Āmid or Diyār-Bakr (Arabic), Diyarbekir or Diyarbakîr (Turkish): town—M1e3: 1.

Amiens (French): city—E3c1: 2.

Amigdala or La Mandelée (medieval): village, probably Amendolara, 65 miles SW of Taranto (H3d5: 3).

'Ammān (Arabic), Philadelphia (classical), Rabbath 'Amman (Israeli): town—L1f4: 7.

Amorgos; Murgo (medieval Italian), Yamurgi (Turkish), Amorgós (modern Greek): island—J1e4: 5.

'Amshīt (Arabic): village 2 miles NNW of Jubail (L1f1: 6).

Anadolu-Hisar (Turkish: castle of Anatolia): fortress—J5d4: 5.

Anagni (Italian): town—G4d4: 3.

Anaphe; Anaphē (classical Greek), Namfio (medieval Italian), Anáfi (modern Greek): island—J1e4: 5.

Anatolia; Asia Minor (Latin), Romania or Rūm (medieval), Anadolu (Turkish): region south of the Black Sea—JKLde: 1, 3, 5.

Anchialus (Latin), Axillo (medieval), Akhyolï (Turkish), Pomoriye (Bulgarian): port—J3d3: 5.

Ancona (Italian): port—G4d2: 2, 3.

Andalusia; al-Andalus (Arabic), Andalucia (Spanish): region of southern Spain—CDe: 2.

Andechs (German): priory on Ammersee, 30 miles SSE of Augsburg (G1c2: 3).

Andreas, Cape, or Cape Saint Andrew; Le Chief (medieval): NE tip of Cyprus—K5e5: 8.

Andros (classical), Andro (medieval Italian), Andria (Turkish), Ándros (modern Greek): island—I5e3: 5.

Angoulême (French): town—E1c5: 2.
Anido: island—see Anydros.
Anjou (French): region of NW France—D5c3: 2.
Ankara (Turkish), Ancyra (classical), Angora (medieval): town, now city—K3e1: 1, 3.
Anopolis (Greek): village—I5e5: 3.
Antalya: port—see Adalia.
Anti-Lebanon; al-Jabal ash-Sharqī (Arabic: the eastern mountain)—L2f1: 6, 7.
Anticythera: island—see Cerigotto.
Antilles: island group in West Indies—not in area mapped.
Antioch; Antiochia (classical), Anṭākiyah (Arabic), Antakya (Turkish): city—L2e4: 1, 6.
Antiparos (classical), Andipáros (modern Greek): island just sw of Paros (J1e3: 5).
Antivari (Italian), Antebarium (Latin), Bar (Serbian): port—H5d3: 3.
Anydros (classical), Anido (medieval Italian), Ánidhros (modern Greek): island—J1e4: 5.
Apamea (classical), Afāmiyah or Qalʻat al-Muḍīq (Arabic): town, now unimportant—L2e5: 6.
Apros (medieval): unidentified port, probably between Kavalla and Rodosto (Jd: 5).
Apulia (classical), Puglia or Puglie (Italian): region of SE Italy—Hd: 3.
Aquileia (Italian): town—G4c5: 3.
ʻAqūrah (Arabic): village—L1f1: 7.
Arabia (classical), Jazīrat al-ʻArab (Arabic): peninsular region east of the Red Sea—LMNgh: 1, 6, 7.
Aragon; Aragón (Spanish), Araghūn (Arabic): region of NE Spain—DEd: 2.
Aral Sea; Aral'skoye More (Russian)—PQcd: 9, 10 (name not shown on maps).
Ararat, Mount (classical), Ağri Daği (Turkish), Massis (Armenian), Kuh-i-Nuh (Persian)—M4e1: 1.
Arcadia (classical), Mesaréa (medieval), Arkadhía (modern Greek): district of northern Morea—I2e3: 4.
Arcadiopolis (medieval), Bergulae (Latin), Bergoulē (classical Greek), Lüleburgaz (Turkish): town—J3d4: 5.
Arcas: town—see ʻArqah.
Archipelago (from Greek Aigaion Pelagos): islands of the Aegean Sea (IJe: 5).
Ardeal: region—see Transylvania.
Argesh; Curtea de Argeş (Rumanian): town—I5c5: 3.
Argolid or Argolis (classical), Argolís (modern Greek): district of eastern Morea—I3e3: 4.
Argos (classical), Árgos (modern Greek): town—I3e3: 3, 4.
Argyrokastron (Greek), Gjirokastër (Albanian): town—I1d5: 4.
Arles (French), Arelas (classical): town—E5d2: 2.
Armalech: town—see Almalyk.
Armenia (classical), Hayastan (Armenian), Ermenistan (Turkish): region north of Lake Van—Md: 1.
Armenia, Cilician: kingdom—KLe: 9.
Armiro: town—see Halmyros.
Arnauti, Cape: western tip of Cyprus—K3e5: 8.
ʻArqah or ʻIrqah (Arabic), Arcas or Irqata (classical), Villejargon (medieval): town—L2f1: 6.
Arsuf; Apollonia-Sozusa (classical), Arsur (medieval), Arsūf (Arabic), Tel Arshaf (Israeli): town, now abandoned for Herzliyya—K5f3: 7.
Arta (medieval), Ambracia (classical), Narda (Turkish), Árta (modern Greek): town—I1e1: 3, 4.
ʻArtāḥ (Arabic), Artesia (classical), Artais (medieval): town, now unimportant—L2e4: 6.

Arthabec (medieval), al-Mughair (Arabic): village—K5f3: 7.

Artois (French): district of northern France—E3b5: 2.

Arzenga: town—see Erzinjan.

Ascalon; Ashkelon (biblical), 'Asqalān (Arabic), Tel Ashqelon (Israeli): port, now abandoned for modern Ashqelon—K5f4: 1, 7.

Ascoli Piceno (Italian): town 52 miles south of Ancona (G4d2: 3).

Asia Minor (classical): region equivalent to western Anatolia.

Assisi (Italian): town—G3d2: 2, 3.

Asti (Italian), Hasta (classical): town—F4d1: 2, 3.

Astypalaea (Latin), Stampalia (medieval), Ustrapalia (Turkish), Astipálaia (modern Greek): island—J2e4: 5.

Athens; Athēnai (classical Greek), Cetines or Satines (medieval), Athínai (modern Greek): city—I4e3: 3, 4.

Athens: duchy—Ie: 9.

Athlith, 'Atlīt: castle—see Château Pèlerin.

Athos, Mount; Áyion Óros (modern Greek): Greek Orthodox monastery—I5d5: 4, 5.

Atlantic Ocean—BCc: 2.

Atlas, High; Aṭlas (Arabic): mountain range—Cf: 2.

Attica (Latin), Attikē (classical Greek), Attikí (modern Greek): district of eastern Greece—I4e3: 4, 5.

Aue (German): village 67 miles SE of Naumburg (G2b4: 3).

Augsburg (German): city—G1c2: 2, 3.

Aulps or Aups (French): village 50 miles NE of Marseilles (F1d2: 2).

Aura (German): village 85 miles NW of Nuremberg (G2c1: 3).

Austria; Ostmark (German): region east of Bavaria, smaller than modern nation—GHc: 2, 3.

Auvergne (French): region of southern France—Ecd: 2.

Auxerre (French): town—E4c3: 2.

Avesnes-sur-Helpe (French): town 40 miles SSE of Tournai (E4b5: 2).

Avignon (French), Avenio (classical): city—E5d2: 2.

Avila; Avela (classical), Ávila de los Caballeros (Spanish): town—D1d5: 2.

Avlona (medieval), Aulon (classical), Valona (Italian), Vlonë or Vlorë (Albanian): port—H5d5: 3, 4.

Ayas (medieval), Lajazzo (Italian), Yumurtalîk (Turkish): port—L1e4: 6.

Ayasoluk: town—see Ephesus.

Ayazmend (Turkish): port—L4e2: 1.

Aydîn (Turkish): district of western Anatolia, equivalent to classical Lydia—Je: 5.

Aydînjîk (Turkish): port—J3d5: 5.

Azarshahr: town—see Dehkharegan.

Azerbaijan; Ādharbādhagān or Āzerbaijān (Persian): region of NW Persia and SE Transcaucasia—Ne: 1.

Azov: port—see Tana.

Azov, Sea of; Azovskoye More (Russian)—Lc: 1.

Baalbek; Heliopolis (classical), Ba'labakk (Arabic): town—L2f1: 6, 7.

Babylon: town—see Fustat.

Badr (Arabic): battlefield—L5h2: 1.

Baffa: castle—see Sigouri.

Baghdad; Baghdād (Arabic): city—M5f2: 1.

Baghrās (Arabic), Pagrae (classical), Gaston (medieval), Bağra (Turkish): town—L2e4: 6.

Baihaq (medieval), Sabzivār (ancient Persian), Sabzevār or Sabzavār (modern Persian): town—P3e4: 12.

Bains (medieval), Castellum Balneorum (Latin): village—K5f4: 7.

Baisān: town—see Bethsan.
Bait Jibrīn (or Jibrīl): town—see Beth Gibelin.
Balaklava: port—see Cembalo.
Baleares (Spanish): island group—Ec: 2.
Balkans: mountain range—Id: 3, 5.
Balkans: peninsular region east of the Adriatic Sea.
Balkhash, Lake—STc: 9, 10 (name not shown on maps).
Baltic Sea—HIab: 2, 3.
Bamberg (German): city—Glcl: 2, 3.
Banyas; Paneas or Caesarea-Philippi (classical), Belinas (medieval), Bāniyās (Arabic): town—Llf2: 7.
Bar: port—see Antivari.
Bar Ṣaumā (Syriac): Jacobite monastery 50 miles ESE of Melitene (L4e2: 1).
al-Bārah: village—see Albara.
Barbary: the coast of North Africa.
Barbastro (Spanish), Barbashtrū (Arabic): town—Eld3: 2.
Barcelona (Spanish), Barcino (classical), Barshilūnah (Arabic): city, port—E3d4: 2.
Bari (Italian), Barium (classical): port—H2d4: 3.
Barīd (Arabic): village—L2e5: 6.
Ba'rīn, Bārīn: fortress—see Montferrand.
Barletta (Italian): port—H2d4: 3.
Barr ash-Sha'm (Arabic), Syria Magna (Latin): region including Syria proper and adjoining territory.
Barrius, Mount: unidentified mountain in the Caucasus.
Baruth: port—see Beirut.
Basel (German), Basle or Bâle (French): city—F3c3: 2, 3.
Bashkent or Kara Hisar (Turkish): battlefield—L5el: 1.
Bashkir; Bascardia (medieval): district of eastern Russia— OPab: 13.
Basra; al-Baṣrah (Arabic): city, port—N3f5: 1.
Bath: city—D3b4: 2.
al-Batrūn: town—see Botron.
Bavaria; Bayern (German): region of southern Germany—Gc: 2, 3.
Beauvais (French): town—E3cl: 2.
Bedford: town—D5b3: 2.
Beirut; Berytus (classical), Bairūt (Arabic), Baruth (medieval): port—Llf2: 1, 6, 7.
Bela Palanka (Serbian): town—I3d2: 3.
Belfort or Beaufort (medieval), Shaqīf Arnūn or Qal'at ash-Shaqīf (Arabic: fort of the rock): crusader castle—Llf2: 7.
Belgrade; Beograd (Serbian: white town): city—IIdl: 3.
Belhacem (medieval), Qal'at Abī-l-Ḥasan (Arabic): village—Llf2: 7.
Belinas: town—see Banyas.
Bellapais or Bella Paise (medieval): monastery—K4e5: 8.
Belmont (French), Dair al-Balamand (Arabic): abbey and castle—Llfl: 6.
Benevento (Italian), Beneventum (Latin): town—G5d4: 3.
Berat (Albanian), Pulcheriopolis (classical), Bellagrada (medieval): town—H5d5: 3, 4.
Bergulae, Bergoulē: town—see Arcadiopolis.
Berry (French): district of central France—Ec: 2.
Besharri: town—Llfl: 7.
Besharri Mountains: range 20 miles east of Botron (Llfl: 7).
Beth Gibelin (medieval), Betogabri or Eleutheropolis (classical), Bait Jibrīn or Bait Jibrīl (Arabic), Bet Guvrin (Israeli): town, now village—K5f4: 7.
Bethany; al-'Azarīyah (Arabic), 'Eizariya (Israeli): abbey and fort—Llf4: 7.
Bethlehem (biblical), Ephrata (classical), Bait Laḥm (Arabic: house of flesh): town— Llf4: 7.

Bethsan or Bessan (medieval), Scythopolis or Bethshan (classical), Baisān (Arabic), Bet She'an (Israeli): town — L1f3: 7.

Béthune (French): town 20 miles wsw of Lille (E4b5: 2).

Beyoğlu: port — see Pera.

Beyshehir; Beyşehir (Turkish): town — K2e3: 1, 3.

Béziers (French): town — E4d2: 2.

Biga or Biğa (Turkish), Pegae (Latin), Pēgai (medieval Greek): town — J3d5: 3, 5.

Bilād ash-Shaqīf (Arabic: land of rock): district of southern Lebanon — L2e5: 6.

Bilbais or Bilbīs (Arabic): town — K2f5: 1.

al-Biqā' (Arabic: the hollow), Coele-Syria (classical), Bekaa (modern): district of central Lebanon — L1f2: 6, 7.

al-Bīrah (Arabic), Mahumeria or La Grande Mahomerie (medieval), Bira (Israeli): fortress, now town — L1f4: 7.

Bisignano (Italian): village — H2e1: 2.

Bithynia (classical): district of NW Anatolia — Jde: 10.

Black Sea: Mare Euxinus (Latin), Kara Deniz (Turkish), Chernoye More (Russian) — JKLd: 1, 3, 5.

Blanchegarde (medieval), at-Tall aṣ-Ṣāfiyah (Arabic: the glittering hill): castle — K5f4: 7.

Blois (French): town — E2c3: 2.

Bnahrān (modern Arabic): probably Benharan, village 12 miles south of Tripoli (L1f1: 6, 7).

Bobalna; district north of Grosswardein — Ic: 3.

Bodrum or Budrum (Turkish), Halicarnassus (classical), Petroúnion (modern Greek): town — J3e3: 5.

Boeotia (Latin), Boiōtia (classical Greek), Voiotía (modern Greek): district of eastern Greece — I4e2: 4.

Bohemia; Čechy (Czech): region north of Austria — GHc: 2, 3.

Bokhārā: city — see Bukhara.

Bolanden (German): castle near Kirchheim, 27 miles ssw of Mainz (F4b5: 3).

Bolgar: town — see Bulgar.

Bologna (Italian): city — G2d1: 2, 3.

Bombay: city and port — S3i2: 12, 13.

Bonditza: town — see Vonitsa.

Bonn (German): town, now city, 15 miles sse of Cologne (F2b5: 3).

Bordeaux (French), Burdigala (classical): city, port — D5d1: 2.

Bosnia; Bosna (Serbian, Turkish): region west of Serbia — Hd: 3.

Bosporus (classical), Karadeniz Boğazı (Turkish: Black Sea strait) — J5d4: 1, 3, 5.

Bosra; Bostra (classical), Buṣrâ (Arabic): town — L2f3: 1, 7.

Botras: unidentified locality, probably in France.

Botron (medieval), Botrys (classical), al-Batrūn (Arabic): town — L1f1: 6, 7.

Bougie: port — see Bugia.

Bouillon (French): town — F1c1: 2, 3.

Boulogne-sur-Mer (French): port — E2b5: 2.

Bourcq: castle — see Le Bourg.

Bourges (French): town — E3c3: 2.

Bourgogne: region — see Burgundy.

Brabant (French, Flemish): district east of Flanders — EFb: 2, 3.

Brandenburg (German): district of northern Germany — Gb: 2, 3.

Braşov: district — see Burzenland.

Bratislava (Slovakian), Pressburg (German), Pozsony (Hungarian): city — H3c2: 3.

Braunschweig: city — see Brunswick.

Bremen (German): city, port — F4b2: 2, 3.

Brescia (Italian): city — G1c5: 3.

Breslau (German), Wrocław (Polish): city — H3b4: 3.

Brienne-la-Vieille (French): village 20 miles ENE of Troyes (E5c2: 2).

Brindisi (Italian), Brundisium (Latin): port—H3d5: 3.

British Isles: England, Wales, Scotland, Ireland, and smaller islands.

Brittany; Bretagne (French), Breiz (Breton): region of NW France—Dc: 2.

Bruges (French), Brugge (Flemish): port, now city—E4b4: 2.

Brunswick; Braunschweig (German): city—G1b3: 2, 3.

Buda (Hungarian), Ofen (German): city, now part of Budapest—H5c3: 3.

Buffavento (medieval): castle—K4e5: 8.

Bugia; Saldae (classical), al-Bijāyah (Arabic), Bougie (French): port—F1e4: 2.

Bukhara; Bokhārā (Persian), Bukhārā (Arabic): city—Q5e1: 12, 13.

Bulgar or Bolgar; Bolgary (Russian, formerly Uspenskoye): town, now village—N5b3: 12.

Bulgaria; Moesia (classical), Blgariya (Bulgarian): region south of the Danube, larger than modern nation—IJd: 1, 3, 5.

al-Buqai'ah (Arabic; the little hollow), La Boquée (medieval French): valley—L1f1: 6.

Burgundy; Bourgogne (French): region of eastern France, extending farther south than now—EFc: 2.

Bursa (Turkish), Prusa (classical), Brusa (medieval): city—J5d5: 1, 3, 5.

Burzenland or Burza (German), Braşov (Rumanian): district of SE Transylvania—IJc: 3.

Buzā'ah (Arabic): town—L3e4: 6.

Byblos: town—see Jubail.

Byzantium: city—see Constantinople.

Caco: fortress—see Qāqūn.

Caen (French): city—D5c1: 2.

Caesarea ad Argaeum or Mazaca (classical), Kayseri (Turkish): city—L1e2: 1.

Caesarea Maritima or Palaestinae (classical), Cesaire (medieval), Qaisārīyah (Arabic), Qesari (Israeli): port, now abandoned for Sedot Yam—K5f3: 7.

Caffa: port—see Kaffa.

Cafresi (medieval): manor near Acre (L1f3: 7).

Cahors (French): town—E2d1: 2.

Caiffa: port—see Haifa.

Cairo: al-Qāhirah (Arabic: the victorious): city—K2f5: 1, 3.

Calabria (Italian): region of SW Italy—He: 3.

Calamona (medieval), Ma'lūlah (Arabic): Greek Orthodox monastery—L2f2: 7.

Calansue: village—see Qalansuwā.

Cambaluc: city—see Khanbaliq.

Cambay or Khambayat: port—S3h3: 13.

Cambrai (French): town—E4b5: 2.

Campomorto (Italian): battlefield SSE of Rome (G3d4: 3).

Candia: island—see Crete.

Candia (medieval), Heracleum (Latin), Iráklion (modern Greek): port—J1e5: 3.

Canea (classical), Khanía (modern Greek): port—I5e5: 3.

Canina (medieval), Bullis or Byllis (classical), Kanine (Albanian): town, now unimportant—H5d5: 4.

Canterbury: town—E2b4: 2.

Canton; Kwangchow or Kuang-chou (Chinese): city, port—AA4g2: 13.

Caorle (Italian): town 29 miles NE of Venice (G3c5: 3).

Capharnaum (medieval), Khirbat al-Kanīsah (Arabic), Shiqmōna (Israeli): village 5 miles SSW of Haifa (L1f3: 7).

Capua (Italian): town—G5d4: 3.

Caransebesh; Caransebeş (Rumanian): town—I3c5: 3.

Carcassonne (French): town—E3d2: 2.

Carinthia; Kärnten (German): region south of medieval Austria—Gc: 2, 3.

Carmel, Mount; Jabal Mār Ilyās (Arabic: Mount Saint Elias), Karmel (Israeli)—K5f3: 7.

Carpas: district—see Karpass.

Carpathians; Carpates (classical), Karpaty (Czech, Polish), Carpatii (Rumanian): mountain range—IJc: 1, 3.

Carpi (medieval), Kerpe (Turkish): port—K1d4: 5.

Carystus (classical), Káristos (modern Greek): town—I5e2: 4, 5.

Casal Imbert (medieval), az-Zīb (Arabic), Tel Akhziv (Israeli): castle—L1f2: 7.

Casius, Mount (medieval), Jabal al-Aqra‘ (Arabic)—L2e5: 6.

Caspian Sea—NOde: 1.

Cassandra; Pallene (classical), Kassándra (modern Greek): peninsula—I4e1: 4.

Castello or Olivolo (Italian): district on the lagoon of Venice (G3c5: 3).

Castellorizzo; Megisto (classical), Meis (Turkish), Castelrosso (Italian), Kastellórizo (modern Greek): island—J5e4: 1, 5.

Castellum Balneorum: village—see Bains.

Castellum Regis (Latin), Chastiau dou Rei (medieval), Mi‘ilyah (Arabic): fortress 2 miles ESE of Montfort (L1f2: 7).

Castile; Castilla (Spanish), Qashtālah (Arabic): region of north central Spain—Dde: 2.

Catalonia; Cataluña (Spanish), Catalunya (Catalan): region of NE Spain—Ed: 2.

Cathay: region—see China.

Catodica (medieval Italian): unidentified port, probably in Albania or Epirus.

Cattaro (Italian), Kotor (Serbian): port—H4d3: 3.

Caucasus; Kavkaz (Russian): mountain range—MNd: 1.

Caymont (medieval), Tall Qaimūn (Arabic): castle—L1f3: 7.

Cayphas: port—see Haifa.

Cembalo (medieval), Balaklava (Russian): port—K4d1: 1.

Central Asia: region extending from the Aral Sea to Mongolia.

Ceos; Keōs (classical Greek, Tziá (medieval), Zea (Italian), Morted (Turkish), Kéa (modern Greek): island—I5e3: 4, 5.

Cephalonia (Latin), Kephallēnia (classical Greek), Kephallōnia (medieval Greek), Kefallinía (modern Greek): island—I1e2: 3, 4.

Cerigo (Italian), Cythera (Latin), Kythēra (classical Greek), Kíthira (modern Greek): island—I3e4: 3, 4.

Cerigotto (Italian), Aegilia or Anticythera (Latin), Andikíthira (modern Greek): island—I4e5: 3.

Cerne: abbey at town of Cerne Abbas—D3b5: 2.

Cesaire: port—see Caesarea.

Cesena (Italian): town 17 miles WNW of Rimini (G3d1: 3).

Cesson: fortress—see Kesoun.

Cetines: city—see Athens.

Centa (Spanish), Septa (classical), Sabtah (Arabic): port—C5e5: 2.

Chalcedon (Latin), Kalkhēdōn (classical Greek), Khalkēdōn (medieval Greek), Kadî-köy (Turkish): town—J5d5: 3, 5.

Chalcidice (Latin), Khalkidikē (classical Greek), Khalkidhikí (modern Greek): peninsula—I4d5: 4.

Chalcis: port—see Negroponte.

Chalon-sur-Saône (French): town—E5c4: 2.

Champagne (French): region of NE France—EFc: 2.

Champlitte (French): town, now part of Champlitte-et-le-Prélot, 30 miles NE of Dijon (F1c3: 2).

Charbon: river—see Alpheus.

Chartres (French): town—E2c2: 2.

Chastel-Blanc (medieval), Burj Ṣāfīthā (Arabic): crusader castle—L2f1: 6.

Chastel-Neuf (French), Ḥūnīn (Arabic), Qiryat Shemona (Israeli): crusader castle – L1f2: 7.

Chastiau dou Rei: fortress – see Castellum Regis.

Château Pèlerin (French), Athlith (medieval), 'Atlīt (Arabic), 'Aṯlit (Israeli): crusader castle – K5f3: 7.

Châteauneuf (French): unidentified castle.

Châtillon-sur-Loing (French): town, now part of Châtillon-Coligny, 32 miles west of Auxerre (E4c3: 2).

Chaydo: unidentified realm, possibly mythical.

Chernomen; Črnomen (Bulgarian), Çirmen, Çermen, or Sîrf Sîndîgî (Turkish: destruction of the Serbs), Orménion (modern Greek): battlefield – J2d4: 3, 5.

Cherson: port – see Kherson.

Cheshme; Çeşme (Turkish): town – J2e2: 5.

Chester: city – D3b2: 2.

Chiarenza: town – see Glarentsa.

China; Cathay (medieval): region of eastern Asia – W/CCe/h: 12, 13.

Chioggia (Italian): port – G3c5: 3.

Chios (classical), Scio (Italian), Sakîz (Turkish), Khíos (modern Greek): island – J1e2: 5.

Chocques (French): suburb just west of Béthune.

Chorlu; Çorlu (Turkish), Tzurulum (Latin): town – J3d4: 5.

Cigiis: unidentified locality, possibly Chioggia.

Cilicia (classical): region of southern Anatolia – KLe: 6.

Cilly; Celje (Slovene): town – H1c4: 3.

Cimolos; Kímolos (modern Greek): island – I5e4: 5.

Circassia: region north of western Caucasus – LMd: 1.

Cîteaux (French): abbey – F1c3: 2.

Citrum (Latin), Lo Kitro (medieval), Kítros (modern Greek): port – I3d5: 3, 4.

Civetot (medieval), Cibotus (classical): port, now abandoned – J5d5: 3, 5.

Clairvaux (French): abbey – E5c2: 2.

Clarence: town – see Glarentsa.

Clermont (French): town, now part of Clermont-Ferrand – E4c5: 2.

Cluny (French): abbey – E5c4: 2.

Coilum: port – see Quilon.

Cologne (French), Colonia Agrippinensis (Latin), Köln (German): city – F2b5: 2, 3.

Comacchio (Italian): town 29 miles ESE of Ferrara (G2d1: 3).

Comana or Placentia (medieval): town, now abandoned – L2e2: 1.

Compostela or Santiago de Compostela (Spanish), Campus Stellae (Latin), Shant Ya'qūb (Arabic): town and shrine – C2d3: 2.

Conches-en-Ouche (French): town, formerly Douville, 33 miles south of Rouen (E2c1: 2).

Constance (French), Konstanz (German): town – F5c3: 2, 3.

Constantinople; Byzantium or Constantinopolis (classical), İstanbul (Turkish): city – J4d4: 1, 3, 5.

Cordova; Córdoba (Spanish), Qurṭubah (Arabic): city – D1e3: 2.

Corfu; Corcyra (Latin), Kerkyra (classical Greek), Corfù (Italian), Kérkira (modern Greek): island – H5e1: 3, 4.

Corice: town – see Cyrrhus.

Corinth; Korinthos (classical Greek; now Palaiá Kórinthos: Old Corinth): city – I3e3: 3, 4.

Corinth, Gulf of; Korinthiakós Kólpos (modern Greek) – I3e2: 4.

Cornwall: region of sw England – CDb: 2.

Coron (medieval), Korōnē (medieval Greek), Koróni (modern Greek): port – I2e4: 3, 4.

Corsica; Cyrnus (classical), Corse (French): island – Fd: 2, 3.

Cortona (Italian): town 24 miles NW of Perugia (G3d2: 3).

Corycus (classical), Goṛigos (Armenian), Le Courc (medieval), Korgos (Turkish): port – K5e4: 1.

Cos; Lango or Stanchio (medieval Italian), Stankoi (Turkish), Kós (modern Greek): island – J3e4: 5.

Cotrone (medieval Italian), Crotone (modern Italian): port – H3e1: 3.

Courtenay (French): village 32 miles WNW of Auxerre (E4c3: 2).

Cracow; Cracovia (Latin), Kraków (Polish): city – H5b5: 3.

Cremona (Italian): town – G1c5: 2.

Crete; Candia (medieval), Krētē (medieval Greek), Kandia (Turkish), Kríti (modern Greek): island – IJef: 1, 3.

Crimea; Gazaria (medieval), Krym (Russian): peninsula – K4c5: 1, 3.

Croatia; Meran (medieval), Hrvatska (Croatian): region north of Dalmatia – Hc: 3.

Croia (Italian), Kroja (Serbian), Akça-Hisar (Turkish), Krujë (Albanian): town – H5d4: 3, 4.

Crotone: port – see Cotrone.

Ctesiphon: town – see Seleucia.

Cursat (medieval), Qal'at az-Zau or Quṣair (Arabic: little castle): castle – L2e4: 6.

Curzola (Italian), Korčula (Serbian): island – H2d3: 3.

Cyclades (classical), Kikládhes (modern Greek): island group – IJe: 3, 5.

Cyprus (Latin), Kypros (medieval Greek), Kîbrîs (Turkish), Kípros (modern Greek): island – Kef: 1, 8.

Cyrenaica (classical), Barqah (Arabic): region west of Egypt – If: 10, 11.

Cyrrhus (Latin), Gouris (Armenian), Corice (medieval), Qūriṣ (Arabic): town – L2e4: 6.

Cythera: island – see Cerigo.

Cythnos (classical), Thermia (medieval), Kíthnos (modern Greek): island – I5e3: 4, 5.

Cyzicus (classical), Kapîdağ (Turkish): town, now abandoned – J3d5: 3, 5.

Dalaman: river – J5e3: 1, 5.

Dalmatia (classical), Dalmacija (Croatian): region east of the Adriatic Sea, equivalent to classical Illyria – Hd: 3.

Damascus (classical), Dimashq or ash-Sha'm (Arabic: the left): city – L2f2: 1, 7.

Damietta; Dimyāṭ (Arabic): port – K2f4: 1.

Danube; Donau (German), Duna (Hungarian), Dunav (Serbian, Bulgarian), Dunărea (Rumanian): river – G5c2, J3d1: 1, 2, 3.

Darb Sarmadā (Arabic), "Ager sanguinis" (medieval): battlefield, pass – L2e4: 6.

Dardanelles; Hellespontus (classical), Çanakkale Boğazî (Turkish): strait – J2d5: 1, 3, 5.

Darum or Daron (classical), ad-Dārum (Arabic): town, now unimportant – K5f4: 7.

Deabolis: town – see Devol.

Dead Sea; Baḥr Lūṭ (Arabic: sea of Lot), Yam Hamelah (Israeli) – L1f4: 1, 7.

Dehkharegan (Russian), Azarshahr (Persian): town – N1e3: 1.

Delhi; Dillī (Hindi), Dihlī or Dehlī (Persian): city – T3g2: 12, 13.

Demetrias; Goritsa or Dēmētrias (medieval Greek), Demetriade (medieval): town, now abandoned – I3e1: 3, 4.

Demotica; Didymoteichon (classical), Dēmotika (medieval Greek), Dhidhimótikhon (modern Greek): town – J2d4: 3, 5.

Denmark; Danmark (Danish): region of Scandinavia, then including southern part of modern Sweden – FGab: 2, 3.

Derkos (medieval): fortress – J4d4: 5.

Devnya, Lake – J3d2: 5.

Devol; Deabolis or Diabolis (medieval): town, now abandoned – I1d5: 3, 4.

Dijon (French): city – F1c3: 2, 3.

Dilmān: town—see Salmas.
Dimashq: city—see Damascus.
Dimilṣā (Arabic): village north of Jubail (L1f1: 6, 7).
Diu: port—S1h5: 13.
Diyār-Bakr (Arabic): region of the upper Tigris—Le: 1.
Diyār-Bakr, Diyarbekir: town—see Amida.
Dnieper; Borysthenes (classical), Dnepr (Russian): river—K3c4: 1.
Dniester; Tyras (classical), Dnestr (Russian), Nistru (Rumanian): river—J5c4: 1.
Dobruja: region east of lower Danube—Jd: 1, 3.
Doha: unidentified realm, possibly mythical.
Dol-de-Bretagne (French): town 75 miles sw of Caen (D5c1: 2).
Domažlice (Czech), Taus (German): town—G3c1: 3.
Domfront (French): town 42 miles ssw of Caen (D5c1: 2).
Don; Tanaïs (classical): river—L5c3: 1.
Donjon: town—see Le Donjon.
Dorylaeum (classical): town, now abandoned in favor of Eskishehir—K1e1: 3.
Douro (Portuguese), Duero (Spanish), Duwīruh (Arabic): river—C3d4: 2.
Drama: town—I5d4: 3, 4, 5.
Dristra (medieval), Durostorum (classical), Silistre (Turkish), Silistra (Rumanian), Silistria (Bulgarian): town—J3d1: 3.
Dubrovnik: port—see Ragusa.
Dulcigno (Italian), Ulcinj (Serbian): port—H5d4: 3
Duluk; Doliche (classical), Dulūk (Arabic), Dülük (Turkish): town—L3e3: 6.
Durazzo (Italian), Epidamnus or Dyrrachium (classical), Draj (Turkish), Dürres (Albanian): port—H5d4: 3, 4.
Durham: city—D4b1: 2.
Dusburg (medieval), Duisburg (modern German): town, now city, 36 miles NNW of Cologne (F2b5: 3).

Ebro (Spanish), Ibruh (Arabic): river—D4d3: 2.
Edessa; Rohais or Rochais (medieval), ar-Ruhā' (Arabic), Urfa (Turkish): city—L4e3: 1, 6.
Edirne: city—see Adrianople.
Edremit: town—see Adramyttium.
Egmund (Dutch): monastery, now town—E5b3: 2.
Egypt; Miṣr (Arabic): region of NE Africa—JKf: 1, 3.
Elbasan (medieval, Albanian): town—I1d4: 3, 4.
Elbe (German), Labe (Czech): river—G2b2: 2.
Elbistan: town—see Albistan.
Eleutheropolis: town—see Beth Gibelin.
Elis; Ēlis or Ēleia (classical Greek), Ilía (modern Greek): district of NW Morea—I2e3: 4.
Elysium (classical): spring at unidentified location in Syria.
Emba (Greek): village—K3f1: 8.
Emel: river—see Imil.
Emmaus; Nicopolis (classical), 'Amwās (Arabic), Imwas (Israeli): village (not biblical Emmaus) 9 miles WNW of Jerusalem (L1f4: 7).
Engedi or En Gedi (Israeli), Engeddi (medieval), 'Ain Jidī (Arabic): village—L1f4: 7.
Engia: island—see Aegina.
England; Britannia (Latin): region—Db: 2.
English Channel; La Manche (French)—CDbc: 2.
Ephesus (classical), Altoluogo (medieval), Ayasoluk (Turkish): city, now unimportant—J3e3: 3, 5.
Epirus (Latin), Ēpeiros (classical Greek), Ípiros (modern Greek): region west of Thessaly—Ie: 3, 4.

Episcopi; Episkopí (modern Greek): town—K3f1: 8.
Eretna (Turkish): district east of Ankara—Ke: 1.
Erlau (German), Eger (Hungarian): city—I1c3: 3.
Erzerum; Theodosiopolis (classical), Garin (Armenian), Erzurum (Turkish): city—
    M2e1: 1.
Erzinjan (Turkish), Arsinga (classical), Arzenga (medieval): town—L5e1: 1.
Estanor: port—see Pera.
Estives: city—see Thebes.
Ethiopia or Abyssinia; Ityopya (Amharic): region of east central Africa—not in re-
    gion mapped.
Euboea (classical), Evripos (medieval Greek), Negroponte (Italian), Egripos (Turk-
    ish), Évvoia (modern Greek): island—I4e2: 3, 4, 5.
Euphrates (classical), al-Furāt (Arabic), Firat Nehri (Turkish): river—N1f4: 1; L4e4:
    6.
Eurotas (classical), Evrótas (modern Greek): river—I3e4: 4.

Famagusta; Ammōkhostos (classical Greek), Famagosta (medieval Italian): port—
    K4e5: 1, 8.
Fano (Italian): port 29 miles NW of Ancona (G4d2: 3).
Far East: region including China, Japan, and Indo-China.
Faran or Pharan: Greek Orthodox bishopric at Mount Sinai (K4g2: 1).
Ferrara (Italian): city—G2d1: 2, 3.
Fertile Crescent: region comprising Palestine, Syria, and Mesopotamia.
Feuchtwangen (German): town 40 miles WSW of Nuremberg (G2c1: 3).
Fez; Fās (Arabic): city—D1f1: 2.
Flanders; Vlaanderen (Flemish): region of northern France and Belgium—EFb: 2.
Florence; Firenze (Italian): city—G2d2: 2, 3.
Florentin (Bulgarian): town—I3d1: 3.
Foglia, Foça: port—see Phocaea.
Fontanella (Italian): village 29 miles east of Milan (F5c5: 3).
Forez (French): district east of Clermont (E4c5: 2).
France: region, smaller than modern nation.
Francières (French): village in Picardy, about 25 miles NW of Amiens (E3c1: 2).
Frankfurt am Main (German): city—F4b5: 2, 3.
Frenk-Yazusu (Turkish): battlefield—K3e3: 1.
Frisia; Friesland (Dutch, German): region of northern Netherlands and NW Germany
    —Fb: 2, 3.
Friuli (Italian): district of NE Italy—Gc: 2, 3.
Fustat; al-Fusṭāṭ (Arabic), Babylon (medieval): town—K2f5: 1.

Gadres: town—see Gaza.
Gaeta (Italian): port—G4d4: 3.
Galilee; Hagalil (Israeli): region of northern Palestine—L1f3: 7.
Galilee, Sea of, or Lake Tiberias; Buḥairat Ṭabarīyah (Arabic), Yam Kinneret (Is-
    raeli)—L1f3: 7.
Gallipoli (medieval), Callipolis (classical), Gelibolu (Turkish): town—J2d5: 3, 5.
Gascony; Gascogne (French): region of SW France—Dde: 2.
Gaston: town—see Baghrās.
Gata, Cape: southern tip of Cyprus—K4f1: 8.
Gaul; Gallia (Latin): classical region roughly equivalent to France.
Gaza (classical), Gadres (medieval), Ghazzah (Arabic): town—K5f4: 7.
Gazaria: peninsula—see Crimea.
Geluth: village—see 'Ain Jālūt.
Genoa; Genua (Latin), Genova (Italian): city, port—F4d1: 2, 3.

Georgia or Grusia (medieval), Sakartvelo (Georgian): region east of the Black Sea and south of the Caucasus—MNd: 1.

Germany; Alamannia or Allemania (medieval), Deutschland (German): region of north central Europe—FGbc: 9.

Germiyan (Turkish): district of west central Anatolia—JKe: 5.

Gezer: hill—see Mont Gisard.

al-Gharb (Arabic: the west): district of western Lebanon—L1f2: 6, 7.

Ghogah or Gogha: town on Kathiawar peninsula 50 miles ssw of Cambay (S3h3: 13).

Ghor; al-Ghaur (Arabic: the bottom): valley of the lower Jordan—L1f4: 7.

Gibelcar: fortress, mountain— see 'Akkar, Jabal 'Akkar.

Gibelet: town—see Jubail.

Gibraltar, Strait of; az-Zuqāq (Arabic)—C5e5: 2.

Giurgiu (Rumanian), San Giorgio (Italian), Szentgyörgy (Hungarian): town—J1d2: 3.

Glarentsa; Chiarenza or Clarence (medieval), Cyllene (Latin), Kyllēnē (classical Greek), Killíni (modern Greek): town—I2e3: 4.

Golden Horn; Chrysoceras (classical), Haliç (Turkish): bay between Constantinople and Pera (J4d4: 5).

Golubats; Golubac (Serbian): town—I2d1: 3.

Good Hope, Cape of: southern tip of Africa—not in area mapped.

Goritsa: town—see Demetrias.

Göynük (Turkish): town—K1d5: 5.

Grado (Italian): town 26 miles sse of Udine (G4c4: 3).

Granada (Spanish), Ighranāṭah or Gharnāṭah (Arabic): city—D2e3: 2.

Greco, Cape—K5f1: 8.

Greece; Hellas (Greek), Graecia (Latin): region west of the Aegean Sea, smaller than modern nation.

Grosswardein (German), Nagyvárad (Hungarian), Oradea (Rumanian): city—I2c3: 3.

Grusia: region—see Georgia.

Guadalquivir (Spanish), al-Wādī al-Kabīr (Arabic: the great river): river—C5e3: 2.

Guadiana (Spanish, Portuguese), Wādī Ānah (Arabic): river—C4e2: 2.

Gujerat or Gujarat: district of western India—Sh: 13.

Gurganj: city—see Urgench.

Györ (Hungarian), Raab (German): town—H3c3: 3.

Gyps (medieval): village near Sidon (L1f2: 7).

Habil (Arabic): village 5 miles ENE of Jubail (L1f1: 6, 7).

Ḥabīs Jaldak (Arabic): cave fortress—L1f3: 7.

Habsburg: castle—see Hapsburg.

Ḥadath (Arabic): village—L1f1: 7.

Haifa; Cayphas or Caiffa (medieval), Ḥaifā (Arabic), Ḥaifa (Israeli): port—L1f3: 1, 7.

Hainault; Hainaut (French), Henegouwen (Flemish): district east of Artois—EFb: 2, 3.

Ḥajīt or Ḥadshīt (Arabic): village 1 mile west of Besharri (L1f1: 6).

Ḥalab, Haleb: city—see Aleppo.

Ḥālāt (Arabic): village 3 miles sse of Jubail (L1f1: 6, 7).

Halberstadt (German): city—G2b4: 2, 3.

Halicarnassus: town—see Bodrum.

Halmyros (classical Greek), Armiro (medieval Italian), Almirós (modern Greek): town—I3e1: 3, 4.

Hamah; Epiphania or Hamath (classical), Ḥamāh (Arabic): city—L2e5: 1, 6.

Hamid (Turkish): district of west central Anatolia—Ke: 5.

Hangchow or Hang-chou (Chinese), Quinsai (medieval): city, port—CC1f5: 13.

Hapsburg; Habsburg (German): castle sw of Brugg, 29 miles east of Basel (F3c3: 3).

Hardīn (Arabic): town 11 miles east of Botron (L1f1: 6, 7).

Harod, Well of — see 'Ain Jālūt.

Harran or Haran (Turkish), Carrhae (classical), Ḥarrān (Arabic): town — L5e4: 1.

Hattin, Horns of; Madon (classical), Ḥaṭṭīn or Ḥiṭṭīn (Arabic): battlefield, hill — L1f3: 7.

Hauran; Ḥaurān (Arabic): district of SE Syria — L2f2: 7.

Hauteville (French): village 55 miles WSW of Caen (D5c1: 2).

Haynis (medieval): fief near Caesarea (K5f3: 7).

Hebron (classical, Israeli), Ḥabrūn or Khalīl (Arabic), Saint Abraham (medieval): town — L1f4: 7.

Hejaz; al-Ḥijāz (Arabic): region of western Arabia — Lgh: 1.

Heldrungen (German): village 73 miles SSE of Halberstadt (G2b4: 3).

Heliopolis: town — see Baalbek.

Hellespont(us): strait — see Dardanelles.

Henneberg (German): village 53 miles NNE of Würzburg (F5c1: 3).

Heraclea or Perinthus (classical), Ereğli or Marmaraereğlisi (Turkish): port — J3d5: 5.

Heracleum: port — see Candia.

Hermannstadt (German), Szeben or Nagyszeben (Hungarian), Sibiu (Rumanian): town — I5c5: 3.

Hermon, Mount; al-Jabal ash-Shaikh or Jabal ath-Thalj (Arabic: the hoary, or snow-covered, mountain) — L1f2: 7.

Herzegovina; Hercegovina (Serbian), Hersek (Turkish): district NW of Montenegro — Hd: 3.

Hierapolis: town — see Mabūj.

al-Ḥijāz: region — see Hejaz.

Himara or Himarë (Albanian), Chimaera (classical), Chimara (Italian): town — H5d5: 4.

Ḥismah (Arabic): region east of Sinai, in NW Arabia — KLg: 1.

Ḥiṣn al-Akrad: fortress — see Krak des Chevaliers.

Ḥiṣn Ziyād or Zaid: fortress — see Kharput.

Hohenlohe (German): district 14 miles SW of Würzburg (F5c1: 3).

Holland (Dutch): region north of Brabant — Eb: 2, 3.

Holy Land — see Palestine.

Homs; Emesa (classical), Ḥimṣ (Arabic): city — L2f1: 1, 6.

Horeb, Mount — see Mount Sinai.

Horneck (German): castle at Gundelsheim, 52 miles SE of Würzburg (F5c1: 3).

Hulda or Huldre (medieval): village — K5f4: 7.

Humairah (Arabic), Homaire (medieval): village — L1f2: 7.

Hungary; Magyarország (Hungarian): region of central Europe — HIc: 3.

Ḥūnīn: castle — see Chastel-Neuf.

Hyères (French): town — F2d2: 2.

Ianina or Janina (medieval), Yanya (Turkish), Ioánnina (modern Greek): town — I1e1: 3, 4.

Ibelin (medieval), Jabneel or Jamnia (classical), Yabnâ (Arabic), Yavne (Israeli): village — K5f4: 7.

Iberia: peninsular region comprising Spain and Portugal.

Iconium: city — see Konya.

Imbros; Lembro (medieval Italian), İmroz (Turkish): island — J1d5: 5.

Imil, Emel, or Yemel (Russian): river east of Lake Balkhash — 12, 13 (name not shown on maps).

India: region of southern Asia — R/Vf/j: 12, 13.

Indian Ocean — M/Xhij: 12, 13 (name not shown on maps).

Indo-China: peninsular region of SE Asia — YZ1m: 12, 13.

Ionian Sea—HIe: 3.
Ios; Nios (medieval), Íos (modern Greek): island—J1e4: 5.
Iraq; al-'Irāq (Arabic): modern nation, approximately equivalent to Mesopotamia.
Ireland; Hibernia (Latin), Eire (Gaelic): island—Cb: 2.
Iskar or Iskŭr (Bulgarian): river flowing past Sofia to the Danube—I5d2: 3.
Iskenderun: port—see Alexandretta.
Isonzo (Italian), Soča (Croatian): river east of Aquileia—G5c5: 3.
Istanbul: city—see Constantinople.
Istria (classical), Istra (Croatian, Slovene): peninsula—Gc: 3.
Italy; Italia (Latin, Italian): peninsular region, now a nation.
Ithaca (Latin), Ithakē (classical Greek), Itháki (modern Greek): island—I1e2: 4.
Izmir: city, port—see Smyrna.
Iznik: town—see Nicaea.

Jabal 'Akkār (Arabic), Gibelcar (medieval): mountain near 'Akkār (L2f1: 6).
Jabal Anṣārīyah (Arabic: mountain of the Nuṣairīs)—L2e5: 6.
Jabal as-Summaq (Arabic: mountain of the sumac)—L2e5: 6.
Jabala; Gabala (classical), Jabalah (Arabic): port—L1e5: 6.
Jaffa or Joppa; Yāfā (Arabic), Yafo (Israeli): port, now joined to Tel Aviv—K5f3: 1, 7.
al-Jafr (Arabic): oasis in Sinai desert (Kg).
Japan; Nippon (Japanese): island nation—not in area mapped.
Jehoshaphat or Josaphat; valley, possibly Kidron, but probably north of Jerusalem
     (L1f4: 7).
Jericho; Arīḥā or ar-Rīḥā (Arabic): town—L1f4: 7.
Jeroschin (German): probably Jarocin, 38 miles SSE of Posen (H2b3: 2).
Jerusalem; Hierosolyma (classical), al-Quds ash-Sharīf (Arabic), Yerushalayim (Is-
     raeli): city—L1f4: 1, 7.
Jidda; Jiddah (Arabic): port—L5h4: 1.
Joinville (French): town 37 miles WSW of Toul (F1c2: 2).
Joppa: port—see Jaffa.
Jordan; al-Urdunn (Arabic): river—L1f3: 1, 7.
Josaphat: valley—see Jehoshaphat.
Jubail (Arabic: small mountain), Byblos (classical), Gibelet (medieval): town—L1f1:
     1, 6, 7.
Judea: region of central Palestine—L1f4: 7.
Judin (medieval), Qal'at Jiddīn (Arabic): fortress—L1f2: 7.

Kadesh (medieval): village—L2f1: 6.
Kadiköy: town—see Chalcedon.
Kafar (Arabic): village near Jubail (L1f1: 6, 7).
Kafarhai (Arabic): village near Botron (L1f1: 6, 7).
Kaffa or Caffa (medieval), Theodosia (classical), Feodosiya (Russian): port—L1c5: 1.
Kaftūn (Arabic): village 5 miles ENE of Botron (L1f1: 6, 7).
al-Kahf (Arabic: the cavern): cave-fortress—L2e5: 6.
Kalden (German): castle at Pappenheim, 40 miles north of Augsburg (G1c2: 3).
Kalocsa (Hungarian): town—H4c4: 3.
Kamchiya (Bulgarian): river—J2d3: 5.
Kanakaria (Greek): village—K4e5: 8.
Kangurlan: town—see Sultaniyeh.
Kantara; al-Qanṭarah (Arabic: the bridge), Kantára (modern Greek): town—K4e5: 8.
al-Karak: fortress—see Kerak.
Karakilissa (medieval Turkish), Karachisia (Armenian), Sisian (Russian): town—
     N2e1: 1.
Karakorum (Tatar), Holin (Chinese): city, now abandoned—Y3c3: 12, 13.

Karaman (Turkish): region of south central Anatolia—Ke: 1.

Karasi; Karasî or Karesi (Turkish): district of NW Anatolia—Je: 5.

Karpass (Greek), Carpas (medieval): peninsular district—K5e5: 8.

Kasrawān or Kisrawān (Arabic): district around Jubail (L1f1: 6, 7).

Kastamonu (Turkish), Castra Comnenon or Kastamuni (medieval): town—K4d4: 1, 3.

Kathiawar or Saurashtra: peninsula on which Diu is located (Sk: 13).

Kavalla; Neapolis Datenon (classical), Christopolis (medieval), Kaválla (modern Greek): port—I5d5: 3, 4, 5.

Kavarna (Bulgarian): resort town—J4d2: 3.

Kayseri: city—see Caesarea.

Kemer or Keramides (medieval), Burhaniye (Turkish): port—J2e1: 5.

Kerak; Kir-hareseth (classical), Krak des Moabites or Krak of Moab (medieval), al-Karak (Arabic): fortress, now town—L1f4: 1, 7.

Kerch: port—see Vosporo.

Kermanshah; Kermānshāh (Persian), Sarmasane (medieval): city—N2f1: 1.

Kerpe: port—see Carpi.

Kerpen (German): village 12 miles WSW of Cologne (F2b5: 3).

Kesoun; Ḳesoun (Armenian), Cesson (medieval), Kaisūn (Arabic), Keysun (Turkish): fortress, now town—L3e3: 6.

Khanbaliq (Mongolian), Chi, Yenking, or Chungtu (classical Chinese), Cambaluc (medieval), Peking, Pei-ching, Beijing, or Peiping (modern Chinese): city—BB1e1: 12, 13.

Kharput or Harput (Turkish), Kharpert (Armenian), Ḥiṣn Ziyād or Zaid (Arabic): fortress, now town—L5e2: 1.

Kherson or Cherson (medieval Russian), Chersonesus Heracleotica (classical), Korsun (Slavic): port, now ruined (not modern Kherson on the Dnieper)—K4d1: 1.

Khirbat Jabatah (Arabic), Jebetzah (Israeli): casal in Palestine.

Khirokitia; Khirokitía or Khoirokitía (modern Greek): battlefield—K4f1: 8.

Khrysokou (Greek): district east of Akamas—K3e5: 8.

Khurasan; Khorāsān (Persian): region of NE Persia—PQe: 12, 13.

Kiev (Russian): city—K1b5: 3.

Kilani (Greek): village—K3f1: 8.

Kilia (medieval), Kiliya (Russian): town—J5c5: 1, 3.

Kilidulbahr (Turkish): fort—J2d5: 5.

Kirchheim unter Teck (German): town 80 miles east of Strassburg (F3c2: 3).

Kiti; Kíti (modern Greek): village—K4f1: 8.

Kiti, Cape—K4f1: 8.

Kîzîl Ahmadlî (Turkish): tribal region in northern Anatolia—Kd: 10, 11.

Knodhara (Greek): village—K4e5: 8.

Koja-ili (Turkish): district around Nicomedia—Jd: 5.

Köln: city—see Cologne.

Kolossi (medieval), Kolóssi (modern Greek): fortress—K3f1: 8.

Konya (Turkish), Iconium (classical, medieval): city—K3e3: 1, 3.

Korčula: island—see Curzola.

Kormakiti, Cape—K3e5: 8.

Kossovo; Kosovo (Serbian): town—I2d3: 3.

Kouklia (Greek): village—K3f1: 8.

Kouris (Greek): river—K3f1: 8.

Kozan: town—see Sis.

Kozlu-Dere (Turkish): port—J2d5: 5.

Kraguyevats; Kragujevac (Serbian): town—I1d1: 3.

Krak de Montréal (medieval), ash-Shaubak (Arabic): fortress, now village—L1f5: 1.

Krak des Chevaliers (medieval), Ḥiṣn al-Akrād (Arabic: stronghold of the Kurds): fortress—L2f1: 1, 6.

Krak of Moab, or des Moabites: fortress – see Kerak.
Kraków: city – see Cracow.
Kreuzburg (German), Slavskoye (Russian): town – I1b1: 3.
Kronstadt (German), Braşov (Rumanian): town (recently called Stalin) – J1c5: 3.
Krushevats; Kruševac (Serbian), Alaja-Hisar (Turkish): town – I2d2: 3.
Kulm (German), Chełmńo (Polish): town – H4b2: 3.
Kumukh; Cumuk (Russian): town – H3d3: 1.
Kurdistan; Kurdistān (Persian, Arabic): region between Armenia and Persia – MNe: 1.
Küstendil; Konstantin-ili (Turkish), Kyustendil (Bulgarian): town – I3d3: 3.
Kutná Hora (Czech), Kuttenberg (German): town – H1c1: 3.
Kwangchow: city, port – see Canton.
Kykkou (Greek): Greek Orthodox monastery – K3e5: 8.
Kyrenia; Cerines (medieval), Kerýnia (modern Greek): town – K4e5: 8.
Kythrea (Greek): spring and town 8 miles NE of Nicosia (K4e5:8).

La Berrie (medieval): desert west of southern Dead Sea – KLf: 7.
La Boquée: valley – see al-Buqai'ah.
La Broquière or La Broquère (French): village 65 miles sw of Toulouse (E2d2: 2).
La Castrie (medieval), Gastría (modern Greek): castle – K4e5: 8.
La Ferté-Alais (French): village 27 miles south of Paris (E3c2: 2).
La Grande Mahomerie: fortress – see al-Bīrah.
La Mandelée: village – see Amigdala.
Laconia (Latin), Lakōnia or Lakōnikē (medieval Greek), Lakonía (modern Greek):
  district of SE Morea – I3e4: 4.
Lagosta (Italian), Lastovo (Serbian): island 60 miles west of Ragusa (H4d3: 3).
Lairon or Laron (French): village 16 miles east of Limoges (E2c5: 2).
Lajazzo: port – see Ayas.
Lajjūn (Arabic), Legio or Megiddo (medieval): village – L1f3: 7.
Lampedusa (Italian): island – G3e5: 3.
Lampron (Armenian), Namrun (Turkish): fortress – K5e3: 1.
Lampsacus (classical), Lapseki (Turkish): village – J2d5: 5.
Lancaster: city – D3b1: 2.
Landorre (French): probably a castle near Rodez, 75 miles NE of Toulouse (E2d2: 2).
Landsberg (German): town – G3b4: 2, 3.
Langensalza: town – see Salza.
Lango: island – see Cos.
Langres (French): town – F1c3: 2, 3.
Languedoc (French): region of southern France – Ecd: 2.
Lannoy (French): town 9 miles NW of Tournai (E4b5: 2).
Laodicea: port – see Latakia.
Laon (French): town – E4c1: 2.
Lapithos; Lapēthos (medieval Greek): town – K4e5: 8.
Larnaca; Lárnaka (modern Greek): town – K4f1: 8.
Lasithi or Lasethi (Greek): district of eastern Crete (Je).
Lastovo: island – see Lagosta.
Latakia; Laodicea ad Mare (classical), al-Lādhiqīyah (Arabic): port – L1e5: 1, 6.
Lausanne (French): town – F2c4: 2, 3.
Le Bourg or Bourcq (French): castle in Vouziers canton, Ardennes, near Rethel, NE
  of Rheims (E5c1: 2).
Le Donjon (French): town 50 miles NE of Clermont (E4c5: 2).
Le Monestra: fortress – see al-Munaiṭirah.
Le Puiset (French): castle 25 miles SE of Chartres (E2c2: 2).
Le Puy-en-Velay (French), Podio (medieval Latin): town – E4c5: 2.
Lebanon; al-Lubnān (Arabic), Liban (French): region, now a nation (Lf).

Lebanon, Mount; Jabal Lubnān (Arabic)—L2f1: 6, 7.
Lefka (Greek): village—K3e5: 8.
Lefkara (medieval Greek): town—K4f1: 8.
Lefkoniko; Lefkonikó (modern Greek): town—K4e5: 8.
Legio: village—see Lajjūn.
Leicester: town—D4b3: 2.
Lelantian plain (medieval), Ambelian plain (modern): in central Euboea (I4e2: 5).
Lemba (Greek): village—K3f1: 8.
Lemnos; Lēmnos (medieval Greek), Stalimene (medieval), Límnos (modern Greek): island—J1e1: 5.
Lentini (Italian): town—H1e3: 3.
Leon; León (Spanish): region of northern Spain—CDd: 2.
Leontes: river—see Litani.
Lepanto (Italian), Naupactus (classical), Epaktos (medieval Greek), Návpaktos (modern Greek): port—I2e2: 3, 4.
Lesbos (classical), Mytilēnē (medieval Greek), Metelino (medieval Italian), Midülü (Turkish), Lésvos (modern Greek): island—J2e1: 5.
Lesh; Lezhe (Albanian), Lissus (classical), Alessio (Italian): town—H5d4: 3, 4.
Leucas or Leukas (classical), Leucadia or Santa Maura (medieval), Levkás (modern Greek): island—I1e2: 3, 4.
Levant: the Near East, sometimes also including Greece.
Lewes: town 43 miles south of London (D5b4: 2).
Liége or (recently) Liège (French), Luik (Flemish): city—F1b5: 2, 3.
Lihfid or Lahfid (Arabic): village—L1f1: 7.
Lille (French), Ryssel (Flemish): city—E4b5: 2.
Limassol; Nemesos (medieval Greek), Lemesós (modern Greek): port—K4f1: 1, 8.
Limburg (Flemish): district east of Liége—Fb: 2, 3.
Limoges (French): city—E2c5: 2.
Lisbon; Lisboa (Portuguese), Ushbūnah (Arabic): city, port— C1e2: 2.
Lisieux (French): town 45 miles wsw of Rouen (E2c1: 2).
Litani; Leontes (classical), al-Lītānī (Arabic): river—L1f2: 7.
Lithuania; Lietuva (Lithuanian): region east of Poland, larger than modern state —IJab: 3.
Livadia; Lebadea or Levadeia (classical), Levádhia (modern Greek): town—I3e2: 5.
Livonia; Livland (German): district NE of Riga—IJa: 3.
Lo Dromiti: town—see Adramyttium.
Lo Kitro: port—see Citrum.
Locedio (Italian): abbey 12 miles WNW of Montferrat (F4c5: 2).
Loire (French): river—E3c3: 2.
Lombardy; Lombardia (Italian): region of NW Italy—Fcd: 2, 3.
London: city, port—D5b4: 2.
Longjumeau (French): town 11 miles ssw of Paris (E3c2: 2).
Lorraine (French), Lothringen (German): region of eastern France—EFc: 2, 3.
Lorraine, Lower: district of southern Belgium (EFbc).
Low Countries: Netherlands and part of Belgium.
Lübeck (German): city, port—G1b2: 2, 3.
Lucca (Italian): town—G1d2: 2, 3.
Lucera (Italian): town—H1d4: 3.
Lucuk (medieval): port on coast north of Matrega (L2c5: 1).
Lüleburgaz: town—see Arcadiopolis.
Lusignan (French): town—E1c4: 2.
Lydda (classical), Saint George (medieval), al-Ludd (Arabic), Lod (Israeli): town—K5f4: 7.
Lyons; Lyon (French): city—E5c5: 2.

Ma'arrat an-Nu'mān (Arabic): town — L2e5: 6.
Mabūj or Manbij (Arabic), Hierapolis (classical), Membij (Turkish): town — L3e4: 6.
Macedonia (classical), Makedhonía (modern Greek), Makedonija (Serbian): region
    west of Thrace — Id: 3, 4, 5.
Machaeras or Makhairas (Greek): Greek Orthodox monastery — K4f1: 8.
Mâcon (French): town — E5c4: 2.
Madeira: island group in the Atlantic Ocean — not in area mapped.
Madras: city, port — U1m2: 12, 13.
Maeander (classical), Büyük Menderes (Turkish): river — J4e3: 5.
al-Maghrib: region — see North Africa.
Mahumeria: fortress — see al-Bīrah.
Maidān (Arabic): plain near Muzairib (L2f3: 7).
Maifūq (Arabic): village — L1f1: 7.
Mainz (German), Mayence (French): city — F4b5: 2, 3.
Majdal: castle — see Mirabel.
Majorca; Mallorca (Spanish), Mayūrqah (Arabic): island — Ee: 2).
Makheras Mountains — north of Larnaca (K4f1: 8).
Makri (medieval), Fethiye (Turkish): port — J5e4: 1, 3, 5.
Maku (Persian): town 125 miles NW of Tabriz (N2e2: 1).
Malabar: coastal region of sw India.
Malamocco (Italian): village 5 miles south of Venice (G3c5: 3).
Malatia, Malatya: city — see Melitene.
Malberg (German): town 21 miles north of Trier (F2c1: 3).
Malea, Cape; Ákra Maléas (modern Greek) — I4e4: 4.
Mallorca: island — see Majorca.
Malmsey, Malvasia: fortress — see Monemvasia.
Malta; Melita (classical), Māliṭah (Arabic): island — G5e5: 3.
Mamistra (medieval), Mopsuestia (classical), Msis (Armenian), Misis (Turkish): town —
    L1e4: 1, 6.
Mamonia (Greek): village — K3f1: 8.
Manbij: town — see Mabūj.
Mansurah; al-Manṣūrah (Arabic): town — K2f4: 1.
Mantua; Mantova (Italian): city — G1c5: 3.
Manzikert; Mandzgerd (west) or Mantskert (East Armenian), Malazgirt (Turkish):
    town — M3e1: 1.
Mappa (medieval), Anapa (Russian): port — L3d1: 1.
Maraclea (medieval), Maraqīyah (Arabic): port — L1e5: 6.
Maragha; Marāgheh (Persian): town — N2e3: 1.
Marash (Armenian, Turkish), Germanicia (classical), Mar'ash (Arabic): town — L2e3:
    1, 6.
Marburg an der Lahn (German): city 47 miles north of Frankfurt (F4b5: 3).
Mardin (Turkish), Māridīn (Arabic): town — M1e3: 1.
Marethasa: valley east of Tylleria (K3e5: 8).
Margat (medieval), al-Marqab (Arabic: the watch-tower): fortress — L1e5: 6.
Marienburg (German), Malbork (Polish): fortress, now town — H5b1: 3.
Maritsa; Hebrus (classical), Evros (medieval Greek), Meriç (Turkish): river — J2d4:
    1, 3, 5.
Marj 'Uyūn (Arabic: meadow of springs): district of southern Lebanon — L1f2: 7.
Marmara, Sea of; Propontis (classical), Marmara Denizi (Turkish) — J4d5: 5.
Maron (medieval), Marūn ar-Rās (Arabic): village just sw of Toron (L1f2: 7).
Maros (Hungarian), Marisus (classical), Mureş (Rumanian): river flowing by Alba
    Julia — IJc: 3.
al-Marqab: fortress — see Margat.
Marrakesh; Marrākush (Arabic): city — C2f4: 2.

Marseilles; Massalia (classical Greek), Massilia (Latin), Marseille (French): city, port
— F1d2: 2.

Martoni (Italian): village near Carinola, 14 miles WNW of Capua (G5d4: 3).

Marturana (medieval), Martirano (Italian): town — H2e2: 3.

Marv: city — see Merv.

Masovia (medieval), Mazowsze (Polish): region of east central Poland — Ib: 3.

Maṣyāf or Maṣyāth or Maṣyād or Miṣyāf (Arabic): fortress — L2e5: 6.

Matapan, Cape; Taenarum (Latin), Metōpon (medieval Greek), Ákra Taínaron (modern Greek) — I3e4: 4.

Matrega (medieval): port, now unimportant — L2e5: 1.

Maugastel (French): unidentified castle near Tyre (L1f2: 7).

Mayence: city — see Mainz.

Mecca; Makkah (Arabic): city — L5h4: 1.

Medina; al-Madīnah (Arabic: the city): city — L5h1: 1.

Mediterranean Sea — D/Ldef: 1, 2, 3, 4, 6, 7, 8.

Megali-Agora (medieval), Malkara or Migal-Kara (Turkish): town — J2d5: 5.

Megara; Mégara (modern Greek): town — I4e3: 4.

Megiddo: village — see Lajjūn.

Meissen (German): town — G4b4: 2, 3.

Melitene (classical), Melden (Armenian), Malatia (medieval), Malatya (Turkish): city
— L4e2: 1.

Melos; Mēlos (classical Greek), Milo (medieval Italian), Degir Menlik (Turkish),
Mílos (modern Greek): island — I5e4: 4, 5.

Menteshe (medieval), Muğla (modern Turkish): region of western Anatolia equivalent to classical Caria — Je: 5.

Mérencourt (French): unidentified locality in France.

Merv or Marv (Persian), Margiana (classical): city — Q2e3: 12, 13.

Mesaoria; Mesaréa (modern Greek): plain around Lefkoniko — K4e5: 8.

Mesaréa: district — see Arcadia.

Mesembria (medieval), Misivri (Turkish), Nesebar (Bulgarian): town — J3d3: 3, 5.

Mesopotamia (classical), al-'Iraq (Arabic): region between the Tigris and the Euphrates
— LMNef: 1.

Messenia; Messēnē (medieval Greek), Messíni (modern Greek): district of sw Morea
— I2e4: 4.

Messina (Italian): port — H1e2: 3.

Messines (French), Mesen (Flemish): village 12 miles NW of Lille (E4b5: 2).

Metelino: island — see Lesbos.

Mézières (French): town, now attached to Charleville, 50 miles NE of Rheims (E5c1:
2).

Micone: island — see Myconos.

Milan; Milano (Italian): city — F5c5: 2, 3.

Milly (French): village 30 miles SSE of Paris (E3c2: 2).

Milo: island — see Melos.

Mirabel (medieval), Majdal (Arabic): castle — K5f3: 7.

Misis: town — see Mamistra.

Miṣr: region — see Egypt.

Mistra (medieval), Myzithra (medieval Greek), Mistrás (modern Greek): town — I3e3: 4.

Moab: biblical region equivalent to Transjordan.

Mocha; Mukhā (Arabic): port — M4j2: 13.

Modon (medieval), Methōnē (medieval Greek), Methóni (modern Greek): port —
I2e4: 3, 4.

Moldavia; Boghdan (Rumanian): region east of the Carpathians — Jc: 3.

Molybdos (classical), Mólivdhos (modern Greek): port — J2e1: 5.

Monastir; Bitolj (Serbian): town — I2d4: 3, 4.

Monemvasia; Minōa (classical Greek), Malvasia or Malmsey (medieval), Monemvasía (modern Greek): fortress, now town—I4e4: 3, 4.
Monferrato: district—see Montferrat.
Mongolia; Meng-ku (Chinese): region north of China—V/BBbcd: 12, 13.
Mont Gisard or Gisart (medieval), Gezer or Gazara (classical), Tall al-Jazar (Arabic): hill 5 miles SE of Ramla (K5f4: 7).
Montaigu-sur-Champeix or Montaigut-le-Blanc (French): castle 10 miles SSE of Clermont (E4c5: 2).
Montbéliard (French): town 36 miles west of Basel (F3c3: 2).
Monte Cassino (Italian): abbey—G4d4: 3.
Monte Corvino or Montecorvino Rovella (Italian): town 11 miles ENE of Salerno (G5d5: 3).
Monte Croce (Italian): village near Florence (G2d2: 3).
Monteil (French): village, now Monteil-au-Vicomte, 30 miles NW of Nice (F3d2: 2).
Montenegro (Italian: black mountain), Crna Gora (Serbian): district north of Albania—HId: 3.
Montferrand (medieval), Ba'rīn or Bārīn (Arabic): fortress—L2f1: 6.
Montferrat (French), Monferrato (Italian): district of NW Italy—F4c5: 2, 3.
Montfort (French), Starkenberg (German), Qal'at al-Qurain (Arabic): castle—L1f2: 7.
Montfort-l'Amaury (French): town 25 miles WSW of Paris (E3c2: 2).
Montmerle-sur-Saône (French): town 24 miles NNW of Lyons (E5c5: 2).
Montmusart or Mont Musard (French): northern suburb of Acre (L1f3: 1, 7).
Montpellier (French): town—E4d2: 2.
Montréal (French): fief around Krak de Montréal (L1f5: 1).
Morava (Serbian): river—I2d2: 3.
Moravia; Morava (Czech): region SE of Bohemia—Hc: 9.
Morea (medieval), Peloponnesus (Latin), Peloponnēsos or Moreas (medieval Greek), Pelopónnisos (modern Greek): peninsular region of southern Greece—Ie: 3, 4.
Morfittes (medieval), Omorphita (Greek), Küçük Kaimakli (Turkish): village—K4e5: 8.
Morocco; al-Maghrib al-Aqṣā (Arabic: the farthest west): region of NW Africa—CDf: 2.
Morphou; Mórphou (modern Greek): town—K3e5: 8.
Mosul; al-Mauṣil (Arabic), Musul (Turkish): city—M4e4: 1.
Muggia (Italian), Milje (Slovene): town—G4c5: 3.
Mühlenbach or Mühlbach (German), Sebeş (Rumanian), Szászsebes (Hungarian): town—I4c5: 3.
al-Munaiṭirah (Arabic: the little lookout), Le Monestre or Le Moinestre (medieval): fortress—L1f1: 7.
Muret (French): town—E2d2: 2.
Murgo: island—see Amorgos.
Muzairib (Arabic): village—L2f3: 7.
Myconos (classical), Micone (medieval Italian), Mokene (Turkish), Míkonos (modern Greek): island—J1e3: 5.
Myrianthoussa (Greek): valley in NW Cyprus.
Myriokephalon (classical), Çardak Boğazỉ (Turkish): pass about 70 miles ESE of Ankara (K3e1: 1).
Mytilene: island—see Lesbos.
Mytilene; Mytilēnē (classical Greek), Mitylēnē (medieval Greek), Mitilíni (modern Greek): town—J2e1: 1, 3, 5.

Nablus; Shechem or Neapolis (classical), Nābulus (Arabic): town—L1f3: 7.
Nabruwah (Arabic): village in the Nile delta 30 miles SW of Mansurah (K2f4: 1).
Nadjivan (Persian), Nakhichevan (Russian): town—N1e1: 1.

an-Nahr al-Kabīr (Arabic: the big river): river, northern boundary of modern Lebanon.

Namfio: island – see Anaphe.

Namur (French): town – E5b5: 2, 3.

Nanking or Nan-ching (Chinese): city – BB4f3: 13.

Naples; Napoli (Italian): city, port – G5d5: 3.

Naples: kingdom – Hd: 9.

Narbonne (French): town – E4d2: 2.

Narenta (Italian), Naro (classical), Neretva (Serbian): river flowing into Adriatic 40 miles NW of Ragusa – H3d2: 3.

Naumburg an der Saale (German): city – G2b4: 2, 3.

Nauplia (classical), Návplion (modern Greek): port – I3e3: 4.

Navarino (Italian), Pylos (classical Greek), Zonklon (medieval): port, now superseded by New Navarino – I2e4: 4.

Navarre (French), Navarra (Spanish): region of northern Spain – Dd: 2.

Naxos; Nicosia (medieval Italian), Naksa (Turkish), Náxos (modern Greek): island – J1e4: 5.

Nazareth; an-Nāṣirah (Arabic): town – L1f3: 7.

Near East: region from Egypt to Persia and Turkey to Aden.

Negroponte: island – see Euboea.

Negroponte (medieval Italian: black bridge), Chalcis (classical), Khalkís (modern Greek): port – I4e2: 3, 4.

Nejd; Najd (Arabic): region of central Arabia – MNg: 1.

Neopatras: duchy – Ie: 9.

Nephin (medieval), Anafah (Arabic): town – L1f1: 7.

Neretva: river – see Narenta.

Nesle (French): village 28 miles ESE of Amiens (E3c1: 2).

Nestos (Greek), Nestus (Latin), Kara Su (Turkish), Mesta (Bulgarian): river flowing into the Aegean opposite Thasos – I5d4: 5.

Neuilly-sur-Marne (French): town 10 miles east of Paris (E3c2: 2).

Nevers (French): town – E4c4: 2.

Newburgh: town – D2a4: 2.

Nicaea (classical), İznik (Turkish): town – J5d5: 1, 3, 5.

Nice (French), Nizza (Italian): port – F3d2: 2.

Nicomedia (classical), İzmit (Turkish): town – J5d5: 1, 3, 5.

Nicopolis (medieval), Nikeboli̇ (Turkish), Nikopol (Bulgarian): town – I5d2: 1, 3.

Nicosia; Levkōsia (medieval Greek), Nicosía (modern Greek): city – K4e5: 1, 8.

Nicosia: island – see Naxos.

Nijmegen (Dutch): town – F1b4: 3.

Nile; Baḥr an-Nīl (Arabic): river – K3g4: 1; K1f4: 3.

Nîmes (French): city – E5d2: 2.

Nios: island – see Ios.

Nish; Niš (Serbian), Niş (Turkish), Naissus or Nissa (classical): town – I2d2: 3.

Nishava; Nišava (Serbian): river flowing past Pirot into the Morava – I3d2: 3.

Nisibin or Nusaybin (Turkish), Nisibis (classical), Naṣībīn or Nuṣaibīn (Arabic): town – M2e3: 1.

Nogent-sur-Marne (French): town 7 miles east of Paris (E3c2: 2).

Normandy; Normandie (French): region of northern France – DEc: 2.

North Africa; al-Maghrib (Arabic: the west): region from Morocco to Cyrenaica, north of the Sahara.

North Sea – DEFab: 2, 3.

Novara (Italian): town – F4c5: 3.

Novgorod (Russian: new city): city – K2a2: 12.

Novi Pazar or Raška (Serbian), Rascia (Latin): town – I1d2: 3.

Nubia (classical): region south of Egypt, equivalent to northern Sudan.

Nuremberg; Nürnberg (German): city — G2c1: 2, 3.
Nymphaeum (classical), Nif or Kemalpaşa (Turkish): town — J3e2: 5.

Ochrida, Lake; Lychnitus Lacus (classical), Ohridske Jezero (Serbian) — I1d4: 4.
Oder (German), Odra (Czech, Polish): river — H1b3: 2.
Oldenburg (German): city — F4b2: 2, 3.
Olives, Mount of, or Olivet; Jabal aṭ-Ṭūr (Arabic): hill east of Jerusalem (L1f4: 7).
Oreus (Latin), Ōreos (medieval Greek), Oreoí (modern Greek): town — I4e2: 4.
Orléans (French): town — E2c3: 2.
Orontes (classical), al-ʿĀṣī (Arabic: the rebellious), Far (medieval): river — L2e5: 1, 6, 7.
Orseln (German): probably Nieder- and Oberursel, 7 miles NNW of Frankfurt (F4b5: 2).
Orshova; Orşova (Rumanian): town — I3d1: 3.
Orthosias (medieval): village — L1f1: 6.
Osterna (medieval), Osternohe (modern German): village 18 miles NE of Nuremberg (G2c1: 3).
Ostia (Italian): port, now village — G3d4: 2, 3.
Otranto (Italian): town — H4d5: 3.
Öttingen (German): village 40 miles SSW of Nuremburg (G2c1: 3).
Oultrejourdain: region — see Transjordan.
Outremer (French: overseas), Ultramare (Latin): the Latin states in Syria and Palestine.
Oxford: town — D4b4: 2.

Paderborn (German): town — F4b4: 2, 3.
Padua; Padova (Italian): city — G2c5: 2, 3.
Palatia (medieval), Miletus (classical), Balat (Turkish): port, now abandoned — J3e3: 3, 5.
Palekythro (Greek): village — K4e5: 8.
Palermo (Italian), Balarm (Arabic): city, port — G4e2: 3.
Palestine; Palaestina (classical), Filistīn (Arabic): region west of the Dead Sea and the Jordan — KLf: 1.
Palma de Mallorca (Spanish) or of Majorca: city, port — E3c1: 2.
Palmiers, Palmaria: oasis — see Segor.
Palmyra or Tadmor (classical), Tadmur, now Tudmur (Arabic): caravan town — L4f1: 6.
Pannonia (classical): region including parts of modern Austria, Hungary, and Yugoslavia.
Papal States — Gd: 9.
Paphos (medieval), Páphos (modern Greek): town — K3f1: 1, 8.
Paris (French): city — E3c2: 2.
Parma (Italian): town 75 miles SE of Milan (F5c5: 2).
Paros; Paro (medieval Italian), Bara (Turkish), Páros (modern Greek): island — J1e3: 5.
Passarowitz (German), Požarevac (Serbian): town 37 miles SE of Belgrade (I1d1: 3).
Passau (German): town — G4c2: 2, 3.
Patmos; Patmo (Italian), Batnos (Turkish), Pátmos (modern Greek): island — J2e3: 5.
Patras (medieval), Pátrai (modern Greek): port — I2e2: 3, 4.
Pavia (Italian): town — F5c5: 2, 3.
Pedhoulas; Pedhoulás or Pedoulás (modern Greek): town — K3f1: 8.
Pedias or Pediaios; Pediás (modern Greek): river — K4e5: 8.
Peking: city — see Khanbaliq.
Pelendria or Pellendri; Peléndria (modern Greek): town — K3f1: 8.
Peloponnesus: peninsular region — see Morea.
Peñaforte (Spanish): castle near Villafranca del Panadés, 25 miles west of Barcelona (E3d4: 2).
Pendayia (Greek): village — K3e5: 8.
Pennedepie (French): village 28 miles NE of Caen (D5c1: 2).

Pentedaktylos (Greek): monastery — K4e5: 8.

Pera or Estanor (medieval), Beyoğlu (Turkish): port — J4d4: 3, 5.

Perche (French): district west of Chartres — E1c2: 2.

Pergamum (classical), Bergamo (Turkish): town — J3e1: 3, 5.

Peritheorium (medieval), Perithearion (Greek): port — I3e3: 4.

Persia (classical), Īrān (Persian): region of sw Asia — NOef: 1.

Persian Gulf; Khalīj-i-Fars (Persian), Khalīj al-ʿAjam (Arabic) — NOg: 12, 13 (name not shown on maps).

Perugia (Italian): town — G3d2: 3.

Petra Deserti (classical): ancient city — L1f5: 1.

Petrich (Bulgarian), Petritzos (medieval Greek): castle — I5d4: 3, 5.

Petrovaradin (Serbian), Peterwardein (German): town — H5c5: 3.

Pharan: bishopric — see Faran.

Philadelphia (classical), Alaşehir (Turkish): town — J4e2: 3, 5.

Philadelphia: town — see ʿAmmān.

Philippopolis (classical), Plovdiv (Bulgarian), Filibe (Turkish): town — I5d3: 1, 3, 5.

Phínika (modern Greek): village — K3f1: 8.

Phocaea (classical), Foglia (Italian), Foça (Turkish): port, now abandoned for New Phocaea — J2e2: 3, 5.

Phocaea, New; Yenifoça (Turkish): port — J2e2: 3, 5.

Phoenicia (classical): region equivalent to modern Lebanon and part of Israel.

Pholegandros (medieval Greek), Folégandros (modern Greek): island — I5e4: 5.

Piacenza (Italian): town — F5c5: 2.

Pian del Carpine or Piano della Magione (Italian), Plano de Carpini (Latin), Planocarpino (medieval): village 9 miles wnw of Perugia (G3d2: 3).

Picardy: Picardie (French): region of northern France — Eb: 2.

Picquigny (French): village 8 miles wnw of Amiens (E3c1: 2).

Piotrków (Polish): town — H5b4: 3.

Pirot (Bulgarian): town — I3d2: 3.

Pisa (Italian): port, now city — G1d2: 2, 3.

Pisanith: port — see Porsico.

Pistoia (Italian): town 20 miles nw of Florence (G2d2: 3).

Placentia: town — see Comana.

Plancy (French): village 20 miles nw of Troyes (E5c2: 2).

Planocarpino: village — see Pian del Carpine.

Podio: town — see Le Puy.

Podolia: region north of Moldavia — Jc: 3.

Poitiers (French): town — E1c4: 2.

Poitou (French): region of western France — DEc: 2.

Pola (Italian), Pula (Croatian): port — G4d1: 3.

Poland; Polska (Polish): region east of Germany — HIb: 3.

Polis (medieval), Arsinoë (classical): town — K3e5: 8.

Pomerania; Pommern (German): region of ne Germany — GHb: 2, 3.

Pomerelia; Pommerellen (German), Pomorze (Polish): district of northern Poland — Hb: 3.

Pont-de-Fer (French): casal in the county of Tripoli.

Porchades (medieval), Parsata (Greek): casal — K4f1: 8.

Pordenone (Italian): town 28 miles wsw of Udine (G4c4: 3).

Porsico or Pisanith (medieval): port on south shore of Black Sea.

Porto (Italian): village 13 miles sw of Rome (G3d4: 3).

Portugal; Lusitania (classical): region west of southern and central Spain, now a nation — Cde: 2.

Posen (German), Poznán (Polish): city — H2b3: 3.

Potamía (Greek): casal in Cyprus, possibly Potamiou.

Potamides (Greek): port on sw coast of Naxos (J1e4: 5).
Potamiou; Potamioú (modern Greek): village—K3f1: 8.
Prague; Praha (Czech): city—G5b5: 2, 3.
Prato in Toscana (Italian): town 12 miles NW of Florence (G2d2: 3).
Prespa, Lake; Brygius Lacus (classical), Brygēis Limnē (medieval Greek), Prespansko Jezero (Serbian)—I1d5: 4.
Prote (Serbian), Prodano (Italian), Barakada (Turkish): island—I2e3: 4.
Provadiya (Bulgarian), Probaton (medieval), Provadi (Turkish): town—J3d2: 5.
Provence (French): region of SE France—EFd: 2, 3.
Provins (French): town 40 miles WNW of Troyes (E5c2: 2).
Prussia; Preussen (German), Prusy (Polish): region of NE Germany—HIb: 3.
Psimolófo (medieval Greek), Psomolóphou (modern Greek): village—K4e5: 8.
Pskov (Russian), Pleskau (German): city—J4a3: 12.
Puglia or Puglie: region—see Apulia.
Pyla, Cape—K4f1: 8.
Pyramus (classical), Chahan (Armenian), Jeyhan (Turkish): river—L1e4: 6.
Pyrenees; Pyrénées (French), Pirineos (Spanish): mountain range—DEd: 2.
Pyrgos (Greek): town—I2e3: 4.

al-Qadmūs (Arabic): fortress—L2e5: 6.
Qalansuwā (Arabic), Calansue (medieval): village—L1f3: 7.
Qal‘at Ja‘bar (Arabic): fortress—L4e5: 6.
Qāqūn (Arabic), Caco (medieval): fortress—L1f3: 7.
al-Qasṭal (Arabic): fortress—L1f4: 7.
Qinnasrīn (Arabic), Chalcis ad Belum (classical): town, now unimportant—L2e4: 6.
Qrna: unidentified town north of Maragha (N2e3: 1).
Quilon or Coilum: port—T2j2: 13.
Quinsai: city—see Hangchow.
Quṣair: castle—see Cursat.

Ra‘āshīn or Rash‘īn (Arabic), Resshyn (medieval): village—L1f1: 6.
Rafanīyah (Arabic): village—L2f1: 6.
Raffiyaḥ (Arabic), Raphia (medieval): village—K5f4: 7.
Ragusa (medieval), Dubrovnik (Serbian): port—H4d3: 3.
Rahova or Rakhova (medieval), Oryakhovo (Rumanian): town—I4d2: 3.
ar-Rainah (Arabic), Raine (medieval): village 4 miles NNE of Nazareth (L1f3: 7).
Rāmallāh (Arabic), Ramelie (medieval): village 9 miles north of Jerusalem (L1f4: 7).
Ramla; Rama or Rames (medieval), ar-Ramlah (Arabic: the sandy): town—K5f4: 7.
Raphia: village—see Raffiyaḥ.
Ravenna (Italian): town—G3d1: 2, 3.
Ravennika (medieval): town, now abandoned—I3e2: 4.
Red Sea; al-Baḥr al-Aḥmar (Arabic)—Lgh: 1.
Regensburg (German), Ratisbon (medieval): town—G3c1: 2, 3.
Resshyn: village—see Ra‘āshīn.
Retesta (medieval): probably Rethel, 23 miles NE of Rheims (E5c1: 2).
Retimo (medieval), Calamona or Rethymnon (classical), Réthimnon (modern Greek): town—I5e5: 3.
Rheims; Reims (French): city—E5c1: 2.
Rhine; Rijn (Dutch), Rhein (German), Rhin (French): river—F3b5: 2; F3c2: 3.
Rhineland: region of the middle Rhine.
Rhodes; Rhodos (classical Greek), Rhodus (Latin), Ródhos (modern Greek): city, port—J4e4: 1, 5.
Rhodes; Rhodos (classical Greek), Rhodus (Latin), Rodos (Turkish), Rodi (Italian), Ródhos (modern Greek): island—Je: 1, 3, 5.

Rhodope; Rhodopē (classical Greek), Rodhópi (modern Greek), Rodopi (Bulgarian): mountain range — I5d4: 5.

Rhone; Rhône (French): river — E5c5: 2.

Ridefort (French): chateau, location unknown.

Riga; Rīga (Lettish): city — I5a4: 12.

Rimini (Italian): town — G3d1: 2, 3.

Rodosto (medieval), Bisanthe or Rhoedestus (classical), Tekirdağ (Turkish): port — J3d5: 5.

Romano d'Ezzelino (Italian): village 36 miles NW of Venice (G3c5: 2, 3).

Romans-sur-Iserre (French): town 11 miles north of Valence (E5d1: 2).

Rome; Roma (Italian): city — G3d4: 2, 3.

Rosetta; Rashīd (Arabic): port — K1f4: 1.

Rothenburg (German): town 40 miles west of Nuremberg (G2c1: 3).

Rouen (French): city — E2c1: 2.

Roussa: town — see Rusion.

Rubruck (Flemish): village 33 miles WNW of Lille (E4b5: 2).

Rugia (medieval), ar-Rūj (Arabic): valley — L2e5: 6.

Rūm: region — see Anatolia.

Rumeli-Hisar (Turkish: castle of Rumelia): fortress — J5d4: 5.

Rumelia; Rumeli (Turkish): Ottoman territory in Europe — 11.

Rusion or Roussa (medieval), Rusköy (medieval Turkish), Keşan (modern Turkish): town 55 miles south of Adrianople (J2d4: 5).

Russano (Italian): probably Rossano, 40 miles NW of Cotrone (H3e1: 3).

Russia; Rus (medieval), Russiya (Russian): region of eastern Europe — JKLMbc: 1, 3.

Ruthenia (medieval): region of eastern Europe, not equivalent to modern (till 1945) Czechoslovakian province — IJc: 3.

Sabina (Italian): district 35 miles north of Rome (G3d4: 3).

Sabkhat Bardawīl (Arabic, now Sabkhat al-Bardawīl): lagoon north of Sinai — K4f4: 1.

Sabran (French): village 24 miles NW of Avignon (E5d2: 2).

Sabzevār or Sabzavār: town — see Baihaq.

Sachsen: region — see Saxony.

Safad; Saphet (medieval), Ṣafad (Arabic), Tsefat (Israeli): town 12 miles north of Tiberias (L1f3: 7).

Sagitta: port — see Sidon.

Sahara; aṣ-Ṣahrā' (Arabic): desert — DEFGfg: 2, 3.

Saiges (medieval); unidentified place, possibly Saignes, 75 miles SE of Limoges (E2c5: 2).

Saint Abraham: town — see Hebron.

Saint Amand (French): town 25 miles south of Bourges (E3c3: 2).

Saint Bertin (French): abbey 17 miles east of Boulogne (E2b5: 2).

Saint Chariton; Khirbat Kharaitūn (Arabic): Greek Orthodox monastery — L1f4: 7.

Saint Euthymius; Khān al-Aḥmar (Arabic): Greek Orthodox monastery — L1f4: 7.

Saint George: town — see Lydda.

Saint George of Khoziba: Greek Orthodox monastery — L1f4: 7.

Saint Gerasimus; Qaṣr Ḥajlah (Arabic): Greek Orthodox monastery 3 miles SE of Jericho (L1f4: 7).

Saint Gilles: village — see Sinjīl.

Saint Gilles-du-Gard (French): village 10 miles west of Arles (E5d2: 2).

Saint Hilarion or Dieudamour (French), Áyios Ilárion (modern Greek): castle — K4e5: 8.

Saint Jean d'Acre: city, port — see Acre.

Saint John; Qaṣr al-Yahūd (Arabic): Greek Orthodox monastery — L1f4: 7.

Saint Lazarus: village 2 miles ESE of Jerusalem (L1f4: 2).

Saint Nicholas (tou Soulouaiy); Áyios Nikólaos (modern Greek): village — K3f1: 8.

Saint Quentin (French): town 26 miles NW of Laon (E4c1: 2).
Saint Sabas; Mār Sābā (Syrian): Greek Orthodox monastery — L1f4: 7.
Saint Simeon (medieval), as-Suwaidīyah (Arabic), Süveydiye (Turkish): port — L1e4: 6.
Saint Theodosius; Dair Ibn-'Ubaid (Arabic): Greek Orthodox monastery — L1f4: 7.
Saint Trond (French): town — F1b5: 2.
Sakarya (Turkish), Sangarius (classical): river — K2e1: 1; K1d5: 5.
Salamanca (Spanish), Salmantiqah (Arabic): city — C5d5: 2.
Salamis (classical), Koulourē (medieval Greek), Koluri (Turkish), Salamís (modern
    Greek): island — I4e3: 4.
Salerno (Italian): port — G5d5: 3.
Salmas, Selmas, or Salamastrum (medieval), Salmās, Dilmān, or Shāhpūr (Persian):
    town — M5e2: 1.
Salona or La Sala (medieval), Amphissa (classical), Amfíssa (modern Greek): town —
    I3e2: 3, 4.
Salonika or Saloníki: city — see Thessalonica.
Salsette: island NE of Bombay, on which Thana (S3i1: 13) is located.
as-Salṭ (Arabic): town — L1f3: 7.
Salza or Langensalza (German): town — G1b4: 2, 3.
Salzburg (German): city — G4c3: 2, 3.
Samaria (classical): district of northern Palestine — L1f3: 7.
Samarkand; Samarqand (Persian, Arabic): city — R2e1: 12, 13.
Samos (classical), Samo (medieval Italian), Susam (Turkish), Sámos (modern Greek):
    island — J2e3: 5.
Samothrace; Samothrakē (classical Greek), Samothráki (modern Greek): island —
    J1d5: 5.
Samsun (Turkish), Amisus (classical), Summiso or Simiso (medieval): port — L2d4: 1.
San Germano Vercellese (Italian): village 22 miles NW of Montferrat (F4c5: 3).
San Gimignano (Italian): town 18 miles SW of Siena (G2d2: 3).
Sancerre (French): town 26 miles NE of Bourges (E3c3: 2).
Sangerhausen (German): town 31 miles SSE of Halberstadt (G2b4: 3).
Sanok (Polish): town — I3c1: 3.
Santalla: unidentified place, probably in Galicia, Spain.
Santiago de Compostela: shrine — see Compostela.
Santorin: island — see Thera.
Saone (medieval), Ṣahyūn or Ṣihyaun (Arabic): crusader castle — L2e5: 6.
Saphet: town — see Safad.
Sapientsa; Sapienza (Italian), Sapiéntza (modern Greek): island — I2e4: 4.
Saragossa; Caesaraugusta (classical), Zaragoza (Spanish), Saraqusṭah (Arabic): city —
    D5d4: 2.
Sarai or Sarai-Batu (Tatar), Sarāi (Persian: palace): town, now abandoned — N3c3: 1.
Sarai-Berke: town — see Aksarai.
Sardenay (medieval), Ṣaidnāyā (Arabic): village — L2f2: 7.
Sardinia; Sardegna (Italian): island — Fde: 2, 3.
Sarepta (medieval), Zarephath (classical), Ṣarafand (Arabic): town — K5f3: 6.
Sargines or Sergines (French): village 35 miles west of Troyes (E5c2: 2).
Saronic Gulf; Saronikós Kólpos (modern Greek) — I4e3: 4.
Sarukhan (Turkish): district of western Anatolia — Je: 5.
Sarus (classical), Sahan (Armenian), Seyhan (Turkish): river — L1e3: 6.
Sarvantikar; Sarouantiḳar (Armenian): fortress — L2e3: 6.
Satalia: port — see Adalia.
Satines: city — see Athens.
Sauvegny (French): probably Sauvigny, 15 miles SW of Toul (F1c2: 2).
Sava or Save (Croatian), Sau (German), Száva (Hungarian): river — H4d1: 3.
Savignone (Italian): village 11 miles north of Genoa (F4d1: 3).

Savoy; Savoie (French): region of SE France—Fc: 2, 3.
as-Sawād (Arabic: the black land): district east of the Sea of Galilee—L1f3: 7.
Saxony; Sachsen (German): region of northern Germany—Gb: 2, 3.
Sayn (German): town—F3b5: 2, 3.
Scandinavia: region comprising Denmark, Sweden, and Norway.
Schuf or Souf (medieval), Shuf or Chouf (modern): district NE of Sidon—L1f2: 6.
Schwaben: region—see Swabia.
Schwanden (German): village 46 miles south of Constance (F5c3: 3).
Schwarzenberg (German): castle 5 miles SE of Aue.
Scio: island—see Chios.
Scotland; Scotia (Latin): region north of England—CDa: 2.
Scutari (Italian), Chrysopolis (classical), Üsküdar (Turkish): port—J5d4: 5.
Scutari (Italian), Scodra (classical), Shkodër (Albanian): port—H5d3: 3.
Scyros: island—see Skyros.
Scythopolis: town—see Bethsan.
Sebastia: city—see Sivas.
Sebastia (medieval), Samaria (classical), Sabasṭīyah (Arabic): village—L1f3: 2.
Sebastopolis (medieval), Gagry (Russian): port—M1d2: 1.
Sebenico (Italian), Šibenik (Serbian): port—H1d2: 3.
Sedinum (medieval), Shadīnah (Arabic): manor—L1f2: 7.
Segni (Italian): town 30 miles ESE of Rome (G3d4: 3).
Segor; Zoar (classical), Palmaria or Palmiers (medieval): oasis—L1f4: 7.
Seine (French): river—E5c2: 2.
Seleucia or Ctesiphon (classical): suburb of Baghdad—M5f2: 1.
Seleucia Trachea (classical), Selevgia (Armenian), Silifke (Turkish): port, now town—
  K4e4: 1.
Selmas: town—see Salmas.
Selymbria (medieval), Silivri (Turkish): port—J4d4: 5.
Senj (Serbian), Segna (Italian), Zengg (German): port—G5d1: 3.
Serbia; Srbija (Serbian): region east of Dalmatia—H1d: 3.
Seriphos (classical), Sérifos (modern Greek): island—I5e3: 4, 5.
Serres (medieval), Sérrai (modern Greek): town—I4d4: 3, 4, 5.
Sevan, Lake (Russian), Gökçe Gölü (Turkish)—N1d5: 1.
Sévérac-le-Château (French): village 70 miles NW of Nîmes (E5d2: 2).
Severin (Rumanian): district north of Orshova—Icd: 3.
Seville; Hispalis (classical), Sevilla (Spanish), Ishbīliyah (Arabic): city—C5e3: 2.
Shaizar (medieval Arabic), Larissa (classical), Saijar (modern Arabic): fortress, now
  town—L2e5: 6.
Shaqīf Arnūn: castle—see Belfort.
ash-Shaubak: fortress—see Krak de Montréal.
Shumen; Šumen (Bulgarian), Şumnĭ (Turkish): town, now Kolarovgrad—J2d2: 3.
Siberia; Sibur (Russian): northern portion of Asia.
Sicily; Sicilia (Italian), Ṣiqillīyah (Arabic), Trinacria (medieval): island—Ge: 2, 3.
Sidon; Sagitta (medieval), Ṣaidā' (Arabic): port—L1f2: 1, 7.
Siebenbürgen: region—see Transylvania.
Siena (Italian): town—G2d2: 2, 3.
Sifanto: island—see Siphnos.
Sígouri or Sívouri (modern Greek), Baffa (medieval): castle—K4e5: 8.
Sikinos; Síkinos (modern Greek): island—J1e4: 5.
Silesia; Schlesien (German), Śląsk (Polish), Slezsko (Czech): region north of Moravia—
  Hb: 3.
Silifke: port—see Seleucia.
Silivri: port—see Selymbria.
Silves (Portuguese), Shilb (Arabic): town—C2e3: 2.

Simiso: port—see Samsun.
Sinai: Sīnā' (Arabic): peninsula—Kfg: 1.
Sinai, Mount, or Mount Horeb; Jabal Mūsâ (Arabic: mountain of Moses)—K4g2: 1.
Sinjar: plain around town of Sinjar (M2e4: 1).
Sinjar; Sinjār (Arabic): town—M2e4: 1.
Sinjīl or Sanjīl (Arabic), Saint Gilles (French): village—L1f3: 7.
Sinope; Sinōpē (medieval Greek), Sinop (Turkish): port—L1d3: 1.
Sion, Mount, or Mount Zion: hill south of Jerusalem (L1f4: 7).
Siphnos (classical), Sifanto (Italian), Sífnos (modern Greek): island—I5e4: 5.
Sis (Armenian, medieval), Kezan (Turkish): town—L1e3: 1.
Sitia or Seteia (Greek): town—J2e5: 3.
Sivas; Sebastia (classical), Sîvas (Turkish): city—L3e1: 1.
Skiathos; Skíathos (modern Greek): island—I4e1: 4.
Skopelos; Skópelos (modern Greek): island—I4e1: 4.
Skoplje: Üsküb (Turkish), Skopje (Serbian): town—I2d4: 3.
Skyros or Scyros (classical), Skíros (modern Greek): island—I5e2: 4, 5.
Slavonia: district east of Croatia—Hc: 3.
Slavskoye: town—see Kreuzburg.
Smyrna (classical), İzmir (Turkish): city, port—J3e2: 1, 3, 5.
Socotra; Suqūṭrâ (Arabic): island—Q4/5j3: 13.
Sofale: unidentified town on coast north of Bombay (S3i2: 13).
Sofia; Sardica (classical), Triaditia (medieval Greek), Sredec (Serbian), Sofiya (Bulgarian): city—I4d3: 3, 5.
Soissons (French): town 20 miles sw of Laon (E4c1: 2).
Soldaia (medieval), Sudak (Russian): port—K5d1: 1.
Solgat: town—see Surgat.
Soli (Greek): town, now abandoned—K3e5: 8.
Sopot (Bulgarian), Scribention (medieval): town—I5d3: 3, 5.
Souf: district—see Schuf.
Sozopolis (medieval), Apollonia (classical), Sözebolî or Uluborlu (Turkish), Sozopol (Bulgarian): town—J3d3: 3, 5.
Spain; Hispania (classical), España (Spanish): region south of the Pyrenees.
Spalato (medieval), Split (Serbian): port—H2d2: 3.
Sparta or Lacedaemon (Latin), Spartē or Lakedaimōn (classical Greek), Spárti (modern Greek): town—I3e3: 4.
Sporades; Sporádhes (modern Greek): island group—IJe: 3, 4, 5.
Sredna Gora (Bulgarian): mountain range—Id: 5.
Stalimene: island—see Lemnos.
Stampalia: island—see Astypalaea.
Stanchio or Stankoi, island—see Cos.
Starkenberg: castle—see Montfort.
Stavrovouni; Stavrovoúni (modern Greek): mountain—K4f1: 8.
Sterviga (medieval): farmland near Nicosia (K4e5: 8).
Strassburg (German), Strasbourg (French): city—F3c2: 2, 3.
Strobilo (medieval Italian): island—J3e4: 5.
Strymon; Strymōn (classical Greek), Strimón (modern Greek), Struma (Bulgarian): river—I4d4: 4.
Styria; Steiermark (German): region of southern Austria—GHc: 3.
Suchem (German): parish, probably Sudheim, near Paderborn (F4b4: 3).
Sudak: port—see Soldaia.
Sudan; as-Sūdān (Arabic: the Negro lands): region south of Egypt—JKh: 1.
Suez; as-Suwais (Arabic): port—K3g1: 1.
Sultaniye (medieval Turkish), Çanakkale (modern Turkish): port—J2d5: 5.
Sultaniyeh; Sulṭānīyeh (Persian), Kangurlan (Mongol): town—N4e4: 1.

Summiso: port—see Samsun.

Ṣūr: port—see Tyre.

Surgat or Solgat (medieval): town, probably in the Crimea (K4c5: 3).

Suzdal (Russian): city—M1a4: 12.

Swabia; Schwaben (German): region of sw Germany—Fc: 2, 3.

Sweden; Sverige (Swedish): region of Scandinavia, smaller than modern nation— GHa: 12, 13.

Syba (medieval): port, now unimportant—L4d1: 1.

Syria (classical), ash-Sha'm or Sūriyah (Arabic): region east of the Mediterranean —Lf: 1.

Syros (classical), Syra (medieval), Síros (modern Greek): island—I5e3: 5.

Szczekociny (Polish): town—H5b5: 3.

Szegedin (Hungarian): city, now Szeged—I1c4: 3.

Tabor, Mount; Jabal Tābūr or Jabal aṭ-Ṭūr (Arabic), Tavor (Israeli)—L1f3: 7.

Tabriz; Tabrīz (Persian): city—N2e2: 1.

Tagliamento (Italian): river flowing into the Adriatic 12 miles east of Caorle—G3c4: 3.

Tagus (classical), Tajo (Spanish), Tejo (Portuguese), Tājuh (Arabic): river—C3e1: 2.

Ta'if; aṭ-Ṭā'if (Arabic): oasis—M1h5: 1.

Tana (medieval), Tanaïs (classical), Azov (Russian): port—L5c3: 1.

Tannenberg (German), Stębark (Polish): village—I1b2: 3.

Tarakli-Yenije; Taraklî-Yenije (Turkish): village—K1d5: 5.

Taranto (Italian): port—H3d5: 3.

Tarsus (classical, Turkish), Darsous (Armenian): city—K5e4: 1.

Tartary: area held by the Mongols at any given time.

Tashkent; Binkāth or Tāshkand (Arabic): city—R5d4: 12, 13.

Taurus (classical), Toros Dağları (Turkish): mountain range—Le: 1.

Taygetus (classical), Pentedaktylon (medieval Greek), Taïyetos (modern Greek): mountain range—I3e3: 4.

Tbilisi; city—see Tiflis.

Tegea (classical): town, now abandoned for Tegía (formerly Pialí) nearby—I3e3: 4.

Tekirdağ: port—see Rodosto.

Tekke (Turkish): region of sw Anatolia, equivalent to classical Pamphylia—Je: 5.

Tell Bashir; Tall Bāshir (Arabic), Turbessel (medieval), Tilbeshar (Turkish): fortress— L3e4: 6.

Tembros or Tembria (Greek): village—K3e5: 8.

Temesvár (Hungarian): district of western Rumania—Ic: 10, 11.

Temesvár (Hungarian), Timişoara (Rumanian): town—I2c5: 3.

Tenduk (medieval), Tozan (Mongol): district of Mongolia—AAd: 13.

Tenedos; Tenedo (medieval Italian), Bozja-ada (Turkish): island—J1e1: 5.

Tenos; Tēnos (classical Greek), Tine (medieval Italian), İstendil (Turkish), Tínos (modern Greek): island—J1e3: 5.

Thabaria: town—see Tiberias.

Thana (medieval): port—S3i1: 13.

Thasos; Thásos (modern Greek): island—I5d5: 3, 5.

Thebes; Thēbai (classical Greek), Estives (medieval), Thívai (modern Greek): city— I4e2: 3, 4.

Theiretenne (French): village—L1f2: 7.

Thera; Thēra (classical Greek), Santorin (medieval), Thíra (modern Greek): island— J1e4: 5.

Therasia; Thirasía (modern Greek): island just NW of Thera (J1e4: 5).

Thermia: island—see Cythnos.

Thessalonica (medieval), Therma (classical), Solun (Macedonian), Salonika (Italian), Thessaloníki or Saloníki (modern Greek): city, port—I3d5: 3, 4.

Thessaly; Thessalia (classical), Vlachia (medieval), Thessalía (modern Greek): region of northern Greece — Ie: 3, 4.
Thessy (French): probably Theix, 65 miles NW of Le Puy (E4c5: 2).
Thrace; Thracia (Latin), Thrakē (classical Greek), Trakya (Turkish), Thráki (modern Greek): region south of Bulgaria — Jd: 1, 3, 5.
Thuringia: Thüringen (German): region of central Germany — Gb: 2, 3.
Tiberias (classical), Thabaria (medieval), Ṭabarīyah (Arabic), Tevarya (Israeli): town — L1f3: 1, 7.
Tiberias, Lake — see Galilee, Sea of.
Tibet: region north of India — UVWfg: 12, 13.
Tibnīn (Arabic): village just west of Toron (L1f2: 7).
Tiflis; Tiflīs (Persian), Tbilisi (Georgian): city — M5d4: 1.
Tigris (classical), Dijlah (Arabic), Dijle (Turkish): river — N2f4: 1.
Tikrit; Tikrīt (Arabic): town — M4f1: 1.
Tine or Tínos: island — see Tenos.
Tirnovo; Ternovum (Latin), Tîrnova (Turkish), Trnovo (Bulgarian): town — J1d2: 1, 3, 5.
Toledo (Spanish), Toletum (classical), Ṭulaiṭulah (Arabic): city — D1e1: 2.
Tolentino (Italian): village 30 miles SSW of Ancona (G4d2: 3).
Torcello (Italian): town 6 miles NE of Venice (G3c5: 3).
Toron (medieval): fortress — L1f2: 7.
Toros: mountain range — see Taurus.
Tortosa; Antaradus (classical), Anṭarṭūs or Ṭarṭūs (Arabic): port — L1f1: 1, 6.
Tortosa (Spanish), Dertosa (classical), Ṭurṭūshah (Arabic): town — E1d5: 2.
Toul (French): town — F1c2: 2, 3.
Toulouse (French): city — E2d2: 2.
Tournai (French), Doornijk (Flemish): town — E4b5: 2.
Tours (French): town — E1c3: 2.
Transcaucasia: region including Georgia and parts of Armenia and Azerbaijan.
Transjordan; Oultrejourdain (medieval French): region east of the Jordan.
Transoxiana: region (QRde) SE of the Aral Sea.
Transylvania; Siebenbürgen (German), Erdély (Hungarian), Ardeal (Rumanian): region SE of medieval Hungary — IJe: 1, 3.
Traù (medieval), Trogir (Serbian): port — G2d2: 3.
Trebizond; Trapezus (classical), Trapezunt (medieval), Trabzon (Turkish): city, port — L5d5: 1.
Trebizond: empire — Ld: 9.
Trefile (medieval): district NE of Acre — L1f3: 7.
Treviso (Italian): town 16 miles NNW of Venice (G3c5: 3).
Trier (German), Trèves (French): city — F2c1: 2, 3.
Trinacria: island — see Sicily.
Tripoli; Oea (classical), Ṭarābulus al-Gharb (Arabic): port — G4f3: 3.
Tripoli; Tripolis (classical), Ṭarābulus (Arabic): city, port — L1f1: 1, 6, 7.
Trogir: port — see Traù.
Troödos; Tróodos (modern Greek): mountain — K3f1: 8.
Troy; Ilium, Ilion, or Troia (classical): site of ancient city, at village of Hisarlik — J2e1: 3, 5.
Troyes (French): town — E5c2: 2.
Tsinkiang: port — see Zaitun.
Tudela (Spanish), Tutela (classical), Tuṭīlah (Arabic): town — D4d3: 2.
Tunis; Tūnis (Arabic): city — G1e4: 2, 3.
Tunisia; Ifrīqiyah (Arabic): region of North Africa — FGef: 2, 3.
Turbessel: fortress — see Tell Bashir.
Turkestan: region NE of Transoxiana.

Turkey; Türkiye (Turkish): modern nation, comprising Anatolia and parts of Thrace, Armenia, and Kurdistan.
Turnu (Rumanian), Drubeta (classical): town, now Turnu-Severin — I3d1: 3.
Tuscany; Toscana (Italian): region of central Italy — Gd: 2, 3.
Tusculum (Latin): town, now abandoned, 12 miles SE of Rome (G3d4: 3).
Tylleria (Greek): district NE of Khrysokou — K3e5: 8.
Tyre; Tyrus (classical), Ṣūr (Arabic), Tyr (Israeli): port — L1f2: 1, 7.
Tyron, Cave of; Shaqīf Tīrūn (Arabic): cave fortress — L1f2: 7.
Tyrrhenian Sea — FGde: 2.
Tzía: island — see Cos.

Udine (Italian): town — G4c4: 3.
Ujlak (Croatian), Ilok (Turkish): village — H5c5: 3.
Ukraine; Ukraina (Russian): region of sw Russia — Kc: 1, 3.
Ultramare — see Outremer.
Upper Egypt: region along the Nile south of Cairo — JKg: 1.
Urfa: city — see Edessa.
Urgench (Russian), Urgenç (Turkish), Gurganj (Persian), al-Jurgānīyah (Arabic), now Kunya Urgench: city, now abandoned for Novo Urgench — Q1d4: 13.
Üsküdar: port — see Scutari.

Valania (medieval), Bulunyās (medieval Arabic), Bāniyās (modern Arabic): port — L1e5: 6.
Valence (French): town — E5d1: 2.
Valencia (Spanish), Balansiyah (Arabic): city, port — D5e1: 2.
Valona: port — see Avlona.
Van, Lake; Van Gölü (Turkish) — M3e2: 1.
Vardar (medieval), Axius (classical): river — I3d4: 4.
Varna (medieval, Bulgarian): port, recently called Stalin — J3d2: 1, 3, 5.
Venice; Venezia (Italian): city, port — G3c5: 2, 3.
Verdun (French): town — F1c1: 2, 3.
Verona (Italian): city — G2c5: 2.
Verrai (medieval), Véroia (modern Greek), Fere or Kara-Ferye (Turkish): town — I3d5: 4.
Via Egnatia (medieval): road across Balkans from Durazzo to Constantinople — HIJd: 4, 5.
Vicenza (Italian): town — G2c5: 2, 3.
Vidin (Bulgarian): town — I3d2: 3.
Vienna; Wien (German): city — H2c2: 3.
Vienne (French): town — E5c5: 2.
Viennois (French): district of sw France, now called Dauphiné — Fc: 2.
Vilk (Serbian): district around the Lab valley.
Villach (German): town — G4c4: 2, 3.
Villefranche-sur-Mer (French), Villafranca (Italian): port — F3d2: 2.
Villehardouin (French): castle near Troyes (E5c2: 2).
Villejargon: town — see 'Arqah.
Vistula; Wisła (Polish), Weichsel (German): river — H5b3: 5.
Viterbo (Italian): town — G3d3: 2, 3.
Vitry-en-Artois (French): village 25 miles south of Lille (E4b5: 2).
Vittoria (Italian): town — G5e4: 3.
Vivar or Bivar or Viver (Spanish): town — D5e1: 2.
Vlachia: region — see Thessaly and Wallachia.
Volga (Russian), Itil (Tatar): river — N3c4: 1.
Vonitsa (medieval Greek), Bonditza (medieval), Vónitsa (modern Greek): town — I1e2: 3, 4.

Vosporo (medieval), Kerch (Russian): port—L2c5: 1.
Vostitsa (medieval), Aegium (Latin), Aíyion (modern Greek): town—I3e2: 4.

Wādī al-Qilt (Arabic): valley sw of Jericho (L1f4: 7).
Wādī Kurn or Wādī al-Karn (Arabic): brook at Montfort (L1f2: 7).
Wādī Ṣadr (Arabic): village—K4g1: 1.
Wādī-t-Taim (Arabic): valley—L1f2: 7.
Wales; Cambria (Latin), Cymru (Welsh): region west of England—Db: 2.
Wallachia; Vlachia (medieval), Valachia (Rumanian), Eflak (Turkish): region north
    of Bulgaria—IJd: 1, 3.
Warwick: town—D4b3: 2.
Wavrin (French): town 18 miles west of Tournai (E4b5: 2).
Wendover: town 34 miles NW of London (D5b4: 2).
Westminster: abbey in London (D5b4: 2).
Wien: city—see Vienna.
Willersleben or Wüllersleben (German): village 70 miles south of Bamberg (G1c1: 3).
Winchester: city—D4b4: 2.
Worms (German): town—F4c1: 2, 3.
Würzburg (German): city—F5c1: 2, 3.

Yangchow or Yang-chou (Chinese): city, port—BB5f3: 13.
Yantra (Bulgarian): river—J1d2: 5.
Yānūḥ (Arabic): village—L1f1: 7.
Yaytse; Jajce (Serbian): town—H3d1: 3.
Yemen; al-Yaman (Arabic: the right hand): region of sw Arabia—MNi: 12, 13.
Ypres (French), Ieper (Flemish): town 17 miles NNW of Lille (E4b5: 2).

Zaitun (medieval), Tsinkiang or Chin-chiang (Chinese): port—BB4h1: 12, 13.
Zante (Italian), Zacynthus (Latin), Zákinthos (modern Greek): island—I1e3: 3, 4.
Zara (Italian), Jadera (classical), Zadar (Croatian): port—H1d1: 3.
Zaragoza: city—see Saragossa.
Zea: island—see Ceos.
Zeitounion; Lamia (classical), Gitonis or Citó (medieval), Zitouni (medieval Greek),
    Lamía (modern Greek): town—I3e2: 3, 4.
Zeitz (German): town—G3b4: 2, 3.
az-Zīb: castle—see Casal Imbert.
Zichne (Greek): town—I4d4: 4, 5.
Zion, Mount—see Sion, Mount.
Znojmo (Czech), Znaim (German): town—H2c2: 3.
Zvornik (Serbian): town—H5d1: 3.

INDEX

553